WEALTH A

KING'S COLLEGE RESEARCH CENTRE
Project on
Political Economy and Society, 1750–1850
(1978–1984)

WEALTH AND VIRTUE

The Shaping of Political Economy
in the Scottish Enlightenment

Edited by
ISTVAN HONT
King's College, Cambridge
and
MICHAEL IGNATIEFF
King's College, Cambridge

CAMBRIDGE UNIVERSITY PRESS
Cambridge
London New York New Rochelle
Melbourne Sydney

Published by the Press Syndicate of the University of Cambridge
The Pitt Building, Trumpington Street, Cambridge CB2 1RP
32 East 57th Street, New York, NY 10022, USA
10 Stamford Road, Oakleigh, Melbourne 3166, Australia

© Cambridge University Press 1983

First published 1983
First paperback edition 1985

Library of Congress catalogue card number: 83-1898

British Library Cataloguing in Publication Data

Wealth and virtue
1. Scotland – Economic conditions   2. Scotland –
Politics and government – 18th century
I. Hont, Istvan   II. Ignatieff, Michael
330.941'1   HC257.S4

ISBN 0 521 23397 6 hard covers
ISBN 0 521 31214 0 paperback

Transferred to digital printing 2001

Contents

	Preface	*page* vii
	List of abbreviations	ix
1	Needs and justice in the *Wealth of Nations*: an introductory essay ISTVAN HONT AND MICHAEL IGNATIEFF (*King's College, Cambridge*)	1
2	Where had the Scottish economy got to by the third quarter of the eighteenth century? T. C. SMOUT (*University of St Andrews*)	45
3	Gershom Carmichael and the natural jurisprudence tradition in eighteenth-century Scotland JAMES MOORE (*Concordia University*) AND MICHAEL SILVERTHORNE (*McGill University*)	73
4	The Scottish professoriate and the polite academy, 1720–46 PETER JONES (*British Library*)	89
5	From applied theology to social analysis: the break between John Locke and the Scottish Enlightenment JOHN DUNN (*King's College, Cambridge*)	119
6	The Scottish Enlightenment at the limits of the civic tradition JOHN ROBERTSON (*St Hugh's College, Oxford*)	137
7	Adam Smith as civic moralist NICHOLAS PHILLIPSON (*University of Edinburgh*)	179
8	The legal needs of a commercial society: the jurisprudence of Lord Kames DAVID LIEBERMAN (*Christ's College, Cambridge*)	203

9 Cambridge paradigms and Scotch philosophers: a study of the relations between the civic humanist and the civil jurisprudential interpretation of eighteenth-century social thought 235
J. G. A. POCOCK (*Johns Hopkins University*)

10 Adam Smith's 'enduring particular result': a political and cosmopolitan perspective 253
DONALD WINCH (*University of Sussex*)

11 The 'rich country–poor country' debate in Scottish classical political economy 271
ISTVAN HONT (*King's College, Cambridge*)

12 John Millar and individualism 317
MICHAEL IGNATIEFF (*King's College, Cambridge*)

13 Scottish echoes in eighteenth-century Italy 345
FRANCO VENTURI (*University of Turin*)

Index 363

Preface

A book such as this would not have been possible without the renaissance in studies of the Scottish Enlightenment which has taken place in the past fifteen years. This new work, associated especially with the names of George Davie, Duncan Forbes, Ronald Meek, James Moore, Nicholas Phillipson, John Pocock, Andrew Skinner and Donald Winch, has made possible a complex new understanding of Scottish jurisprudence, moral philosophy and political economy, and their origins in Scottish provincial culture and metropolitan politics. At the same time, new scholarship on Hobbes and Locke and the political philosophy of the three British revolutions of 1641, 1688 and 1776, on the continental natural jurisprudence tradition and on the English neo-Harringtonian forms of Machiavellian civic humanism, have made possible a new degree of precision in siting Scottish political economy on the map of the main traditions of European political, moral and legal philosophy. This book is an attempt to take stock of these achievements in scholarship. The specific occasion which gave rise to it was a colloquium held at King's College, Cambridge, in May 1979 on Scottish political economy and the civic humanist tradition. The papers by Istvan Hont, Nicholas Phillipson, John Pocock, John Robertson and Franco Venturi were originally delivered at that colloquium; the rest were given at the seminar series which preceded it or were commissioned for the volume. Each paper has been rewritten and extended for publication. The joint essay which opens the volume is not intended as a conventional introduction to the collection, but it does highlight what turned out to be a major interpretative issue for the volume as a whole – the relative weight which ought to be given to the civic humanist and natural jurisprudence traditions in the constitution of the language of Scottish political economy.

In putting this book together, we have incurred numerous debts of gratitude: to the Provost and Fellows of King's College, as well as to the Managers of the Research Centre, and especially to John Dunn and Gareth Stedman Jones, for the decision to support a research project on the history of political economy in the first place and for the unfailing intellectual companionship they have shown as it proceeded; to Patricia Williams and Stephen Barr of Cambridge University Press for their forbearance and understanding during this book's long gestation; to Sylvana Tomaselli for invaluable editorial assistance; and to Mrs Hazel Clark, secretary of the Research Centre, for patience and skill in typing the manuscript. We would like to record our thanks to those who presented papers at our seminar series on the Scottish Enlightenment: Thomas Campbell, Jeremy Cater, John Christie, George Davie, Thomas Devine, Duncan Forbes, David Kettler, Aladár Madarász, Rosalind Mitchison, Charles Munn and Andrew Skinner.

We wish to dedicate this book to a teacher and friend who supported our research and who, to our deep regret, did not live to see its first fruits: Professor Sir M. M. Postan.

ISTVAN HONT
MICHAEL IGNATIEFF

Abbreviations

WORKS OF DAVID HUME

Philosophical Works   *The Philosophical Works of David Hume*, ed. T. H. Green and T. H. Grose, 4 vols. (London, 1874–5)
Treatise   *A Treatise of Human Nature*, ed. L. A. Selby Bigge, 2nd edn, rev. P. H. Nidditch (Oxford, 1979)

WORKS OF ADAM SMITH*

ED   '"Early Draft" of Part of the *Wealth of Nations*', in *LJ(A)*
EPS   *Essays on Philosophical Subjects*, ed. W. P. D. Wightman and J. C. Bryce with Dugald Stewart's 'Account of Adam Smith', ed. I. S. Ross (Oxford, 1980)
TMS   *The Theory of Moral Sentiments*, ed. D. D. Raphael and A. L. Macfie (Oxford, 1976)
LJ(A)   *Lectures on Jurisprudence. Report of 1762–3*, ed. R. L. Meek, D. D. Raphael, P. G. Stein (Oxford, 1978)
LJ(B)   *Jurisprudence or Notes from the Lectures on Justice, Police, Revenue, and Arms delivered in the University of Glasgow by Adam Smith, Professor of Moral Philosophy. Report dated 1766*, ed. R. L. Meek, D. D. Raphael, P. G. Stein (Oxford, 1978)
WN   *An Inquiry into the Nature and Causes of the Wealth of Nations*, ed. R. H. Campbell, A. S. Skinner and W. B. Todd, 2 vols. (Oxford, 1975)
Correspondence   *The Correspondence of Adam Smith*, ed. E. C. Mossner and I. S. Ross (Oxford, 1977)

* References to these works follow the practice adopted by the editors of *The Glasgow Edition of the Works and Correspondence of Adam Smith*, citing not the page number but the relevant section and paragraph (i.e. *WN* I.X.b.1 = *The Wealth of Nations*, Book I, Chap. X, Section b, §1).

1 Needs and justice in the *Wealth of Nations*: an introductory essay

ISTVAN HONT and MICHAEL IGNATIEFF

> Since...according to Smith, a society is not happy, of which the greater part suffers – yet even the wealthiest state of society leads to this suffering of the majority – and since the economic system (and in general a society based on private interest) leads to this wealthiest condition, it follows that the goal of the economic system is the *unhappiness* of society.
>
> Karl Marx, 'Economic and Philosophical Manuscripts of 1844'

> No society can surely be flourishing and happy, of which the far greater part of the members are poor and miserable...
>
> Compared, indeed, with the more extravagant luxury of the greater, [the labourer's] accommodation must no doubt appear extremely simple and easy – and yet it may be true, perhaps, that the accommodation of an European prince does not always so much exceed that of an industrious and frugal peasant, as the accommodation of the latter exceeds that of many an African king, the absolute master of the lives and liberties of ten thousand naked savages.
>
> Adam Smith, *Wealth of Nations* (Bk I, Chs. I and VIII)

No clear definition of the identity of political economy in eighteenth-century Scotland can be given unless an account is offered of the central questions which Adam Smith was trying to answer when he wrote the *Wealth of Nations*. This in turn requires that we should be able to understand the relation between Smith's concerns as a moral philosopher, as a professor of jurisprudence and as a political economist. The claim made in this paper is that there was a central question about modern 'commercial society' which Smith identified in his moral philosophy, in his jurisprudence lectures and in the 'early draft', and which the final version of the *Wealth of Nations* was intended, above all other purposes Smith might have had in mind, to answer. Commercial societies were more unequal in their distribution of property than any previous stage of society, and yet they remained capable of satisfying the basic needs of those who laboured for wages. Primitive societies, by contrast, were more equal, but miserably poor. Why was it that the 'productive labourers' of a commercial society were able to carry such a huge burden of 'unproductive labourers' upon their backs and still manage to provide adequately for their own needs? For

Smith this was a question about the unique productivity of modern forms of labour. Why, moreover, were free labourers, who depended for their subsistence on markets in labour and food, more productively employed and better fed than slaves, whose subsistence was the responsibility of their masters, or savage tribesmen, who retained the whole produce of their labour? Smith's division of labour theory and his natural price model – the central core of his economic argument – were deployed, so we argue, to explain the compatibility of economic inequality and adequate subsistence for the wage-earner within a free market system. These new economic arguments, we maintain, were developed in the context of an intense eighteenth-century debate about the inequality and luxury of modern commercial societies, and, as arguments, were designed as a defence of modernity against those who condemned commercial society from the vantage point, either of the classical civic humanist ideal of a virtuous republic which delegated productive labour to slaves, or of the Christian ideal of society as a positive community of goods.

Our argument is that the *Wealth of Nations* was centrally concerned with the issue of justice, with finding a market mechanism capable of reconciling inequality of property with adequate provision for the excluded. Smith was simply transposing into the language of markets an ancient jurisprudential discourse, carried into modernity by Grotius, Pufendorf and Locke, about how to ensure that private individuation of God's dominion would not deny the propertyless the means of satisfying their needs. Yet the answer which Smith gave to this problem – that a system of competitive markets in food and labour could guarantee adequate subsistence to the labouring poor – was a scandal in his own time, to those, even within the ranks of political economists themselves, who insisted that government should 'police' the market in subsistence goods, and to those who believed that the poor had rights to subsistence which must have priority over the property claims of the possessors. This sentiment was still at work in the later anti-Malthusian quip that political economy was a 'dismal science'. Yet Smith's arguments were designed to show how an economy of abundance could be created in which this ancient jurisprudential antinomy between the needs of the poor and the rights of the rich could be transcended altogether.

I. *The paradox of commercial society*

The very first pages of the *Wealth of Nations* – the 'introduction and plan' – clearly identify the feature of commercial society which Smith selected as the starting point of his analysis. It was a feature, he explained, which emerged clearly from a comparison between commercial society and the 'savage nations of hunters and fishers' which had preceded it in the history of human refinement. In the savage nations, the population was not divided into productive and unproductive classes. 'Every individual who is able to work is more or less employed in useful labour' and endeavours to provide both for his family and for those unable to work for themselves.[1] In such societies, as he had explained to his students in his jurisprudence lectures, there were 'no landlords, no usurers, no tax gatherers'.[2] Everyone retained the produce of his labour. In so-called civilized societies, on the other hand, Smith mordantly observed in the 'early draft' of the *Wealth of Nations*:

> the poor provide both for themselves and for the enormous luxury of their superiors. The rent which goes to support the vanity of the slothful landlord is all earned by the industry of the peasant. The monied man indulges himself in every sort of ignoble and sordid sensuality, at the expence of the merchant and the tradesman to whom he lends out his stock at interest. All the indolent and frivolous retainers upon a court are, in the same manner, fed, cloathed and lodged by the labour of those who pay the taxes and support them.[3]

In a civilized society, the poor wage-labourer, 'he who as it were supports the whole frame of society and furnishes the means of the convenience and ease of all the rest', was rewarded with a 'very small share' from his own productive labour and was 'buried in obscurity', 'thrust down into the lowest parts of the earth'.[4] He and the artisan bore on their backs not only landlords and monied men, but also a mass of 'unproductive labourers', whom Smith listed in the *Wealth of Nations*: menial servants, churchmen, lawyers, physicians, men of letters of all kinds; players, buffoons, musicians, opera-singers, opera-dancers, etc.; not to mention the most onerous burden of all, a standing army and 'the sovereign with all the officers of justice and war'.[5]

In primitive societies, however, although each retained the whole produce of labour, everyone was so 'miserably poor' that 'from mere want they are frequently reduced or at least think themselves reduced to the necessity sometimes of directly destroying and sometimes of abandoning their infants, their old people and those afflicted with lingering diseases to perish with hunger or to be devoured with wild beasts'.[6] Such societies were egalitarian, but theirs was the equality of poverty; they were incapable of freeing their populations from the grip of natural scarcity.

In commercial society, on the other hand, the division of produce was 'by no means made in proportion to the labour of each individual: on the contrary those who labour most get least'.[7] Yet 'in the midst of so much oppressive

---

[1] *WN* (1).4. The *Oxford English Dictionary* defines one of the meanings of the word 'paradox' as a statement contrary to received opinion, belief or expectation.
[2] *LJ(A)* vi.24.
[3] '"Early Draft" of Part of *The Wealth of Nations*' in A. Smith, *Lectures on Jurisprudence*, ed. R. L. Meek, D. D. Raphael, P. G. Stein (Oxford, 1978), 4; see also *LJ(B)* 213.
[4] *LJ(A)* vi.28; *ED* 6.   [5] *WN* II.iii.2.
[6] *WN* (1).4.   [7] *ED* 5; see also *WN* I.viii.5.

inequality', Smith asked, how was it possible to 'account for the superior affluence and abundance commonly possessed even by [the] lowest and most despised member of civilized society, compared with what the most respected and active savage can attain to?'[8] Why was it, as Smith said in the *Wealth of Nations*, that the 'industrious and frugal peasant' in a commercial society was able to live better than an 'African king, the absolute master of the lives and liberties of 10,000 naked savages?'[9] There was no economic mystery in the material well-being of 'the rich and powerful'. In any society he 'who can at all times direct the labours of 1000's to his own purposes' could be expected to live well. The distinctive feature of 'commercial society' was that those who 'provide both for themelves and for the enormous luxury of their superiors' should themselves be able to retain from the produce of their labour both the necessities and many of the simpler conveniences of life. This was the central question laid bare by any inquiry into the conjectural history of progress – why was it that a modern society which did not return the whole produce of labour to the labourer provide a better standard of living for the very poorest than the societies of the past? How was extreme inequality of distribution in modern society compatible with the satisfaction of the needs of its poorest working members?

For Smith the answer to this question lay in the distinctive productivity of modern division of labour. As he put it in the 'early draft', 'the division of labour by which each individual confines himself to a particular branch of business can alone account for the superior opulence which takes place in civilized societies and which, notwithstanding the inequality of property, extends itself to the lowest members of the community'. It was the division of labour which explained why 'so great a quantity of everything is produced that there is enough both to gratify the slothful and oppressive profusions of the great and at the same time abundantly to supply the wants of the artizan and peasant'. The division of labour accounted for the fact that in opulent societies labour was 'dear' while work or goods were 'cheap'.[10] In such societies, therefore, a 'liberal reward for labour' was a 'natural symptom of increasing national wealth' and not, as mercantilists and civic moralists alike supposed, a sign of incipient corruption.[11] Since the epoch of Colbert,

---

[8] *ED* 5–6.   [9] *WN* I.i.11; see also *LJ(A)* vi.21, 23; *LJ(B)* 212; *ED* 3.
[10] *ED* 11; see also *LJ(A)* vi.28; *LJ(B)* 213; *WN* I.i.1–11; on the relation between the division-of-labour analysis and the rhetoric of social inequality in Smith, see Andrew Skinner, *A System of Social Science: Papers Relating to Adam Smith* (London, 1980), p. 149n; also Donald Winch, *Adam Smith's Politics: An Essay in Historiographic Revision* (London, 1978), pp. 88–9.
[11] *WN* I.viii.42–4; on the reasons why real, and not merely money wages were increasing, in Smith's view, see *WN* I.viii.35, 52; on luxury and its corrupting effect on the poor's industry, see Ellen Ross, 'The Debate on Luxury in Eighteenth-Century France: A Study in the Language of Opposition to Change' (Ph.D. thesis, University of Chicago, 1975); S. M. Wade, Jr, 'The Idea of Luxury in Eighteenth-Century England' (Ph.D. thesis, Harvard University, 1968); John Sekora, *Luxury: The Concept in Western Thought, Eden to Smollett* (Baltimore, 1977).

advocates of the 'mercantile system' had insisted that keeping down wage costs was the key to maintaining competitive prices in international markets. Low wages, moreover, enforced the industry of the poor. Those few observers who believed that the labouring poor would respond to higher wages with higher output were unable to explain how the unit prices of goods sold abroad could be kept competitive with those manufactured in low-wage economies.[12] What Hume had found insupportable about low-wage strategies for economic growth was that a nation's progress was purchased at the expense of the 'happiness of so many millions of its own labourers'.[13] In his polemic with Josiah Tucker, he had argued for a world free-trade system in which rich countries would specialize in high-price, high-wage goods, while poor countries would concentrate on primary production, using their low-wage advantages to give them a toe-hold in the international division of labour. Smith emphatically accepted Hume's endorsement of a high-wage economy for the sake of its advantages for the labourer, and he was convinced that rich, high-wage countries could compete successfully against low-wage countries by reducing the unit price of their goods through the application of the division of labour. So decisive were the advantages of rich countries which resorted to the division of labour that only the commission of some 'great error' in their 'commercial police', such as loading taxes on subsistence goods and artificially driving up the price of labour, could cause them to forfeit their lead over poor countries.[14]

Smith was neither the first philosopher to point out the paradox of commercial society, nor the first to identify the division of labour as its solution. Anticipations of these themes can be found in the economic pamphlets of the post-Restoration period as well as in the natural jurisprudence tradition. Locke's property chapter in the *Second Treatise* and Mandeville's *Fable of the Bees*, for example, both contained the rudiments of a division of labour theory.[15]

---

[12] On 'mercantilist' wage policy, see T. E. Gregory, 'The Economics of Employment in England, 1660–1713', *Economica*, 1 (1921), 37–51; E. S. Furniss, *The Position of the Laborer in a System of Nationalism: A Study in the Labor Theories of the Later English Mercantilists* (New York, 1920); M. T. Wermel, *The Evolution of the Classical Wage Theory* (New York, 1939); Peter Mathias, 'Leisure and Wages in Theory and Practice', in his *The Transformation of England* (London, 1979), pp. 148–62; on political economy and the wages of the labouring poor, see A. W. Coats, 'Changing Attitudes to Labour in the Mid-Eighteenth Century', in M. W. Flinn and T. C. Smout (eds.), *Essays in Social History* (Oxford, 1974), pp. 78–99; and 'The Classical Economists and the Labourer', in A. W. Coats (ed.), *The Classical Economists and Economic Policy* (London, 1974), pp. 144–79; Richard C. Wiles, 'The Theory of Wages in Later English Mercantilism', *Economic History Review*, 2nd ser., 21 (1968), 113–26.

[13] David Hume, 'Of Commerce', *Philosophical Works*, iii, p. 267.

[14] *ED* 13; *LJ(A)* vi.34–5; *LJ(B)* 215; *WN* 1.i.4.

[15] See William Petty, *Political Arithmetick*, in C. H. Hull (ed.), *The Economic Writings of Sir William Petty*, 2 vols. (Cambridge, 1899), i. p. 260; John Locke, *Two Treatises of Government*, 2.5.42–3; [Henry Martyn], *Considerations on East India Trade* (London, 1690); Bernard Mandeville, *The Fable of the Bees*, ed. F. B. Kay, 2 vols. (Oxford, 1924), ii, p. 284. See also W. Letwin, *The Origins of Scientific Economics: English Economic Thought 1660–1776* (London, 1963); J. O. Appleby, *Economic Thought and Ideology in 17th-Century England* (Princeton, N.J., 1978).

Yet in the case of Mandeville, the argument was not linked to a vindication of a high-wage economy. Mandeville's strongly Augustinian insistence on the corrupting influence of luxury led him to conclude that rich countries would be pulled into a cycle of decline unless they used low wages to compel the poor to be industrious. Smith's decisive contribution was twofold: he provided an analytical demonstration that a high-wage economy, employing the division of labour, was not threatened with the Polybian cycle of decline into corruption; and he used this argument to invalidate those critiques of commercial modernity which appealed to the Christian ideal of the positive community of goods or to the slave republics of the virtuous classical past. He admitted the living force of 'levelling' and egalitarian ideology in his own time when he said that modern people were apt to look on a man of 'huge estate' as a 'pest to society, as a monster, a great fish who devours up all the lesser ones'.[16] Such a man, he insisted, 'eats no more than what any other man does' – i.e. his consumption of necessities did not deny the poor theirs, while his 'accumulation of stock' made it possible to extend the division of labour which rendered labour 'dear' and work 'cheap'. To be sure, he admitted, 'rent and profit eat up wages and the two superior orders of the people oppress the inferior one'.[17] But because modern economies were the first capable of sustained 'improvement', because they were the first to draw themselves beyond the cycle of luxury, corruption and decline, the share of the labourer could continue to grow in absolute terms, even though the oppression of the superior orders might prevent it from increasing in relative terms.

Smith's concern with inequality should be traced to his engagement with the natural jurisprudence tradition, rather than to the Anglo-Irish civic humanist discourse on political personality. In this latter discourse, inequality was a problem only in so far as the new fortunes created by commerce and speculation threatened the 'balance of the constitution'. The Country party and Commonwealthman opposition to the Walpolean ascendancy argued, for example, that the Court and the Ministry had entered into a corrupt alliance with the speculators enriched by the system of funded debt, to buy elections and subvert the independence of the Parliament. The focus of this discourse was upon maintaining equality among the political nation of franchise-holders, not between them and the unenfranchised poor.[18]

The central commitment of civic discourse, moreover, was to 'virtue', to

---

[16] *LJ(A)* iii.135; *TMS* IV.1.10.
[17] *WN* IV.vii.b.3; *WN* v.1.b.2; *WN* 1.xi.9.
[18] Caroline Robbins, *The Eighteenth-Century Commonwealthman: Studies in the Transmission, Development and Circumstance of English Liberal Thought from the Restoration of Charles II until the War with the Thirteen Colonies* (Cambridge, Mass., 1961); F. Raab, *The English Face of Machiavelli* (London, 1964); J. G. A. Pocock, *The Machiavellian Moment: Florentine Political Thought and the Atlantic Republican Tradition* (Princeton, N.J., 1975); I. Kramnick, *Bolingbroke and his Circle: The Politics of Nostalgia in the Age of Walpole* (Cambridge, Mass., 1963).

political activism among the propertied elite, while the central commitment of Hume and Smith was to justice. In civic discourse, the societies of Europe were compared in terms of their forms of government and of the degrees of political liberty they afforded to their political nation. In Humean and Smithian analysis, societies were to be compared on the basis of how securely they grounded rights of property and how adequately they met the needs of their labourers. This set of preferences is clear enough in Smith's dictum that no society could be considered happy 'if the far greater part of its members are poor and miserable'.[19] Hume had written that even the absolute monarchy of France, whom English Commonwealthmen and radical Whigs execrated as a despotism, was no less a 'regular government' than the English. Like the English, it guaranteed property and it met the needs of its poorest inhabitants. As Duncan Forbes has pointed out, the Humean line on 'regular government' pricked the balloon of the 'vulgar Whig' contrast between continental despotism and English liberty.[20]

Civic discourse, especially in its Scottish Fletcherian form, lamented the attenuation of martial virtue and the absorption in private self-interest of commercial peoples, exemplified in their delegation of martial functions to standing armies.[21] Smith's division of labour argument enabled him to take a radically different position on the historical development of the privatized personality of commercial men. In Book V, he took over the format of the history of property within the natural jurisprudence tradition and developed it into an account of the progressive delegation of civic and martial duties to state functionaries and standing armies as societies progressed from the hunting and gathering stage to the agricultural and commercial stages. Against those who lamented the loss of the undivided personality of the civic republics of ancient times, Smith insisted that it was only in 'the barbarous societies' that men could be at once both a producer and a 'statesman, a judge, a warrior'.[22] In the natural progress of opulence, men's increasing interdependence in the division of labour forced them to delegate civic and martial functions. Such a delegation

---

[19] *WN* I.viii.36.
[20] Duncan Forbes, *Hume's Philosophical Politics* (Cambridge, 1975), pp. 145–72; 'Sceptical Whiggism, Commerce and Liberty', in A. Skinner and T. Wilson (eds.), *Essays on Adam Smith* (Oxford, 1976), pp. 179–202; 'The European, or Cosmopolitan, Dimension in Hume's Science of Politics', *British Journal for Eighteenth-Century Studies*, 1 (1978), 57–60.
[21] Andrew Fletcher, 'A Discourse of Government with Relation to Militias', in *Selected Political Writings and Speeches*, ed. D. Daiches (Edinburgh, 1979). On the militia debate in England and Scotland, see L. G. Schwoerer, '*No Standing Armies!*': *The Antiarmy Ideology in Seventeenth-Century England* (London, 1974); J. R. Western, *The English Militia in the Eighteenth Century: The Story of a Political Issue* (London, 1965); John Robertson, 'The Improving Citizen: Militia Debates and Political Thought in the Scottish Enlightenment' (D.Phil. thesis, University of Oxford, 1980), and also his essay in this volume, pp. 137–78 below; Nicholas Phillipson, 'The Scottish Enlightenment', in R. Porter and M. Teich (eds.), *The Enlightenment in National Context* (Cambridge, 1981), pp. 19–40.
[22] *WN* V.i.a.1–20; *LJ(A)* iv.79; *LJ(B)* 335.

of unproductive functions by productive labour was crucial to increasing the yield of labour itself. Book V demonstrated that the disintegration of the undivided personality was irrevocably linked to commercial society's best feature – its capacity to feed and clothe its poorest members. For all his undoubted sympathy for the civic ideal of undivided personality and his advocacy of martial education to combat the stupefying and privatizing effects of the division of labour, Smith was convinced that it was impossible to restore human beings to an integrated identity as productive labourers and soldier-citizens.[23] Justice to the needs of the poor ought to have priority over civic virtue.

II. *The invisible hand*

Smith was concerned to theorize the resolution of the paradox of commercial society not only in economic terms – i.e. in the language of the division of labour – but also to explain a 'benevolent' result – i.e. the satisfaction of the basic needs of the poor – without imputing 'benevolent' intention to any of the contributory actors. In a market society, as he explained in his lectures and in the introductory chapters of the *Wealth of Nations*, although a 'man has almost constant occasion for the help of his brethren, it is in vain for him to expect it from their benevolence only'. To impute benevolence as a motive or a cause of the distributional results of modern society was to fail to take man as he really was, and also to neglect the fact that in commercial society these relations of benevolence were significantly weaker than they were in feudal society.[24] How was it exactly that in modern society we could count on our dinners by appealing not 'to the humanity' of the 'butcher, the brewer or the baker' but to their self-love?[25]

His other, and related, problem was to assess the moral quality of the mechanism – the generalized pursuit of material wealth – by which the end which he clearly endorsed – the liberal reward for labour – was achieved. It would be plausible to assume that he who valued the end would value the means. Certainly, Smith attached immense positive significance to the plain facts of a modern labourer's material abundance and he dissented strongly from the civic moralist jeremiads on the impact of luxury upon the morals and industry of the poor. Yet it is notorious, from his contemptuous references in the *Wealth of Nations* to the medieval lord's fascination for the 'baubles and trinkets' of trade goods, and from his sardonic strictures in the *Theory of Moral Sentiments* on men's passion for accumulating objects of 'frivolous utility', that he believed material prosperity was purchased, more often than not, at the price of a measure of what he himself called 'deception'.[26] At first sight, it is

[23] *WN* V.i.f.50–3; Pocock, *Machiavellian Moment*, pp. 458, 498.
[24] *WN* III.iv.13–16 on the conversion of feudal lords' expenditure from 'hospitality' to 'baubles and trinkets'; also *WN* II.ii.42.
[25] *WN* I.ii.2; *LJ(A)* vi.46; *LJ(B)* 220.   [26] *TMS* IV.1.6–10; *WN* III.iv.10.

not an easy task to reconcile his evident distaste for the vulgar materialism of the 'great scramble' of commercial society with his clear endorsement of economic growth. In the last edition of the *Theory of Moral Sentiments*, completed in the months before his death, he added a chapter which argued that 'the great and universal cause of the corruption of our moral sentiments' lay in the 'disposition to admire and almost to worship the rich and the powerful and to despise or at least to neglect persons of poor and mean conditions'.[27] This disposition was at the root of commercial men's material insatiability. Basic needs were capable of satisfaction, but the desire for pleasure, channelled in commercial society into the accumulation of 'baubles and trinkets', was 'altogether endless'.[28] These material desires were insatiable because men judged their individual satisfaction in comparison to those higher or lower in the ranks system of an unequal society. It was inequality in conditions of economic progress which fuelled the particular material 'avidity' of modern commercial men. Smith and Hume were careful to historicize this propensity: in more equal and backward societies, the incentives and opportunities for material accumulation were limited. Hume explained in 'Of Commerce' that exclusively agricultural societies were fated to remain locked in backwardness and 'indolence' as long as incentives, in the form of manufactured goods, were lacking to induce farmers to produce marketable surpluses.[29] Smith agreed: 'our ancestors were idle for want of a sufficient encouragement to industry'. As residents themselves of a poor country on the periphery of European economic development, they were both made keenly aware that, far from being able to take 'economic man' for granted in their analysis, they had to explain his historical possibility as a psychological type.[30] Only in commercial societies, with the emergence of a town–country division of labour, as Smith explained

---

[27] The 'great scramble of human society' is at *LJ(A)* iv.163. For the whole argument, see the whole of Part 1, section III, chapter 11 of *TMS*, 'Of the Origin of Ambition, and of the Distinction of Ranks'.

[28] *WN* I.xi.c.7.

[29] Hume, 'Of Commerce', p. 203. See Eugene Rotwein's 'Introduction' to David Hume, *Economic Writings*, ed. E. Rotwein (Edinburgh, 1955), ch. 2, 'The Outlines of the Natural History: Hume's Economic Psychology', pp. xxxii–liii.

[30] *WN* II.iii.12; also *LJ(B)* 207–9. On the influence of Scotland's status as a province upon Scottish thought, see N. Phillipson, 'Culture and Society in the 18th Century Province: The Case of Edinburgh and the Scottish Enlightenment', in L. Stone (ed.), *The University in Society*, 2 vols. (Princeton, N.J., 1974), ii, pp. 407–48; on Scottish economic backwardness and its periphery status in the metropolitan economy, see T. C. Smout, 'Centre and Periphery in History; with Some Thoughts on Scotland as a Case Study', *Journal of Common Market Studies*, 18 (1980), 256–71; and also his 'Scotland and England: Is Dependency a Symptom or a Cause of Underdevelopment?', *Review*, 3 (1980), 601–30, and Immanuel Wallerstein's answer, 'One Man's Meat: The Scottish Leap Forward', *Review*, 3 (1980), 631–40; also E. J. Hobsbawm, 'Scottish Reformers of the 18th Century and Capitalist Agriculture', in E. J. Hobsbawm (ed.), *Peasants in History: Essays in Honour of Daniel Thorner* (Calcutta, 1980), pp. 3–29. On Highland backwardness, see A. T. Youngson, *After the Forty-Five: The Economic Impact on the Scottish Highlands* (Edinburgh, 1973).

in the 'baubles and trinkets' passage of Book III, had the purely privatized drive for the accumulation of commodities become the ruling principle of every individual.

Yet this distinctively modern pursuit of 'baubles and trinkets', not for themselves but for the esteem they would bring, not for their real utility but for their symbolic or aesthetic signification, was built upon a deception – that wealth would bring happiness. The game, Smith insisted, was hardly worth the candle. 'Power and riches' were enormous 'machines' which required the labour of a lifetime to create and which, while made to give their possessors happiness, could not protect them from the real sorrows of life:

They keep off the summer shower, not the winter storm, but leave him always as much, and sometimes more exposed than before, to anxiety, to fear and to sorrow; to diseases, to danger and to death.[31]

This is Smith at his most darkly Stoic. It was the Stoics, he said, who had rightly taught that 'happiness was altogether or at least in great measure independent of fortune'.[32] Besides the classic Stoic texts – Zeno, Epictetus, Cicero – Smith had also meditated upon the modern discourses on the 'vanity of human wishes', chief among these being Rousseau's *Second Discourse*, which Smith examined at length in his *Edinburgh Review* article of 1755. Rousseau is an important if unavowed interlocutor in the passages in the *Theory of Moral Sentiments* which Smith devoted to the pursuit of wealth in modern society.[33]

Smith broke decisively with the modern Stoic and Rousseauian critique of modern deception. 'It is well that nature imposes upon us in this manner', he wrote. Were the majority of human beings capable of Stoic *ataraxia*, were they capable of seeing through the lure of baubles and trinkets, and were they to act upon their occasional flights of nostalgia for a life of detached and Stoic simplicity, the species would have been condemned to an eternity of egalitarian barbarism. It was the ever-receding lure of happiness in material things which 'first prompted men to cultivate the ground, to build houses, to found cities and commonwealths and to invent all the sciences and arts which ennoble and embellish human life'. It was true, as moralists charged, that the rich 'sought only the gratification of their own vain and insatiable desires', but their stomachs were no bigger than those of poor men. They could not, by their own consumption of food, starve the poor of their necessities, as Rousseau supposed when he painted a picture of the 'privileged few gorging themselves with superfluities, while the starving multitude are in want of the bare necessities of life'. The consumption of rich and poor in basic necessities was not a 'zero-sum game'. The demand of the rich set in motion a cycle of production and

---

[31] *TMS* IV.1.8.
[32] *TMS* VII.ii.1.20–1; on Stoicism in Smith, see A. L. Macfie, *The Individual in Society: Papers on Adam Smith* (London, 1967), pp. 72–81; J. Ralph Lindgren, *The Social Philosophy of Adam Smith* (The Hague, 1973), p. 35.
[33] 'Letters to the Editors of the *Edinburgh Review*' (1755), in *EPS* 13.

employment which 'by an invisible hand' led a commercial society 'to make nearly the same distribution of the necessaries of life which would have been made had the earth been divided into equal portions among all its inhabitants'. Thus, 'without intending it, without knowing it' and certainly without benevolently desiring it, the rich 'advance the interest of society and afford means to the multiplication of the species'.[34]

The 'invisible hand' passage in the *Theory of Moral Sentiments* explained the paradox of commercial society as an outcome of unintended consequences – the subsistence needs of the poor being served through a machine kept in motion by the blind cupidity of the rich. This has sometimes been taken as a Mandevillian solution – justifying private vice in terms of its public benefits. In his reply to Berkeley, however, Mandeville made it clear that his was not an argument from unintended consequences. Public benefits could only be drawn forth from private vice if there was a statesman at the helm constantly regulating the circulation of private interest.[35] Smith himself took pains to reject the Mandevillian position which, he argued, had labelled as 'vice' a range of private activities which could only be justly regarded as vicious if pursued in excess or with harm to others. Mandeville was in fact a strict moralist, condemning commercial society by an ascetic standard of virtue to which in everyday life no ordinary mortal could aspire.[36] The task of a realistic account of moral sentiments was to explain, not how 'a perfect being' should act, but 'how so weak and imperfect a creature as man actually and in fact' acts. In practice, ordinary men's self-interest was constrained by their need for the approval of others. Since men, as Malebranche and Hume had said, were mirrors to each other, each man's self-respect, his *amour de soi* as Rousseau had called it, depended on the approving gaze of the other.[37] This need for approval

---

[34] The passage from Rousseau is from *A Discourse on the Origin of Inequality*, in J. J. Rousseau, *The Social Contract and Discourses*, trans. G. D. H. Cole, rev. J. H. Brumfitt and J. C. Hall (London, 1973), p. 105. All of the quotations from Smith are from the 'invisible hand' passage in *TMS* IV.1.10; see also *WN* IV.ii.9; on the Smith–Rousseau relationship, see E. G. West, 'Adam Smith and Rousseau's *Discourse on Inequality*: Inspiration or Provocation?', *Journal of Economic Issues*, 5 (1971), 56–70.

[35] B. Mandeville, *A Letter to Dion, Occasion'd by his Book call'd Alciphron, or the Minute Philosopher* (London, 1732), pp. 36–7. For a commentary, see Jacob Viner, 'Introduction to Bernard Mandeville, "A Letter to Dion" (1732)', in *The Long View and the Short: Studies in Economic Theory and Policy* (Glencoe, Illinois, 1958), pp. 332–42; and George Davie, 'Berkeley, Hume, and the Central Problem of Scottish Philosophy', in D. F. Norton, N. Capaldi and W. L. Robison (eds.), *McGill Hume Studies* (San Diego, Calif., 1979), pp. 43–62.

[36] *TMS* VII.ii.4.6–13.

[37] Rousseau, *Discourse on Inequality*, p. 66n; Hume, *Treatise*, p. 365. For a discussion of similar ideas in Malebranche and their influence on Hume, see Forbes, *Hume's Philosophical Politics*, pp. 8–10, and 'Hume and the Scottish Enlightenment', in S. C. Brown (ed.), *The Philosophers of the Enlightenment*, Royal Institute of Philosophy Lectures, xii (Hassocks, Sussex, 1979), pp. 99–101. For an interesting discussion of the origins of the *amour de soi–amour propre* dualism in French philosophical and moral thought, see Nannerl O. Keohane, *Philosophy and the State in France: The Renaissance to the Enlightenment* (Princeton, N.J., 1980).

was the check which self-interest imposed upon itself. It guaranteed that ordinary men could be counted on to obey society's rules of propriety. Mandeville had called this need for the approval of others 'vanity' and in doing so, Smith argued, he had confused the 'frivolous desire of praise at any rate', which was simply selfishness by another route, with the desire to 'deserve' the praise of others, which was necessary to a human being's self-esteem. Men, Smith went on, were neither incapable of, nor indifferent to, the distinction between winning and deserving praise. They did indeed seek to deserve praise, and this guaranteed that the competitive search for social esteem was not simply a game of vain deception and self-deception.

Moreover, Smith contended that 'the passion for present enjoyment', the often 'violent' and essentially insatiable pursuit of material 'baubles and trinkets', had to be distinguished from the 'calm and dispassionate' desire for self-improvement. The latter 'interest', Smith argued, 'seems not only to predominate, but to predominate very greatly' over the 'passion' for present enjoyment. Were this not so, Smith maintained, we could not give any account of the immense accumulation of capital and stock in modern commercial societies. The predominance of the principle of 'frugality' over the principle of 'expense' in commercial men's vocabulary of motives indicated that they were capable of self-restraint in the pursuit of self-betterment and were not simply swept away in a deluded scramble after things.[38]

Against Mandeville, and Rousseau, Smith insisted that economic self-interest did check itself, through self-imposed observance of the rules of propriety and the calculus of saving for the future. The pursuit of 'baubles and trinkets' by a whole society was deluded, but its moral quality was validated by its immensely positive unintended result, provided of course that economic self-seeking was constrained by the disciplines of free competition. Smithian propriety required for its enforcement a free market society. The road to virtue and the road to fortune, he explained, were one and the same in those ranks where market success itself depended on a reputation for probity and propriety – i.e. among the independent professional men, manufacturers, and tradesmen of the middling sort.[39] The chief danger to propriety in a market society came from those great merchants and monopolists whose market power enabled them to 'widen the market and narrow the competition' against the public interest.[40] The 'system of natural liberty' which Smith advocated thus had the normative purpose of guaranteeing the economic conditions of competition necessary for the enforcement of common rules of propriety in market relations.

[38] *WN* II.iii.28; *WN* I.xi.c.7. Albert Hirschman argues that Smith collapses the distinction between self-love and self-esteem; see A. O. Hirschman, *The Passions and the Interests: Political Arguments for Capitalism before Its Triumph* (Princeton, N.J., 1977), pp. 100–13.
[39] *TMS* I.iii.3.5.
[40] *WN* IV.iii.c.9; I.x.c.27; I.x.p.10.

III. Moral economy, police and political economy: the grain trade debate

If, as Smith had argued in the 'invisible hand' passage of the *Theory of Moral Sentiments*, the moral legitimacy of distribution in commercial society lay in the fact that those who were 'left out in the partition' of property, i.e. the wage-earning poor, received adequate subsistence, it remained for him to explain in the *Wealth of Nations* exactly how this was achieved. In a commercial society, wage-labourers were 'independent': that is, they did not depend upon their masters to provide them with subsistence, and their rate of remuneration was determined by the supply and demand for labour and by the customs of their trade, and only ultimately by what was necessary for their bare subsistence. Smith and Hume gave the strongest positive endorsement to modern 'independence': it was this praise of independence which put a distance between them and the civic humanist nostalgia for a classical ideal of citizenship which was economically dependent upon the delegation of productive labour to slaves.[41] Yet those who did consider the example of the classical ideal as well as the more recent heritage of 'feudal dependency' – Andrew Fletcher, John Millar and, in some measure, Robert Wallace and James Steuart – pointed out that the subsistence of dependents had been guaranteed by their masters, and asked how the subsistence of modern wage-labourers was to be guaranteed.[42] Given the recurrence of dearth, even famine, and the omnipresence of underemployment in the European economies of their day, it was natural for even those who styled themselves political economists to suppose that the subsistence of the labouring poor could only be safeguarded by a 'police' of the market in grain, by magistrates and central authorities, to ensure adequate stockpiling in case of famine and to regulate subsistence prices even in high-price years. The 'police' of grain was the central element of 'mercantilist' regulation of the economy in all *ancien régime* societies; no society, as Polanyi once said, can be considered a fully market society until

---

[41] David Hume, 'Of the Populousness of Ancient Nations', *Philosophical Works*, iii, p. 385. Speaking about domestic slavery, Hume remarked: 'Some passionate admirers of the ancients, and zealous partizans of civil liberty, (for these sentiments, as they are, both of them, in the main, extremely just, are found to be almost inseparable) cannot forbear regretting the loss of this institution; and whilst they brand all submission to the government of a single person with the harsh denomination of slavery, they would gladly reduce the greater part of mankind to real slavery and subjection.' Compare this with *LJ(A)* vi.6.

[42] Andrew Fletcher, 'The Second Discourse Concerning the Affairs of Scotland Written in the Year 1698', in *Selected Political Writings*, ed. D. Daiches, pp. 46–58; Robert Wallace, *A Dissertation on the Numbers of Mankind in Antient and Modern Times; in which the Superior Populousness of Antiquity is Maintained. With an Appendix, Containing Additional Observations on the Same Subject, and Some Remarks on Mr Hume's Political Discourse, Of the Populousness of Antient Nations* (Edinburgh, 1753), pp. 22–4; James Steuart, *An Inquiry into the Principles of Political Oeconomy*, ed. A. S. Skinner, 2 vols. (Edinburgh, 1966), i, p. 51; John Millar, 'The Origin of the Distinction of Ranks', in W. C. Lehmann, *John Millar of Glasgow 1735–1801: His Life and Thought and his Contributions to Sociological Analysis* (Cambridge, 1960), pp. 300–4.

it dismantles such a structure and allows a free market in subsistence goods. To question the necessity of a 'police' in grain was to challenge the 'right to subsistence' of the labouring poor which *ancien régime* governments had always been obliged to honour and which the French Revolution only reiterated for modern times as a natural right.[43] This was precisely the cluster of assumptions which Smith's 'system of natural liberty' seemed to put into question. The most radical of all his theoretical claims, both in his own day and since, was that if the market for labour and the market in food were freed of meddling interventions, in the long run the price of labour and the price of food would balance out in such a way that the labouring poor would never go hungry. It was this claim which earned Smith the reputation, even in his own day, of being a dogmatic 'projector' for the application of long-term models of natural market processes as a guide for practical policy.[44] The European grain-trade debates of the 1760s, in which Smith's thought took shape, were a crucial battleground for the reception of the idea of natural economic order. The debates divided *philosophes* and *économistes* into those like Smith and the Physiocrats who believed that food should be a 'natural' commodity like any other, which should be left to find its own price, and those like James Steuart and Abbé Galiani who believed that food was a 'political' commodity whose price should be regulated, in situations of grave necessity at least, by the government. The debate was not only about how far market forces should be left to themselves; it was also about property. Since the grain clearly belonged to somebody, the crucial issue was whether the government should align the force of law with the property rights of grain merchants or with the claims of the poor in distress? The debate was also about the uses of natural modelling itself. Since human beings starve in the short term rather than in the long, the problem of guaranteeing food supply in a free market was the sharpest possible practical challenge to the correctness of long-term natural models as guides for practical policy.

Edward Thompson would have us understand the debates over bread prices and the grain trade in eighteenth-century England as an encounter between the new political economy and a 'moral economy' of the crowd which was a popular reflection of a paternalist body of regulation dating back to the days of Elizabeth.[45] This structure of market supervision and consumer protection

---

[43] Karl Polanyi, 'The Economy as Instituted Process', in K. Polanyi, C. M. Arensberg and H. W. Pearson (eds.), *Trade and Market in the Early Empires: Economies in History and Theory* (New York, 1957), p. 255.

[44] See, for example, the critique by James Anderson, *Observations on the Means of Exciting a Spirit of National Industry* (Edinburgh, 1777), p. 355; also *A Letter from Governor Pownall to Adam Smith* [1776], in Smith, *Correspondence*, p. 340.

[45] E. P. Thompson, 'The Moral Economy of the English Crowd in the Eighteenth Century', *Past and Present*, no. 50 (1971), 76–136; also A. W. Coats, 'Contrary Moralities: Plebs, Paternalists and Political Economists', *Past and Present*, no. 58 (1973), 130–3; Elizabeth Fox-Genovese, 'The Many Faces of Moral Economy: A Contribution to a Debate', *Past and Present*, no. 58

was infrequently enforced, lapsing during times of good harvest and moderate prices, but invoked again in crisis years. It was by no means a dead letter, and whenever magistrates were slow to act or resistant to enforcing its provisions, the crowd was quick to exert the pressure of demonstration and riot to force the magistrates to regulate the market place. If magistrates refused, the poor took the matter in their own hands, intercepting shipments of grain, breaking open granaries and distributing supplies at 'just' prices. By recovering the moral economy of the poor and the regulatory system to which they made appeal, Thompson has set the iconoclasm of the Smithian position in sharp relief, crediting him with the first theory to revoke the traditional social responsibility attached to property. Yet the antinomy – moral economy versus political economy – caricatures both positions. The one becomes a vestigial, traditional moralism, the other a science 'disinfested of intrusive moral imperatives'. To the extent that favouring an adequate subsistence for the poor can be called a moral imperative, it was one shared by paternalists and political economists alike. Smith's case for dismantling the Assize of Bread, for example, was not based on dogma for its own sake, but on the claim that the Assize had kept the price of loaves above their natural competitive price. Likewise, he opposed export bounties because they distorted the price of corn for the benefit of the farmer at the expense of the consumer.[46] On the other hand, to call the moral economy traditionalist is to portray it simply as a set of vestigial moral preferences innocent of substantive argument about the working of markets. In fact, so-called traditionalists were quite capable of arguing their position on the same terrain as their political economist opponents. Indeed, and this is the crucial point, debate over market or 'police' strategies for providing subsistence for the poor divided philosophers and political economists among themselves no less deeply than it divided the crowd from Smith. Indeed, it makes no sense to take Smith as typical of the range of opinion within the European Enlightenment camp. This becomes apparent if one moves beyond the English context, to which Thompson confines his discussion, and considers the debate in its full European setting. The crucial context for Smith's 'Digression on Grain' was not the encounter with the English or Scottish crowd, but the French debates over the liberalization of the internal trade in 1764–6, which occurred, it should be remembered, when Smith himself was in France.

Between May 1763 and July 1764, the police of the grain trade in France was withdrawn by a series of edicts allowing anyone to deal in grain, ending the requirement of public-market sale, abolishing the intendants' power to

---

(1973), 161–8; and P. S. Atiyah, *The Rise and Fall of Freedom of Contract* (Oxford, 1979), pp. 62–5. On the European context, see Charles Tilly, 'Food Supply and Public Order in Modern Europe', in C. Tilly (ed.), *The Formation of National States in Western Europe* (Princeton, N.J., 1975), pp. 380–445.

[46] *WN* I.x.c.62; *WN* IV.v.a.6.

commandeer grain supplies in times of dearth and freeing the import and export of grain up to a certain price threshold.[47] As was the case in England, free trade in grain was not a contentious issue as long as harvests were adequate. Thus, prior to these edicts, the royal administration had adopted a policy of benign neglect towards the grain market in good years. The issue at stake was whether they should continue to step in to suspend the property rights of grain merchants and landowners when high prices threatened to cause hardship and unrest among poor consumers.

The liberalization of the internal trade had been proposed throughout the eighteenth century, but it was the Physiocrats who made the most complete analytical case in economic terms. Their argument was that the freedom of the trade would raise agricultural prices and draw investment into agriculture away from what Quesnay called 'the improper employment of men and wealth in the manufacture of luxury goods.'[48] With a strong agriculture, France could become fully self-sufficient in food, using grain exports to purchase 'sterile' luxury goods manufactured in countries like Holland and Switzerland which could not produce enough food of their own. High agricultural prices would increase the productivity of agriculture and improve supply. As Quesnay put it, 'abundance plus dearness equals opulence'. High prices would not endanger the wage-earning poor because their money wages would rise in equivalent amounts, while the productivity effects of high prices would guarantee that farmers' profits, proprietors' revenue and the king's tax income would all increase ahead of the increase in wage costs. The key to Quesnay's whole argument was his insistence on inverting the old commonplace which equated good times with cheap prices. 'Enforced poverty', he insisted, was 'not the way to render the peasants industrious'. He wanted to lift the whole economy out of its low-price equilibrium which he saw as a cycle of perpetual poverty. Quesnay's economic arguments in turn were supported, as he made clear in his *Encyclopédie* article on 'natural right', by the contention that absolute property right, in this case in grain, was crucial to creating the incentive for improvements to agricultural productivity. Systems of police which requisitioned grain from their owners fatally compromised these incentive effects.

[47] Steven L. Kaplan, *Bread, Politics and Political Economy in the Reign of Louis XV*, 2 vols. (The Hague, 1976), i, pp. 90-101; on French 'police' in general, see Olwen Hufton, *The Poor of Eighteenth-Century France* (Oxford, 1974). For a description of the general European 'mercantilist' provisioning policy, see Eli F. Heckscher, *Mercantilism*, trans. M. Shapiro, 2 vols. (London, 1935), ii, pp. 80-112.

[48] The cited material is from Quesnay's *Encyclopédie* article, 'Corn', and from the 'General Maxims for the Economic Government of an Agricultural Kingdom', as translated in Ronald L. Meek (ed.), *The Economics of Physiocracy: Essays and Translation* (Cambridge, 1963), pp. 84-6, 235, 255-9; for the original texts, see *François Quesnay et la Physiocratie*, 2 vols. (Paris, 1958); see also Elizabeth Fox-Genovese, *The Origins of Physiocracy: Economic Revolution and Social Order in Eighteenth-Century France* (Ithaca, N.Y., 1976); Georges Weulersse, *Le Mouvement physiocratique en France (de 1756 à 1770)*, 2 vols. (Paris, 1910).

Quesnay's model and the French policy experiment which it supported turned out to be vulnerable to the stubborn niggardliness of eighteenth-century grain supply. As long as harvests were adequate, protests against liberalization were muted, but once harvests went short in 1768–9 and prices began to rise sharply, many philosophers who had been 'friends of liberty' drew back from their earlier enthusiasms. The ensuing debate – which pitted Galiani, Diderot, Voltaire, Necker, Grimm, Linguet and Mably against Quesnay, Baudeau, Roubaud, Dupont, Mercier, Morellet and Condorcet – split the 'party of humanity' down the middle, between those who insisted that government must stabilize prices in the short term to prevent harm to the poor and those who maintained that such interference jeopardized a long-term solution to the recurring crises in agricultural productivity.[49] This was not a debate between modernity and traditionalism. Many of those who spoke for liberty in every other sphere drew back on the question of liberty in grain. Diderot, for example, supported Turgot on the abolition of artisanal corporations, but not on the grain trade.[50]

The most influential attack on liberalization came from someone who was himself a political economist, author of a formidable treatise on money, Abbé Galiani. His *Dialogues sur le Commerce des Bléds* of 1770 can be read as a rueful reconsideration of the virtues of natural liberty which his earlier economic writing had celebrated. Franco Venturi suggests in fact that it was Galiani's experience of the Tuscan famine of 1764–5 which caused him to rethink his earlier enthusiasms.[51] The skeletal poor covered with sores and vermin whom he had seen in the street with his own eyes left him convinced that subsistence could not be left either to the 'natural' force of the harvest or the market place.

[49] Kaplan, *Bread, Politics and Political Economy*, i, pp. 152–7, vol. 2, pp. 591–606; see also Keith M. Baker, *Condorcet: From Natural Philosophy to Social Mathematics* (Chicago, 1975); I. F. Knight, *The Geometric Spirit: The Abbé de Condillac and the French Enlightenment* (New Haven, Conn., 1968); Robert D. Harris, *Necker: Reform Statesman of the Ancien Régime* (Berkeley, Calif., 1979); James J. McLain, *The Economic Writings of Du Pont de Nemours* (New York, 1977); Darline Gay Levy, *The Ideas and Careers of Simon-Nicolas-Henri Linguet* (Chicago, 1980); Ira O. Wade, *The Structure and Form of the French Enlightenment*, 2 vols. (Princeton, N.J., 1977), particularly the chapter on '"Moeurs", "Lois", and Economics', i, pp. 435–515.

[50] For Diderot's positions on the law of corporations, see W. H. Sewell, *Work and Revolution in France: The Language of Labour from the Old Régime to 1848* (Cambridge, 1980), pp. 65–72; also A. Strugnell, *Diderot's Politics: A Study of the Evolution of Diderot's Political Thought* (The Hague, 1973); H. C. Payne, *The Philosophes and the People* (New Haven, Conn., 1976), p. 146.

[51] Ferdinando Galiani, *Dialogues sur le Commerce des Bleds* (London, 1770), p. 2. On Galiani, see Kaplan, *Bread, Politics and Political Economy*, vol. 1, pp. 594–606; and his 'Introduction' in *La Bagarre: Galiani's 'Lost' Parody*, ed. S. Kaplan (The Hague, 1979); Franco Venturi, 'The Position of Galiani between the Encyclopedists and the Physiocrats', in *Italy and the Enlightenment: Studies in a Cosmopolitan Century*, trans. S. Corsi (London, 1972), pp. 180–97; M. Minerbi, 'Diderot, Galiani e la polemica sulla fisiocrazia (1767–1771)', *Studi Storici*, 14 (1973), 148–63; Philip Koch, Introduction and Appendix B, 'The Dialogues after Publication', in Fernando Galiani, *Dialogues entre M. Marquis De Roquemaure, et Ms. Le Chevalier Zanobi: The Autograph Manuscript of the 'Dialogues sue le Commerce des Bleds'*, ed. P. Koch (Frankfurt-on-Main, 1968), pp. 1–51, 316–41.

The objective of modern policy, he said, was not to submit to nature's laws but to use human reason to ensure that society was never at her mercy. Nothing was truer in theory, he said, than that a system of free internal trade would allow grain to flow naturally from areas of surfeit to areas of scarcity, seeking the highest price and thus bringing supply and demand into balance. Yet such theories of the natural long-term process were dangerous because they simply ignored short-term frictions. Any failure of local supply, be it a delay of as little as a week, could bring starvation in its wake. Men, he said pointedly, eat real bread, not potential bread. If free exportation were allowed, the triggering mechanism of the ceiling price might not operate quickly enough to redirect supplies from export to areas of domestic dearth, especially in an economy dogged with poor transport. If national grain dealers were allowed unlimited freedom of purchase in local markets, they would buy up all of the grain before the needs of the local poor were met. Galiani was not opposed to freedom of trade in years of plentiful supply. In such times, national purchasing agents served a useful purpose in equilibrating supply among regions. Yet free trade was positively dangerous in high-price years. It was all very well to consider 'letting the sails free to the wind' when the sea was calm; but any prudent helmsman of state 'would trim his sails when the sea got rough'. Accordingly, he insisted that the state retain its authority to commandeer supplies and to force local farmers to sell in small lots to the local poor before disposing of the surplus to grain dealers. In essence, his position was that once the priority of distributive justice had been served, the property rights of landlords and merchants could be allowed their head. It was this position, and not that of the Physiocrats, which carried the day. The administration of Terray introduced a national grain police between 1769 and 1774.[52] After Turgot's attempt to return to free trade in grain was exploded in the *guerre des farines* of 1775, the Physiocratic school disintegrated and the police of the grain trade was brought back.[53] It endured until the Revolution. By 1776, Smith remained the only standard-bearer for 'natural liberty' in grain.

These French debates were closely paralleled in Scotland. James Steuart had been educated in the language of continental natural jurisprudence and had spent some of his years as a Jacobite exile in Tübingen, where he became familiar with the German science of 'police' – *Polizeiwissenschaft*.[54] In the

[52] René Girard, *L'Abbé Terray et la liberté du commerce des grains, 1769–1774* (Paris, 1924).
[53] Kaplan, *Bread, Politics and Political Economy*, ii, p. 606; on Turgot, see Condorcet, *The Life of M. Turgot* (London, 1787); D. Dakin, *Turgot and the Ancien Régime in France* (London, 1939); R. L. Meek (ed.), *Turgot on Progress, Sociology and Economics* (Cambridge, 1973).
[54] On Steuart's sojourn in Germany, see Paul Chamley, *Documents Relatifs à Sir James Steuart* (Paris, 1965); Andrew Skinner's 'Introduction' to his edition of Steuart's *Political Oeconomy*, (Edinburgh, 1966); on *Polizeiwissenschaft*, see F. L. Knemeyer, 'Polizei', *Economy and Society*, 9 (1980), 168–96; A. W. Small, *The Cameralists* (Chicago, 1909); M. Walker, 'Rights and Functions: The Social Categories of Eighteenth-Century German Jurists and Cameralists', *Journal of Modern History*, 50 (1978), 234–51.

Scottish context of recurrent arguments from the mid 1750s until the 1770s about how to provision the towns and how to regulate the import and export of grain and oatmeal, Steuart took a line consistent with *Polizeiwissenschaft* and with the Galiani position. While he is often understood as a paternal traditionalist, he was nearly as accomplished an analyst of the economy as a natural process as Smith. What he denied insistently was that the 'natural course of things' in the long term should constitute the definitive guide for the 'art' of economic policy. He said that natural causes should never be allowed to run unchecked when the effects would be followed by injustice.[55] It was the local government's job to make economic circumstances conform to justice. Nowhere was the intervention of 'the statesman' more necessary than in the market of subsistence goods. Even if prices were self-correcting in the long term, in the short term panic-buying, hoarding and speculation could cause real misery to the poor and unleash the avoidable disorders of 'meal mobs'.[56] It was to prevent such 'sudden revolutions in the prices of markets' that Steuart proposed the public stockpiling of grain in state granaries and the orderly sale of this grain in times of high price. As an additional measure of price stabilization, he endorsed a duty on imported grain and a bounty on exports. He had no quarrel with the argument that high prices were the key to increasing agricultural productivity, but insisted on a mechanism to reconcile high prices with regular subsistence for both the labouring poor and those dependent on charity.

While Steuart's public granary scheme would have required more administrative capacity than most local governments of the time were capable of, his import and bounty proposals were closer to the common sense of his day. Such a system had been a feature of English Corn Law legislation since the Restoration, and the most recent act of 1772 instituted a bounty and import system which shut off exports and allowed in imports whenever the domestic price rose above 48 shillings per bushel. This was designed to reconcile high agricultural prices for producers with price stability and adequate supply for consumers. The act also repealed Elizabethan legislation against forestalling

[55] Steuart, *Political Oeconomy*, ii, p. 238; also *ibid.*, p. 254.
[56] James Steuart, 'A Dissertation on the Policy of Grain With a View to a Plan for preventing Scarcity of Exorbitant Prices in the Common Markets of England' and 'Considerations on the Interests of the County of Lanark in Scotland', in *Works, Political, Metaphisical, and Chronological of the Late Sir James Steuart of Coltness, Bart.*, 6 vols. (London, 1805), v, pp. 347-77, 286-345. For similar plans in Scotland in the period, see the pamphlet *The Causes of the Scarcity of Oat-Meal in the Public Market of Glasgow; with an easy Method proposed for preventing that Evil in Time coming, in a Letter to a Friend* (Edinburgh, 1763). On Scottish grain prices, see Rosalind Mitchison, 'The Movements of Scottish Corn Prices in the 17th and 18th Centuries', *Economic History Review*, 2nd ser., 18 (1965), 278-91; on the response amongst landowners, see Rosalind Mitchison, 'Scottish Landowners and Communal Responsibility in the 18th Century', *British Journal for Eighteenth-Century Studies*, 1 (1978), 41-5; and T. C. Smout, 'Famine and Famine-relief in Scotland', in L. M. Cullen and T. C. Smout (eds.), *Comparative Aspects of Scottish and Irish Economic and Social History 1600-1900* (Edinburgh, 1976), pp. 21-31.

and regrating – the practices, that is, of speculative purchasing and avoiding local markets by direct purchase from farmers. The act, in other words, steered a middle course between liberalization and 'police'.[57]

If the act of 1772 incarnated the cautious common sense of the day, Smith's comments on it indicate how far beyond the common sense consensus his advocacy of 'natural liberty' had taken him. The act, he said resignedly, was 'the best which the interest, prejudices and temper of the times would admit of'.[58] Import duties were a political inevitability, given the prejudices and influence of the farmers, but 'were all nations to follow the liberal system of free exportation and free importation', he wrote, the whole continent's agricultural production would come to be specialized where yields were greatest. Smith insisted that protectionism actually 'aggravate[d] the unavoidable misfortune of a dearth into the dreadful calamity of a famine' by obstructing the free flow of grain to where it was needed most.[59]

Smith's endorsement of freedom in the internal trade was no less uncompromising. He regarded the laws against speculation in grain and those regulations requiring farmers to sell first in local markets as nothing less than an invasion of the rights of property:

> To hinder...the farmer from sending his goods at all times to the best market, is evidently to sacrifice the ordinary laws of justice to an idea of publick utility, to a sort of reasons of state – an act of legislative authority which ought to be exercised only, which can be pardoned only in cases of the most urgent necessity.[60]

Hume had taken it for granted that magistrates had the right to open private

---

[57] 13 George III, c. 43 (1772).
[58] *WN* IV.v.b.53. It was in connection with the free importation clauses of the Corn Bill for Scotland of 1777, an amendment to the 1772 British Corn Law, that James Steuart found that the 'Glasgow Theorists' had taken the advice of Smith, who in the *Wealth of Nations* had 'pointed in favour of free Importation'. See Steuart's memorial on the corn laws, 14 October 1777, in Appendix B to A. Skinner's edition of the *Political Oeconomy*, ii, pp. 737–8. For the arguments of the Glasgow manufacturers, see the following pamphlets: *Memorial for the Merchants, Traders and Manufacturers of Glasgow* (n.p.; n.d.) [Glasgow, 1777]; *Corn-Bill Hints in Answer to the Memorial for the Merchants, Traders and Manufacturers of the City of Glasgow* (Glasgow, n.d. [1777]); *Thoughts Occasioned by Reading a Memorial for the Merchants, Traders and Manufacturers of Glasgow, dated 2d May 1777, respecting the Proposed New Corn Bill, presently depending in Parliament* (Edinburgh, n.d. [1777]). In connection with the debate on the Corn Law Amendment, Thomas Reid, Smith's successor as Professor of Moral Philosophy at the University of Glasgow, also wrote an interesting paper answering the Literary Society's question: 'Whether the Storing and Warehousing of foreign Grain or Meal for Reexportation be highly prejudicial to the Interest of this Country, and whether it ought to be prevented if possible?', Aberdeen University Library, Birkwood MSS., MS. 306113, fols. 1–13.
[59] *WN* IV.v.b.39.
[60] *WN* IV.v.b.39. The traditional theory of justice framing Smith's discourse of free trade in subsistence goods during dearth and famines has been overlooked by both Salim Rashid, 'The Policy of Laissez-faire during Scarcities', *Economic Journal*, 90 (1980), 493–583, and Amartya Sen, *Poverty and Famines: An Essay on Entitlement and Deprivation* (Oxford, 1981); Smith's discourse was not about the conditions of actual famines, which belonged to the discourse on grave necessity which 'breaks all laws'.

granaries and distribute grain to the poor at set prices, not merely in a situation of actual starvation, but 'even in less urgent necessities'. He had used this example to argue that the 'rules of equity or justice depend entirely on the particular state and condition in which men are placed'.[61] In situations of 'extreme necessity' it was 'perfectly useless' to insist on maintaining an unlimited right of private property. Smith followed this line, but seems to have closed off the case of 'less urgent' necessities. Only actually impending starvation appears to qualify as the 'case of most urgent necessity' which would justify the suspension of property right in grain.

Even more striking was his endorsement of the role of grain merchants in rationing supply. By holding back supply in expectation of higher price, merchants helped to restrict demand and conserve supply for periods of still more acute shortage. Smith admitted it was 'avarice' to 'raise the price of corn somewhat higher than the scarcity of the season requires', but this at least prevented the premature dumping of grain at low prices, which would result in famine when supplies ran out at the end of the season.[62] Now, as Smith himself said, not even stock-jobbing drew more odium to the whole market system of a commercial society than grain speculators. To endorse such speculation was to go further in justifying the ways of the invisible hand than anyone but the Physiocrats dared to go.

The adequate subsistence of the poor, like everything else in the Smithian system, depended on growth led by increasing productivity in manufacturing. The only way agricultural surplus could be induced was if manufacturing sectors of the town produced goods which would serve as an incentive for production of food for sale.[63] A manufacturing country could free itself of dependence on the uncertain bounty of its own domestic harvest cycle by developing manufactured goods to trade for food in the international market. The ability of the domestic wage-labourers to purchase this imported food depended in turn on investment in the division of labour in manufacturing. Only if the unit labour costs of manufactured goods for export were driven down could the real wages of the poor continue to rise. If landlords and poor consumers alike paid less for their manufactured goods at home, they had more income available for agricultural investment and consumption of food. The proper role of the state, therefore, was not to regulate prices but to remove obstacles like the bounty and the import duty system which would upset the proper division of labour between town and country, driving investment capital into agriculture away from manufacturing. The Smithian solution to

[61] David Hume, *An Enquiry Concerning the Principles of Morals*, ed. L. A. Selby-Bigge, 3rd edn, rev. P. H. Nidditch (Oxford, 1975), p. 186; see also *LJ(A)* iii.144: 'But in time of necessity the people will break through all laws. In a famine it often happens that they will break open granaries and force the owners to sell at what they think a reasonable price.'
[62] *WN* IV.v.b.3.
[63] *WN* IV.ix.48-9; also *WN* III.iv.1-6; also *WN* I.xi.p.4.

agricultural productivity, therefore, was profoundly counterintuitive – to expand the manufacturing sector and to induce the agricultural sector to produce surpluses in exchange for finished goods. While almost all of his contemporaries, even the Physiocrats, were obsessed by the vulnerability of the economy to the vagaries of the harvest cycle and the uncertain bounties of the earth, Smith was looking forward to an international division of labour in which developed economies like England would use their manufacturing capacity to draw themselves forever beyond the closed limits of nature. In his view, the key to growth lay in a natural distribution of resources and a division of labour between town and country. Neither the Colbertists nor the Physiocrats had understood the delicate interdependence of manufacturing and agricultural sectors; the one bent the rod of policy too far towards agriculture, the other bent it too far towards manufacture.[64] In the 'natural course of things' the optimum distribution of labour and investment between sectors would establish itself of its own accord. Such an analysis, it hardly needs saying, simply dismissed as misguided moralizing the entire civic moralist and Country party jeremiad on the 'parasitical' and 'corrupting' growth of towns.[65]

The Smithian case for 'natural liberty' was never conducted only on economic grounds. The second plane of his argument was jurisprudential. As we have seen, he insisted on the all but absolute priority of the property rights of grain merchants and farmers over the claims of need made by poor labourers. Lest it be thought that the Smithian position on property was simply a reflection of the naturalized common sense of his time, it should be recalled that in the French debates on grain the equivalent position had been regarded as a scandal. Diderot thought the Physiocratic position on property when applied to famine conditions a 'cannibal principle', and he exclaimed, 'Isn't the sentiment of humanity more sacred than the right of property?'[66] Linguet, for his part, had gone so far as to argue that the needs of the distressed constituted a claim of right as binding as the rights of property, and Morelly had grounded this argument in the ancient jurisprudential hypothesis that the world had been originally granted to men in positive community of goods, to which state it reverted in conditions of necessity.[67] In claiming relief of their

[64] *WN* IV.ix.4.
[65] See for example Kramnick, *Bolingbroke and his Circle*, p. 56; Raymond Williams, *The Country and the City* (London, 1973); Robert Wallace, *A Dissertation on the Numbers of Mankind*, pp. 22–3; Lord Kames, 'A Great City', in *Sketches of the History of Man*, 4 vols. (4th edn, Edinburgh, 1788), iii, pp. 126–34; Hume, 'Of the Populousness of Ancient Nations', p. 432; also 'Of Public Credit', pp. 364–5, for discussion of the impact of the public debt system in drawing 'a mighty confluence of people and riches to the capital, by the sums levied in the provinces to pay the interest'.
[66] Kaplan, *Bread, Politics and Political Economy*, ii, p. 609.
[67] On Linguet, see Levy, *The Ideas and Careers of Simon-Nicolas-Henri Linguet*, pp. 105, 106, 121; Kaplan, *Bread, Politics and Political Economy*, pp. 476, 479. The *économiste* Abbé Roubaud wrote in his *Représentations aux magistrats, contenant l'exposition raisonnée des faits relatifs à la liberté du commerce des graines* (n.p.) in 1769 that 'needs are not rights at all, and rights are before

distress from the property of the rich, in other words, the poor were merely reclaiming what was theirs, as common members of the human species, in the first place.

Smith's position, like Morelly's, drew upon the long-established vocabulary of natural jurisprudence. It was not simply carpentered together to provide justification for the economic interests which his analysis endorsed. Following Hume's analysis, Smith simply took it for granted that institutions of property had emerged historically because of their utility and necessity. Had human beings been naturally endowed with 'generosity' and 'benevolence' towards their fellow beings, and had there been no limits on nature's bounty, no institutions of property would have been necessary.[68] It was the facts of limited human benevolence and natural scarcity which required the elaboration of rules of private individuation. Without such rules, security of human life would have been out of the question. As Hume put it, it was 'by establishing the rule for the stability of possession' that the 'insatiable, perpetual and universal avidity of acquiring goods and possessions' was rendered compatible with social order and stability.[69] Moreover, and this was a crucial argument, absolute security in private possession was the necessary precondition for pushing back the scarcity limits of nature. Without a guarantee that a man could keep what he had improved, he would have no incentive to make improvements.[70] This guarantee, Hume insisted, had to be 'perfect': property right, to be a right at all, could not admit of qualification. Doubtless, Hume admitted, the parcelling out of the world into exclusive individuation 'must frequently prove contradictory both to men's wants and desires – and persons and possessions must often be very ill adjusted'. Specifically, possession was rarely correlated with virtue or desert: the idle unmarried bachelor, if he had a better title, would accede to property ahead of the virtuous poor man with a numerous family. Yet any system which allocated property according to need or desert or some ideal of distributive justice was infinitely contestable, since every man had a different estimation of his own or another's merit. Any attempt to distribute according to such principles would be fatal to the stability of possession necessary to social order and the improvement of economic conditions.

---

everything, and everything that violates rights is violence and tyranny... I will add that the right of a single person must prevail over the interests of all without rights, because justice is the supreme, universal and unique law', pp. 395, 399–400. Linguet's answer in his 'Suite de la lettre de M. Linguet à M. L'Abbé Roubaud' was that right was not in property, but in life: 'The most vital of all properties is that in life. There are no longer any rights, there no longer can be any when it is compromised by hunger.' (See Levy, *Linguet*, p. 121.)

[68] Hume, *Treatise*, p. 494; Hume, *Enquiry Concerning the Principles of Morals*, pp. 146–7; see also David Miller, *Philosophy and Ideology in Hume's Political Thought* (Oxford, 1981); K. Haakonssen, *The Science of a Legislator: The Natural Jurisprudence of David Hume and Adam Smith* (Cambridge, 1981); Forbes, *Hume's Philosophical Politics*; James Moore, 'Hume's Theory of Justice and Property', *Political Studies*, 24 (1976), 103–19.

[69] Hume, *Treatise*, pp. 492–3.   [70] *Ibid.*, p. 497.

Particularly pernicious would be distribution according to 'ideas of perfect equality'. 'Render possessions ever so equal, men's different degrees of art, care and industry will immediately break that equality.' Worse, any attempt to restrain these differences in human talent would destroy incentives and thus 'reduce society to the most extreme indigence'. Instead of preventing starvation and beggary, the equal partition of possessions would 'render it unavoidable to the whole community'.[71]

Yet if property must be absolute, how then were those excluded from the partition of the world to be provided for? Smith's answer to this question made reference to the distinction in natural jurisprudence between 'perfect rights', such as property, which were enforceable at law, and 'imperfect obligations', such as charity, which was a moral duty incapable of legal enforcement. This distinction between 'justice' and 'benevolence' had the effect of denying that the excluded poor had a perfect right to the charity of the rich. As Smith told his students, 'a beggar is an object of our charity and may be said to have a right to demand it – but when we use the word right in this way it is not in a proper but a metaphoricall sense'.[72] The law had no business commanding men to be benevolent: in any case, benevolence must be freely given or else it was not a virtue at all. The proper province of justice was the enforcement of *suum cuique*, 'to each his own', i.e. the rules of property. Without such rules, 'the immense fabric of human society must crumble into atoms'. Without benevolence, on the other hand, society would doubtless be a mean and harsh place, but it could subsist 'as among different merchants, from a sense of its utility, without any mutual love or affection'. Yet Smith believed, as did Hume, that even in a market society, pity and compassion towards the unfortunate would remain natural and unprompted motives of action. It was to this discretionary sentiment that they looked to the relief of the necessities of the poor in any emergency.[73] Yet, as we have tried to show, the whole burden of the analysis of the *Wealth of Nations* was intended to demonstrate that by stimulating agricultural production in a system of competitive markets, the adequate subsistence of the labouring poor would cease to be a matter either of benevolence or of the drastic justice of grave necessity. Neither the generosity of individuals nor the interventions of the magistrate would be required.

This position effectively excluded 'distributive justice' from the appropriate functions of government in a market society. Smith insisted that the only appropriate function of justice was 'commutative'; it dealt with the attribution

---

[71] Hume, *Enquiry Concerning the Principles of Morals*, p. 194.
[72] *LJ(A)* i.14–16; also *LJ(A)* v.142; see also Winch, *Adam Smith's Politics*, pp. 51–2.
[73] *TMS* II.ii.1–10; also *TMS* II.ii.3.4. On 'natural' virtues of pity and generosity, see Hume, *Treatise*, p. 482; *Enquiry Concerning the Principles of Morals*, the whole of Section III, Part I, 'Of Justice'; also 'Of the Original Contract', *Philosophical Works*, iii, pp. 454–5, and 'Of Refinement in the Arts', p. 300.

of responsibility and the punishment of injury among individuals.[74] Distributive justice, which dealt with the allocation of superfluity according to claims of need, or desert, or merit, was not properly in the domain of law, but of morality.

The essential function of government was to protect property 'from the indignation' of the poor. Smith was under no illusions that the existing distribution of property in a market society could legitimize itself to the excluded: 'It is only under the shelter of the civil magistrate that the owner of that valuable property, which is acquired by the labour of many years, or perhaps of many successive generations, can sleep a single night in security.'[75] Yet in denying that the poor's needs constituted a claim of right against the property of the rich, Smith did not extrude the question of justice from his political economy. On the contrary, he transposed the question from the terrain of jurisprudence and political theory to the terrain of political economy, using natural modelling to demonstrate that by raising the productivity of agriculture, commercial society could provide adequately for the needs of the wage-earner without having to resort to any form of redistributive meddling in the property rights of individuals. Growth in conditions of 'natural liberty' would explode the whole antinomy between needs and rights.

To be sure, Smith knew full well that 'to insist upon establishing, and upon establishing all at once, and in spite of all opposition', any systematical plan of reform, specifically a system of natural liberty, 'must often be the highest degree of arrogance'. If a reformer could not 'conquer the rooted prejudices of the people by reason and persuasion', it was quite wrong for him 'to attempt to subdue them by force'. He must accommodate himself 'as well as he can' to the 'confirmed habits and prejudices of the people'.[76] Yet Smith's model itself was not any less uncompromising an argument for 'natural liberty'. Its structural properties were not altered in any way by Smith's awareness of the practical difficulties standing in the way of its implementation. These structural properties, as we have seen, were given by property theory: property was either 'perfect' and absolute or it was meaningless; and while in cases of real famine, necessity must overturn property, this was an exception and in no sense a

---

[74] *TMS* VII.ii.1.10: Smith's discussion of the distinction in Grotius between strict justice or *justitia expletrix*, 'which consists in abstaining from what is another's, and in doing voluntarily whatever we can with propriety be forced to do', and *justitia attributrix*, 'which consists in proper beneficence, in the becoming use of what is our own, and in the applying it to these purposes either of charity or generosity, to which it is most suitable in our situation, that it should be applied'.

[75] *WN* V.i.b.2.

[76] *TMS* VI.ii.2.16–18; *WN* IV.ii.43: 'To expect, indeed, that the freedom of trade should ever be entirely restored in Great Britain, is as absurd as to expect that an Oceana or Utopia should ever be established in it.' Hume's own defence of the usefulness of theoretical models in politics is in 'The Idea of a Perfect Commonwealth', *Philosophical Works*, iii, p. 481; see also the introduction to 'Of Commerce'.

permanent qualification of property right; to grant the distressed a right to the property of the rich would be to overturn all stability of possession, even in normal times, and would compromise the incentive effects which stability of possession provided for improvement. Accordingly, government must concern itself with commutative, rather than with distributive justice. To regard this argument as the contingent legitimation of interest would be to ignore the fact that its terms can be traced back to a tradition which antedated 'commercial society' and political economy alike. Smith himself left no doubt that in crafting his argument for a 'system of natural liberty', he was deploying terms whose provenance had to be traced to Grotius, the founder of modern natural jurisprudence, and to his reformulation of the heritage of Aristotle and the Schoolmen. It was Grotius, he said, who had been the first to make a rigorous distinction between 'the laws of police' and 'those rules of natural equity which ought to run through, and be the foundation of the laws of all nations'.[77] It was by thinking in these categories that Smith developed a conception of political economy's task as criticizing the contingent, historical structure of 'police' by the criterion of a 'system of natural liberty'. Even more important, the natural jurisprudence philosophers were the first to propose that the theoretical reconciliation of the claims of the propertied and the claims of the excluded could be achieved by shifting the terms of analysis from a language of rights to a language of markets. It is to this tradition and to this constitutive move in the making of classical political economy that we now turn.

IV. Political economy and natural jurisprudence

The story begins with Aquinas, because it was he who set the terms of the argument on the origins and limits of property right in the grain-trade debates of mid-eighteenth-century Catholic Europe.[78] For Aquinas the world was God's property and had been given to the collective stewardship of the human

---

[77] *TMS* VII.iv.37; *LJ*(*A*) 1.1–4; *LJ*(*B*) 5, 203.
[78] The Catholic origins of the debate were evident to Condorcet when he accused Necker of endorsing the 'Jesuit' principle of endorsing theft in times of necessity. See Baker, *Condorcet*, p. 61. On the Jesuits, see J. Brodrick, *The Economic Morals of the Jesuits* (Oxford, 1934). In Galiani's case, Raymond de Roover called attention to his schooling in scholastic jurisprudence and trade theory; see Raymond de Roover, *Business, Banking, and Economic Thought in Late Medieval and Early Modern Europe*, ed. J. Kirshner (Chicago, 1974), pp. 327, 334. There was an important Jesuit–Jansenist debate on the obligation of charity, the memory of which was still alive in eighteenth-century France; see Robin Briggs, 'The Catholic Puritans: Jansenists and Rigorists in France', in D. Pennington and K. Thomas (eds.), *Puritans and Revolutionaries: Essays in Seventeenth-Century History Presented to Christopher Hill* (Oxford, 1978), pp. 333–54. On the impact of this debate in England, see Margaret Sampson, 'Property and Poverty in Mid-Seventeenth-Century England: An Intellectual History with Particular Reference to Doctrines Permitting Theft in Cases of Extreme Necessity' (unpublished fellowship dissertation, Cambridge University, 1980).

species as a community of goods. In addition to this 'competence' as trustees of the world's resources, individuals had a second 'competence' to care for and distribute these resources. This second competence rendered private possession legitimate, for under private possession 'each person takes more trouble to care for something that is his sole responsibility than what is held in common by many'. Under communal property, there was no reliable incentive to labour and no reliable means of adjudicating the quarrels which were inevitable when things were held in common. Following Aristotle, therefore, Aquinas argued that 'the individual holding of possession is not...contrary to natural law; it is what rational beings conclude as an addition to the natural law'. Aquinas thus qualified the radical line in earlier Church thinking which, in the writing of St Basil, for example, had denied that it was legitimate to preclude others from the use of common property. It was individuation which made possible a responsible and productive management of God's estate, both for those with property and those without. In the extreme case of famine, however, property was to be overruled altogether, and the poor could reclaim their original share in the community of goods:

> If, however, there is so urgent and blatant a necessity that the immediate needs must be met out of whatever is available as when a person is in imminent danger and he cannot be helped in any other way, then a person may legitimately supply his own wants out of another's property, whether he does it secretly or flagrantly.[79]

The history of European natural law can be understood as a series of attempts to re-arrange the elements of the puzzle left by Aquinas. It was possible either to posit an original community of goods and then to limit individual property right accordingly, by the hypothesis of a return to the original condition of a community of goods in times of necessity, or alternatively to insist on the necessity of private property for the productive management of man's resources and for ensuring peace in conditions of scarcity. The logical corollary of the first position was that men should restrict their needs to what

---

[79] St Thomas Aquinas, *Summa Theologiae*, vol. 38, ed. M. Lefebure, general ed. T. Gilby (London, 1975), 2a.2ae.q.66.a.7, in answer to the question 'Is theft justifiable in cases of necessity?' The key texts on property in the *Summa* are 2a.2a.q.66 and 1a.2ae.q.105. The passages in Aristotle on which Aquinas had drawn are *Politics*, 1262b and 1265a. The radical statement of St Basil of Caesaraea discussed here was a paraphrase and interpretation of the Stoic example of the public theatre: '"Rich people who regard common property as their own simply because they have been the first to occupy it are like those who prevent others from coming to the public games by arriving at the arena first and so appropriating what is meant for common use." But it is not legitimate to preclude others from using common property.' 2a.2ae.q.66.a.2. M. Lefebure, '"Private Property" According to St Thomas and Recent Papal Encyclicals', in Aquinas, *Summa*, vol. 38, pp. 271–83. See also A. Parel, 'Aquinas' Theory of Property', in A. Parel and T. Flanagan (eds.), *Theories of Property: Aristotle to the Present* (Calgary, 1979); R. Tuck, *Natural Rights Theories: Their Origin and Development* (Cambridge, 1979), ch. 1. For a modern influence of Aquinas on the moral theory of famines, see Peter Singer, 'Famine, Affluence and Morality', in Peter Laslett and James Fishkin (eds.), *Philosophy, Politics and Society*, 5th ser. (Oxford, 1979), pp. 30–2.

was natural and necessary in order always to have superfluity to distribute to the needy, while the corollary of the second position was that private property created the incentive for improving God's dominion in such a way that everyone's needs could be satisfied without a system of austerity.

Grotius, the founder of modern natural jurisprudence, took up and transformed these polarities in the Aristotelian and Thomist tradition. He agreed with Aquinas that 'if a man under stress of such necessity takes from the property of another what is necessary to preserve his own life, he does not commit a theft'. The reason for this, he explained, was not that the owner was bound 'by the rule of love' or common humanity, but that 'all things seem to have been distributed to individual owners with a benign reservation in favour of the primitive right'.[80] In times of necessity, private property was suspended according to this 'benign reservation' and primitive community of goods returned, giving the poor an absolute right in the superfluity of the rich.

This theory was linked to a historicization of Aquinas's two 'competences'. This historicization is the origin of Scottish conjectural history.[81] In the original community of goods, man's competence as a trustee of God's resources held in common was to the fore. Common ownership of goods could only be maintained, Grotius continued, as long as 'men continued in great simplicity or...lived on terms of mutual affection such as rarely appears'. The distribution of individual use rights in the common could only remain stable and peaceful so long as needs were constrained. 'Men did not, however, continue to live this simple and innocent life', Grotius went on, beginning to historicize the picture. Aquinas's second competence, man's ability to decide on exclusive private possession of scarce resources, came into play. As new needs emerged which could only be satisfied by labour, movable objects were hived off from common ownership; lands for grazing were divided up among separate tribes; and land was individuated by families within the same tribe. Disputes were bound to develop as each family applied its industry to the land, and to put an end to these disputes, a compact, either accepting existing occupation or explicitly dividing what had formerly been common, became necessary. This first division by compact was a unique act and could not be repeated. Anything

[80] Hugo Grotius, *Of the Law of War and Peace, in Three Books*, trans. F. W. Kelsey, 3 vols. (Oxford, 1927), Book 2, ch. 2, 'Of Things Which Belong to Man in Common', particularly 2.2.6.4; also Richard Tuck, *Natural Rights Theories*, ch. 3, especially p. 80, and James Tully, *A Discourse on Property: John Locke and his Adversaries* (Cambridge, 1980), ch. 4, 'The Background to Chapter Five of the Second Treatise'. Our account of property theories in the natural jurisprudence tradition has relied heavily on the guidance provided by these two latter books. See also James Tully, 'Current Thinking About Sixteenth- and Seventeenth-Century Political Theory', *Historical Journal*, 24 (1981), 475–84. On Grotius, see Richard Schlatter, *Private Property: The History of an Idea* (London, 1952), ch. 6; Francis De Pauw, *Grotius and the Law of the Sea* (Brussels, 1965); Karl Olivecrona, *Law as Fact* (2nd edn, London, 1971).

[81] R. L. Meek, *Social Science and the Ignoble Savage* (Cambridge, 1976), pp. 12–16, and in a broader sense Forbes, *Hume's Philosophical Politics*, ch. 1, 'The Experimental Method in Morals: The Natural Law Forerunners'.

not then divided was turned into private property thereafter by the rule of first occupation.[82] This property, once instituted by compact, became a full or perfect right which everyone else had to respect. It was this exclusive or absolute right which alone deserved the name of property, Grotius said. Such was the poverty of language that the word was applied indiscriminately to rights to use of common property as well. In a major clarification of jurisprudential language, he insisted that the term be applied solely to the modern type of exclusive dominion over things.[83]

In order to provide for those without property, however, Grotius had to argue that in times of necessity history stopped, as it were, and the movement away from community of goods was reversed temporarily. He also had to give an account of 'just price' – of the jurisprudence which ought to govern the markets in subsistence goods. While accepting that freedom of trade and commerce were derivatives of natural law, he insisted that such freedoms should be constrained by natural equity. In particular, freedom to trade in grain should be limited by the requirement that the price remain within reach of the poor. 'We affirm, therefore', Grotius wrote, 'that all men have the right to buy such things at a fair price; unless they are needed by the person from whom they are sought; thus in times of extreme scarcity, the sale of grain is forbidden.' This meant that grain should not be exported in times of dearth and should be offered for sale instead in the province where it was produced. Similarly, the right of engrossing ought to be controlled.[84] Positive or municipal law, he believed, should set limits to man's natural liberty of trade.

Grotius thus placed great stress on the role of strict justice in regulating social life. But he took society as it was, operating beyond the constraints either of natural equity or artificial simplicity. The proper domain of justice was expletive, rather than distributive. It was properly concerned, not with desert or need, but with *suum cuique*. Expletive justice was about 'perfect rights', the chief of which were rights of property. Distributive or attributive justice was about 'imperfect rights', such as 'generosity, compassion and foresight in matters of government'. Imperfect rights did not entail a strict reciprocal obligation: they were commanded by humanity, not by law. A perfect right was one which could be defended by force if need be.[85] Here is the seed-bed of Smith's treatment of distributive justice. The distinctive feature of Grotian jurisprudence lay in so reducing the scope of distributive justice that the right of theft in necessity or the right to buy grain at a fair price – rights of desert and claims of need – were theorized as exceptions, rather than as rules, as they had been in Thomist jurisprudence. A man had a right only to what was his

---

[82] Grotius, *Of the Law of War and Peace*, 2.2.2.1–5.
[83] Hugo Grotius, *Of the Law of Prize and Booty*, trans. G. L. Williams (Oxford, 1950), ch. 12, 'Justness of the Case if the War were Private'. See also Tuck, *Natural Rights Theories*, pp. 60–1.
[84] Grotius, *Of the Law of War and Peace*, 2.2.19.   [85] *Ibid.*, 1.1.2.5.

own. He had no right to what was his due. His imperfect right to be treated with humanity only hardened into a perfect right under conditions of gravest necessity.

Grotius left two major problems for his heirs. His claim that the parcelling out of the common into private property required a contract was ridiculed by his critics, among them the English monarchical absolutist Filmer, who found it entirely implausible that the whole structure of modern dominion could be traced back to an actual moment of collective consent.[86] More plausible, his critics insisted, was the hypothesis that God had granted dominion to Adam and to each of the sovereigns who had succeeded him, leaving it to the positive institution of the sovereign what the laws of property should be. To rebut such legitimations of the system of private property, the defenders of natural jurisprudence had to find a theory of the origin of property which avoided the embarrassment of a contract. The second difficulty was the Grotian thesis of the suspension of private property and the temporary return of community goods in times of necessity. Most natural-law theorists found this hypothesis dangerous: if the need claims of the poor were given priority over property, society could be reduced to a state of anarchy even in times of relative plenty. Pufendorf took up this problem. Against Grotius's theory, Pufendorf argued that the obligations of the rich were better explained

if we say that a man of means is bound to come to the aid of one who is in innocent want, by an imperfect obligation which no one should, as a rule, be forced to meet; and yet the urge of supreme necessity makes it possible for such things to be claimed, on the same ground as those which are owed by a perfect right, that is, a special appeal may be made to a magistrate, or, when time does not allow anything of the sort, the immediate necessity may be met by taking the thing through force or stealth.[87]

[86] R. Filmer, *Observations Concerning the Originall of Government upon Mr Hobs 'Leviathan', Mr Milton against 'Salmasius', H. Grotius 'De Jure Belli'*, in *Patriarcha, and other Political Works*, ed. Peter Laslett (Oxford, 1949), pp. 273–4. On Filmer, see James Daly, *Sir Robert Filmer and English Political Thought* (Toronto, 1979), and John Dunn, *The Political Thought of John Locke: An Historical Account of the Argument of the 'Two Treatises of Government'* (Cambridge, 1969), ch. 6.

[87] Samuel Pufendorf, *On the Law of Nature and Nations*, 2.6.6; also his earlier *The Elements of Natural Jurisprudence*, trans. W. A. Oldfather (Oxford, 1931), Bk. II, Observation IV, section 2. Pufendorf was incensed by the Grotian idea that the case of necessity should be theorized only as an exception: 'when the necessity has merely to do with the property of the other, or when our life can be saved only by the property of the other, there is scarcely any doubt but that, when no other means are available, this property can be appropriated by force, and against the will of the owner, who is not under pressure of the same necessity. And this is not on the basis of some exception, added or understood in the pact establishing private ownership in the first instance, namely, that, in the case of necessity, community of goods was to return.' It is important to note that the most authoritative Scottish legal textbook of the time, Viscount Stair's *The Institutions of the Law of Scotland* (first published in 1681, second, enlarged edition in 1693), contained an endorsement of the Grotian tradition of legitimate use of force in case of grave necessity in a way which was moving closer to Pufendorf's formulation and away from Grotius's 'benign reservation' theory: 'There is also in property implied an obligation of commerce, or exchange, in case of necessity; every man cannot have actually all necessaries without exchange, which being denied in cases of necessity, or where there is no common

By means of this distinction between 'perfect rights' and 'imperfect obligations', Pufendorf managed to find a way to provide for the poor without granting them, as Grotius did, a property right in the goods of the rich in times of necessity. In his theory, the poor simply came into a right by default of someone else's obligation. This obligation derived not from the law of property, but from the natural law of humanity. The shift between Grotius and Pufendorf is decisive. In one, the focus was upon the rights of the poor, while in the other, it was upon the voluntary obligations of the rich. The implied nexus of relations between rich and poor shifted from the grounds of law to that of moral sentiment, benevolence on one side, gratitude on the other.[88] This rhetoric obliterated the linguistic possibility of expressing the poor's right of desert in the property of the rich.

Having redefined the basis of provision for the excluded without recourse to a community of goods, Pufendorf was in a position to streamline the Grotian account of the history of property. He poured scorn on theorists who derived modern property right from the hypothesis of an original donation by God of exclusive dominion to Adam and his heirs. Likewise, he rejected the Hobbesian argument that property right was a natural relation between human individuals and things and hence the origin of that conflict in the state of nature which the creation of a sovereign was designed to stop. Property, Pufendorf insisted, involved consent, a man to man relationship, established after God's initial grant of the earth to mankind in common in order to secure concord in the individuation of the world. Its purpose was to pre-empt the Hobbesian war of all against all, by requiring men to recognize that all human rights entailed correlative duties to abstain from the property of others.[89]

authority, it may be taken by force...yea, there is implied in property, an obligation to give, in cases of necessity, to these who have not wherewith to exchange, and cannot otherwise preserve their life, but the obligation of recompense when they are able...and this is the ground of the obligation, to aliment the poor, which though it also floweth from the obligation of charity, yet...that obligation hath no determinate bounds, but is left to the discretion of the giver, not of the demander, and so can be no warrant for taking by force, and without the proprietor's consent' (James Dalrymple, Viscount of Stair, *The Institutions of the Law of Scotland* (1693), ed. D. M. Walker (Edinburgh and Glasgow, 1981), 2.1.6).

On Pufendorf's position, see Peter Stein, *Legal Evolution* (Cambridge, 1980); Hans Medick, *Naturzustand und Naturgeschichte der bürgerlichen Gesellschaft: Die Ursprünge der bürgerlichen Sozialtheorie als Geschichtsphilosophie und Sozialwissenschaft bei Samuel Pufendorf, John Locke und Adam Smith* (Göttingen, 1973); H. Welzel, *Die Naturrechtslehre Samuel Pufendorfs* (Berlin, 1958); Iring Fetscher, 'Der gesellschaftliche "Naturzustand" und das Menschenbild bei Hobbes, Pufendorf, Cumberland, und Rousseau: ein Beitrag zur Standortbestimmung der politischen Theorie Rousseaus', *Schmollers Jahrbuch für Gesetzgebung, Verwaltung, und Volkswirtschaft*, 80 (1960), 650–5; Horst Denzer, *Moralphilosophie und Naturrecht bei Samuel Pufendorf, Eine geistes- und wissenschaftgeschichtliche Untersuchung zur Geburt des Naturrechts aus der Praktischen Philosophie* (Munich, 1972). [88] Pufendorf, *Law of Nature*, 3.3.5; 3.3.15–17; 3.4.6.

[89] *Ibid.*, 3.5.3. A man–thing relationship thus could not be construed as a right, since 'things are under no obligation to present themselves for man's use'. A right thus presupposed a response by other men, i.e. their expressed or tacit consent. On the correlativity principle, see David Lyons, 'The Correlativity of Rights and Duties', *Nous*, 4 (1970), 45–55; Tuck, *Natural Rights Theories*, pp. 159–60.

Yet like all natural-law theorists, Pufendorf had to explain both how individuation had occurred and whether it was consistent with God's original intentions when he granted the world to man's use. In thinking through these questions, Pufendorf made use of a distinction developed by the Spanish Jesuit Suarez between 'preceptive' and 'permissive' natural law. Had God granted the world to man 'preceptively', that is, with specific injunctions in natural law as to how it was to be individuated; or had he granted it to man 'permissively', without express stipulations? Pufendorf agreed with his Spanish forerunner that 'proprietorship' could not be considered to have been a command of preceptive natural law from the beginning. Proprietorship was introduced 'as the peace of men seemed to require'. A 'quiet and decorous society' could not exist 'without distinct dominions of things'. Pufendorf reduced the range of preceptive natural law to a minimum: 'no man should hurt another', and no man should take what rightly belonged to another. Men had the liberty to initiate such forms of individuation as were consonant with these precepts.[90]

This distinction between 'preceptive' and 'permissive' natural law entailed a rethinking of the nature of God's initial grant of the world to mankind. Using these concepts, Pufendorf argued that the 'donation of God, described in the Sacred Scriptures, sets forth not a definite form of dominion, but only an indefinite right to apply things to uses which are reasonable and necessary'. Accordingly, in the beginning, things were lying '"open to any and every person", in the same sense [that] such things are said to be nobody's, more in a negative than in a positive sense; that is, they are not yet assigned to a particular person'. In the beginning, therefore, the world belonged to the community of mankind, but it was no one's in particular; it belonged neither to an individual Adam, nor to a primitive group of men. It was in a 'negative' rather than a 'positive' community, to use Pufendorf's terminology.[91] If men chose subsequently to institute community of goods, they could do so, but they

---

[90] Pufendorf, *Law of Nature*, 4.4.14; 4.6.6. Pufendorf did not refer to Suarez openly, but simply remarked that the difficulty involved 'has long ago been met by learned men, who have drawn a distinction between a preceptive and a permissive law of nature, and pointed out a different meaning of the expression "law of nations"'. For Suarez's discussion of the different meanings of natural law, see Francisco Suarez, *A Treatise on Laws and God the Lawgiver*, trans. G. L. Williams, A. Brown and J. Waldron (Oxford, 1944), 2.14.2–16. See Filmer's criticism of Suarez in *Patriarcha*, pp. 74–8, and of Grotius in *Observations Concerning the Originall of Government*, p. 266; Dunn, *The Political Thought of Locke*, p. 60 and pp. 60–1n. On Suarez, see Reijo Wilenius, *The Social and Political Theory of Francisco Suarez* (Helsinki, 1963); Tuck, *Natural Rights Theories*, pp. 54–6; Quentin Skinner, *The Foundations of Modern Political Thought*, 2 vols. (Cambridge, 1978), ii, ch. 5, 'The Revival of Thomism', pp. 151–4, 158–61, 176–7; also Tully, *A Discourse of Property*, pp. 66–8. For the problem of subjective rights, see M. Villey, *La Formation de la Pensée Juridique Moderne* (Paris, 1968) and Tuck's amendment of Villey's position in *Natural Rights Theories*, ch. 1, 'The First Rights Theory'; especially on Aquinas, pp. 16–17.

[91] Pufendorf, *Law of Nature*, 4.4.2; see O. Gierke, *Natural Law and the Theory of Society, 1500 to 1800*, trans. E. Barker, 2 vols. (Cambridge, 1934), i, p. 103, and note in ii, pp. 293–4.

had to arrive at some explicit arrangement distributing individual use rights to the soil and to the products of nature. Such a system of distributive justice in a particular, positive community, moreover, could only remain stable and uncontentious, Pufendorf argued, as long as needs were confined to the same limited standard. This was both his and Grotius's reply to the European tradition of nostalgia for the Golden Age of primitive communism, exemplified in More's *Utopia* and Campanella's *City of the Sun*.[92] Such communities could only persist as long as their inhabitants remained content to live at the same equal and rude standard. Pufendorf, moreover, firmly banished such communities to the historical past, arguing that 'as mankind multiplied and living conveniences were increased by industry, the necessity of preserving a social life led to the introduction of dominion'. The division of the earth did not begin all at once, with a contract, as Grotius supposed; rather there was a gradual passage from individuated use rights, which did not require the dissolution of a negative community, to exclusive property rights, which did require compact.[93] In the hunting and gathering stage, only a 'tacit convention' was required for men to appropriate natural produce for use. Thus, 'An oak tree belonged to no man, but the acorns that fell to the ground were his who had gathered them.' A tacit convention of this kind, permitting promiscuous use, could only persist 'without disturbance to the common peace',[94] Pufendorf argued, as long as men lived in 'great simplicity'. Nor was full dominion required in the shepherding and agricultural stages as long as land and pasture remained in abundance and no individual was yet excluded. Full dominion came in only when land became scarce relative to population, and occupiers sought to push back the limits of scarcity by applying the labour of improvement to their plots. Following the line of argument in Aristotle, Pufendorf maintained that property right did away with the quarrels which were inevitable 'if all men should labour in common and should lay up their earnings in common'. Those who did not labour were rightfully excluded. 'It was improper that a man who had contributed no labour should have right to things equal to his by whose industry a thing had been raised or rendered fit to service.'[95] Yet in an economy without money, men had no incentive to appropriate more than they needed, and hence individuation into exclusive dominion did not, as yet, exclude others from the means of subsisting. In an economy without money, 'envy and craving for more than they need' had no means to develop.

[92] Pufendorf, *Law of Nature*, 4.4.7. 'I suppose', remarked Pufendorf, that 'perfect men are more easily imagined than found'. Pufendorf depicted the state of nature as inhabited by men who were like miserable animals (2.1.8) and declared that 'the complaint of the masses about the burdens and drawbacks of civil states could be met in no better way than by picturing to their eyes the drawbacks of a state of nature' (2.2.2).
[93] Pufendorf, *Law of Nature*, 4.4.12–13; for a critique of the Grotian first division story, see 4.6.2.
[94] *Ibid.*, 4.r.13; 4.4.9.
[95] *Ibid.*, 4.4.6–7. Pufendorf's account of the departure from negative community was drawing here on Aristotle's critique of the Platonic positive community of property in *Politics*, 1263a.

'Unlettered agricultural peoples', Pufendorf argued, 'were still ignorant of the enticements of the appetite, an easy living.'[96]

Money was introduced, so Pufendorf argued, not because men were innately greedy, but because their needs began to expand once labour began to generate surpluses. Initially, these needs could be satisfied by barter, but since natural produce perishes, barter provided no mechanism for avoiding future scarcity. Following Aristotle, Pufendorf argued that money was introduced in order to break through the constraint on accumulation entailed in the natural spoliation of unused produce. 'As long as wealth lay only in stores of grain, herds and the like, the desire for unlimited gain was ultimately quenched by the work involved in such things, the difficulty of handling them and the further fact that they were easily destroyed.' But 'upon the introduction of gold and silver money', Pufendorf explained, 'it is easy for avarice to amass even millions'.[97]

In this analysis of the coming of money, natural jurisprudence gave itself the occasion for a discourse on modern luxury parallel to that found in the civic humanist vernacular. Pufendorf did not deny that modern commerce had brought with it 'luxury', avarice, restlessness and inequality. Yet exchange in a money economy made it possible for societies to push back the limits on improvement posed by natural scarcity and the spoliation of natural produce. At the same time, Pufendorf did argue that the inequality occasioned by the emergence of money and commerce could only be justified in terms of natural law if those without property in the means of subsistence could continue to satisfy their needs. This was the burden of his insistence that consent, expressed or presumed, and not only the rule of first occupation, was required in the passage from use rights to exclusive property. 'It is impossible to conceive how the mere corporal act of one person – one man's appropriation of a thing – can prejudice the faculty of others, unless their consent is given, that is, unless the pact intervenes.' Man's natural faculty to acquire dominion through occupation had its own natural boundaries. Consent limited individuation to what could be used:

Such was the generosity of God towards men that He supplied them abundantly with what serves their needs. But reason prescribed to men such bounds of possession, as would leave them content upon acquiring what would be likely to meet the needs of themselves and of their dependents. Nor yet does it want them to take no thought for the future, provided their envy and craving for more than they need do not prevent others from providing for their own necessities. If any person ranges too far afield and

---

[96] Pufendorf, *Law of Nature*, 4.4.7–8.
[97] *Ibid.*, 5.1.14. Pufendorf cites Aristotle, *Nicomachean Ethics*, 1133a–b and *Politics*, 1257a; see *Law of Nature*, 5.1.12. On Pufendorf's condemnation of luxury, see *ibid.*, 2.4, 'The Duties of Man Towards Himself', section 10: 'what has been secured should not be regarded as anything but helps for our need and means for deserving well of others. On no account should the mind be solely concerned or satisfied with the mere possession and care of property, and the infinite concern of accumulating it.'

heaps up superfluous wealth by the oppression of others, the rest will not be blamed if, when opportunity affords, they undertake promptly to bring him into line.[98]

Yet if property had to serve the interest of all human beings and not merely the propertied, how were those excluded from the means of subsistence to satisfy their needs? A consistent theorist was required by this question to engage with the legitimacy of the money system in which the subsistence goods of the have-nots were priced. What was the 'just price' at which such goods should exchange in a free market? Pufendorf was in no doubt that, in a market of free agents, the just price was the price the market would bear. Even if 'I should set an outrageous price upon a thing of mine', Pufendorf said, 'no one can complain about it' since they were free to refuse my offer of exchange. A merchant had a right to demand a profit in the commerce in subsistence goods, but he could be blamed for inhumanity if he 'either refuses to sell to one in need, or else is willing to part with them only upon very hard terms'. The avaricious merchant offended against his 'imperfect obligation' to act humanely, and not against the law, except of course if he actually caused someone to starve to death.[99]

The only way to ensure justice as between haves and have-nots in a commercial economy, Pufendorf believed, was to guarantee the productivity of agricultural land by keeping market prices of agricultural commodities high. 'If in time of great abundance of money the price of land and its products should be low, the cultivators of the soil must needs be ruined, while if money is scarce and the price of land high, the other class of men must labour in want.'[100] Interfering with market prices in the interests of distributive justice for the sake of the poor consumer would only weaken the incentives to producers. The long-term interests of both required market prices to be set by the price of agricultural produce in lean years.

While Locke's property theory belongs squarely within the continental natural jurisprudence tradition, he wrote in the vernacular of English property debates and did not follow Grotius's and Pufendorf's restriction of the use of the term 'property' to its modern meaning of exclusive and absolute right of dominion. In the vernacular which Locke employed, property meant not only the absolute 'right in' something, but also common right to use. The term also referred to man's natural right to the means of his own self-preservation. A man's life was also his property and as such was inalienable. This usage has created the impression that Locke was a positive-community theorist, arguing that God's gift of the earth to mankind in common conferred a property right

[98] Pufendorf, *Law of Nature*, 4.5.9. But compare this with 4.4.6, where Pufendorf agrees that the initial abundance is at best a very short-lived phenomenon. See also 4.4.7. On the requirement of corporeal occupation by persons, see 4.4.5; 4.5.8; 4.6.8–9; 4.9.7.
[99] Pufendorf, *Law of Nature*, 5.1.8–10.
[100] Pufendorf, *Law of Nature*, 5.1.15. The products of land could have a stable price only, argued Pufendorf, if their price was 'sufficiently fixed by a full year compensating for a lean one'.

to the means of self-preservation to each and every man.[101] Yet Locke was quite explicit that this inalienable right to preservation did not presume a world given to mankind in positive community. The great common of the earth was open to any taker: it was a negative community, neither individuated to Adam, nor given to a positive community.[102]

Locke, like Pufendorf, should be seen as attempting to defend Grotian natural law by reformulating those parts of it, especially the doctrine of consent, which had been exposed by Filmer, his primary interlocutor in the *Two Treatises*. Locke improved on Pufendorf by eliminating the theoretical necessity of consent in the gradual emergence of private property. He did so by assuming that in the state of nature, land and natural produce were in such abundance relative to population that men had no rational reason either to contend with each other or to be required to make explicit arrangements as to their division.[103] 'In the beginning', as Locke said in a famous passage, 'all

[101] On the interpretation of the meaning of 'property' in Locke, see Tully, *A Discourse on Property*, pp. 11–12, 61, 111–16 and 122. Tully claims that the very first lines of chapter 5, 'Men, being once born, have a right to their Preservation, and consequently to Meat and Drink, and such other things, as Nature affords for their subsistence', make mankind who are collectively in receipt of the world as God's gift a positive community (*A Discourse on Property*, p. 130). He argues that this interpretation was needed by Locke as a consistency requirement for Locke's theory of revolution (*ibid.*), that Locke was a radical, and 'it is only with a natural standard of property to appeal to that a radical can criticise and justify opposition to prevailing forms of property' (*ibid.*, p. 89), and that Locke in fact differed from Aquinas in using doctrine of the positive community for radical purposes, since Aquinas's natural standard mirrored the existing property relations in order to justify them (*ibid.*, pp. 120–1). Locke would have accepted the negative-community interpretation had he wished 'to justify unlimited accumulation' as Macpherson suggested he did (*ibid.*, pp. 152–3). Locke's natural standard for the distribution of property rights had to be a positive community and cover more than grave necessity and dire need, because his commitment that happiness required plenty and security would have led him 'to a conservative theory if the inference is made that only some can, or do, have the requisite plenty' (*ibid.*, p. 101). It is not clear, however, that even if we could accept Tully's claim that Locke was an unambiguously radical thinker who systematically made these contentions, we should designate this normative package a positive community theory. One should not forget that the negative community theory was still meant to be a new interpretation of community theory ('mankind in common') against Adamite private property theories.

[102] Among modern commentators Locke's theory of property in the state of nature was understood as a negative-community theory by Schlatter, *Private Property*, p. 153; Dunn, *The Political Thought of John Locke*, pp. 67–8n.: 'In place of the crude antithesis between everything belonging to everybody (with its logical incoherences so doggedly mocked by Filmer) or everything belonging to Adam or his heir, the world is presented as belonging to nobody but available for the appropriation of all.' See also Patrick Kelly, 'Locke and Filmer: Was Laslett So Wrong After All?', *Locke Newsletter*, no. 8 (1977), pp. 84 and 90n. Richard Tuck, who sees Locke's theory as Grotian in shape, seems strongly to support a negative-community reading of Locke *via* his insistence that Locke and James Tyrell were aware of each other's work on property theory and that Tyrell's *Patriarcha non Monarcha* of 1681 in fact incorporated some of Locke's ideas on property; see Tuck, *Natural Rights Theories*, pp. 154–5, 169–72, 169–70n. As for Barbeyrac, he did not use the scholastic language of communities, but he did not object to Pufendorf's formulation in any of his notes, despite its conspicuous place in the Pufendorfian text. See Pufendorf, *Law of Nature*, 4.4.3.n.2 and also 4.6.2.n.1; 4.4.9.n.2.

[103] Locke, *Two Treatises*, 2.5.33: 'Nor was this appropriation of any parcel of Land, by improving it, any prejudice to any other Man, since there was still enough, and as good left; and more

the world was America': 'the Inhabitants were too few for the Country and want of People and Money gave men no Temptation to enlarge their Possession of Land or contest for a wider extent of Ground'.[104]

His second improvement was to specify more clearly than Pufendorf the natural boundaries which individuated shares would confine themselves to in the state of nature. In Pufendorf, this boundary was given by the extent of produce or land which any individual and his family could occupy and cultivate. Locke defined the natural limits of individuation in terms of a 'use' and 'spoliation condition'. God gave the world to man to use, not to abuse or waste, and in the pre-money stage, he had no reason to accumulate anything beyond what he could use to satisfy his basic needs. Accordingly, 'the exceeding of the bounds of his just property' did not lie 'in the largeness of his Possession, but the perishing of anything uselessly in it'.[105] Locke also simplified the jurisprudential legitimation of private property by arguing that the act of first occupation – the taking of an acorn or the settling of a piece of ground – conferred a right to exclusive use because the act was a process of labour. Previous jurisprudential theory had always separated the entitlement created by first occupation from that created by labour. 'The measure of Property', the natural boundary of what each man could rightfully individuate to his own use, was set by his labour. 'No Man's Labour could subdue, or appropriate all: nor could his Enjoyment consume more than a small part; so that it was impossible for any Man, this way, to intrench upon the right of another.'[106]

The major question about Lockian theory, for our purposes, is whether he theorized man's right of self-preservation as conferring on the excluded a perfect or imperfect right in the property of the rich. 'God has not left man', Locke wrote, 'so to the Mercy of another that he may starve him is he please.' In case of necessity, 'Charity gives every Man a Title to so much out of another's Plenty, as will keep him from extream want when he has no means to subsist otherwise.'[107] Yet this obligation on the part of the rich was left to the individual. It was a side-constraint, rather than a structuring condition, on whatever property arrangements happened to be in force. As a side-constraint, moreover, it was not constantly applied but only in necessity. 'We are not obliged', Locke argued, 'to provide with shelter and to refresh with food any and every man, but only when a poor man's misfortune calls for our alms and our property supplies means for charity.'[108] Locke added that the

than the yet unprovided could use.' John Dunn has suggested that the abundance hypothesis in Locke might have originated in an aside in Filmer's critique of Hobbes: Filmer, *Observations concerning the Originall of Government*, p. 242; Dunn, *The Political Thought of John Locke*, p. 71n.

[104] Locke, *Two Treatises*, 2.5.49. For Locke, as for Grotius and Pufendorf, it was 'the Ocean, that great and still remaining Common of Mankind', which represented the uncorrupted survival of negative community: *ibid.*, 2.5.30.9–10.

[105] Locke, *Two Treatises*, 2.5.4.6; also 2.5.3.1.   [106] *Ibid.*, 2.5.36.

[107] *Ibid.*, 1.4.42; 2.6; 3.132; Tully, *A Discourse on Property*, pp. 131–2.

[108] Locke, *Essays on the Law of Nature*, ed. W. von Leyden (Oxford, 1954), Essay 7, 'Is the Binding Force of the Law of Nature Perpetual and Universal?', p. 195. On Locke's personal attitude

poor only had a right to appeal to the rich when they themselves had fulfilled their duty towards God to labour in a calling. Nobody had a right to live comfortably from other people's labour. Nor were those in necessity entitled to be relieved in comfort. Only their bare necessities were to be relieved. Locke's position on charity was neither more nor less generous than Pufendorf's.[109]

Like Pufendorf too, Locke believed that the just price in any market was simply the price which that market would bear. This was the case even with subsistence goods. The free play of supply and demand, as he argued in a note entitled 'Venditio', would necessarily result in just prices in the long run. In 'the mutual and perpetually changing wants of money and commodities, the buyer and the seller comes to a pretty equal and fair account'. If free trade were to be obstructed, for example by some measure specifying 'the utmost justifiable profit, there would be no commerce in the world, and mankind would be deprived of the supply of foreign mutual conveniences of life'. High prices in time of famine would draw forth supply. A merchant, faced with the choice between sending corn to Ostend where it could fetch 5 shillings or to Dunkirk where famine prevails and corn fetches 20 shillings, would send it to Dunkirk. Examination of the morality of this sort of transaction had been a feature of classical jurisprudence at least since Cicero.[110] But where Cicero condemned anyone who exploited or profited from another's distress, both Locke and Pufendorf simply took it for granted that economic allocation was best served if someone's hardship was another's gain. Discrimination towards the poor in markets was indeed charitable, but it was not 'what strict justice requires'. Indeed, discrimination in their favour was an infringement against

to the poor, see Lady Masham's testimony in M. Cranston, *John Locke: A Biography* (London, 1957), p. 426; 'Poor Law Reform Proposal' [1697], in H. R. Fox-Bourne, *The Life of John Locke*, 2 vols. (London, 1876), ii, pp. 376-93.

[109] John Dunn, *The Political Thought of John Locke*, p. 217. See also Locke's statement in his note on 'Moralists': 'Justice the greatest and difficultest duty being thus established the rest will not be hard. The next sort of virtues are those which relate to society and so border on Justice but yet are not comprised under direct articles of contract such as are Civility, Charity, Liberality.' T. Sargentich (ed.), 'Locke and Ethical Theory: Two MS. Pieces', *Locke Newsletter*, no. 5 (1974), p. 28. C. B. Macpherson's claim in his *The Political Theory of Possessive Individualism* (Oxford, 1972), p. 221, that in Locke the 'traditional view that property involved social obligations' was undermined seems to be misplaced. For a critique of Macpherson's ahistorical and now technically dated analysis, see Alan Ryan, 'Locke and the Dictatorship of the Bourgeoisie', *Political Studies*, 13 (1965), 219-30; Edward J. Hundert, 'The Making of Homo Faber: John Locke Between Ideology and History', *Journal of the History of Ideas*, 33 (1972), 33-44; Richard Ashcraft, 'The *Two Treatises* and the Exclusion Crisis: The Problem of Lockean Political Theory as Bourgeois Ideology', in J. G. A. Pocock and R. Ashcraft, *John Locke: Papers read at a Clark Library Seminar, 10 December 1977* (Los Angeles, 1980), pp. 25-114.

[110] The 'Venditio' (1695) is reprinted in Dunn, 'Justice and the Interpretation of Locke's Political Theory', *Political Studies*, 16 (1968), 84-7. Locke was paraphrasing the classical parable of the Alexandrian grain merchant who sails to the famine-ridden but rich island of Rhodes and who has to choose whether or not he should tell the Rhodians that other ships are also on their way. See Cicero, *De Officiis*, 3.1.2, and Pufendorf, *Law of Nature*, 5.3.4, and also Jean Barbeyrac's note on Pufendorf's passage.

strict justice which has 'but one measure for all men'. Like Pufendorf, Locke admitted that merchants who exploited scarcity offended against the law of humanity, but he argued that they would only offend against strict justice if they actually caused someone to starve.

Where Locke differs from Pufendorf is in the historical account of the origins of the modern money-economy. Pufendorf, as we have seen, explained the origin of barter and money in terms of the emergence of scarcity, which in turn required the creation of property by consent. Wishing to avoid the necessity of a consent theory, Locke theorized the state of nature as one of abundance. Why then, if each man had more than enough for his needs, should he want to trade and barter? Locke, unlike Pufendorf, had to assume a natural covetousness in men, which operated even in the state of primitive simplicity. 'The Root of all Evil', the 'Desire of having more than we need of' (which Locke elsewhere insisted was evident in children 'as soon almost as they are born'), took hold of men and caused them to agree 'that a little piece of yellow Metal, which would keep without wasting or decay should be worth a great piece of Flesh or a whole Heap of Corn'. By consenting to put an artificial use-value on an almost useless commodity like gold, men were able to cheat the natural law limiting property to what one could use. Now they could trade away their perishable surpluses and hoard money in return, claiming that the possession of money qualified as 'use'. By agreeing to create a money system, men agreed, in effect, to create a system of inequality:

But since Gold and Silver, being little useful to the Life of Man in proportion to Food, Rayment, and Carriage, has its value only from the consent of Men, whereof Labour yet makes, in great part, the measure, it is plain, that Men have agreed to disproportionate and unequal Possession of the Earth, they having by a tacit and voluntary consent found out a way, how a man may fairly possess more land than he himself can use the product of, by receiving in exchange for the overplus, Gold and Silver, which may be hoarded up without injury to any one, these metals not spoileing or decaying in the hands of the possessor.[111]

Even before money was introduced, 'the different degrees of Industry' between men were 'apt to give Men Possessions in different Proportions'.[112] The inequality created by the emergence of money was a faithful reflection of natural differentials in human industry. Such inequality could only have been contained if either God or man had determined that needs should be constrained. Yet Locke was adamant that God had given the world to mankind, not merely to satisfy their basic needs, but for 'the support and

---

[111] Locke, *Two Treatises*, 2.5.50; 2.5.37; 2.5.46. Note that the consent of mankind establishing money did not, in practice, extend its validity to cases of necessity: 'in a siege silver may not be of equal value to gunpowder and in a famine gold may not be worth its weight in Bran', 'Locke's Early Manuscript on Interest' [1688], in William Letwin, *The Origins of Scientific Economics: English Economic Thought, 1660–1776* (London, 1963), p. 279.

[112] Locke, *Two Treatises*, 2.5.48.

Comfort of their being'. 'It cannot be supposed', he said, that God intended that the world 'should always remain common and uncultivated' as it would have been had human needs been constrained from the beginning. God had given the world 'to the industrious and rational' to improve without limit; he had not given it 'to the fancy or covetousness of the Quarrelsom and Contentious'.[113] Once, however, land became scarce relative to population and the excluded and landless faced the 'rational and industrious', then a pact creating government and the positive laws of property became necessary to prevent the 'rapin and force' which were sure to break out. Such laws stipulated that those excluded were 'not to meddle with what was already improved by another's Labour: If he did 'tis plain he desired the benefit of another's pains, which he had no right to.'[114] Locke's improvement on Pufendorf, as Barbeyrac observed, was to have pushed back the moment in history when contract became necessary by virtue of a hypothesis of initial abundance, and then to have theorized the emergence of the inequality which would make necessary a pact establishing government.[115]

Locke's distaste for modern inequality and covetousness was genuine enough. In other parts of his writing he sharply criticized modern man's 'fantastical uneasiness (as itch after Honour, Power, or Riches etc.)' which the 'luxury of the Courts' was apt to implant among the industrious sort to the detriment and dishonour of the 'useful and mechanical arts'.[116] Such comments,

---

[113] *Ibid.*, 2.5.34.   [114] *Ibid.*, 2.5.34.

[115] See Barbeyrac's footnotes to Pufendorf, *Law of Nature*, 4.4.3.n.4; 4.4.4.n.2; 4.4.9.n.2; 4.6.2.n.1. See also Gershom Carmichael, *De Officio Hominis et Civis et juxta Legem Naturalem, Libri Duo. Supplementis et Observationibus in Academicae Juventutis usum auxit et illustravit Gerschomus Carmichael* (Edinburgh, 1724), Note 1 to 1.12. Carmichael understood the original community of mankind in receipt of God's gift as a negative community and criticized Pufendorf for hesitating in the matter. He accepted Locke's labour theory of the basis of private ownership. Barbeyrac sharply criticized this move despite his general admiration for Locke's theory of property; see Barbeyrac's censures on Carmichael's n. 6 to Pufendorf, *De Officio*, 1.2.6 in his own n. 2 to Pufendorf, *Law of Nature*, 4.6.2. On Carmichael, see the essay of James Moore and Michael Silverthorne in this volume, pp. 73–87 below.

See also George Turnbull's note to J. C. Heineccius, *A Methodical System of Universal Law: or, The Laws of Nature and Nations deduced from Certain Principles, and applied to Proper Cases*, trans. G. Turnbull, 2 vols. (London, 1743), 1.9.235–6 and notes. Smith used H. Coccejus, *Hugonis Grotii de Jure Belli ac Pacis Libri Tres, cum Annotatis Auctoris, nec non J. F. Gronovii Notis, et J. Barbeyracii Animadversionibus, Commentariis in super locupletissimus Henr. L. B. Cocceii*, published as *Grotius Illustratus* by his son, Samuel L. B. De Coccejus, adding to it his own *Novum Systema Institutiae Naturalis et Romanae in quo Universum Ius Romanum Nova Methodo ad artem Redigitur*, 5 vols. (Lausanne, 1751). This edition directed the reader to those of Barbeyrac's notes on Pufendorf's *Law of Nature* which included the famous references to Locke. The comments of the elder Coccejus on Grotius's 2.2.1–6 discuss the problem of negative community in an interesting way, with reference to Pufendorf's 4.4.13 and the exclusion from property in land (Coccejus, vol. ii, pp. 72–97).

[116] John Locke, 'Note on Labour' (1693), Bodleian Library, Lovelace Collection, MS. Film 77, fols. 310–11, as reproduced almost in entirety in Dunn, *Political Thought of John Locke*, pp. 231n, 235–6n. Note Locke's contrast between 'the arts and instruments of Luxury and Vanity' and 'honest and useful industry', pp. 235–6n.

as we have seen in the case of Pufendorf, show that a critical discourse on modern luxury was by no means a monopoly of civic humanist thought. Yet Locke theorized covetousness as innate to human nature and not simply as a contingent historical curse of a commercial society. Its effects could be counteracted, chiefly by the laws of property themselves, but it could not be extirpated by a return to primitive simplicity. More positively, Locke argued that, however ungodly the modern scramble after money, the society which resulted from the scramble did not violate God's natural law that all men ought to enjoy the means of their own self-preservation. Indeed, those who had no property but in their own labour had a more secure hold on their subsistence than their virtuous but impoverished ancestors. Exclusive dominion created the incentives necessary to increase the productivity of soil and to push back the limits of scarcity. Almost all of the conveniences of modern life were created by the application of human labour to God's original gift. 'If we rightly estimate things as they come to our use', Locke said, 'and estimate what in them is purely owing to Nature and what to labour, we shall find that in most of them 99/100 are wholly to be put on the account of labour.'[117] Moreover, in modern times, labour was distinctively divided and therefore distinctively productive. It was this division of labour which explained, too, why 'numbers of men are to be preferred to largenesse of dominions', why, in other words, countries with relatively weak natural resources were able to feed their populations without recourse to conquest. Increasing the productivity of land, Locke stressed, was 'the great art of government' in modern states. This was best achieved by giving 'protection and incouragement to the honest industry of mankind' by means of laws of property. 'There cannot be a clearer demonstration', Locke said, of the productivity of modern labour than the fact that the American tribes who possessed almost unlimited land 'have not one hundredth part of the Conveniences we enjoy'. A king of one of their large territories, Locke concluded, 'feeds, lodges and is clad worse than a day labourer in England'.[118]

With this comparison between the English day labourer and the savage king, we return full circle to the paradox of commercial society as Smith had described it, in almost identical terms, in the introduction and plan of the *Wealth of Nations*. As a participant in the economic pamphleteering in the 1690s, in the reformulation of Grotian natural jurisprudence, and in the philosophical

[117] Locke, *Two Treatises*, 2.5.40. In contrast to Rousseau, Locke celebrated the invention of iron-melting and labour-saving machines. See the entry in his diary for 8 Feb. 1677 in Lord King, *The Life of John Locke with Extracts from his Correspondence, Journals and Commonplace Books*, 2 vols. (London, 1830), pp. 162-3. Compare this with Rousseau, *Discourse on Inequality*, pp. 83-5, and the fragments on machines and needs in 'Fragments Politiques' in *Oeuvres Complètes*, ed. B. Gagnebin and M. Raymond, iii (Paris, 1964), pp. 525-6. Locke's later statements on the productivity of human labour constitute an amendment of his earlier 'zero-sum game' image of the world in Essay 8, 'Is Every Man's Own Interest the Basis of the Law of Nature?', in *Essays on the Law of Nature*, p. 211.   [118] Locke, *Two Treatises*, 2.5.40.

inquiry into the moral implications of luxury in a commercial society, Locke's work exemplifies the three major discourses in which the paradox of commercial society was first posed in the seventeenth century. In one of the important economic pamphlets of Locke's day, one finds, for example, this explicit statement of the paradox:

> Among the wild Indians of America, almost every thing is the labourer's, 99 parts of a 100 are to be put upon the account of Labour. In England perhaps the Labourer has but 2/3 of all the conveniences of Life, but then the Plenty of these Things is so much greater here that a King of India is not so well lodg'd and fed and cloathed as a Day Labourer of England.[119]

Yet in none of this economic pamphleteering was the paradox posed as a problem of justice – of reconciling property claims against need claims. It was primarily as a problem in justice that the paradox came to occupy such a central place in Smith's thought as the *Wealth of Nations* took shape during his period as a professor of jurisprudence during the 1750s and early 1760s. Thus, it is essentially in the natural jurisprudence tradition, rather than in the 'economic' pamphleteers usually described as Smith's predecessors, that the central question in the *Wealth of Nations* was set up. Moreover, it was within that tradition that we can see the preparation of a specifically 'market' solution to the paradox, and to its key problem: how to enjoy the benefits of exclusive dominion without excluding the propertyless wage-earners from the means of subsistence. In both Pufendorf's and Locke's discussion of the necessity of high prices to call forth adequate supplies of subsistence, and in Locke's specific identification of property and the division of labour as the key to increasing the productivity of land, we can see how the natural-law theorists had shifted the problem of adjudicating the need claims of the poor and the property claims of the rich beyond a juridical plane and had begun to consider how a market system could be run in such a way that the scarcity constraints forcing a choice between the claims of need and the claims of property could be overcome altogether. Once this key move had been made, it was possible for Smith to short-circuit the laboured jurisprudential account of the origins of a world divided into labourers and the propertied. As long as Western thought on property was dominated by the idea that the world had originally been given to mankind in common, each account of the actual private property of the modern world had been forced to provide a conjectural history which both accounted for and legitimated exclusive individuation. The Pufendorfian and Lockian account of the initial condition of the community as 'negative' rather than 'positive', and Locke's elimination of even tacit consent as a necessary moment in the individuation of the common, cleared the way for Smith to take the distribution of property in his society as historically generated and to move

---

[119] [Henry Martyn], *Considerations upon East India Trade* (London, 1701), in *Select Collection of Early English Tracts of Commerce*, ed. J. R. McCulloch (London, 1856), pp. 593–4.

on to a clear analytical demonstration of how markets in subsistence goods and labour could balance themselves out in a manner consistent with strict justice and the natural law of humanity. This becomes clear enough if we look at the entirely cursory way Smith pauses to consider the possibility of a world in which the 'whole produce of labour' could belong to the labourer. In the beginning of the wages chapter, he says that such a state could only occur 'in that original state of things, which precedes both the appropriation of land and the accumulation of stock'. Had such a state continued, Smith argued, the labourer would have reaped all the productive benefit of the division of labour, but, he tersely concluded, such a state would not have made improvements in the division of labour in the first place, lacking the necessary incentives to capital accumulation. Hence, he said, 'it would be to no purpose to trace further'[120] what would have happened had the world not come to be divided into labourers, capitalists and landlords. The world whose economic problems Smith set out to solve was a world where land was already private property; while he certainly used the 'conjectural history' embedded in jurisprudential theories of property in his lectures and in Book V, they themselves enabled him to conclude that a world 'before mine and thine' was a distant historical chapter of no direct relevance to the modern world.

Natural jurisprudence – particularly its distinction between 'strict' and 'distributive' justice – provided Smith with the language in which his theory of the functions of government in a market society took shape. In this tradition, liberty was defined primarily in a passive sense, as the perfect right to enjoy and improve one's property free from the encroachments of others. In such a conception, individuals could be virtuous – *The Theory of Moral Sentiments* showed they were at least capable of propriety – but the society as a whole, as the unintended outcome of discrete acts of self-interest, could not be virtuous. It could stand for 'strict justice', for the rigid enforcement of 'to each his own' – indeed, this was the pillar, as Smith said, which held up the whole edifice. But market society could not guarantee anything more than strict justice. As John Millar put it, justice was the sole allegiance of a 'people engrossed by lucrative trades... whose great object is gain, and whose ruling principle is avarice'. Yet this was 'not that nice and delicate justice, the offspring of refined humanity, but that coarse though useful virtue, the guardian of contrasts and promises, whose guide is the square and the compass, and whose protector is the gallows'.[121]

---

[120] *WN* 1.viii.5. On Smith's position on the conjectural history of property in a Lockean perspective, see James Moore, 'Locke and the Scottish Jurists', unpublished paper presented to the 'John Locke and the Political Thought of the 1680s' symposium of the Conference for the Study of Political Thought and the Folger Institute for Renaissance and Eighteenth-Century Studies, Washington, D.C., 21–23 March 1980.

[121] John Millar, 'Political Consequences of the Revolution', in *An Historical View of English Government*, 4 vols. (London, 1812), iv, p. 94.

In the Renaissance civic paradigm, on the other hand, liberty was defined primarily in an active sense, not only as the enjoyment of rights, but as the exercise of active life and citizenship. In such a society, virtue consisted in the restraint of self-interest in the interests of civic good. History in the civic paradigm was understood, not as an account of the unintended consequences of private interest, but as the struggle of civic institutions of republican self-government to survive the cycle of corruption initiated by the republic meeting its *fortuna*. In such an account, if a society's individuals were suffused with civic virtue, the society as a whole could be virtuous. The social structure as such could be moralized. It could stand for and embody the ideal of civic participation.[122]

Both of these paradigms exerted a profound hold on the imagination of the Scottish Enlightenment, and on Smith in particular. Yet he never ceased to insist that the civic ideal had rested ultimately on an invidious and unjust delegation of productive labour to slaves. These ancient republics, like the primitive tribes also celebrated for their martial virtue and simplicity of manners, were in fact barbarously poor. There could be no 'paradox of the ancient republics' as there could be a paradox of commercial society. As Smith observed sardonically, in the 'ideal republick described in the laws of Plato', the productivity of labour would have been so low that it would have required a 'territory of boundless extent and fertility' simply to maintain those guardians of martial virtue, the 'five thousand idle men (the number of warriors supposed necessary for its defence) together with their women and servants'.[123] Modern commercial society was unequal and unvirtuous but it was not unjust. It did not purchase civic virtue at the price of misery for its poorest members. However unequal men might be, in property and citizenship, they could be equal in access to the means to satisfy basic need. In this set of preferences, it is clear that Smith was choosing strict justice over civic virtue, passive liberty over active. These were the preferences of the natural jurisprudence tradition.

[122] The active and passive distinction in respect of liberty is brought out well in J. H. Hexter, 'Republic, Virtue, Liberty, and the Political Universe of J. G. A. Pocock', in *On Historians* (London, 1979), pp. 255–303; see also J. G. A. Pocock's reflections on the relation between jurisprudential and civic humanist discourse in the introduction to the Italian edition of the *Machiavellian Moment*, published in English as '*The Machiavellian Moment* Revisited: A Study in History and Ideology', *Journal of Modern History*, 53 (1981), 49–72; and the same author's 'Reconstructing the Traditions: Quentin Skinner's Historians' Theory of Political Thought', *Canadian Journal of Political and Social Theory*, 3 (1979), 95–114; 'Virtues, Rights and Manners: A Model for Historians of Political Thought', *Political Theory*, 9 (1981), 353–68; and 'Authority and Property: The Question of Liberal Origins', in Barbara C. Malamont (ed.), *After the Reformation: Essays in Honor of J. H. Hexter* (Manchester, 1980), pp. 331–54. See also Pocock's essay in this volume, pp. 235–52 below.

[123] *WN* III.ii.9; compare with Hume, 'Of Commerce', p. 290. The general question 'Can a Body Politick be virtuous as a Collective body?' had been discussed by the Select Society in Edinburgh. See the 'Minutes of the Select Society', National Library of Scotland, Adv. MS. 23.1.1.

2 Where had the Scottish economy got to by the third quarter of the eighteenth century?*

T. C. SMOUT

I

The purpose of this essay is to delineate the economic position of Scotland immediately prior to the publication of the first books of the *Wealth of Nations* in 1776 and to inquire to what extent Scotland in this period was experiencing growth, who (if anyone) was becoming richer, and how was it coming about. To pose these questions in a book of this nature is not to imply that the early Scottish political economists were really writing about Scotland (or mainly about Scotland) when they proposed general models. But it would be wilful not to recognize that part of their intellectual equipment was the experience of the contemporary Scottish economy and recent economic history, and that if we want to understand them it may help to understand this experience also.

It is appropriate to begin by considering the seventy-five years or so that preceded 1750. The conventional picture of this period is one of deep stagnation in which very little economic growth or benevolent change occurred.[1] On the one hand, in the late seventeenth century the economy had been bedevilled by commercial crisis in overseas export markets and by famines[2] which were themselves indicators both of a relatively backward and stagnant agriculture and of the inability of the country to earn sufficient foreign exchange to import enough food to cover a shortfall. On the other hand, the Parliamentary Union of 1707 cured nothing in the short run, owing to Scottish

---

* I am most grateful to Tom Devine, Istvan Hont, Rosalind Mitchison and Sylvia Price for reading the text and making many helpful suggestions. All remaining faults are my own.
[1] This interpretation was established for the eighteenth century by Henry Hamilton, *The Industrial Revolution in Scotland* (Oxford, 1932), and *An Economic History of Scotland in the Eighteenth Century* (Oxford, 1963), and R. H. Campbell, *Scotland since 1707* (Oxford, 1965); for the seventeenth century by T. C. Smout, *Scottish Trade on the Eve of Union, 1660–1707* (Edinburgh, 1963). Recent texts, such as S. G. E. Lythe and J. Butt, *An Economic History of Scotland 1100–1939* (Glasgow, 1975), Bruce Lenman, *An Economic History of Modern Scotland, 1660–1976* (London, 1977), and R. H. Campbell, *The Rise and Fall of Scottish Industry 1707–1939* (Edinburgh, 1980), follow this view with only minor modifications.
[2] The latest study of the famines is in M. W. Flinn (ed.), *Scottish Population History from the Seventeenth Century to the 1930s* (Cambridge, 1976), pp. 164–86.

inability to improve the performance of the linen industry or the cattle trade, which had their principal external markets in England, and a similar failure before the 1740s to make much of the opening of the tobacco trade from the Chesapeake. Only around and after the Jacobite rising of 1745 was there a perceptible quickening of activity, marked both by limited agricultural improvement and by certain advances in the linen industry.

While there is no reason to think this is basically wrong, the traditional view now stands in need of modification and amplification. It has been argued that the agricultural sector, in particular, was not anything like as unresponsive as was once believed. Ian Whyte has shown how the seventeenth century (especially its closing decades) was marked by significant changes in land management, notably the widespread practice of granting leases for a fixed term of years (36 per cent of 2,900 surviving seventeenth-century leases were for ten years or more) and the consolidation of joint-farms into single tenancies (more than 90 per cent of written leases were for single-tenant farms). There was apparently more enclosure and emparking at least round the great houses than had been thought, especially in the east of Scotland, facilitated by the Parliamentary Acts to divide run-rig and the commonties, and a good deal of attention was paid after the Restoration to forestry and planting – so important in the wind-ravaged open fields of the Lowlands.[3] At the same time there was extensive cultivation of legumes and wheat and a certain amount of genuine new husbandry involving the introduction of liming (from the 1620s at least) and experiments with various rotations, so that the early heroic figures among the improvers like Cockburn of Ormiston and Grant of Monymusk must now be seen as part of a wider movement with pre-Union origins. This picture of early agrarian change is confirmed in detail for Roxburghshire and Berwickshire in the first part of the eighteenth century by the work of R. A. Dodgshon.[4]

The question of course remains as to how significant all this was in terms of productivity gains, and that is unlikely to be resolved without systematic long-run studies of agricultural yields. Whyte has made a useful start on this, but shows a great range of yields rather than any conclusive upward trend.[5] No one, moreover, is yet claiming that Scotland had a Kerridge-type agricultural revolution before the middle of the eighteenth century or that

---

[3] Ian Whyte, *Agriculture and Society in Seventeenth Century Scotland* (Edinburgh, 1979). See also M. L. Parry and T. R. Slater (eds.), *The Making of the Scottish Countryside* (London, 1980). This is a collection of important revisionist essays by historical geographers, including Whyte, Dodgshon and Adams.

[4] R. A. Dodgshon, 'Farming in Roxburghshire and Berwickshire on the Eve of Improvement', *Scottish Historical Review*, 54 (1975), 140–54. His book on Scottish agrarian history before the Improvers, *Land and Society in Early Scotland* (Oxford, 1981), deals with the subject at length, confirming and amplifying Whyte's work.

[5] Whyte, *Agriculture and Society*, pp. 74–9.

Scottish husbandry was anything other than backward in comparison to Dutch or English at the time of the Union: and in particular the seventeenth-century Scots appear to have ignored leys, sown grasses, hay-making and the other essentials of 'up-and-down husbandry'. On the other hand, it has also long been realized that one of the distinguishing features of the period 1680–1750 was that, despite the climatic accidents that led to famine in the 1690s, the Scots did normally produce and export a substantial surplus of grain.[6] There can be explanations for this other than agricultural progress, of course: the easing of population growth and a possible long-run amelioration in the weather, for example.[7] But, whatever the cause, the fact was that Scottish farms began to produce more food than the Scots could normally eat, and its disposal became a problem that worried landowners and statesmen to such a degree that it may even have inhibited further productivity changes on the land. What was the point of spending capital to produce more food if you could not sell what you already had? To put it in the contemporary language of a Scottish landowner in 1705, 'We are yearly improving our landes to produce more and more grain [but]... unless we alter our methods or fall on some nieu wayes of export our corns will become such a drug on our handes we shall never be able to pay our publick dues.'[8] The problem of surplus which (in general terms) so interested all early political economists was more familiar in real life to Scots farmers than the problem of dearth.

Another feature of this period which needs emphasis relates to internal communications and markets, the improvement of which must have gone some way to offset the apparently poor performance of external trade.[9] As Ballard pointed out as long ago as 1916, and as Whyte has recently re-emphasized,[10] the half-century before the Union was a great age for new markets: Parliament authorized 97 burghal and non-burghal markets and fairs between 1571 and 1660, but no fewer than 298 between 1660 and 1707, of which 246 were in non-burghal country sites. On the face of it this suggests an extraordinary explosion of buying and selling, even if some of the foundations may have been

---

[6] T. C. Smout and A. Fenton, 'Scottish Agriculture before the Improvers: An Exploration', *Agricultural History Review*, 13 (1965), 73–93.

[7] For Scottish climatic history, see M. L. Parry, 'Secular Climatic Change and Marginal Agriculture', *Transactions of the Institute of British Geographers*, no. 64 (1975), 1–13.

[8] J. Buchan to the Earl of Seafield, 23 June 1705, in J. Grant (ed.), *Seafield Correspondence 1685–1708*, Publications of the Scottish History Society, 2nd ser., iii (Edinburgh, 1912), p. 415.

[9] Even the poor performance of external trade in the first half of the eighteenth century may be exaggerated: rough calculations comparing the value of domestic exports per capita (including exports to England) suggest that they approximately doubled between 1698–1700 (when Scottish trade was in a particularly sorry plight) and 1755. See L. M. Cullen and T. C. Smout (eds.), *Comparative Aspects of Scottish and Irish Economic and Social History 1600–1900* (Edinburgh, 1976), 'Introduction', pp. 4–5.

[10] A. Ballard, 'The Theory of the Scottish Burgh', *Scottish Historical Review*, 13 (1916), 16–29; Ian Whyte, 'The Growth of Periodic Market Centres in Scotland 1600–1707', *Scottish Geographical Magazine*, 95 (1979), 13–26. See also Whyte, *Agriculture and Society*, chs. 7 and 9.

more nominal than real. And, although little is yet known in detail, it is very likely that Scotland experienced something of the contemporary revolution in internal transport that John Chartres has recently drawn attention to in England.[11] It is hard to imagine how otherwise the striking differences in regional grain prices of the seventeenth century came to be so substantially reduced by the second quarter of the eighteenth century,[12] and the vigour of inland commerce has been illustrated by a recent study of the first Scottish turnpikes, the important Edinburgh network established by the act of 1713.[13] Lenman's recent study on the Jacobites emphasizes the extent to which quite remote Highland chiefs were enmeshed, even by 1715, in the trading economy (and also, incidentally, the polite culture) of the Lowlands, so it becomes hard to sustain Insh's old theory that the risings represent an elemental clash between the old patriarchal forces of the hills and the new capitalist forces of the plain.[14] This integration increased rapidly in the first half of the eighteenth century, with consequent improvement in the number and quality both of drove roads and military roads, and in the multiplication of shipping services all the way round the Highland coast from Thurso to the Clyde.

The short-term impact of the Union on Scottish internal and external trade remains uncertain. Lenman argues for quite severe short-term dislocation, but much of his evidence is drawn, *faute de mieux*, from the statements of disappointed or rebellious men who could equally be reflecting, not decline, but the continuing failure of the economy to recover from its pre-Union depression. The only statistical material yet known on Scottish shipping that spans the Union period is embedded in the shipping lists of Dundee – the third or fourth port of Scotland, and located on the east coast where decay was complained of more than on the west. Analysis of a run of seven years before the Union compared with seven years afterwards shows a negligible decline in the tonnage of arrivals from outside Scotland of 1.5 per cent, and a modest increase in coastwise tonnage of 10 per cent.[15]

Some indirect support for the view that the Scottish economy had made somewhat better progress in the first four decades of the eighteenth century

[11] John Chartres, *Internal Trade in England 1500–1700* (London, 1977).
[12] Rosalind Mitchison, 'The Movements of Scottish Corn Prices in the Seventeenth and Eighteenth Centuries', *Economic History Review*, 2nd ser., 18 (1965), 278–91.
[13] R. G. Heddle, 'Road Administration in Midlothian in the Early Eighteenth Century' (unpublished MS.). I am grateful to Mr Heddle for permission to cite it. The tolls on the turnpikes coming into Edinburgh were 'rouped' (auctioned yearly) and rose in value by some 25 per cent between 1721 and 1730. There are no earlier statistics, and none later than 1733.
[14] Bruce Lenman, *The Jacobite Risings in Britain, 1689–1746* (London, 1980), especially ch. 6. G. P. Insh, *The Scottish Jacobite Movement: A Study in Social and Economic Forces* (Edinburgh, 1952).
[15] These details are from my own unpublished research on the lists, which are in the archives of Tayside Regional Council, Dundee. I am also grateful to the archivist of Aberdeen for the information on the shore dues accounts, which show a 4 per cent increase in the value of the farm, comparing similar pre- and post-Union periods.

than is generally allowed is provided by the events of 1740-1, when a very serious failure of the harvest (compared by contemporaries to the shortfall in the tragic years of 1697 and 1699) threatened a mortality crisis on the scale of those of the seventeenth century: none occurred, just as none occurred in subsequent similar harvest failures later in the eighteenth century.[16] There is little doubt that a major reason in 1740 was the superior organization of emergency relief by local heritors and magistrates: but improvements in market organization and in transport would make it easier to distribute grain, and perhaps there was a slightly wealthier elite of lairds and burgesses from whom the marginal charitable pound could be more easily extracted.[17] Whatever the reason, this crisis clearly marks that important watershed in national history between a society too economically and socially primitive to cope with famine and one able to overcome bad harvests without measurable demographic costs.

II

The period 1750-75 can be fruitfully examined in the light of such statistical series as are available: these are not as numerous or always as directly apposite as the historian would wish, but they can be made to serve.

Let us consider first those graphed in Figure 1, which are useful in giving a perspective that runs back to 1730: they show imports of tobacco (Scotland's major item in overseas commodity trade), the volume of linen stamped for sale (the major industrial product) and the East Lothian fiars price of oats (the principal food grain). It is obvious at a glance that there are no very clear turning points either at 1750 or elsewhere, the tend line climbing fairly steadily from the start of the period, and, apart from tobacco, also climbing fairly gently. The tobacco trade, of course, was a spectacular success based on American imports re-exported to France and the Netherlands, and Scottish merchants took most of the incremental growth of total Chesapeake traffic in the third quarter of the eighteenth century while their English commercial rivals stagnated in London. This was due in no small degree to 'a steady improvement in transport utilisations, in the number of voyages per ship, in the reduction of turn-round times and in the quantity of tobacco carried per unit'.[18] There has been much discussion among Scottish historians as to the

---

[16] See Flinn, *Scottish Population History*, pp. 216-23.
[17] See T. C. Smout, 'Famine and Famine Relief in Scotland', in Cullen and Smout, *Comparative Aspects*, pp. 25-6; R. Mitchison, 'Local and Central Agencies in the Control of Famine in Pre-Industrial Scotland', *Proceedings of the Seventh International Economic History Congress, Edinburgh, 1978*, 2 vols. (Edinburgh, 1978), ii, pp. 365-405; Flinn, *Scottish Population History*, pp. 216-23.
[18] See J. M. Price, 'The Rise of Glasgow in the Chesapeake Tobacco Trade', in P. L. Payne (ed.), *Studies in Scottish Business History* (London, 1967), pp. 299-318, and 'The Economic Growth of the Chesapeake and the European Market, 1697-1775', *Journal of Economic History*, 24

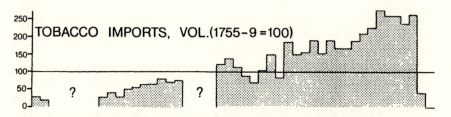

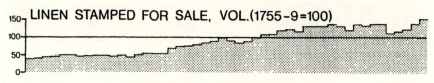

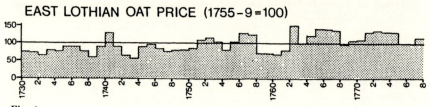

Fig. 1

Sources

Tobacco: *Historical Statistics of the United States, Colonial Times to 1957* (U.S. Bureau of the Census, Washington, D.C.), ch. 2

Linen: Henry Hamilton, *An Economic History of Scotland in the Eighteenth Century* (Oxford, 1963), Appendix III

Oat price: M. W. Flinn (ed.), *Scottish Population History from the Seventeenth Century to the 1930s* (Cambridge, 1976), Appendix B

precise economic significance of this trade: few would now consider it the equal of the linen industry in its capacity to create multiplier effects over a wide area, but few, too would now regard its beneficial influence as solely confined to a Glasgow enclave. T. M. Devine's careful studies have led to the broad and cautious conclusion that 'while not directly responsible for accelerated growth in the later eighteenth century' the tobacco trade was 'among the series of influences which helped to raise the impoverished economy of the early 1700s to the threshold of industrialisation' and was 'crucial to the emergence of the west-central region to a dominating position in the Scottish economy'.[19]

In considering the curves of linen output and oat price it is worth noticing first how their relationship appears to confirm Adam Smith's critical comments

(1964), 496–511; T. M. Devine, *The Tobacco Lords* (Edinburgh, 1975); and Richard F. Dell, 'The Operational Record of the Clyde Tobacco Fleet, 1747–1775', *Scottish Economic and Social History*, ii (1982), from which the quotation is drawn.

[19] T. M. Devine, 'Colonial Commerce and the Scottish economy c. 1730–1815', in Cullen and Smout, *Comparative Aspects*, p. 186; see also the same author, 'The Colonial Trades and Industrial Investment in Scotland', *Economic History Review*, 2nd ser., 29 (1976), 1–13.

on the backward-sloping supply curve for labour;[20] there is, as he remarked, no correlation between the high price of subsistence (oatmeal) and greater output in the staple industry, since the biggest increases in food price are associated either with slight rises or quite significant decreases in linen output. Even if the results are lagged by one year there is no obvious relationship. But it is equally difficult to find any support in the series for Adam Smith's alternative explanation of linen production determined by export demand,[21] since the highest peak of the long trend upwards is reached in 1777 during the American War of Independence, when external trade was seriously dislocated,[22] and there is also no correlation on a year-to-year basis with tobacco imports, though one might have expected to find one if the quantity of linen exported depended on the Virginians' purchasing power, which in turn would depend on American ability to sell to Glasgow.[23] The thrust of modern research has been to indicate that although foreign trade was important, sales in Scotland and in England substantially exceeded them.[24]

Overall, the impression obtained from the graph of linen stamped for sale is a soft but persistent upward trend, stagnating for almost two entire but separate decades between 1734 and 1744, and between 1763 and 1772 and with serious falls in some years, 1754–5, 1762, 1768 and in 1773 (the last in the wake of the Ayr Bank crisis), but nevertheless expanding from an index figure of under 50 to one of over 150 in half a century. The oat-price graph indicates greater relative fluctuations but a less clearly marked trend. The bad year 1740 stands out, as do 1756–7 and 1762. It is perhaps significant that the period 1762–74 emerges as a markedly higher plateau in grain prices than anything that had gone before. This, as we shall see, seems to have been important in respect to structural change in agriculture.

III

Tables I and II should next be considered together: they are designed as a quinquennial series covering the quarter-century, Table I showing actual

---

[20] *WN* I.viii.45–9. [21] *WN* I.viii.50.
[22] M. L. Robertson, 'Scottish Commerce and the American War of Independence', *Economic History Review*, 2nd ser., 9 (1956), 123–31; J. Butt, 'The American War of Independence and the Scottish Economy', in O. D. Edwards and G. Shepperson (eds.), *Scotland, Europe and the American Revolution* (Edinburgh, 1976), pp. 57–60.
[23] The relationship is not even very good between tobacco imports and direct linen exports from Scottish ports: it is true that peaks in 1758 and 1771 coincide, but other peaks in linen exports in 1764, 1767 and 1777 do not, and troughs in 1762, 1766, 1773 and 1775 bear no relation to the tobacco curve. Nor is there any clear upward trend in the direct linen export figures between 1755 and 1775. See Hamilton, *An Economic History of Scotland in the Eighteenth Century*, pp. 410–11.
[24] Alistair Durie, *The Scottish Linen Industry in the Eighteenth Century* (Edinburgh, 1979), especially ch. 8. Durie draws attention to the degree to which other Scottish contemporaries assumed there *was* a backward-sloping supply curve; see pp. 75–6.

52   T. C. Smout

Table I. *Volumes and values, by quinquennia*

Prices	1750–4	1755–9	1760–4	1765–9	1770–4
1 East Lothian oats (lib Scots per boll)	6.02	6.10	6.32	7.59	7.96
2 Lanark oatmeal (lib Scots per boll)	6.50	6.48	6.54	8.50	8.62
3 Perth oatmeal (lib Scots per boll)	5.61	6.02	6.38	7.62	8.66
4 Kintyre bullocks (shillings per head)	25.0	18.5	19.0	28.0	27.0
5 Kintyre cows (shillings per head)	40.0	30.0	30.0	40.0	43.0
Wages					
6 Midlothian day labourer (shillings per week)	3.5	4.0	4.0	5.0	5.0
7 Midlothian day labourer (oatmeal equivalent in oatmeal pecks)	5.015	5.260	5.260	5.304	5.304
Taxes					
8 Yield of 'old duty' on beer (£000)	37.9	37.0	37.3	29.8	26.1
9 Yield of 'old duty' on malt (£000)	25.8	21.7	22.3	20.4	19.9
Industrial production					
10 Paper (000 lbs) stamped for sale	146	206	336	470	558
11 Linen (000,000 yards) stamped for sale	8.51	9.58	12.05	12.80	12.36
12 Linen (value £000)	398	398	328	628	558
13 Flax imports (tons)	—	2065	2708	3325	3379
Trade (official values)					
14 Home-produced exports	—	344.5	409.0	415.9	487.8
15 Tobacco imports	—	178.6	281.3	324.6	452.3
16 Other imports (all £000)	—	387.5	517.3	716.2	773.2
Agricultural change					
17 Land surveyors at work (men per year)	20.8	27.8	37.2	46.6	65.0

Sources for Tables I and II

1–3; M. W. Flinn (ed.), *Scottish Population History from the Seventeenth Century to the 1930s* (Cambridge, 1976), Appendix B.

Table II. *Index figures, by quinquennia*

Prices	1750–4	1755–9	1760–4	1765–9	1770–4
1 East Lothian oats	99	100	104	124	130
2 Lanark oatmeal	100	100	101	131	133
3 Perth oatmeal	93	100	105	127	143
4 Kintyre bullocks	135	100	103	151	146
5 Kintyre cows	133	100	100	133	143
Wages					
6 Midlothian day labourer (money)	88	100		125	
7 Midlothian day labourer (oatmeal equivalent)	95	100		101	
Taxes					
8 Yield of 'old duty' on beer	103	100	101	81	71
9 Yield of 'old duty' on malt	118	100	103	94	92
Industrial production					
10 Paper	71	100	163	228	271
11 Linen (volume)	89	100	126	134	129
12 Linen (value)	100	100	133	158	140
13 Flax imports	—	100	131	161	164
Trade (official values)					
14 Home-produced exports	—	100	119	121	142
15 Tobacco imports	—	100	158	182	253
16 Other imports	—	100	133	185	200
Agricultural change					
17 Land surveyors	75	100	134	168	235

4–5: Eric Cregeen, pers. comm., from estate records of Campbell of Knockbuy.
6–7: George Robertson, *Rural Recollections* (Irvine, 1829).
8–9: S.R.O., E 904/3.
10: A. G. Thomson, 'The Paper Industry in Scotland' (Ph.D. thesis, University of Edinburgh, 1965), Fig. 2.
11–12: Henry Hamilton, *An Economic History of Scotland in the Eighteenth Century* (Oxford, 1963), Appendix IV.
13: Alistair Durie, 'The Scottish Linen Industry in the Eighteenth Century', in L. M. Cullen and T. C. Smout (eds.), *Comparative Aspects of Scottish and Irish Economic and Social History, 1600–1900* (Edinburgh, 1976), p. 89.
14–16: Hamilton, *Economic History of Scotland*.
17: Ian Adams, 'Economic Process and the Scottish Land Surveyor', *Imago Mundi*, 2nd ser., I (1975), 14.

volumes and values, Table II expressing the same as index figures, using 1755–9 as 100 because that is when foreign trade statistics begin.

Grain and cattle price statistics occupy columns 1–5. Grain prices turn out to be a little more buoyant outside East Lothian than inside, especially the Perthshire series, a fact which possibly reflects the increasing activity of a market economy towards the Highland edge and in an area where textiles were making marked progress. The cattle price statistics are drawn from a single estate, that of Campbell of Knockbuy in Kintyre, Argyll; they represent the prices the laird allowed his tenants for animals that he himself ultimately marketed. I am obliged to Eric Cregeen for providing them from his own notes: as far as I am aware these (necessarily inadequate though they may appear to be) are the only consistent series of cattle prices from one place available from anywhere in Scotland. Taken at their face value they do not suggest that cattle prices moved ahead much faster than grain prices during this particular quarter of a century, a finding that is both interesting and surprising.

It is indeed worth pausing over the business of cattle price. Adam Smith claimed in a well-known and oft-quoted passage that the threefold rise in the price of Highland cattle was the biggest benefit the Scots had obtained from the Act of Union,[25] but it is extremely difficult to find evidence of an increase of this magnitude. English customs statistics valued Scottish cattle between 1696 and 1703 between £1 and £2 at 'prime cost', but Clerk of Penicuik writing in 1733 from Edinburgh put the average price of black cattle for export at about £1 10s and said that this was 'one third higher' than twenty years before.[26] Malcolm Gray examining a wide range of diverse quotations for three-year-olds in his study of the Highland economy concluded that in the 1740s their price was around £1 or less, in the 1750s and 1760s about £1 10s, in the 1770s about £2.[27] Cregeen also notes that Campbell of Knockbuy was obtaining bullocks in the earlier 1730s for 13s or 14s, rising to £1 or £1 5s through the 1740s, and ultimately to £1 12s in the quinquennium 1775–9. The last is more than a doubling, but the mid 1730s were extremely depressed and there is no reason to believe that prices around the time of the Union were so low in Kintyre. Much Scottish meat ended up in London; Cregeen found that during the 1730s and 1740s the Beveridge series on what the Navy Victualling Board paid for beef moved in step with prices in Argyll: it was £1 1s per cwt in 1690–4, 17s 6d in 1750–4, £1 4s 9d in 1770–5, which is 35 per cent above 1755 but even less above the pre-Union price.[28] It may be, of course,

[25] *WN* I.xi.6.8; *WN* I.xi.1.3.
[26] Donald Woodward, 'A Comparative Study of the Irish and Scottish Livestock Trades in the Seventeenth Century', in Cullen and Smout, *Comparative Aspects*, p. 164n; 'Sir John Clerk's Observations', ed. T. C. Smout, *Miscellany of the Scottish History Society*, x, Publications of the Scottish History Society, 4th ser., ii (Edinburgh, 1965), pp. 175–212.
[27] Malcolm Gray, *The Highland Economy 1750–1850* (Edinburgh, 1957), p. 142.
[28] Eric Cregeen, 'The Tacksmen and their Successors', *Scottish Studies*, 13 (1969), 93–144, especially pp. 135–6 and the graph. William Beveridge, *Prices and Wages in England from the Twelfth to the Nineteenth Century* (London, 1939), pp. 568–71 (price tables).

that as the search for animals penetrated further and further into the crevices of the Highlands, prices on remote estates entering the pull of the external market for the first time did indeed multiply by a factor of three; cattle prices doubled on the Macleod estates in both Harris and Skye between the late seventeenth century and 1754, and no doubt they rose thereafter here as elsewhere.[29] But at present there seems little indication that Smith's figure was *generally* true.

Nevertheless, a glance at Table III shows that there is some evidence for suggesting that, whatever happened to price, the cattle trade did grow substantially in volume, possibly by 50 per cent in the third quarter of the eighteenth century. Therefore Smith's classic account of how a rising market for cattle could break the old cycle of infertility by encouraging the tenant to keep more stock and thereby providing more manure for both arable land and pasture, which in turn can be used to raise more cattle, may not have been out of place. It is one of the relatively few parts of the *Wealth of Nations* that is given an explicitly Scottish context, in this case by a lucid description of how the old Lowland mode of infield–outfield farming had been limited and indeed determined by the shortage of dung, and was now slowly being replaced by improved farming which rested on heavier stocking ultimately made possible by a higher return for cattle since the Union: 'It has not only raised the value of all Highland estates, but it has, perhaps, been the principal cause of the improvement of the low country.'[30]

Yet the whole question of the developmental effects of a trade in cattle is full of uncertainties in respect to the location of the benefits that may occur. Charles Kindleberger has pointed out that meat-exporting does not necessarily have dynamic effects in the raising area because it is land-intensive 'and flourishes with a feudal type of society that does not encourage consumption'. It often takes place on poor land as some form of ranching, and does not encourage close settlement: the result is that it may be 'impossible to achieve settlements dense enough to establish villages, which are a prerequisite for efficiency in distribution and administration, and hence in development'.[31] He

---

[29] These were conversion prices for produce rents. The price of a mart in Harris was:

1680–1703:	14s 5d
1703–1706:	16s 8d
1706–1720:	14s 5d
1735–1753:	17s 6d
1754:	£1 6s 9d

In Skye prices for mart were:

1706–20:	16s 8d
1724:	17s 6d
1744:	23s 6d
1754:	£1 13s 4d

See C. L. Horricks, 'Economic and Social Change in the Isle of Harris' (Ph.D. thesis, University of Edinburgh, 1974), pp. 290 1.   [30] *WN* I.xi.1.3.

[31] Charles Kindleberger, *Foreign Trade and the National Economy* (New Haven, Conn., 1962), p. 199.

Table III. *Miscellaneous statistics*

1 *Population*
   1755   1,265,400 (Webster)
   1775   Two estimates: 1,376,000
           or   1,398,250
   The latter is favoured, and is a 10.5% increase on 1755.

2 *Bank statistics*

	Assets (£)	Assets/head (£)	Note issue (£)	Bank offices
1744	329,000	0.27	55,000	12
1772	3,147,000	2.33	864,000	37

3 *Cattle exports from Scotland to England*
   1723   30–37,500
   1724   40,000
   c. 1740   40,000
   1770   62,500
   c. 1780   60,000
   These figures must be the most tentative in the series.

4 *Population of five large towns*

	Edinburgh	Glasgow	Dundee	Aberdeen	Paisley	Total
1755	57.2	23.5	12.0	10.5	4.2	107.4
1775	70.4	31.2	15.0	14.0	9.3	139.9

Sources for Table III

Population: The 1775 estimate was kindly made for me by Rosalind Mitchison: compare Flinn, *Scottish Population History*.

Banking: S. G. Checkland, *Scottish Banking, A History, 1695–1973* (London, 1975), p. 722.

Cattle: This table was originally compiled by A. J. Youngson in an unpublished paper, but, while kindly willing to allow me to use it, he was unwilling to take responsibility for its accuracy. The sources he used were:

D. Defoe, *Tour Through Great Britain in 1724* (6th edn, 1762), i, p. 60.
A. R. B. Haldane, *The Drove Roads of Scotland* (1952), pp. 173, 181, 205.
W. Nimmo, *History of Stirlingshire* (1777), p. 457.
T. Pennant, *A Tour in Scotland and Voyage to the Hebrides, 1772* (1776), ii, p. 230.
A. Porteous, *The History of Crieff* (1912), p. 235.
J. A. Symon, *Scottish Farming Past and Present* (1959), p. 132.

Town Population: *Old Statistical Account*. The 1755 figures originate in Webster: those for 1775 (apart from Edinburgh, which was estimated in 1775) are derived from figures for the 1780s given in the OSA for other towns.

cites the examples of Texas, Argentina and Africa, but that of the Highlands and indeed of Lowland Galloway are very relevant in the eighteenth-century Scottish context, as these are generally believed to have been the main cattle-producing areas, but they remained notoriously backward throughout the period.[32]

Indeed, agrarian advance before 1775 was still largely confined to the east coast south of Aberdeen and less markedly to Ayrshire and the counties abutting on Glasgow – certainly not areas devoted to breeding animals for the English market. This does not imply that improved areas were not carrying heavier stocks of beasts or that their manure was not breaking the infertility cycle in exactly the way Adam Smith described: but what was the origin and market of those animals?

The conventional picture (which no scholar has attempted to revise) is of the cattle ranched in the upland areas and sold at Crieff, Dumfries or Falkirk Trysts as lean stock driven into England for fattening before slaughter: when young they therefore dropped their dung uselessly on the barren moor, when older the benefits of their manure accrued to Yorkshire or East Anglian husbandry, not to that of Lothian, Fife or Lanarkshire.[33] There is no reason to suppose that this needs modification in respect to beasts sold in England, and Adam Smith's remarks in respect to the effect of the Union at first sight seem misleading.

On the other hand, they need not be if there was a substantial and growing demand for meat in the Scottish towns, due to an expanding bourgeois population with increasing *per capita* incomes and a concomitant appetite for steak. In the absence of the droving trade to England this could no doubt have been cheaply met from Highland leanstock, but, with Highland animals now siphoned off to the south, prices remained high and Lowland farmers themselves turned to more intensive husbandry which increasingly approximated to English models. It was the Lothians especially which were in the van of agricultural change before 1790, raising more animals, going over to

---

[32] Galloway in the 1780s was 'much behind eastern counties in improvements' despite its early enclosures that triggered the Levellers' Revolt in 1724. J. E. Handley, *Scottish Farming in the Eighteenth Century* (London, 1953), pp. 199, 212.

[33] See A. R. B. Haldane, *The Drove Roads of Scotland* (Edinburgh, 1952), p. 57: 'The agriculture of those parts of Scotland capable of fattening stock was till the early years of the nineteenth century largely an agriculture of crop cultivation, and not till then did new farming methods, based on the growing of artificial grasses and turnips, turn the attention of Scottish farmers towards stock fattening.' It is true that Hamilton, *The Industrial Revolution in Scotland*, pp. 62–5, gave the impression that fattening cattle in the east-coast counties from Angus north to Moray and Nairn was practised from soon after the '45 rebellion, but all the sources he cites relate to a period later than the third quarter of the eighteenth century, and the latest thrust of research has been to place the large-scale introduction of turnips and sown grasses necessary to feed such cattle into the period after 1790. See Malcolm Gray, 'Scottish Emigration: The Social Impact of Agrarian Change in the Rural Lowlands 1775–1875', *Perspectives in American History*, 7 (1973), pp. 95–174.

artificial grasses and turnips for fodder, alternating 'green' crops with 'white', and using the increase in dung (supplemented by cart-loads of human excrement from Edinburgh) to grow more wheat as well as other grains.[34]

The importance of Edinburgh as a growth point in the third quarter of the eighteenth century was indeed considerable, and has been insufficiently emphasized in the standard accounts of Scottish economic history. Population in the metropolis grew by a quarter. The college was gaining rapidly in reputation, especially under the leadership of Principal William Robertson from 1762 and with teachers like Adam Ferguson and Joseph Black: it was accompanied by a great growth in facilities for private education by private tutors and in schools and academies of many kinds, bringing wealthy families into the town for the education of their children.[35] The 'Proposals' for the construction of a New Town were published in 1752, and their author, Sir Gilbert Elliot of Minto, dwelt at length on the economic justifications for expansion:

> The national advantages which a populous capital must necessarily produce, are obvious. A great concourse of people brought within a small compass, occasions a much greater consumption than the same number would do dispersed over a wide country. As the consumption is greater so it is quicker and more discernible. Hence follows a more rapid circulation of money and other commodities, the great spring which gives motion to general industry and improvement. The example set by the capital, the nation will soon follow. The certain consequence is, general wealth and prosperity: the number of useful people will increase; the rents of land rise; the public revenue improve; and, in the room of sloth and poverty, will succeed industry and opulence.[36]

The development of George Square and the Georgian southside proceeded apace in the 1760s; the Exchange was completed about 1760, the North Bridge was opened in 1765 and Register House begun in 1774, though other developments to the north hardly became significant before the 1780s. Edinburgh's intellectual life, exemplified by the foundation of the Select Society in 1754, also had a magnetic effect on the gentry and nobility, who wished to acquire polish from consorting with the literati as much as the literati desired status from the patronage of the social elite. Alexander Carlyle reported how the landed class flocked to its meetings: 'though few of them took any share in the debates [they] thought themselves so well entertained and instructed that they gave punctual attendance'. The attraction of the clubs had an economic as well as a social effect, in bringing visitors into the town to spend as well as to attend.[37]

[34] T. C. Smout, introduction to *The Lothians, Statistical Account of Scotland*, new edn, D. J. Withrington and I. R. Grant (general eds.), ii (Wakefield, 1975); Gray, 'Scottish Emigration'.
[35] D. B. Horn, *A Short History of the University of Edinburgh 1556–1889* (Edinburgh, 1967); Alexander Law, *Education in Edinburgh in the Eighteenth Century* (Edinburgh, 1965).
[36] Quoted in A. J. Youngson, *The Making of Classical Edinburgh* (Edinburgh, 1966), p. 11.
[37] N. T. Phillipson, 'Culture and Society in the 18th Century Province: The Case of Edinburgh and the Scottish Enlightenment', in L. Stone (ed.), *The University in Society*, 2 vols. (Princeton, N.J., 1974), ii, pp. 442–6.

Much of the development was due initially to the vision of a single man, Provost George Drummond, who was seeking to create an urban setting to which men of taste and income would be attracted. Though not himself a merchant (but a civil servant), he stood at the apex of the Edinburgh merchant guild, traditionally by far the most numerous and opulent body of traders in Scotland, whose importance was only just beginning to be rivalled by that of their counterparts in Glasgow. Equally, the prosperity of Edinburgh surely also reflected the rent increases of landowners, including Highland lairds enriched by their augmented cattle rents and thus enabled to support the economic needs of the lawyers, their offspring and their establishments. Edinburgh's charms had a redistributive effect, with much of the surplus from Highland trade ending up not in the glens but in the High Street, its impact on Lothian farmers appearing in turn when it was spent on local meat and white bread.

Scots might be glad that this was occurring in Edinburgh rather than in London, where the multiplier effects of their incomes would be lost. After the middle of the century less is heard of the kind of complaint Clerk of Penicuik made in 1730: 'our want of money may be ascribed to many of this country who, without business either at Court or in the Parliament, live in London and drain off their rents for supporting them there. If this way of living was general, all manner of improvements here would be neglected.'[38] It was a situation Sir Gilbert Elliot was reflecting when he commented that, while only a few great families chose to reside in London, many others go occasionally: 'and if their stay be long, and their expense by consequence greater than this country can well bear, it must be entirely imputed to the present form and situation of Edinburgh. Were these in any tolerable degree to be remedied, our people of rank would hardly prefer an obscure life at London, to the splendour and influence with which they might reside at home.' There is a counterfactual problem here which is hardly capable of definitive solution; would more families have spent more time in London if Edinburgh had not been a reconstructed and expanding town? The answer is not necessarily positive, yet the prosperity of the city in the third quarter of the century suggests that Elliot had his analysis right.[39]

IV

Who gained from the limited improvements in agricultural prices and markets that we have examined so far? Henry Hamilton argued that 'between the middle of the century and the early nineties when the *Statistical Account* was compiled wages rose substantially. Some ministers reckoned the increase to be

[38] 'Sir John Clerk's Observations', pp. 207–8.
[39] Quoted in Youngson, *The Making of Classical Edinburgh*, p. 10. I can find little evidence for Nicholas Phillipson's assertion in 'Culture and Society', p. 443, that 'throughout the 1750s and 1760s the drift [of landowners] away from Edinburgh to London became increasingly noticeable', though I concede this might be true by the 1780s.

threefold, others fourfold.'[40] He may be right for the last two decades, but our evidence suggests that the first part of this period, to 1775, was probably not a quarter-century of rising wages at least for day labourers, even those on Edinburgh's doorstep, where any benefit of rising incomes was likely first to become apparent.[41] Certainly there was a rise in money wages (Tables I and II, column 6) but only a quite trivial one of about 5 per cent in real wages, as measured in the amount of meal the wage would buy (column 7). The figure is calculated from data in George Robertson's *Rural Recollections* and runs back to the 1640s. Very interestingly, the money wage did not vary at all over the first hundred years: plainly it was a traditional fixed wage, not a market wage. Then it began to creep forward, a process no doubt marking the modernization and monetization of the local economy in the third quarter of the eighteenth century. Real wages, of course, had been far from stagnant over the period, owing to the variation in grain price moving against a fixed money wage. Robertson suggests that the worst decade was 1645-54, when the day labourer's income would only buy 4 pecks, the best 1686-94, when it rose to 6.5 pecks. The purchasing power of 5.304 pecks of 1765-74 is therefore in the middle of previous experience, and it was not until the last quarter of the century that the best seventeenth-century experience was improved upon.[42]

On the other hand, such day labourers formed only a relatively small proportion of the total permanent work force on Scottish farms. It was farm-servants (and 'unpaid' family labour) which contributed most of the labour input, and servants were paid wholly or partly in kind. It was common at the time of the *Statistical Account* for servants in and around towns and villages to send to market that part of their payment in kind which they did not need for subsistence, so rising grain prices would actually tend to their benefit. We know too little of the trend in their earnings to be sure whether or not they gained much before 1775; it seems unlikely that the trend in their payments would deviate far from that of day labourers, even if payment-in-kind would give them a slight advantage. Nor should one forget that this was a period in which benefit could arise among the rural working-classes as a whole from the increase in women's employment.

This impression of the third quarter of the eighteenth century being an unremarkable time for labour is superficially strengthened by a look at the tax yields on beer and malt, since drink was the main consumer good of the poor. Rates were raised in 1761, but document E904/3 in the Scottish Record Office

---

[40] Hamilton, *Economic History of Scotland in the Eighteenth Century*, pp. 352-3.
[41] See Smith's observations on high wages in the neighbourhood of great towns, including Edinburgh, *WN* I.x.c.19.
[42] It is very unlikely that these figures are invalidated by a proportion (or a varying proportion) of the wage being paid in kind: in the Lothians, though the hind (ploughman) was usually paid partly or largely in kind, day labourers were paid in cash.

divides the yield thereafter into 'old duty' (i.e. minus the incremental rate) and 'new duty': columns 8 and 9 in Tables I and II give the yield of the 'old duty' as a better proxy for the amounts of beer and malt produced. Both index figures show substantial falls over the period, so the question arises as to whether tax evasion on a large scale could be a better explanation of the decline than falling consumption.

The story of the whisky industry in this period suggests that over 500,000 gallons a year (virtually all for home consumption) were charged with excise in the early 1750s, but following a temporary prohibition on legal distilling in the bad harvest of 1756–7 there was an enormous increase in illicit distillation, especially in the towns: by the 1760s only 50,000 gallons a year was being excised, and by 1779 there were reckoned to be up to 400 illegal distilleries in Edinburgh alone. How much did they make? One estimate by an excise officer (in 1784) put the annual output of the illegal distilleries in Scotland at 500,000 gallons, which certainly suggests not an enormous net increase in production but rather a switch from legal to illegal stills. We do know, however, that it was during this quarter-century that whisky became a popular addition to beer and wine, being drunk alone, instead of mixed with punch and cordials, by the landed gentry; and there was also a substantial increase in the consumption of cheap rum from the West Indies.[43]

If there is little decisive evidence that the labouring classes were gaining appreciably in this period, nevertheless there is reason to suppose that improvement in personal incomes was occurring, and was being concentrated in the pockets of middle and higher social groups. One shred of evidence in that direction is column 10 of Tables I and II, showing almost a fourfold increase in paper production within Scotland. Paper was not, of course, an

[43] For the whisky trade, see Michael S. Moss and John R. Hume, *The Making of Whisky* (Ashburton, 1981), ch. 2. Ian Donnachie, *A History of the Brewing Industry in Scotland* (Edinburgh, 1979), carefully considers the problem of tax yields in relation to brewing, but his table of the yield of the malt tax is less useful for our purposes as it gives the figures after deduction of administrative costs. Henry Hamilton, *Economic History of Scotland in the Eighteenth Century*, p. 105, gives the total yield of the malt tax and the excise. From this the table shown below can be constructed. The raising of the rates from 1760 and 1761 is clearly reflected in the table, but the improvement in yield is seen to be only temporary. Alexander Murdoch, '*The People Above*': *Politics and Administration in Mid-Eighteenth-Century Scotland* (Edinburgh, 1980), provides additional information on the customs and excise system, evasion and the political machinations that surrounded appointments.

	1750–4	1755–9	1760–4	1765–9	1770–4
Yield of Malt Tax (£000)	25.8	23.8	33.5	30.7	29.9
Yield of Excise (£000)	37.9	36.3	54.4	44.4	38.5
Yield of Malt Tax (index: 1755–9 = 100)	109	100	140	129	125
Yield of Excise (index: 1755–9 = 100)	104	100	143	122	106

important industry on the scale of linen textiles, but it did take off in the 1750s from a level of output that had been relatively stagnant for two decades,[44] and paper was *par excellence* a consumption good of the bourgeois (which is not to deny that in Scotland the peasantry was also a literate class). Part of this surge in production was import substitution, both of English paper and of English books: a recent thesis has shown how the Edinburgh book trade flourished in the 1750s and 1760s, with the partnership of Gavin Hamilton and John Balfour alone publishing about 400 titles between 1750 and 1762.[45]

The growth of the paper industry was also, however, part and parcel of the growth of the middle- and upper-class consumer goods industries and service industries of the capital, ranging from books and coaches to perfumeries and coaching inns. William Creech's Edinburgh contribution to the *Statistical Account* is full of odds and ends of statistical statements, mainly comparing 1763 with 1783, illustrating this process.[46] One example was that the quantity of wheat made into flour at the Water of Leith in mills belonging to the Incorporation of Bakers increased from 23,000 bolls in 1750 to 43,000 bolls in 1770,[47] an 87 per cent increase over a period when the population of Edinburgh and Leith grew only by about 23 per cent. Wheat and meat were the food of the well-to-do, but meal and potatoes remained the food of the Edinburgh poor. That statistic demonstrates as well as any the rising standards of the bourgeoisie.

V

The next three columns (11–13) in Tables I and II relate to linen, the staple manufacture of the country; as a recent commentator has observed, 'the importance of the linen trade can hardly be exaggerated for eighteenth-century growth'.[48] Certain features in the statistical series are particularly worth noting. Firstly, flax imports (column 13) grew substantially faster than the volume of linen stamped for sale (column 11), the reason being that an increasing proportion of linen was woven from imported flax.[49] That was a matter of some importance, as it marks a point of divergence between Scottish and Irish industrial history. In Scotland even in the second quarter of the

---

[44] Alistair G. Thomson, 'The Paper Industry in Scotland 1700–1861' (Ph.D. thesis, University of Edinburgh, 1965).

[45] Warren MacDougall, 'Gavin Hamilton, John Balfour and Patrick Neill: A Study of Publishing in Edinburgh in the Eighteenth Century' (Ph.D. thesis, University of Edinburgh, 1974).

[46] See *The Lothians* in *Statistical Account*, ii, pp. 20–59. See also Lorna Weatherill, 'Marketing English Pottery in Scotland, 1750–1820', *Scottish Economic and Social History*, ii (1982), 18–43, for a study of the start of the penetration of the Scottish market by one English consumer good.

[47] *Ibid.*, pp. 42–3. The context makes it clear that this was only about a third of the wheat consumed in the city, but the other mills 'have increased their quantities in proportion'.

[48] Lenman, *An Economic History of Modern Scotland*, p. 89.

[49] By the last quinquennium of the century the index figures for linen production (1755–9 = 100) had reached 229, but that for flax imports 341.

century less than half the linen was made from home-grown flax,[50] but in Ireland almost all was home-grown. Flax did not grow particularly well in Scotland, and the efforts of the Board of Trustees for Manufactures to improve and subsidize its cultivation were of comparatively little avail in the long run. The consequence of this divergence was that Scotland progressively separated linen production from farming, and ultimately developed a proletariat skilled in textile production but divorced from the land and ready to work in towns and villages – small-holdings were generally discouraged by landowners. Ireland went the other way, and the proto-industrial family there became tied to a small farm, with subdivisions of holdings encouraged by landlords wherever the industry flourished; flax was grown, spun and woven in the same household, with consequent rural congestion and ultimate lack of flexibility that contributed not a little to the tragedy of nineteenth-century Ireland.

The linen trade more than any other manufacture must have been the industry that Adam Smith was most familiar with, as it was successful and widespread throughout most of the Lowlands, not least in the Fife villages near Kirkcaldy. It was still a domestic and cottage industry, even if divorced from agricultural production, and this small-scale mode of production seems most to meet with his approval. Almost the only thing Smith had to say about 'large manufactories' was that they frequently ruined the morals of the workers:[51] Kindleberger has interpreted this paucity of references as an indication that the author of the *Wealth of Nations* was out of touch with the most exciting contemporary developments of the Industrial Revolution,[52] but in the third quarter of the eighteenth century apart from Carron there simply were no large manufactories in Scotland; the growth points of the economy lay in the cottage.

Almost the whole of Smith's discussion of industrial work and payment in Book I relates to the domestic system and could have been drawn from his observations of the linen trade – for example, 'a poor independent workman will generally be more industrious than even a journeyman who works by the piece. The one enjoys the whole produce of his own industry; the other shares it with his master... the superiority of the independent workmen over those servants who are hired by the month or by the year... is likely to be still greater.'[53] Another remark that seems to rest on the same experience is his comment that in years of dear food independent workers will enter a master's employment to work for wages but leave again in cheap years to work on their own account, and that in cheap years many women spin for their own families and craftsmen work on a bespoke basis for their neighbours rather than coming to the market, so that 'the produce of their labour... makes no figure in those

---

[50] Durie, *The Scottish Linen Industry*, p. 35.   [51] *WN* I.viii.48.
[52] Charles Kindleberger, 'The Historical Background: Adam Smith and the Industrial Revolution', in T. Wilson and A. S. Skinner (eds.), *The Market and the State: Essays in Honour of Adam Smith* (Oxford, 1976), pp. 1–6.   [53] *WN* I.viii.48.

public registers of which the records are sometimes published with so much parade'.[54] It is a relevant warning against taking the Board of Trustees' figures of linen 'stamped for sale' as too exact a proxy for output.

Apart from its direct contribution to national income the linen industry had an important structural effect on the Scottish economy. Estimates of the numbers employed varied, and are probably unreliable; Naismith suggested that there might have been 20,000 weavers in the 1760s, while David Loch actually enumerated over 12,000 looms at work in the mid 1770s on a tour of the country that omitted to count those at certain important centres like Edinburgh and Cupar: 15,000 weavers by then would seem a basic minimum. Estimates of spinners ranged from Lord Deskford's guess in the mid 1750s that 180,000 women were employed from time to time, to Naismith's estimate in the 1780s of 170,000 who found their 'chief employment' by spinning. These would suggest that about four-fifths of the adult female population were involved, which seems an improbably high proportion. If one allows four or five spinners to keep each weaver employed (probably on the low side), there must have been at a very minimum almost 100,000 hands in the industry, equivalent to one person in every second or third family in the country. What is self-evident is that very large numbers were employed, and that as the industry grew they found that an increasing proportion of their time could be more profitably spent in industry than in agriculture or housekeeping. As Alistair Durie puts it: 'Whereas a weaver in 1700 might have been hard put to find enough work for (say) six months in the year, his son fifty years later would probably have been able to get enough for eight, and the grandson in the 1790s could work virtually the year round, if he so desired, and the same probably held on the distaff side.'[55]

In so far as this process was taking these workers wholly or partly out of the agricultural-producer pocket (where their marginal productivity was close to zero) and into the industrial-worker-cum-food-consumer pocket it was performing a useful service by making 'farmers' into 'free-hands', to use Steuart's language. Hume and Steuart foresaw such a transfer as vital to balanced growth but they also seemed to think it would only come about through the growth of 'luxury', the domestic spending of the rich. Smith seems to have believed specifically in relation to linen that the demand growth was export lead. Durie's authoritative book on the industry stresses the market in England and abroad as probably more important even in this period than the market in Scotland: he estimates that between 19 per cent and 30 per cent of output was exported from British ports, and accepts that another 30 per cent of linen cloth (and about half the yarn) may have been sold in England.[56]

[54] *WN* I.viii.51.
[55] Durie, *The Scottish Linen Industry*, pp. 158–9, implies mid-century employment of this order of magnitude at least. [56] *WN* I.viii.54; Durie, *The Scottish Linen Industry*, pp. 144–55.

It is also worth considering whether the earnings of the women engaged in spinning linen might not have been the main source of any gains in working-class real incomes as there were in this period, as 80 per cent or more of the workers in the industry were spinners, whose opportunity for income was otherwise low, even though their earnings in the trade were themselves small – as Smith said, 'they earn but a very scanty subsistence who endeavour to get their entire livelihood by [spinning]. In most parts of Scotland she is a good spinner who can earn twenty pence a week.' One commentator explained that the putters-out in Angus gave the spinners 'credits for meal, butter, cheese, hardfish, coals, lint, lintseed and such like things'. The interesting thing about this list is the inclusion of 'butter, cheese, hardfish, coals', items of diet or fuel slightly superior to the traditional basic necessities of oatmeal, milk and furze or peat. It looks as if this improvement in household incomes was being partly spent on marginal items where there was (at this level) a high income-elasticity of demand.[57]

In a similar fashion, the movement of men from agriculture to weaving would also be a gain that would not show up in wages indices, as it was essentially a 'shifting-up' from less well paid to better paid employment.

VI

Columns 14–16 in Tables I and II relate to official values of overseas trade through Scottish ports: statistics relating to the traffic only start in 1755, and as we have no knowledge of the coasting trade with England or trans-Border traffic we cannot take these to be the equivalent of a statement of all Scottish external commerce. The official values appear to represent rough market values around 1755 but were not varied in succeeding years, so they provide an index of volumes at 1755 prices rather than a true index of value.

The composition of the 'home-produced exports' of column 14[58] was studied by analysing the manuscript returns for four individual years, 1755, 1760, 1765 and 1770.[59] Textiles were always by far the largest single group, accounting for 40–50 per cent of the total. Linen was obviously dominant among textiles, producing at least three-quarters of that sum, and probably considerably more (there is a problem of deciding what fabric or fibre 'haberdashery' and some 'stockings' were really made of). Woollen goods seem regularly to have run at 5–10 per cent of total exports. The next most important export group was fish, at 21 per cent of the total in 1755, 9 per cent in 1760, 15 per cent in 1765

---

[57] Durie, *The Scottish Linen Industry*, pp. 39, 60, 76 7; *WN* I.x.b.48 52.
[58] Some of these 'home-produced exports' no doubt originated in England (the customs books distinguish Irish goods from British but not English from Scottish), as some commodities were moved coastwise to the Clyde to make up export cargoes for the plantations.
[59] 'Ledgers of the Inspector General for Imports and Exports', S.R.O., RH 2/4. (These are photocopies of the volumes in Public Record Office, Customs 14.)

and 13 per cent in 1770 – salmon and herring led the group, with cod a poor third: the vigour of the eighteenth-century fisheries is not always appreciated. Lead began at 18 per cent in 1755 and fell steadily to 5 per cent in 1770 – it was sent to Holland, almost entirely from the one mine at Leadhills in Lanarkshire. Exports of grain and meal were usually slight and tending to fall, but in 1760 could still account for 8 per cent of total exports. Norway was the main destination.

The period of the early 1770s seems to have been quite good for home-produced exports as a group, and they bore up well under the impact of the Ayr Bank crisis of 1772. The two decades as a whole saw a larger growth of home-produced exports from Scottish ports than from English: if we compare 1755-64 with 1765-74, it is clear that Scottish home-produced exports rose by 22 per cent, English by only 2 per cent, but the better performance still only increased Scotland's overall share of the trade from 4.2 per cent to 4.6 per cent of the English total.[60] England had between four and five times greater value of home-produced exports per head leaving her ports than Scotland; itself a crude measure of the gap between the commercial economies of the two countries, even though no allowance is made for the coasting trade and mutual re-exports of each other's manufactures.

Column 15 relates to tobacco import figures; they speak for themselves, and complement the more detailed picture in Figure 1. Most of the tobacco was re-exported, and its value in the official statistics increased from $2\frac{1}{2}d$ to $5d$ a pound, so that the 'official value' of tobacco on its way out to final markets in Europe far eclipsed the values placed on all home-produced exports towards the end of the period.[61] Such valuations took no account of real changes in market price and in the terms of trade, but it is probably significant that 'other imports' (column 16) remained in value well above 'home-produced exports', presumably because the re-exports of tobacco paid for an excess of imports without running Scotland into chronic balance-of-payment problems on her foreign seaborne trade.

The composition of the import parcel[62] reflects the great importance of the colonial trades, tobacco accounting for between a third and two-fifths of imports by value in most years, with sugar and rum accounting for another 9-15 per cent: rum was becoming distinctly more popular towards the end of the period. The next-largest items were a group of raw materials for industry and construction, amounting together to 20-30 per cent of imports: flax (10-15 per cent), wood (5-8 per cent), and iron (3-4 per cent), along with linseed

---

[60] English figures from Phyllis Deane and W. A. Cole, *British Economic Growth 1688-1959* (Cambridge, 1967), p. 48. But note the 'official values' of English exports are based on 1697-1703 prices, those of Scottish, c. 1755.
[61] Because of this (apparently arbitrary) revaluation, it is impossible to subtract the value of re-exports from those of imports to obtain a figure of 'retained imports'.
[62] S.R.O., RH 2/4, volumes for 1755, 1760, 1765, 1770.

and dyestuffs that were generally a little less important. Manufactured imports were fairly diverse, but only linen textiles were at all prominent in terms of value – they ranged between 5 per cent and 12 per cent. Probably some of these would be destined in turn for the overseas market as re-exports. There can be little doubt, however, that England provided her less-developed northern neighbour with most of the manufactures she could not produce herself, especially woollen textiles and metal goods of all kinds.

The developmental effect of all this miscellaneous commercial activity on the urban sector was quite striking. In Table III the estimates of the population of five large towns indicate that their growth was at three times the rate of the national average population increase during the quarter-century. Edinburgh, though it had the largest aggregate increase of the five, had actually the smallest in percentage terms. Paisley, a textile town with an inclination towards the finer linens and silks and therefore probably selling a smaller proportion of its output abroad, had the largest percentage growth. But Glasgow, Aberdeen and Dundee all grew by a quarter to a third over the period, and were all significant ports in which the direct impact of trade and shipping must have been considerable. Glasgow, for example, in 1775 imported 46 million pounds of tobacco, or approximately 21,000 tons; as ships probably only managed one trans-Atlantic voyage a year this must have employed a similar quantity of shipping, apart from the volume employed on re-export and on the other trades of the city; but in the half century before the Union of 1707 the total shipping of the entire kingdom of Scotland probably never exceeded 20,000 tons burden. When the effects of external trade on this scale is added to the booming internal trade in small communities, it is no wonder this was an age of urban and market growth. And the economic effects of the growth of towns and villages was another subject on which Adam Smith waxed eloquent, no doubt drawing on the visible experience around him.[63]

VII

To measure structural change in agriculture it would be best to have statistics of output or at least of acreage enclosed: nothing of this kind is available, but Ian Adams has been able to throw a little light on the problem by measuring the number of land surveyors at work each year (Table II, column 17). The profession of land surveyor was a new one in the eighteenth century; very few had been at work in Scotland before 1730, but there was a clear surge in numbers after 1750; the peak of numbers at work in the 1770s was not surpassed again until after 1810. Their job was essentially to survey an estate prior to enclosure and reorganization: it was a first step towards basic agrarian

---

[63] 'How the Commerce of the Towns contributed to the Improvement of the Country'. *WN* III.iv.

change, but not itself a change, since enclosure might not immediately follow and agricultural productivity might not be enhanced by their activities. Adams has been able to show, however, that it was not an isolated phenomenon. For one thing, legal processes for 'division of commonty' (enclosure of the commons is the rough English equivalent) increased from 8 in 1740s to 23 in the 1750s and 40 in the 1760s, and was never surpassed later. For another, the foundation of planned villages that so often went hand in hand with schemes for restructuring the local rural economy and redeploying the local population, grew from 2 in the 1740s to 15 in the 1750s and 45 in the 1760s, and was also never surpassed later.[64]

What all this adds up to is evidence of the busy activity of the improving landlords (not necessarily their effectiveness) as they started to try to force structural change on the countryside. It also testifies to the affluence of the improvers, for surveying, dividing commonty and planning new villages were expensive pastimes; the accumulation of the necessary capital was probably made easier by the price tendencies for agricultural and other produce noted above.

What we are seeing is a first step, the manifest willingness of an elite to attempt to lead Scotland towards modernization. This is the collective enthusiasm of the Edinburgh-centred literati wedded to that of the landowners, who together supported the Honourable Society of Improvers and the Select Society, translated into action in the countryside. It was to finance processes like these that the Faculty of Advocates began in 1764 to lead a national campaign to reform the law of entail, a campaign readily interpreted as being in favour of the smaller and middle-sized landowners who wished to free the land-market and raise loans in a commercial way, and against the interests of the greatest families whose primary concern was in keeping dynastic lands intact. All equally made obeisance to the ideological god of improvement, but Adam Smith for one was sceptical of the sincerity and effectiveness of such grandees – 'it seldom happens that a great landowner is a great improver', he wrote in the *Wealth of Nations*,[66] and in a private letter to Shelburn in 1759 he was even more frank:

We have in Scotland some noblemen whose estates extend from the east to the west sea, who call themselves improvers, and are called so by their countrymen, when they cultivate two or three hundred acres round their own family seat while they allow all

---

[64] Ian Adams, 'Economic Process and the Scottish Land Surveyor', *Imago Mundi*, 2nd ser., 1 (1975), p. 14.

[65] The only consistent series of rents which has yet been extracted from the enormous volume of Scottish estate papers of this period is the work of Leah Leneman, and will be forthcoming in her Edinburgh Ph.D. thesis on the Atholl estates, 1680–1780. She shows that on one group of Perthshire estates, where sales of linen yarn (as well as cattle) were an important determinant of total tenant payments, rent rose by 80 per cent between 1750 and 1775.

[66] *WN* III.ii.7.

the rest of their country to lie waste, almost uninhabited and entirely unimproved, not worth a shilling the hundred acres, without thinking themselves answerable to God, their country and their Posterity for so shameful as well as so foolish a neglect.[67]

The criticism, note, is not directed against the efforts of improving landlords *per se*: the passage is prefaced by a reference to 'the very noble and generous work which your Lordship has been employed in in Ireland'. It was an objection to the tokenism of great families. The Argylls, Sutherlands and Buccleuchs might feel themselves offended by such a comment, but hardly Lord Kames or the 'middling sort' of 'gentry' in whom Smith felt the virtue of a country resided.[68]

VIII

The last statistic we should notice relates to the growth of banking assets (Table III): in a sense it is the most dramatic of all, as it is the only one in which a change in the order of magnitude is involved. Over 90 per cent of the assets in question were loans. S. G. Checkland explains that there is no systematic information available on the directions of Scottish bank lending. Landed estates and their rent rolls were effective security: from 1770 even entailed estates could borrow for improvements to the extent of six years' rental, and in any case three-fifths of the land was not encumbered by entail. Loans on heritable bonds seem largely to have been used for agricultural improvements and for building stately homes.[69]

Banks also lent widely to drovers in the cattle trade, and to certain industrial and commercial concerns such as whaling and the grain trade. The most unusual and significant industrial banking venture was the British Linen Company, founded in 1746 both to provide credit in an industry beset with liquidity problems and to assist sales and marketing – the former function almost completely displaced the latter by 1770.[70] The British Linen Company was the only chartered bank in the United Kingdom that had as its purpose industrial development; but it was a characteristic product of the Scottish age

---

[67] *WN* III.ii.7; Smith to Lord Shelburne, 4 April 1759, in Smith, *Correspondence*, p. 32.
[68] See the paper by Nicholas Phillipson, pp. 179–202 below. There is a puzzle as to who 'the gentry' might be in a Scottish context, but any future analysis of the Scottish landowning classes will be very much assisted by the spade-work done by L. Timperley, 'The Pattern of Landholding in Eighteenth-Century Scotland', in Parry and Slater, *The Making of the Scottish Countryside*, pp. 137–54, which outlines the anatomy of landownership *c*. 1770. At that date the 'great landlords' controlled just over 50 per cent of total agrarian wealth, though with enormous regional variation; the 'lairds' controlled 41.6 per cent, and the 'bonnet lairds' (owner occupiers) 5 per cent – but the last-named were still the most numerous. There had been some growth of large estates and attrition of middle-sized estates in the first half of the century, but it had been halted in the second: bonnet-lairds, however, suffered 'a continuous diminution' in their numbers until towards the end of the century.
[69] Checkland, *Scottish Banking*, pp. 226–7.
[70] *Ibid.*, p. 228; Durie, *The Scottish Linen Industry*, ch. 7.

of the improvers, in that its foundation was regarded as a patriotic objective calling on and receiving the disinterested support of landowners and great merchants.[71]

The obverse of bank assets is liabilities, and the most striking figure on that side was the fifteenfold growth of note issue between 1744 and 1772. When one considers the Scottish tradition, going back to John Law, of interest in the relationship between issuing paper money and the encouragement of economic growth, and the fact that in this third quarter of the eighteenth century the extension of paper money did go hand-in-hand with growth, the fascination of Hume, Steuart and Smith with note issue and banks is easily understood.[72] Not that the system worked without juddering: it was rocked by the crisis of 1761–2, rocked again by the small-note mania that was in turn stabilized by the Bank Act of 1765, and shaken much more fundamentally by the collapse of the Ayr Bank in 1772. For anyone taking an active interest in economic affairs these events provided the most absorbing spectacle that anyone could observe in contemporary Scotland. Thus Hume wrote to Smith at the time of the Ayr Bank crisis, speaking of

Continual bankruptcies, universal loss of credit, and endless suspicions...Mansfield has paid away £40,000 in a few days...the case is little better in London. It is thought that Sir George Colebrook must soon stop; and even the Bank of England is not entirely free from suspicion. Those of Newcastle, Norwich and Bristol are said to be stopped. The Thistle Bank has been reported to be in the same condition. The Carron Company is reeling...Do these events anywise affect your theory? Or will it occasion the revisal of any chapters?[73]

It is hard to believe in the face of evidence like this that the Scottish political economists were not aware of and interested in their country's own particular economy; but it was banks, not factories, that mattered at that moment.[74]

IX

'I have little faith in Political Arithmetic', said Adam Smith on one occasion,[75] and he was equally sceptical about the publication of commercial records 'from which our merchants and manufacturers [and now he might justly wish to add "economic historians"] would often vainly pretend to announce the prosperity or declension of the greatest empires'.[76] Nevertheless our tables suggest some simple conclusions.

(1) In this quarter-century there must have been a modest yet distinct

[71] For a comparable but much less successful near-contemporary body, see Jean Dunlop, *The British Fisheries Society, 1780–1863* (Edinburgh, 1978).
[72] See the paper by Istvan Hont, pp. 271–315 below.
[73] David Hume to Smith, 27 June 1772, in Smith, *Correspondence*, p. 162.
[74] This paper takes a different emphasis from Kindleberger 'The Historical Background: Adam Smith and the Industrial Revolution', especially pp. 6–7.
[75] Smith to George Chalmers, 10 November 1785, in Smith, *Correspondence*, p. 288.
[76] *WN* I.viii.51.

improvement in Scottish GNP per capita, which was not sudden but was pleasing.

(2) The benefits of this probably accrued much more to the landowners and the bourgeoisie than to the common people, for whom there is little evidence of gain except from employment in domestic industry.

(3) Growth occurred over a range of sectors and was associated with improvement both in internal and external demand, so that the old problems of surplus that had so concerned the early political economists were cured. The strength of internal demand was demonstrated in the buoyancy of grain prices (for wheat as well as oats) and in the market for meat and textiles, where the role of Edinburgh and other towns was significant. The role of external demand, including English, was shown for cattle, linen and re-exported tobacco and probably deserves primacy, though the relative strength of the two pulls has yet to be determined.

(4) A secondary effect of the initial phase of growth was to redistribute labour (perhaps especially female labour) away from agriculture, where it had very low marginal productivity, towards the linen industry on the one hand and to town services of all kinds on the other. This further improved the internal market for foodstuffs and assisted balanced growth.

(5) In these circumstances landowners took the opportunity to play the improver by surveying and reorganizing their estates, and by moving against the small tenantry. This can be regarded as one step in the long road by which the Scottish landowner ceased to regard his tenants as subjects (ruled as in feudal times under a set of mutual obligations and known customs and wooed for military service) and began to consider them as objects (as means or obstructions to the rational maximization of estate income). This further improved the labour supply outside the agricultural sector and increased the incentive to move to towns and villages. It is doubtful, however, if there is evidence to suggest that landowners actually produced an 'agricultural revolution' in the shape of dramatically improved productivity per acre.

(6) To a considerable extent what happened can be summed up as a greater spread of monetization through the economy, during which growth was facilitated and sometimes disrupted by the relatively lavish issue of paper money by the banks.

This is not a quarter-century of 'industrial revolution', but it can be not inaptly described as an era of pre-industrial growth, during which Scotland resembled a number of late-eighteenth-century European countries (Denmark, for example, and some of the German states) rather more than her precocious yoke-fellow in the Union, England. The fact that Scotland so quickly plugged into the dynamic current of the English industrial revolution at the end of the century and quickly made it a British phenomenon, should not blind us to the peculiar characteristics of her own economy up to that point.

For this reason some aspects of Sir James Steuart's economic theory perhaps seem more apposite than Adam Smith's. Steuart emphasized the need to raise effective demand for agriculture, which happened in Scotland in this period with the switch from stagnant to rising food prices; he stressed the role of aspirations, the 'taste for luxury', and in Scotland's case in these years the desire to imitate and follow England could be important; he also stressed the importance of the physical circulation of money in facilitating choice, which was exactly in Scottish experience; finally he believed that the government had a duty to intervene in order to increase agricultural productivity and to find ways to absorb the ensuing surplus – in Scotland the government was hardly placed to be able to intervene in this way, but the improvers, as a patriotic class, took upon themselves a quasi-governmental function in trying to do exactly that, through enclosure on the one hand and village building on the other. To say that what Steuart was writing about had relevance to Scotland is not to say that Steuart was writing about Scotland or that he had a major influence in Scotland – it is merely to remark that his models had a good deal to do with economies like those of his native country at this time.

With Smith the case is different: it is not difficult to find in the *Wealth of Nations* and other writings evidence of extensive knowledge about the economy of his native country, but often his intellectual preoccupations seem to have had less immediate relevance to its problems than Steuart's did. Smith was interested in capital accumulation, not a serious problem as far as we can see in eighteenth-century Scotland, with the single but important exception of the linen trade. He was further interested in the division of labour and in technical change, but in Scotland between 1750 and 1775 it would be difficult to argue that such growth as there was rested upon sophisticated modes of organization or a new technology. Smith, of course, wrote a decade and a half later than Steuart, and in these intellectual concerns pointed more (as far as Scotland was concerned) to the problems of the future than of the present or of the past. His interests were in some respects more relevant to the industrial revolution itself than to this earlier phase. Consequently, it was to appear by 1800 to be (in Dugald Stewart's interpretation) of the greatest concern to a Scotland that had then reached the stage of take-off. But that position had not been reached in Scotland in the quarter-century prior to the publication of the *Wealth of Nations*.

3 Gershom Carmichael and the natural jurisprudence tradition in eighteenth-century Scotland*

JAMES MOORE and
MICHAEL SILVERTHORNE

No discussion of the origins of the Scottish Enlightenment would be complete without an expression of homage to Gershom Carmichael, the first occupant of the Chair of Moral Philosophy at the University of Glasgow and the predecessor of Francis Hutcheson and Adam Smith. He has sometimes been called, following Sir William Hamilton, 'the real founder of the Scottish school of philosophy', but it is not entirely clear what Sir William Hamilton intended to convey by this pronouncement.[1] His teaching and writings have been characterized more cautiously but perhaps more judiciously by James McCosh as 'the bond which connects the old philosophy with the new in Scotland'.[2] Clearly Carmichael was a transitional thinker of some importance; but McCosh's description, like Sir William Hamilton's, continues to beg the question: in what respect may Carmichael be considered an innovator in his teaching and in his writing? He was not a philosopher of common and of moral sense like the 3rd Earl of Shaftesbury and Francis Hutcheson; Carmichael was aware of this development in moral philosophy in the early eighteenth century and he rejected it. He did not claim to be an experimental philosopher or to be the Newton of the moral sciences; this distinction was claimed by and for later thinkers of the Scottish Enlightenment, more sceptical in their approaches to moral and political philosophy than Carmichael. Indeed, considering that he wrote and taught entirely in Latin, and that for most of his teaching career

---

* This paper was presented to the Political Economy Seminar, King's College Research Centre, Cambridge University, 4 December 1980. An earlier version was read at a meeting of the Canadian Society for Eighteenth-Century Studies. This paper appears in the first volume of the proceedings of that society: *Man and Nature*, ed. Roger Emerson, Gilles Girard and Roseann Runte (London, Ont., 1982). The authors wish to thank the Social Sciences and Humanities Research Council of Canada and the Faculty of Graduate Studies and Research of McGill University for their support.

[1] This cryptic but often-cited remark was made by Sir William Hamilton in a note to Dugald Stewart's 'Account of the Life and Writings of Thomas Reid, D.D.', in *The Works of Thomas Reid*, 2 vols. (Edinburgh, 1846), i, p. 30n.

[2] James McCosh, *The Scottish Philosophy: Biographical, Expository, Critical, from Hutcheson to Hamilton* (London, 1875), p. 36.

he was a regent in the old system of Scottish university education,[3] it might be more appropriate to locate him in what might be called the pre-Enlightenment in Scotland than in the luminous company which was soon to follow.[4] But in one crucial respect at least Carmichael's career as a teacher and writer of moral philosophy was the source of much that was distinctive and of enduring significance in the Scottish Enlightenment. For it was above all Carmichael who was responsible for establishing the natural jurisprudence tradition in the Scottish universities. It was not just his decision to make Pufendorf's smaller work, *De Officio Hominis et Civis*, the set text in moral philosophy at Glasgow, a practice also followed at Glasgow by John Loudon and later at Edinburgh by Sir John Pringle, and continued at Glasgow by Francis Hutcheson. It was rather the notes and supplements which Carmichael appended to the text, and which Hutcheson considered of more value than the text itself, which supplied many of the moral and political ideas that lie behind the numerous treatises, tracts and lectures on jurisprudence which were to prove such a fecund source of speculation on human nature and society in eighteenth-century Scotland. In order to appreciate the distinctive turn given the study of moral philosophy and natural jurisprudence in Scotland by Carmichael it may be helpful to provide some (albeit fragmentary) biographical details about him.

Gershom Carmichael was born in London in 1672, the son of a Presbyterian clergyman, Alexander Carmichael, who had been deprived of his church in Scotland and exiled to England earlier in the same year. There the elder Carmichael became minister of a congregation of expatriate Scots Presbyterians.[5] He and his wife appear to have been acutely sensible of the alien

---

[3] John Veitch, 'Philosophy in the Scottish Universities', *Mind*, 2 (1837), 74–91 and 207–34, locates Carmichael at the beginning of the era of independent philosophical inquiry in Scotland which followed upon the termination of the regenting system: 'Remarkably enough with the first man appointed to the professoriate in Glasgow, we have the commencement of independent investigation...Both by date and habit of thought, Carmichael may be taken as the link between the regenting and the professoriate, between the old thought and the new. (p. 209)'

[4] For a description of Carmichael's teaching and of the reputation he enjoyed in his own time, see Robert Wodrow, *Analecta: Or Materials for a History of Remarkable Providences*, 4 vols. (Edinburgh, 1842–3), iv, pp. 95–6, and David Murray, *Memoirs of the Old College of Glasgow* (Glasgow, 1927), pp. 506–8. For more recent discussion of Carmichael, there is a short article by W. L. Taylor, 'Gershom Carmichael: A Neglected Figure in British Political Economy', *South African Journal of Economics*, 13 (1955), 252–5, which is devoted mainly to his contribution to the theory of value or of the natural price of commodities. Hans Medick, *Naturzustand und Naturgeschichte der bürgerlichen Gesellschaft: Die Ursprünge der bürgerlichen Sozialtheorie als Geschichtsphilosophie und Sozialwissenschaft bei Samuel Pufendorf, John Locke und Adam Smith* (Göttingen, 1973), pp. 296–305, also contains useful material. The reader may wish to approach the latter through a review article by David Kettler, 'History and Theory in the Scottish Enlightenment', *Journal of Modern History*, 48 (1976), 95–100.

[5] Hew Scott, *Fasti Ecclesiae Scoticanae: The Succession of Ministers in the Church of Scotland from the Reformation* (Edinburgh, 1928), iii, p. 319, vii, p. 489, and Philip O. Williams, 'The Founders' Hall Meeting', *Journal of the Presbyterian Historical Society of England*, 2 (1972), 133–8.

condition of their life in England, as may be inferred from their choice of the name Gershom for their son, which derives from the name of Moses' son mentioned at Exodus viii.22, 'a stranger born in a strange land'. The elder Carmichael died in 1677, leaving behind a tract which was published as *Believers Mortification of Sin by the Spirit or Gospel-holiness advanced by the power of the Holy Ghost...* (London, 1677; Glasgow, 1730), a document as dour as the title would suggest. Gershom's mother married another clergyman, Sir James Fraser of Brea,[6] who brought the family back to Edinburgh in 1687, where Gershom enrolled at the University of Edinburgh and graduated with an M.A. in 1691.[7] Gershom Carmichael was appointed a regent at St Andrews in 1693 but resigned later in the same year to obtain an M.A. from Glasgow, where he became a regent in 1694, a position he held until 1727 when he became Professor of Moral Philosophy at the same university.[8] He died in 1729.

Gershom Carmichael was a vigorous supporter of the Revolution of 1688 and the Hanoverian succession. His convictions were reinforced, no doubt, by those of his patrons; in particular, he owed his appointment at Glasgow in part to the patronage of a distant kinsman, Lord Carmichael, who had been made Chancellor of the University of Glasgow in 1692 and Secretary of State for Scotland in 1696.[9] In helping to arrange the appointment of Gershom Carmichael, Lord Carmichael was not merely obliging a distant relative, he was contributing to the religious and political realignment of the Scottish universities which occurred at the Revolution. By an Act of Parliament (4 July 1690) all principals and regents were required to subscribe an oath of allegiance and to declare their belief in the articles of faith of the Presbyterian Church of Scotland.[10] Gershom Carmichael liked to contend (particularly in one notable riposte to Sir Richard Steele) that such subscription in no way inhibited members of the university in their inquiries.[11] And his own theological views were sufficiently unorthodox (as we shall see) that we must take him at

---

[6] Fraser of Brea enjoyed a certain reputation in Presbyterian circles through the eighteenth century for the sanctity of his life and writings, particularly for his memoirs, or *Memories of the Life of Sir James Fraser of Brea, written by himself* (Edinburgh, 1738). See also Scott, *Fasti Ecclesiae Scoticanae*, v, pp. 15–16.

[7] *A Catalogue of the Graduates of the Faculties of Arts, Divinity, and Law of the University of Edinburgh since its Foundation*, ed. David Laing (Edinburgh, 1858), p. 141.

[8] *Munimenta Alme Universitatis Glasguensis*, ed. C. Innes, 4 vols. (Glasgow, 1854), iii, p. 396. Robert Wodrow, *Analecta*, iv, pp. 95–6, and Murray, *Memoirs of the Old College of Glasgow*, pp. 506–8.

[9] *Munimenta*, iii, pp. 309, 583.

[10] James Coutts, *A History of the University of Glasgow* (Glasgow, 1909), pp. 165–72. See also R. L. Emerson, 'Scottish Universities in the Eighteenth Century, 1690–1800', *Studies on Voltaire and the Eighteenth Century*, 167 (1977), 453–74.

[11] Gershom Carmichael, *De Officio Hominis et Civis juxta Legem Naturalem, Libri Duo. Supplementis et Observationibus in Academicae Juventutis usum auxit et illustravit Gerschomus Carmichael* (Edinburgh, 1724), 'Greeting to the Reader' (*lectori benevolo*), pp. xiv–xvn. A review of Carmichael's edition of Pufendorf in *Acta Eruditorum* (Leipzig), 58 (1727), 45–8, takes Carmichael's response to Steele as its point of departure and goes on to examine the implications of Carmichael's theological ideas for his natural jurisprudence, focussing particularly on his theory of the family.

his word, on this point at least. As a regent he was responsible for teaching his students moral philosophy, natural philosophy, logic and metaphysics. He published two sets of philosophical theses (on which his students were examined, in 1699 and 1707, on metaphysics and moral philosophy respectively)[12] and three major works: his edition of Samuel Pufendorf's *De Officio Hominis et Civis juxta Legem Naturalem* (Glasgow, 1718; Edinburgh, 1724); an introduction to logic, *Breviuscula Introductio ad Logicam* (Glasgow, 1720; Edinburgh, 1722); and *Synopsis Theologiae Naturalis* (Edinburgh, 1729), which contained, he said, the most important part of metaphysics and of that discipline known in eighteenth-century Scotland as pneumatology. He insisted, he tells us in the preface to the last of these works, that his teaching be confined in his later years to natural theology and moral philosophy, which he took to be nothing but natural jurisprudence. In the sequel, the discussion will focus upon these two closely related aspects of his thought.

In the preface to his edition of *De Officio Hominis et Civis* Carmichael remarked on the great advances in human knowledge which had occurred since the beginning of the seventeenth century. No one with the least tincture of learning could be ignorant, he said, of the remarkable progress made in natural philosophy in the previous century, but no less striking was the improvement in moral philosophy in the same period. It was the incomparable Grotius who had restored moral philosophy to the splendour it had enjoyed in ancient times. And from that time, the most erudite and celebrated scholars of Europe, as if aroused by the sound of a trumpet, had vied with one another in the pursuit of moral knowledge. He mentions Selden and Hobbes in this connection, not without profound reservations, however, since Selden's work was confined by his preoccupation with Hebrew learning, and Hobbes, he said, set out not to improve the study of the law of nature but to corrupt it. It was Pufendorf who put the materials of Grotius in a more logical order, adding what was necessary to produce a systematic treatise in moral philosophy. The publication of Pufendorf's *De Jure Naturae et Gentium* (1672) and the compendium of that work, his *De Officio Hominis et Civis* (1673), persuaded many that the study of moral philosophy or ethics properly understood was nothing but the study of natural jurisprudence or the demonstration of the duties of man and the citizen from knowledge of the nature of things and the circumstances of human life.

Pufendorf's works were widely adopted by professors of moral philosophy for the use of students in European universities. They became best known, perhaps, in the translations of those works by Jean Barbeyrac, Professor of Civil Law and History of the College of Lausanne (1710–17) and later Professor of Jurisprudence at the University of Groeningen (1717–44).[13] But there were

---

[12] *Theses Philosophicae...Sub Praesidio Gerschomi Carmichael, P.P.* (Glasgow, 1699) and *Theses Philosophicae...Sub Praesidio Gerschomi Carmichael, P.P.* (Glasgow, 1707).

[13] Samuel Pufendorf, *Le Droit de la Nature et des Gens...traduit du Latin par Jean Barbeyrac avec des notes du traducteur et une preface qui sert d'introduction à tout l'ouvrage* (Amsterdam, 1706). Subsequent

many annotated editions and discussions of Pufendorf's work, particularly of *De Officio Hominis et Civis*, and in 1709 a dozen of these commentaries were collected in a single volume. One comment in that volume had a particular impact on readers generally and on Carmichael in particular. It was an extended critique of the philosophical principles on which Pufendorf had chosen to base his study of the law of nature. The commentator, the famous Leibniz, held that Pufendorf's first principles were basically unsound; this did not prevent the work from having substantial value for the reader, he hastened to acknowledge, since much of the argument in the book did not logically follow from the first principles. There were three basic mistakes in the premises of Pufendorf's discussion of natural law. The first was Pufendorf's insistence that the study of the law of nature should be confined to this life, without consideration of the prospect of happiness or misery after death. Secondly, Pufendorf's understanding of natural law was limited to the external manifestations of human conduct with insufficient consideration of the spirit in which men act, their motives and intentions. Thirdly, given these deficiencies in Pufendorf's understanding of the law of nature, it was not surprising that he had an unsatisfactory notion of the efficient cause of natural law or of what obliges us to obey the law of nature. Leibniz concluded his criticism of Pufendorf on this note:

This has not a little relevance for the practice of true piety: it is not enough, indeed, that we be subject to God just as we would obey a tyrant; nor must He be only feared because of His greatness, but also loved because of His goodness... To this, lead the best principles of universal jurisprudence which collaborate also with wise theology and bring about true virtue.[14]

Leibniz's proposal that any attempt to offer an understanding of the law of nature more satisfying than Pufendorf's would be well advised to search for it in the collaboration of wise theology with natural jurisprudence found a most receptive reader in Carmichael. He had been remodelling Pufendorf's natural jurisprudence on just these lines in his moral philosophy lectures from the turn of the century. In his edition of Pufendorf, Carmichael advised his readers that he had

taken particular care that the obligations imposed by the law of nature be deduced from the existence, the perfection and the providence of the deity: so that the manifest bond between moral knowledge and natural theology might be clearly exhibited.[15]

---

references to this work will be to the fourth edition, trans. B. Kennett, *Of the Law of Nature and Nations... to which are added all the large notes of Mr Barbeyrac, translated from the best edition* (London, 1729). Barbeyrac's translation of Pufendorf's smaller work, *Les Devoirs de l'Homme et du Citoyen, tels qu'ils lui sont prescrits par la loi naturelle*, was published in Amsterdam in 1707.

[14] G. W. Leibniz, 'Opinion on the Principles of Pufendorf' (1706), in *The Political Writings of Leibniz*, trans. and ed. Patrick Riley (Cambridge, 1972), p. 72.

[15] *De Officio Hominis et Civis*, 'Greeting to the Reader', p. xvi.

He also tells us that the first and second supplements which he had added to the text, and which contained a demonstration of the law of nature, its derivation from the supreme being, and its principal maxims or prescriptions, were offered by way of response to the criticisms of Pufendorf's theory of natural law made by the excellent Leibniz. Unlike Jean Barbeyrac, who defended Pufendorf's separation of natural religion and natural jurisprudence, Carmichael, in an initiative which would have significant consequences for the teaching of moral philosophy in eighteenth-century Scotland, insisted that the two were inseparable. 'I have asserted more than once', he said in his *Synopsis Theologiae Naturalis*

> that a genuine philosophy of morals must be built upon natural theology as its foundation, as it were, and that every well founded distinction of good and evil in our actions... must be deduced from the perceived relation of those actions to God, that is, to our knowledge of the existence, perfections and providence of the supreme being.[16]

It is worth underlining that it was natural theology which was to serve as the foundation for a system of natural jurisprudence. Carmichael was not concerned to link natural jurisprudence to Christian theology or the study of the revealed word. It was an error, he said, to suppose that one could discover the rights and duties of men and citizens from consultation of holy scripture; in fact, the revealed law, or as he prefers to call it, the positive law of God, offered little guidance in these matters. And for that reason he had always opposed, he said, the teaching of what is popularly called Christian ethics in the universities.[17] Because the scriptures provided little guidance for the citizen and for the ruler, they had to be supplemented by observations unsystematically culled from pagan writers, and the resulting mish-mash (*farraginem*) had engendered entirely fallacious ideas of government such as the ideas of divine and indefeasible hereditary right, which Carmichael also characterized by the term *hallucinatio*. Much better to have followed the lead of the natural theologians and natural jurists who did not attempt to find guidance in holy writ on subjects where the scriptures remain silent but who sought direction instead from the nature of things and of man.

What were the sources of Carmichael's natural theology? In his *Synopsis Theologiae Naturalis* he appears to combine three distinguishable traditions. He made use of what Hume was to call experimental theology, or arguments for the existence of a supreme being from evidence of design in the physical world. He made reference to the plethora of writings on this subject, mentioning works by Cheyne, Pelling, Ray, Derham and Nieuwent, which one encounters everywhere, he said, and which indicate continued progress in our knowledge

---

[16] Gershom Carmichael, *Synopsis Theologiae Naturalis, sive Notitiae, De Existentia, Attributis et Operationibus, Summi Numinis, ex ipsa rerum Natura, Studiosae Juventutis usibus accommodata* (Edinburgh, 1729), p. 9.

[17] De Officio Hominis et Civis, 'Greeting to the Reader', pp. x–xi.

of natural things and the confirmation this knowledge affords of the existence of a supreme architect or designer.[18] In this connection, he observed that one might as well suppose that Virgil's *Aeneid* was composed by the ink flowing fortuitously down the pages as suppose that matter somehow accommodated itself to laws of nature without the intervention of an intelligent world orderer; an observation which may bring to mind the remark of the sceptic in Hume's *Dialogues*, that our experience of the creation of universes is so slight that, faced with the argument from design, we are in much the same position as an illiterate person who is shown a copy of the *Aeneid* and is asked to form a judgement about the existence and the abilities of the poet.[19] But Carmichael does not attach overriding importance to the argument from design in the physical or corporeal world; he finds more weighty the argument from design in the moral and political world, underlining in particular the description by Malebranche of the way the human mind, by the mediation of the feelings and instincts of the body, unites itself with the perceptible world and with the minds of other men by the instinctive tendency to imitate and sympathize with the feelings of others. Since the ability of men to live in society and in peace with others depends so much upon natural instincts and feelings of this kind which human beings could never have invented for themselves, we must conclude that our instinctive propensities for social life are better traced to the providence of the supreme being.[20] In a third line of argument which proves the most important ingredient in Carmichael's natural theology, we find him calling attention to the imperfections of matter, which would lack both form and motion, he tells us, if it were not shaped and moved by a superior immaterial cause. Even human beings cannot be said to generate their nobler and more sublime modes of thought from their corporeal or material natures. We find rather in man a longing or aspiration to think in ways unbounded by his material existence:

he arrives by long chains of reasoning at knowledge of the most abstract and recondite truths, not only of things past but of infinite vistas of possible things; thought ascends in its meditations beyond the bounds of earth to contemplate the idea of a perfect being, it aspires to beatific enjoyment of this vision of perfect being...[21]

The third element in Carmichael's natural theology is the theology of the Schoolmen; the ideas and the language are more reminiscent of Aquinas than of writers in the Presbyterian canon, and, however paradoxical it may seem,

---

[18] *Synopsis Theologiae Naturalis*, p. 18.
[19] David Hume, *Dialogues Concerning Natural Religion*, ed. J. V. Price (Oxford, 1976), p. 191.
[20] *Synopsis Theologiae Naturalis*, p. 22. Nicholas Malebranche, *De La Recherche de la Vérité*, ed. Geneviève Rodis-Lewis, *Oeuvres complètes*, general ed., A. Robinet, 21 vols. (Paris, 1958–70), i, p. 120.
[21] *Synopsis Theologiae Naturalis*, p. 20.

Carmichael was quite explicit about his indebtedness to this earlier theological tradition:

> I cannot avoid confessing that the doctrines of the Scholastics, at least of the more ancient ones, seem to me to be more correct and more consistent with reason and even with Sacred Scripture in this, by far the gravest part of philosophy; in particular, in the articles concerning the unity of God, the simplicity and the other communicable attributes thence flowing, likewise concerning the knowledge and decrees of God, and concerning his providence as ruler and preserver than are those opinions which are opposed to them today...and are very much worn in the hands of the student body: whence I have not been ashamed to introduce to them other ideas...and I have not refrained from use of words and phrases which are Scholastic, although they may grate on more delicate ears, when a more Latin mode of signifying the sense with equal precision did not occur to me.[22]

Carmichael attached great significance to this element in his natural theology. The principle of aspiration, of longing for complete fulfilment (*beatitudo*) in this life and in the hereafter, was the principle that would answer Leibniz's question of the end or aim of the study of the law of nature: the end of the study was knowledge of how one must conduct one's life if one would enjoy eternal happiness.[23] The same principle also pointed to the appropriate inspiration of moral conduct: one must act in a spirit of love and reverence for the supreme being. And finally, it supplied the efficient cause or motivation for observance of the law of nature in a way that avoided the impious notion of the supreme being as a tyrant who enjoys authority over men only because of the penalties he will impose for disobedience. The authority which God enjoys over human beings is authority over rational beings and is properly called *majestas* or *imperium* as distinct from His power over other creatures and things which is properly called *dominium*.[24] The significance of this distinction between *imperium* and *dominium* will become evident when we consider Carmichael's contribution to the theory of property and the theory of allegiance to government. It may be advisable to turn directly to these topics.

Both the theory of property and the theory of allegiance as one discovers them in Carmichael's writings and lectures are noteworthy above all because they bring to bear upon the thought of Pufendorf and the natural jurisprudence tradition the political ideas of John Locke. We do not know what prompted Carmichael to take up Locke's *Two Treatises of Government* and employ them extensively as a gloss upon the argument of Pufendorf. But as early as his lectures of 1702–3 on ethics, which take the form of a commentary on

---

[22] *Ibid.*, pp. 7–8.
[23] *De Officio Hominis et Civis*, Supplement I, pp. i–xi, 'Greeting to the Reader', p. xvii and notes to author's preface, sect. 6 n. 1 and n. 3.
[24] *Synopsis Theologiae Naturalis*, pp. 70–1.

Pufendorf, we find him referring to the *Second Treatise of Civil Government* for a discussion of property which was found to be preferable to the discussions of property in Pufendorf and Grotius.[25] The date is significant, for there would be no problem in accounting for the use of Locke's *Second Treatise* to provide a corrective for Pufendorf's theories of property and allegiance to government after 1706; for Barbeyrac's work was published in that year, and Barbeyrac, through his associations with Pierre Coste, Jean Le Clerc and the Huguenot community in Amsterdam, was well acquainted with Locke's political ideas, and Barbeyrac corresponded with Locke in the last years of Locke's life.[26] There is no evidence of this kind which connects Carmichael directly with Locke or with the friends of Locke in Holland. But there seems nonetheless some reason to suppose that it was the Dutch connection with the Scottish universities and the fact that the *Second Treatise* was widely acclaimed in Holland in the 1690s that would have called it to the attention of Carmichael. This would be consistent with the close connections between the Dutch and Scottish universities in the seventeenth and eighteenth centuries, a connection which was responsible, it has been said, for the great emphasis on Roman law in Scottish legal education in this period, and it would also be consistent with the attempt of William Carstares (the leading adviser on Scottish policy to King William) to reform Scottish university education along Dutch lines.[27] But whatever the source of Carmichael's attachment to Locke's *Second Treatise*, it was his use of that text (along with Barbeyrac's use of it to much the same end) which not only made Locke a political thinker of some importance in the Scottish Enlightenment, but also recast Locke's ideas in ways that would stimulate inquiry in new directions among later Scottish thinkers. The recasting was due in part to Carmichael's retention of the frame of reference of Pufendorf's jurisprudence and in part to the Scholastic orientation of his natural theology and jurisprudence.

The immediate attraction of Locke's theory of property for Carmichael was that it allowed him to explain how men could have acquired a right of ownership in things not yet owned by anyone. It was a problem which had arisen from the description by Pufendorf of the state of nature or original condition of things as a condition of negative community, as contrasted with the condition of positive community in which things were shared by men in accordance with the agreement or consent of all members of the community.

---

[25] 'Ethicae sive Jurisprudentiae Naturalis Compendiosum Certamen. Magistro autore Gershomo Carmichael, 1702–03', Glasgow University Library, MS. Gen.168, fol. 152a; and Medick, *Naturzustand und Naturgeschichte*, pp. 301–3.

[26] Bodleian Library, MS. Locke, C.3, fols. 140–4. On Barbeyrac's friendship with Le Clerc, Coste, etc., see Annie Barnes, *Jean Le Clerc, et la Republique des Lettres* (Paris, 1938).

[27] Peter Stein, 'The Influence of Roman Law on the Law of Scotland', *The Juridical Review*, N.S., 8 (1963), 205–45, and Emerson, 'Scottish Universities in the Eighteenth Century'.

What appeared paradoxical to Carmichael was Pufendorf's contention that ownership of property in negative communities depended on the same kind of agreement or consent. A much better explanation of the origin of property in the state of nature or of negative community had been provided by Locke: men may be considered to own those things they have occupied by their labour, without waiting upon the agreement or consent of others.[28]

Now it has come to be regarded as controversial whether Locke ever supposed that the state of nature was a negative community in Pufendorf's sense. It has been argued that Locke's theory of the state of nature was a theory of positive not of negative community, that his labour theory of property was a theory of the way men mix their personalities with the things of the common, that it was a theory of individuation not of occupation in the classical juridical sense.[29] But whatever Locke's intentions may have been in elaborating this theory of property, the labour theory of property was recognized in eighteenth-century Scotland by moral philosophers like Francis Hutcheson and George Turnbull, who adopted it, and by critics of the labour theory like David Hume, as a theory of occupation, as a theory of the way men may be supposed to occupy rightfully a previously unoccupied world. It was this formulation of the theory which prompted Adam Smith, Henry Home and others to ask what kind of labour or what sort of occupation men might have engaged in when they began to occupy a hitherto unoccupied world.[30] The form in which the question came to them derives immediately from Francis Hutcheson. But Hutcheson's natural jurisprudence (not his moral psychology) was in turn taken over very largely from the work of Carmichael, as Hutcheson generously acknowledged:

The learned will at once discern how much of this compend is taken from the writings of others, from Cicero and Aristotle; and to name no other moderns, from Pufendorf's smaller work, *De Officio Hominis et Civis*, which that worthy and ingenious man, the late Professor Gershom Carmichael of Glasgow, by far the best commentator on that book, has so supplied and corrected that the notes are of much more value than the text.[31]

Remarkably, perhaps, the labour theory of property became so closely identified with the commentators on Pufendorf's natural jurisprudence in the early eighteenth century, specifically with the names of Barbeyrac and Carmichael, that, in some texts (as in translations of Bishop Cumberland's *De Legibus Naturae*), Locke's authorship of the labour theory drops entirely from

---

[28] *De Officio Hominis et Civis*, 1.2.2.n.1. See also Barbeyrac's discussion in Pufendorf, *Law of Nature*, 4.4.4.n.4.

[29] James Tully, *A Discourse on Property: John Locke and his Adversaries* (Cambridge, 1980).

[30] This discussion is developed more fully in James Moore, 'Locke and the Scottish Jurists', unpublished paper presented to the 'John Locke and the Political Thought of the 1680s' symposium of the Conference for the Study of Political Thought and the Folger Institute for Renaissance and Eighteenth-Century Studies, Washington, D.C., 21–23 March 1980.

[31] Francis Hutcheson, *A Short Introduction to Moral Philosophy* (Glasgow, 1747), p. i.

sight and reference is made only to the presentations of Barbeyrac and Carmichael.[32]

One other feature of Carmichael's formulation of the labour theory of property remains to be mentioned. It is one of the notable features of theories of commercial society in Britain in the eighteenth century that such theories are formulated typically – by Bernard de Mandeville, David Hume, Adam Smith, John Millar, and others – without reference to Locke and his labour theory of property.[33] But if Hume, Adam Smith and the later thinkers of the Scottish Enlightenment formed their ideas of Locke's political thought from compendiums of natural jurisprudence like Carmichael's, then their diffidence concerning Locke's theory of property may be readily explained and appreciated. For Carmichael's construction of the labour theory of property and his use of Locke's political ideas generally remained within the conceptual horizons of the Scholastic tradition, with its insistence on the duties of human beings to limit possessions and transcend attachments to material things.

Carmichael's clearest articulation of these duties appears in his third supplement to the first book of *De Officio*, entitled 'On the Duties of Man to His Own Mind'. Here he reminds the reader that while external things are needed to preserve life and to provide for the needs of others, no man requires more than a finite and small amount of such things for himself and for his family. Any man who misapplies his mind in the accumulation of wealth is engaged in a purposeless or literally endless activity alien to the nature of man. We have a duty to ourselves not to be overly concerned about our possessions, for such things may be lost or stolen or destroyed; we have a duty to avoid appropriation in excess of our immediate and foreseeable needs, for the surplus will surely spoil and thereby frustrate the end of property, which is simply to sustain life; we have, at all times, the overriding duty to maintain ourselves in a spirit of reverence for the supreme being, a mental inclination which cannot fail to direct the mind to higher concerns when we have provided by our labour for the needs of ourselves and those dependent on us.[34] In this highly Scholastic account of human duties with respect to external things, one finds little support for a reading of the labour theory of property which would be of service to a theorist of commercial society. It was a monastic or ascetic construction of the labour theory which could only apply in a society characterized by relations of production and exchange very different from those typical of commercial

[32] Richard Cumberland, *A Treatise of the Law of Nature*, trans. John Maxwell (London, 1727), p. 315, and *Traité Philosophique des Loix Naturelles*, trans. Jean Barbeyrac (Amsterdam, 1744), pp. 346–8.

[33] See J. G. A. Pocock, 'The Mobility of Property and the Rise of Eighteenth-Century Sociology', in A. Parel and T. Flanagan (eds.), *Theories of Property: Aristotle to the Present* (Waterloo, Ontario, 1979), pp. 146ff.; Donald Winch, *Adam Smith's Politics: An Essay in Historiographic Revision* (Cambridge, 1978); Thomas Horne, *The Social Thought of Bernard Mandeville: Virtue and Commerce in Early Eighteenth-Century England* (London, 1977).

[34] *De Officio Hominis et Civis*, Supplement III, pp. 98–9.

societies. In order to recognize the kind of society Carmichael had in mind when he conceived his theories of property and morality, we must turn to his description of the manner in which any legitimate society may be supposed to have begun.

Carmichael's account of the origin of civil or legitimate societies took its point of departure from Pufendorf's theory of the original contract, amended, or so he claimed, by Locke's theory of consent. Here the problem addressed by Carmichael had been posed by the sceptical and historical; critics of the original contract theory (notably Bayle), who had contended that neither human nature nor history afforded grounds for the belief that societies and governments had their beginnings in agreements or contracts: the origins of all societies were to be found in a perception of the utility or convenience of submission to the craft or force of ambitious men.[35] This sceptical critique of the original contract theory had made an impression on at last two of the commentators on Pufendorf's work: Gerhard Gottlieb Titius (of Leipzig) and Jean Barbeyrac both conceded to the sceptics that the idea of a social contract or original agreement to live peaceably in society was indeed a mistake. But both commentators went on to insist that the sceptical arguments applied only against the first of the contracts in Pufendorf's account of the origin of societies and governments; there was a second contract in Pufendorf's scheme, between members of the society and their sovereign or ruler, and in relation to it, the first contract was nothing more than 'what scaffolds are with respect to the structure of...buildings'.[36] The second or political contract, the contract of allegiance, had a foundation in history as well as in human nature, and the entire case for the theory of the original contract might be best supposed to rest upon it.

This concession to the sceptical critique of the original contract theory by such eminent men (*clarissimi viri*) as Titius and Barbeyrac seemed to Carmichael a most unfortunate lapse on the part of those distinguished jurists. There could be no doubt that crafty and ambitious men were involved in the beginnings of societies, but such men could expect to enjoy support for their schemes only if they presented arguments which seemed persuasive to the people they hoped to induct into the society.[37] The presumption that force could be used to establish a society begged the question: for the presence of armed force presupposed established social arrangements; those who employ force must already enjoy power (*imperium*). And in order to discover the source of power (*imperium*) one must find it in human relations which are quite different from the relations characteristic of the exercise of force, the relations of command

---

[35] P. Bayle, *Nouvelles Lettres à l'occasion de la Critique générale du Calvinisme de Maimbourg*, Lettre XVII, sect. 2, cited by Barbeyrac in his notes to Pufendorf's *Law of Nature*, 7.1.7.n.1.
[36] Gerhard Gottlieb Titius, *Observationes in Samuelis de Pufendorf De Officio Hominis et Civis Juxta Legem Naturalem* (Leipzig, 1703), Observ. 555, sect. 6, pp. 562-3, and Barbeyrac's note in Pufendorf, *Law of Nature*, 7.2.8.n.1.   [37] *De Officio Hominis et Civis*, 2.5.7.n.1.

and obedience. In pursuit of this theoretical goal Carmichael embarked upon an extended gloss upon the Roman law distinction between *imperium* and *dominium*.

There is a natural power which great landowners or landlords may enjoy which can be called *imperium soli* or power derived from the land. The landlord acquires this power by his willingness to acknowledge that anyone who lives on the land has the right to occupy and work the land and establish a household there. The obligation to acknowledge this right of *dominium* in the land plainly followed from God's gift of the earth to men to occupy and use it for the preservation of themselves and their families and the corresponding duty of men to limit their occupancy of the earth so that others may enjoy *dominium* in it. The concession of parts of his estate to others was bound to diminish the wealth of the landlord, but such diminution was entirely consistent with the duties of men with respect to external things: it could not fail, however, to engender a sense of obligation in all his beneficiaries. And this was the source of natural power derived from the land or *imperium soli*. There was no need then to look with the sceptics and historians for the origin of *imperium* in force or in the craft and guile of ambitious men; it was already present in those heads of households who enjoyed recognition and support from all those they had obliged.[38] On this basis, the beginnings of civil power (*imperium civile*) could be readily explained: it must be presumed to have originated in an agreement or contract among men already in enjoyment of natural power to live in society, to establish a government and, finally, to transfer their powers or *imperia* to the ruler or rulers by particular promises of allegiance. The entire transaction might be distinguished into three separate pacts as Pufendorf had done or more conveniently described as one original contract which contained the force of the various pacts described by Pufendorf. In either case, there could be no doubt that the origin of all legitimate societies and governments could be traced to an original contract or contracts, and the concessions made by earlier jurists to the sceptics and historians should be withdrawn.

Now Carmichael thought that his presentation of the theory of the original contract was consistent with Locke's theory of consent as presented in the *Second Treatise*, chapter VIII. And his belief that his natural jurisprudence was supported by the authority of Locke was reinforced, no doubt, in the minds of the later generations of natural jurists and moral philosophers in eighteenth-century Scotland, by Francis Hutcheson's repeated linking of Carmichael's work with Locke's. But just as Carmichael's version of the labour theory of property was found to differ in crucial respects from Locke's formulation of the theory, one finds a similar divergence in their theories of the original contract. One of the most distinctive constituents of Locke's model, his theory of trust, is conspicuously lacking: instead, Carmichael supposed, with Pufendorf,

[38] *Ibid.*, 2.6.9.n.1.

that governments derived their authority from an exchange of promises; and this version of the original contract theory was the version criticized by Hume, Adam Smith and others. Secondly, Carmichael believed that the original contract theory was corroborated in history and experience, as did Francis Hutcheson and the Scottish critics of the theory, notwithstanding the allowance made by Locke himself that arguments taken from history to prescribe how governments ought to be conducted, 'from what has been to what should of right be', have 'no great force'. And finally, it would seem to have been Carmichael's elaborate derivation of civil power from the natural or moral power of the obliging landowners, an argument which may have been suggested to him in part by Locke, as he claimed, but also by Grotius and by Pufendorf himself, which prompted Hutcheson to conclude that the parties to the original contract were independent landowners and that ownership of land was the best foundation for civil government and for the maintenance of high standards of civic virtue.[39]

Hutcheson had his own reasons for supposing that land was the material foundation of government, inasmuch as his political thinking was strongly influenced (as Carmichael's was not) by the political writings of Harrington and the classical republican tradition. But Hutcheson's subscription to Carmichael's version of the theory of the original contract, and his insistence, with Carmichael and Locke, on the natural independence of individuals and societies, identified for later Scottish jurists and political theorists a tradition in which liberty or independence was supposed to be best secured by an original contract entered into by men who enjoyed independence as owners of land. It was a tradition which was soon challenged in eighteenth-century Scotland. And in this light one may perhaps recognize in the critiques of the theory of the original contract by David Hume in his *Political Discourses* and Adam Smith in his *Lectures on Jurisprudence* one element in the more general argument of both thinkers that the societies which offered the most favourable conditions for liberty or independence were not, as their immediate predecessors had claimed, landed societies. A better prospect for the liberty of individuals and societies was afforded by commercial societies, notwithstanding the deleterious effects of commerce on other aspects (mental, moral and military) of social life.[40]

In the revised and quite distinctive form in which Carmichael presented the natural jurisprudence tradition, one may find then at least some of the problematic formulations which were taken up by later thinkers of the Scottish Enlightenment. It would be necessary, to be sure, in any treatment of Carmichael's work which aspired to be more comprehensive, to consider still other features of his natural jurisprudence: his formulation of the law of nature

---

[39] Hutcheson, *Short Introduction*, pp. 286, 310.
[40] Smith, *LJ(A)* v.777-79; *LJ(B)* 14-18. *WN* III.iv.4; Winch, *Adam Smith's Politics*, chs. 3, 4 and 5.

and the manner in which he proposed to reconcile the duties of sociability and
self-preservation; his theory of the family and of the duties of parents with
respect to the education of their children; a denunciation of slavery and the
right of conquest which claimed the authority of Locke, but was in fact more
thoroughgoing in its opposition to slavery and in its defence of the land and
the liberty of conquered people than anything written by Locke. And we have
seen that it was Carmichael's construction of the labour theory of property and
the theory of the original contract (indebted to the theories of Pufendorf and
of Locke but differing from both) which was carried over into the moral
philosophy of Francis Hutcheson and which challenged the more sceptical and
more historically minded philosophers of a later generation. In the range of
his concerns, Carmichael was indeed representative, as Dugald Stewart
observed at the end of the eighteenth century, of the natural jurisprudence
tradition which dominated the study of moral and political philosophy in the
Scottish universities early in the century.[41] But in the particular turn which
Carmichael gave that tradition – in his attempt to ground natural jurisprudence in natural theology, in his concern for the independence of individuals
and societies, in his (no doubt idiosyncratic) use of the political thought of John
Locke – he must be regarded as an original thinker (perhaps not of the first
rank) whose ideas formed an indispensable part of the movement of thought
that culminated in the Scottish Enlightenment.

[41] Dugald Stewart, *Dissertation: Exhibiting the Progress of Metaphysical Ethical and Political Philosophy since the Revival of Letters in Europe*, in *Collected Works*, ed. Sir William Hamilton, 10 vols. (Edinburgh, 1854–60), i, pp. 177–8.

4 The Scottish professoriate and the polite academy, 1720–46

PETER JONES

The Darien scheme, viewed with the benefit of hindsight, can be seen as a do-or-die attempt on the part of its instigators to win the Scottish polity a firm economic base. If so, it had a patriotic equivalent in the cultural sphere – the Visitation of the Scottish universities in the 1690s. The 'presbyterian and whiggish crew' (as seen by the jaundiced eye of Dr Archibald Pitcairne) came once more into their own after the Revolution of 1688, determined on a thoroughgoing policy to restore the godly republic heralded by Knox and Melville. The instruments to hand for this cultural revolution were the Scottish universities, preordained by Melville as suppliers of a godly ministry. The spirit in which Principal Hadow of St Andrews and his fellow visitors approached their task was that of renewers of the well-springs of Calvinist orthodoxy; consequently they were zealous not only in hunting out those professors suspected of lukewarmness or worse, but in examining and pronouncing on the curriculum. Their aim was to establish a set of texts which would be the agreed and established basis of the arts curriculum in particular. It proved very difficult to settle on proper authors and texts, so that the colleges were required to go away and each draft a suitable text of their allotted part of the curriculum. This enterprise ran into the sands, however, as authorship by committee often does, and the texts were not delivered on schedule or subsequently adopted universally, as had been hoped. In the same way as the Darien scheme, it proved much more difficult to carry the business through than to set it up in the first place.

But the setback was not just temporary; for the spirit which had sustained the Visitation could not survive in the atmosphere of post-Union Scotland. In the period from the Union to the '45, the drive to make the universities fitting training-grounds for a godly ministry was irretrievably lost. Two major factors seem to have been involved: firstly, the worsening economic position of the clerisy, which made a ministerial vocation less attractive, and with which I am not directly concerned here; and secondly, a counter-revolution on the part of the professoriate, who kicked over the traces of clerical supervision and control, and established a new ethos for the colleges. This ethos, well-established by 1745, owed much to outside sources in England and Ireland, not least in the language in which it found expression. Its literary inspiration was the 'Commonwealth' or 'Real Whig' canon (particularly later exponents such as Shaftesbury, Toland and Molesworth), but it was adopted less as a political creed than as a manifesto for an authentically 'republican' culture which would reinvigorate the liberal arts curriculum of the colleges. In this perspective, the liberal arts were not to be indulged as ornamental accomplishments, but as a vital forming-process for the character of citizens in a modern Scottish *res publica*. In the course of promulgating these ideals, the professoriate often found itself at odds with those amongst the orthodox who wished to reclaim the Scottish universities, not for a gentlemanly republican culture with overtones of secularism, but for schools of godliness and good learning. The professors branded their critics as bigots, narrow-minded enthusiasts, ignorant and intolerant, using for Presbyterians the epithets applied by their literary mentors to High Tory and Anglican Oxford. As allies and patrons the professors looked to the landed proprietors, whom the Commonwealthmen taught them to admire as the backbone of any true republic, and whom they flattered by association in their clubs and societies, dedicated to the patriotic tasks of improvement and refinement.

In one half-century, between 1707 and 1754, Edinburgh was transformed from the capital city of a Scottish *res publica* to the capital of a republic of letters. Before the Union of 1707 Edinburgh was the political, administrative and religious capital of Scotland. What persuaded Scotland's political nation to embark on the Union, or at least served to legitimize the adventure, was the hope that the *res publica* would emerge from its comparative barbarism into civility as a British province. The price Edinburgh had to pay for this adventure was the loss of her capital status. But the first fifty years of the Union did not bring about the economic and social leap forward which its champions had anticipated. The first twenty years were little better in economic terms than the bleak 1690s, and a real break with the terms of the seventeenth-century agricultural economy did not begin until the 1720s. The institutions which had formerly sustained Edinburgh's social life took a bad knock from the Union: not only the balls and assemblies which used to accompany the Parliamentary season but the more 'serious' cultural activities which depended on aristocratic patronage. The era of the virtuosi, like Sir George Mackenzie and Sir Robert Sibbald, was past, along with their aspirations for a revival of learning which would embellish status and promote courtliness. Yet by 1754 Edinburgh was well on its way to becoming the 'Athens of the North', though it was never a culture of learned individuals but a republic of letters in the most palpable sense, with its own forum, the Select Society, and a bias towards practical eloquence rather than mere learning.

This modern republic of letters was not brought to birth easily and if anybody can lay claim to the role of midwife, it must be the Scottish professoriate. Just as the 'Gentlemen, Farmers, and Lovers of their Country' on whose behalf Thomas Hope of Rankeilor approved the publication of the *Select Transactions of the Honourable the Society of Improvers in the Knowledge of Agriculture in Scotland* (1743) banded together in their improving societies from the 1720s onwards, so the professors began at the same period to exhibit a spirit of voluntary and co-operative endeavour for improvement in the sphere of belles lettres and philosophy. The role of the pupils of Boerhaave in the founding of the Edinburgh medical school and publishing the *Medical Essays and Observations* (1737) has been widely acknowledged,[1] but the role of their colleagues in the arts faculties of all the Scottish universities, and particularly at Edinburgh, Glasgow, and the Marischal College, Aberdeen, has been less often noticed. This may be simply because so many of the arts professors died or disappeared prematurely from the scene (most notably Francis Hutcheson and Colin MacLaurin). But in respect of their importance as intellectual leaders and influence as teachers we have abundant testimony in the memoirs of their pupils. Take an intellectually lightweight though much respected professor such as John Stevenson, who taught logic and rhetoric at Edinburgh. By the time of his long-delayed and much-anticipated retirement in 1775 he had not only outlived all his former colleagues but also his usefulness as a teacher; yet he was the subject of eulogies by Alexander Carlyle, John Ramsay of Ochertyre, William Robertson, Thomas Somerville and Dugald Stewart. This is the impression Stevenson made on Carlyle, who entered his class in 1736 and who later became a leading figure in the Select Society:

I went to the Logic class, taught by Mr. John Stevenson, who, though he has no pretensions to superiority in point of learning and genius, yet was the most popular of all the Professors on account of his civility and even kindness to his students, and at the same time the most useful, for being a man of sense and industry he had made a judicious selection from the French and English critics, which he gave at the morning hour of eight, when he read with us Aristotle's *Poetics* and Longinus *On the Sublime*. At eleven he read Heineccius' *Logic*, and an abridgement of Locke's *Essay*; and in the afternoon at two – for such were the hours of attendance in those times – he read to us a compendious history of the ancient philosophers, and an account of their tenets. In all these branches we were carefully examined at least three times a week. Whether or not it was owing to the time of life at which we entered this class, being all about fifteen years of age or upwards, when the mind begins to open, or to the excellence of

[1] J. R. R. Christie, 'The Origins and Development of the Scottish Scientific Community, 1680–1760', *History of Science*, 12 (1974), 122–41; J. B. Morrell, 'The Edinburgh Town Council and Its University, 1717–1766', in R. G. W. Anderson and A. D. C. Simpson (eds.), *The Early Years of the Edinburgh Medical School* (Edinburgh, 1976), pp. 46–65. Morrell argues that the spectacular rise of the faculty of medicine stemmed from the professorial appointments of the 1720s, and that the arts faculty benefited too.

the lectures and the nature of some of the subjects we could not then say, but all of us received the same impression – viz., that our minds were more enlarged, and that we received greater benefit from that class than from any other. With a due regard to the merit of the professor I must ascribe this impression chiefly to the natural effect which the subject of criticism and of rational logic has upon the opening mind.[2]

This testimony may stand as representative, speaking as it does less of the matter of what was taught than of the manner in which Stevenson opened up for his pupils vistas of authors and texts which afforded delightful relief from the aridities of grammar and scholasticism, but which also presented a challenge to them as would-be citizens of the intellectual world. Ramsay of Ochertyre recalled that ever after he was liable to the temptations of literature as an escape from his law-books, just as his younger friend Walter Scott found in his turn; both, however, left their destined profession to pursue the avocation of man of letters. Stevenson made the most of the opportunities offered by the circumstances of the book trade in Scotland: his pupils could obtain the many books he recommended to them because of Scotland's close relationship with the booksellers of Antwerp and other continental towns. From this period, too, dates that entrepreneurship in the production of cheaper texts which so infuriated the Company of Stationers in London; and what Ruddiman and Gavin Hamilton could do at home, Andrew Millar found that he could carry to London, thus revolutionizing the British book trade.[3] There was a far wider range of books available, and at a lower price than when the commissioners of the Visitation of the Scottish universities in the 1690s had been driven to the conclusion that the colleges must unite to provide a single philosophy textbook published under their aegis. Stevenson gloried in the eclecticism which these circumstances permitted him to indulge, and his colleagues profited in like manner.

But this eclecticism went hand in hand with determined efforts by the professors themselves to break down the walls of the pedagogic ghetto which had grown up around the universities. Robert Hepburn in his short-lived *Tatler of the North* which appeared at Edinburgh in 1711 had made fun of the professoriate as menial clerics who taught 'a Company of Boys and Children'.[4] From the point of view of the pseudonymous Donald Macstaff the universities were making no contribution to the spread of polite and civilized values in North Britain. A new generation of professors set out to change that, despite the seemingly insuperable obstacle of the youth and inexperience of the

[2] *Autobiography of Dr Alexander Carlyle of Inveresk 1722–1805*, ed. J. H. Burton (Edinburgh, 1910), pp. 47-8.
[3] Warren McDougall, 'Gavin Hamilton, Bookseller in Edinburgh', *British Journal for Eighteenth-Century Studies*, 1 (1978), 1-19.
[4] Edinburgh University Library, MS. Df.2.47, ' *The Tatler*...by Donald MacStaff of the North' (Robert Hepburn), no. 26, from Saturday 7 April to Wednesday 11 April 1711. This copy has manuscript annotations by Hepburn.

students whom they taught. Their very ambition to open up the universities to the influence of a wider society infected their pupils with a sense of intellectual excitement. One manifestation was a readiness to plunge their pupils into the midst of current intellectual and literary debate – the foundations of Newtonian fluxional calculus, the paradoxes of Berkeley, or the comparative merit of English Augustan and French neo-classical literature. But the universities financially, and ultimately in terms of the benefits of prestige themselves adopted a more active and responsible role in the affairs of the wider community. They were prominent in the forming of societies for cultural and improving purposes from the 1720s onwards.[5] Professors of arts as well as those of theology spoke in the General Assembly, notably on the great issue of Professor John Simson's right to profess his close-to-heretical opinions. Most significant of all, perhaps, was the appearance of the professors in polite society, and their acceptance into the circles of those landed gentlemen who wished to be thought of as cultured and progressive. The personal links thus formed with the higher ranks of Scottish society were immediately useful to the universities financially, and ultimately in terms of the benefits of prestige accrued as a result of the flattering interest taken in their activities. It was to these private patrons that the colleges addressed their appeals for the donation of astronomical instruments (Professor MacLaurin of Edinburgh set his sights on nothing less than a fully-equipped observatory) and for college buildings. These were developments which would have very much surprised the editor of the *Tatler of the North*; it is to the professors themselves that we must turn to explain how these things came to pass.

I

In July 1722 Robert, Viscount Molesworth relinquished his responsibilities as a member of the secret committee of investigation into the South Sea Bubble and as a leader of the Parliamentary opposition to Walpole, and retired to his seat of Brackenstown near Dublin. There, while keeping in touch with Parliamentary matters, he devoted himself to his estates and to the patronage of a coterie of young men who shared his enthusiasm for philosophy and belles lettres. One of those to whom he extended his help was Francis Hutcheson, lately arrived in Dublin to found an academy. But in the months immediately after his establishment at Brackenstown he entered into correspondence with several young Scots who were, like Hutcheson, to play a considerable part in the fortunes of the Scottish universities. One of them was George Turnbull,

---

[5] For these activities, see D. D. McElroy, 'Literary Clubs and Societies of Eighteenth-Century Scotland' (Ph.D. thesis, University of Edinburgh, 1952); Roger L. Emerson, 'The Social Composition of Enlightened Scotland: The Select Society of Edinburgh', *Studies on Voltaire and the Eighteenth Century*, 114 (1973), 291–329; and 'The Philosophical Society of Edinburgh, 1737–1747', *British Journal for the History of Science*, 41 (1979), 154–91.

who, as he informed Molesworth, had just been appointed Professor of Philosophy at Marischal College, Aberdeen. Another was William Wishart the younger, then a licensed preacher in Edinburgh, where his father was Principal of Edinburgh University.[6] Turnbull was to leave his mark as the teacher of Thomas Reid and as the author of works on education and moral philosophy; Wishart became in his turn an active Principal of Edinburgh University. At the time of their correspondence with Molesworth, both still had careers to make, and were keen to enlist as protégés of the leading Parliamentarian who was also the one-time teacher of Shaftesbury and author of the *Account of Denmark* (1692). Accordingly, the enthusiasm they professed for the writings of Shaftesbury and Molesworth knew no bounds; but Wishart also acknowledged his indebtedness to Molesworth for reintroducing him to the works of George Buchanan – now encountered as patriot and champion of liberty rather than the poet of Wishart's schooldays. Evidently Wishart also thought that Molesworth was the author of Cato's letters in the *London Journal*, whose final attack on the Walpole administration was delivered on 8 September 1722.[7]

In any case Wishart and Turnbull were not slow in finding practical applications closer to home for the doctrines they found in the canon of Commonwealth writers to which Molesworth acted as guide. They both dwelt on the activities of students at Glasgow University, and Wishart wrote:

I have the happiness to share with Your Lordship in the joy you have conceived from the dawnings of a revival of ancient virtue and the love of true liberty, particularly in this country. I do indeed think the proofs of that noble spirit, which the learned youth of the university of Glasgow have lately given, deserve commendation.[8]

Turnbull's friend, James Arbuckle, was one of the student leaders, and himself wrote to Molesworth soliciting his support. The students' main grievance was that their statutory right of election of the rector of the university had been arbitrarily ignored by Principal Stirling and his allies. The flashpoint of the trouble in 1722 was the expulsion of a student called John Smith 'for kindling a bonfire on intelligence of Lord Molesworth's election as a Member of Parliament reaching Glasgow'.[9] Arbuckle asked Molesworth's advice as to

[6] George Turnbull to Molesworth, 3 August 1722, pp. 343–4; William Wishart to Molesworth, 13 October 1722, pp. 347–9; George Turnbull to Molesworth, 5 November 1722, p. 352; George Turnbull to Molesworth, 14 May 1723, pp. 360–1; William Wishart to Molesworth, 7 November 1723, pp. 366–7; in Historical Manuscripts Commission, *MSS. in Various Collections* (London, 1913), viii, pp. 343–67. This correspondence is placed firmly in the context of a classical republican tradition by Caroline Robbins, '"When It Is That Colonies May Turn Independent": An Analysis of the Environment and Politics of Francis Hutcheson (1694–1746)', *William and Mary Quarterly*, 3rd ser., 11 (1954), 234.
[7] Wrongly, as revealed by C. B. Realey, *The London Journal and Its Authors, 1720–1723* (Laurence, Kansas, 1935).
[8] William Wishart to Molesworth, 13 October 1722 in H.M.C., *Various Collections*, viii, p. 347.
[9] *Munimenta Alme Universitatis Glasguensis*, ed. C. Innes, 4 vols. (Glasgow, 1854), ii, pp. 424–5. But see R.M. [Col. Richard Molesworth] to Hon. John Molesworth, 22 March 1722, in H.M.C., *Various Collections*, viii, p. 334, for Molesworth's final withdrawal before the Westminster election.

whether the students should renew their petition to the House of Commons for a restoration of their rights. Although Robert Wodrow suggests that Molesworth did recommend the students' case to the King, it was not until 1727 (two years after Molesworth's death) that a Royal Commission was appointed to visit Glasgow University and inquire into the continuing disruption there. What is most remarkable about the whole episode is that Arbuckle, Turnbull and Wishart were so successful in dramatizing the students' case as the cause of liberty and virtue that not only the students themselves but national political leaders took them seriously.

Part of the explanation for this success was that the tradition of Commonwealth literature of which Molesworth regarded himself as an expositor had always tended to a preoccupation with virtuous culture rather than with republicanism as a political programme. The polemical preface to Molesworth's own *Account of Denmark* had singled out education as the 'very foundation stone of the publick liberty' – a foundation which 'has been of late years committed to the sole management of such as make it their business to undermine it; and must needs do so unless they will be false to their fortunes, and make the character of *priest* give place to that of true *patriot*'.[10] Molesworth went on to attack the constitution of the English universities which encouraged the fellows of colleges to put their own interests before those of the public. He held the constitution of the universities responsible not only for the entrenched positions they offered to High Tories and Non-jurors, but for the survival of scholasticism and barbaric uncouthness, and indeed for

the prejudices and wrong notions, the stiffness and positiveness in opinion, the litigiousness and wrangling, all which the old philosophy breeds, besides the narrow spiritedness, and not enduring of contradiction, which are generally contracted by a monastick life [and] require a great deal of time to get rid of.[11]

In the same year that Molesworth was carrying on his correspondence with Scotland, Nicholas Amhurst was bringing out his bi-weekly satires on Oxford university, later published as *Terrae filius* (London, 1726), and that institution's reputation reached its nadir. Amhurst compared the heads of the Oxford colleges to the directors of the South Sea Company.

But the preoccupation with the university constitution which had so nearly borne fruit in a Universities Bill in 1717–19 did not preclude those polemicists who looked to the original Commonwealthmen for their inspiration indulging themselves in a vision of the virtuous culture which a modern university ought to provide. The political and scientific millenarianism shared by Samuel Hartlib and his circle had of course vanished, but Milton's discontent with the liberal arts curriculum was well-known and still quoted a hundred years later.

[10] Robert Molesworth, *An Account of Denmark as it was in the year 1692*, 5th edn (Glasgow, 1745), p. xi.
[11] *Ibid.*, p. xxii.

As Charles Webster has noted, Milton's criticisms were 'completely assimilated into a humanistic framework', in contrast to Francis Bacon's 'Great Instauration'.[12] Milton's educational prescriptions had little to do with enlarging man's dominion over nature or fulfilling prophecy; he was concerned with the training of orators who would do their civil duty in war and peace. Shaftesbury in particular had elaborated some of Milton's themes into a critique of that scholastic education which was totally inappropriate to the needs of a polite gentleman, since it inculcated servility rather than independence of mind, and ignored those useful arts which bred a gentleman. This school of thought had its Scottish representatives before the Union, too. In 1704 a pamphlet was printed anonymously in Edinburgh entitled *Proposals for the Reformation of Schools and Universities, in order to the better education of Youth, Humbly offer'd to the Serious Consideration of the High Court of Parliament*. The author complained of the 'great Decay of Learning in this Kingdom for many years', and isolated one main cause in the cheapness and ease of obtaining a university education so that 'the mechanicks and poorer sort of people, are encouraged to remit their sons to schools and universities, finding a very little money, and little time sufficient to make what we call a scholar'. The younger sons of nobles and gentlemen were kept idle at home or sent abroad and as a consequence entered into the business of life with no pretensions to useful learning. 'And in one word, the natural tendence of our present methods, is to unfit a scholar for a gentleman and to render a gentleman asham'd of being a scholar. And till we reconcile the gentleman with the scholar [a favourite Shaftesburian motif], tis impossible learning should ever flourish.'[13] There are strong strains of anticlericalism and elitism in this outlook, which harked back to an educational archetype of philosopher and noble youth.

It is with Milton, Shaftesbury and Molesworth in mind that the letters of Turnbull and Wishart in 1722 must be read. It is nevertheless somewhat curious to find these Scottish Whigs and Presbyterian preachers attacking their own universities in identical terms to those used of Jacobite and High Tory Oxford. Turnbull exclaimed in a letter of 3 August 1722:

But Oh! My Lord, education in this country is upon a miserable footing; and why should I say in this country, for is it not almost everywhere? And must it not be so, while philosophy is a traffic, and science is retailed for a piece of bread.[14]

Wishart complains in similar vein of the obstacles in the way of the inculcation of true virtue, namely savage zeal, fierce bigotry and dire superstition, all of which play on those corrupt passions and inveterate prejudices of men's minds which favour the designs of the priests. Arbuckle pointed out that if the

[12] Charles Webster, *The Great Instauration; Science, Medicine and Reform 1626–1660* (London, 1975), p. 190.
[13] As reprinted in *The Harleian Miscellany*, 12 vols. (London, 1808–11), x, pp. 561–3.
[14] H.M.C., *Various Collections*, viii, p. 344.

constitutional grievances of the students were not redressed then the labour of those masters who were men of good learning and fit to train up the youth of a free people would be rendered useless. Turnbull, who doubtless considered himself just such a master, felt that his work at Marischal College, Aberdeen, was no less in jeopardy than that of his like-minded colleagues at Glasgow. The students in Aberdeen had very similar grievances to those in Glasgow, though they were more circumspect in their actions, as the Aberdeen colleges had been subjected to a visitation to inquire into their loyalty following the '15. Turnbull despaired of a return of philosophy to the academies:

All this surely is mere romance and enthusiasm. For how can it be so, while our colleges are under the inspection of proud domineering pedantic priests, whose interest it is to train up the youth in a profound veneration to their senseless metaphysical creeds and catechisms, which for this purpose they are daily inured to defend against all doubters and enquirers with the greatest bitterness and contempt, in a stiff formal bewildering manner admirably fitted indeed to enslave young understandings and to beget an early antipathy against all free thought.[15]

How far should these professions of faith be taken seriously? After all, these young men had careers to make. Arbuckle became a leading member of the Molesworth coterie when he moved to Dublin in 1724, and acted as general editor of their mouthpiece, *The Dublin Journal*. Wishart was spared the need to seek patronage by an opportune legacy from his uncle, Admiral Sir James Wishart. Turnbull added a footnote to his letter of 23 May 1723; 'I do not know, my Lord, if I should venture upon so short and distant an acquaintance with Your Lordship to desire of you to recommend me, if it fall your way, to go abroad governor to a young gentleman.'[16] He at least had every reason for pandering to the known preconceptions of Molesworth; they were all evidently flattered by his notice. Nevertheless, Turnbull's views on educational topics had not changed by the time he came to write his *Observations upon Liberal Education* (London, 1742), in which he enlisted ancient and modern authorities to support his model of a virtuous education. William Wishart, despite his comfortable circumstances, proved the most dynamic Principal of Edinburgh University since William Carstares, and had the librarian draw up a pioneering advertisement in the *Scots Magazine* for August 1741 which dwelt at length on the attention given to philosophy and belles lettres in the arts curriculum. The sense of being members of a select band dedicated to the extension of Molesworthian principles into the educational sphere never seems to have disappeared, even when the young men came to hold important professional appointments. This sense of comradeship, which, as we shall see, played such a significant role in fostering their clubbability, was not likely to disappear whilst their rigidly orthodox clerical enemies posed a formidable threat, which

[15] George Turnbull to Molesworth, 5 November 1722, in *ibid.*, p. 352.
[16] *Ibid.*, pp. 352 and 361.

they continued to do until the victories of the Moderates in the General Assembly in the 1750s.

The mission of Turnbull and Wishart and their friends looked very different from the standpoint of Presbyterian orthodoxy. This standpoint was personified by Robert Wodrow, minister of Eastwood, who chronicled in his *Analecta* Wishart's career in particular with a kind of fascinated horror. He began by noting that Wishart was ordained in Glasgow in September 1724 over the heads of the people by the magistrates, who, he reflected, were asserting their patronage in the towns as the landed gentlemen had done in the country. In January 1725 Wodrow recorded:

> At Glasgow the debates among the Students continue, and make no little noise. There seems to be a humour getting in among them of opposing confessions, and exalting reason, under pretence of search after truth. The triuphenian club they say is renewed with new vigor there, and they talk [of] Mr Harvey...writing in defence of Mr Wallace's Sermon upon reason. They say Mr Wishart meets with the club; which, if true, is a strange step, and he is ill-advised. The Non-subscribers in Ireland give it out that he is the minister of Scotland they have their eye most upon, and one of the brightest men in it.[17]

By February the club had been renamed the Sophocardian Club, in honour of Wishart (since his namesake George Wishart had been affectionately so dubbed by the patriot George Buchanan). Wishart's dissemination of the new ideas amongst the students was bad enough, but he was also preaching that revelation and religion served but to teach us our duties to one another as members of society, which was worse. Wodrow suspected Wishart and the students of using the Molesworth connection to good advantage; he retails a story that a student expelled from the college in March 1725 as a result of the rectorship disturbances went to Ireland and with Molesworth's help got a paper drawn up which passed by way of Bishop Hoadley to the King. Wodrow thought that this precipitated the Royal Commission of Visitation in 1726–7. Wishart played a major part in protecting Professor John Simson from the ecclesiastical authorities, and it was with a sense of relief that Wodrow recorded his dimission and undertaking of the charge of the Scots congregation in London. In Wodrow's eyes, Wishart ran the whole gamut of unpalatable liberalism: from stirring up the students, to defending Simson, banishing declamatory effusions and Scotticisms from his sermons, crying up good works and downgrading the doctrine of election, working hand-in-glove with the forces of patronage, and sponsoring free-thinking clubs. Wodrow's relief at getting rid of Wishart to London was only tempered by the rumour reaching him of Wishart's being so close with the Earl of Islay as to have a claim on the principalship of Edinburgh University when that became vacant.

[17] Robert Wodrow, *Analecta, or Materials for a History of Remarkable Providences; Mostly Relating to Scotch Ministers and Christians*, 4 vols. (Edinburgh, 1842–3), iii, p. 178.

But in any case the torches lit at Molesworth's flame of liberty and virtue had already been used to light others. One of the most famous of the early Scottish clubs was the Rankenian, which had for its nucleus Wishart, Turnbull and a group of their friends soon to be closely connected with Edinburgh University. The club had been founded in 1717, and was named after the tavern at which it met. Other members included Wishart's brother George, Dr Robert Wallace, John Stevenson, Charles Mackie and Colin MacLaurin, the last three subsequently professors of Edinburgh University. The club's historian, Dr George Wallace, recorded that 'The object was mutual improvement by liberal conversation and rational enquiry' and that 'the Rankenians were highly instrumental in disseminating throughout Scotland, freedom of thought, boldness of disquisition, liberality of sentiment, accuracy of reasoning, correctness of taste, and attention to composition'.[18] It may well have been as members of the Rankenian that Turnbull and Wishart first made contact with Molesworth, just as they are supposed to have entered into correspondence with Bishop Berkeley before his departure for Bermuda in 1728. Unfortunately, there is no record of the proceedings of the Rankenian, but it seems to have been distinguished by the determination of its members to put Scotland in the van of intellectual developments. This was the channel into which the energies generated by the catchwords of liberty and virtue were directed. Since so many of the club were, or soon became, professors, they had no difficulty in finding auditors.

The teaching of the liberal arts at Edinburgh University, which had shown no immediate effects as a result of the change from the regenting system to the professorial in 1708, was galvanized in the 1720s and the 1730s by a new generation of professors. Mackie, MacLaurin and Stevenson, later abetted by Wishart as Principal, brought the concerns of the Rankenian into the classroom – a trifle incongruously, since to begin with at least most of their students were 'the Boys and Children' who had provoked Robert Hepburn's taunt. Luckily a unique body of evidence exists which enables us to trace the influence of the Rankenian on professorial teaching in Edinburgh. One of the members of the club closely linked to Wishart in particular by personal friendship was John Stevenson, who took over the teaching of logic and rhetoric from 1730. In Edinburgh University Library there is a bound volume of student essays, thirty-seven in all, dating from 1737 to 1750. They were composed by students on topics allocated to them by Stevenson, and were intended to be read before the assembled class. The extant essays are in the handwriting of the students, but are evidently those Stevenson thought most worthy of preservation. The authors include William Robertson, David Dalrymple (Lord Hailes), Gilbert Elliot of Minto, John Erskine the evangelical leader, a clutch of future law lords, and a number of others who were to become

---

[18] George Wallace, 'Memoirs of Dr Wallace of Edinburgh', *Scots Magazine*, 33 (1771), 340-1.

members of the Select Society in its heyday from 1754 to 1763. Curiously, the essay of Hugh Blair, known to have been admired by Stevenson, is not among the collection. Dugald Stewart, another of Stevenson's auditors not represented here, recalled that Stevenson was very fond of reminding his pupils of his membership of the Rankenian.[19] Certainly the ideas of Shaftesbury, Molesworth and Berkeley are found everywhere in the essays, indeed dominate them. Gilbert Elliot's essay 'De pulchro', for instance, leans heavily on Shaftesbury's *Characteristics*, arguing that beauty is defined as what of its own nature is praiseworthy, but is more easily understood from the common consent of mankind 'who attempt the most hazardous Actions, and prefer the noblest undertakings, only because Honourable, Beautiful, and Becoming'.[20] Whole sentences are lifted straight from the *Characteristics*, and Shaftesbury's view that the man of taste marked by this 'true relish for virtue' is the real patriot is heartily endorsed. When Shaftesbury is not quoted, his style is closely imitated.

Similarly, the correspondence of Rankenian members with Molesworth is reflected in several essays which harp on the need for a virtuous education to counteract the effects of luxury and corruption. The essays on ancient education, of which there are six, amount to an attack on the degeneracy of modern social *mores* and on the trivialities of scholastic education. Adam Carlyle followed Molesworth in his dictum 'The Basis of Government is inseparably connected with a virtuous Education.'[21] For their source material on ancient education, the students relied on the well-known texts of Cicero's *De Oratore* and *Brutus* and Quintilian's *Institutio Oratoria*, but they played down the *ars dicendi* in favour of the dependence of liberty on the right acquisition of philosophy and eloquence. While priestly authoritarianism did not loom so large as a bugbear as in Molesworth's writings (probably because so many arts students went on to Divinity), the essayists argued that political tyranny and a free traffic in education and learning were incompatible. In fact Cicero and Quintilian are glossed in the spirit of the 'Cato' of the *London Journal*. The role of education is to make good citizens and thus it is the cornerstone of a virtuous polity. Carlyle ends his essay with the pious exhortation: 'Let us therefore, while we enjoy the opportunities of a virtuous Education, attend carefully to the wise Instructions of our Teachers, Learn Wisdom from their Mouths, Coppy after their Example...lest our Nation become a Reproach among our Enemies.'[22] In drawing lessons from ancient education, Stevenson seems to have impressed on his students the role of the professoriate as intellectual midwives of a learned and virtuous Scottish polity.

[19] Dugald Stewart, *Dissertation Exhibiting the Progress of Metaphysical, Ethical and Political Philosophy since the Revival of Letters in Europe*, in *Collected Works*, ed. Sir William Hamilton, 10 vols. (Edinburgh, 1854-60), i, pp. 350-1.
[20] Gilbert Elliot, 'De Pulchro', in 'Class Essays by Students of Moral Philosophy (Doctor John Stevenson), 1737-50', E.U.L., MS. Dc.4.54, fol. 59.
[21] Adam Carlyle, 'Of the Education of the Youth of Athens', 'Stevenson Class Essays', fol. 223.
[22] *Ibid.*, fol. 228.

The part played in the Stevenson essays by the theories of Bishop Berkeley has already been illuminated by George Davie.[23] He points out that the student essays share with the published works of Turnbull and MacLaurin a characteristic Rankenian concern with refuting materialism while sometimes baulking at the Berkeleian solution of disposing of matter altogether. What the student essayists do, which the formal philosophical constraints on Turnbull and MacLaurin prevent them doing, is to bring out the practical consequences of adopting what they took to be the Spinozist or Berkeleian positions. Francis Garden held that materialism necessarily undermines belief in the principles of mathematics and artillery, particularly in the infinite divisibility of matter and the infinity of space. For this reason he devoted the last section of his essay to a eulogy of Stevenson's friend MacLaurin, the 'admiration and ornament of all his intelligent countrymen'.[24] MacLaurin in his work on fluxions had, according to Garden, eschewed dogmatic extremism in favour of a proper respect for the inscrutability of God's purposes, and a practical concern for carrying on the business of the investigation of nature. Another of the essayists, John Carre, argued that Berkeley's paradoxes could not alter the fact that we do in the course of ordinary life act as if our perceptions are pictures of material existence. His main concern was the psychological consequences of giving credence to immaterialism: 'the just order and balance of things being lost, it is necessarily succeeded by great uneasiness and many anxieties which are no other than the strong efforts of Nature to restore and recover herself to her former original condition'.[25]

If Stevenson's essays are anything to go by, the Rankenians never lost sight of the requirements of virtue even in their enthusiasm for metaphysical inquiry. As well as the psychological unease induced by scepticism, which distracts the individual from his moral responsibilities, other essayists diagnosed a pathology in civil society brought about by an insatiable demand for proofs. Robert Liston in his essay 'Of Moral Certainty' warned

Take away this moral evidence, and the dissolution of all society in general would be the immediate consequence. For as mutual confidence, and the trust that Men repose in One Another, is one of the chief Bonds of all Societies and Communities, if this be taken away So that One Man must give Credit to what Another says, then Jealousy and Suspicion must reign in every place.[26]

The anarchic condition thus conjured up by Liston and his fellows is clearly in Stevenson's view a disease not only of the republic of letters but of the *res publica* itself. It is characteristic of these essays to take philosophic and literary

[23] G. E. Davie, 'Berkeley's Impact on Scottish Philosophers', *Philosophy*, 40 (1965), 222-34.
[24] Francis Garden, 'Whether Matter has any real or absolute existence distinct from being perceived', 'Stevenson Class Essays', fol. 58.
[25] John Carne, 'Of the Certainty of External Existence', *ibid.*, fol. 120.
[26] Robert Liston, 'Of Moral Certainty', *ibid.*, fol. 254.

issues so seriously – as if the fate of liberty and virtue depended on the liberal arts.

From a purely professional point of view the Rankenian professors must have been keen to advertise their rejection of the scholastic curriculum in favour of the sorts of liberal studies appropriate to citizens of a free commonwealth. In August 1741 William Wishart, now Principal of Edinburgh University, gave them their head by instigating the publication in the *Scots Magazine* of 'A short account of the University of Edinburgh, the present Professors in it, and the several parts of learning taught by them'. It was drawn up by the librarian Robert Henderson, who gave a brief account of the set books used by each professor, and the heads of his lectures. Much more space was given to the professors of the arts faculty, in particular MacLaurin, Mackie, Stevenson and John Pringle, than to professors of Divinity, Law or Medicine. Whereas professors of those faculties were simply alloted a list of textbooks, the courses of the arts professors were described in sufficient detail to indicate that, taken together, they constituted a programme of practical and liberal studies to suit a landed gentleman. Practical matters like surveying and fortification were mentioned as forming an integral part of the natural philosophy course, but strictly vocational studies like law and medicine were by comparison underemphasized. This advertisement for the arts faculty was well-designed to exploit the market of fee-paying students in the new conditions of *Lernfreiheit*[27] which had developed out of the collapse of the degree requirements. It did not take long for other colleges, notably Marischal College, Aberdeen, and Benjamin Franklin's new college at Philadelphia, to imitate the Edinburgh example.

II

There was no direct equivalent of the Rankenian Club in Glasgow, though like-minded professors belonged to a number of literary and improving clubs. But those who saw themselves as changing the face of university teaching did have what was almost an institutional base in the household of the Mures of Caldwell. Evidence for the existence of this base can be found in the Caldwell papers, where, apart from the correspondence, there is the sprightly memoir of Elizabeth Mure, which begins by describing the change of manners in Scottish society which she remembered as having happened around 1730. In particular she recalled that

> taste for good morals, which was improved by a set of teachers established among us, most of whom had their education abroad or had travelled with young gentlemen. As

---

[27] For *Lernfreiheit*, see J. B. Morrell, 'The University of Edinburgh in the Later Eighteenth Century: Its Scientific Eminence and Academic Structure', *Isis*, 62 (1971), 168–9. Only prospective Divinity students had to take all the elements of the arts course, and then in no particular order.

every body at this period went regularly to church, I may justly mention ministers as teachers: Prof. Hamilton and the two Mr. Wisharts at Edinburgh, Prof. Hutcheson; Craig, Clark and Principal Leechman in the West; they taught that whoever would please God must resemble him in goodness and benevolence, and those that had it not must affect it by politeness and good manners. Those lectures and sermons were attended by all the young and gay. They were new and entertaining and matter for conversation and criticism.[28]

The ministers in the Caldwell group were in the end less important than the professors, though they were responsible for introducing the new style of polite preaching to the West. Alexander Clark was regarded by the Mures as the most promising of all, but though he was librarian of Glasgow University 1727–31 and was appointed to the living of Neilston four miles from Caldwell in 1733 by the Earl of Dundonald, he died young in 1736. His nephew William Craig stepped into his shoes, and his sermons were sufficiently well thought of to justify their printing by the Foulis brothers. William Leechman, the future Professor of Divinity and Principal at Glasgow, was presented to Beith, the parish in which the Caldwells lived, in 1736; simply by his longevity he was enabled to carry over the educational and theological principles of the Caldwell circle into the generation of Smith and Reid. But Francis Hutcheson, was the 'philosophical monitor' and prime mover of the liberals in the university, as well as being an intimate friend of the Baron of the Exchequer, William Mure. He brought over the political, religious and philosophical outlook of the Molesworth coterie from Dublin to Glasgow in 1730. Chief amongst his early allies was Alexander Dunlop the Professor of Greek, whose second marriage in 1729 was to Abigail Mure of Caldwell. According to Robert Wodrow, Dunlop was largely responsible for Hutcheson's appointment; they were relatives, and Dunlop had taught Hutcheson when the latter was himself a student at Glasgow. In any case Dunlop and Hutcheson worked together in the university to make sure that the right sort of professors were appointed, and to manage all its business affairs. The key appointment in Hutcheson's view, one that crowned his efforts with success and was intended to change the face of theology in Scotland, was that of Leechman to the Professorship of Divinity in 1743.[29] Hutcheson's own activities were soon to be curtailed by his early death in 1746 but he was already sure of the victory of his party and principles in Glasgow University, where it mattered, though the capture of the General Assembly by the younger Moderate leaders did not take place until the 1750s.

By the 1740s the Caldwell household was becoming virtually a faculty club for the university. Younger members of the circle were James Moor, appointed

[28] Elizabeth Mure, 'Some remarks on the change of manners in my own time. 1700–1790', *Selections from the Family Papers preserved at Caldwell*, 3 vols. (Glasgow, 1854), i, pp. 267–8.
[29] Francis Hutcheson to Mure, 23 November 1743, *Caldwell Papers*, i, pp. 53–4.

successor to Dunlop as Professor of Greek in 1746, and William Rouet, later Professor of Oriental Languages (1751) and afterwards of Church History (1752). Both Moor and Rouet were highly commended by Hutcheson in a list of promising candidates he sent to Lord Minto in 1744, when the Professorship of Moral Philosophy at Edinburgh which Hutcheson himself later turned down (and Hume lost) became vacant.[30] Alexander Carlyle wrote of Moor that he was 'a very lively and witty man, a famous Grecian, but a more famous punster'.[31] Besides editions of Greek authors for Foulis, Moor was author of *Essays; read to the Literary Society; at their Weekly Meetings, within the College at Glasgow* (1759). The essay titles indicate his predilection for Shaftesbury and his range of concerns: 'An Essay on the influence of Philosophy upon the Fine Arts', 'An Essay on the Composition of the Pictures described in the Dialogue of Cebes', 'An Essay on Historical Composition'. Rouet was a cousin of the Baron of the Exchequer, and wrote a lively series of letters to Mure while on the Grand Tour with Sir John Maxwell of Pollock's son. He seems to have enjoyed this kind of tutorial work, not least for its financial rewards, rather more than the exercise of his professional function. In May 1759 the Earl of Hopetoun was to offer £400 to the university if leave of absence was granted for four years to Rouet, and though the offer was refused, his friends were powerful enough to put off his resignation until 1762. His surviving notes on his continental tours and on ancient printing, modern history and the politics of the Polish question, demonstrate an enthusiasm for republican principles in politics and a secular delight in the liberal arts for their own sake.[32] Other professors allied to the members of the Caldwell group included Robert Simson, the celebrated geometer, and George Rosse, Professor of Humanity 1735–54, who was a close friend and correspondent of the learned Dr Pearce, Bishop of Bangor. Starting as a beleaguered minority in the bitter struggles of university politics at the time of the Visitation of 1727, Hutcheson's allies had by the 1750s become numerous and powerful enough to be sure of such appointments as that of Adam Smith.

Edinburgh and Glasgow professors were by no means cut off from each other. As we have seen, Wishart moved in both circles, keeping up a voluminous correspondence with his brother George while in Glasgow. Although they were unable to tempt him from Glasgow to Edinburgh, Edinburgh University and its patrons, the town council, were well aware of Hutcheson's gifts, and he must have been respected in particular by the Rankenians. Colin MacLaurin wrote to him in the most adulatory terms, declaring that personally he was 'always

[30] Francis Hutcheson to Sir Gilbert Elliot (Lord Minto), 4 July 1744, National Library of Scotland, MS. 11004, fol. 57.
[31] Alexander Carlyle, *Autobiography*, p. 89.
[32] William Rouet to Earl of Hopetoun, 26 September 1759, N.L.S., MS. 4941, fol. 298; Rouet, 'Journal of a tour through Holland, France, and Italy, c. 1741', N.L.S., MS. 4990–1; 'Lecture Notes, c. 1751–60', N.L.S., MS. 4992.

zealous for the moral sense and fond of improving it'.³³ Hutcheson also kept up a correspondence with Wishart.³⁴ In general, Edinburgh and Glasgow professors pursued very similar aims in similar circumstances, prevented only by indifferent communications (Wishart was always waiting anxiously for parcels of books from his brother in Edinburgh) from making common cause. The universities of King's College and Marischal College, Aberdeen, were of course far more cut off than their southern counterparts, but there is evidence to show that there were those who wished to follow a parallel course once they were back on an even keel after the '15 and the subsequent purges. George Turnbull was a Professor of Philosophy at Marischal College from 1721 to 1727, taking an LL.D. there in 1727. A fellow Rankenian, MacLaurin, was Professor of Mathematics at the same college from 1717 to 1725. Turnbull taught Thomas Reid (who maintained later that Turnbull and David Fordyce were authors of the best books on the theory of liberal education), before leaving Aberdeen to travel and begin a career of authorship in London. The Aberdonians, at least before 1758 when the Aberdeen Philosophical Club was founded, seem to have had no central focus like the Rankenian in Edinburgh or the Caldwell circle in Glasgow. If anything, they have have thought of Aberdeen as a place of exile or a stepping-stone to better things. Thomas Blackwell the younger, Principal of Marischal College, wrote in 1730 to Sir John Clerk of Penicuik that the liberal professors there deserved support because 'we can do particular service in the heart of a disaffected country'.³⁵ Like Wishart in Edinburgh, Blackwell followed his father as principal, but belonged to a different ecclesiastical party and held very different views about the purposes and means of university education. Blackwell was a devout follower of Shaftesbury, and was reckoned by Thomas Birch to have been an ardent republican in his political principles, on the basis of his *Memoirs of the Court of Augustus*. His relation David Fordyce, who had been his pupil, himself became a regent in 1742, after some years in England as student and apprentice of Philip Doddridge at his academy at Northampton. The effect of this in providing him with a model of a liberal education is to be seen in his *Dialogues concerning Education* (1745).³⁶ Blackwell and Fordyce were jointly responsible for obtaining the award of D.D. to James Foster in 1748, and kept up contacts with other dissenting leaders such as Isaac Watts and Benjamin Avery in London. Fordyce was another who died early, drowned off the coast of Holland in 1751, but he was succeeded in his post by his pupil Alexander Gerard, who

[33] Colin MacLaurin to Francis Hutcheson, 23 October 1728, Scottish Record Office, RH. 1/2/497.
[34] Francis Hutcheson letters, n.d. [1735], in Wishart papers, E.U.L., MS. La II. 235, fols. 114, 115.
[35] Thomas Blackwell to Sir John Clerk, 1 April 1730, S.R.O., GD. 18/5036. See also the article on 'Blackwell, Thomas', in *Biographia Brittania*, ed. Andrew Kippis, 2nd edn (London, 1778-93). [36] David Fordyce, *Dialogues concerning Education*, 2 vols. (London, 1745).

with Thomas Reid shaped the Aberdeen Philosophical Club (or Wise Club).

It was Gerard, in fact, who was responsible for the statement of faith of the liberal professors at Marischal College, when, sponsored by Principal Blackwell and his colleagues, he drew up the *Plan of Education in the Marischal College and University of Aberdeen* (1755). It was an attempt to go one better than Edinburgh, in that 'The Order of teaching in the Marischal College' published in the *Scots Magazine* for December 1752 was now supplemented by the reasons for the new dispensation. Gerard expanded on their declared intention 'to render the study of the sciences more natural and progressive, and to fit their students to be *useful in life*'.[37] He began with a thorough critique of the scholastic order of education, which, according to him, equipped the student by means of logic and ontology with a technical but artificial language, fit only to subject his understanding to the arbitrary scholastic systems of natural and moral philosophy. By demoting logic and metaphysics to the end of the course, Gerard believed that the student would be enabled to draw general conclusions in moral and natural philosophy from his own experience and observation, thus making him subject to no other authority than his own understanding. Gerard hoped to persuade his readers of the virtues of this new plan by invoking the warrant of Bacon, and claimed that as a result of the new plan the masters of Marischal College 'have already begun to experience the public approbation by the increase of the number of their students'.[38] The plan was soon translated into German, and became well-known in America as well as Europe. The Marischal reforms afforded a useful blueprint for the makers of colleges in America; William Smith, the Provost of the Academy at Philadelphia, certainly drew on them in his pamphlet *A General Idea of the College of Mirania* (1753), which was a highly influential statement of the new liberal principles.[39]

Gerard and his colleagues showed no real inclination to meddle with pedagogic practice beyond changing the order in which the established curriculum was taught. The components of the arts curriculum remained basically unchanged in the Scottish universities throughout the eighteenth century. The 'Statistical Account of the University of Glasgow' supposed to have been drawn up in 1794 by Thomas Reid outlines a curriculum of five parts: the Latin and Greek languages, logic, moral philosophy and natural philosophy.[40] Although these classes were by then the province of specialist professors, they comprise the same heads as those taught by regents who before

[37] 'The Order of Teaching in the Marischal College', *Scots Magazine*, 14 (1752), 606.
[38] Alexander Gerard, *Plan of Education in the Marischal College and University of Aberdeen* (Aberdeen, 1755), pp. 34–5.
[39] A. F. Gegenheimer, *William Smith, Educator and Churchman, 1727–1803* (Philadelphia, 1943); Douglas Sloan, *The Scottish Enlightenment and the American College Ideal* (New York, 1971), pp. 82–5.
[40] Thomas Reid, 'Statistical Account of the University of Glasgow', *The Statistical Account of Scotland; drawn up from the Communications of the ministers of the different Parishes*, ed. Sir John Sinclair, 21 vols. (Edinburgh, 1791–9), xxi, Appendix 1.

1727 took each class through the whole curriculum. The picture was substantially the same for Edinburgh, Marischal College, Aberdeen, and St Andrews (King's College, Aberdeen, retained its regenting system throughout). As Professor David Ritchie of Edinburgh University remarked in his evidence to the Royal Commission on the Scottish Universities of 1826: 'the four regents taught just those sort of subjects which have been taught all along'.[41] The curriculum retained a sort of unity because it was required that each prospective Divinity student take all its parts, although the practice of graduating in arts virtually died out. But if the institutional structure survived intact from the scholastic era, this was actually because the skeleton could be clothed with the flesh of a rounded gentlemanly education; each professor judged his own teaching by its success in attracting sufficient numbers of gentlemen and sons of gentlemen willing to pay the class fee (normally two or three guineas). Adam Smith set his seal of approval on this academic entrepreneurship, regarding it as the best way of ensuring that the educational requirements of the civic community were met, and as resembling the ancient model most nearly. He argued that the Scottish universities had already achieved a signal superiority over English and continental universities in this respect.[42] Certainly by the 1750s they had left far behind the attempts of the visitation of Gilbert Rule in the 1690s to determine minutely just what each regent should teach.

Apart from the natural desire to give the fee-paying patrons what they wanted, the only real pedagogic principle which seems to have governed the liberal professors was the rejection of scholasticism in all its forms. Even so, changes in the practice of university teaching were probably less the result of a principled commitment than of factors such as the availability of books. The Commissioners who had attempted to draw up a *cursus philosophicus* for all the Scottish colleges in the 1690s had agreed that the practice of dictation was slow, laborious and left the students little time to reflect on what they had copied down.[43] Nevertheless, the practice lingered on, and was replaced only as individual professors began to devise their own lecture courses, and use set books for illustration and reference rather than simply as a unique exposition of the subject. Dictation came to be seen as an infringement of the independence of the individual, on his liberty to abide by his own judgement in matters of science and taste. Similar connotations brought about the decay of disputation as a means of testing the student's knowledge of his subject. It smacked too much of the wrangling of scholastics, although the practice of a ceremonial disputation at graduation remained.

[41] 'Evidence of Prof. David Ritchie', in *University of Edinburgh, Evidence, Oral and Documentary, taken and received by the Commissioners appointed by His Majesty George IV July 23 1826...for visiting the Universities of Scotland*, i, p. 139.
[42] *WN* V.i.f.7–50; Adam Smith to William Smith, 24 August 1740, *Correspondence*, p. 7, and Smith to William Cullen, 20 September 1774, *ibid.*, p. 173.
[43] *Munimenta Alme Universitatis Glasguensis*, ii, pp. 518–28.

English replaced Latin as the language of instruction in the arts curriculum in a haphazard fashion: Turnbull, Hutcheson and Stevenson have all been hailed as originators on the basis of student testimony and surviving lecture notes. What is clear is that there were very good pedagogic reasons for retaining Latin, as giving it up meant cutting off students from the European language of scholarship. In the seventeenth and early eighteenth centuries, Scottish universities could with justification be considered as full members of a family of European Protestant academic institutions, even if there was a net export of students. The transition to English meant a break with the Dutch universities which had served as pedagogic models, though individual Scottish professors like Charles Mackie and George Rosse continued to correspond in Latin with their Dutch masters and colleagues. But steadily the Scottish universities disengaged themselves from the European academic scene (although the process advanced much faster in the arts than the other faculties). Instead of Latin, English was embraced as the language of politeness – some like Blackwell carrying their enthusiasm so far as to favour the ornate style of the 3rd Earl of Shaftesbury. Anything less appropriate for the Scottish student on purely pedagogic grounds can hardly be imagined, yet even the student societies purged their proceedings of Scotticisms along with Latinity. Augustan English certainly put as many difficulties in the way of composition and comprehension as did continental Latin, but it had the inestimable advantage of representing a clean break with scholasticism. The innovatory professors pursued no vision of pedagogic efficiency comparable to that of George Jardine in his *Outlines of Philosophical Education* (1825) or Dugald Stewart, though the changes they were responsible for were at least as far-reaching.

If a widely admired work like David Fordyce's *Dialogues concerning Education* (1745) is anything to go by, the professors aspired to the creation of an entire community organized as an ideal academy, rather than simply to a more efficient form of university education. Fordyce's work met with immediate success. Robert Dodsley commissioned Fordyce and an Aberdeen colleague William Duncan to write the contributions on moral philosophy and logic respectively in his famous compendium *The Preceptor*, which appeared in 1748 with a preface by Dr Johnson. The other Samuel Johnson, D.D. and President of King's (later Columbia) College in America, maintained that the *Dialogues concerning Education* was 'the prettiest thing in its kind, and the best system – both in physical, metaphysical and moral philosophy as well as the conduct of life that I have seen'.[44] Benjamin Franklin was sufficiently impressed to attribute it to Francis Hutcheson.[45] The tributes on both sides of the Atlantic may seem strange now, as the Shaftesburian dialogue form and bursts of rhapsodic prose

---

[44] Samuel Johnson to Benjamin Franklin, 14 December 1750, *Papers of Benjamin Franklin*, ed. L. W. Labaree, iv (New Haven, Conn., 1961), p. 79.
[45] Benjamin Franklin to William Smith, 3 May 1753, *ibid.*, iv, p. 476.

obscure for us the import of the book. But aside from the useful reading-lists and occasional disquisitions on fashionable subjects like female education, the core of the book is the description of the workings on an ideal academy which, as we shall see, subsumes all the activities of a civic rather than merely educational community.

The *Dialogues* are introduced by a first-person narrator, Simplicius, who journeys to the pretty town of N**** in order to finish his education at the Academy presided over by Euphranor: 'I was very agreeably surprised with the sight of so many young gentlemen, some of them of rank and fortune, who were come hither from all quarters to imbibe the principles of science and virtue, in order to qualify them for the service of their friends and country'.[46] This experience is based on Fordyce's own, as after completing his M.A. at Marischal College, Aberdeen, he had gone to the dissenting academy run by Philip Doddridge at Northampton.[47] However, the Academy of Euphranor aspires to rather more than a denominational or postgraduate status; it is more like the model of a perfect commonwealth in miniature. Each member has the right to propose, determine and vote whatever he please, and elect to and stand for any of the offices within the Academy. In order to benefit from these privileges, Simplicius has on arrival to enter the chamber of initiation, and swear a solemn oath. The chamber is dominated by a throne, with a statue of Virtue on the right, Liberty on the left. Around the room are busts of ancient lawgivers, inventors, improvers, assertors of liberty and masters of politics (Plato, Aristotle, Sir Thomas More, Harrington and Sidney among others). Surrounded by these momentous icons, Simplicius swears the oath of initiation, quoted in full:

I swear in the name of the all-seeing Deity, and before these witnesses, that I will henceforth be a slave to no sect or party of men; – that I will espouse no principles, but such as I believe true, and submit myself only to reasonable authority; that I will always look upon myself as a part of the society to which I belong, and therefore bound to promote its most extensive interest above all private or personal views; though still in subordination to the two grand societies of my country and mankind. I likewise solemnly declare, that I consider myself as a citizen of the intellectual world, and subject to its almighty Lawgiver and Judge; that by him I am placed upon an honourable theatre of action, to sustain, in the sight of mortal and immortal beings, that character and part which he shall assign me, in order to my being trained up for perfection and immortality; and shall, therefore, from this time forth devote my life to the service of God, my country, and mankind. As I observe this oath, may I be acceptable to God.[48]

Thus Simplicius, in return for a voluntary commitment to these intellectual

---

[46] Fordyce, *Dialogues*, i, p. 13.
[47] *Correspondence and Diary of Philip Doddridge*, ed. John Doddridge Humphreys, 5 vols. (London, 1830), iii, p. 5. Fordyce addressed Doddridge as 'Mon Révérent et cher Père'.
[48] Fordyce, *Dialogues*, i, pp. 34–5.

and cultural goals, is vested with the rights and responsibilities of a citizen of this republic of letters.

Simplicius soon finds that the main engines of Euphranor's drive for improvement are the conversational clubs into which the Academy breaks up. The members of the Academy choose to join such clubs as cater for their interests: poetical, mathematical, political, and artistic. Their only rules as regards what they may or may not discuss are that they avoid idle gay chatter about love intrigues or fashion on the one hand, and debates on matters of state and party politics on the other. Just such clubs and societies had of course sprung up in Edinburgh, Glasgow and Aberdeen, particularly from the 1720s onwards, and these very rules were commonly adopted (by the Rankenian Club, for instance). The club to which Simplicius is introduced by his friend Sophron is the Philosophical Club, and he is told it is 'a picture of the Academy in miniature'.[49] This might be regarded as a blueprint for the Aberdeen Philosophical Society, better known as the Wise Club, one of whose founder members in 1758 was Alexander Gerard, Fordyce's best-known pupil and successor. Sophron reassures Simplicius that the young gentlemen of the club are 'conversable' rather than 'metaphysical' by inclination; moreover, they reason for their own improvement rather than to dictate to others. Sophron is also keen to stress that Euphranor would never interfere, or attempt to direct philosophical debates, for fear that he should breed the same 'spirit of adulation and servility' which marked the French Academy once it was taken under Richelieu's protection. Any interference with the delicate mechanism of intellectual exchange between independent agents, by which the purposes of mutual improvement in knowledge and virtue are served, would corrupt the clubs as voluntary institutions.

Another aspect of the affairs of the model Academy is that its members are treated as adults in accordance with their status as 'citizens of the intellectual world'. Conversely, adults are in as much need of improvement through conversation as youths; 'gentlemen of the first rank, in the town and neighbourhood' frequently visit the Academy and take part in the conversations of its clubs.[50] The Academy is not only an institution where students act the part of citizens, but where citizens may come to improve themselves as befits their moral status as progressive and rational beings. Fordyce chooses to blur the distinction between student and citizen by imposing on both an obligation to better themselves in knowledge and virtue. This process of self-improvement is depicted as the main business of life, besides which party politics, commerce and other mundane activities in general, pale into insignificance. This vision of the Academy clearly builds on Fordyce's experiences at Northampton, his knowledge of the French and other continental academies, and his classical reading; but none of these can have supplied him with its outstanding feature,

[49] *Ibid.*, pp. 65–6.   [50] *Ibid.*, p. 25.

its function as the mainspring or engine of civic improvement. To judge by the approbation the *Dialogues* met with, this vision must have been highly sympathetic, not least because it could offend no creed or political ideology and yet carried such a charge of uplifting moral sentiment. But despite its English and American success, the work also provided a rationale for the activities of the Scottish liberal professoriate to which Fordyce himself belonged. By implication they were all true Scottish patriots, heirs of Buchanan as well as of Andrew Melville (Fordyce's niece, the wife of Samuel Bentham, called Fordyce himself a second Crichton).[51] The Scottish landowning elite were asked to endorse professional initiatives, and to act as patrons of this cultural drive. They were to be partners with the professors in creating the republic of letters, on the same lines as the landowning retired politician Atticus who worked with Euphranor in the *Dialogues*.

III

What the relationship between professor and patron might amount to in practice is well illustrated by the papers of Charles Mackie in the Laing collection in Edinburgh University Library, and in the Leven–Melville papers at the Scottish Record Office. Mackie was Professor of Universal and Civil History at Edinburgh effectively from 1719 to 1754, a post he first obtained through the good offices of his uncle, Principal William Carstares. He published little, though he did contribute occasional papers to the societies of which he was a member, including the Rankenian and the Philosophical Society.[52] His main interests seem to have been Roman law and antiquities, which must have been of some use to those of his auditors with a legal career in mind, and chronology. He left behind him no great reputation for eloquence or learning, unlike his friends Stevenson and MacLaurin. But what his correspondence reveals is that he acted as a sort of clearing-house in the business of matching tutors to pupils for the Grand Tour. His own ex-pupils often applied for such posts, and Mackie was usually able to put them in touch with landed gentlemen who had sons of the right age. Mackie also operated a profitable boarding service for those young gentlemen, English or Scottish, who could afford it, and built at his own expense a large room in his house where he conducted private classes. No doubt his close association with his more famous colleagues and his sociability helped in all this. But his enviable position

---

[51] 'Notice by Lady Bentham of her descent from Fordyce of Fordyce', British Library, Add. MS. 33,553, fol. 66.

[52] Mackie's papers in E.U.L. are described by L. W. Sharp, 'Charles Mackie, the First Professor of History at Edinburgh University', *Scottish Historical Review*, 41 (1962), 23–45; Leven–Melville MSS., S.R.O., GD. 26/13/602. Mackie was also a member of the Associated Critics, committed to producing a text of Buchanan's works which would do justice to his republicanism, in competition with the edition of Thomas Ruddiman.

depended probably in the first place on his relationship with Alexander, 5th Earl of Leven. Leven had his own 'doer' in Edinburgh, John Russell, but he used Mackie as his eyes and ears when he was in London serving as one of the Scottish representative peers. Apart from Mackie's handling of the education of his sons, Leven relied on him for political information, social gossip and advice on estate matters.

But Mackie had still more to offer Leven than this. Leven was flattered to be a member of the professorial circle in Edinburgh. In particular he was proud of providing material in 1733 for an article on lightning in the *Philosophical Transactions* which he wanted Colin MacLaurin to write. Leven had invited Professors Mackie and MacLaurin to his country seat to inspect the damage caused by a lightning bolt, refusing his servants permission to clear up the mess until it had been properly investigated. Leven's enthusiasm serves to show how far the professors' vision of a polite society dedicated to the cause of patriotic improvement in knowledge and virtue had struck a responsive chord amongst the nobility and gentry. It would be a mistake of course to exaggerate the ideological element in the Mackie–Leven relationship; primarily, Mackie was Leven's confidant and adviser on practical matters. But they did share a set of assumptions about their respective roles as executant and patron in the important sphere of culture and improvement. Those other nobles, gentlemen and professors who played so dominant a role in the Philosophical Society and the Select Society subscribed to the same assumptions.

But not all observers saw the mutual embrace of professors and landed patrons with the indulgence of David Fordyce; or the development of the Scottish arts curriculum with the complacency of Adam Smith. In the rather more jaundiced eyes of William Thom of Govan, for instance, high-flown liberal sentiments and fawning on the gentry had elevated professorial status at the cost of losing touch with the educational needs of Glasgow's citizens. In his *Letter from Pr--f--r ------- to H------- M-------, Esq. Airshire, explaining the motives which have determined the University of Glasgow to desert the Blackfriar Church and betake themselves to a Chapel*, he puts into the mouth of the professor a candid explanation of the gap which had grown up over fifty years between professors and burgesses. In his letter the good professor declares to his patron:

ever since you put your son to both my classes, I have held you in great esteem; and I beg leave to tell you, that when I reached out my hand to you, I scarce expected so large an honorarium as you generously gave me. My heart warms whenever I think of you; and many times when we meet in faculty, we comment and regret deeply, that so few who send their children to our college have your liberal and gentlemanly turn of mind. You, Sir, know the value of ancient and solid literature, and have the heart to encourage those who instil it into the minds of our North-British youth.[53]

The motives he attributes to the professors for wishing to have their own

[53] *The Works of the Rev. William Thom, late minister of Govan...* (Glasgow, 1799), pp. 231-2.

The Scottish professoriate and the polite academy 113

chapel are: first, that they might avoid the unwarranted disgrace under which they labour for smiling, sleeping and otherwise showing their superiority to the instruction they receive in church; second, to demonstrate their independence, in particular of the city; third, to suit the dignity of their increased incomes; fourth, because of their distaste for ordinary Presbyterianism; fifth, to act the gentleman without incurring censure at kirk-session; sixth, to divert resentment against the private lives of the professors to its proper object, ignorance and contempt of philosophy; seventh, and most important of all, to raise a profit by letting seats to the citizens. Thom harps again and again on the worldly profits the professors have garnered as a result of their pretensions to instilling the principles of virtue and liberty. He compares this with the situation before 1720:

> Fifty years ago we were but in low estimation; there might be now and then a professor, who, upon account of merit and personal dignity, was confessedly above most clergymen; but in truth, Sir, we were generally looked upon as in a middle rank between parish ministers and country school-masters; and, at that time, no minister in town, and scarce one in the country, would have chosen to throw up his charge for the sake of one of our professorships.[54]

But by 1764, when Thom wrote this pamphlet, he reckoned that the dignity assumed by the professors was itself paying a dividend, in that gentlemen felt obliged by the show of it to raise their *honorariums* still further.

But Thom did not rest his case there. He challenged the professors on their own ground, on the merit of their liberal education. He found the continued teaching of logic and metaphysics indefensible, and explicable only as a means of keeping knowledge mysterious and so overawing students (the same criticism that the liberal apologists launched against scholasticism). Even in their much vaunted moral philosophy the professors were not safe from Thom's attacks. In his *Letter to J------- M-----, Esq. on the defects of a university education and its unsuitableness to a commercial people; with the expediency and necessity of erecting at Glasgow an academy for the instruction of youth*,[55] Thom disputed the need for disquisitions on the foundations of morality after the fashion of Hutcheson and Smith. Would not the students be better off in having explained to them the nature of the different virtues without puzzling their understandings with philosophical controversy? In place of the liberal curriculum, Thom wanted to see one adapted to the needs of a commercial people rather than to the taste of fine gentlemen. He looked for practical mathematics, history in general, the history of Scotland and its neighbours, natural history, geography, the history of commerce, and practical morality. He quoted the plan of Gerard for Marischal College, only to declare that the professors had in fact continued to teach in the liberal fashion rather than really putting into practice Bacon's

[54] *Ibid.*, p. 235.   [55] *Ibid.*, pp. 263-301.

prescriptions. The only solution was to give up hope for the universities, and to follow the example of Perth in setting up an academy which *would* meet the needs of a commercial people. Thom pursued a vigorous vendetta against Glasgow University, and his views must not be taken as wholly representative of local opinion; nevertheless, he appeals with sufficient frequency to resentment against the professoriate to make it reasonably certain that he could expect a good deal of support from the Glasgow citizenry.

But despite Thom's diatribes, professional credit remained unharmed where it counted most, and indeed went from strength to strength. The events of 1745 gave the liberal professoriate a wonderful opportunity to show themselves the true patriots they had always aspired to be. Whereas the town councils of Edinburgh and Glasgow were distinctly reluctant to take any measures to oppose the Pretender that would put property and lives at stake, the professors were vociferous in their calls for action. In both towns the professors and their students wished to join the bands of volunteers formed to offer a defence against the Pretender's army. We are fortunate in that Professor Colin MacLaurin not only wrote a long letter to Lord President Forbes on 9 December 1745, recording his personal part in these events, but also composed a 'Journal of what passed relating to the defence of Edinburgh from Monday September 2 till Monday September 16'.[56] This journal shows the zeal and civic virtue of the volunteers in a very creditable light, by contrast with the lukewarmness and delays of the Provost and town council. On September 2 a group of about twenty met at Mrs Clark's and agreed to make a fresh application to the Provost to put the town in a state of defence; Baillie Stuart and MacLaurin were deputed to wait on the Provost the next morning. They put it to him 'our doing something was requisite to save the report of the town, to divert the enemy from coming this way and to raise a spirit in the country'. MacLaurin seems to have thought of the activities of the volunteers largely as a propaganda exercise; the journal itself was probably conceived of as such. The formal association of volunteers took place on September 5; MacLaurin was made overseer of the fortifications; and a broadsheet was drawn up announcing the association of volunteers 'to encourage others to join and rouse the lethargic spirit of the country'. MacLaurin subscribed for the keep of a dozen volunteers personally and pushed on with work on the fortifications; but he soon had cause to complain of the paltry help he was getting from the Provost and council. Alexander Carlyle recalled visiting him at the fortifications, and was urged to apply himself to learning the use of arms.[57] Some of the hot-headed volunteers,

---

[56] Colin MacLaurin to Lord President Forbes, 9 December 1745, N.L.S. MS. 2629, fol. 46; 'Journal of what passed relating to the defence of Edinburgh from Monday September 2 till Monday September 16', N.L.S., MS. 299, fols. 2–13. The two following quotations are also taken from the 'Journal'.

[57] Alexander Carlyle, *Autobiography*, pp. 123–4.

notably William Cleghorn the Professor of Moral Philosophy, rode out from the city to try to make contact with Sir John Cope's forces, which were making a leisurely advance on Edinburgh. A Dutch fleet was rumoured to be about to enter the Forth. However, the town council proved less interested in a display of civic virtue than in preserving lives and property. A bargain was struck with the Pretender's army while the volunteers were off the scene, and MacLaurin and his colleagues were presented with a *fait accompli*. MacLaurin continued nevertheless to live quietly in town until he was required to make a formal submission, when he made his way to England, and stayed with the Archbishop of York.

A very similar pattern of events unfolded in Glasgow, where again the professors put themselves in the forefront of patriotic resistance to the invader. More was at stake than political loyalties, for Jacobitism meant a return to the feudal state from which the Lowlands at least were just now emerging. The Highlanders represented an atavistic challenge to modern polite values, with which the professors themselves were most closely associated. Consequently they were absolutely committed to the Hanoverian cause and the Union with England, and did as much to advertise the fact as discretion would allow. The universities were very quick to present their congratulations to George II on his deliverance, and to remind him of their unwavering loyalty and efforts on his behalf. The defeat of the rebellion was an endorsement of professorial values, and enhanced their prestige with the followers of the Duke of Argyle who were now back in power, and in polite society generally.

MacLaurin died unexpectedly of a chill in 1746, which was afterwards attributed to his exertions in the fortification of Edinburgh, on top of the strain of many years of intensive teaching. He was prevented by an early death, like Hutcheson and Fordyce, from seeing the professoriate and the universities moving into an era of consolidation. The capture of the leadership of the General Assembly by a group of younger ministers of a liberal persuasion meant that the Kirk would no longer attempt to discipline professors with unorthodox opinions. Indeed by the time that Principal William Robertson took over leadership of the Moderates, the sort of liberalism for which Hutcheson and the Rankenians had stood was no longer controversial. It was the manners of the Moderates which gave offence now to the orthodox, rather than their pronouncements as professors or authors; or it was their large incomes by comparison with those of ordinary ministers, which so infuriated Thom. But such resentments were by then of little account. The Select Society, founded in 1754, was the nearest Scotland came to developing a single forum for its republic of letters, and had a full professorial representation. It devoted its attention to improvement in philosophy and eloquence, and to more material improvement in agriculture and industry, offering prizes for the fine and for the practical arts. It is not surprising that the Select Society inherited the objectives of the liberal arts professoriate, as so many of its members were the first generation of pupils of those professors.

As Adam Smith appreciated, it is characteristic of institutions which have developed their own momentum that those who belong to them worship the beauty of utility, and pursue the aim of functional efficiency, rather than the original purposes for which they were instituted. The professors appointed to the arts faculties of the 1720s and 1730s had found a new purpose for the universities to replace the training up of a godly ministry, which had motivated the Visitation of the 1690s. They had a vision of apotheosis in the 'Academy' of David Fordyce, a cultural generator rather than a pedagogic institution, one which would supply the energies of improvement in virtue and civility vital to the Scottish nation. But the vision faded as the reputation of the colleges grew, and as the Shaftesburian language in which the vision had been expressed came to seem outmoded. By the 1750s *Lernfreiheit*, a fact of life which the earlier generation of professors had learned to live with and to exploit, was coming to be recognized as a guarantee of pedagogic excellence. The pedagogic efficiency of Scottish university education was now widely known, even advertised. In these circumstances it is not surprising that the professoriate no longer saw the universities primarily as vehicles for patriotic cultural aspirations but as institutions with interests of their own to advance or protect. There is no room here to explore these developments further. But one consequence was the dispelling of the notional unity afforded to the arts curriculum by the ideal of a virtuous gentlemanly education, and its eventual replacement as an organizing principle by the more rigorous mental philosophy of Reid, Stewart and their successors. Their teaching was the inspiration of a second generation of imitators of the Scottish model in European and American universities of the early nineteenth century.

But there was also a change after the mid-century in the relations between the professoriate and the landowners. Perhaps once the professors had found their feet, a more critical attitude on their part towards their patrons was inevitable. In any case, some aspects of the Scottish landholding system came in for sharp criticism by the professors, in particular the entailing of estates, which Smith and others supposed contributed to the less efficient management of land in Scotland. For their part, the landowners looked askance at the professors' vociferous advocacy of increased ministerial (and of course professional) stipends, a cost which would necessarily fall on the heritors and elders. But if the honeymoon was over, then the marriage itself had perforce to be lived through; even when both parties had established to their own satisfaction their separate identities as vital members of the North British polity. There was a good deal of active professional interest in the Poker Club and its agitation for a Scottish militia, showing that faith in the landowning and arms-bearing gentry as the backbone of the *res publica* was far from extinguished.

The landowners certainly demonstrated their faith in the efficacy of the liberal arts curriculum, in so far as they sent their sons to Scottish universities rather than as before to Leiden or Göttingen (even if many finished their education abroad). The bid made by the professoriate earlier in the century for recognition and for an improved status in the eyes of the Scottish landowning community, proved a lasting rather than an ephemeral success.[58]

[58] See further Peter Jones, 'The Polite Academy and the Presbyterians, 1720-1770', in *New Perspectives on the Politics and Culture of Early Modern Scotland*, ed. J. Dwyer, R. A. Mason and A. Murdoch (Edinburgh, 1982), pp. 156-78.

5 From applied theology to social analysis: the break between John Locke and the Scottish Enlightenment

JOHN DUNN

The duty of mankind, as God's creatures, to obey their divine creator was the central axiom of John Locke's thought. The entire framework of his thinking was 'theocentric'[1] and the key commitment of his intellectual life as a whole was the epistemological vindication of this framework.[2] It is still a controversial question precisely what the religious opinions of David Hume and Adam Smith in fact were. But it would certainly be a profoundly implausible claim to make in relation to either that the *framework* of their thinking was in any sense 'theocentric'. Whether or not either was in any theoretical sense an atheist, it is fair to describe each as being, as David Gauthier terms Hobbes,[3] 'a practical atheist': someone for whom, if God does exist, at least his existence makes no practical difference to the sane conduct of human life. It is scarcely surprising that the acquaintance of a practical atheist like Hume should have troubled the neurotic and credulous James Boswell, whose conduct even when Hume was virtually on his deathbed fully merited the latter's lapidary rebuke on an earlier occasion that 'it required great goodness of disposition to withstand the baleful effects of Christianity'.[4] But it is historically more striking and more illuminating to notice that their (on the whole very discreet) practical atheism would certainly in Locke's eyes have put Hume and perhaps even a wholly honest Smith,[5] at least in later life, beyond the pale of toleration:

---

[1] David Gauthier, 'Why Ought One Obey God? Reflections on Hobbes and Locke', *Canadian Journal of Philosophy*, 7 (1977), 425–46, especially p. 432.

[2] John Dunn, *The Political Thought of John Locke: An Historical Account of the Argument of the 'Two Treatises of Government'* (Cambridge, 1969); James Tully, *A Discourse of Property: John Locke and his Adversaries* (Cambridge, 1980).   [3] Gauthier, 'Why Ought One Obey God?', p. 435.

[4] Ernest Campbell Mossner, *The Life of David Hume* (Edinburgh, 1954), pp. 586–7. Even during this final illness Hume retained the capacity to tease Boswell with the greatest finesse. See the account of their last meeting in Boswell's journal, 3 March 1777, in *Boswell in Extremis, 1776–1778*, ed. Charles M. Weis and Frederick A. Pottle (London, 1971), pp. 11–15, especially p. 11: 'He then said flatly that the Morality of every Religion was bad, and I really thought, was not jocular when he said that when he heard a man was religious, he concluded he was a rascal, though he had known some instances of very good men being religious.'

[5] The question of Smith's theological beliefs is an extremely intricate one. Jacob Viner, for example, *The Role of Providence in the Social Order* (Philadelphia, 1972), ch. 3, especially pp. 79,

'Promises, covenants, and oaths, which are the bond of human society, can have no hold upon or sanctity for an atheist; for the taking away of God, even only in thought, dissolves all.'[6] Hume certainly had little hesitation in subtracting God in thought; and there is some evidence that Smith became increasingly ready to do so (or perhaps merely increasingly ready to acknowledge having done so) towards the end of his life. But each of them set himself with considerable determination to establish that the bonds of human society, human moral sentiments, neither depended nor needed to depend for either their prevalence or their rationally binding force upon an authority external to human society or to the human race as a whole.

In their earliest major works both Hume and Smith explain, painstakingly and determinedly, that so far from its being true that everything (and in particular all human obligation) is dissolved by considering such obligation independently of the purposes of a concerned creator, all that human society requires in order to be causally viable is the dependable genesis of the sense of such obligation in individuals, as these become socially adult. In lieu of theological reassurance, their readers were offered what we today would see as *sociological* reassurance, sophisticated, modern and disenchanted, an offer still readily applauded as 'scientific'. By contrast, Locke's views on the untrustworthiness and the objectively intolerable attributes of atheists are normally passed over with some discomfort by modern commentators[7] who, even if they are not all now theoretically atheists to a man, are certainly apt all to be practical atheists (and in so far, for example, as they elect to keep their promises, would be most unlikely to mention their beliefs about God in listing their reasons for doing so). Few would now be prepared to regard Locke's views on this topic as an index of much sociological acumen. But it should at least be easy enough to perceive historically that this sociological obtuseness was not a matter of mere intellectual oversight, indeed that Locke had the deepest and

---

81–2 and also p. 60, lays considerable emphasis on the providentialist dimension of Smith's social thought. It is certainly easy enough to find such themes articulated by Smith in his earlier writings and in the early editions of the *Theory of Moral Sentiments*. In later life, however, Smith appears to have become considerably more sceptical (or considerably less discreet). Special attention must be paid to the so-called 'Passage on Atonement' in Appendix II, *TMS*, pp. 383–401. See also notes 67 and 68 below.

[6] John Locke, *Epistola de Tolerantia*, ed. and trans. R. Klibansky and J. W. Gough (Oxford, 1968), p. 135. (See also the Latin text of the whole of paragraph 4, p. 134). It is not, however, clear that Locke's views on this matter were wholly consistent. Why, on this view, should promises and oaths 'tye the infinite Deity'? (*Two Treatises of Government*, ed. Peter Laslett (Cambridge, 1960), 1.2.6 line 6). And see the, at first sight, slightly more naturalistic drift of: 'Truth and keeping of Faith belongs to Men, as Men, and not as Members of Society.' (*Two Treatises*, 2.2.14 lines 17–19.)

[7] See, for example, the introductions by Klibansky and Gough to Locke, *Epistola de Tolerantia*, esp. pp. xxxv, 40–1, etc. For a very helpful historical survey of attitudes towards disbelief in God in seventeenth-century England, see G. E. Aylmer, 'Unbelief in Seventeenth-Century England', in Donald Pennington and Keith Thomas (eds.), *Puritans and Revolutionaries: Essays in Seventeenth-Century History Presented to Christopher Hill* (Oxford, 1978), pp. 22–46.

most closely considered reasons for refusing to regard descriptive sociology as an appropriate standard for human practical reason. For Hume and Smith, all there normatively is to individual human existence and to the reproduction of human society is the *fact* that human beings individually (and thus collectively) hold certain beliefs, the internal reasons with which history has furnished individuals, constrained in their individual distribution by the mechanisms of social reproduction.[8] Property, justice, allegiance, loyalty, duty, fidelity, all human rights and all human duties, are in the last instance functions of opinion.

In considering the development of political economy in eighteenth-century Scotland – a special and theoretically powerful aspect of the systematic causal analysis of society to which Hume and Smith committed themselves – it may thus be illuminating to see their adoption of this analytical project very directly in contrast with the thinking of Locke. For to do so does not merely have the merit of historical relevance (in that both Hume's and Smith's moral thinking was initially much preoccupied with remedying what they saw as the defects of Locke's thought and the politically deplorable consequences of its vulgarization). It also offers an imaginative backcloth against which it should be easier to see clearly the relations between the intellectual dynamic of Hume's and Smith's thinking and the historical limits of their comprehension. It is hard for us even today to grasp the profundity of this caesura in the history of liberalism. But if we commence our efforts to grasp it from the fact that Locke had, in a sense, consciously set himself to *establish* it, we may contrive to draw some assistance in grasping it from the forceful and highly explicit reasons which led him to do so.

Both Hume and Smith, in different ways, vindicate an extremely strong theory of human practical reason: the theory, that is, that the rational grounds for human action are, within the laws of physical nature, reasons internal to individuals,[9] restrained from chaos or arbitrariness solely by the causal processes of society. All *good* reasons for human action and human effort are founded on this single blunt (if complicated) fact that human beings hold certain beliefs. And any reasons for human action and human effort which are not founded on this fact cannot be good reasons.[10] This is certainly a very modern view; and there is some reason to suppose that both Hume and Smith

---

[8] For Hume, see particularly David Gauthier, 'David Hume, Contractarian', *Philosophical Review*, 88 (1979), 3–38.

[9] See e.g. Gauthier, 'Why Ought One Obey God?'; and the very clear analysis given by Bernard Williams, 'Internal and External Reasons', in Ross Harrison (ed.), *Rational Action* (Cambridge, 1979), pp. 17–28.

[10] See Philippa Foot, 'Morality as a System of Hypothetical Imperatives', *Philosophical Review*, 81 (1972), 305–16, and 'Reasons for Action and Desires', in Joseph Raz (ed.), *Practical Reasoning* (Oxford, 1978), pp. 178–84; and John McDowell, 'Are Moral Requirements Hypothetical Imperatives?', *Proceedings of the Aristotelian Society*, supplementary vol. 62 (1978), 13–29.

were sharply aware of its modernity. But what they cannot have been aware of was the degree to which Locke's thought by contrast was devoted precisely to its rejection. The break in social thought between Locke and the great Scottish thinkers was not in essence (as the effortless Whig perspective on history inclines us to see it) a break strenuously established by the latter. Rather, it was a break established prophylactically by Locke himself, a refusal of the *future* as it was to come to be. To speak anachronistically, both Hume and Smith in effect subordinate human practical reason to the contingencies of sociology, seeing history as real causal process, and value for human beings as engendered within this process, and setting themselves to identify the logic of this process. History, they supposed, very much in the modern view, must be taken as it comes. Locke, by contrast, chose (and chose very early in his life) to devote his intellectual energies to shoring up human practical reason *against* the contingencies of sociology. Indeed at a purely personal level it is biographically correct to say (though it is, of course, not something which he would have said for himself) that his *purpose* in setting himself to vindicate epistemologically the theocentric framework of his thought was precisely to uphold human practical reason against the contingencies of sociology.

It is important to be clear about the implications of this endeavour. It was not that Locke was in any sense less interested than Hume or Smith were in the social causation of human beliefs, any more than it is true, for example, that he was uninterested in the causal properties of the British monetary system.[11] He did not hesitate to apply moral categories not merely to human rights,[12] but also explicitly to market exchange as such.[13] There is, indeed, no single theme in Locke's intellectual life as a whole about which he thought as hard and long and into which he inquired as systematically as the social processes which sustain moral and religious beliefs.[14] But what was crucial in determining

[11] See particularly Patrick Kelly, 'Locke on Money: An Edition of John Locke's Three Pamphlets on Money Published in the 1690s' (unpublished Ph.D. thesis, University of Cambridge, 1973). Joyce Oldham Appleby, *Economic Thought and Ideology in Seventeenth-Century England* (Princeton, N.J., 1978), esp. pp. 221-54, 258, and 'Locke, Liberalism and the Natural Law of Money', *Past and Present*, no. 81 (1976), 43–69, offers an illuminating discussion of the internal mechanisms of Locke's theory of the determinants of the value of coined gold and silver. But her efforts to relate his adoption of this theory to the trajectory of seventeenth-century English economic thought in general and more particularly to explain his abandonment of the more homogeneously causal theories of his predecessors and opponents is neither clear nor compelling. See also William Letwin, *The Origins of Scientific Economics: English Economic Thought 1660-1776* (London, 1963), ch. 6, esp. pp. 147–8.

[12] For an important clarification of the implications of his doing so (which corrects many influential misunderstandings) see Tully, *A Discourse of Property*.

[13] See John Locke, 'Venditio' (1695), printed in John Dunn, 'Justice and the Interpretation of Locke's Political Theory', *Political Studies*, 16 (1968), 84–7.

[14] This preoccupation can be traced in his writings from the *Two Tracts on Government*, ed. Philip Abrams (Cambridge, 1967), onwards. William G. Batz, 'This Historical Anthropology of John Locke', *Journal of the History of Ideas*, 34 (1974), 663–70, gives some interesting information on one range of Locke's sources for these inquiries, though he shows little understanding of

the significance of his inquiries was not the degree of his preoccupation or the extent of the inquiries to which this preoccupation led him but, rather, the single-mindedness with which he rejected any conception of the causal processes of human belief as a self-subsistent locus of value.[15] His fiercely reductive view of socially realized human belief as intrinsically ideological in character set the problem which, in varying forms, all his major works from the *Two Tracts of Government* to the *Reasonableness of Christianity* sought to resolve epistemologically. Naturally all men everywhere are born cognitively free. But in real social history all men everywhere are reared in credal chains. Natural freedom (the candle of the Lord which presumptively shines bright enough for all ethically legitimate human purposes) and social servitude are reconciled theoretically throughout his thinking by a highly unstable balance of social explanation and individual moral blame.[16] Within his social theory, social explanation came close in effect to entailing moral blame. True beliefs reflected the use of the cognitive capacities with which God had endowed all human beings, undeflected by the abuse of the moral freedom with which he had also elected to endow them.[17] False beliefs reflected the abuse of these cognitive capacities, an abuse which in the field of morality he explained by the socially institutionalized or the individually devised distortion of experience, in both cases under the pressure of discreditable desires. The field in which Locke's necessarily rather intricate[18] 'ethics of belief'[19] was worked out most elaborately was the assessment of religious belief systems; and the clearest insight into his conception of the potential for human individuals to transcend the disorder of human credal history comes in his extensive correspondence with those few friends whom he profoundly trusted and who shared his commitment to the intellectual and practical battle to extend religious toleration.[20]

the relation which Locke himself claimed for his anthropological evidence to the theoretical structure of his argument.

[15] Not reason, but 'passion and Superstition' 'share the bulk of mankinde and possesse them in their turnes'. (Bodleian Library, MS. Locke, fols. 5, 59.) Within Locke's moral psychology the predominance of this affective state necessarily implied that most men's moral beliefs were erroneous. See Hume, *Treatise*, pp. 552–3.

[16] See the interpretative and practical dilemma described by P. F. Strawson in 'Freedom and Resentment' in his *Studies in the Philosophy of Thought and Action* (London, 1968), pp. 71–96.

[17] Locke acknowledged frankly to his friend William Molyneux his incapacity to grasp how such moral freedom is in fact possible: letter to William Molyneux, 20 January 1693, *The Correspondence of John Locke*, ed. E. S. de Beer, iv (Oxford, 1979), pp. 625–6.

[18] For the factors dictating this intricacy, see Dunn, *Political Thought of John Locke*, esp. chs. 4 and 14. And for an important correction of the context of these discussions, see Michael Ayers, 'Analytical Philosophy of History and the History of Philosophy', in Jonathan Rée *et al.*, *Philosophy and its Past* (Hassocks, Sussex, 1979), pp. 46–7.

[19] On the idea of an 'ethics of belief' generally, see E. M. Curley, 'Descartes, Spinoza and the Ethics of Belief', in Eugene Freeman and Maurice Mandelbaum (eds.), *Spinoza: Essays in Interpretation* (La Salle, Illinois, 1975), pp. 159–89, and see Bernard Williams, 'Deciding to Believe', in *Problems of the Self* (Cambridge, 1973), ch. 9.

[20] See particularly the correspondence with Philippus van Limborch, William Popple and Benjamin Furley in Locke, *Correspondence*, iii and iv.

124   John Dunn

In a letter of 1659, earlier than any of his formal writings, Locke sets out with great force this sense of the epistemically treacherous relation between human desire and human belief. He also makes it plain that he conceives this relation not simply as a theoretical puzzle in academic philosophy but as an urgent problem of practical reason and a pressing threat to the constitution and sustaining of a viable sense of identity.

...tis Phansye that rules us all under the title of reason, this is the great guide both of the wise and the fooleish, only the former have the good lucke to light upon opinions that are most plausible or most advantageous. Where is that Great Diana of the world Reason, every one thinkes he alone imbraces this Juno, whilst others graspe noething but clouds, we are all Quakers here and there is not a man but thinks he alone hath this light within and all besids stumble in the darke. Tis our passions that bruiteish part that dispose of our thoughts and actions, we are all Centaurs and tis the beast that carrys us, and every ones Recta ratio is but the traverses of his owne steps. When did ever any truth settle it self in any ones minde by the strength and authority of its owne evidence? Truths gaine admittance to our thoughts as the philosopher did to the Tyrant by their handsome dresse and pleaseing aspect, they enter us by composition, and are entertaind as they suite with our affections, and as they demeane themselves towards our imperious passions, when an opinion hath wrought its self into our approbation and is gott under the protection of our likeing tis not all the assaults of argument, and the battery of dispute shall dislodge it? Men live upon trust and their knowledg is noething but opinion moulded up betweene custome and Interest, the two great Luminarys of the world, the only lights they walke by. Since therefor we are left to the uncertainty of two such fickle guides, lett the examples of the bravest men direct our opinions and actions; if custome must guide us let us tread in those steps that lead to virtue and honour. Let us make it our Interest to honour our maker and be usefull to our fellows, and content with our selves. This, if it will not secure us from error, will keepe us from loseing our selves, if we walke not directly straite we shall not be alltogeather in a maze.[21]

At least on occasion, in his later life, Locke expressed remarkable optimism over the extent to which human beings could hope to secure themselves from error. The truth needs no assistance from the holders of power and authority amongst mankind and can be confidently expected to prevail through its own force.[22] There are few purely theoretical issues on which the honest and impartial will disagree if only they take the trouble to make themselves clearly intelligible to one another.[23] But for the most part his expectations of men's actual cognitive and moral performance remained considerably more despondent throughout his life.

[21] Letter to Tom [Thomas Westrowe?], 20 October 1659. According to the editor of the Locke correspondence it is not likely that the letter was ever dispatched. (Locke, *Correspondence*, vol. 1, p. 123.)   [22] Locke, *Epistola de Tolerantia*, p. 122, lines 8–14.
[23] Locke to William Molyneux, 26 December 1692: 'being fully persuaded there are very few things of pure speculation, wherein two thinking men who impartially seek truth can differ if they give themselves the leisure to examine their hypotheses and understand one another'. (Locke, *Correspondence*, vol. iv, p. 609.)

It was this despondent view of how on most occasions most of his fellow men would probably behave which made it easy for his contemporaries to assimilate his views to those of Thomas Hobbes. (More recently it has led others to make the same error.)[24] In the eyes of Locke's contemporaries, the thought of Hobbes himself – and still more its vulgarized ideological outcome, 'Hobbism' – amounted in essence to a union of two theoretical components: an extremely pessimistic descriptive social psychology (which emphasized mutual untrustworthiness as being fundamental to human nature) and a decisive abandonment of the theocentric framework of thought. The relation between these two components, none too clear in Hobbes's own thought,[25] was not conspicuously clarified either by Locke's contemporaries or by his successors of the early eighteenth century.[26] In the case of Hobbes himself this residual opacity may have been simply a consequence of the author's own prudence. But in the case of later thinkers it was plainly almost entirely a product of intellectual

---

[24] See Richard H. Cox, *Locke on War and Peace* (Oxford, 1960).

[25] On Hobbes's theology, see Leopold Damrosch, Jr, 'Hobbes as Reformation Theologian', *Journal of the History of Ideas*, 40 (1979), 339–52: R. W. Hepburn, 'Hobbes on the Knowledge of God', in Maurice Cranston and Richard S. Peters (eds.), *Hobbes and Rousseau* (Garden City, N.Y., 1972), pp. 85–108; Willis B. Glover, 'God and Thomas Hobbes', in K. C. Brown (ed.), *Hobbes Studies* (Oxford, 1965), pp. 141–68; J. G. A. Pocock, 'Time, History and Eschatology in the Thought of Thomas Hobbes', in his *Politics, Language and Time* (London, 1972), pp. 148–201; Gauthier, 'Why Ought One Obey God?' For the response to Hobbes as essentially a religious menace, see Samuel I. Mintz, *The Hunting of Leviathan* (Cambridge, 1962), and John Bowle, *Hobbes and his Critics* (London, 1951). For more complex placing of Hobbes as philosopher and political theorist in the intellectual context of his time, see the work of Quentin Skinner, particularly 'The Context of Hobbes's Theory of Political Obligation', in Cranston and Peters, *Hobbes and Rousseau*, pp. 109–42, and 'Conquest and Consent: Thomas Hobbes and the Engagement Controversy', in G. E. Aylmer (ed.), *The Interregnum: The Quest for Settlement 1646–1660* (London, 1972), pp. 79–98. See also Richard Tuck, *Natural Rights Theories: Their Origin and Development* (Cambridge, 1979), ch. 6.

[26] See particularly the views of Locke's pupil the 3rd Earl of Shaftesbury, who decisively conflated the implications of his tutor's rejection of innate ideas with the fundamental tendency of Hobbes's thought. See his letter to Michael Ainsworth, 3 January 1709: 'It was Mr Locke that struck the home blow: for Mr Hobbes's character and base slavish principles in government took off the poison of his philosophy. 'Twas Mr Locke that struck at all fundamentals, threw all order and virtue out of the world, and made the very idea of these (which are the same as those of God) *unnatural* and without foundation in our minds... Then comes Mr Locke with his Indian, barbarian stories of wild nations...' (*The Life, Unpublished Letters, and Philosophical Regimen of Anthony, Earl of Shaftesbury, Author of the Characteristicks*, ed. Benjamin Rand (London, 1900), p. 403.) But also see his November 1709 letter to General Stanhope: 'Locke, whose *State of Nature* he supposes to be chimerical, and less serviceable to Mr Locke's own system than to Mr Hobbes's that is more of a piece, as I believe.' (*Life, Unpublished Letters*, p. 415.) Shaftesbury's views on this question are not easy to disentangle and have been considerably misunderstood. See e.g. Jason Aronson, 'Shaftesbury on Locke', *American Political Science Review*, 53 (1959), 1101–4. The most illuminating brief formulation of his attitude is perhaps his *Second Characters or the Language of Forms*, ed. Benjamin Rand (Cambridge, 1914), pp. 106, 173–8 and esp. p. 178. For the sense of the pervasiveness of Hobbism as an ideological menace and its extremely vague theoretical specification, see e.g. Margaret C. Jacob, *The Newtonians and the English Revolution 1689–1720* (Hassocks, Sussex, 1976), pp. 24, 52, 65, 67, 198–9, 232, 238, and more broadly John Redwood, *Reason, Ridicule and Religion: The Age of Enlightenment in England 1660–1750* (London, 1976).

confusion. On this issue at least, however, Locke himself was certainly far from confused. Not merely did he succeed with some ease in distinguishing the two components of vulgar Hobbism from one another, he in fact premised his entire intellectual project on the need to keep the distinction absolute. It was not simply that, in large measure, he shared Hobbes's views of the empirical properties of human beings as such but happened nevertheless to dissent from Hobbes's views of the place of the deity in specifying what is of value for man. Rather, he set himself to vindicate a conception of what is rationally of value for man which centred on the will of a benevolent and omnipotent creator because, in the face of human beings as he experienced them, he could see no other way in which to guarantee a sense of meaning in his own life or of assurance in the stability of his own identity.[27]

His sense of the inherent untrustworthiness of human performance was not focussed, as with Hobbes, on men's individual psychological properties (their ineluctable concern with the imperatives of their own preservation and, in many instances, their fundamental mutual malignity) but on the arbitrariness of their *social* relations, however these were institutionalized. Hobbes saw the attaining of social order for a creature so disorderly in its individual properties as unambiguously a good. But for Locke, whatever social order was attained through institutional design and the causal mechanisms of human belief and human passion, although it might and did vary considerably in moral acceptability, afforded under all circumstances too shaky a basis on which to found a sound sense of moral identity. A viable moral identity depended upon stable and unambivalent goods – goods which could not be derived from the properties of (and which will at best be very imperfectly realized within) human social institutions. He expressed this fundamental refusal to accord value to the social specification of purely human power (a refusal which formed the core of his later rejection of the political theory of Filmer) very early in his life, in bitter response to the political misfortunes of his father and to the strains and indignities of his personal situation of social dependence:

it will teache me this caution, to withdraw my dependences from such windy props, to forbid my hopes and feares a commerce with their frowns, or promises, and to use them as they use us, only as long as serviceable. I cannot overvalue those accidentall differences that chance doth place on men, and are noe reall ones, but as they are usd.[28]

The determination to use the nexus of patronage and cliental dependence in a purely instrumental spirit was not, or course, in any sense a choice to eschew whatever facilities for enhancing his personal social mobility (within the limits

---

[27] See, more extendedly, J. Dunn, 'Individuality and Clientage in the Formation of Locke's Social Imagination', in Reinhard Brandt (ed.), *John Locke Symposium, Wolfenbüttel 1979* (Berlin, 1981), pp. 43–73.

[28] Locke to John Locke, sen., 6 April 1658, Locke, *Correspondence*, i, p. 60.

set by his own moral susceptibilities) which that nexus could be induced to offer: as his Somerset friend John Strachey put it, 'a man of parts, lett him study but complyance, hee need want noe preferment'.[29] Nor, once such investments had been made, did it preclude the human relations which embodied these from coming to carry a heavy load of moral responsibility.[30] But what was moralized was in each instance a relation of reciprocity between individual agents and never the social matrix itself within which this relation was set. It is clear both theoretically and biographically that in this rejection of the substance of social relations as a foundation for human value, Locke was in part simply affirming the intimations of his familial religious background, however decisively his subsequent thinking was to transform the implications of this heritage in a consequentially more secular direction.[31] (No human being can pluck a moral identity out of thin air.) It is also clear that both affirmation and rejection are actively present in the deep significance which, in his later life, Locke attached to the practice of friendship.[32] Friendship is the only psychically worthwhile form of terrestrial riches because it is the only relationship between human beings in which moral solidarity may be depended upon. Seen in this light, his persistent determination to construe churches as voluntary associations appears not as a further instance of his sociological ineptitude or as a mere ideological convenience in the battle to make the social world safer for his personal religious beliefs, but rather as a forlorn attempt to stretch human moral solidarity to its limit. If the irrelevances of force and power could be extruded from religious institutions and the latter could be confined to their true end, what would a church be but a tissue of somewhat overextended friendship?

From an existential point of view it would be hard to exaggerate the precariousness of this synthesis. But if it was inherently evanescent as a historical possibility, its theoretical consequences are nonetheless clear. For Locke, to put this theocentric framework in jeopardy was to imperil the rationality of human existence in its entirety.

A dependent intelligent being is under the power and direction and dominion of him

---

[29] John Strachey to Locke, 13 November 1663, Locke, *Correspondence*, i, p. 215.
[30] 'when it was paid for with all that I had got in attending on him ten or a dozen of the best years of my life': Locke, *Correspondence*, iv, p. 411. For the context of this sense of injury see other letters in vol. iv, pp. 383, 398–9, 406–7, 412–13, 422–4, 452, 455–6, 698–9, 768, 773–4.
[31] For a helpful account of this impact, see Paul Marshall, 'John Locke: Between God and Mammon', *Canadian Journal of Political Science*, 12 (1979), 73–98. For further treatment of the rejection of the substance of social relations as a foundation for value, see Dunn, 'Individuality and Clientage'.
[32] See e.g. his claim to William Molyneux: "The only riches I have valued or laboured to acquire has been the friendship of ingenious and worthy men", as cited in Patrick Kelly's interesting discussion, 'Locke and Molyneux: The Anatomy of a Friendship', *Hermathena*, no. 126 (1979), p. 43.

on whom he depends and must be for the ends appointed him by that superior being. If man were independent he could have no law but his own will, no end but himself. He would be a god to himself and the satisfaction of his own will the sole measure and end of all his actions.[33]

By the same token, to specify value for human beings was in the last instance to construe the implications of the theocentric framework. Even in 1790 Adam Smith appears to have been little, if any, more enthusiastic than Locke at the prospect of dispensing with belief in a benevolent deity:

...the very suspicion of a fatherless world, must be the most melancholy of all reflections; from the thought that all the unknown regions of infinite and incomprehensible space may be filled with nothing but endless misery and wretchedness. All the splendour of the highest prosperity can never enlighten the gloom with which so dreadful an idea must necessarily over-shadow the imagination.[34]

Nor was he any more attracted than Locke was to discrete 'internal reasons' conception of the character of value for man:

A wise man...does not look upon himself as a whole, separated and detached from every other part of nature, to be taken care of by itself and for itself. He regards himself in the light in which he imagines the great genius of human nature, and of the world, regards him. He enters, if I may say so, into the sentiments of that divine Being, and considers himself as an atom, a particle, of an immense and infinite system, which must and ought to be disposed of, according to the conveniency of the whole. Assured of the wisdom which directs all the events of human life, whatever lot befalls him, he accepts it with joy, satisfied that, if he had known all the connections and dependencies of the different parts of the universe, it is the very lot which he himself would have wished for. If it is life, he is contented to live; and if it is death, as nature must have no further occasion for his presence here, he willingly goes where he is appointed.[35]

What was theoretically crucial, however, was that Smith's rejection of the moral and epistemic sufficiency of individual internal reasons did not depend, as Locke's did, on 'entering into the sentiments of the divine Being', but derived more directly from his treatment throughout his analysis, both in the *Theory of Moral Sentiments* and in the *Wealth of Nations*, of sociology and psychology as theoretically coordinate terms. Because his approach never centred upon, and was never theoretically extrapolated from, God's purposes, but instead was concerned throughout with the systematic causal analysis of social relations and social systems, it failed to shift at all drastically (let alone to narrow, as Locke's would have done, to a nihilistic individualism), when Smith in later life experienced greater difficulty in entering into the deity's

---

[33] Bodleian Library, MS. Locke c.28, fol. 141, 'Ethica B', as quoted in Dunn, *Political Thought of John Locke*, p. 1; and also see there: 'Happiness is a continuation of content without any molestation. Very imperfect in this world. No body happy here certain.'
[34] *TMS* VI.ii.3.2.   [35] *TMS* VII.ii.1.20.

sentiments. This fundamental choice gave to Locke on the one side and to Hume and Smith on the other two drastically different fields for the deployment of their imaginative energies. At the centre of one field lay the vindication of the intelligibility and validity of the purposes of a divine creator and the interpretation of the implications which these purposes bore for the life of man. At the centre of the other lay the identification and explanation of the causal properties of human societies and economies and the systematic analysis of the services and hazards to a life which was genuinely good for human beings which these economies and societies presented.

This division of imaginative attention comes out very clearly in the differing attitudes of Locke on the one side and Hume and Smith on the other towards the rational basis of political obligation. For Locke the duties of most human beings towards terrestrial political authority are in the first instance altruistically prudential specifications of their duties, as common creatures of God, towards their fellow men.[36] The celebrated central argument of the *Two Treatises of Government* is not merely an ideological defence of the legitimacy of resistance to political authority, where the latter is abused. It is also a decisive theoretical defence of the categorical limits of the rights of political authorities and a demonstration of the consequent asymmetry between the scope of these rights and the markedly more extensive scope of the politically relevant duties of subjects. It was *not* Locke's theory that all human political duties were necessarily exclusively derived from consent; and it indisputably was his theory that all valid human political duties were rationally to be interpreted as specifications of God's purposes for man. Political duty was a theoretical derivative of natural theology. Both Hume and Smith criticize Locke's *Two Treatises* severely, taking it as symptomatic of the provincial superstitions of vulgar Whiggism[37] and developing at some length an alternative analysis of the nature of allegiance which they presume to be both less superstitious and more cosmopolitan. Neither was at all a careful critic of Locke's text and neither appears to have grasped even the essentials of its argument,[38] though each certainly mounts an intellectually and polemically effective enough critique of vulgar Whig shibboleths. Neither in particular appears to have grasped the theoretical dependence of Locke's entire analysis upon natural theology, though it is plain

[36] See particularly J. Dunn, 'Consent in the Political Theory of John Locke', in Dunn, *Political Obligation in its Historical Context* (Cambridge, 1980), pp. 29-52, and more generally in Dunn, *Political Thought of John Locke*.
[37] See the added footnote identifying Rapin, Locke, Sidney, Hoadley as the authors of 'Compositions the most despicable, both for style and matter' which Hume complained 'have been extolled, and propagated, and read; as if they had equalled the most celebrated remains of antiquity' (Hume, *History of England*, 8 vols. (London, 1778), viii, p. 323). Compare it with the earlier edition, Hume, *The History of Great Britain*, vol. II. *Containing the Commonwealth, and the Reigns of Charles II and James II* (London, 1757), p. 445.
[38] For a helpful treatment of Hume's misunderstanding, see Martyn P. Thompson, 'Hume's Critique of Locke and the "Original Contract"', *Il Pensiero Politico*, 10 (1977), 189-201.

enough that both of them would, if anything, have regarded such a theoretical dependence as an aggravation rather than a mitigation of the intrinsic intellectual weakness of his position.[39]

Hume's critique is developed particularly in Book III of the *Treatise of Human Nature*, the *Enquiry concerning the Principles of Morals*, and in the famous essay 'Of the Original Contract'. He takes the Lockean account as claiming that men are only politically obliged as a result of promises and that their existence within the borders of a state constitutes such a promise. He has no difficulty in demonstrating that this view bears little resemblance to most men's understanding of political obligation and that it does little justice to the facts of their political situation: 'it being certain that there is a moral obligation to submit to government, because every one thinks so; it must be as certain that this obligation arises not from a promise; since no one, whose judgment has not been led astray by too strict adherence to a system of philosophy, has ever yet dreamt of ascribing it to that origin'.[40] The theoretical basis of his criticism was the analysis of justice as an artificial virtue, an analysis which rendered absurd any attempt by contractarian theorists to 'mount higher'[41] and resolve the obligation of allegiance into the obligation of fidelity. Thinking both causes men's acceptance of moral obligations and furnishes the rational grounds for their accepting these in practice. Obligation, property and right in human society all depend upon the stability of possessions.[42] All of them are natural in the sense that they are made necessary by the intrinsic characteristics of human beings. But all of them are also artificial in the sense that they do not arise directly out of human emotions, do not intuitively accord fully with these, but are effectively inculcated by determined social indoctrination. Property right is presented as the outcome of an essentially arbitrary process of allocation, rationalized only in the most perfunctory manner. What is important about property right is simply that it be clear and well-defended in practice. The social function of government, above all the protection of property, is the institutionalized protection of men's individual and collective long-term self-interest against their individual short-term self-interest, an instrument for securing the command of their calm over their violent passions.

---

[39] See *WN* V.i.f.31: 'a debased system of moral philosophy, which was considered as immediately connected with the doctrines of Pneumatology, with the immortality of the human soul, and with the rewards and punishments which, from the justice of the Deity, were to be expected in a life to come'. For Hume, see particularly his *Dialogues concerning Natural Religion* and Duncan Forbes, *Hume's Philosophical Politics* (Cambridge, 1975), chs. 1 and 2, esp. pp. 45, 65, 80, and 'Hume's Science of Politics', in G. P. Morice (ed.), *David Hume: Bicentenary Papers* (Edinburgh, 1977), pp. 39–50, esp. pp. 46–7; E. C. Mossner, 'The Religion of David Hume', *Journal of the History of Ideas*, 39 (1978), 653–63, and 'Hume and the Legacy of the *Dialogues*', in Morice, *David Hume: Bicentenary Papers*, pp. 1–22.

[40] Hume, *Treatise*, p. 547. For the argument as a whole, see Bk. III, pt. II, sect. VIII, 'Of the source of allegiance'. For a placing of this arguement, see Forbes, *Hume's Philosophical Politics*, pp. 91–101.

[41] Hume, *Treatise*, pp. 542–3.   [42] Hume, *Treatise*, p. 491.

From applied theology to social analysis 131

Government is the greatest of all civilizing agencies.[43] The duty of allegiance is securely grounded in prevailing human sentiment, a sound criterion of its moral validity[44] and a causally effective guarantee of its furnishing any government of any practical merit with the political support which it both deserves and requires. In the *Treatise* itself Hume expounds his own view, revelling in its originality and its intellectual radicalism.[45] It was not until he turned to a more explicitly political attack on 'vulgar Whiggism' that he took the trouble to develop his position as an explicit criticism of Locke.[46] But in the essay 'Of the Original Contract' of 1748 he made clear his assimilation of the positions criticized in the *Treatise* to those which he now assailed in Locke's work.[47]

Smith's moral theory, like that of Hume, was an essentially naturalistic theory of the character and causation of human moral sentiments. Both the duty to obey a government and the right to resist one must rest upon the realized psychic conditions of human beings. Once any form of effective rule has been established in a particular society, most men in most countries at most times simply do in fact recognize a duty of allegiance towards it.[48] In so doing they accept, compulsively but also rationally,[49] the 'principle of authority'.[50] The

---

[43] Forbes, *Hume's Philosophical Politics*, esp. pp. 190, 192, 322.

[44] Hume, *Treatise*, p. 552. 'The general opinion of mankind has some authority in all cases; but in this of morals it is perfectly infallible. Nor is it less infallible, because men cannot distinctly explain the principles on which it is founded.'

[45] See his own anonymous puff for the work: David Hume, *An Abstract of a Treatise of Human Nature*, ed. J. M. Keynes and P. Sraffa (Cambridge, 1938), esp. p. 4; 'the Author seems to insinuate, that were his philosophy receiv'd, we must alter from the foundation the greater part of the sciences'.

[46] But for direct evidence that he regarded Locke as a representative intellectual proponent of the error which he wished to correct, see his letter of 1743 to Francis Hutcheson on the latter's new *Philosophiae Moralis Institutio Compendiaria*: 'P.266.1.18 & quae seq: You imply a Condemnation of Locke's Opinion, which being the receiv'd one, I cou'd have wisht the Condemnation had been more express.' (*The Letters of David Hume*, ed. J. Y. T. Grieg, 2 vols. (Oxford, 1932), i, p. 48.)

[47] See 'Of the Original Contract', in Hume, *Philosophical Works*, iii, p. 460. Hume continued to alter this essay throughout his life, adding one of its most important passages in the final and only posthumously published edition. The Locke references were included in the first publication of 1748. See also his letter of 8 January 1748 to Lord Elibank about this essay: 'I shall be very much mortify'd, if you do not approve, in some small degree, of the Reasonings with regard to the original Contract, which, I hope, are new and curious, & form a short, but compleat Refutation of the political Systems of Sydney, Locke, and the Whigs, which all the half Philosophers of the Nation have implicitely embrac'd for near a Century; tho' they are plainly, in my humble Opinion, repugnant to Reason & the Practice of all Nations.' ('New Hume Letters to Lord Elibank', ed. E. C. Mossner, *Texas Studies in Language and Literature*, 4 (1962), 437.)

[48] For Smith's political theory in general, see especially the characteristically trenchant and illuminating article by Duncan Forbes, 'Sceptical Whiggism, Commerce and Liberty', in A. S. Skinner and T. B. Wilson (eds.), *Essays on Adam Smith* (Oxford, 1975), pp. 179–201, and a more extended treatment by Donald Winch, *Adam Smith's Politics: An Essay in Historiographic Revision* (Cambridge, 1978). For Smith's analysis of political obligation see *LJ(A)* v.103–49, and *LJ(B)* 12–19, 91–7, and commentary in Winch, *Adam Smith's Politics*, pp. 50–5.

[49] *LJ(A)* v.102–12.   [50] *LJ(A)* v.119–23.

rational component of their acceptance is in part[51] simply a matter of immediate egocentric prudence, but it is also in part a matter of the reflective and socially responsible judgement of the long-term advantages and disadvantages of resistance to governmental authority.[52] The principle of authority is solidly rooted in the pre-reflective zones of human psychology, 'in the natural modesty of mankind'.[53] But it is balanced by the more detached and rationally critical criterion of utility,[54] a criterion which in some instances firmly vindicates the legitimacy of popular resistance: 'No one but must enter into the designs of the people, go along with them in all their plots and conspiracys to turn them out, is rejoiced at their success, and grieves when they fail.'[55] The balance between these two criteria varies in accordance with the social and political realities of a society, since different structures of power within a society engender different distributions of popular sentiment, and different distributions of popular sentiment within a society in their turn[56] causally modify its structure of power. Different forms of regime have different causal properties, different social psychologies and correspondingly different ranges of objective moral entitlement to the allegiance of their subjects. How far this is a coherent and theoretically determinate position is a very open question in modern political philosophy.[57] But it is easy to see how firmly it distances Smith's political vision from that of Locke. For Smith, 'Every morall duty must arise from some thing which mankind are conscious of.'[58] A contractarian theory of political obligation, however firmly endorsed by 'the generallity of writers on this subject (as Locke and Sidney, etc)',[59] cannot meet this test. Belief in such a theory 'is confined to Britain, and had never been heard of in any other country'.[60] Even 'here it can have influence with a very small part of the people, such as have read Locke, etc. The far greater part have no notion of it, and nevertheless they have the same notion of the obedience due to the sovereign power.'[61] Even within its own terms the version of the contractarian theory associated with Locke and the Whigs fails, as Hume had pointed out, to resolve a number of the difficulties with which it was devised to deal.[62] For

---

[51] $LJ(A)$ v.120.
[52] $LJ(A)$ v.131–2.
[53] $LJ(A)$ v.121.
[54] $LJ(A)$ v.123–7.
[55] $LJ(A)$ v.126.
[56] $LJ(A)$ v.129–49.
[57] See J. Dunn, 'Political Obligations and Political Possibilities', in Dunn, *Political Obligation in its Historical Context*, pp. 243–99. It is possible that, clearly understood, the position dictates a rigorous pragmatism, which begins from Smith's sardonic note: 'one who is to consider this matter must set out anew and upon his own bottom. All disputes of this sort have been decided by force and violence. If the sovereign got the better of the subjects, then they were condemned as traitors and rebels; and if the subjects have got the better of the sovereign, he is declared to be a tyrant and oppressor not to be endured.' $LJ(A)$ v.103–4; but denies the legitimacy of his subsequent reservation in $LJ(A)$ v.104: 'Sometimes the decision has been right and sometimes wrong.'
[58] $LJ(A)$ v.127.
[59] $LJ(A)$ v.114.
[60] $LJ(A)$ v.115; and see $LJ(B)$ 15.
[61] $LJ(A)$ v.116; and see v.118.
[62] $LJ(A)$ v.116–19.

Smith, political obligation rests psychically on non-rational deference, the principle of authority, and it rests rationally on utility. But its main weight in practice plainly falls causally on the principle of authority. For him political duties, as men actually experience them, are preponderantly vertical obligations to sovereigns, not, as they are with Locke, horizontal obligations to our fellows.[63]

It is a queasy type of intellectual project to seek the roots of these differences of attitude in the social and personal experience of the three men, even if it can hardly be the case that these roots simply lie elsewhere. One very simple contrast can, however, be drawn with some confidence. Locke's social thinking, we know, began from his experience of the moral arbitrariness of vertical obligations, obligations which pervaded the social texture of the world in which he lived and on which his own individual prospects of social mobility abjectly depended.[64] Both Hume and Smith were fortunate enough to avoid any such sense of dependence, Hume in particular expressing for it a disdain which Locke himself amply shared but which, unlike Hume, he was never able to afford to express in practice. In comparison with Locke, it is plain, both Hume and Smith were very much at ease in their society and well able to take both it and their own membership within it very much for granted. Approaching it with an imaginative calm which Locke could never emulate, they found themselves free to press the causal understanding of its properties very far indeed. Each of them also, at least at some points in their lives, perhaps displayed, as an accompaniment to the imaginative calm which made their intellectual achievements possible, a certain moral complacency over the social and economic realities of the society in which they were so much at home.[65] But in Smith at least this complacency had been left far behind by the end of his intellectual life. It is historically correct to think of him as the inventor of ideological materials of extraordinary power, materials whose ideological force was a direct function of their intellectual depth. But it is historically preposterous to think of him as the ideological spokesman of his society. Indeed, the same deepening of causal understanding which enabled him to invent such ideologically powerful conceptions served to dissolve much, if not most, of the moral plausibility of his own society in his eyes. As his studies deepened,[66] and

---

[63] Cf. Michael Walzer, *Obligations: Essays on Disobedience, War and Citizenship* (Cambridge, Mass., 1970), esp. p. 207; Dunn, 'Political Obligations and Political Possibilities'; Carole Pateman, *The Problem of Political Obligation* (London, 1978).

[64] See notes 27 and 28 above.

[65] This was not, of course, a simple failure in personal sensitivity or humanity – and least of all so in contrast with Locke. But it was a decisive shift in the angle of imaginative attention to the properties of society, in effect the disappearance of an entire dimension of assessment.

[66] '...my own schemes of Study leave me very little leisure, which go forward too like the web of penelope, so that I scarce see any Probability of their ending.' (Smith to Lord Hailes, 15 January 1769, Smith, *Correspondence*, p. 140.) It is a decidedly more illuminating fact about the tone and content of much of the *Theory of Moral Sentiments* than it is for example of those

as he moved in consequence from the slightly fussy moral didacticism perhaps incumbent on a young Scots Professor of Moral Philosophy into the imaginatively chillier ambiance of a cosmopolitan theorist of the historical process, his serenity in the face of prevailing social deference shifted to a mood of pronounced moral distaste.[67]

In conclusion we may note a discomfiting historical possibility. Locke presumed that there were strict theoretical implications between the abandonment of theocentrism, the acceptance of a purely internal conception of human rational agency and the resting of all human rights and duties upon the contingencies of human opinion. He presumed this, in essence, because he put no faith in the autonomous causal processes of social reproduction. Both Hume and Smith in contrast, despite their impressive insight into the dynamics of the capitalist economy, distinctly overestimated the long-term prospects for combining the dynamics of capitalist development with the deferential socializing capacities of pre-capitalist society. In their vision, we as human beings are society's creatures at any time only in so far as society has contrived to make us such. The limits of our social duties are the limits of its socializing capabilities. Hume's views of the socializing powers which can be imputed to all societies were absurdly eupeptic – at least outside the domain of religious belief. Smith certainly thought much more deeply about, and saw much more clearly, than either Locke or Hume the ways in which the individual distribution of beliefs in eighteenth-century Britain was constrained by the mechanisms of social reproduction. But even he misjudged the implications of this observation, identifying an evanescent contingency of social history with a quasi-biological property of the human species, 'the natural modesty of mankind'.[68] Today even admirers of Hume and Smith can no longer take the causal processes of social reproduction trustingly for granted.[69] The development of a purely internal conception of rational agency has left human individuals impressively disenchanted and undeceived. But it has also left them increasingly on their own and devoid of rational direction in social or political action, prisoners in games of self-destruction to which, on these terms, there may well be no rational solutions.[70] It is easier, perhaps, now to see the connections between these menaces. If there is indeed nothing rationally to human

of the *Wealth of Nations* that each in a very extended sense began as a set of edifying university lectures.
[67] See *TMS* I.iii.3.1–8. For an account of the different editions of this work, see D. D. Raphael and A. L. Mackie, 'Introduction', *TMS*, pp. 34–52.
[68] See *LJ(A)* v.121; *TMS* I.iii.2.1–4. Smith's beliefs on this matter were in obvious tension with some other aspects of his thought, notably his sophisticated sociological conception of changes in relations of dependence which is set out most elaborately in the *Wealth of Nations*.
[69] See F. A. Hayek, *New Studies in Philosophy, Politics, Economics and the History of Ideas* (London, 1978); Keith Joseph and Jonathan Sumption, *Equality* (London, 1979).
[70] David Gauthier, 'The Social Contract as Ideology', *Philosophy and Public Affairs*, 6 (1977), 130–64; Dunn, 'Political Obligations and Political Possibilities'.

existence, individually and socially, but opinion,[71] it will certainly be bad news if opinion ever falters. Locke's serried forty-year defence of theocentrism is a very distant battle. But its purpose, to preserve the rationality for humans of an irrational and heartless world, is disturbingly close. The real anguish which lay behind it is an anguish which we still have coming to us and which will be truly ours when we at last learn to feel what now we know. In their imaginations Hume and Smith certainly inhabited a world which was far closer to ours than Locke's world was. It is clear that, on the whole, they were well content to do so. But it is not clear that they understood its deeper structures very well.[72] Locke, on the other hand, though he devoted his intellectual life to its rejection, seems to have understood these deeper structures all too well. It has taken us nearly three centuries to begin to catch up with him.

[71] Compare this with Gauthier, 'David Hume, Contractarian', esp. p. 38: 'Opinion is all; there is and can be no appeal against the present established practice of the age.'
[72] See Hume's verdict on the political judgement of the ancients: "These people were extremely fond of liberty; but seem not to have understood it very well.' ('Of the Populousness of Ancient Nations', *Philosophical Works*, iii, p. 403.)

6 The Scottish Enlightenment at the limits of the civic tradition*

JOHN ROBERTSON

I

Few societies have experienced more acutely the problem of a conflict between established political institutions and the demands of economic development than eighteenth-century Scotland; few thinkers have reflected on that problem as thoroughly as those of the Scottish Enlightenment. In 1707 Scotland effectively faced a choice: either the nation preserved its existing political institutions at the cost of severely restricting its economic opportunities, or it yielded up its institutional independence and accepted union with England in return for free trade across the border and access to the English commercial empire. Whatever the motives of the politicians immediately responsible for the Union, there is no doubt that Scotsmen were aware of the significance of the decision then taken. For some ten years before 1707 the critical economic and political condition of the country had been the subject of intense public debate; and from this had emerged widespread agreement that the root of the crisis lay in the failure of Scotland's political institutions – its parliament above all – to generate economic improvement.

Within half a century of the Union, what had then been discussed as a problem for Scotland in particular is to be found at the centre of the Scottish Enlightenment's inquiry into 'the progress of society' in general. For the Enlightenment philosophers, none more so than the two greatest, David Hume and Adam Smith, the potentially contradictory relation between political institutions and economic development presented a major challenge to the aspiration to elaborate an integrated theory of society; with hindsight, their confrontation with the problem may also be regarded as one of their most important contributions to the creation of the intellectual space in which would emerge 'liberal' or 'classical' political economy. In this paper I wish therefore to examine the Scottish confrontation with the problem of institutions and

* Among several who have kindly read and commented on successive versions of this paper, I would like particularly to thank those who have helped at every stage: Lord Dacre, Istvan Hont and Nicholas Phillipson. I would like also to express gratitude to the Dean, Canons and Students of Christ Church for electing me to a Research Lectureship between 1975–80, when the paper was conceived and written.

economic development in some detail; and I propose to do so, as any historian must, in the terms in which the problem was formulated by the Scots themselves – the terms of the civic tradition.

The 'civic tradition' I take to be that body of political ideas, classical and specifically Aristotelian in origin, concerned with the phenomenon of political community in its secular and historical particularity. The tradition's principal characteristics may be briefly, if crudely, summarized as follows. Political community is defined first and foremost in institutional terms. Its necessary conditions are a regular constitution which distributes legislative, executive and judicial powers among assemblies and offices open to citizens, and a military force which involves all citizens in the community's defence. In principle such a regular constitution is a republic or commonwealth, and the proper form of its defence a militia; the opportunity with which citizens are provided to participate in the government and defence of the community is what makes possible political liberty. Conversely the antitheses of political community are the irregular, strictly unconstitutional states of despotism and anarchy, dependent for their defence on mercenary arms. In these the people are condemned to political slavery.

In the perspective of the civic tradition, however, a regular constitution and a militia are not in themselves sufficient for a free political community. There are moral and material as well as institutional conditions to be satisfied. Morally citizens must possess the public spirit or virtue to participate actively in the community's government and defence: only thus can they realize the political liberty which the community's institutions make possible. The practice of such participatory virtue in turn depends on a material condition: at the economic level, citizens should be independent or autonomous, which was classically interpreted to mean that they be free from the need to engage directly in productive activity. There should be a clear line of demarcation in society at large between citizens, who are exempt from material pursuits, and producers, whose function is simply to satisfy economic needs. If, however, those who ought to be devoting themselves to citizenship are led by necessity or choice to put private, material interests before public virtue, then, in the view of the civic tradition, the political community will be threatened by corruption. Corruption is a dynamic, destructive force which constantly endangers the entire edifice of political community. Dissolving the moral commitment of citizens to participate, it leads to the neglect of institutions and the consequent loss of political liberty.

It is the idea of corruption, moreover, which gives the civic tradition's otherwise generalized concern with political community its historical sense and practical urgency. The fear of corruption requires those who think in the terms of the tradition to be alert to the secular forces of change which may undermine the material base and moral and institutional superstructure of the political community. The same fear also renders the civic tradition highly prescriptive. Its analyses serving simultaneously as injunctions to sustain or renew the institutional, moral and economic fabric of the community in the face of corruption, the civic tradition provides both the concepts of intellectual reflection and the imperatives of political debate.

It will be obvious, not only from this bare summary, but from the analysis I shall develop, how much my understanding of the civic tradition is indebted to the magisterial investigations of J. G. A. Pocock.[1] I have, however, deliberately chosen to use the simple description 'civic tradition', rather than one of Pocock's several alternative designations – civic humanist, Machiavellian or Harringtonian. Important though the *quattrocento* humanists, Machiavelli and later Harrington were to its development, I believe that identifying the tradition with any one of them produces too specific an historical definition of the form in which it reached eighteenth-century Scotland. This may seem to leave a very abstractly defined tradition. And indeed it must, I think, be acknowledged that the civic tradition had not the canonical and academic coherence of such other prominent traditions in early modern political thought as natural, civil and even customary jurisprudence. There was no equivalent in the civic tradition of the corpus of authority, commentary and historiography by which the jurists consolidated and transmitted their intellectual inheritance, and it would be misleading to seek to supply one.

The civic was, moreover, a tradition whose boundaries are particularly hard to fix. As J. H. Hexter, reviewing Pocock, has observed, the tradition was 'open' in at least two important directions.[2] On the one hand, the civic tradition was from the Renaissance closely related to republicanism – Italian, Dutch and English – as a political cause, and derived much of its continuing intellectual vitality from the association. Conceptually, it should be emphasized, the tradition is not reducible to such republicanism: it is not altogether impossible to treat monarchy in civic terms as a regularly constituted government. But the accommodation was never an easy one, and by the late seventeenth century the generic terms republic and commonwealth were commonly regarded as designating a particular form of government antagonistic to monarchy.[3] Yet historically little less difficult to separate from the civic tradition are, on the other hand, post-Aristotelian Stoic and Ciceronian

---

[1] J. G. A. Pocock, *The Machiavellian Moment: Florentine Political Thought and the Atlantic Republican Tradition* (Princeton, N.J., 1975).

[2] J. H. Hexter, 'Republic, Virtue, Liberty, and the Political Universe of J. G. A. Pocock', *On Historians* (London, 1979), pp. 292–303.

[3] The difficulty of accommodating monarchic government within the civic perspective is evident from its earliest formulation, in Aristotle's failure in the *Politics* to account for the Persian monarchy, of which the Greeks were by this time well-informed. To Aristotle too can be traced the ambiguous use of a single term, *politeia*, as both the generic description of a regular constitution and the specification of one favoured form of government. It is to avoid falling directly into such ambiguity that I do not speak of a 'classical republican' tradition.

accretions which pointed in a direction quite different from political republicanism. These offered an alternative definition of society as a community in cultural terms; and their political tendency, where not simply elevating the ideal of private contemplation against public participation, was towards the universalism of natural and Roman law. Through Stoic and Ciceronian mediation, therefore, the civic tradition was opened in the direction of just those jurisprudential traditions which, increasingly centred upon the concept of sovereignty, regarded monarchy as the exemplary, because unitary, form of government. Those were traditions, moreover, which postulated another concept of liberty – liberty not as freedom *to* participate in government, but as freedom *from* authority, liberty not as the good of the community as a whole, but as the natural or historical right or property of the individual.

Thus to concede the abstractness of the civic tradition, and the uncertainty of its boundaries, as it reached eighteenth-century Scotland is by no means to diminish its significance. On the contrary, it may be argued, it was precisely these qualities which rendered the civic tradition so adaptable to the concerns of the Scots, and to consideration of the problem of institutions and economic development in particular. Unencumbered with academic apparatus, the civic tradition provided the Scots with an accessible reservoir of concepts presupposing the interdependence of institutions and society in history. At the same time the openness of the civic tradition to political republicanism on one side and to Ciceronianism and its jurisprudential affiliations on the other ensured that use of its concepts imposed no intellectual straightjacket. To think in civic terms was to confront the actual division of Europe into republics and monarchies; but it need not imply automatic hostility to monarchy as a form of government, or denial of the existence of another concept of liberty.

The following account of the eighteenth-century Scottish response to the problem of institutions and economic development is in two parts. I begin by establishing a reference point in the political writings of Andrew Fletcher, the outstanding figure in the debate on Scotland's predicament before the Union. Not only did Fletcher clearly recognize the interdependence of Scotland's political and economic difficulties; but he formulated a response in exemplary civic terms, making, I shall argue, a remarkable attempt to incorporate the imperative of economic development within a stringently civic conception of political community. At much greater length, I then consider the treatment of the problem in the Scottish Enlightenment, and specifically in the work of David Hume. Hume can be seen to have drawn extensively on the conceptual resources of the civic tradition both to analyse and to resolve the problem; but he did so by exploiting the tradition's openness, and thus, I shall contend, modified the civic concepts' usage and transformed their implication. Acknowledging both the superiority of monarchies over republics in modern Europe, and the historical interrelation of the two concepts of liberty, Hume recognized that commercial society entailed a definitive break with the classical ideal of political community to which Fletcher adhered. The Scottish Enlightenment's confrontation with the problem of institutions and economic development does not of course end with Hume: the story should – and will elsewhere – be carried forward to Adam Smith. But I have chosen here to concentrate in detail on the arguments of Hume, and the contrast they present with Fletcher's. Relatively neglected, Hume's achievement was yet Smith's starting point: with Hume the Scottish Enlightenment came to the limits of the civic tradition.

II

Born in 1653, Andrew Fletcher of Saltoun emerged to lead Scottish political debate in the late 1690s, just as the crisis which was to culminate in the Union broke upon the country. The significance of Fletcher's intervention is only beginning to be appreciated by historians: for too long it has been obscured by a nationalistic posterity's preoccupation with his supposed role as leader of patriotic opposition to the Treaty of Union.[4] In fact, it is clear that Fletcher was ill-fitted for any conventional political role. He positively alarmed his contemporaries. Not only had he a violent past; he was secular, cosmopolitan and formidably learned, the possessor of a magnificent library; perhaps most disturbing of all, he was utterly ingenuous. Isolation was the natural price of such qualities – isolation from those whose views were close to his own as much as from opponents. Reputed a militant republican, his connections with republican circles are shadowy; and despite his fearless criticisms of the crown's ministers, he never had an organized political following in the Scottish Parliament. But Fletcher's impact is not properly measured in narrow political terms. What distinguished him was the passionate intelligence he brought to bear on Scotland's predicament: for this his fellow countrymen tempered their alarm with genuine respect. To a remarkable extent Fletcher's writings can be seen to have established the framework for the debate on 'the condition of Scotland' in the years preceding the Union: those who were to support the Union no less than its opponents adopted Fletcher's analysis of the crisis as their starting point.[5]

[4] There is no adequate biography of Fletcher, about whose political activities and intellectual formation much remains obscure. The known facts are contained in *DNB*. Justice has not been done to his writings: the recent *Selected Political Writings and Speeches*, ed. David Daiches (Edinburgh, 1979), has woefully missed the opportunity for a proper edition. Scholars must continue to work from the complete eighteenth-century editions of *The Political Works of Andrew Fletcher* (London, 1732 and 1737, Glasgow, 1749). But because the new edition is the most accessible, I have reluctantly decided to give references to it.
[5] For a first recognition that Fletcher's contemporary significance was intellectual rather than political, see two pioneering essays by Nicholas Phillipson: 'Culture and Society in the 18th Century Province: the Case of Edinburgh in the Scottish Enlightenment', in L. Stone (ed.),

Two economic disasters, the collapse of the Darien venture and a succession of harvest failures, precipitated Scotland's crisis and provided the occasion for Fletcher's first Scottish writing, the *Two Discourses Concerning the Affairs of Scotland*, which he published in Edinburgh in 1698. Horrified as he was by the suffering which the disasters brought his fellow countrymen, however, Fletcher was at pains to emphasize that the problems involved were not temporary but structural. The Darien expedition had assumed such importance precisely because Scotland had been almost the only nation in Europe not to apply itself to commerce.[6] The harvest failures exposed much more than the inadequacy of provision for poor relief in emergencies. Scotland, Fletcher was convinced, already faced a chronic problem of vagabondage and insubordinate servants. Most damaging of all – 'the principal and original source of our poverty' – Scottish agriculture was crippled by the practices of racking the lands and charging rent in kind, compound evils which effectively inhibited investment.[7]

Fletcher's second contribution to the debate on the condition of Scotland was in response to a political turn in the crisis. In the absence of an acceptable Stuart successor to the sickly Queen Anne, the question of Scotland's future relation with England became in 1702 a matter of urgent concern on both sides of the border. Fletcher seized the opportunity to develop his analysis of Scotland's predicament in a series of vigorous speeches before the Scottish Parliament of 1703.[8] Once again he insisted that the present crisis was but the culmination and reflection of deep-seated problems; and he explicitly connected Scotland's political with its economic difficulties.

From its inception, Fletcher argued, the Union of the Scottish and English Crowns under the Stuarts had been disastrous for Scotland. Exploiting the country's poverty, English ministers had been able to bribe the necessitous Scottish aristocracy into subservience, and had reduced the nation as a whole to a condition 'more like a conquered province than a free, independent people'. At the same time, Fletcher held the Union of the Crowns itself principally responsible for Scotland's economic plight. The poverty and distress of the people, he declared, have no other cause but the ill-constitution of our government, and this has no root but our dependence on the English court. Specifically, Fletcher blamed the English court for the Darien fiasco, for the drain of Scotland's wealth south to purchase courtly luxuries instead of native manufactures, and for the enlistment of Scots for mercenary service

---

The University in Society, 2 vols. (Princeton, N.J., 1974), ii, pp. 417–20; and 'The Scottish Enlightenment', in R. Porter and M. Teich (eds.), *The Enlightenment in National Context* (Cambridge, 1981), pp. 22–6. Phillipson, however, is pursuing the possibilities thus opened towards a socio-cultural interpretation of the Scottish Enlightenment, a direction rather different from the one I now propose.

[6] 'First Discourse Concerning the Affairs of Scotland', *Selected Writings*, p. 31.
[7] 'Second Discourse Concerning the Affairs of Scotland', *Selected Writings*, pp. 46–7, 54–5, 58–61.
[8] First published as *Speeches by a Member of the Parliament which began at Edinburgh the 7th of May, 1703* (Edinburgh, 1703).

in the armies of Holland and England. To Fletcher the last article of the charge was the most serious of all. Not merely did standing armies threaten Scotland, as any nation, with political slavery, but they were particularly oppressive in a country which could not even afford the economic burden. Economic backwardness and political dependence were thus, on Fletcher's analysis, mutually reinforcing.[9]

In both his interventions, Fletcher did not hesitate to match analysis with prescription; and in line with his insistence on the structural character of the crisis the reforms he proposed were explicitly aimed at the long-term reconstitution of Scotland's economy and government. For each of the economic problems identified in the *Two Discourses* Fletcher enjoined a specific remedy. To develop Scotland's trade, the revenue of the land tax should be applied as credit for the national trading company. To relieve poverty and deal with the fundamental problems of vagabondage and insubordination among servants, a regime of domestic servitude should be imposed on the entire labouring class. Every man of a certain estate in Scotland should be obliged to support and employ a proportionate number of servants and their families, with the right to sell them when he ceased to have work. Finally, to stimulate Scottish agriculture Fletcher recommended an ambitious programme of directed investment. Great proprietors should be compelled to sell the lands which they were unable or unwilling to cultivate under their own supervision; and with the proceeds they should be encouraged to buy half-shares in the profits of the farms of small-holders. In this way all the land would be cultivated by its possessors, and the small-holders would be provided with capital for stock and improvements.

Where these economic remedies were put forward in pamphlet form, Fletcher was able to present his political proposals directly to the Scottish Parliament. In an *Act for the Security of the Kingdom*, Fletcher urged the placing of clearly defined 'Limitations' upon the power of all future Scottish monarchs. The 'Limitations' fall under two principal heads. First, they would recast the relation between legislative, executive and judiciary in Scottish government. The Scottish Parliament itself was to be reformed by the introduction of annual elections, conducted by ballot rather than by vote; and the members of the reformed Parliament were then to choose their own standing committee and appoint the executive officers of state. The judiciary, meanwhile, was to be independent, disqualified both from sitting in the legislature and from holding executive office. Second, the Limitations made strict provision for the nation's military organization. The maintenance of standing or mercenary forces without parliamentary consent would be prohibited, and a national militia raised instead, its officers appointed by Parliament.[11]

[9] 'Speeches', nos. ii, iv, v, vii and xiv, *Selected Writings*, pp. 70-2, 79-80, 81, 83-4, 95-7.
[10] 'First Discourse', p. 33; 'Second Discourse', pp. 55-6, 62-4.
[11] 'Speeches', no. iii, pp. 74-6.

Although his own analysis emphasized the interdependence of the economic and political problems facing Scotland, Fletcher did not explicitly connect his successive prescriptions for resolving the crisis. However, he explained and justified the various economic and political proposals in distinctive terms; and elsewhere, in works not specifically addressed to Scotland's crisis, he made it clear that any solution must be seen in wider European and historical perspective. From these indications, I would now argue, there does emerge a single consistent vision of an economically and politically viable Scotland. It is a vision founded upon the principles of the civic tradition, casting Scotland as a materially self-sufficient, free and independent political community.

Anticipating criticism of their severity, Fletcher went to some length to explain the proposals of the *Two Discourses*. He insisted on the need for public enterprise to initiate reform in all three spheres of trade, labour and agriculture, observing in the case of the last that bad custom could only be overcome by 'the public authority'.[12] More particularly, Fletcher was most concerned to deny that the proposed regime of domestic servitude was tantamount to slavery. Slavery, he argued, was properly a political condition of subjection to despotism; but as long as a servant's life, limb and family were protected at law, he was personally 'free'.[13] What Fletcher had in mind, in fact, was a return to the strictly domestic master–servant relation which had prevailed in pre-Christian antiquity. He extolled the advantages which the ancients had derived from the system. Not only had it eliminated poverty and unemployment among the servants themselves, but it had encouraged their masters to regard wealth as a public rather than a private good. Instead of consuming their estates in conspicuous private consumption like the moderns, the ancients, Fletcher recalled in wonderment, had used it

> to perform those great and stupendous public works, highways, aqueducts, common shores, walls of cities, seaports, bridges, monuments for the dead, temples, amphitheatres, theatres, places for all manner of exercises and education, baths, courts of justice, market places, public walks, and other magnificent works for the use and conveniency of the public, with which Egypt, Asia, Greece, Italy and other countries were filled; and to adorn them with stately pillars and obelisks, curious statues, most exquisite sculpture and painting...[14]

Commenting also (if at less length) on his proposals for agricultural reform, Fletcher vigorously defended their abolition of all legal relations of superiority

---

[12] 'Second Discourse', p. 61.
[13] *Ibid.*, pp. 49–52: 'A slave properly is one, who is absolutely subjected to the will of another man without any remedy: and not one that is only subjected under certain limitations, and upon certain accounts necessary for the good of the commonwealth, though such an one may go under that name. And the confounding these two conditions of men, by a name common to both, has, in my opinion, been none of the least hardships put upon those who ought to be named servants.'
[14] *Ibid.*, pp. 52–4.

and dependence between proprietors and small-holders. But he would nonetheless insist on a continued distinction between the ranks: husbandmen were to be discouraged from aspiring to live in the manner of men of great estates.[15]

Fletcher's evident anxiety that the severity of his prescriptions be not misunderstood can, I believe, be taken seriously. The proposals were deliberately exemplary, less important for themselves than for the principles which they embodied. In what are recognizably the terms of the civic tradition, Fletcher would have Scotland satisfy the material conditions of political community. In the first place, the Scots must recognize that economic development was a public responsibility. This meant not only that development be carried out by public enterprise, but that its object, once poverty had been eliminated, be regarded as the creation of public wealth. Only if the public good was made the economic priority could the Scots again assert their independence – let alone embellish their country with public works and monuments after the manner of the ancients. Ensuring the priority of the public good depended in turn, however, on a second civic principle: there must be a definite hierarchy of ranks within Scottish society, clearly distinguishing the producers from those who, without full-time economic engagements, were free for public duties. Present by definition in the avowedly classical proposal of domestic servitude, this principle can equally be seen to underlie the plan for agricultural reform. Landowners might supervise the work of their servants on as much of their estates as they could cultivate; but by leaving the rest to independent husbandmen, they should be free to devote most of their attention to public affairs.

Fletcher's initial justification of his political demands, in his *Speeches*, was both simpler and rather different in its terms. The demands were presented as but a matter of restoring the freedom and independence which the Scots had historically enjoyed before the Union of the Crowns. Until that Union overthrew 'our ancient constitution', Fletcher declared to Parliament, no monarchy in Europe had been more limited, and no people more jealous of liberty, than the Scottish. The 'Limitations' simply embodies the most essential liberties of 'our ancestors'.[16]

The language of ancient or ancestral constitutionalism may seem far removed from the civic principles evident in Fletcher's economic prescriptions. Nevertheless, it is arguable that the incongruity was much more apparent and rhetorical than real. For one thing, Fletcher was relatively imprecise in his use of a language commonly all too specific in its historical references. The most important version of ancient Scottish constitutionalism was that elaborated by George Buchanan in the late sixteenth century and subsequently espoused by the Covenanting opposition to Charles I. But even though his Limitations

[15] *Ibid.*, pp. 64–5.
[16] 'Speeches', nos. iii and iv, pp. 72–4, 79.

were very similar to the Covenanters' legislative programme of 1641, Fletcher was quite unequivocal in repudiating association with that cause. The 'peevish, imprudent, and detestable conduct of the presbyterians' had only compounded the damage done by 'the prelatical party'.[17] In fact, the ancestral liberties to which Fletcher referred were not exclusively Scottish at all (even if the Scots had enjoyed them to an unusual degree). A militia, he reminded Parliament, was 'the principal part of the constitution of any free government'.[18] And in a work published a year later, Fletcher stated clearly that the Limitations were only such as had 'formerly existed in most of the limited monarchies of Europe'.

This further work, *An Account of a Conversation concerning a Right Regulation of Governments for the common Good of Mankind. In a Letter to the Marquiss of Montrose, the Earls of Rothes, Roxburg and Haddington, from London the first of December 1703* (Edinburgh 1704), is perhaps the most revealing of the underlying framework of Fletcher's constitutional thinking. Addressed to the young Scottish nobles who had been his closest supporters in the Parliament of 1703, the pamphlet was presented as a record of a conversation in London between Fletcher, the Earl of Cromarty (a Scottish ministerialist), Sir Christopher Musgrave and Sir Edward Seymour (both English Tories, the latter vigorously Scotophobic). Defending his own and his young supporters' parliamentary conduct, Fletcher first simply reiterated the case for Limitations in terms of Scotland's dependent relation with England. But he then proceeded to add an entirely new dimension to his argument by setting the Limitations in the context of a plan for the reform of government throughout Europe.

Ideally, Fletcher envisaged a Europe divided into ten natural geographical areas, each further divided into ten or twelve territories around prominent cities. In each of the geographical areas the cities would unite for their common defence, under either a great council of delegates or a single prince (but preferably the latter, for better military coordination). The cities themselves, however, were to be 'sovereign', by which Fletcher meant that they would be 'the capitals of sovereign and independent kingdoms or countries', housing the administration of justice and the seat of government in their territory. The result of this division of Europe, Fletcher argued, would be a balance of power between both the individual cities and the larger unions, checking the natural inclination of all societies to exceed each other, and thus securing at last universal peace. So many seats of government would, moreover, ensure the most convenient administration of justice, encourage virtue in the conduct of public affairs, and tend to the improvement of all arts and sciences. In Fletcher's view the islands of Britain were well-placed to form one of the unions,

---

[17] 'Speeches', no. iii, p. 73. William Ferguson, *Scotland's Relations with England: A survey to 1707* (Edinburgh, 1977), pp. 190-2, 209, emphasizes the similarity between the Limitations and the 1641 legislation, but overlooks Fletcher's repudiation of the Covenanters.

[18] 'Speeches', no. xiv, p. 98.

and the kingdom of Scotland would constitute one or possibly two 'distinct sovereignties' within it.[19]

Fletcher gave no hint of an ancient constitutionalist inspiration for this plan, and indeed professed to be aware of no previous statesman or writer who had contrived such a scheme for the general good of mankind. However, he did point to the constitution of the Achaian League as approaching what he had in mind, and he praised the governability and cultural vitality of the ancient Greek cities.[20] Recalling the classical precedent which Fletcher cited for his proposal of domestic servitude, these references are, I believe, indicative in the same way of an essentially civic argument. Indeed, I would now suggest, it was civic principles which gave coherence and precision to Fletcher's constitutional thinking as a whole. They were the foundation not only of his plan for Europe, but equally of his avowedly ancient constitutional proposals for Scotland.

Projecting the civic principles of balance and participation into a federal framework, Fletcher would remedy the problem of Scotland's dependence on England within a solution to the general problem of relations between provinces and great monarchies throughout Europe. By dividing Europe into a certain number of balanced unions of provinces, Fletcher would turn the existence of provinces from a cause of rivalry into a security for peace. Within each union, he would then balance the power of each participating province, ensuring that none established a metropolitan predominance at the expense of the others by constituting each a 'distinct sovereignty' with its own freedom and independence. In Scotland's case this might be presented as a restoration of ancestral liberties; but behind the patriotic rhetoric the same civic principles are still evident.[21] In specifying a strict balance between legislature, executive and judiciary, and provision for citizens to participate freely in regular parliaments and a national militia, the Limitations did but specify the essential requirements of regular, free government on the civic model.[22]

---

[19] 'An Account of a Conversation Concerning the Right Regulation of Governments for the Common Good of Mankind', *Selected Writings*, pp. 127–37. In a list of a possible twelve capital cities in the British Isles, Fletcher named Stirling and Inverness in Scotland, neatly dividing the country into lowland and highland. He had previously expressed the view that Edinburgh was thoroughly ill-situated for a capital: 'Second Discourse', p. 65.

[20] 'An Account of a Conversation', pp. 132, 134, 136.

[21] Ancient constitutionalism being exploited, in variant forms, by Jacobite as well as Presbyterian writers at this time, Fletcher's vaguely-worded rhetoric was presumably intended to appeal to the mainstream of patriotic sentiment in the Estates. But his vagueness was probably also a tacit acknowledgement of the thinness of pretensions to an ancient constitution in a nation as institutionally weak as Scotland.

[22] In strict civic principle, Fletcher would reconstitute Scotland a republic. But Fletcher was evidently well aware of the pejorative connotations the term had acquired, for in the 'Account of a Conversation' he explicitly forestalled the identification of the free and independent provinces with republics. One of his interlocutors, Sir Edward Seymour, raised the issue: 'But you talk...of sovereign cities; I fancy you mean republics; which is nothing to us, who live

So interpreted, Fletcher's political response to Scotland's predicament emerges fully consistent with his economic remedies: the crisis was to be resolved by the simultaneous establishment of the economic and constitutional order of a civic political community. The point of this vision, however, is not fully apparent until one further dimension of Fletcher's thought is considered – the historical.

In the first and most densely argued of all his writings, his tract on militias and standing armies, Fletcher had essayed a civic history of European government. The tract originally appeared as a contribution to the English standing army controversy in 1697, but Fletcher subsequently revised it to include references to Scotland and had it republished in Edinburgh in 1698 under the title *A Discourse of Government with relation to Militias*.[23] Adopting as his standard 'those excellent rules and examples of government which the ancients have left us', Fletcher set himself to explain 'the alteration of government which happened in most countries of Europe about the year 1500', when the limited monarchies of the Gothic middle ages were replaced by the tyrannies of modern times. The causes of the alteration, which he emphasized was impossible to reverse, Fletcher found in the revival of ancient learning and the inventions of printing, the compass-needle and gunpowder.[24] The recovery of ancient learning and the invention of printing had bred in Italians and subsequently in Europe as a whole the desire to enjoy the 'refined and expensive pleasures' of the ancients; and to such pleasures the ocean navigation made possible by the compass had enabled the moderns to add the luxury of Asia and America. The unprecedented knowledge and 'expensive way of living' thus acquired had brought, Fletcher conceded, great gains. But it had also brought corruption, transforming the military organization of almost all European societies, and thereby removing the most essential limitation on their rulers' power.

under the benign influence of monarchy.' Fletcher promptly replied: 'You may suppose those cities...to be the capitals of sovereign and independent kingdoms or countries. For of such sovereignties, united under one monarch, we have many examples.' And when Seymour triumphantly observed that the divers sovereignties would be better united under one prince than a council of delegates, Fletcher was delighted: 'I am very glad...that you think such united governments more suitable to monarchies than to commonwealths; for if that be true, there will be greater hopes of introducing them into the world.' ('Account of a Conversation', pp. 131–2.) In civic terms, Fletcher's federal solution to the problem of provinces and great monarchies may be seen as a remarkable attempt to elide the distinction between a republic and a monarchy.

[23] This edition is reprinted in the *Selected Writings*. For classic expositions of the pamphlet: J. G. A. Pocock, 'Machiavelli, Harrington and English Political Ideologies in the Eighteenth Century', in his *Politics, Language and Time* (London, 1972), pp. 138–40; and *The Machiavellian Moment*, pp. 427–32.

[24] Pocock, 'Machiavelli, Harrington and English Political Ideologies', p. 139, notes that none of these causes is in Harrington. Lord Dacre has pointed out to me that the three inventions were in Bacon, *Novum Organum* (1620), Bk. 1, no. cxxix, and before him in Cardano, *De Subtilitate* (1550), Ch. XVII. Significance was attached to these particular inventions as being exclusively modern, and unknown to the ancients.

Before 1500, Fletcher argued, the sword had been in the hands, not of the king, but of his subjects, the barons and their vassals. The advent of the new way of living, however, had led the barons to compound the military service of their vassals for rent; and a people grown rich by trade had allowed themselves to be taxed heavily by their monarchs. The princes of Europe had thus acquired the freedom and the means to raise mercenary armies, and with the invention of gunpowder prolonging the conduct of war so that it became 'a constant trade to live by', those armies were retained on a permanent basis. Since it was precisely possession of the sword which had hitherto protected the liberties of subjects, its transfer to mercenary, standing armies henceforth assured princes of arbitrary power. For particular reasons, indeed, the nations of England and Scotland had until recently remained exempt from this European pattern: their island situation and Scotland's poverty had made it unnecessary for the one and impossible for the other to maintain standing forces. But with both nations now being called upon to raise such armies, they too, Fletcher was convinced, must be in imminent danger of succumbing to 'a French fashion of monarchy'.[25]

Even as Fletcher published *A Discourse of Government* in 1698 he was turning his attention specifically to Scotland's crisis in the *Two Discourses*.[26] What then was the relation between the Scottish predicament and the continental European history of corruption and arbitrary government? If Scotland was indeed threatened with 'a French fashion of monarchy', it was clearly not owing to internal corruption. As Fletcher indicated in the *Discourse of Government*, and emphasized at length in the 'First Discourse' on Scotland, the country had been and still was too poor to raise armies of any size. It was England which, through the Union of the Crowns, was imposing standing armies on Scotland. But that the Scots had to suffer such an imposition only demonstrated that while their poverty might prevent them corrupting themselves, it left them wide open to corruption from outside. Far from exempting the country from the European pattern of corruption, in short, poverty actually rendered Scotland more vulnerable, placing its liberties, its very independence, at the mercy of its richer (and increasingly corrupt) neighbour. In civic historical perspective, therefore, Scotland's predicament was peculiarly urgent; and the imperative of the economic development and political reform which Fletcher so passionately advocated could not have been clearer.

[25] 'A Discourse of Government with Relation to Militias', *Selected Writings*, pp. 2–18.
[26] But not to Scotland exclusively: in this year Fletcher also published his remarkable *Discorso delle Cose di Spagna*, the one of his major writings not discussed here. Even so, as I hope to show elsewhere, this work was by no means unconnected with Fletcher's Scottish concerns, bearing as it did the imprint 'Napoli', and analysing the relation between a great monarchy and its provinces. Reprinted in the 1732 and 1737 editions of the *Political Works*, and translated in the 1749 edition, it is excluded by Daiches for parochial reasons from the *Selected Writings*.

Yet the very urgency of Scotland's predicament also constituted, in civic terms, an historic opportunity. Still in a state of poverty, Scotland had not yet lost the chance to develop in a manner that would secure it from corruption and arbitrary government. If, as Fletcher proposed, Scotland undertook economic improvement within a social framework which made public wealth the priority and maintained a strict distinction of ranks, and if at the same time Scotland's liberty and independence were renewed by the essential institutions of free government, a parliament and a militia, then not only would the nation escape the trap of poverty and break the chains of its dependence on England; but it could attain, without corruption, a level of prosperity, culture and political virtue surpassing even that of classical antiquity. In Fletcher's words to Parliament, it was a 'golden opportunity': would the Scots but act now, they could render the nation 'for many ages easy and happy'.[27] And so acting, they would set an example to the world. For Fletcher's proposals, while inspired – as he frankly acknowledged at the end of *An Account of a Conversation* – by concern for Scotland's happiness in particular, were nevertheless designed to render 'not only my own country, but all mankind as happy as the imperfections of human nature will permit'.[28] Truly was Scotland's crisis the Fletcherian Moment.

Unfortunately, Fletcher failed at the first hurdle: his fellow countrymen were not convinced. Urgent, opportune, exemplary – his prescriptions were yet generally regarded as visionary. Virtually no Scot indeed defended the social and political *status quo*, and many hoped for reforms which would both promote economic development and revive the nation's political institutions. But the particular proposals of Fletcher's *Two Discourses*, not least that of domestic servitude, were discounted as bizarre; and though the idea of Limitations, with its ancient constitutional resonances, attracted more support, Fletcher's specific demands were soon set aside by the Estates as impractically radical. Fletcher himself acknowledged the charge of visionary,[29] but would not compromise; and after 1704 he made no further published contribution to the debate.[30] His moment, it seemed, had soon passed.

In his chosen terms, however, Fletcher had every justification for his uncompromising stand. For he was well aware that whatever the wish for reforms, Scots were increasingly tempted, with ministerial encouragement, to incorporate their parliament with England's in return for access to England's markets. Committed by civic principles to holding free institutions no less important than economic improvement, Fletcher could not but regard such

[27] 'Speeches', no. iv, pp. 76–7.
[28] 'Account of a Conversation', p. 136. Once again Fletcher was responding to a challenge by Seymour.
[29] In both the 'Second Discourse' and the 'Account of a Conversation', pp. 65, 114, 135.
[30] At least, no reports of his later speeches in Parliament have survived. Several later pamphlets have been attributed to Fletcher, but on doubtful grounds.

an exchange as 'the bait which covers the hook'.³¹ At the same time, his own diagnosis of Scotland's predicament entailed that nothing short of a wholesale transformation of the nation's social and political order would secure both its institutional independence and its economic development. Fletcher's civic vision, in other words, was actually the sole alternative to the choice towards which the nation was being led. Unless the Scots were willing to seize the moment to realize Fletcher's prescriptions in full, they would indeed have to sacrifice either their parliamentary institutions or their prospects of economic development.

III

David Hume was almost certainly familiar with the issues and arguments of the Union debate; and it may well be supposed that he held in particular respect the contribution of one he once described as 'a man of signal probity and fine genius'.³² The generation of the Enlightenment, indeed, was no less keenly committed to Scotland's progress than its predecessor at the time of the Union; and Hume was a leading participant in the renewed debate on the country's economic and political development fostered by the formation of the Select Society. Between the Union and the Enlightenment, however, there had been a decisive change of perspective. Where Fletcher had set Scotland's predicament in the forefront of his analysis, placing it in a broad historical and comparative framework the better to highlight its peculiar urgency and potential, Hume subsumed the case of Scotland within a consciously universal inquiry. As a philosopher of the progress of society in general, not simply a commentator on the condition of Scotland or even Britain in particular, he regarded an understanding of the common problems of developing, commercial societies as the prerequisite for dealing with the specific affairs of his own country.

In turning to consider Hume's treatment of the problem of institutions or government and economic development, therefore, we encounter a very different form of argument. The problem, we shall see, is formulated as one characteristic of every commercial society, and is illustrated by reference to the widest appropriate range of evidence. So too, it is clear that Hume derived the terms of his inquiry from a comprehensive knowledge of the civic tradition, its classical antecedents and jurisprudential affiliates. While there are obvious

---

³¹ 'Account of a Conversation', p. 118. Fletcher in fact thought that free trade with England was no solution to Scotland's economic problem either.

³² Hume's interest in the Union is attested by his notes in 'Hume's Early Memoranda 1729–40: The Complete Text', ed. E. C. Mossner, *Journal of the History of Ideas*, 9 (1948), notes 80-2 (from John Law) and 106-7 (from the Articles of Union), pp. 507-9. The description of Fletcher occurs in the account of Monmouth's invasion in *The History of England*, 8 vols. (London, 1778), viii, p. 228.

similarities in the conceptual structure of his arguments, Hume acknowledged no specific intellectual debt to the participants in the Union debate. The extent of the direct continuity between the Union debate and the Enlightenment inquiry is not, however, at issue in this essay, and does not affect my argument. Though both may be implied, neither Fletcher's 'influence' nor a concern on the part of Hume to reconsider the issues of the Union is presupposed. In the story told here, the significance of Fletcher's contribution is strictly structural and contextual. By the coherence with which he applied civic principles to remedying the Scottish condition of institutional dependence and economic backwardness, Fletcher provides a point of intellectual reference and contrast for assessment of the subsequent response of Hume to the general problem of institutions and economic development.[33]

A commitment to economic development was integral to Hume's moral and political philosophy from its earliest formulation in Book III of the *Treatise of Human Nature* (1740). Given the natural constraint of scarcity, the improvement of the goods mankind acquires by industry and fortune is, Hume wrote, 'the chief advantage of society'. Society makes possible such improvement by overcoming the weaknesses of men as individuals. Gathering men in sufficient numbers to permit both the combination of their forces and the division of their employments, and providing mutual security, society gives rein to the individual's 'interest' – his 'insatiable, perpetual, universal' passion for acquiring goods and possessions for himself and his nearest friends and family.[34]

Of the social conditions of economic development, it was of course the third, mutual security, which particularly concerned Hume in the *Treatise*. As he immediately observed, this 'insatiable, perpetual, universal' passion for acquisition is 'directly destructive of society' unless regulated and restrained so as to ensure the stability of possession.[35] Such stability of possession is provided by justice, which establishes the rules of property, its transference by consent and the obligation of promises. By itself, Hume believed, justice does not entail the existence of government: it is only when society has to provide for its external as well as mutual security by defending itself against acquisitive strangers that this emerges. The need for leadership in war is what accustoms men to the exercise of the 'authority' required by government.[36] If at first created specifically for defence, however, government will tend to assume responsibility

---

[33] It is thus not my purpose to make a case for the existence of a pervasive civic 'language' of politics and social inquiry in eighteenth-century Scotland: such is already the object of a series of studies by Phillipson, although the language which he identifies is more Ciceronian than (on my definition) strictly civic. Nor is it my concern to analyse the 'ideological' relation between Scottish experience and the thought of the Scottish Enlightenment. These limitations are not simply pragmatic. They reflect my convictions that the identification of a single civic 'language' threatens to blur critical distinctions within Enlightenment thinking, and that the attempt to reconstitute an encompassing 'ideology' for eighteenth-century Scotland is likely to end in reductionist simplification.

[34] *Treatise*, pp. 485–8, 491–2.   [35] *Treatise*, pp. 491–2.

[36] *Treatise*, pp. 501–34, 539–41.

for justice also as soon as the society has acquired any considerable wealth. Men will recognize that it is in their long-term interest to place the execution and decision of justice, along with the organization of defence and the provision of public works, in the hands of particular persons whose own interest (for those in government must be supposed to be still motivated by interest) is then identified with the impartial performance of those functions.[37] Arguing with and within the tradition of natural jurisprudence, Hume thus established government, providing by its authority defence and justice, as the necessary condition of the progress of society; and simply from the need and utility of such government he derived the obligation of allegiance to it.[38]

The assumption of the *Treatise* that those in government would act upon the interest of society as a whole was subject, however, to a critical qualification in the first volume of the *Essays Moral and Political* (1741). Hume was obliged to accept it as 'a just political maxim, that every man must be supposed a knave', since by acting together in parties those in power are able to pursue separate interests free from the normal constraints of public opinion.[39] Hume did not of course reduce the phenomenon of party or faction simply to the expression of distinct 'interests'. He was acutely aware of the potency of personal divisions, particularly in small states, and, still more, of the lethal violence of factions from principle, especially religious principle, and from mere 'affection'.

Nevertheless, he found factions from interest the most reasonable and excusable, 'considering that degree of selfishness implanted in human nature', and doubted whether they could ever be entirely prevented. He observed too that interest was commonly the real motive of the priests who led religious parties, even if their followers acted from principle. The consequences of such factions were potentially disastrous. Conflicting factions, Hume wrote, 'subvert government, render laws impotent, and beget the fiercest animosities among men of the same nation, who ought to give mutual assistance and protection to each other'. Where one faction is dominant, as in a despotic government, the effect is yet more pernicious, the more powerful oppressing the weaker with impunity.[40]

[37] *Treatise*, pp. 534–9. 'Magistrates find an immediate interest in the interest of any considerable part of their subjects. They need consult nobody but themselves to form any scheme for the promoting of that interest... Thus bridges are built; harbours open'd; ramparts rais'd; canals form'd; fleets equip'd; and armes disciplin'd; everywhere, by the care of government, which, tho' compos'd of men subject to all human infirmities, becomes, by one of the finest and most subtle inventions imaginable, a composition that is, in some measure, exempted from all these infirmities' (pp. 538–9).

[38] On the Natural Law foundations of Hume's theory of government and allegiance: Duncan Forbes, *Hume's Philosophical Politics* (Cambridge, 1975), chs. 1–3 - a work to whose challenge I am greatly indebted. Cf. James Moore, 'Hume's Theory of Justice and Property', *Political Studies*, 24 (1976), pp. 103–19. It is worth observing, however, that while in Hume's account 'authority' is an essential attribute of government, sovereignty is not.

[39] 'Of the Independency of Parliament', *Philosophical Works*, iii, pp. 118–19.

[40] 'Of Parties in General', *Philosophical Works*, iii, pp. 127–33.

With such consequences, it would seem that faction could not but imperil government's capacity to fulfil its original purpose of securing economic development. Even so, Hume did not focus upon this implication of separating the interest of those in government from the interest of society as a whole until his second collection of essays, the *Political Discourses* of 1752. He then did so, however, suggesting that the increase in a society's wealth actually intensifies the temptation to those in government to pursue a separate interest. The prosperity of a society, Hume observed in the first of these essays, 'Of Commerce', is represented by the proportion of its inhabitants not directly engaged in agriculture and the manufactures necessary to it. It is this pool of labour which manufactures 'the finer arts, which are commonly denominated the arts of luxury', whose possession constitutes the happiness of society's individual members. But, Hume continued, the superfluities of agriculture must also support the power of government: and herein lies the temptation. Instead of ministering to private luxury, it might be argued, would not society's surplus labour be better employed in manning large fleets and navies for the defence and aggrandizement of the state? Such, after all, was the policy of the greatest states of the ancient world, the republics of Sparta and Rome.[41]

Hume succinctly exposed the danger of succumbing to this temptation. In requiring farmers to yield their surplus entirely to the public, the ancient policy was, he argued, 'violent, and contrary to the more natural and usual course of things'; only by 'an extraordinary concurrence of circumstances' had it succeeded. The natural interest of those engaged in agriculture is to exchange their surplus for manufactured luxury goods; if this is made impossible, there will be no incentive for them to produce more than their own subsistence. But then, Hume pointed out, there will no longer be the means to meet the demands of the public: unless its armies make sudden and violent conquests, they must disband for want of subsistence, and society will be left without a regular means of attack or defence. Properly understood, Hume insisted, the interests of government and society in relation to trade and manufactures are united. The greater the scope for individuals to pursue their natural interest in the production and exchange of luxuries, the greater the resources available for the public to draw on in emergencies. On such occassions the sovereign can by taxation oblige the people to retrench on what is least necessary to their subsistence, and thus acquire the means and the surplus man-power to raise an army for as long as the danger lasts.[42]

On the whole, modern governments did not maintain the large military establishments which were Hume's particular target in 'Of Commerce'. But the temptation to separate the interests of government and society had not been overcome: for public credit, the subject of another of the *Political Discourses*,

[41] 'Of Commerce', *Philosophical Works*, iii, pp. 288–91.
[42] *Ibid.*, pp. 291–5.

was only a more insidious modern form of the same unnatural aggrandizement of public power. In direct contradiction to the natural policy of retrenchment by extraordinary taxation, public credit was an expedient to mitigate the immediate economic impact of war at the cost of a long-term misdirection of resources. Its adverse effects, according to Hume, were to increase artificially the wealth of the capital at the expense of the provinces, to raise prices by acting as paper money, to intensify the burden of taxation on labour, and to render the situation of the idle rentier more attractive than that of the productive investor. Not only was public credit thus injuring commerce and industry, however: again, but more explicitly and (with the addition of several paragraphs in 1764) at greater length, Hume emphasized the self-destructive consequences of such government aggrandizement. If the system of credit continued to expand, he foresaw a subversion of the social order such that the authority of government could only be maintained by mercenary armies and wholesale electoral corruption. Unless the sovereign could then place the whole income of every individual entirely at his mercy – 'a degree of despotism, which no oriental monarchy has ever yet attained' – government, Hume concluded, most in the long run dissolve upon the creditors' refusal to support it further.[43]

There was no sign that extraordinary circumstances would intervene providentially to save the modern world from public credit as they had the ancient (at least for a considerable period) from its over-large armies. Yet although Hume was certainly alarmed, it is important to recognize that he did not present public credit as spelling the inevitable doom of modern commercial societies. Throughout the essay his argument was strictly conditional: he acknowledged that its premises were suppositions, and stated his conclusions in the form of tendencies.[44] If his language was unusually vehement, it was precisely because, even in the absence of extraordinary circumstances, the danger could still be averted.

Together, therefore, the essays 'Of Commerce' and 'Of Public Credit' confirm a deep uncertainty in the relation established in the *Treatise* between government as the necessary condition for the progress of society, and economic improvement, the 'chief advantage' of society and motor of its progress. The problem diagnosed by Hume may be summarized thus. Government is the prerequisite of economic improvement because by its authority it provides the conditions of security in which individuals can freely pursue their interest in material betterment. In the natural course of things, furthermore, the relation between government and economic improvement is complementary: as members of society acquire more goods and possessions, so they have more need of the legal and military security which government provides, while their goods

[43] 'Of Public Credit', *Philosophical Works*, iii, pp. 360–74.
[44] *Ibid.*, pp. 367, 369.

constitute an increasing store of surplus resources on which government may draw in emergencies. However, the very increase in a society's wealth also makes the natural relation between government and economic activity ever more difficult to sustain. Those in government are tempted to divert this wealth to enhance their own power at the expense of what appears to be the unnecessary 'luxury' of society: acting as they do in parties, they pursue their own immediate interest, and are blinded to the fatal long-term consequences of their unnatural policy. These are to render the institutions of government more and more oppressive; to deprive the people of any incentive to increase their wealth; and ultimately to undermine the material basis of government's own existence. From the necessary condition of the society's progress, in short, government is turned into the efficient cause of its regression: and the society, if it is not conquered and absorbed by another, will revert eventually to a condition of primitive barbarism. This end is not indeed inevitable; there is no necessary cycle of progress and regression. But if the possibility is to be forestalled, and the uncertainty of progress diminished, it is imperative to frame government so that it will meet society's increasing demand for security with the minimum possible diversion of resources, and thus will continue to ensure the maximum freedom for individual members of society to pursue their own interest.[45]

So formulated, the problem of government and economic development remains within the essentially jurisprudential framework from which Hume began in the *Treatise*. The authority of government requires to be as much and no more as is necessary to secure property, so leaving the individual with the largest possible degree of liberty *from* its power. It may also be noted that this formulation of the problem embodied a more or less explicit rejection of the civic concept of wealth as a public good. Andrew Fletcher, it will be recalled, eloquently identified wealth with the noble array of public works and monuments found in antiquity; for Hume, by contrast, the public wealth of the ancients is identified with oppressive standing armies. A minimum diversion of resources into justice, defence and even certain public works is, Hume believed, always necessary; and in emergency government may appropriate the greater part of these resources. But it is the wealth of individuals and their families which constitutes the happiness – the progress – of society. We are, it seems, in the classic liberal world of 'possessive individualism'.

[45] There is a very similar account of Hume's problem, making it the starting point for an interpretation of his political thought as a whole, in G. Giarrizzo, *David Hume Politico e Storico* (Turin, 1962), pp. 23–39. My account differs from Giarrizzo's however, in that it does not extend to society Hume's distinction between the 'existence' and 'perfection' of government (as Giarrizzo appears to do on pp. 24–5). Beyond its most primitive, pre-governmental state, as I understand it, society is for Hume permanently subject to conflicting tendencies of progress and regression: a government which simply assures the 'existence' of society, without facilitating its 'perfection' or progress, must in the long run tend to cause its regression. As will become evident, this disagreement leads me to a less conservative interpretation of Hume's theory of government than Giarrizzo's.

Hume, however, did not leave the problem of government and economic development at that. While taking individual economic betterment as its baseline, his concept of progress extended thence to embrace, as integral features of civilization, the maturing of social relations and refinement of moral values which result from the general growth of wealth. In turn these further dimensions of progress set the role of government in a wider context. There is a first indication of their significance in 'Of Commerce', where Hume commented favourably on the greater equality resulting from the extension of wealth. If possible, he believed, every person ought to enjoy 'the fruits of his labour, in full possession of all the necessaries, and many of the conveniencies of life'. None can doubt, he continued, but such an equality is 'most suitable to human nature', subtracting much less from the happiness of the rich than it adds to that of the poor; at the same time it augments the power of the state by broadening its tax base.[46]

The next of the *Political Discourses*, 'Of Luxury' (from 1760 retitled 'Of Refinement in the Arts'), was addressed directly to the social and moral consequences of economic improvement, and their implications for government. Not only does luxury ensure an expanding material basis for government, but, Hume now argued, it creates an increasingly favourable social and moral environment for political life. Aware that the second clause of this argument no less than the first conflicted with ancient wisdom, Hume dismissed the hackneyed commonplace that Rome's decline had been caused by importing 'Asiatic' luxury: in reality an ill-modelled government and unlimited conquests were to blame. (In other words, the unnatural preponderance of the public power had ultimately taken its toll.) Properly, he argued, 'a progress in the arts is rather favourable to liberty, and has a natural tendency to preserve, if not produce a free government'. In the first place, it fosters a stable, graduated social order. In 'rude unpolished nations' there are only two classes, proprietors of land and their vassals or tenants, the latter absolutely dependent, the former exercising a petty tyranny. Where luxury nourishes commerce and industry, however, the peasantry can become rich and independent, and tradesmen and merchants may acquire a share of property. Authority and consideration are thus drawn to 'that middling rank of men, who are the best and finest basis of public liberty', because most interested in the rule of law and security of property. The moral consequences of luxury are as positive as the social. Here Hume plainly had more in mind than the diffusion of polite manners and the encouragement of the useful and liberal arts, for he explicitly emphasized the benefit also to men's public, military and political virtues. Habits of industry and discipline, he argued, give added force to martial spirit, while politics are conducted with a new mildness and moderation. 'Factions are then less inveterate, revolutions less tragical, authority less severe, and seditions less frequent.' The legislative and administrative capacity of the

[46] 'Of Commerce', pp. 296–7.

people is enhanced, application to the vulgar arts of commerce and manufactures being the prerequisite, Hume observed, for perfecting laws and police.[47]

With such implications, the social and moral aspects of progress necessarily set the problem of government and economic development in a fresh perspective. For if economic improvement depends upon government being able to provide security for members of society to pursue their interest, it clearly also creates conditions in which members of society will be able – and will expect – to contribute to the conduct of government. In these circumstances it will not be enough to frame government simply to ensure private property and safeguard individual liberty under the law: it will be necessary also to take account of the people's enhanced political capacity and expectations by recognizing a freedom *to* participate in public affairs. Requiring government to respond in this way suggests, however, that it is to serve a purpose which was historically understood in civic terms: that of satisfying the institutional conditions of political community. How does this accord with the jurisprudential account of government's purpose which Hume developed from the *Treatise* – an account whose basic individualism, as we have already seen, entailed a clear rejection of the civic concept of wealth as a public good?

The answer appears to lie in a radical revision of the traditional civic conception of political community's material and moral premises. This revision can be traced in two stages, the first of which was contained within an observation on the actual development of commercial societies, and the second of which was a projection thence into their future. The first, empirical stage of the revision was the abandonment of that rigid line of distinction between the free and the unfree, the political and the economic classes of society, which was so important to a traditional civic theorist such as Fletcher (and underpinned the civic concept of wealth as a public good). According to Hume, it is only in poor and backward societies that so rigid a distinction is to be found: with the onset of commerce it is overridden by the emergence of a 'middling rank' of farmers, tradesmen and merchants.[48] As the very concept of a 'middling rank', indicates, Hume by no means imagined commerce to abolish all social division: the greater equality which he welcomed in 'Of Commerce' is not an absolute equality.[49] But the existence of an ever-growing commercial

---

[47] 'Of Refinement in the Arts', *Philosophical Works*, iii, pp. 299–306.

[48] It seems likely that the gentry, as independent landholders, would fall within the definition of the middling rank in 'Of Luxury'; in 'Of Public Credit' it is 'landholders' who constitute the 'middle power' between king and people (p. 368). But as Forbes, *Hume's Philosophical Politics*, pp. 176–8, has cautioned, Hume's usages here and elsewhere are not entirely consistent.

[49] The difference between the equality of which Hume wrote favourably in 'Of Commerce' and absolute equality is clarified in a passage of *An Enquiry Concerning the Principles of Morals*, ed. L. A. Selby-Bigge, 3rd edn, rev. P. H. Nidditch (Oxford, 1975), pp. 193–4. Perfect equality such as the Levellers preached and the Spartans and Romans attempted to practise is criticized as both 'impracticable' and 'pernicious': it would stifle improvement and, by destroying all subordination, weaken extremely the authority of the magistracy.

class whose interest it is to insist upon the rule of law is sufficient to ensure that the economic classes of society can no longer be kept in the state of dependence presupposed by the traditional civic idea of political community.

The second stage of Hume's revision of the premises of political community is an inference from the first. What Hume appears to suggest is that within the framework of continuing social division, commerce will in the long run make it possible for every individual to satisfy the material and moral requirements of citizenship. In so far as commerce can ultimately bring sufficiency and independence to all, all may eventually attain that economic autonomy which in civic terms was the material condition of free political activity. Concurrently, with the general improvement and diffusion of martial and political virtues resulting from the industrious pursuit of luxury, it should become possible for everyone to cultivate the basic moral attributes of citizenship. These are both, it must be emphasized, projections into the future: on Hume's own account, no society had yet approached the level of economic development required for them to be realized. As projections, moreover, they are not elaborated in any detail, but are left rather as implications than as explicitly stated conclusions of the analysis of the social and moral dimensions of progress. Hume undertook no extended investigation of the conditions of individual political 'independence' in modern commercial society. Nor, apparently, did he reach the point of asking whether even as commerce makes it possible for the great majority to achieve moral fulfilment, it does not also create new forms of degradation and corruption. Even if no more than an undeveloped projection, however, the suggestion that commerce has the potential to universalize citizenship was sufficient to enable Hume to realign the civic ideal of political community with the individualism of his jurisprudential theory of government. Quite simply, it was Hume's contention that as every individual is motivated by interest, so, by achieving the material sufficiency and independence for which interest strives, every individual may also be capable of the virtue required of a citizen.[50]

From this projected reconciliation of citizenship with individualism follows a corresponding integration of the civic and jurisprudential concepts of liberty. On the one hand, it is clear that liberty under the law, by enabling the

---

[50] Thus the observation by James Moore, in his article 'Hume's Political Science and the Classical Republican Tradition', *Canadian Journal of Political Science*, 10 (1977), pp. 820–1, that Hume's insistence on the universality of interest undermines the traditional civic assumption of virtue in politics is one-sided, missing the extent to which Hume at once retains and transforms the civic ideal. For Hume, virtue cannot indeed be presupposed in politics, but with the progress of commerce it becomes increasingly possible, and calls for institutional recognition.

It may also be suggested that if, as Pocock contends (*The Machiavellian Moment*, pp. 462–7), there was a 'dialectic' in eighteenth-century debate between the 'ancients' who adhered to the agrarian ideal of the economically independent, virtuous freeholder, and the 'moderns', whose defence of commerce sacrificed virtue and independence to passion and self-interest, then Hume's argument effectively transcends it: commerce, interest, independence and virtue are interrelated.

individual to pursue his interest in security and thus to acquire material independence, is the precondition of enjoying the civic freedom to participate. With the growth in a society's wealth, on the other hand, the individual's liberty under the law, in the sense of his freedom from government, will itself be increasingly better secured by making institutional provision for the liberty to participate. For if the growing political capacity and virtue of society at large can be harnessed in government, it will ensure a closer identification of the interests of magistrates and people, checking the influence of faction and forestalling the increasing temptation to aggrandize government at the expense of society. Fully to resolve the problem of government and economic improvement, therefore, requires that both forms of liberty, the civic as well as the jurisprudential, must be acknowledged and provided for. What form of government did Hume believe could achieve this?[51]

It must be acknowledged that Hume never explicitly offered to 'solve' the problem of government and economic development. He did not, however, evade it: a response, indirect but definite, can be reconstructed from his political essays. To effect this reconstruction, a fresh theme in Hume's political inquiry requires to be introduced, and examined in some detail: the history and influence of the different forms of government. First elaborated in its own right in the earlier *Essays Moral and Political*, this theme converges in the *Political Discourses* with the problem of government and economic development – to the point, I shall suggest, at which the conclusion or model derived from the one serves also, by implication, as a solution to the other. Thus reconstructed, it will be clear that Hume's response to the problem of government and economic development was still framed in the terms of the civic tradition: but the radical revision of civic concepts already evident in the problem's formulation was, I shall conclude, confirmed and extended.

Returning to the discussion of government in the early *Essays*, Hume's response there to the problem of faction reveals a clear commitment to

---

[51] It will be obvious that civic, participatory liberty is given a rather larger place in my argument than in most studies of Hume's political thought. But it is important to note that the difference is as much one of perspective as of substance. Explicitly adopting 'a social historian's perspective', Phillipson has suggested that Hume be seen as addressing the middle ranks of contemporary provincial societies such as Scotland: in this context, Phillipson argues, Hume effectively reduces participatory liberty to a neo-Ciceronian 'liberty of indifference', cultivation of which will serve to isolate metropolitan faction and so secure the rule of justice ('Hume as Moralist: A Social Historian's Perspective', in S. C. Brown (ed.), *The Philosophers of the Enlightenment*, Royal Institute of Philosophy Lectures, xii (Hassocks, Sussex, 1979), p. 149). Forbes is more bluntly dismissive of participatory liberty, treating it throughout *Hume's Philosophical Politics* as a very secondary, if not vulgar, ideal. But Forbes has no interest in the possibility of abstract, tendential argument in Hume: he explicitly excludes Hume's economics from his consideration, and claims that an 'historical' approach must be limited to Hume's discernible intentions in the context of eighteenth-century British politics ('Introductory Preface', *Hume's Philosophical Politics*, p. vii). This seems to me much too narrow a basis for an historical understanding of Hume.

identifying the institutional framework which would ensure a harmony of interest between government and society. It was, he believed, the test of a 'wise and happy' government that by a skilful division of power among the separate courts and orders of men within it, the separate interest of each 'must necessarily, in its operation, concur with the public'.[52] Faced with the phenomenon of factions from principle and affection as well as interest, Hume emphasized also that government must exercise a general responsibility for the manners and character of society at large: 'general virtue and good morals in a state, which are so requisite to happiness... must proceed entirely from the virtuous education of youth, the effect of wise laws and institutions'.[53] The importance of these objectives was reflected in Hume's high estimate of the office of legislator.

> Of all men, that distinguish themselves by memorable achievements, the first place of honour seems due to LEGISLATORS and founders of states, who transmit a system of laws and institutions to secure the peace, happiness, and liberty of future generations.[54]

It was moreover precisely the capacity of institutions to regulate political behaviour and shape society's moral values which, Hume supposed, made it possible to reduce politics to a science. Such is the force of laws and particular forms of government 'that consequences almost as general and certain may sometimes be derived from them, as any which the mathematical sciences afford us'.[55]

Hume's most extensive discussion of the different forms of government and their influence is contained in 'Of the Rise and Progress of the Arts and Sciences', published in the second volume of the *Essays Moral and Political* in 1742. At the outset Hume made it clear that he was specifically choosing the rise and progress of learning to illustrate the scientific pretensions of politics because the history of commerce was more easily accounted for;[56] nevertheless, the essay's argument indicates that essentially the same conditions were required for the development of both.

Hume began with the observation that neither learning nor any significant commerce could have originated among the primitive tyrannies which served as governments in the first ages of the world. The value of general laws and regular political institutions was then unknown; and there was no reason to suppose that a barbarous monarch would ever have set up as a legislator to restrict the exercise of arbitrary power either by himself or, still more important, by his subordinate ministers. Under such a government, accord-

---

[52] 'Of the Independency of Parliament', p. 119.
[53] 'Of Parties in General', p. 127.
[54] *Ibid.*
[55] 'That Politics may be reduced to a Science', *Philosophical Works*, iii, p. 99.
[56] 'Of the Rise and Progress of the Arts and Sciences', *Philosophical Works*, iii, p. 176.

ingly, a people 'are slaves in the full and proper sense of the word, and it is impossible that they can ever aspire to any refinements of taste or reason. They dare not so much as pretend to enjoy the necessaries of life in plenty or security.'[57] It was only, Hume continued, with the elaboration of the principles of law in 'free governments' or 'republics' that the improvement of society could properly begin. To restrain their magistrates and secure their liberty, citizens of republics had pioneered the orderly regulation of authority by the rule of law. The security which law alone can provide had in turn stimulated men's curiosity, and republics had thereby led in the encouragement of knowledge and learning.[58] In a second observation, Hume added that the external relations of the earliest republics, forming a balance of 'neighbouring and independent states, connected together by commerce and policy', were a further cause of the rise of politeness and learning. Referring particularly to the republics of ancient Greece, Hume observed that the rivalry of such small states prevented the development of the uniform, stifling system of authority characteristic of large governments.[59] Thus, Hume concluded, laws and institutions, stability and order – the preconditions of learning and commerce alike – were originally 'the sole growth of republics'.[60]

Turning from the rise to the subsequent progress of the arts and sciences, Hume's third observation was that having once taken root in republics, the necessary conditions for the further advance of civilization could then be transplanted into other forms of government. In particular, he pointed to the way in which the rule of law, the product of order and liberty, had subsequently been incorporated in what he termed the 'civilized monarchies'. These monarchies were quite different from the first barbarous despotisms. In a civilized monarchy the prince alone possessed an unbounded power, and even that was restrained by custom, example and the sense of his own interest; his subordinate ministers, meanwhile, were fully subject to the general laws of society. The people might still be dependent on their sovereign for the security of their property, but the distance set between them ensured that such dependence was barely felt. Only in 'a high political rant' could this regime be described as tyranny; and Hume in fact believed civilized monarchy to be a form of government which 'by a just and prudent administration, may afford tolerable security to the people, and may answer most of the ends of political society'. Hume did not thereby suggest that all distinction between the republican and monarchic governments had disappeared. Republics, he believed, typically reward those who make themselves useful by industry and knowledge, and are thus a form of government more favourable to the sciences. Monarchies, by contrast, tend to honour those who cultivate wit and civility, thus encouraging the polite arts – whose contribution to civilization was no less

[57] *Ibid.*, pp. 178–9; and cf. p. 185.
[58] *Ibid.*, pp. 179–81.
[59] *Ibid.*, pp. 181–2.
[60] *Ibid.*, p. 186.

important.[61] Hume was confident, however, that the emergence of the large civilized monarchies alongside republics would rather reinforce than disrupt a balance in external relations. The nations of modern Europe were 'a copy at large of what GREECE was formerly a pattern in miniature'.[62]

'Of the Rise and Progress of the Arts and Sciences' requires careful interpretation, for the argument, though uncharacteristically repetitive, is unevenly elaborated. Nevertheless, the analysis of the influence of the different forms of government yields two important propositions. In the first place, the emergence of republics is presented as marking a decisive break in the history of government. Although Hume does not detail the circumstances of the republics' origin, it would seem that they developed in small states, in which it was possible for the people to throw off the yoke of monarchy relatively early, while the fortunate coincidence of a cluster of similarly small states in ancient Greece enabled the republics to avoid subordination to larger neighbours. The republics thus possessed two essential attributes of 'free governments'. By regulating the authority of their magistrates, they ensured the rule of law; and by maintaining a balance of power in relations with each other, they made the best provision for their external security. In contrast, the primitive monarchies, as the original form of government, had provided only an irregular security. Uncertain in the provision of justice, and, it is implied, with a proclivity for conquest inimical to a settled system of peaceful relations with neighbours, they remained despotisms or tyrannies, under which the people were no better than 'slaves'. Since such conditions offered no encouragement to the arts and sciences, or even to commerce, their rise must be ascribed to republics alone.[63]

The second proposition of the arts and sciences essay is that modern monarchies are closer, in essentials, to republics than to their primitive monarchic forbears. There are still indeed distinct republican and monarchic forms of government in the modern world. But there is no longer, on Hume's analysis, a fundamental distinction of principle between them. For the 'civilized' monarchies have successfully adopted the original attributes of republics, and constitute regular if not entirely free governments. The authority

[61] *Ibid.*, pp. 186-7. [62] *Ibid.*, p. 183.
[63] The 'decisive break' which I have identified is not, however, the same as the 'logical gap' which Forbes found between the account of the original monarchic form of government given in the *Treatise* and the claims made on behalf of the first republics in the arts and sciences essay (*Hume's Philosophical Politics*, p. 318). Assuming, as seems reasonable, that the primitive monarchies of the essay are the original monarchies of the *Treatise*, it is not necessary, as Forbes supposed, to invoke the intervention of a founding Legislator to create the first republics. Although Hume does not rule out the initiative of a single legislator in a small state, the emphasis in the essay is upon the collective action of the people to bridle the power of monarchy, and thus set the rule of law for the first time on a firm foundation. This is quite consistent with the summary statement in the *Treatise*, p. 540, that 'republics arise only from the abuses of monarchic and despotic power'.

of all subordinate magistrates is restrained, and the rule of law thereby assured. At the same time, the existence of these large monarchies has not proved to be necessarily incompatible with maintaining the principle of the balance of power in external relations. In these circumstances it is plainly mere rhetoric to describe the civilized monarchies as tyrannies or despotisms: such categories may be relegated to the barbarous pre-history of government. The civilized monarchies have shown themselves in their own way as fitted as republics to promote the progress of learning and, it may be inferred, commerce.

Hume of course commented on forms of government throughout the *Essays* and in the later *Political Discourses*. Ranging over governments ancient and modern, republican and monarchic, these more particular observations not only throw further light on the propositions of the arts and sciences essay, but focus increasingly upon the specific relation between forms of government and economic development.

The assessment of the famous republics of classical antiquity to be found elsewhere in Hume's work sets the very generalized analysis of the arts and sciences essay firmly in perspective. In the earlier *Essays*, Hume repeatedly drew attention to the ancient republics' political limitations. Despite instituting the rule of law, the republics had been disorderly and ill-policed, while their prized political liberty had been marred by virulent factional division, made worse by the absence of any system of representation.[64] By comparison, economic conditions received less notice, Hume simply remarking on the indifference to commerce implicit in the fact that scarcely any ancient writer had regarded trade as an important affair of state.[65] In the *Political Discourses*, however, Hume spelt out and emphasized the republics' economic limitations, explicitly connecting them with their political defects. As we have seen, 'Of Commerce' stressed the unnaturalness of putting the demands of the state for military power before individual economic betterment, while 'Of Luxury' ridiculed the attempt to suppress private refinement in the name of an artificially severe private virtue.[66]

The 'extraordinary concurrence of circumstances' which had made those policies possible, and their damaging consequences, were the subject of further commentary later in the *Political Discourses*, in that perhaps most remarkable of all Hume's essays, 'Of the Populousness of Ancient Nations'. Looking for the conditions which might be supposed favourable to population, Hume pointed to the direct connection between the political liberty, small size and

---

[64] 'Politics a Science', 'Parties in General', and 'Of Civil Liberty' - first published in 1741 under the title 'Of Liberty and Despotism' and renamed in 1758: *Philosophical Works*, iii, pp. 99-100, 128-9, 161.
[65] 'Of Civil Liberty', *Philosophical Works*, iii, p. 157; although in a conventional way Hume numbered ancient Tyre, Athens, Syracuse and Carthage at the head of a list of free governments under which commerce had flourished (*ibid.*, p. 160).
[66] 'Of Commerce', 'Of Refinement in the Arts', pp. 290-2, 305.

social equality of the ancient republics: 'each man had his little house and ...
to himself, and each county had its capital, free and independent'.[67] When his
attention turned to the potential hindrances to population, however, it was to
reveal the critical flaws in that apparently desirable conjunction of circumstances. First, the liberty of citizens was based on the continuing domestic
slavery of the servant class – a denial of real liberty, Hume sharply observed,
far more serious than any occurring under the most arbitrary government of
modern Europe, and the most probable reason for 'the severe, I might say,
barbarous manners of ancient times'.[68] Second, the degree of equality
maintained between citizens effectively prevented the development of trade
and manufactures, and thus made impossible the emergence of a middling
rank.[69] In the resulting absence of a stable, graduated social hierarchy, it was
no wonder that the government of the ancient republics knew no medium
between 'a severe, jealous Aristocracy, ruling over discontented subjects; and
a turbulent, factious, tyrannical Democracy'.[70]

In a final revision of the ancient populousness essay, Hume added a sentence
immediately following the last-quoted judgement on the classical republics,
declaring the republics of modern Europe the equal or even the superior of
their most celebrated ancient predecessors in 'justice, lenity, and stability'.
'Almost all of them are well-tempered Aristocracies.'[71] A well-tempered
aristocracy implied a regular social order such as only economic development
could bring; and, Switzerland apart, the modern republics Hume had in mind
were clearly commercial.[72] In one of his earliest essays, Hume identified the
commercial nobility of Venice as the paradigm of a stable republican
aristocracy, expressly contrasting it with the impoverished, anarchic nobility
of that archetype of Gothic backwardness, Poland.[73]

Yet despite the advance registered by the modern republics over their
ancient predecessors, these governments too suffered from serious limitations.

---

[67] 'Of the Populousness of Ancient Nations', *Philosophical Works*, iii, p. 398.

[68] *Ibid.*, p. 385. Hume's denunciation of slavery might have been directed specifically at Andrew Fletcher: 'Some passionate admirers of the ancients, and zealous partisans of civil liberty, (for these sentiments, as they are, both of them, in the main, extremely just, are found to be almost inseparable) cannot forbear regretting the loss of this institution; and whilst they brand all submission to the government of a single person with the harsh denomination of slavery, they would gladly reduce the greater part of mankind to real slavery and subjection.'

[69] *Ibid.*, pp. 410–13. Hume now stressed the 'inconsiderable' extent of Athenian commerce.

[70] *Ibid.*, p. 409. As Hume observed, p. 404: 'The utmost energy of the nervous style of *Thucydides*, and the copiousness and expression of the *Greek* language, seem to sink under that historian, when he attempts to describe the disorders, which arose from faction throughout all the *Grecian* commonwealths. You would imagine, that he still labours with a thought greater than he can find words to communicate.' (In memory, C. W. Macleod.)

[71] *Ibid.*, pp. 409–10. The addition appeared in the posthumous 1777 edition of the collected *Essays and Treatises on Several Subjects*.

[72] And even Switzerland was populous: 'Of the Populousness of Ancient Nations', p. 399.

[73] 'Politics a Science', p. 100; cf. the derisive comment on the Poles in 'Of Refinement in the Arts', pp. 305–6.

Their faults were closely related to the circumstances of their commercial success. With their mercantile wealth, the Dutch had been the first to contract a public debt, and, Hume observed, 'have well-nigh ruined themselves by it'. Since in a popular government public creditors will commonly have the highest offices, it is virtually impossible for such a state to resort to a bankruptcy to clear its debt.[74] A still more fundamental weakness derived from the republics having attained commercial prosperity in despite of natural disadvantages, by exploiting the priority of foreign trade in European economic development.[75] For as commerce became more general, their small size must in the long run become a liability. Even the Dutch, Hume observed, lacked the resources of land and commodities to rival the larger territorial states in sustained economic growth. That republic could indeed continue to prosper for a considerable period by 'art and industry'; but its relative weight among the powers of Europe had already declined.[76]

Hume's favourable opinion of the modern civilized monarchies was clear even before the appearance of the essay on the arts and sciences. In the essay originally published in 1741 as 'Of Liberty and Despotism', he affirmed that:

though all kinds of government be improved in modern times, yet monarchical government seems to have made the greatest advances towards perfection. It may now be affirmed of civilized monarchies, what was formerly said in praise of republics alone, *that they are a government of Laws, not of Men*. They are found susceptible of order, method and constancy, to a surprising degree. Property is there secure, industry encouraged; the arts flourish; and the prince lives secure among his subjects, like a father among his children.

In this class, 'the most perfect model of pure monarchy' was France. Not only was the security of property there assured; but such a monarchy had the advantage over popular governments of possessing sufficient authority to protect the individual against oppression by special interests. If the King of France and his minister would but recognize that only the *financiers* gained by the present expensive and arbitrary method of collecting taxes, not to mention the public debt, Hume was confident that these abuses could be speedily and painlessly remedied. The difference between absolute monarchy and free government in relation to commerce would then be narrowed even further than it had been already.[77]

That such a difference still existed, however, Hume did not seek to deny: their progress notwithstanding, the civilized monarchies were subject to limitations of their own. In 'gentleness and stability' they were still inferior to popular

---

[74] 'Of Civil Liberty', p. 163.
[75] 'Of Taxes', *Philosophical Works*, iii, p. 356. The modern republics mentioned are Genoa, Venice and Holland. 'Of Commerce', p. 295.
[76] 'Of the Jealousy of Trade', *Philosophical Works*, iii, pp. 347-8.
[77] 'Of Civil Liberty', pp. 161-2.

or free governments; and they did not sufficiently 'honour' commercial activity, but continued to encourage traders to throw up commerce in order to purchase the privileges of title and place. Insisting upon a subordination of ranks as 'absolutely necessary to the support of monarchy', they refused recognition to a commercial middling rank.[78] Later, when considering the balance of power in modern Europe, Hume also attributed to the French monarchy the potential ambition, at least, of universal monarchy. Should the Bourbons be thus tempted, however, he warned that they would face the nemesis which had struck all enormous monarchies since the Roman, of succumbing to the inevitable revolt of their provinces.[79]

If the civilized monarchy of France was still inferior to a free government in the encouragement of commerce, and vulnerable to the lure of universal empire, would it not be reasonable to suppose that the mixed monarchy of Britain was uniquely advantaged? Hume certainly believed England to be ahead of any nation in the world in agriculture and commerce, and Britain to enjoy the freest of governments; and he acknowledged that since 1688 the nation's achievements in public liberty, in commerce, in arts and sciences and in war had spread its glory throughout Europe.[80] Yet even as he admitted all this of the present, he displayed a persistent scepticism about the future. As Forbes has led us to appreciate, Hume ever regarded Britain's vaunted liberty as dangerously precarious.[81]

The very mixture of republican and monarchic elements in Britain's government was a source of weakness as much as strength. Of the two, Hume believed the republican component to predominate, and in one early essay he suggested that Britain was not far from being a 'pure' republic. It would become one, he wrote, of perhaps 'no inconvenient form', if parliamentary representatives were required to accept instructions from their constituents, like the Dutch, so permitting a measure of participation without opening government to the direct influence of 'popular currents'.[82] However, when Hume thereupon set himself to answer the question 'whether the British Government inclines more to Absolute Monarchy or to a Republic', he argued that the only sort of republic which was in practice likely to develop out of Britain's limited government would be tantamount to an anarchy. He therefore concluded that he would prefer the British government to end in an absolute monarchy.[83] The conviction that the balance of limited monarchy tended to permit a dangerous excess of republican liberty only hardened in

---

[78] *Ibid.*, pp. 160–2.
[79] 'Of the Balance of Power', *Philosophical Works*, iii, pp. 355–6.
[80] 'Of Commerce', 'Of the Protestant Succession', *Philosophical Works*, iii, pp. 297–8, 475–6.
[81] Forbes, *Hume's Philosophical Politics*, chs. 5–6.
[82] 'Of the First Principles of Government', *Philosophical Works*, iii, pp. 112–13.
[83] 'Whether the British Government inclines more to Absolute Monarchy, or to a Republic', *Philosophical Works*, iii, pp. 122–6.

Hume's later essays. The most dramatic illustration of the danger was provided by the national debt. Under the prevailing form of government, Hume believed, it would be difficult or dangerous for any minister to venture on a bankruptcy to clear the debt; but without such a measure, Britain's economy and constitution could eventually be overwhelmed, and the nation left at the mercy of a conqueror.[84] Celebrated Britain's mixed constitution might be, therefore, but it by no means guaranteed Britain's continued pre-eminence, or even further economic development.

Summarized in this way, Hume's particular observations on forms of government can be seen both to clarify and to move beyond the general propositions of the arts and sciences essay. Clarification of the significance to be attached to those propositions is to be found principally in the earlier *Essays*. In the case of the classical republics, Hume leaves no doubt that the peculiar circumstances which enabled them to inaugurate regular, free government must also restrict their significance for posterity. Natural limitations of size having been exacerbated by the unnatural constraints of slavery and excessive equality, the ancient republics had restricted commerce and suffered from severe political instability. There was therefore no special virtue in their being the first free government: the classical republican was no model to which to seek to return. Hume's full assessment of modern governments, on the other hand, makes it equally clear that these mark a definite advance over the ancients: both in republics and in monarchies, authority is now better regulated, liberty under the law more assured, and hence commerce more thriving. Of the two, furthermore, it is evidently the advance of the civilized monarchies which is of the greatest significance. The republican form of government, despite its improvement, is still a prisoner of size: in the modern as in the ancient world it has proved appropriate only for small states, whose potential for growth is necessarily limited. The mixed government of Britain has, it is true, republican features; but, present favourable appearances notwithstanding, Hume regarded the outcome of the attempt to combine these with monarchy as deeply uncertain. By contrast, the civilized monarchies have successfully established regular government in large territories, and bid fair to overtake the free governments in wealth and influence.[85]

By no means all of Hume's observations on forms of government, however, serve simply to clarify the propositions of the essay on the arts and sciences. Increasingly, they illustrate also Hume's specific concern with the relation between government and economic development. Predominant in the *Political Discourses*, but anticipated in a few earlier essays, this concern can be seen to

---

[84] 'Of Public Credit', pp. 373–4.

[85] At this point Hume's argument can be read as a powerful counter to the favourable view of republican government, and its supposed British adaptation in particular, which Montesquieu made fashionable among writers of the European Enlightenment. On these: Franco Venturi, *Utopia and Reform in the Enlightenment* (Cambridge, 1971), chs. 1–3.

have sharpened Hume's assessment of the various forms of government to a point where all, including the monarchies, are found wanting. The ancient republics present a paradigm of the unnatural aggrandizement of government at the expense of society, with the consequent frustration of liberty in both economic and political life. The modern republics have compounded their deficiency in size by engaging in similar unnatural aggrandizement through public credit; and both in the republics, and still more, in the mixed government of Britain, the disproportionate influence of the financial interest appears likely to prevent the remedy of a bankruptcy. The presumed ability of the civilized monarchies to override the financiers' interest is the principal reason for their better prospects of development; but in other respects they too are judged defective. They remain liable to the temptation of universal monarchy (and thus to burdening themselves with military expenditure and oppressing their provinces and neighbours); and by their insistence on a continued subordination of ranks they are inhibiting the emergence of a commercial middle rank, and preventing the attainment of the fullest degree of political liberty and stability. In short, if some forms of government have historically proved more favourable to commerce than others, not one has offered to satisfy the 'natural' requirements of an economically developing society. None has combined the minimum diversion of resources with flexible adaptation to social change, so as to ensure both the maximum liberty under the law and an increasing freedom to participate. Under none, therefore, can the progress of society be perfectly assured.

That Hume would be content to leave his analysis of the forms of government thus open-ended, without indicating how they might best be rendered equal of the demands of economic development, is unlikely. Hume was of course no advocate of violent, revolutionary changes in government, holding as he did a theory of customary legitimacy which denied a right of resistance against any but the worst tyrannies.[86] Reform, however, as distinct from revolution, was perfectly proper and desirable: as we have seen, Hume held the office of legislator in high esteem. In a large modern state this was no longer – if indeed it ever had been – an office that could be fulfilled by a solitary, heroic individual; but it was one for which, Hume was confident, an ever larger proportion of the people were being equipped by the habits and values associated with commercial activity. If, however, modern legislators were to provide future generations with a form of government appropriate for commercial society, they must possess a standard or model by which to direct their reforms.

It was just such a model, I would now suggest, that Hume was proposing in the last essay of the *Political Discourses*, the 'Idea of a perfect Commonwealth'. And thereby, it will be argued, this essay brings to an issue both Hume's

[86] *Treatise*, pp. 551–3; 'Of Passive Obedience', *Philosophical Works*, iii, pp. 460–2.

historical analysis of governmental forms and his concern with the problem of government and economic development.

Introducing the 'Idea of a perfect Commonwealth', Hume was at pains to delimit his purpose. He began with a warning of the danger of tampering with an established government 'merely upon the credit of supposed argument and philosophy'. Nevertheless, Hume suggested, just as Huygens had experimented to find which figure of a ship was most commodious for sailing, so one might as well inquire which form of government was the most perfect. The question was not only worthy of curiosity, but also potentially useful. Either the dissolution of an old government or the combination of men to form a new one 'in some distant part of the world' might in future afford an opportunity to reduce the theory to practice. In all cases, moreover,

> it must be advantageous to know what is most perfect in the kind, that we may be able to bring any real constitution or form of government as near it as possible, by such gentle alterations and innovations as may not give too great disturbance to society.

Hume then explicitly distinguished his proposal from those previous plans of government which, by supposing 'great reformation in the manners of mankind', were plainly imaginary. Of this kind were Plato's *Republic* and More's *Utopia*. In fact, Hume declared, 'the only valuable model of a commonwealth, that has yet been offered to the public', was Harrington's *Oceana*; and even *Oceana* was flawed in presupposing the maintenance of an unnatural degree of material and moral equality among citizens.[87]

Hume gave his perfect commonwealth a federal structure. At its base would be a certain number of 'county' assemblies, preferably one hundred. The members of these would be annually elected from each parish by qualified freeholders and urban householders. (The voting qualifications, which Hume twice revised upwards, were designed to ensure an electorate of 'fortune and education', as opposed to 'an undistinguishing rabble, like the ENGLISH electors'.)[88] In turn, the county representatives would annually elect from their number both local magistrates and a member of the national senate. Defeated candidates for the senate with more than one-third of the votes were to form an official opposition 'court of competitors'. The county assemblies were to be the ultimate legislative power, but every new law would first be debated in the senate. The senate would also have full executive authority, choosing by 'an intricate ballot, such as that of VENICE or MALTA', a protector, two

[87] 'Idea of a perfect Commonwealth', *Philosophical Works*, iii, pp. 480–2. The specific defects of *Oceana* were its insistence upon rotation in public office, its agrarian law (which would be made unenforceable by concealment), and its concentration of power in the senate.

[88] Thinking nonetheless in terms of English qualifications, Hume initially accorded the vote to all freeholders, and those paying scot and lot in the towns. Within two years (by 1754), he had restricted the franchise to £10 freeholders, and urban householders worth £200; and in 1768 these qualifications were raised again, to £20 and £500 respectively. ('Perfect Commonwealth', p. 482 and note.)

secretaries of state, commissioners of the treasury and councillors of state (foreign affairs), religion, learning, trade, laws, war and the admiralty. In emergencies these executive bodies could assume dictatorial powers for six months. The third branch of government, the judicial power, would be divided between the counties and the senate, with the court of competitors having the right of accusation before them. There were additional stipulations for the perfect commonwealth's defence and religious organization. It was to be defended by a militia on the Swiss model, twenty thousand men being called out annually in rotation for training. The national church would be presbyterian, and formally subordinated to the civil power through having its ministers appointed by local magistrates. In a series of aphorisms designed to explain the plan, Hume insisted particularly on its capacity both to allow a measure of popular participation without confusion and to regulate the authority of the senate, preventing it either combining against the people, or dividing into faction. The perfect commonwealth would thus have 'all the advantages of both a great and a little commonwealth'.[89]

Hume concluded with observations on the scheme's feasibility. He enumerated the relatively few alterations which it would require in the governments of the United Provinces and Great Britain, although in the latter case he reiterated his intense suspicion of limited monarchy. More generally, Hume was explicit in discounting the conventional wisdom that a commonwealth was incompatible with large states such as France or Britain. A republican or free government in an extensive territory, he argued, would be more stable in the long run, if initially less easy to establish, than one in a city.

> In a large government, which is modelled with masterly skill, there is compass and room enough to refine the democracy, from the lower people, who may be admitted into the first elections or first concoction of the commonwealth, to the higher magistrates, who direct all the movements. At the same time, the parts are so distant and remote, that it is very difficult, either by intrigue, prejudice or passion, to hurry them into any measures against the public interest.

Even in a large state, the perfect commonwealth could not of course be assured of permanence: 'rust may grow to the springs of the most accurate political machine'. But if preserved from enthusiasm, faction and the pursuit of empire, Hume was confident that it might flourish for many ages.[90]

To interpret, as I wish to do, the 'Idea of a perfect Commonwealth' as a model form of government for modern commercial society requires the demonstration of two points. The first concerns the relation between the essay and Hume's historical analysis of the forms of government. To constitute a model (as opposed to an *a priori* speculation), the perfect commonwealth must, by Humean definition, comply with custom: its principles must be derived from

---

[89] *Ibid.*, pp. 482–90.   [90] *Ibid.*, pp. 490–3.

historical and existing forms of government, and be applicable in the various circumstances in which governments are actually established. The second point to be demonstrated is the compatibility of the 'Idea of a perfect Commonwealth' with Hume's analysis of the demands which economic development naturally imposes upon government. The perfect commonwealth must, this is, both be able to secure individual liberty under the law with the minimum necessary diversion of resources, and be sufficiently flexible to extend political recognition and freedom to participate to an increasing proportion of commercial society's members.

Hume's own careful presentation of the 'Idea of a perfect Commonwealth' renders its alignment with his historical analysis of the forms of government relatively straightforward. The essential principles of the scheme are explicitly acknowledged to be of republican origin. As republics have been from the first, the perfect commonwealth is founded upon the principle of participation as the means to regulate the conduct of those in authority, and hence to ensure the rule of law. At the same time, the federal structure of the perfect commonwealth incorporates the principle, exemplified in the external relations of the earliest republics, of maintaining a balance between small, neighbouring social units. While embodying such principles, however, it is clear that the perfect commonwealth transcends the restrictive conditions to which the republican form of government has historically been subject. Above all, the perfect commonwealth will not be fitted only for states of small size, as the republican form of government has been in both the classical and the modern worlds: its federal constitution enables it to join neighbouring 'counties' or provinces within a large territory. In combining regular government with large territory, indeed, the perfect commonwealth draws rather upon the example of the civilized monarchies: and it seems, if anything, to be adapted more completely to their circumstances than to those of the republics. Fewer changes, it is true, may be required to bring the republican United Provinces and the semi-republican mixed government of Britain into line with the perfect commonwealth; but as the prospects of the civilized monarchies are even now better than those of the republics, so, in the long run, the perfect commonwealth would be more securely established in a large state. Deriving its principles, therefore, from both the republican and the civilized monarchic forms of government, the 'Idea of a perfect Commonwealth' may be seen to constitute a single, composite model of regular, free government, applicable as well to the actual circumstances of the monarchies as to those of the republics – ultimately, in fact, rather better.

To serve as a model for the reform of any government in the modern commercial world, however, the 'Idea of a perfect Commonwealth' must also be equal to the natural requirements of an economically developing society. Although this was not a point to which Hume directly addressed himself, more than one recent historian has noticed that the perfect commonwealth at least presupposes relatively advanced economic and social conditions;[91] and I would now contend that it is positively designed for commercial society. By the provision of security of person and property for all, the perfect commonwealth will ensure the universal enjoyment of that individual liberty under the law which is the first condition of economic opportunity and political independence. With liberty under the law, the perfect commonwealth will combine a measured freedom to participate in the assemblies and offices of government. A certain level of wealth and education is required to exercise this second freedom, but these are qualifications which an ever larger proportion of the members of commercial society can be expected to attain. To protect the two forms of liberty, moreover, the perfect commonwealth makes strict institutional provision against the abuse of government by personal or partisan interests. A clear division of legislative, executive and judicial power between several assemblies and offices is complemented by the requirements for annual elections and intricate ballots. Perhaps most significant, however, is the distribution of powers and functions between the centre and the localities, ensuring that the scope for factious misuse of governmental authority is checked by the relative autonomy of the provinces.

The connection of the two forms of liberty is further strengthened by the perfect commonwealth's military and religious institutions. Entrusting defence to a universal militia, which can be called out as necessary in emergencies, will obviate the need for a permanent establishment of any size, and thereby ensure the minimum diversion of the nation's resources. At the same time the involvement of all citizens in the defence of their families and property will harness the improved martial spirit fostered by commercial habits of industry and discipline, while the possession of arms will provide the people with the surest guarantee of their political liberty. The assertion of lay control over an established church, on the other hand, ought to prevent the priestly manipulation of society's values, and the exploitation of popular liberty in furtherance of factious clerical interests.

Thus, it may be argued, does the 'Idea of a perfect Commonwealth' satisfy the two criteria of a model form of government for commercial society. Not only is it abstracted from the historical experience of government, and applicable to the existing circumstances of both republics and monarchies; it it also compatible, as no actual government has been hitherto, with the 'natural' demands of economic development. So interpreted, the essay can be seen to draw two major themes in Hume's political inquiry together to a

[91] On this see first of all the acute though brief comments of Douglass Adair in '"That Politics may be Reduced to a Science": David Hume, James Madison and the Tenth *Federalist*', *Huntington Library Quarterly*, 20 (1956–7), p. 350 and note. Now also, Moore, 'Hume's Political Science and the Classical Republican Tradition'.

conclusion. On the one hand, by combining the positive attributes of both republics and monarchies, it consolidates the lessons derived from the study, begun in Hume's earlier *Essays*, of the historical evolution and influence of those different forms of government. On the other, by matching the requirements of a fully commercial society, it responds to what was, by the time he wrote the *Political Discourses*, Hume's paramount concern with the relation between government and economic development: in effect, it is Hume's 'solution' to that problem.

So interpreted, moreover, the 'Idea of a perfect Commonwealth' suggests that Hume's political thinking remained to the end within the framework of the civic tradition. That such was the essay's lineage was indicated by Hume himself, when he introduced it as intended to improve upon Harrington's *Oceana*; and its essential features – the strict division of legislative, executive and judicial powers within a federal structure, the citizen's militia – were those traditionally constitutive of the civic concept of regular, free government. In two distinctive respects, moreover, the essay may be thought to have had a closer and more recent predecessor even than Harrington's *Oceana*. In its aspiration to join the vitality characteristic of small 'free and independent' provincial societies with the resources of scale associated with monarchies, and to harmonize regular, free government with the pursuit of economic development, Hume's plan of a perfect commonwealth resembles above all that stringently civic scheme of government for Scotland and Europe outlined in Andrew Fletcher's Limitations and *Account of a Conversation concerning a Right Regulation of Governments*.

If the 'Idea of a perfect Commonwealth' thus reveals a continuing civic derivation for Hume's concept of government, however, it also measures the transformation he wrought upon the civic inheritance. It is, furthermore, precisely the apparent marks of affinity with Fletcher which prove, on closer examination, to be the critical points of difference. When Fletcher recognized the need to meet the particular problem of Scotland's dependence on England within a solution to the European problem of relations between a great monarchy and its provinces, he still regarded 'the excellent rules and examples of government which the ancients have left us' as his standard; he still held the monarchies of modern Europe to be tyrannies or despotisms. By contrast, when Hume sought to combine the resources of large states with the benefits of provincial autonomy, it was in the confident conviction that modern forms of government were already far in advance of the ancient. The emergence of the ancient republics out of the earliest barbarous monarchies had indeed, Hume argued, been a decisive break in the history of government, establishing for the first time the rule of law. But the governments which have since grown up in the modern world, monarchies as well as republics, have absorbed and improved upon the classical republics' achievement. In particular, Hume argued, the modern civilized monarchy bears no resemblance to its barbarous namesake. Far from being a despotism, the civilized monarchy now provides a degree of security under the law and protection from special interests unobtainable in a republic: it constitutes the best and surest basis on which to build a perfect commonwealth.

No less critical was the revision of the traditional civic concept of government entailed by Hume's very different understanding of economic development. When Fletcher urged the pursuit of economic improvement as the only means by which Scotland, as a poor country in the modern corrupt world, could secure its liberty and independence, he assumed that such improvement would occur within and reinforce a social order in which wealth was deemed a public good, and in which there was a clear distinction between the producing and the citizen classes, with the latter alone capable of the virtue required for political life. He presupposed, in other words, the traditional material and moral premises of political community, and consequently identified regular, free government with the participatory liberty of an exclusive citizen class. When, however, Hume recognized in economic development the ultimate reason for every society's existence and the motor of its progress, he also recognized that development will only occur through the individual pursuit of personal and family interest, in conditions of the universal security of property and the minimum necessary diversion of resources to public ends. At the same time, he saw that if these conditions are met, economic development will then tend to bring an ever larger proportion of society within reach of material independence and moral fulfilment - and thus will tend to universalize the capacity for citizenship. On these premises, the liberty to be provided by regular, free government must take not one but two forms. Priority must initially be given to the 'jurisprudential' form of liberty: liberty under the law, liberty *from* neighbours and government. But as economic and moral betterment diffuses the capacity for citizenship ever wider, so in the perfect commonwealth the civic liberty *to* participate will in the end become equally important and extensive.

Thus transforming the definition of regular, free government, the 'Idea of a perfect Commonwealth' transformed also, finally, the perspective in which such government is to be realized. Fletcher, seeking to restore a past ideal, had called upon his fellow Scots to seize an historic opportunity: in the best civic tradition, the attainment of political community was presented as a matter of the moment. Hume's perfect commonwealth being by contrast a projection into the future, its realization is a matter of time. Not only is no major government in modern Europe so tyrannical as to justify immediate revolution; but the economic and social conditions required for the full realization of regular, free government have nowhere yet been attained. Despite the security enjoyed by its subjects, the civilized monarchy of France still sustains social conventions which militate against the achievement of political freedom, while in Britain the level of material and moral development is certainly not yet sufficient to ensure that participatory liberty can be extended without danger of factious abuse. The perfect commonwealth, therefore, is not (at least in Europe) an immediate possibility,[92] but simply a model or 'idea', towards which legislators might seek to bring 'any real constitution or form of government as near...as possible'.[93]

In the end, it is not even certain that Hume regarded the full realization of his concept of regular, free government as, in principle, possible. Concluding what has been described as his 'political testament', 'Of the Origin of Government' (1774), Hume wrote:

> The government, which, in common appellation, receives the appellation of free, is that which admits a partition of power among several members, whose united authority is no less, or is commonly greater than that of any monarch; but who, in the usual course of administration, must act by general and equal laws, that are previously known to all the members and to all their subjects. In this case, it must be owned that liberty is the perfection of civil society; but still authority must be acknowledged essential to its very existence: and in these contests, which so often take place between the one and the other, the latter may, on that account, challenge the preference.[94]

It is clear that no government, however regular and free, would be exempt from that tension. Not only does liberty under the law, and hence the independence which is the prerequisite of the freedom to participate, presuppose the existence of authority and the obligation to obey. But in conditions of universal citizenship, the freedom to participate itself will in important respects be inseparable from an obligation: in the perfect commonwealth that traditional guarantee of civic freedom, a citizens' militia, is to be recruited by general conscription. Liberty, it seems, must ever remain a compromise or balance, both with authority and between its two forms.

But if this conclusion suggests scepticism as to whether the 'Idea of a perfect

---

[92] Nor is there any evidence that Hume anticipated the perfect commonwealth's suggested application by Madison to the making of the revolutionary American constitution (on which see Adair, 'David Hume, James Madison and the Tenth *Federalist*'), even though he observed that the formation of a new government 'in some distant part of the world' would provide an opportunity to reduce the theory to practice.

[93] With this perspective, it is not necessary to regard Hume's vigorous private distaste for the Wilkesite reform movements of the 1760s and 1770s as evidence of a last flight into conservatism, as does Giarrizzo, *Hume Politico e Storico*, pp. 92–5. To Hume the Wilkesite campaigns were the most extreme example yet of the factious licence to which Britain's mixed government was peculiarly prone: in conjunction with the unceasing growth of the national debt, the reformers' demand for an extension of political or participatory liberty only threatened to set partisan interest over the rule of law.

[94] 'Of the Origin of Government' (written in 1774 and first published posthumously in the 1777 edition of the collected *Essays and Treatises*), *Philosophical Works*, iii, pp. 116–17. The description of the essay as a 'political testament' is Giarrizzo's, *Hume Politico e Storico*, p. 96; cf. Forbes, *Hume's Philosophical Politics*, p. 192.

Commonwealth' will ever be realized, it does not devalue the essay's significance.[95] It is a commonplace that Hume's was a sceptical politics: but just as too narrow a choice of historical context may limit the asssessment of his politics, so indifference to its intellectual content may vulgarize the quality of his scepticism. From the *Treatise* through the *Essays* and *Political Discourses*, the historical evolution of forms of government, from primitive to civilized monarchies by way of republics, and the implications of commerce for the morals and institutions of society were two subjects of Hume's sustained theoretical reflection; and the reflection was conducted throughout in close confrontation with the traditional civic concepts of wealth, virtue and free government. As at once an historically derived model form of government and a balance of the legal and participatory liberties, the 'Idea of a perfect Commonwealth' was the outcome of that reflection and that confrontation: thereby it stands at the limits of the civic tradition.

IV

Lest such a conclusion seem misleadingly conclusive, two forward glances yield a moderating epilogue. More immediately, this was not the end of the story within the Scottish Enlightenment. Adam Smith should be seen as the heir to Hume's encounter with the problem of government and economic development. Smith's formulation of the problem in the *Wealth of Nations* amplified that of Hume. To the danger of government aggrandizement he added a class dimension (in the shape of the mercantile interest); and he suggested that if the individual liberty from government essential to economic development was to be ensured in future, the labouring classes must positively be educated to exercise that freedom to participate for which their increasing material independence would qualify them. Still more radical were the implications of Smith's response to the problem. Not only was Smith's argument, unlike Hume's, direct and systematic, Book V of the *Wealth of Nations* elaborating an explicit model of economical and free government for commercial society. But in the process Smith quietly abandoned the constitutional principles of the civic tradition. In their stead Smith substituted (albeit piecemeal) others of a quite different character, deriving from the newly emergent British doctrine of parliamentary sovereignty.[96]

Even then, in the longer term, the Scottish Enlightenment did not signal

---

[95] Hume, it may be noted, did not withdraw the essay on writing 'Of the Origin of Government': the 'Idea of a perfect Commonwealth' continued to appear at the end of the collected *Essays and Treatises*. And, as Forbes has pointed out (*Hume's Philosophical Politics*, p. 135), when Hume devoted such care to the revision of his essays, he may be presumed to have adhered to what he left standing.

[96] J. Robertson, 'The Scottish Enlightenment beyond the Civic Tradition: Adam Smith on Government and Economic Development', *History of Political Thought* (forthcoming).

the end of the civic tradition. Quite apart from its ever tenacious undergrowth of moralism, several of what I have defined as the tradition's primary, constitutional principles would be born again in the political thought and political economy of the nineteenth century. Mere Scottish reason might determine the limits of the civic tradition: but a combination of Americans and Marxists, ever reviving antique ideals of direct participation and a citizens' militia, made certain that no reason was enough.

7 Adam Smith as civic moralist*
NICHOLAS PHILLIPSON

In this paper I present Adam Smith as a practical moralist who thought that his account of the principles of morals and social organization would be of use to responsibly-minded men of middling rank, living in a modern, commercial society. In this account Smith will appear as a philosopher who was concerned with the principles of propriety as well as with those of virtue and valued the spirit of independence and sense of ego of commercial man rather than the libertarian civic virtues of the classical republican. He will, above all, appear as the philosopher who saw the province as the true source of the opulence, freedom and political wisdom that was needed to maintain the fabric of a commercial polity in a modern age.

I

It is now customary to think of the Scottish social philosophers as moral philosophers who were anxious to introduce the methods of the natural into the moral sciences.[1] As an intellectual historian, I prefer to think of them as practical moralists who had developed a formidable and complex casuistical armoury to instruct young men of middling rank in their duties as men and as citizens of a modern commercial polity. Hutcheson, Smith, Ferguson, Reid and Stewart were professors of moral philosophy who saw their curricula as devices to teach their pupils to 'adorn your souls with every virtue, prepare yourselves for every honourable office in life and quench that manly and laudable thirst you should have after knowledge'.[2] Hume and Kames preferred

---
* I am very grateful to J. H. Burns, Istvan Hont, Michael Ignatieff, John Pocock, Quentin Skinner and Donald Winch for comments on this paper at various stages of its production.
[1] See, for example, G. Bryson, *Man and Society: The Scottish Inquiry of the Eighteenth Century* (Princeton, N.J., 1945); L. Schneider, *The Scottish Moralists on Human Nature and Society* (Chicago, 1967); R. L. Meek, *Social Science and the Ignoble Savage* (Cambridge, 1976), chs. 1 and 4; A. S. Skinner, *A System of Social Science: Papers relating to Adam Smith* (Oxford, 1979); A. Swingewood, 'Origins of Sociology: The Case of the Scottish Enlightenment', *British Journal of Sociology*, 21 (1970), 164–80.
[2] F. Hutcheson, *A Short Introduction to Moral Philosophy* (Glasgow, 1747), p. iv.

to use the polite Addisonian essay which, in Hume's hands, developed as a sophisticated and flexible mode of moral discourse, capable of attracting an intelligent salon and coffee-house readership as well as philosophers and men of letters. And both agreed with Robertson, Smith, Ferguson and Millar that philosophical history was an instrument which could be used to teach men to understand the origins of their ideas of morality, justice and politics so that they could better understand their roles as citizens and legislators of a commercial polity. Taken together, the purpose of this moralistic armoury was to instruct men in the principles of practical morality which Dugald Stewart usefully defined as

> ... all those rules of conduct which profess to point out the proper ends of human pursuit, and the most effectual means of attaining them; to which we may add all those literary compositions, whatever be their particular form, which have for their aim to fortify and animate our good dispositions, by delineations of the beauty, of the dignity, or of the utility of Virtue.[3]

Not much notice has been taken of the casuistical framework of Scottish philosophy, although it is true that Smith scholars – notably Joseph Cropsey and Ralph Lindgren – have been more sensitive to its existence than most.[4] But it is one which we would do well to recognize. It was as practical moralists that the Scottish philosophers presented themselves to their contemporaries and received, in return, the distinctively pre-eminent civic status that they enjoyed in contemporary polite Scottish society.[5] It was as such that they acquired a Shaftesburian distrust for those inquiries about the science of man that seemed to be irrelevant or positively harmful to the principles of practical morality. It was this, for example, that encouraged Hume to turn away from systematic philosophizing in the manner of the *Treatise* to essay-writing in the manner of Addison. For this seemed to be a more appropriate vehicle for discussing the principles of politics and civic morality in a way which would be of use to ordinary citizens.[6] Paradoxically, the same concern led Reid and the Aberdonian philosophers to develop that critique of Humean scepticism

---

[3] Dugald Stewart, 'Account of the Life and Writings of Adam Smith LL.D.', in Smith, *EPS*, p. 278.

[4] J. Cropsey, *Polity and Political Economy: An Interpretation of the Principles of Adam Smith* (The Hague, 1957); J. R. Lindgren, *The Social Philosophy of Adam Smith* (The Hague, 1973). Notwithstanding our different approaches to Smith, I must acknowledge my debt to Ralph Lindgren's meticulous and perceptive study.

[5] See Phillipson, 'Towards a Definition of the Scottish Enlightenment', in P. Fritz and D. Williams (eds.), *City and Society in the Eighteenth Century* (Toronto, 1973), pp. 125–47; 'Culture and Society in the 18th Century Province: The Case of Edinburgh and the Scottish Enlightenment', in L. Stone (ed.), *The University in Society*, 2 vols. (Princeton, N.J., 1974), ii, pp. 407–48; 'The Scottish Enlightenment', in R. Porter and M. Teich (eds.), *The Enlightenment in National Context* (Cambridge, 1981), pp. 19–40.

[6] Phillipson, 'Hume as Moralist: A Social Historian's Perspective', in S. C. Brown (ed.), *The Philosophers of the Enlightenment*, Royal Institute of Philosophy Lectures, xii (Hassocks, Sussex, 1979), pp. 140–61.

which was to play so important a part in shaping higher education in ~~~~~
and France at the turn of the eighteenth century. And it was because Reid
himself was felt to be too abstruse and unsystematic a critic of Hume that
Beattie and Stewart were led to reformulate and extend his principles in order
to suit the casuistical needs of a modern age.[7]

However, it is impossible to understand Smith's approach to the principles
of practical morality without taking into account the revolution which Hume
had brought about in the understanding of the principles themselves. By
demonstrating that moral distinctions are matters of sentiment, Hume had,
at a single stroke, undermined the credibility of the entire casuistical tradition
in the ancient and modern world. Hitherto, casuists had thought of virtuous
conduct as the pursuit of universal goals. They had described the faculties of
human nature on which their achievement had rested and prescribed the moral
exercises necessary to cultivate them. But no matter how attractive the
prescriptions of these casuists might be – and, as far as Stewart was concerned,
it was a matter of some historical interest that many of them had been
universally admired throughout the ages – in a post-Humean world they
seemed to be arbitrary and dependent on the whims of their authors rather
than on a just appreciation of the principles of human nature.[8] Hume's
revolutionary insight was an injunction to serious moralists to shift their
attention from the study of ends to the study of means; to the principles which
explain how we acquire moral sentiments and ideas of virtue and to the lessons
which a virtuously-minded agent could hope to draw from a study of his own
moral history and that of mankind in general.

This taught moralists to think of the moral wisdom men acquire in the course
of ordinary life as the rock upon which a life of virtue must be founded. This
concern with the relationship between wisdom and virtue, framed by a
renewed interest in Cicero and Stoic morality in general, was to play an
increasingly important part in shaping the Scottish philosophers' understanding
of the principles of morals, politics and history. Certainly, as I shall try to show
here, it was of integral importance to Smith. Indeed I propose to show why
Smith thought that stupidity made a man more contemptible than cowardice
in a civilized society.[9] In commercial civilization wisdom rather than the classic
martial and political virtues was the true touchstone of virtue.[10]

II

Smith's theory of morals was founded on his theory of sympathy and I want
to review his treatment of this subject in order to show how closely casuistry

---

[7] Phillipson, 'James Beattie and the Defence of Common Sense', in B. Fabian (ed.), *Festschrift für Rainer Gruenter* (Heidelberg, 1978), pp. 145–54.
[8] Stewart, 'Account of Smith', *EPS*, p. 279; *TMS* VII.iv.6.
[9] *WN* V.i.f.61.   [10] Compare *TMS* I.iii.3.1–3.

and moral science were interwoven and to demonstrate the force of Dugald Stewart's remark that in his early work Smith 'aimed more professedly at the advancement of human improvement and happiness'.[11] I shall also want to suggest that his theory is best seen, not as a general theory of morals, but as an account of the process by which men living in a commercial society acquire moral ideas and may be taught how to improve them. This is not simply to say that Smith preferred modern examples to those drawn from the experience of primitive societies or that he reserved some of his most subtle discussion for a consideration of the effect of wealth and poverty on the formation of moral sentiments. It is simply that his theory is redundant outside the context of a commercial society with a complex division of labour.

Smith's theory of sympathy was designed to explain why we derive intense pleasure from what he calls 'mutual sympathy' and distress from discord. It was what Hume called 'the hinge of your system' and Smith summed it up like this:

Whatever may be the cause of sympathy, or however it may be excited, nothing pleases us more than to observe in other men a fellow-feeling with all the emotions of our own breast; nor are we ever so much shocked as by the appearance of the contrary.[12]

Tactically, he seems to have decided to proceed in this discussion by presenting his readers (like the audience of fourteen- and fifteen-year-old students who had originally heard his lectures) with a large number of examples to remind them of the pleasure and pain which different types of social encounter could cause. These 'illustrations' as Burke called them[13] were homely and literary in character and rooted in the social experience of a commercial civilization. Many of them also belonged to the common stock of moral data about which contemporary Addisonian moralists were accustomed to philosophize; no doubt that is exactly why Smith chose them. Here is an example.

When we have read a book or poem so often that we can no longer find any amusement in reading it by ourselves, we can still take pleasure in reading it to a companion. To him it has all the graces of novelty; we enter into the surprise and admiration which it naturally excites in him, but which it is no longer capable of exciting in us; we consider

---

[11] Stewart, 'Account of Smith', *EPS*, p. 314. There are useful discussions of the theory of sympathy in T. D. Campbell, *Adam Smith's Science of Morals* (London, 1971), esp. chs. 4 5; Lindgren, *Adam Smith*, chs. 2–3. The best introduction is still that given in Stewart's 'Account of Smith'.

[12] *TMS* I.i.2.1. Hume was uneasy about Smith's treatment of this central point and regretted that he had not 'more particularly and fully prov'd that *all kinds of Sympathy are necessarily Agreeable* [my italics]. This is the Hinge of your system, & yet you only Mention the Matter cursorily on p. 20.' That was indeed Smith's contention and it is interesting that he regarded his collection of homely Addisonian illustrations as a strong enough foundation on which to raise this central argument. Hume to Smith, 28 July 1759, in *Letters of David Hume*, ed. J. Y. T. Greig, 2 vols. (Oxford, 1932), i, p. 313. See also Campbell, *Adam Smith's Science of Morals*, pp. 103 6.

[13] Edmund Burke to Smith, 10 September 1759, in Smith, *Correspondence*, p. 46.

all the ideas which it presents rather in the light in which they appear to him, than in that in which they appear to ourselves, and we are amused by sympathy with his amusement which thus enlivens our own. On the contrary, we should be vexed if he did not seem to be entertained with it, and we could no longer take any pleasure in reading it to him.[14]

These examples were designed to show that encounters which end in the pleasure of experiencing mutual sympathy could be found in most of the ordinary areas of everyday life and the rhetoric suggests that Smith was anxious to legitimize the pleasure that such an experience brought by encouraging his readers to cultivate the social skills that were necessary to produce them.[15]

As far as Smith was concerned, the search for mutual sympathy was a complex and demanding activity. He believed that human beings were naturally curious about each others' behaviour and that they were naturally disposed to interpret it in the only way they knew – by imaginatively conceiving 'what we ourselves should feel in the like situation'.[16] Now what is curious and distinctive about Smith's theory is that he does not think that we simply put ourselves in another man's shoes in order to see whether, were we him, we would approve of what he was doing. That would have introduced an element of egotism into the theory which he was particularly anxious to avoid.[17] In his account we exercise our imaginative curiosity quite hard in order to achieve what we judge to be a genuinely critical detachment in our understanding of another man's behaviour. Thus, to take a particularly graphic Smithian example, a man does not ask what he would suffer if he were a woman in labour; he tries to imagine what it would be like to be a woman in labour.[18] Only after we have undergone this demanding imaginative and critical exercise and acquired what we feel is a satisfactory degree of detachment, do we decide whether or not to bring the encounter to a close by offering our sympathetic approval of the other man's behaviour. For it is a cardinal principle of Smith's theory that

> To approve of the passions of another...as suitable to their objects, is the same thing as to observe that we entirely sympathize with them; and not to approve of them as such, is the same thing as to observe that we do not entirely sympathize with them.[19]

---

[14] *TMS* I.i.2.2.

[15] Thus, 'Mankind, however, more readily sympathize with those smaller joys which flow from less important causes. It is decent to be humble amidst great prosperity; but we can scarce express too much satisfaction in all the little occurrences of common life, in the company with which we spent the evening last night, in the entertainment that was set before us, in what was said and what was done, in all the little incidents of the present conversation, and in all those frivolous nothings which fill up the void of human life. Nothing is more graceful than habitual cheerfulness which is always founded upon a particular relish for all the little pleasures which common occurrences afford. We readily sympathize with it: it inspires us with the same joy, and makes every trifle turn up to us in the same agreeable aspect in which it presents itself to the person endowed with this happy disposition.' (*TMS* I.ii.5.2.)

[16] *TMS* I.i.i.2.   [17] *TMS* VII.iii.i.4.

[18] *Ibid.*   [19] *TMS* I.i.3.1.

urse this process is likely to become a reciprocal one and recognizing the fact structures the encounter. Smith used a vivid musical metaphor to describe it. Each actor sharpens or flattens the pitch of his natural response to the other in order eventually to reach a 'concord' of sentiments.[20] It is a concord which terminates an encounter set in motion by actors who are anxious to experience, once again, the pleasures of mutual sympathy. The encounter has been hedged around by an apprehension of the pain that is felt when it is impossible to offer sympathetic approval of another's actions. It has ended because each actor has come to believe that his imaginative and critical understanding of the behaviour of the other is sufficiently informed and objective to allow him to offer that sympathetic approval he is now pretty sure will be returned. As Smith puts it, 'though they will never be unisons, they may be concords, and this is all that is wanted or required'.[21] Putting it less metaphorically and in Smith's own technical language, the stern capacity for self-command and the more generous and sentimental capacity for humanity have been brought into play in order to allow the two actors to reach a state of mutual sympathy which appeals to their sense of propriety and gives them pleasure because it does so.

And hence it is, that to feel much for others and little for ourselves, that to restrain our selfish, and to indulge our benevolent affections, constitutes the perfection of human nature; and can alone produce among mankind that harmony of sentiments and passions in which consists their whole grace and propriety. As to love our neighbour as we love ourselves is the great law of Christianity, so it is the great precept of nature to love ourselves only as we love our neighbour, or what comes to the same thing, as our neighbour is capable of loving us.[22]

One of the most striking features of Smith's account of sympathy is that while he allows that our natural, or as we would say spontaneous, instincts always incline us to seek the approval of others and to offer our own in return if we possibly can, our imaginative and critical faculties often seem to intervene, holding them in check in order to allow a complex evaluative process to take place before approval is offered. In this respect, the pleasure we get from mutual sympathy smacks as much of the relief we feel when the anxieties generated by the encounter are over as of disinterested or spontaneous pleasure. Smith's discussion of the principles of sympathy in the first part of the *Theory of Moral Sentiments* is devoted exclusively to an examination of this demanding and self-conscious mode of interaction and is designed to highlight the psychological demands that the search for critical understanding and detachment places on men who are nevertheless naturally sociable. His theory takes no account at all of those forms of interaction which are, so to speak, spontaneous and

---

[20] *TMS* I.i.4.7. [21] *Ibid.* Compare this with *TMS* VII.iv.28.
[22] *TMS* I.i.5.5.

non-reflective, in which approval is sought and given uncritically without interruption that the attempt to acquire an imaginative understanding of the situation involves. Indeed, Smith took some trouble to demonstrate that there was scarcely any place for such responses in ordinary social intercourse. For every human passion about which ancient and modern philosophers had philosophized could be regulated by the principles of sympathy. And it is particularly striking that he avoids any discussion of relationships within the family or in simpler and more primitive forms of social organization which might be thought to be activated by less sophisticated principles.[23] Indeed, one of the most striking differences between the social thought of Smith and Adam Ferguson is that the latter continually returns to these simpler and less sophisticated forms of social bonding in an attempt to criticize a theory which he feared would weaken the moral fabric of society and expose it to the forces of luxury and despotism.[24] Ralph Lindgren, using the word in a slightly different context, calls this simpler and unsophisticated form of interaction *empathy* and I shall do the same.[25] As we shall see, the distinction between sympathy and empathy which is implicit in the first part of the *Theory of Moral Sentiments* surfaces in Smith's discussion of commercial versus pre-commercial civilization in the *Lectures on Jurisprudence* and the *Wealth of Nations*. However, the force of the distinction becomes sharper in the later sections of the *Theory of Moral Sentiments* in which Smith sets out to show how the external circumstances of ordinary life in commercial society teach us the hard way to value the warier principles of sympathy more than the simpler principles of empathy. Indeed, Smith's theory is designed to show that the happiness and prosperity that accompany a life of propriety and virtue can only come to those who have managed to escape from a world of empathy by cultivating an understanding of the principles of sympathy.

This becomes clear from Smith's discussion of the impartial spectator which Professor Raphael has suggested may well have been developed some years

---

[23] Smith's only extended discussions of savage morality deal with the remarkable capacity of savage people for stoic forbearance in the face of hideous torture: *TMS* V.2.9–15; VII.ii.1.34–5.

[24] Ferguson's critique of Smith is implicit rather than explicit, and directed towards his discussion of propriety. Ferguson does not deny that spectators and considerations of propriety are of great importance in shaping men's moral sentiments in a commercial age. It is simply that there is more to explaining the principles of social action and morality than this. In his view, moralists like Smith could be criticized for defining happiness in terms of the absence of pain and social anxiety. Ferguson thought that men were capable of experiencing a higher form of happiness which was generated by their aggressive instincts, their love of conflict and their restless search for perfection. This higher and purer form of pleasure could only be fully experienced when it was fully realized that it was an activity which leads men to identify their interests with those of 'groupes', 'communities', 'nations', etc. And it is in experiencing the pure pleasure of empathetic relationships in such groups that men become capable of virtue. On which, see Duncan Forbes's introduction to Ferguson's *History of Civil Society* (Edinburgh, 1966), and D. Kettler, *The Social and Political Thought of Adam Ferguson* (Ohio, 1965), esp. ch. 6.   [25] Lindgren, *Adam Smith*, pp. 21–6.

after the theory of sympathy had first been formulated.[26] His theory is founded on the premise that 'the chief part of human happiness arises from the consciousness of being beloved' and it is designed to consider the paradox that 'we desire both to be respectable and to be respected', 'not only to be loved, but to be lovely; or that thing which is the natural and proper object of love'.[27] And it is Smith's leading contention that while we cannot ever be absolutely sure of winning the approbation of others, we can certainly learn to behave in such a way that we feel we are worthy of it.[28] The desire to be praiseworthy is an acquired, not an innate, need. It is an extension of our desire to achieve an imaginative detachment in our understanding of our own actions as well as those of others.[29] The impartial spectator is a mental construct we invent in order to help us to achieve detachment and understanding in complex social situations which present us with a potentially bewildering variety of possibly conflicting sentiments. At a simple level, impartial spectator is a title we confer on an actual person in an actual situation. Such a man is 'the attentive spectator', 'every reasonable man', 'every impartial bystander', and we deem his approval of our behaviour to be worth all the pain that the disapproval of other spectators will cause us.[30] At a more complex and ambiguous level the impartial spectator seems to lie more within the breast than in the real world – he is 'the real or supposed spectator of our conduct'.[31] At the most complex level of all, he is completely internalized, 'the abstract and ideal spectator',[32] the man, the tribunal or even 'the demi-god within the breast',[33] an ideal spectator whose approval is worth more than the disapproval of every real spectator, whose authority is underwritten by a lively conscience and a system of punishments that is so severe that we prefer the most terrible physical and social torments to the wrath of these 'avenging furies'.[34] For the sake of clarity, I shall call this curious device the man within the breast. He is an *alter ego*, called into existence in response to the rigours of a complex social life. Smith writes of him like this:

When I endeavour to examine my own conduct, when I endeavour to pass sentence upon it, and either to approve or condemn it, it is evident that, in all such cases, I divide myself, as it were, into two persons; and that I, the examiner and judge, represent in a different character from that other I, the person whose conduct is examined into and judged of.[35]

---

[26] D. D. Raphael, 'The Impartial Spectator', in A. S. Skinner and T. Wilson (eds.), *Essays on Adam Smith* (Oxford, 1975), pp. 87–8. See also Campbell, *Adam Smith's Science of Morals*, ch. 6.
[27] *TMS* I.ii.5.1; I.iii.3.2; III.ii.1.
[28] *TMS* III.2.7–8.
[29] *TMS* II.ii.1; III.i.1–7.
[30] *TMS* I.i.1.4; II.i.2.3; II.i.2.2.
[31] *TMS* III.3.20.
[32] *TMS* III.3.38.
[33] *TMS* III.2.31 (note); III.2.33; III.3.4.
[34] *TMS* III.2.9; I.iii.2.10–12.
[35] *TMS* III.1.6. Cf. Smith's characterization of the austere, stoic qualities that the truly virtuous man will possess: 'The man of real constancy and firmness, the wise and just man who has been thoroughly bred in the great school of self-command, in the bustle and business of the

In this carefully-worded metaphor, there is no distinction at all between the socialized and the selfish self. One is as real as the other, each acting as a natural check on the other, each performing that most basic of services 'to keep [us] out of harm's way'.[36]

At this point I would like to consider what I take to be the central assumption of Smith's theory. It is that men's social experience is complex and potentially demanding, requiring specific skills which have to be cultivated and refined in order to maximize the chance of happiness and minimize the chance of the pain a disordered social existence can cause. What is more, according to Smith's theory, it is in the process of acquiring that moral knowledge that we acquire a sense of moral identity. It is the character of that moral world and Smith's concern with the quality of that moral identity that concern me here. As Dugald Stewart first noticed, the theory of the impartial spectator is designed to explain the moral behaviour of those who have learned the hard way that they cannot live happily simply by seeking the approval of actual spectators.[37] No doubt when we are members of tightly-knit familial groups we can be pretty confident that there will never be any serious conflict between our own values and those of the others, and so we are unlikely to think much about the opinions of an impartial spectator. But it is more difficult to know how to act in looser, more complex situations when we are exposed to the company of those we don't know, those whose moral education has been acquired in very different circumstances to our own, and those who may even want to sow the seeds of discord.[38] Such situations encourage us to turn to an impartial spectator for help. Smith never discusses systematically when and how we acquire our moral education. He tells us that it is in the family that we first become aware that we are the objects of attention and learn that self-command is a useful habit to acquire in the search for approval, but he only deals in passing with the social experience we undergo thereafter.[39] However, his language is suggestive;

> world, exposed, perhaps, to the violence and injustice of faction, and to the hardships and hazards of war, maintains this control of his passive feelings upon all occasions; and whether in solitude or in society, wears nearly the same countenance, and is affected very nearly in the same manner. In success and in disappointment, in prosperity and in adversity, before friends and before enemies, he has often been under the necessity of supporting this manhood. He has never dared to forget for one moment the judgement which the impartial spectator would pass upon his sentiments and conduct. He has never dared to suffer the man within the breast to be absent one moment from his intention. With the eyes of this great inmate he has always been accustomed to regard whatever relates to himself. This habit has become perfectly familiar to him. He has been in the constant practice, and, indeed, under the constant necessity, of modelling, or of endeavouring to model, not only his outward conduct and behaviour, but, as much as he can, even his inward sentiments and feelings, according to those of this awful and respectable judge. He does not merely affect the sentiments of the impartial spectator. He really adopts them. He almost identifies himself with, he almost becomes himself that impartial spectator, and scarce even feels but as that great arbiter of his conduct directs him to feel.' (*TMS* III.3.25.)

[36] *TMS* VI.i.1.
[37] Stewart, 'Account of Smith', *EPS*, pp. 287-9.
[38] *TMS* I.ii.4.1.
[39] *TMS* III.3.22; *LJ(A)* iii.5.

outside the family, the capacity for self-command and the rarer capacity for humanity is acquired in 'societies', 'associations', 'companies', 'clubs'. It is the product of the 'ordinary commerce of the world',[40] in which we seek 'the wise security of *friendship*'[41] by means of 'conversation' which helps us to acquire ideas of 'independence' and even of 'liberty'. I shall have more to say about the voluntarist associations of this terminology in due course. Here it is instructive to compare it with its opposite, as it appears in the *Lectures on Jurisprudence* and the *Wealth of Nations*. There, the sociable world of friendship is contrasted with that of the 'tribe', 'clan', 'family' and 'nation'.[42] It is associated with ideas of patriarchal authority and 'dependence' and with the servile values of feudal civilization, of which Smith remarks in a classic aside:

Nothing tends so much to corrupt and enervate and debase the mind as dependency and nothing gives such noble and generous notions of probity as freedom and independency. Commerce is one great preventative of this custom. The manufacturers give the poorer sort better wages than any master can afford; besides it gives the rich an opportunity of spending their fortunes with fewer servants, which they never fail of embracing. Hence it is that the common people of England who are alltogether free and independent are the honestest of their rank anywhere to be met with.[43]

In remarks like these Smith was, of course, contrasting the value system of a commercial and a feudal age. But he was also contrasting a system of social bonding which was based on sympathy with one which was based on empathy, recommending one at the expense of the other. If the *Theory of Moral Sentiments* is seen in this perspective, it appears not simply as an account of moral behaviour in general but as an account of the peculiar moral constraints which are placed on the citizens of a commercial society, and it was offered in the belief that it would help them to learn how to turn their social experience to their advantage as moral agents who were anxious to maximize their happiness and preserve their sense of self-respect.

This is to place Smith's discussion of the principles of sympathy in the context of a discussion about the principles of practical morality which had begun with Addison and Steele's *Tatler* and *Spectator*. Nothing is more characteristic of Addison and Steele's teaching than their recognition that commercial society was bewilderingly complex and potentially disconcerting for ordinary citizens who were simply anxious to know how to lead useful, happy and virtuous lives.[44] In Mr Spectator's world, sociability was a skill to be cultivated and

[40] *TMS* III.3.8.   [41] *TMS* VI.ii.18.
[42] *LJ(A)* ii.1; iii.6–7; iv.9; iv.63–5; iv.112–14.
[43] *LJ(A)* vi.6–7. Smith is at pains to insist on the importance of feelings of equality in generating sympathetic relationships: 'The farmer...considers his servant as almost on an equall with himself [*sic*], and is therefore the more capable of feeling with him' (*LJ(A)* iii.109).
[44] Addison's moral writing has received surprisingly little attention. But see D. F. Bond's introduction to his edition of *The Spectator*, 5 vols. (Oxford, 1965); and also E. A. and L. D. Bloom, *Joseph Addison's Sociable Animal: In the Market Place, on the Hustings, in the Pulpit*

valued for the sake of the ease and sense of ego it could provide. In a commercial age men's appetites were constantly aroused by the bewildering variety of objects that were placed before them. They were constantly in danger of becoming prisoners of fashion and prejudice, creatures of fantasy rather than reason. Mr Spectator taught the absurdity of trying to escape from this world by adopting an austere life of stoic virtue. That was advice fit only for the saint, hero and eccentric; it was of no practical help to the ordinary citizen. He showed that in a commercial society men could only live virtuously by constructing a social world which lay outside the family and away from the world of fashion and affairs. In the coffee-houses, taverns and salons, men from different walks of life confronted each other as friends and equals and learned that conversation which was the instrument that forged the bonds of friendship. By cultivating the arts of conversation and friendship they would learn to value tolerance, detachment, moderation and a respect for the value of consensus as a means of maintaining the bonds of society.

Hume once called Addison's essays 'triffling' and although he owed more to Addison than historians have been accustomed to admit, it is not hard to see why.[45] For one thing, Addison had no developed theory of morals, politics aesthetics or religion. For another he could be accused, quite properly, of confusing the lofty idea of virtue with the more modest idea of propriety. Viewed with Smithian hindsight, Addison could be said to have done little more than admit that men found it surprisingly easy to internalize the values of the world in which they lived, thinking of them as values that they had chosen freely. Like Hume, Smith thought that it was quite improper to think of this as virtue. There was, he wrote, 'a considerable difference between virtue and mere propriety; between those qualities and actions which deserve to be admired and celebrated, and those which simply deserve to be approved of'.[46] In Smithian terms, Addison had merely written about men whose actions were directed by the impartial spectator and not by the man within the breast. No doubt a life lived according to such principles allowed men to acquire ideas of self-respect and independence which were necessary and desirable for the conduct of ordinary life. Indeed, as we shall see, Smith was to argue that one of the principal glories of life in commercial society was that it enabled artisans,

(Providence, Rhode Island, 1971). My discussion of Addison has some affinity with the general interpretation of the history of manners offered by N. Elias in *Über den Prozess der Zivilisation* (Basle, 1939), recently translated under the title *The Civilizing Process: The History of Manners*, trans. E. Jephcott (Oxford, 1978). Elias rather surprisingly ignores Addison.

[45] Hume to William Strahan, 7 February 1772, *Letters of David Hume*, ii, p. 257. See also Phillipson, 'Hume as Moralist: A Social Historian's Perspective'. James Moore's important essay, 'The Social Background of Hume's Science of Human Nature', in D. F. Norton, N. Capaldi and W. L. Robison (eds.), *McGill Hume Studies* (San Diego, Calif., 1979), also deals with Hume's concern with politeness. Moore does not tackle the Addisonian dimension of the question but his analysis is of the greatest relevance to it.

[46] *TMS* I.i.5.7.

shopkeepers and servants as well as men of rank, property and education to live decently according to the principles of propriety. But he was under no illusions about the limitations of a life lived according to the principles of propriety, and he never failed to be struck by the ease with which men could internalize even the most horrible social values, like child-murder, slavery and, more insidiously, an uncritical reverence for wealth and power. This last, 'though necessary both to establish and to maintain the distinction of ranks and the order of society is, at the same time, the great and most universal cause of the corruption of our moral sentiments'.[47] More important, he was struck, as Hume had been, by the ease with which men were able to adopt the values of the class or profession, 'the different orders and societies', to which they belonged.[48] Thus while a careful study of the principles of propriety could transform our understanding of morality, justice, economic and political behaviour, and while they could help men to live happier and more decent lives, it was self-evident that men still possessed ideas of virtue which were, qualitatively, quite different from those of propriety. As Smith put it:

To act according to the dictates of prudence, of justice, and proper beneficence, seems to have no great merit where there is no temptation to do otherwise. But to act with cool deliberation in the midst of the greatest dangers and difficulties; to observe religiously the sacred rules of justice in spite both of the greatest interests which might tempt, and the greatest injuries which might provoke us to violate them; never to suffer the benevolence to our temper to be damped or discouraged by the malignity and ingratitude of the individuals towards whom it may have been exercised; is the character of the most exalted wisdom and virtue.[49]

This was to raise the question of the meaning of virtue and its relation to propriety. If I understand Smith's theory of virtue properly, it was men's capacity to admire 'those qualities and actions which deserve to be admired and celebrated', those astonishing displays of self-command and humanity of which few are capable, that allowed them to check the hold which the principles of propriety exercised over their conduct.[50] The imaginative understanding that was necessary to comprehend the behaviour of those whose lives were directed by the man within the breast; the anxious effort that was involved in acting so as to earn the sympathetic approval of such remarkable men was, Smith thought, the necessary condition to encourage men to convert the moral knowledge they had painstakingly acquired in ordinary life into a moral wisdom. This moral wisdom would stem from a recognition of the limitations of a life lived according to the rules of propriety and an appreciation of the pleasure that was to be derived from a stoic

[47] *TMS* I.iii.1 and 3; V.2.15–16; *LJ(A)* iii.100–1.
[48] *TMS* V.2; Hume, 'Of National Characters', *Philosophical Works*, iii, pp. 244–5.
[49] *TMS* VI.iii.11.
[50] Cf. Lindgren, *Adam Smith*, pp. 48–50, and D. A. Reisman, *Adam Smith's Sociological Economics* (London, 1976), p. 79.

understanding of the moral framework of the social universe. What is more, without such wisdom there could be no virtue.

A disposition to admire and cultivate wisdom and virtue was doubtless admirable and natural even if it was, regrettably, rare.[51] But of what consequence was it to society at large? Was it possible to conceive of a commercial society which was regulated by the principles of propriety alone? This question troubled Smith. His discussion of propriety and virtue in the first and last editions of the *Theory of Moral Sentiments* suggests that he was alert to the problem in 1759, and that it remained with him at the end of his life. But he reserved his consideration of the political dimension of the problem for the *Wealth of Nations*.

III

Smith's thinking about the social structure of commercial society was governed by two principles. The first was contained in his understanding of the economic mechanisms which governed the progress of the division of labour. The second was his belief in the moral value of the process of 'higgling and bargaining' which took place in the market places of a free commercial society. For this was the best means of generating the opulence, freedom and sense of independence and self-respect that men possess when they live their lives according to the principles of propriety.[52] His thinking about social structure rested on his understanding of land, labour and capital, 'the three great, original and constituent orders of every civilized society from whose revenue that of every other order is ultimately derived'.[53] Like Hume, he took it for granted that 'the understandings of the greater part of men are necessarily formed by their ordinary employments',[54] and he thought it absurd to expect ordinary men to see 'that the prosperity and preservation of the state required any diminution of the powers, privileges and immunities of [their] own particular order or society'.[55] Such political wisdom could only be expected from the few. The question was whether the three constituent orders of society could resonably be expected to generate the wisdom necessary to preserve the fabric of a modern commercial polity. Put technically, it was a matter of discovering which men could be expected to have the imaginative and moral resources to be guided by the man within the breast rather than by the impartial spectator.

[51] *TMS* I.iii.3.2.
[52] *WN* I.v.4–6; II.iii.36; III.iv.1–4. Smith had already insisted on this point in passing in *LJ(A)* vi.4–7 and 56–7. There is an excellent summary of his views on persuading and the moral education which can be thus acquired in *TMS* VII.iv.25–8. And his views on the political, moral and cultural consequences of this education are sharply characterized in *LJ(A)* vi.16–24.
[53] *WN* I.xi.p.7.
[54] *WN* V.i.f.50. Cf. *TMS* VI.ii.2.7 – added in 1790. The sentiment is Humean; cf. 'Of National Characters', *Philosophical Works*, iii, pp. 244–58.   [55] *TMS* VI.ii.10.

Characteristically, Smith did not deal at length with the *mentalités* of the three 'great, original and constituent orders'. Nevertheless, it was a subject to which he continually returned in all his writing and always with the problem of identifying those groups with a capacity for political wisdom in mind. In his discussion of the landowners in the *Wealth of Nations*, he distinguished between the nobility and the gentry. He wrote of the former with lofty contempt. They were the descendants of a feudal baronage that had even survived the modern age in Scotland.[56] They had maintained a social system in a state of servile dependence and had eventually frittered away their power in luxury.[57] Nowadays, although their true interest, like that of all landowners, 'is strictly and inseparably connected with the general interest of society', their wealth, their rank, their deplorable education and the deference they commanded had rendered them indolent, uninterested in agricultural improvement and incapable of understanding the relationship the interest their order bore to that of society at large. What was worse, they had no idea at all how best to preserve it.[58] Smith was less contemptuous of the gentry. Although they necessarily shared many of the vices of the great, their limited wealth and modest rank had made them more gregarious, communicative and industrious.[59] Indeed 'a small proprietor...who knows every part of his little territory, who views it with all the affection which property, especially small property, naturally inspires, and who upon that account takes pleasure not only in cultivating but in adorning it, is generally of all improvers the most industrious, the most intelligent and the most successful'.[60] As we shall see, limited wealth, the intelligent husbanding of resources, hard work and sociability marked out the gentry as a class which could be expected to stock part of that 'natural aristocracy' of men of middling rank which was capable of acquiring political wisdom.

Smith also believed that it was impossible for the interests of labour to be at odds with those of society at large, for the wages paid to labour depended upon its economic performance. Nevertheless, he was struck by the labourer's limited understanding of his own interest and that of society at large. '[His] condition leaves him no time to receive the necessary education and his education and habits are commonly such as to render him unfit to judge even though he was fully informed'.[61] Some of the labourers who appear in the *Wealth of Nations* were, however, at least capable of living according to the rules of propriety. Such men were skilled labourers, journeymen and servants,[62] frugal, industrious, God-fearing and literate; if they were lucky, they had also been educated at a Scottish parish school. The rest, however, were, or might

---

[56] *WN* V.iii.89.
[57] *WN* III.iv.5-9. But a new *locus classicus* will surely prove to be *LJ(A)* iv.164-6. Cf. *ibid.*, i.130-2.
[58] *WN* I.xi.p.8.
[59] *WN* IV.ii.21.
[60] *WN* III.iv.19. Cf. III.ii.7 and III.ii.20.
[61] *WN* I.xi.p.9.
[62] *WN* I.viii.36-43.

soon become, brutalized by the excessive division of labour. Their po
the nature of their employment rendered them 'stupid' and 'benumbed' and
they had even lost the capacity for sympathy.[63] They were lost to the world
of sympathy and could only look forward to lives which were governed by the
principles of empathy and dependence.

It was the third order, that of the merchants and manufacturers, which was
responsible for debasing the moral condition of the labouring poor. Its interest,
Smith thought, could never be exactly the same as that of society at large, for
the capitalists' stock was, by its very nature, moveable. As he once remarked,
merchants were not citizens of any particular country.[64] It was the capitalists'
intelligence that seemed to strike Smith most and his remarks about their order
are periodically sharpened by the indignation he felt at high intelligence used
to pervert the public interest.[65] To be sure, some merchants were genuinely
capable of wisdom; such men had invested their profits in land and turned
themselves into country gentlemen, tempering their natural spirit of enterprise
with the natural caution of the landowner. As Smith observed from the vantage
point of his Glasgow years, 'whoever has had the fortune to live in a mercantile
town, situated in an unimproved country, must have frequently observed how
much more spirited the operations of merchants were in this way than those
of mere country gentlemen'.[66] But these only received passing attention. The
rest, animated by 'the wretched spirit of monopoly', sought to exploit the
gullibility of government and the landed classes and the vulnerability of the
poor to construct a commercial system which interrupted the free flow of labour
and capital, distorted the natural price of labour and commodities and even
threatened to unsettle the very foundations of commercial society itself. These
'tribes' of monopolists 'like an overgrown standing army' had become
formidable to government and Parliament.[67] Even when they had been placed
in charge of government, as had happened in India, the spirit of monopoly
had been unchallenged by any sense of the interests of Indian society at large.[68]
As Smith observed in a celebrated passage,

> The proposal of any new law or regulation of commerce which comes from this order,
> ought always to be listened to with great precaution, and ought never to be adopted
> till after having been long and carefully examined, not only with the most scrupulous,
> the most suspicious attention. It comes from an order of men, whose interest is never
> exactly the same with that of the public, who have generally an interest to deceive and
> even to oppress the public, and who accordingly have, upon many occasions, both
> deceived and oppressed it.[69]

[63] *WN* V.i.f.50–1.
[64] *WN* III.iv.24.
[65] See, for example, the critique of the East India Company, *WN* IV.vii.c.
[66] *WN* III.iv.3.
[67] *WN* IV.ii.43.
[68] *WN* IV.vii.c.103; IV.vii.b.11.
[69] *WN* I.xi.10.

Smith's critique of the capitalist and the spirit of monopoly was animated by a desire to legitimize a particular conception of a commercial polity. Its structure was never formally defined but the language Smith used suggests that the values it embodied had some status in the political *mentalité* of his readers. Ralph Lindgren has come nearest to identifying the structure of this model, and what follows owes much to his discussion.[70] Smith's discussion of the progress of opulence hinged on the story of the rise of towns. But it was designed to demonstrate the origins of a set of loosely defined regional economic systems each of which was founded on a dynamic economic, political and cultural relationship between town and country.

The great commerce of every civilized society, is that carried on between the inhabitants of the town and those of the country. It consists in the exchange of rude for manufactured produce, either immediately, or by the intervention of money, or of some sort of paper which represents money. The country supplies the town with the means of subsistence, and the materials of manufacture. The town repays this supply by sending back a part of the manufactured produce to the inhabitants of the country.[71]

In this model the town serves primarily as 'a continual fair or market' for the region, as a source of investment for the surplus wealth of its inhabitants and, most important of all, as a source of order, government

and with them, the liberty and security of individuals, among the inhabitants of the country, who had before lived almost in a continual state of war with their neighbours, and of servile dependency upon their superiors. This, though it has been the least observed, is by far the most important of all their effects. Mr Hume is the only writer who, so far as I know, has hitherto taken notice of it.[72]

Smith was studiously vague in his choice of terminology to describe this regional structure. Significantly he avoided words with narrowly political associations like 'province' or 'country'; the former was reserved almost exclusively for American colonies, Scotland, Ireland and Holland and the regions of France and Spain. The latter was not used at all. 'Country', 'nation' and occasionally 'society' were generally used synonymously with polity. As a rule, however, Smith chose 'society' or, interestingly, 'neighbourhood'. The first carried voluntarist associations and indicated a community regulated by the principles of sympathy. The second recognized the interaction between town and country on which Smith's conception of regionality depended, and was fluid enough to contain the problem of defining the extent of the market system on which its economic life depended. For example, 'there is in every society or neighbourhood an ordinary or average rate both of wages and profit in every different employment of labour or stock'. Or, 'the town, indeed may

---

[70] Lindgren, *Adam Smith*, chs. 5 6, esp. pp. 125 8. Cf. P. J. McNulty, 'Adam Smith's Concept of Alienation', *Journal of the History of Ideas*, 34 (1973), 365.
[71] *WN* III.i.1.   [72] *WN* III.iv.4.

not always derive its whole substance from the country in its neighbourhood, or even from the territory to which it belongs, but from very distant countries and this... has considerable variations in the progress of opulence in different ages and nations'.[73]

Smith's failure to develop a precise vocabulary to discuss regionalism is interesting. He was understandably anxious not to use terms which had political associations. He was clearly anxious to reserve space in his discussion for the sort of region whose economic life depended upon activity which extended beyond the frontiers of its immediate geographical neighbourhood. And, as he demonstrated in his discussion of the corn trade, he knew perfectly well that, in the case of this commodity at least, market mechanisms could only be properly discussed in national rather than in regional terms. Nevertheless, Smith clearly believed that market relationships operating within a regional framework had a significance which was of consequence to the modern civic moralist. As Lindgren has noticed, he assumed that the process of 'higgling and bargaining' that took place within these neighbourhoods would stimulate the sympathetic capacities of men of all ranks, strengthening the sense of independence and deference upon which the stability, opulence and happiness of the nation as well as the neighbourhood depended.[74] Smith's desire to think of a region as more than a market and less than a province raises the question of the exact political meaning he attached to a form of organization which could not be defined in constitutional terms but nevertheless formed the foundation stone upon which the opulence and happiness of ordinary people depended. As we have seen, Smith's regions had no constitutional identity. Nevertheless, his account of the rise of the towns out of which the regions had grown was designed to emphasize their power and their success in establishing and preserving their 'independence'. In the struggle for power between the king and barons the towns '[had arrived] at liberty and independence much earlier than the occupants of land in the country'.[75] In Italy and Switzerland they 'generally became independent republics'.[76] In France and England, although they never became 'entirely independent', they were so 'considerable' that they were untaxable without their consent.[77] In the modern age, the values of the town had penetrated the country, creating a society with a coherent identity based on these principles. And, as we shall see, it was out of such societies that Smith hoped that a class of citizen would emerge which was capable of acquiring political wisdom and exercising it so as to preserve the liberties of a free commercial polity.

There are echoes, no more, no less, in Smith's remarks about regionality which recall the work of Smith's two most influential Scottish predecessors in the field of political writing, Andrew Fletcher of Saltoun and David Hume.

[73] *WN* I.vii.1; III.i.2. Cf. I.xi.b.5 and 11.
[74] See Lindgren, *Adam Smith*, pp. 125-8.
[75] *WN* III.iii.3.
[76] *WN* III.iii.10.
[77] *WN* III.iii.11.

Both writers had bypassed traditional ideas of regionalism based on the parish and county and had presented new models of commercial society which recognized the importance of local power and the interests of local communities in preserving liberty and happiness. Fletcher thought of modern Britain as a country divided into four or five huge militia camps which would be instruments for limiting the power of the crown and releasing the virtue of a citizen class.[78] These camps would be 'the true mothers of cities', to use Hume's important phrase.[79] Their capital cities would become centres of law, government and culture and, according to some of Fletcher's disciples, trade. And they would form the keystone of a 'happy union' between the regions and government.[80] Hume, for his part, had always been anxious to emphasize the necessary 'wonderful mixture of manners and characters in the same nations speaking the same language and subject to the same government'.[81] And his model of a perfect commonwealth insisted on the importance of local communities in the creation of a constitution which would flourish 'for many ages'. It was to this end that he proposed remodelling the institutions of central and local government in order to ensure that 'the counties...are not so independent of each other, nor do they form separate bodies'.[82]

Fletcher and Hume saw the region as a *zoon* in which men could live happily and even acquire a certain sense of virtue by learning how to preserve its independence. It seems not unlikely that Smith, whose debt to Hume's political thought was considerable, conceived of regionality in much the same way. The progress of opulence had created regions which could be defined in market terms but could offer their citizens the chance of living their lives according to the principles of sympathy. No doubt the ideas of justice and the institutions upon which this social system depended were informal in constitutional terms. Nevertheless, their existence could be explained in terms of natural principles and it was only by respecting the sense of regional independence which they aroused that the opulence and happiness of the subject and the liberty of the state could be preserved.

But the wretched spirit of monopoly threatened this pleasing prospect at every level. Monopoly capitalism, by tampering with natural patterns of competition, necessarily threatened the equilibrium of this regional market system. The price of labour and commodities, being determined by forces which lay outside the control of the regional market system, would begin to seem

---

[78] See his 'A Discourse of Government with Relation to Militias' and 'Speeches by a Member of the Parliament which began at Edinburgh the 6th of May, 1703', in Andrew Fletcher, *Selected Writings*, ed. David Daiches (Edinburgh, 1979), pp. 1–26, 67–103.
[79] Hume, *Treatise*, pp. 540–1.
[80] 'Happy Union' was the invention of one of Fletcher's disciples: J. Hodges, *The Rights and Interests of the Two British Monarchies Inquir'd into, and Clear'd with a Special Respect to An United or Separate State* (London, 1703), preface.
[81] 'Of National Characters', *Philosophical Works*, iii, p. 251.
[82] *Ibid.*, pp. 490–1, 493.

arbitrary and contrary to the ideas of fair play and justice upon which sympathetic relationships within a community ultimately depended. Only in the particular case of the corn trade, where the workings of the market discouraged and even prevented the growth of monopoly, could there be any real security that its baneful spirit would be held in check by natural forces.[83]

Smith's problem was whether such a society, whose three natural orders were confined by ideas of propriety, could generate enough political wisdom to preserve its liberty. As we have seen, Smith thought that the imaginative understanding out of which wisdom was born was to be found only among those who had unusual opportunities to exercise their powers of self-command and humanity. In ordinary life that was only to be expected from those who had lived their lives on the margin of different sorts of social existence, for this was the only sort of experience which could teach men the advantage of relying on the man within the breast rather than the impartial spectator. The 'natural aristocracy' which Smith believed had a natural capacity for wisdom were just such men. They were the ambitious, marginally-minded men, educated in the middling and inferior ranks of society, who had been carried forward by their own abilities and industry 'into the highest office' and had presumably escaped the misfortune of becoming dependent on the great.[84] The most significant members of this group were the merchants who had become landed proprietors and were 'the least subject to the wretched spirit of monopoly'.[85]

Given the social and political realities of modern Britain, this meant that Smith pinned what hopes he had for the survival of a free society upon the intelligent and commercially-minded gentry whose very circumstances ensured that they would be responsible to a model of a commercial polity whose regions were far enough from the capital, from 'the great seat of scramble of faction and ambition', to be 'more indifferent and impartial spectators of the conduct of all'.[86] Seen in this perspective, the regions of Britain appear in Smith's model as the impartial spectators of a body politic which was animated by the class-based pursuit of opulence.

[83] *WN* IV.v.b.3-4.
[84] *TMS* I.iii.2.5.   [85] *WN* IV.ii.21.
[86] *WN* V.iii.90. It must be stressed that Smith's use of 'province' to imply regions as well as the colonies, Scotland and Ireland is momentary. Its relevance for this discussion takes its stand on Smith's obvious recollection of Hume's discussion of the problem of controlling the disruptive force of political faction in large and small states and his observation that provinces, remote from centres of power, have an important role in stabilizing large and regionally complex polities. Hume develops this point in 'That Politics may be reduced to a Science' and 'Idea of a perfect Commonwealth'. For a fascinating discussion of the importance of these essays in shaping American political thinking, and that of Madison in particular, see D. Adair, '"That Politics may be reduced to a Science": David Hume, James Madison and the Tenth *Federalist*', *Huntington Library Quarterly*, 20 (1956-7), 343-60. If my own suggestions are tenable, it is interesting to reflect that these two essays serve as sources for Smithian and Madisonian discussions about the structure of a unitary British polity and a federal American polity.

IV

Smith's moral and political writing could be said to be a discourse on the social and ethical significance of face-to-face relationships between independently-minded individuals. His analysis was designed to show how such relationships could be cultivated and how they enabled men to acquire moral sentiments, a sense of justice, a sense of political obligation and even a sense of personal identity. His discussion of commercial society shows how deeply he distrusted social and economic organizations which were too large to be able to support the sense of identity of those who belonged to them. But the face-to-face relationships he admired were the product of sympathy, not empathy, and were sustained by the curiously self-conscious pattern of interaction that the theory of sympathy embodied. As I have already pointed out, sympathetic relationships implied the existence of a system of voluntary relationships which could be described by terms like 'society', 'association', 'club' and so on, rather than by the terminology Smith reserved for the involuntary relationships which governed the life of pre-commercial society. Indeed, Smith's interest in voluntarist terminology recalls Hume's remark that there was no reason why we should not use the club as a model for the moral history of society itself.

But why, in the greater society or confederation of mankind, should not the case be the same as in particular clubs and companies.[87]

The language of eighteenth-century voluntarism has never received the attention it deserves, and my own understanding of it is confined by my Scottish interests.[88] But it is clear that Addison and Steele played a crucial part in its formation. Before the Seven Years' War, that great watershed in eighteenth-century British history, the most popular voluntary institution must have been the sort of club which was modelled on Addison and Steele's Spectator Club. These clubs, which met in the taverns and coffee-houses of countless provincial towns and cities, were small, semi-formal institutions, drawing their members from the ranks of the middling classes of these local communities. Historically, the function of these clubs was to transmit the culture of the metropolis to the provinces, adapting it to local needs and ensuring that it would support and not threaten the sense of identity of increasingly prosperous provincial communities. As such, the Spectator Club was to become an important mechanism in establishing a consensual relationship between court and country to replace the adversary relationships which had soured and unsettled the political life of seventeenth-century Britain. At a

[87] David Hume, *An Enquiry Concerning the Principles of Morals*, ed. L. A. Selby-Bigge, 3rd edn, rev. P. H. Nidditch (Oxford, 1975), p. 281.
[88] The concluding section of this paper is based on my essays 'Culture and Society in the 18th Century Province: The Case of Edinburgh and the Scottish Enlightenment' and 'The Scottish Enlightenment'.

surface level, these clubs were concerned with the niceties of taste and deportment. However, as we have shown, they can also be seen as instruments designed to establish a framework of social relationships governed by the principles of friendship and propriety. As such, they would provide their members with a sense of moral autonomy and a capacity, for what Addison so misleadingly called virtue. To put it another way, the pursuit of propriety had become an alternative to the pursuit of virtue, and the voluntary society and the coffee-house had emerged as an alternative to the *polis* in this world of provincial morality.

This is to suggest that the Addisonian perspective that I have already referred to in the discussion of Smith's moral theory can be extended still further to Smith's moral and political writing as a whole. For he appears as a philosopher who was anxious to inquire into the basis of moral preoccupations which were of consuming interest to many of his contemporaries. At the same time he explored the principles of political economy which underlay the provincial world of spectatorial morality, showing that it was by 'higgling and bargaining' in regional market places, rather than by participating in the activities of voluntary societies that men's ideas of independence were formed. And he was able to show that such activity strengthened the economic as well as the moral fabric of commercial society at large. To put it another way, Smith had substituted a language of political economy for a language of politics and framed it with a new voluntarist language of provincial morality.

Nowhere did the language of eighteenth-century voluntarism take deeper root than in Scotland. The *Tatler* and *Spectator* essays were reprinted in Edinburgh immediately after they had appeared in London, and they were to be discussed and imitated throughout the century by local moralists. Indeed, it is not without significance that the last great exercise in Addisonian moralizing, Henry Mackenzie's *Mirror* and *Lounger*, and the style of moral journalism that was to replace it, Francis Jeffrey's *Edinburgh Review*, were the work of Edinburgh men. Voluntary societies proliferated in the city throughout the century, creating a complex network of sympathetic relationships which extended from an aristocratic social elite through the professions to the population of young, upwardly mobile men of humbler origins which every centre of government and politics necessarily attracts. Some of Edinburgh's clubs and societies were devoted to the improvement of manners *tout court*. But others were devoted to economic engineering and to the pursuit of polite letters. Some, like the Easy Club (1712–16), were small, informal Spectator clubs composed of young men of relatively humble rank. Others, like the Honourable the Society for the Improvement in the Knowledge of Agriculture (1723–45) and the Select Society (1754–64) of which Smith was a founder member, were highly formal societies attracting men of rank, property and position in public life. As I have shown elsewhere, the political and intellectual life of enlightened

Scotland was tightly meshed into this voluntarist social system and it is interesting to notice that its activities were deeply penetrated by a patriotic language as well as by the language of Addisonian voluntarism. For club after club seemed anxious to insist on its importance in preserving the independence of Scotland and releasing the civic virtue of its governing elite in a post-Union world.

In fact this association between the moral language of Addison and a political language which insisted upon the importance of preserving Scottish independence is of some significance. For it marks an important stage in the evolution of a distinctive and curious political language whose structure is of considerable interest to a historian who is anxious to locate Smith's moral and civic discourse in a peculiarly Scottish context. This language has been completely ignored by historians and its history can only be touched on here.[89] It was a variant of a language of virtue and corruption associated with Harrington and the militia controversialists of the 1690s. Its most distinctive characteristic was that the idea of virtue and corruption had, so to speak, been eased apart from its political frame and relocated in a framework of social relationships that were defined in social, economic and cultural terms. And for this, an underdeveloped constitution, an intractable economy and a long history of uncertain Anglo-Scottish relations were responsible. By the time of the Union, Scottish political discourse was more concerned with 'independence' than with 'liberty', and Scotsmen feared 'dependence' on the English more than 'despotism'. Indeed, it was taken for granted that in the modern age, a kingdom without independent provinces could not possibly be said to be free. Independence was an idea with a long history. Its roots lay in the Wars of Independence, the Declaration of Arbroath and the belief that the act of resisting the English by force was enough to release the virtue of the patriotic Scot. By 1707, however, no one wanted to fight the English and no one believed that Scottish 'independence' could possibly be preserved simply by participating in a political process whose structure was defined by an undeveloped and perilously insecure constitution. At the same time it was recognized that Scotland's independence was embodied in a pattern of social relationships

[89] As the essays in this volume demonstrate, there is a lack of agreement about the precise structure of the civic language used by the Scots to discuss the principles of morals, politics and history. My debts to John Pocock and Donald Winch, pioneers in this treacherous field, will be obvious. My approach differs from theirs mainly (although not exclusively) because I see Scottish civic language as a *variant* of the language of virtue and corruption on which their analysis depends. I think that the Scots' concern with politeness and the 'civic potential' of Addisonian moral discourse was the principal instrument employed in resolving the problems contained in the political language they employed to debate the Union question. My disagreement with John Robertson is that although I am in broad sympathy with his understanding of the purely political structure of the Scottish language of virtue and corruption, I do not think his model takes enough account of those modes of economic and cultural activity which the Scots believed were instrumental in shaping the civic personality and determining the structure of a commercial polity in a modern age.

which was better defined in economic and moral than political terms. The conclusions were obvious, if unusual. Scotland's independence could best be preserved by strengthening the economic and moral bonds of Scottish society. And the act of participating in such a process would be sufficient to release the virtue of the patriot.

To discuss Scottish politics in these terms was to suggest a question of profound importance. For it did not necessarily follow that a civilized society was one which had to be defined in terms of its constitution. Nor did it mean that civic virtue need necessarily be defined in terms of participating in a political process. What forced this question into the centre of debate was the offer by the English of what contemporaries called an Incorporating Union which was based on the principle of exchanging Scotland's free political institutions for the right of free access to English markets at home and abroad. This, it was hoped, would stimulate economic growth in Scotland and so help to preserve the country's independence. But what would Scotland's place in such a polity be? And how exactly would her independence be preserved? Political writers had no difficulty in agreeing on the general principles on which this polity should be founded. It would be a limited monarchy which was no more than the sum of the nations which composed it. But while it was assumed that a largely English Parliament would remain the custodian of its laws and liberties, it was nevertheless taken for granted that such an arrangement would only work if law was made and administered on the principle of respecting the political, economic and cultural integrity of its constituent nations. But how could that integrity be guaranteed? For traditionalists like Andrew Fletcher of Saltoun it went without saying that an independent province without a free parliament was a contradiction in terms. Others were less sure. William Seton of Pitmedden and Daniel Defoe, two of the most articulate and intelligent of contemporary writers, saw no reason why Scotland should not remain independent without a parliament providing her governing elite had enough virtue to discover new ways of preserving the economic and moral fabric to guarantee her independence. The astonishing proliferation of voluntary societies devoted to economic engineering and to polite letters was evidence that they were not alone in sharing this view. For these societies appear as spontaneous, pragmatic attempts by virtuously-minded Scotsmen to find para-political alternatives to the old Scots Parliament to undertake the work of preserving Scotland's independence and release their own virtue.

The curious history of this political language suggests that the Scots, in their search for an understanding of the principles of civic morality which was appropriate to their age and circumstances, had been obliged to recognize that the structure of a commercial polity was more complex than conventional political wisdom allowed. But if they had managed to ease virtue from its political base, they had also succeeded in relocating it in a framework of moral and economic relationships. At the same time, their understanding of the moral and economic framework of commercial society was framed by an understanding of the principles of morality which flowed from the voluntaristic principles of Addison. In the process, they had laid the foundations of a language of civic morality which was of peculiar interest to those provincial communities which had sprung up in the commercial age.

When his thought is seen in this context, Smith appears as a moralist who philosophized about a pattern of social relationships and ideas of civic virtue which were deeply embedded in the political language of his own society. No doubt this language was related to that of metropolitan England, but it was subtly different from it, and it was intellectually provocative in a way that the 'vulgar' language of contemporary English politics was not.[90] And if Smith employed it to analyse the foundations of commercial civilization and of civilization itself with a devastating clarity, it is worth remembering, too, that he was also able to employ it as a moralist who was anxious to remind the political community at large that provincial propriety was embodied in a *mentalité* on which the opulence, liberty, wisdom and virtue of commercial civilization might depend.

[90] I use Duncan Forbes's excellent phrase. D. Forbes, 'Sceptical Whiggism, Commerce and Liberty', in Skinner and Wilson, *Essays on Adam Smith*, pp. 179-201.

8 The legal needs of a commercial society: the jurisprudence of Lord Kames*

DAVID LIEBERMAN

I

Even in his own lifetime, Lord Kames often appeared to have earned greater distinction as a patron and publicist for the Enlightenment in Scotland than as one of its leading philosophical spokesmen. 'He did more to promote the interests of *belles lettres* and philosophy in Scotland than all the men of law had done for a century before', reported John Ramsay of Ochtertyre; and this achievement alone entitled him to a 'distinguished place' in any review of Scottish letters during the period.[1] Kames's own literary output was of course prodigious, both in size and range of subject matter, spanning a publication period of over fifty years and comprising nearly half as many volumes. Yet even in his most impressive works, the philosopher–judge rarely achieved the concentrated philosophical depth of Hume or Smith, or the stylistic grace of Robertson. It is perhaps indicative of the general character of his publications that only the *Elements of Criticism*, the study of aesthetics for which Kames received greatest contemporary acclaim, has managed to sustain critical scrutiny for its theoretical merits; while the rest of his corpus has generally attracted more loosely historical consideration, as a representative product of that aggressive cultivation of the intellect which we have come to term the Scottish Enlightenment.[2]

* I am indebted to J. H. Burns, Istvan Hont and Michael Ignatieff for their generous comments and criticisms of this paper; my preliminary research was supported by research fellowships from the American Bar Foundation and the Institute of Historical Research, University of London.

[1] J. Ramsay of Ochtertyre, *Scotland and Scotsmen in the Eighteenth Century*, ed. Alexander Allardyce, 2 vols. (Edinburgh, 1888), i, p. 179. Adam Smith may have had the same achievement in mind when he offered the handsome, if possibly ambiguous, compliment, 'we must every one of us acknowledge Kames for our master'; cited in I. S. Ross, *Lord Kames and the Scotland of his Day* (Oxford, 1972), p. 97.

[2] For the literature on Kames's *Elements of Criticism*, see Ross, *Lord Kames*, pp. 261–2n. Ross also provides the most complete bibliography of Kames's published works. In addition to his study, there is another recent biography by W. C. Lehmann, *Henry Home, Lord Kames, and the Scottish Enlightenment* (The Hague, 1971). Considerable additional material is also provided in A. F. Tytler, Lord Woodhouselee, *Memoirs of the Life and Writings of the Honourable Henry Home of Kames, one of the senators of the College of Justice, and one of the lords commissioners of judiciary in Scotland: containing sketches of the progress of literature and general improvement in Scotland during the greater part of the eighteenth century*, 2 vols. (Edinburgh, 1807).

This study examines Kames's legal thought, particularly as developed in his *Historical Law Tracts* and *Principles of Equity*.[3] Both works stem from the most dramatic period of Kames's long and active public career, the years circumscribed by the 1751 publication of the *Essays on the Principles of Morals and Natural Religion* and the appearance in 1762 of the *Elements of Criticism*. It was during these years that Kames received appointment to the Court of Session, effectively promoted the academic fortunes of Smith and John Millar, and weathered the threat of excommunication at the hands of the Evangelical Party in the General Assembly. During this period his published works were still untouched by the exasperating readiness to discourse upon virtually any subject at virtually uncontrollable length.

Kames's contributions to legal scholarship, moreover, represent the most substantial part of his literary production and provided the setting in which he could display the greatest professional competence and interpretative skill. And it was in these works, notably in the *Historical Law Tracts*, that Kames first revealed the same general sociological interests exhibited by Smith in the *Lectures on Jurisprudence* or Millar in *The Origin of the Distinction of Ranks*. It is characteristic of Kames's approach that when he wrote of the need to establish law as a 'rational science' suitable for 'every person who has an appetite for knowledge', he referred to a twofold task of having the law's 'principles unfolded' and its 'connection with manners and politics' surveyed.[4] That Kames should have presented 'manners and politics' as a required topic for a rational, scientific treatment of law will by now perhaps seem unsurprising; for much of the recent work on the eighteenth-century Scottish philosophers has drawn attention to the juridical context from which their moral and social theories emerged.[5] Indeed, one of the earliest accounts of Scottish philosophical history, supplied by one of its most striking practitioners, was similarly concerned to identify its origins in legal speculation. Thus, John Millar in the *Historical View of English Government* depicted the researches of Montesquieu, Smith and Kames as an attempt to refashion the natural law theory of Grotius and his successors as a 'natural history of legal establishments'. To this end, 'speculative lawyers' were led to examine 'the first formation and subsequent advancement of civil society', the 'development and cultivation of arts and sciences', the 'acquisition and extension of property in all its different modifications', and their 'combined influence' upon 'the manners and customs, the institutions and laws of any people'.[6]

[3] The *Historical Law Tracts* was first published in two volumes in Edinburgh in 1758 and reached a fourth edition in 1792. Quotations here are from the first edition, hereafter cited as *Law Tracts*. The *Principles of Equity* was published in Edinburgh in 1760. Quotations here are from the expanded second edition of 1767, hereafter cited as *Equity*.

[4] Kames, *Elucidations respecting the Common and Statute Law of Scotland* (Edinburgh, 1777), p. xiii.

[5] See, in particular, Duncan Forbes, *Hume's Philosophical Politics* (Cambridge, 1975), pp. 3–90; and Donald Winch, *Adam Smith's Politics* (Cambridge, 1978), pp. 46–69.

[6] J. Millar, 'The Progress of Science relating to Law and Government', *An Historical View of the English Government*, 4th edn, 4 vols. (London, 1812), iv, pp. 284–5.

If Kames's legal writings thus identify him with a broader tradition of Scottish social theorizing, what distinguished his studies was a special concern to bring moral theory and philosophical history to bear on the technical detail of Scots law; or what Hume in an often quoted letter to Smith sceptically identified as the attempt to make 'an agreeable Composition by joining Metaphysics & Scotch Law'.[7] This effort, in turn, relates his legal publications to another major intellectual enterprise of eighteenth-century Scotland. This was the process by which Scots law received its first systematic exposition in textbook form, what legal historians describe as the 'classical' or 'institutional' period of Scottish legal development. As Peter Stein has pointed out, although the philosophers and institutional law writers occupied overlapping scholarly provinces and regularly drew upon the same legal authorities in their works, there appears to have been little direct intellectual commerce between the groups.[8] Kames, however, ignored this division of scholarly labour and contributed prolifically to both traditions. The point was nicely captured by William Smellie when he placed Kames alongside Hume and Smith in his *Literary and Characteristical Lives*, and then went on to praise the judge's 'law writings' by noting, inaccurately, that they enjoyed the same status 'as those of Coke and Blackstone in the courts of England'.[9]

The more technical character of Kames's law studies plainly reflects his professional position. In this sense, the contrast between his researches and those of Smith and Millar can be posed in terms of the differing concerns of a Session judge and a university professor. But the contrast also reflects another crucial matter, that of Kames's unrivalled devotion to the cause of Scots law reform. As his protégé and first biographer, Alexander Fraser Tytler, stressed, Kames 'was sensible that the Law in Scotland was in many of its branches in a state of great imperfection'; and this awareness, as Tytler further perceived, deeply coloured his interests 'in the science of General Jurisprudence'.[10]

In the discussion here special emphasis is given to the manner in which Kames related his legal and historical researches to this concern for legal improvement in Scotland. One reason for adopting this approach is to highlight that part of Kames's jurisprudence which was directed at an

---

[7] Hume to Smith, 12 April 1759, *Letters of David Hume*, ed. J. Y. T. Greig, 2 vols. (Oxford, 1932), i, p. 304.

[8] See P. Stein, 'Law and Society in Eighteenth-Century Scottish Thought', in N. T. Phillipson and R. Mitchison (eds.), *Scotland in the Age of Improvement* (Edinburgh, 1970), p. 159; and P. Stein, 'The General Notions of Contract and Property in Eighteenth-Century Scottish Thought', *Juridical Review*, N.S., 8 (1963), 1-2, 10. For an introductory account of the Scottish 'institutional' legal authorities, see A. C. Black, 'The Institutional Writers 1600–1826', in *An Introductory Survey of the Sources and Literature of Scots Law*, Stair Society Publications, i (Edinburgh, 1936), pp. 59–69, and T. B. Smith, *British Justice: The Scottish Contribution* (London, 1961), pp. 1-21.

[9] W. Smellie, *Literary and Characteristical Lives* (Edinburgh, 1800), p. 128.

[10] Tytler, *Life of Kames*, i, p. 156.

examination of the character of law in a specifically commercial society, thereby making it possible to view his legal ideas as another substantial contribution to the Scottish exploration of civil society in its commercial form. But it is also hoped that this perspective might illuminate another question raised by several of the contributors to this volume: the question of recovering the historical identity of a distinctly Scottish preoccupation with considering man's moral and social nature in terms of the operation and advance of civil society. Kames's writings provide a formidable indication of the more practical, if cruder, implications of this sort of sociologically informed moral philosophy. And this further suggests that the attempt to account for the emergence and appeal of this style of social inquiry should consider not only its attractions for the self-consciously detached examiner of human nature, but also its usefulness for a pragmatic and impatient reforming judge. Such an approach, in itself, could never hope to capture so complex and diverse a prize as eighteenth-century Scottish social theory. But, at the least, it points to the value of considering what happened to this social theory at the hands of the philosopher whose commitment to Scottish improvement, in Ramsay's apt phrase, 'was almost apostolical'.[11]

Kames introduced his *Historical Law Tracts* with a clear and aggressive call for an historical examination of legal subjects. 'Law in particular', he maintained, became 'only a rational study when it is traced historically, from its first rudiments among the savages, through successive changes, to its highest improvements in civilized society'. And, given his further claim that legal studies were 'seldom conducted in this manner', it becomes important not to mistake the novelty of this methodological declaration. Kames himself cited Bolingbroke's corresponding judgement that law would never 'deserve to be ranked among the learned professions' until lawyers abandoned 'the little arts of chicane' and ascended to the higher 'vantage ground' of 'historical knowledge'. Bolingbroke, in turn, had supported the claim by invoking the instructive examples of Bacon and Clarendon;[12] and historical speculations were already a common and prominent feature of much of the legal literature produced in Britain throughout this period. Such attention to legal history resulted, in England at least, from the continued ideological importance ascribed to representing the fundamentals of the legal system as a body of ancient laws and ancient customs. But it also reflected a more mundane recognition of the difficulty confronting any attempted exposition of current legal practices which ignored matters of historical origins and development. As an English lawyer confidently explained in 1774, 'an infinite number of questions receive the only light they are capable of from the reflection of history...it is necessary to know the original of the matter in question,

[11] Ramsay, *Scotland and Scotsmen*, i, p. 195.
[12] *Law Tracts*, i, pp. v, xi.

what the present state of things succeeded, and what has been its progress'.¹³

Probably the most influential example of this use of legal history is found in Blackstone's *Commentaries on the Laws of England,* which originated in a set of lectures Blackstone first delivered at Oxford some five years before the appearance of Kames's *Law Tracts.* The design of these lectures, as of the four-volume *Commentaries* which succeeded them, was to provide 'a general map of the law' in England for the student beginning his legal training and the general reader.¹⁴ In surveying this legal terrain Blackstone regularly turned to historical considerations to account for its peculiar landmarks and highly technical boundaries, on occasion introducing these historical explanations in explicit repudiation of the unhistorical accounts advanced by earlier legal authorities.¹⁵ Moreover, Blackstone was prompt to draw upon the researches of Scottish historians such as Hume, Robertson and Kames to support his more general comments on England's legal development. Nonetheless, Blackstone's exploitation of these sources did not bar him from perpetuating in the *Commentaries* many of the most insular and dubious specimens of conventional English historiography. Thus, for example, he treated trial by jury as an ancient common law right, insisted that William I had not ruled by right of conquest, and presented Magna Carta as a straightforward confirmation of Saxon liberties.¹⁶ Nor did Blackstone's concern with matters of historical development extend much beyond the immediate task of delineating the contemporary system of law in England.¹⁷

On both these points Blackstone's position contrasts with that of the Scottish

---

¹³ [Edward Wynne], *Eunomus: or, Dialogues concerning the Law and Constitution of England,* 4 vols. (London, 1774), i, pp. 59–60.

¹⁴ W. Blackstone, *Commentaries on the Laws of England,* 9th edn, ed. R. Burn, 4 vols. (London, 1783), i, p. 35; hereafter cited in the form 1 *Comm.* 35.

¹⁵ See, for example, Blackstone's treatment of the rule of inheritance that estates 'shall lineally descend' but 'never lineally ascend', where he insists that it is necessary to 'consider the time and occasion of introducing the rule' to show 'it to have been grounded upon very substantial reasons', and rejects the 'quaint' explanation 'of Bracton, adopted by Sir Edward Coke, which regulates the descent of lands according to the laws of gravitation' (2 *Comm.* 211–12).

¹⁶ Blackstone, 4 *Comm.* 414 (on trial by jury); 2 *Comm.* 48–51 (on William I's title); 4 *Comm.* 420–5 (on Magna Carta). For the political significance of Blackstone's historical treatment of these and related topics, see Forbes, *Hume's Philosophical Politics,* pp. 251–3.

¹⁷ Despite Blackstone's many comments on England's political and constitutional history, most of the historical writing in the *Commentaries* is directed at more restricted matters such as forms of action, common law remedies, judicial procedures and the like. A characteristic example is found in Blackstone's concluding remarks on 'our system of remedial law'. There he seeks to explain how the common law judges transformed the 'old feudal actions' after the decay of the 'military tenures' so as to accommodate the succeeding 'commercial mode of property' which required 'a more speedy decision of right to facilitate exchange and alienation'. Blackstone, in these remarks, seems to indicate that the process reflected major changes in English society as a whole. Still, the point of the account was to explain the 'system of remedial law' and not the historical changes themselves, and Blackstone does not attempt to relate this episode directly to concurrent changes in other parts of the legal system; 3 *Comm.* 265–8.

'speculative lawyers' and philosophical historians, Kames included. Still, it is easy to exaggerate the contrast; and in the case of Kames's earliest historical law studies, what seems to distinguish his efforts is the sophistication with which he handled his sources, rather than any distinctive conception of the historical approach to legal practices. A useful example of this is contained in his 1747 collection of *Essays on Several Subjects concerning British Antiquities*, where Kames explored the well-rehearsed arguments regarding the introduction of feudal law in Scotland. In opposition to legal orthodoxy, Kames argued for a later dating of the development, in part relying on the seventeenth-century researches of Spelman and Craig for the suggested revisions. However, the critical insight he brought to the discussion rested on the claim that the introduction of feudal tenures evinced an increase of royal power at the expense of the nobles, and that therefore it was mistaken to treat the phenomenon as an isolated event or as a result of a mutually advantageous agreement between king and nobles.[18] If this insight enabled Kames to formulate a less narrowly legalistic scenario for the introduction of feudal law, it in turn contrasts with the richer, more generally sociological explanation unveiled by Smith in the *Lectures On Jurisprudence*. There Smith likewise emphasized the manner in which a full extension of feudal tenures entailed a weakening of the position of the great lords. But he presented this change in landholding as part of a broader system of connected social developments which he characterized as the transition from allodial to feudal government.[19]

With Smith's treatment of the issue it becomes easier to discern a rather different notion of an historical approach to legal practices, such as that which Millar identified in the enterprises of the natural historians of legal establishments or which Kames in the *Historical Law Tracts* believed capable of placing legal studies on an altogether new footing. Whereas other writers, such as Blackstone, were concerned to deploy historical data in order to explicate individual, if extensive, features of the existing legal system, Smith was concerned with the way in which changes in the law reflected larger processes in society's development. And whereas Blackstone turned to legal history because of the complexity of England's legal inheritance, Smith turned to legal practices because of the law's predominance as an historical source and because of its special value as an indicator of the character of man's social nature at a particular stage of society's advance. Smith's inquiry into the history of legal practices thus centred on the question of the general progress of civil society, what Duncan Forbes has taught us to recognize as 'the hall-mark and organizing principle of Scottish "philosophical" history'.[20]

Furthermore, it is in the light of this special concern with the progress of

---

[18] Kames, *Essays upon Several Subjects concerning British Antiquities composed anno 1745*, 3rd edn (Edinburgh, 1763), pp. 19–23.
[19] Smith, *LJ(A)* iv.114–34.   [20] Forbes, *Hume's Philosophical Politics*, p. 298.

civil society as a whole that Kames's more ambitious pronouncements regarding the purposes served by an historical consideration of the law can best be regarded. In these comments, he advanced from the slightly unspectacular claim that history would render legal studies rational to the more radical doctrine that the law itself could be judged rational in terms of its historical aspect. In this sense the lawyer needed to become sensitive to history since this provided the proper means for assessing the merits of any particular system of law:

The law of a country is in perfection when it corresponds to the manners of the people, their circumstances, their government. And as these are seldom stationary, the law ought to accompany them in their changes. An institute of law accordingly, however perfect originally, cannot long continue so... The knowledge, therefore, of the progress of law and of its innovations is essential...[21]

Kames, as we shall see, was quick to point out how this understanding of 'the progress of law' bore on the issue of legal improvement. But, aside from these polemical considerations, he was equally aware that this understanding furnished an indispensable heuristic device for treating the inconsistencies and irregularities manifest in virtually all systems of national jurisprudence. This was a feature of legal rules which Scottish and English commentators regularly acknowledged as a peculiarly pressing problem for legal theory, given the shared and commonplace emphasis on the clarity and certainty of those natural moral principles upon which legal rules were held ultimately to be based. If, as Kames alleged, the dictates of natural justice were 'simple and clear' even to the 'most ignorant', then it became rather unclear why the legal obligations to which they related should be so complex and confusing even to the most enlightened.[22] Or, as William Paley expansively observed, 'why since the maxims of natural justice are few and evident' and 'the principles of the law of nature...simple' and 'sufficiently obvious', should there 'exist nevertheless in every system of municipal laws...numerous uncertainties and acknowledged difficulty'?[23]

Kames's response was to insist that the matter demanded historical scrutiny. The progress of society, in other words, provided the framework for explaining the various ways in which particular nations had translated moral imperatives into positive duties, and the particular history of any given state could account for the disparate and contradictory elements in its legal system. He developed the point in one of his first collections of Session decisions, an appropriate

---

[21] Kames, *Select Decisions of the Court of Session, from the Year 1752 to the Year 1768*, 2nd edn (Edinburgh, 1799), p. iii.
[22] Kames, 'Principles and Progress of Morality', *Sketches of the History of Man*, 4th edn, 4 vols. (Edinburgh, 1788), iv, pp. 80–1; hereafter cited as *Sketches*.
[23] W. Paley, *The Principles of Moral and Political Philosophy* (London, 1785), p. 511.

setting since few legal sources provided such vivid evidence of the irregularity and complexity of positive laws as an edition of historical law reports. Kames nevertheless insisted that there would be found 'little clashing among our decisions', particularly in the light of the fact that Scots law was 'scarce past its infancy'. To demonstrate this he distinguished between genuine '*antinomies* of law' and those 'opposite decisions in different ages' which resulted necessarily from 'an alteration of circumstances'. To adopt his own example, in former periods the courts refused to admit the testimony of 'moveable tenants' on behalf of their masters, whereas 'at present they are admitted'. The apparent inconsistency simply reflected the fact that in earlier periods the 'common people of Scotland were little better than slaves'. Now they were 'more independent', and thus their testimony was no longer biased on account of their 'want of safety'. Such cases, he concluded, 'cannot be reckoned among the *antinomies* of the law; on the contrary, the law of that country is wrong which does not accommodate itself to the fluctuating manners of the people'.[24]

Kames's concluding point was aimed directly at the law of Scotland, and reveals a final purpose served by legal history. This was to indicate the need for legal change by demonstrating the antiquated nature of inherited legal practices. John Pocock has noted in general of the Scottish 'sociological historians' that their 'great achievement' lay in 'the recognition that a commercial society had rendered obsolete much that had been believed about society before'.[25] The corollary to this in Kames's case was the recognition that commercial society had rendered the historic Scots law inadequate to its present social purposes. When Tytler observed Kames's preoccupation with the imperfections in Scots law, he pointed out that this referred both to those legal doctrines which were 'irreconcilable to principle', and to the many others 'which originally had their foundation in expediency' but had become 'to the lapse of time... both inexpedient and contrary to material justice'.[26] Kames was thus concerned to marshal his historical discussion of legal practices to the cause of legal improvement. Indeed, as Peter Stein suggests, the limits of his historical vision were generally set by his reforming ambitions.[27] As Kames declared in one such work, in phrases more often associated with Bentham, 'my intention is only to give examples of reasoning, free from the shackles of authority. I pretend not to say what our law is, but what it ought to be.'[28]

Having observed the procedures Kames advised for a correct examination of legal practices, it is also necessary to consider his moral theory before turning to the substance of his legal doctrines. He presented a system of ethics inspired

[24] Kames, *The Decisions of the Court of Session, from its first Institution to the present Time, abridged and digested under proper Heads, in Form of a Dictionary*, 2 vols. (Edinburgh, 1741), i, p. iii.
[25] J. G. A. Pocock, 'Machiavelli, Harrington and English Political Ideologies in the Eighteenth Century', in *Politics, Language and Time* (London, 1972), p. 146.
[26] Tytler, *Life of Kames*, i, p. 156.
[27] Stein, 'Law and Society', p. 158.
[28] Kames, *Elucidations respecting the Law of Scotland*, p. xiii.

principally by Hutcheson's moral theory.[29] Man was viewed as a hedonistic creature for whom morally correct actions were agreeable and vicious actions disagreeable. Man discerned the moral character of actions through his '*moral sense* or *conscience*'; and the dictates of this moral sense could be construed as laws of nature, which for Kames included notions of divine purposes and final causes. The content of morally correct actions, moreover, could be specified in consequentialist terms:

> The general tendency of right actions is to promote the good of society, and of wrong actions, to obstruct that good. Universal benevolence is indeed not required of man...But for promoting the general good, everything is required of him that he can accomplish.[30]

One of the critical features of this ethical theory for Kames's jurisprudence was the distinction drawn between actions which were morally just and those which were simply morally correct. Justice related to situations of perfect rights and correlative duties, and entailed a precise moral imperative. As Kames explained, 'right actions are distinguished by the moral sense into two kinds, what *ought* to be done and what *may* be done, or left undone'. In the former case, the individual found himself under 'the necessity' to act which 'is termed *duty*'. Such duties implied 'a *right* in some person to exact performance of that duty'; and this in turn distinguished just actions from other virtuous actions: 'Duty is twofold; duty to others and duty to ourselves. With respect to the former, the doing what we ought to do is termed *just*: the doing what we ought not to do, and the omitting what we ought to do, are termed *unjust*.'[31]

The best known, and indeed most articulate, formulation of this notion of justice was advanced by Smith in *The Theory of Moral Sentiments*. And it is of some interest that Smith drew attention to Kames's theory when distinguishing justice from beneficence.[32] This distinction impinged on legal theory at several crucial points. First, because justice was unlike other moral virtues, the rules of justice were susceptible to precise formulation in a manner inapplicable to other moral precepts. Thus Kames presented the dictates of justice as three specific rules derived from the fundamental principle not to harm the innocent: the duty of veracity; the duty to perform promises and covenants; and the duties created by special relationships, as those between parent and child.[33] In legal theory, it was vital to observe this distinction, and not treat all moral questions in terms of those precise rules which were actually relevant only to

---

[29] Kames presented three versions of his moral theory, in *Essays on the Principles of Morality and Natural Religion* (Edinburgh, 1751); *Principles of Equity*, 2nd edn (Edinburgh, 1767); and *Sketches of the History of Man*, 1st edn (Edinburgh, 1774). The account and quotations below are taken from the fourth edition of the *Sketches* (1788), which contains the 'Last Additions and Corrections of the Author', and can thus be said to provide Kames's final views on the subject.
[30] 'Principles and Progress of Morality', *Sketches*, iv, pp. 10–14, 78–94, 46.
[31] *Ibid.*, pp. 14–15.   [32] *TMS* II.ii.1.4–2.4.
[33] 'Principles and Progress of Morality', *Sketches*, iv, pp. 31–9.

the consideration of justice. According to Smith, the failure to observe the distinction had undermined all previous attempts to elaborate natural systems of jurisprudence, which in consequence had degenerated into casuistry.[34]

Secondly, the distinction between justice and other virtues also regarded the historical treatment of legal practices. For although justice, in Smith's famous phrase, was merely a 'negative virtue' which could often be fulfilled 'by sitting and doing nothing', it was indispensable for any social existence.[35] 'Without it', wrote Kames, 'society could never have existed', and 'here the moral sense is inflexible'.[36] Thus any society would provide some mechanism, if only an elementary, retributive one, for the preservation of 'natural' justice. But with regard to other moral actions, the moral sense was more pliant, and itself developed with the progress of society. As Kames maintained, 'the moral sense is born within us', yet 'require[s] much cultivation'. 'Among savages' it was 'faint and obscure', and only slowly and never inevitably progressed 'toward maturity'.[37] Accordingly, the standards for morally correct behaviour would vary considerably between nations, and between the historical epochs of a single nation. Therefore, the law, which had 'to accommodate itself to the fluctuating manners of the people', would likewise vary according to the progressive refinement of the moral sense.

Finally, because justice was an absolute prerequisite for any effective social existence, and because the maintenance of justice furthered 'the general good of mankind' more effectively than any other virtue, its profound social utility could be clearly and easily discerned. But for Kames, like Smith and in contrast to Hume, this did not mean that justice could be explained in entirely utilitarian or consequentialist terms. Rather, doing justice remained an immediate and uncalculated response to the moral sense.[38]

Kames thus approached legal theory equipped with two main philosophical doctrines: an ethical theory which indicated the need to promote 'the general good' of society; and a theory of historical development which enabled him to evaluate the relative suitability of legal practices to a particular society. His *Historical Law Tracts* can be read as an extended and critical application of these principles, for which his first tract on the 'History of the Criminal Law' provides an excellent case in point.

Kames began the history by maintaining that the criminal law must ultimately derive from some law of nature. This he identified with the natural passion for 'revenge' which invariably followed 'injury or voluntary wrong';

---

[34] *TMS* VII.iv.7–15, 34. See also Millar, 'Of Justice and Generosity', *Historical View*, iv, pp. 235–6, and 'The Progress of Science relating to Law and Government', pp. 267–72.
[35] *TMS* II.ii.1.10; and see II.ii.3.1–6.
[36] 'Principles and Progress of Morality', *Sketches*, iv, p. 33.
[37] 'Origin and Progress of Arts', *Sketches*, i, pp. 196–7; and see also 'Principles and Progress of Morality', *Sketches*, iv, pp. 127–90.
[38] 'Principles and Progress of Morality', *Sketches*, iv, pp. 45–6, 80–3.

the right of the injured to 'revenge' such wrongs being construed as 'a privilege bestowed by the Law of Nature'. Since this privilege obtained in cases of injustice, 'the first Law of Nature regarding society, that of abstaining from injuring others' was 'enforced by the most efficacious sanctions'.[39]

The natural system for revenging wrongs could operate because of the shared moral consciousness of the offender and his victim. Indeed, for the 'passion' of resentment to be 'fully gratified', 'the person injured must inflict the punishment' and 'the criminal must be made sensible not only that he is punished for his crime, but that the punishment proceeds from the person injured'.[40] But while man's shared moral sense made this possible, the natural system itself was deeply flawed, particularly when viewed in terms of social harmony. It was likely that the morally conscious offender and his morally conscious victim would disagree over the infamy of the crime and the appropriate degree of revenge. Even if such disputes did not ensue, there was always something socially disruptive in this sort of natural vigilanteism. Hence, Kames argued that government could 'never fully attain its end where punishment in any measure is trusted in private hands'. But given the essentially private nature of natural punishment, the required shift from personal revenge to criminal law entailed 'a revolution...contrary to the strongest propensity of human nature'. It could therefore only occur through 'slow' and 'gradual' 'progressive steps', and could only be explained historically in terms of more general social development.[41]

Kames pointed to two particular steps which enabled governments to appropriate the business of punishing. The first related to the several expedients adopted for the direction of personal revenge. Most noteworthy among these was the appearance of 'primitive magistrates' who assisted in the identification of criminals. Punishment itself remained the exclusive right of the injured party.[42] More important was the second step: the emergence of fluid forms of property which accompanied the economic advance of agrarian societies. This enabled individuals to substitute pecuniary compensation for corporal punishments, a process which greatly facilitated the socialization of revenge. By 'the temptation of money' men were led 'to stifle their resentments', and this served as a 'fine preparation for transferring the power of punishment to the magistrate'.[43] The magistrate began punishing still later, when a positive sense of a community interest allowed for the recognition of social crimes, such as disturbing the king's peace, for which there was no assignable victim. As these offences lacked individual victims, the magistrate himself was called upon to punish the criminal. Once this was achieved, the magistrate's role was

---

[39] 'History of the Criminal Law', *Law Tracts*, i, pp. 6–7. Kames's history of the criminal law closely parallels Smith's discussion in the *Lectures on Jurisprudence*; see esp. *LJ(A)* ii.94–104, 144–55; iv.25–9.
[40] 'History of the Criminal Law', p. 10.   [41] *Ibid.*, p. 31, and see too p. 64.
[42] *Ibid.*, pp. 37–40.   [43] *Ibid.*, pp. 54–5.

extended to punishing purely private wrongs 'by imagining every atrocious crime to be a public as well as a private injury'. And thus punishment ceased to be a matter of private action altogether.[44]

With regard to the public administration of punishment, Kames again pointed to several separate stages of historical development. At first magistrates inflicted light pecuniary fines owing to the weakness of public government. Then, as government gained in authority, it exacted heavier penalties including corporal punishments. Finally, 'when a people have become altogether tame and submissive, under a long and steady administration, punishments being less and less necessary, [they] are generally mild and ought always to be so'. Moreover, since punishment had now fully evolved into a public institution with primarily social purposes, and since Britain was 'tame and submissive', it became proper to model the criminal law (and generally to reduce penalties) in accordance with these social circumstances. Hence, Kames concluded his history by rehearsing the arguments for criminal law reform presented by Montesquieu, and soon to be developed systematically by Beccaria and Bentham:

To preserve a strict proportion betwixt a crime and its punishment is not the only or chief view of a wise legislator. The purposes of human punishments are, first, to add weight to those which nature has provided, and next, to enforce municipal regulations intended for the good of society... Hence in regulating the punishment of crimes, two circumstances ought to weigh, *viz.* the immorality of the action, and its bad tendency, of which the latter appears the capital circumstance; for this evident reason, that the peace of society is an object of much greater importance, than the peace, or even the life, of many individuals.[45]

The reaction in Scotland and England to this examination of the criminal law offers a revealing commentary on the special character of Kames's discussion: the commitment to an analysis of law based on an account of society's development, and the case for legal change generated by this approach. Dugald Stewart, for example, in describing the Scottish advances in '*theoretical or conjectural history*' which followed Montesquieu's seminal contributions, promptly cited the 'excellent specimens' of the genre produced by 'Lord Kames in his *Historical Law Tracts*', and singled out the essay on the history of criminal law for special recommendation.[46]

But it was not the method of Kames's inquiry so much as the ease with which his conclusions could be assimilated within the arguments for criminal law reform that attracted the interests of such English reformers as William Eden

---

[44] *Ibid.*, pp. 56–61.
[45] *Ibid.*, pp. 72–5. The consequentialist features of this formula are qualified by Kames's distinction between 'punishment' and 'reparation' which regards the question of intentionality; see 'Principles and Progress of Morality', *Sketches*, iv, pp. 66–78.
[46] Dugald Stewart, 'Account of the Life and Writings of Adam Smith LL.D', *EPS*, pp. 294–5.

and Jeremy Bentham. Eden introduced his *Principles of Penal Law* with a sketchy history of the criminal law, joining Kames in locating its origins in 'the gratification of private resentment' and its development in a process whereby 'the selfish passions' came to be 'softened' through 'an habitual acquiescence' to law and government. For the body of his discussion, however, Eden simply 'assumed' a 'period of perfect civilization', and thereby effectively relegated Kames's analysis to the position of an isolated prologue to a more rigorous critique of existing penal legislation.[47] Similarly, Bentham enthusiastically welcomed the *Historical Law Tracts*, depicting the work as a vital corrective to Blackstone's apologetics. And, in a splendid case of mistaken prophecy, he described Kames's history of the criminal law as that 'ingenious and instructive essay', which not only deserved, but would probably enjoy, 'permanent currency'.[48] Yet it remains doubtful just what sort of impact Bentham was prepared to allow Kames on his own legal doctrines. The extent of Bentham's patience with the historical treatment of legal practices is perhaps better indicated by the early pronouncement that he would proceed 'by diving at once into the recesses of the human understanding with Locke and with Helvetius', and not 'by wandering about in the maze of history in search of particular facts, often ill-authenticated or disguised'.[49] Nor did he seek to qualify his own theory of criminal deterrence in the light of Kames's point that the origins of criminal law lay in private retribution. Indeed, from this standpoint, Bentham's highly selective and pragmatic reading of Kames provides something of a parallel to the more famous instance of his response to Adam Smith. There again Bentham was eager to parade his enthusiasm for Smith's science of political economy, even though this appeared not to require any careful consideration of the style of social inquiry which produced the *Wealth of Nations*.

Kames's study of the criminal law established him as a participant in a movement for law reform which extended well beyond Scotland. But his interest in legal improvement in this field pales into near insignificance when compared with his support for the most controversial proposal for law reform canvassed in eighteenth-century Scotland: the abolition of entails.[50] Entails, Kames argued, had converted 'one of the greatest blessings of life', landed property, 'into a curse', and constituted the most easily identifiable obstacle to Scottish improvement.[51] The survival of the law supporting entails repre-

---

[47] [W. Eden], *Principles of Penal Law* (London, 1771), pp. 1–3. Eden later cites Kames's essay at pp. 62, 166.
[48] University College London, Bentham MSS., UC. xcvi. 75. For Bentham's favourable report on the *Law Tracts*, see J. Bentham, *A Comment on the Commentaries and A Fragment on Government*, ed. J. H. Burns and H. L. A. Hart (London, 1977), pp. 313–14n, 330, 430n.
[49] Bentham MSS., UC., xxvii. 95.
[50] For the campaign to abolish entails, see N. T. Phillipson, 'Lawyers, Landowners, and the Civic Leadership of Post-Union Scotland', *Juridical Review*, N.S., 21 (1976), pp. 97–120.
[51] 'History of Property', *Law Tracts*, i, p. 219.

sented an unpardonable retreat of reason before legal authority, and sharply contrasted with the manner in which English judges had effectively manipulated this area of their law.[52] It was easy to prove that entails violated 'nature and reason' and were a source of profound social mischief. But again Kames was concerned to show that they were also an anachronism, a sinister vestige of the feudal law, that 'violent and unnatural system'.[53]

The first part of Kames's argument was to characterize entails as a perverse extension of the principles of feudal property law. In many instances he implied that the label 'feudal' was sufficient condemnation in itself,[54] but here he was concerned to go further. Entails, which enabled individuals to preserve 'their name, family and estate in strictest union, if possible, to the end of time', followed directly 'from the very nature of the feudal system'. For the feudal system not only provided for 'a perpetual succession' to a single heir, but also prevented the 'dilapidation' of the estate by heirs because the 'vassal's right' was a 'liferent and usufruct only'. This system, in turn, 'unluckily suggested a hint for gratifying this irrational appetite' to control the inheritance of an estate forever. The appetite for such control produced the 1685 Statute of Entails, which even at the very moment of its enactment represented a reactionary move by the great landowners to resist the pressures of commercial exchange.[55]

Once the feudal character of entails was perceived, it became possible to appreciate how antithetical they were to the property relations required by a commercial society. The rationale of feudal land tenure related entirely to the peculiar techniques by which political authority and military service were identified with the possession of land. The disadvantage of this rather unstable system of authority was that it withdrew 'land from commerce' – a 'hardship' which went unnoticed 'in times of war', but which became apparent when the emergence of 'regular government' in Britain 'made the arts of peace prevail'.[56] Once the political reasons for a strict succession of estates to a single heir had been rendered obsolete by the passing of feudal society itself, the only remaining consequence of such forms of landholding was to hinder commerce and improvement. This occurred because the heir to an entailed estate was unable to improve his land effectively, and more especially because entails removed large amounts of property from circulation.[57] As Kames maintained, 'no circumstance tends more to the advancement of commerce than a free

---

[52] *Elucidations respecting the Law of Scotland*, pp. 378–9, and 'Scotch Entails considered in Moral and Political Views', *Sketches*, iv, p. 450.   [53] 'History of Property', p. 198.

[54] For examples, see 'Progress of the Female Sex', *Sketches*, ii, p. 83; 'Military Branch of Government', *Sketches*, iii, p. 11; 'Principles and Progress of Morality', *Sketches*, iv, p. 157.

[55] 'History of Property', pp. 197–9, 218.

[56] *Essays concerning British Antiquities*, pp. 135–40, 156–8, and 'History of Property', pp. 197–9.

[57] 'Scotch Entails', *Sketches*, iv, pp. 447–63. Again, Kames's historical and economic analysis parallels that advanced by Smith; see $LJ(A)$ i.116–33, 160–ii.2, and WN III.ii.3–8.

circulation of the goods of fortune from hand to hand'.[58] These economic conditions required that the real property law provide legal powers for 'splitting land-property' into 'many parts' as was 'favourable to commerce'. Such legal powers, Kames admitted, left the land law 'intricate', but these 'inconveniences' were 'unavoidable in a commercial country'.[59] Accordingly, when entails were judged by the standards of social welfare, they appeared as a fundamental economic liability. And when they were judged in terms of historical development, they appeared as an antiquated relic of feudalism inappropriately lodged in a commercial country. As Kames stressed in discussing another remnant of Scotland's feudal inheritance, 'when the substantial part of the feudal law has thus vanished, it is to be regretted that we should still lie under the oppression of its forms'.[60]

Kames reserved his heaviest guns for use in his *magnum opus*, the four-volume *Sketches of the History of Man*, which was supplied with a separate appendix on 'Scotch entails considered in Moral and Political Views'. He first argued that entails were contrary 'to nature and reason', for the desire to control property 'for ever to certain heirs' was the work of a 'diseased fancy' and 'distempered appetite', utterly 'repugnant to the frail state of man'. He next explored the pernicious economic consequences of entails at length, demonstrating how they hindered commerce, industry, improvement and population.[61] Lastly, he claimed that entails threatened the very fabric of social and political life in Britain. In this context, he produced a new set of arguments, which were again drawn from the Scottish historical interpretation of the recent past. Here he highlighted the implications of the fact that large entailed estates undermined the economic position of 'gentlemen of moderate fortune'. These gentlemen had not only brought opulence to Britain, but had also improved 'manners' and encouraged 'arts and sciences'. More importantly, the present system of political liberty and constitutional forms was dependent on such gentlemen. 'In such only', he alleged, 'resides the genuine spirit of liberty.' The owners of entailed estates, however, were likened to a 'feudal oligarchy', whose immoderate land holdings produced 'an irregular and dangerous influence on the House of Commons'. 'In a word', Kames concluded, 'the distribution of land into many shares, accords charmingly with the free spirit of the British constitution; but nothing is more repugnant to that spirit, than overgrown estates in land'.[62] Thus, entails were both an economic disaster and an ominous political menace; both these evils followed from the historical demonstration

---

[58] *Equity*, p. 259.
[59] 'History of Securities upon Land', *Law Tracts*, i, pp. 223–4.
[60] *Ibid.*, p. 246.
[61] 'Scotch Entails', *Sketches*, iv, pp. 448–9, 452–9.
[62] *Ibid.*, pp. 460–2. For other contemporary accounts of the relationship between commerce and liberty, see the editorial note to Smith, *WN* III.iv.4 (note 6).

that they represented an area of Scots law which had plainly failed to 'accommodate itself to the fluctuating manners of the people'.

II

For Kames the lessons of legal history and the claims of social welfare both pointed to the need for legal change. In responding to this need Kames presented the Court of Session as an appropriate agency for implementing Scots law reform. In support of this, the most arresting feature of his strategy for legal improvement, Kames provided an historical analysis of the Session's judicial authority and an elaborate theory of equity jurisprudence. But his advocacy of this judicial route to law reform also reflected less theoretical matters. These relate largely to Scotland's political circumstances in the period following the Union.

Amongst the more disquieting consequences of the 1707 Union of the two kingdoms were the difficulties created for securing legislation in Scotland's behalf. In the absence of a native legislature, Scotland's legislative fortunes were now located in the less than predictable political arena at Westminster, where Scotland itself was under-represented in the British Parliament and where major Scottish bills generally depended upon ministerial support for their enactment. All this made legislating for Scotland a rather laboured and potentially precarious business, a state of affairs of which Kames had personal experience. Despite his confidence in the courts' powers to effect legal change, Kames recognized that the Scots law of entails could only be altered by statutory amendment. Accordingly, he drafted legislation for their abolition, had his bill published, and solicited political backing in England, particularly from the former Chancellor, Lord Hardwicke, in 1759. But in the absence of any active sponsorship in England, his legislative effort failed to move forward. Even when in 1764 the Faculty of Advocates assumed the leadership of the campaign against entails (and produced a bill virtually identical with that drafted by Kames), their enterprise quickly collapsed once the Scottish M.P.s divided at Westminster.[63]

The Union of 1707 had not, of course, rendered Scotland politically impotent, and it would be mistaken to ignore the various systems of patronage and connection which enabled Scottish politicians to achieve their goals at Westminster. It was not, after all, the absence of English support, but the lack

[63] For Kames's correspondence on entails and legislative proposals, see Tytler, *Life of Kames*, i, pp. 210–14, 222–8. Lehmann cites one of Kames's letters to Hardwicke as well as the text of his proposals; see Lehmann, *Henry Home, Lord Kames*, pp. 327–32. Kames himself published some of his correspondence with Hardwicke in his *Elucidations respecting the Law of Scotland* (pp. 381–8), and outlined his bill in the *Sketches* ('Scotch Entails', iv, pp. 462–3). For the legislative effort of the Faculty of Advocates in 1764, see Phillipson, 'Lawyers, Landowners, and the Civic Leadership of Post-Union Scotland'.

of consensus in Scotland, which ultimately thwarted the legislative attempts to abolish Scottish entails. Nevertheless, there was still nothing in the legislative procedures of the British Parliament to ensure that the legal leadership of Edinburgh could effectively control the fate of any law reform proposal once it reached Westminster. And this, it appears, often provided sufficient inducement for curbing that leadership's legislative ambitions.

In the winter of 1737, Duncan Forbes, the newly appointed Lord President of the Court of Session, wrote to Hardwicke, then Lord Chancellor, on the question of Scots law reform. He noted that 'thirty years experience since the Union' had revealed 'many blemishes' in the law, and proposed that the Session judges produce a bill to remove these blemishes, which could then be placed under Hardwicke's supervision at Westminster. But he also shared his fears that such a bill might be vulnerable in Parliament to 'alterations from hands that may not be so well acquainted with the subject', and stressed that the proposition would have to depend on the likelihood of these fears being realized:

If I could with reason hope that a bill so settled there would pass unaltered, I would set about it without loss of time... but if I may not rely on that, I should rather choose to jog on as we are, than to risk amendments... by unskilled hands...

Hardwicke replied within a fortnight, announcing his support and willingness to serve. Yet notwithstanding his own experience and success as a legislative manager, he could provide no reassurance on the problem which most disturbed the Scottish judges:

As to the Bill passing *without alterations*, your Lordship, who [has] had long experience of our parliament's genius, and of the disposition to amend the English law, and of some attempts relating to your own, can judge, as well as I, of the probability of such an event.

Hardwicke went on to mention a further problem, that 'unless some of your countrymen here are taken in to the original project, many obstacles may arise'.[64] In the face of these hazards, the project was dropped, leaving the Scottish judges to 'jog on' as before. But Kames insisted that another option remained for reforming Scots law, one resting on the equitable authority of the Court of Session itself.

The same institutional arrangement which deprived Scotland of any untroubled access to legislative law reform, also enhanced the institutional importance of the Scottish courts. Aside from the Church, the most socially potent survivor of the Union with England was the Scots law and legal establishment, and the Scottish judges doubtless served a much broader political function than their counterparts in England. Kames's ascribing to the

[64] Cited in P. C. Yorke, *The Life and Correspondence of Philip Yorke Earl of Hardwicke*, 3 vols. (Cambridge, 1913), ii. pp. 532–4.

Court of Session powers competent to reform Scots law in some sense exploited the ambiguities in this situation. If English lawyers, such as Blackstone, viewed his doctrines as violating constitutional norms, then this in part reflected the difficulty of applying these norms, especially any notion of a strict separation of powers, to the actual governing of contemporary Scotland.[65]

At this level, Kames's view of the judicial office can be accommodated fairly readily within the historical space Nicholas Phillipson has identified for the Scottish Enlightenment as a whole. Phillipson argues that many of the most distinctive ideas and activities of the Scottish intelligentsia should be read as part of a process whereby a provincial society which had lost its political identity with the abolition of the Scottish Parliament turned to other institutions to advance an already established programme of improvement – a process evinced in the creation of new bodies such as the learned societies of Edinburgh and the strengthening of older institutions such as the universities, and in the moral values and social goals these institutions were hoped to further.[66] Kames's position thus presents a legalistic version on this theme: a programme of legal improvement which urged Scotland to follow an English lead; and a programme whose realization depended on the initiative of a native institution, in this case Scotland's premier civil court.

Kames, however, did not seek to defend his notion of the judicial office on the basis of mere political necessity. In the first place he was confident of the substantive superiority of that law produced through judicial deliberation. He developed this point in his original collection of Session decisions, after noting the relative paucity of statute in Scots law. This, he claimed, 'was once our misfortune', as it allowed the judges excessive freedom in their determinations. The problem, however, was removed as the law 'came to be more and more ascertained in the course of practice'; and by comparing the relative merits of common law and statute it became obvious that 'what was originally our misfortune, will turn out to our advantage':

> Statutes, though commonly made with a view to particular cases, do yet enact in general upon all similar cases; and as man is but short sighted with regard to consequences, 'tis odds but, in remedying one evil, a greater is produced. A court of justice determines nothing in general; their decisions are adapted to particular circumstances...They creep along with wary steps, until at last, by induction of many cases...a general rule is with safety formed.[67]

Kames's position in these remarks deserves some expansion, as he had

[65] Blackstone's criticisms of Kames's equity theory are at 3 *Comm.* 433, where Kames is referred to as 'a very ingenious author in the other part of the island'. This reference was dropped in the eighth edition of the *Commentaries* (1778).
[66] N. T. Phillipson, 'Culture and Society in the 18th Century Province: The Case of Edinburgh and the Scottish Enlightenment', in L. Stone (ed.), *The University in Society*, 2 vols. (Princeton, N.J., 1975), ii, pp. 407–46.
[67] Kames, *The Decisions of the Court of Session*, i, p. iii.

telescoped several legal doctrines which underpinned much of the contemporary scepticism in both England and Scotland over the efficacy of legal change produced through legislative intervention. His argument in part evokes an orthodox premise of equity theory which held that man was necessarily 'short sighted with regard to consequences' in that he could never construct a system of legal rules which would fulfil its intended purposes or the demands of justice in all possible cases.[68] The argument also draws on an equally orthodox understanding of the special merits of legal rules which were ascertained through the practice of the courts: a type of law which having been formulated 'by induction of many cases', each 'adapted to particular circumstances', came to embody (in Blackstone's phrase) 'the accumulated wisdom of ages', and thereby attained a level of excellence unavailable in any single instance of legislative rule-making. This conception of legal development forms a familiar theme in English common law theory, though there has perhaps been some tendency to treat it as a peculiarly or exclusively English doctrine of legal traditionalism. Richard Tuck's recent discussion of John Selden as a seminal contributor to this understanding of legal development in itself suggests a wider setting for the formulation of this doctrine in the natural law tradition of the continental jurists.[69] In any case, a Scottish lawyer would have encountered the same view of customary law in Stair's *Institutions*. There Stair likewise stressed the superior virtues of a law 'wrung out from...debates upon particular cases', in which 'the conveniences and inconveniences thereof, through a tract of time, are experimentally seen'. And, as Kames was later to do, he immediately contrasted this to the situation in statute law, where 'the law-giver must at once balance the conveniences and inconveniences', and therefore 'may, and often doth, fall short'.[70]

Kames, at the same time, also refers to the actual experience of eighteenth-century legislating, and particularly to the retrospective character of so many parliamentary statutes. On most occasions, he observes, the legislature acted 'with a view to particular cases', and in this sense functioned in a manner similar to a judge. The difficulty with statute was that although the legislature looked to a particular case, it automatically produced a general rule guiding future cases; thus, the effects of its actions extended well beyond the circumstances which had directed its original deliberation.[71] One solution to this

---

[68] This theory of equity is set out below, pp. 225-6.
[69] R. Tuck, *Natural Rights Theories: Their Origin and Development* (Cambridge, 1979), pp. 84, 132.
[70] James Dalrymple, Viscount of Stair, *The Institutions of the Law of Scotland* (1693), ed. D. M. Walker (Edinburgh and Glasgow, 1981), 1.1.15.
[71] The retrospective character of parliamentary statutes was especially striking in the case of penal legislation, and formed the basis of Bentham's splendid lampoon on British legislative practice: 'the Country Gentleman who has had his turnips stolen, goes to work and gets a bloody law against stealing Turnips: it exceeds the utmost stretch of his imagination that the next year the same catastrophe may happen to his potatoes. For the two general rules in...modern British legislation are, never to move a finger till your passions are inflamed, nor ever to look

difficulty, in essence Bentham's response, was to seek a system of legal arrangement and classification which might enable the legislator to see all the potential consequences of his legislative actions immediately. But Kames only raised the problem in order to indicate the inherent superiority of the judicial process as a mechanism for developing legal rules. He further believed the claim easily vindicated by a direct appeal to the actual condition of Scots law:

> Let any one who is curious run over our law in this view, and he will find that those branches of it which have been modelled by the court are generally speaking brought nearer to a standard than those upon which statutes are most frequent.[72]

In addition to invoking these legal doctrines, Kames also sought to restrict the scope for legislation through another set of arguments, those which John Pocock has elucidated as the civic humanist themes in Scottish social theory.[73] Kames plainly shared the preoccupations of civic humanism, and his *Sketches* in particular contain incessant reminders of the need to maintain patriotism, of the threats to virtue posed by commercial life, and of Britain's desperate vulnerability to the forces of luxury, corruption and profligate manners. Patriotism, he explained, was the most exalted of the 'social affections', the 'great bulwark of civil liberty', and the chief support to any state's political and material prosperity: 'A nation in no other period of its progress is so flourishing as when patriotism is the ruling passion of every member.' Thus, although 'successful commerce' was socially 'advantageous' in bringing 'wealth and power', it proved 'hurtful ultimately in introducing luxury and voluptuousness, which eradicate patriotism'. Under conditions of wealth and luxury, the 'social affections decline', 'selfishness becomes the ruling passion', and 'every man studies his own interest'. Such conditions, Kames repeatedly warned, were already subverting British manners and public life. 'The epidemic distempers of luxury and corruption are spreading wide in Britain'; the nation hovered perilously 'on the brink of a precipice!'[74]

Kames was hardly at his most original or indeed most attractive in discussing patriotism and the forces which undermined it. But it is worth noting how he developed these social doctrines at the expense of the legislative office. Initially, of course, his very commitment to the 'important doctrine' that 'patriotism

---

further than your nose'; Bentham MSS., UC. cxl. 92. For more conventional criticisms of parliamentary law-making, see Blackstone, 1 *Comm.* 9–11; Daines Barrington, *Observations on the More Ancient Statutes*, 5th edn (London, 1796), pp. 557–64; Richard Burn, *The Justice of the Peace and Parish Officer*, 9th edn, 3 vols. (London, 1764), i, pp. viii–ix, and iii, pp. 567–8.

[72] Kames, *Decisions of the Court of Session*, i, p. iii.

[73] J. G. A. Pocock, *The Machiavellian Moment: Florentine Political Thought and the Atlantic Republican Tradition* (Princeton, N.J., 1975), pp. 493–505.

[74] 'Rise and Fall of Patriotism', *Sketches*, ii, pp. 319–42, and 'Manners', *Sketches*, i, pp. 347–8, 403–13; see also 'Origin and Progress of Arts', *Sketches*, i, pp. 186–95; 'Progress and Effects of Luxury', *Sketches*, ii, pp. 152–4; 'War and Peace compared', *Sketches*, i, pp. 294–316; 'Military Branch of Government', *Sketches*, iii, pp. 1–65; 'Principles and Progress of Morality', *Sketches*, iv, pp. 164–72.

is the cornerstone of civil society'[75] entailed a devaluing of legislation and public institutions generally as a source of social welfare. Thus he maintained that though government 'will advance men to a high degree of civilization', not even 'the very best government' could 'preserve them from corruption'.[76] The point was further strengthened by adopting Montesquieu's analysis that legislation represented only one of many causes determining the character of any community.[77] This again tended to narrow the sphere for positive legislative action in that the legislator needed to recognize the large range of social practices which could only be improved by customs, manners, education and the like. As Kames observed in his principal didactic tract, 'manners, depending on an endless variety of circumstances, are too complex for law; and yet upon manners chiefly depends the well-being of society'. In such areas, legislation could 'do little' and the sovereign had to proceed by 'example and precept'.[78] On this basis, in the *Sketches*, he roundly criticized various recent parliamentary statutes as misguided attempts to solve problems incapable of legislative cure. And such laws, even if unenforced, were 'never innocent with regard to consequences', for 'nothing' was 'more subversive' of morality and patriotism 'than the habit of disregarding the laws of our country'.[79]

Kames's utilization of this argument in fact sits rather uneasily alongside his own devotion to public projects for social improvement. Whatever his sensitivity to the complex and organic nature of social life, this did not prevent his proposing such visionary pieces of social engineering as, for example, a plan to close down most of London in the interests of public morals.[80] Nonetheless, this social theory obviously proved useful in censuring Parliament, and these criticisms dovetail with his general insistence on the superiority of judge-made law. For according to this social theory, any judicial attempt to create patriotism through legal rules would equally be doomed to failure. But the judicial procedure, as understood by Kames, was unlikely to generate this sort of misguided and ultimately pernicious law-making. The statute book, however, testified to the frequency with which the legislature had succumbed to the temptation to intervene in areas of social life beyond the reach of law.

At all events, Kames was confident of the considerable advantages enjoyed

[75] 'Progress and Effects of Luxury', *Sketches*, ii, p. 155.
[76] 'Manners', *Sketches*, i, p. 402, and see 'Principles and Progress of Morality', *Sketches*, iv, p. 180.
[77] Montesquieu was Kames's principal source for much of the social theory in the *Sketches*; see 'Manners', *Sketches*, i, pp. 314–15; 'Different Forms of Government Compared', *Sketches*, ii, p. 249.
[78] Kames, *Loose Hints upon Education, chiefly concerning the Culture of the Heart* (Edinburgh, 1781), pp. 21–2.
[79] 'Principles and Progress of Morality', *Sketches*, iv, p. 177, and see 'Manners', p. 381 (laws against swearing); 'Finances', *Sketches*, ii, pp. 396–9 (laws multiplying judicial oaths); 'Public Police with respect to the Poor', *Sketches*, iii, pp. 87–8, 95–7 (poor laws).
[80] 'A Great City considered in Physical, Moral and Political Views', *Sketches*, iii, pp. 120–37 (esp. pp. 135–6).

by legal rules derived from the practice of the courts. 'Matters of law', he emphasized, 'are ripened in the best manner by warmth of debate at the bar and coolness of judgment on the bench'.[81] He was equally certain, as we have seen, that all legal rules needed to keep pace with historical development and social change, and that the legal rules of the historic Scots law had often failed to fulfil this requirement. Hence his special concern to explain the manner in which the courts were now to develop the law in response to new social circumstances, a concern which underlined much of the discussion in his *Principles of Equity*. But the first step towards this analysis regarded another consideration, that of correctly identifying the nature of the Court of Session's judicial authority. This task was first undertaken in the *Historical Law Tracts* where Kames, characteristically, explored the question by considering the 'History of Courts'.

Kames's historical investigations revealed that 'no defect in the constitution of a state' deserved 'greater reproach' than that of 'giving license to wrong without affording redress'. Accordingly, in every properly constituted state a 'supreme court' would be empowered 'to redress wrongs of all sorts, where a peculiar remedy is not provided' in the usual legal forms. In Scotland, this power had originally been lodged in the Privy Council. When that court was abolished, its authority 'devolve[d] upon the court of session', giving it a 'new branch of jurisdiction' distinct from its original status 'as a court of common law'. This new 'extraordinary' judicial power was indicated by the Court of Session's acknowledged, if often misunderstood, '*nobile officium*'; and the sort of judicial function the court now served might be identified by comparison with its institutional counterpart in England:

The rule I am contending for, seems to be adopted by the English court of chancery, in its fullest extent. For every sort of wrong...is redressed in the court of chancery, where a remedy is not otherwise provided by common or statute law. And hence it is, that the jurisdiction of this court, confined originally within narrow bounds, has been gradually enlarged over a boundless variety of affairs.[82]

In seeking to relate the judicial authorities of the Session and Chancery courts, Kames recalled an objective he had raised in the preface to these *Law Tracts*. This was the hope that legal studies might in future be conducted in such a way as to promote a better understanding of the two systems of national jurisprudence which had survived the union of the two kingdoms.[83] Kames's ambitions in this regard were shared by several Scottish legal writers of the period, among them Lord Bankton, James Dalrymple and George Joseph Bell. Indeed, several years prior to the appearance of Kames's own discussion, Bankton in his *Institutes* had likewise drawn the comparison between the Court

---

[81] 'History of Courts', *Law Tracts*, i, p. 324, and see Kames, *Remarkable Decisions of the Court of Session From the Year 1730 to the Year 1752* (Edinburgh, 1766), preface.

[82] 'History of Courts', pp. 320–6.   [83] *Law Tracts*, i, p. xiii.

of Session's equity jurisdiction and the practice at the English Court of Chancery.[84]

But Kames had further practical designs in these remarks. For he had previously observed that the Court of Session's 'extraordinary powers' were but imperfectly perceived, and therefore failed to exercise the proper impact on the court's deliberations. By introducing the English Court of Chancery into his discussion he was thus displaying before his judicial colleagues an imposing example of a fully developed and systematic exercise of extraordinary judicial authority. In the *Principles of Equity* this tactic was taken a step further, when Kames cited Chancery decisions in support of his account of equity jurisprudence; a device which perhaps best exposes the programmatic character of the work, since Chancery precedents were never a very likely feature of a purported statement of equity in Scots law.[85] Thus, to understand Kames's claims at this point in his argument it is necessary to consider more closely what was implied in this tendentious identification of the Court of Session with England's leading equity court.

Despite the highly unusual nature of English equity, most eighteenth-century commentators on this part of the English legal system approached the subject in rather conventional terms, viewing equity as a species of judicial discretion which enabled a judge to avoid a mechanical application of the general rules of law in particular harsh cases. Blackstone, for example, in his initial account of equity in the *Commentaries*, provided an orthodox statement, citing Grotius's Aristotelian definition of equity as 'the correction of that, wherein the law (by reason of its universality) is deficient'. Since in law 'all matters cannot be foreseen or expressed', the legal system required a 'power' for defining 'those circumstances, which (had they been foreseen) the legislator himself would have expressed. And these are cases, which according to Grotius, "*lex non exacte definit, sed arbitrio boni viri permittit*".'[86]

This classical notion of equity was adopted and expanded in the more systematic works on equity jurisprudence which first appeared in England during this period. These accounts invariably introduced the topic as Blackstone had done, by insisting upon the utter impossibility of constructing a system of legal rules which might achieve the ends of justice in every possible case. Given this inevitable shortcoming, John Fonblanque, in his late-eighteenth-century edition of *A Treatise of Equity*, explained that it was necessary 'in every well-constituted government' to provide a power 'for supplying that which is defective, and controlling that which is unintentionally harsh, in the application

---

[84] A. McDouall (Lord Bankton), *An Institute of the Laws of Scotland in Civil Rights*, 3 vols. (Edinburgh, 1751–3), ii, pp. 516–20 (Bk. iv. Tit. vii. 23–31).
[85] For Kames's general inflating of the Court of Session's equity practice and his use of Chancery precedents, see David M. Walker, 'Equity in Scots Law', *Juridical Review*, 66 (1954), 18.
[86] Blackstone, 1 *Comm.* 61–2.

of any general rule to a particular case'.[87] In these difficult cases a judge ruled directly according to those principles of natural justice which supported the positive legal edifice. Thus, John Mitford, in his authoritative treatise on Chancery pleadings, described equity as a 'resort to natural principles'; while the author of *A Treatise of Equity* identified it with 'the whole of natural justice' and the 'law of God and nature'.[88] These authors, moreover, were rehearsing doctrines well-known in Scottish law. As Stair had explained, it was only because equity comprehended 'the whole law of rational nature' that it was at all possible to 'give remeid to the rigour and extremity of positive law in all cases'.[89] In the *Historical View of English Government*, John Millar set out this conventional understanding of equity at length:

> It is necessary... to forego in many cases the benefit of that uniformity and certainty derived from the strict observance of a general rule, and by introducing an exception from the consideration of what is equitable in particular circumstances, to avoid the hardship which would otherwise fall upon individuals.[90]

As the English legal writers appreciated, the orthodox notion of equity referred to a form of rational, judicial discretion which any judge was empowered to exercise. But in England, famously, equity was the province of specific courts, the most important in the eighteenth century being the Court of Chancery. And these writers further recognized that the separation of law and equity had introduced elements into English equity practice strikingly unlike anything suggested in the orthodox notion. As Blackstone shrewdly noted, 'Grotius or Puffendorf' would scarcely be able 'to discover by their own light the system of a court of equity in England'.[91] Like Blackstone, these writers were concerned to attend to these special features of English equity, although it often remained unclear how they were to be reconciled with the formal theory of equity with which their accounts began.

One such difference related to the manner in which the normal need to balance the claims of equity against the stability of legal rules had, in England, been transformed into a constitutional issue regarding the extent to which Chancery might interfere with and overrule the common law system. This jurisdictional struggle was largely resolved in the seventeenth century, but not

---

[87] *A Treatise of Equity*, ed. J. Fonblanque, 2 vols. (London, 1793–4), i. p. 6 (Fonblanque's note). For other contemporary versions of this doctrine, see [Richard Francis], *Maxims of Equity* (London, 1727), 'To the Reader', p. 2 (pagination added); Richard Wooddeson, *Systematical View of the Laws of England*, 3 vols. (London, 1792), i, pp. 192-4; John Mitford (Lord Redesdale), *A Treatise on the Pleadings in suits in the Court of Chancery*, 5th edn (London, 1847), p. 8.

[88] Mitford, *Pleadings in Chancery*, p. 3; *Treatise of Equity*, ed. Fonblanque, i, p. 9.

[89] Stair, *Institutions of the Laws of Scotland*, 1.1.6, and see Bankton, *Institute of the Laws of Scotland*, iii, pp. 93–6 (Bk. iv. Tit. xlv. R. 40).

[90] Millar, 'The Progress of Science relating to Law and Government', *Historical View*, iv, p. 278.

[91] Blackstone, 3 *Comm.* 433.

without effect upon subsequent developments in English equity. Eighteenth-century judges in Chancery remained extremely circumspect in asserting the nature of their discretionary powers and took particular care to dissociate equity from an authority to invade the jurisdictions of other courts. The consequence of such restraint, as Blackstone pointed out, was the many areas of law where the equity court failed to give relief even in the face of inadequate common law remedies.[92] Hence, it became extremely difficult to deduce any theoretical principle which governed the extent of English equity. As Mitford acknowledged, 'it is not a very easy task accurately to describe the jurisdiction of our courts of equity'. And thus Francis Hargrave, for example, chose to characterize English equity in entirely historical terms, as a 'power for dispensing with positive rules of law' which had now become 'generally confined' to 'those cases in which length of time has almost sanctified the practice'.[93]

In addition, what was more peculiar and ultimately more important about English equity was that in the majority of cases Chancery judges did not proceed by invoking the dictates of natural justice or by attending to the special circumstances of an individual harsh case. Rather, they decided cases by applying general rules which had been settled by previous Chancery precedents. The development of English equity into a consolidated system of Chancery case law was by no means complete in the eighteenth century. But the development was sufficiently pronounced to earn the attention of legal commentators. Mitford noted that 'principles of decision...adopted by the courts of equity, when fully established...are considered by those courts as rules to be observed with as much strictness as positive law'. Or, as Blackstone more vigorously put it:

The system of our courts of equity is a laboured connected system, governed by established rules, and bound down by precedents, from which they do not depart although the reason of some of them may perhaps be liable to objection.[94]

In highlighting these features of Chancery practice – its jurisdictional restraint and its status as 'a laboured connected system' – English lawyers were eager to explain how the presence of independent equity courts did not serve to disrupt the certainty of the law, the liberty of the subject, or the primacy of the common law within the legal system as a whole. But whatever the considerable comfort afforded by such insights, these at the same time had to be qualified by further considerations. The first was simply the unmistakable fact of the Chancery's institutional success and profound impact on the system of law in England. This was the point Kames enthusiastically reported in the

---

[92] Blackstone, 3 *Comm.* 429–30.
[93] Mitford, *Pleadings in Chancery*, p. 5n; Hargrave's comment is cited in Yorke, *Life of Hardwicke*, ii, pp. 422–3.
[94] Mitford, *Pleadings in Chancery*, p. 4n; Blackstone, 3 *Comm.* 432.

Historical Law Tracts, and it figured critically in Chief Baron Gilbert's more testy description of Chancery as a court of 'very small beginning', employing judicial procedures 'totally before unheard of', and which 'though it was very much impugned even towards its first original creation... is now grown to that degree, that it has swallowed up most of the other business of the common law courts'.[95] Second was a general awareness that the likely course of future developments in English law would, if anything, further enhance the position of England's equity court. As Lord Chancellor Hardwicke explained at length in his correspondence with Kames:

New discoveries and inventions in commerce have given birth to new species of contracts, and... new contrivances to break and elude them, for which the ancient common law had adapted no remedies; and from this cause, courts of equity, which admit of greater latitude, have... been obliged to accommodate the wants of mankind.[96]

In the event, Hardwicke was preaching to the converted. For when Kames came to elucidate the character of equity in Scots law, he was at pains to demonstrate how its character had been formed specifically in response to the 'new discoveries and inventions in commerce'.

III

In the *Historical Law Tracts* Kames alleged that the general misperception of the Court of Session's 'extraordinary powers' had improperly stunted the practice of the court. The business of raising Scotland's legal consciousness was eagerly tackled in his *Principles of Equity*.

Kames introduced the work, as he had argued in the *Law Tracts*, by drawing a sharp distinction between the Court of Session's original function as a court of common law and its comprehensive authority as an equity court. 'One operation of equity universally acknowledged', he maintained, 'is to remedy imperfections in the common law, which sometimes is defective and sometimes exceeds just bounds'. In this sense, 'equity is constantly opposed to common law' in that it 'commences at the limits of the common law'. In England, 'where the courts of equity and common law are distinct', it was an easy matter to identify this point of equity's commencement. But in Scotland, where equity and law were administered in the same court, the matter was more difficult. Many elements in the court's practice, originally derived from equity, had in the course of time become 'considered as common law'. However, since equity comprehended 'every matter of law that by common law is left without remedy', it was possible to identify the actual province of equity by way of 'historical deduction'; that is, by an examination of the contents of the historic

---

[95] Jeffrey Gilbert, *The History and Practice of the High Court of Chancery* (London, 1758), p. 14.
[96] Cited in Yorke, *Life of Hardwicke*, ii, p. 555.

common law so as to determine which legal remedies already existed in this part of the legal system.

Accordingly, Kames embarked on a brisk assessment of the Scots common law, promptly declaring it the law of 'our rude ancestors', which provided only 'regulations to restrain individuals from doing mischief and to enforce performance of convenants', and which altogether ignored 'the more refined duties of morality'. Hence, in the case of Scotland, common law required a massive dose of equitable correction:

> Law, in this simple form, cannot long continue stationary; for in the social state...law ripens gradually with the human faculties...[and] many duties formerly neglected are found to be binding in conscience. Such duties can no longer be neglected by courts of justice; and...they come naturally under the jurisdiction of a court of equity.[97]

Kames next examined those legal principles which were to guide the actions of the equity court, and which he derived from the 'moral laws of society'.[98] The first of these was the principle of justice, which meant the court was responsible 'to make right effectual' and 'to redress wrong'.[99] Kames's position here was reasonably orthodox; as we have seen, equity was regularly identified with 'natural justice' and the need to avoid violating individual just claims in difficult cases. But Kames went on to specify another principle guiding the equity court, one which, he observed, most commentators had overlooked:

> All the variety of matter hitherto mentioned is regulated by the principle of justice solely...But, upon more narrow inspection, we find a number of law-cases into which justice enters not, but only the principle of utility. Expediency requires that these be brought under the cognisance of a court; and the court of equity...takes naturally such matter under its jurisdiction.

Moreover, given the essentially social purposes served by the legal system, when these two principles were found 'in opposition', the court was to sacrifice justice to utility: 'Equity when it regards the interest of a few individuals only, ought to yield to utility when it regards the whole society.'[100]

The point of this theoretical construction was made clearer when Kames turned to the actual practice of the equity court and to the areas of Scots law demanding equitable amendment. He first considered those topics where equity pursued the dictates of justice. At the centre of this discussion was the law of contract and quasi-contract, and here Kames presented what in England were commonplace points of contrast between common law and equity practice. Thus, equity was able to direct the specific performance of a

---

[97] Kames, *Equity*, pp. 38 42, 44, 49. Throughout the discussion Kames uses the term 'common law' as in England, though this was not its sole or original usage in Scots law; see Stair, *Institutions of the Laws of Scotland*, I.1.11, 16, and Bankton, *Institute of the Laws of Scotland*, i, p. 24.
[98] A separate discourse under this title was added in the second edition, pp. 1 37.
[99] *Equity*, p. 249.   [100] *Ibid.*, pp. 44, 47.

contract, where common law could only provide pecuniary damages. Similarly, equity enjoyed a more extensive authority for construing deeds and covenants. Common law was confined to adhering strictly to the letter of an agreement, even in the case of feigned instruments like 'double-bonds'. But equity was authorized 'to follow the dictates of refined justice' and to interpret every contract 'in its true light of a mean employed to bring about some end'.[101]

A second category of cases comprised legal matters for which the principle of justice proved an indecisive guide, and the court determined according to the principle of utility. A leading illustration was found in the question of a *bona fide* payment of debt to the wrong creditor, a major topic in the law covering negotiable paper. This situation resulted from the basic need in a commercial country to allow for 'a free and expedite currency' of property as was required for 'the advancement of commerce'. The cost of maintaining this system of fluid property exchange was the difficulty created for a debtor, particularly in the case of bonds or other negotiable notes, in identifying the true creditor to his debt. Often a debtor might make payment to the wrong individual, a situation Kames declared 'extremely nice in point of equity'. If the court refused to sustain the mispayment, the debtor would then suffer by having to pay twice on the same debt. But if the payment was sustained, the creditor would sacrifice his right through no fault of his own. As Kames put it, 'here the scales hang even', since the principle of justice could not determine the issue. The principle of utility, however, was absolutely decisive and exerted 'all its weight' on the debtor's scale. For unless a debtor was 'secure by voluntary payment', 'no man would venture to pay a shilling' without first going to court, 'and how ruinous to credit this would prove, must be obvious without taking a moment for reflection'.[102]

Lastly, Kames turned to those cases where justice and utility clashed and where utility had to predominate. Again, the question referred to the special legal demands created by commerce. His example was the case 'where a transaction extremely unequal is occasioned by error'. In this situation, Kames acknowledged that 'the justice of affording relief is obvious' and that many legal systems did provide such relief. Nevertheless, the court of equity had to 'yield to utility', as the justice of the case violated 'the interests of the public': 'for if complaints of inequality were indulged, law-suits would be multiplied, to the great detriment of commerce'.[103]

This analysis of how the principle of utility guided the court's determinations in those areas of law affecting the 'advancement of commerce' represented only part of Kames's account of the operation of utility in the practice of the equity

---

[101] *Ibid.*, pp. 42-4, 118-21, 151-2. For the English accounts of the differing treatment of contract in common law and equity, see *Treatise of Equity*, ed. Fonblanque, i, pp. 24-33; Gilbert, *History and Practice of Chancery*, pp. 219-21; John Joseph Powell, *Essay upon the Law of Contract and Agreements*, 2 vols. (London, 1790), ii, pp. 1-4.
[102] *Equity*, p. 259. [103] *Ibid.*, p. 268.

court. The principle of utility also dominated his treatment of the question 'whether a court of equity be, or ought to be, governed by general rules'. This question, as we have seen, was frequently aired by English legal writers in accounting for developments in the Court of Chancery's equity practice. Kames, who had identified the equity practice of the Court of Chancery and the Court of Session, likewise endorsed the development, insisting that the equity court should adjudicate by reference to general rules. He warned that 'men are liable to prejudice and error', and hence all courts relied on general rules 'to preserve uniformity in judgment'. Equity was 'a happy invention to remedy errors in common law', but it 'must stop somewhere', and there could be no adequate 'check upon a court of equity but general rules'. Furthermore, in adhering to general rules the equity court again fulfilled the dictates of utility and the consequent need to sacrifice the 'interests of a few individuals' when they opposed 'the whole society': 'It is for that very reason that a court of equity is bound to form its decrees upon general rules, for this measure regards the whole society in preventing arbitrary proceedings.'[104]

Not only was the equity court to employ general rules, Kames further argued that 'however clear a just claim or defence may be', the court was not to intervene 'unless the case can be brought under a general rule'. This restriction discouraged law-suits, a crucial priority in a commercial country, and it precluded 'the hazard of making judges arbitrary'. Indeed, it followed 'from the very nature of a court of equity' that it adhered to general rules 'even at the expense of forbearing to do justice'. The court was after all empowered to perfect the 'distribution of justice' because this 'promote[d] the good of society'. And 'the means ought to be subordinate to the end'. Therefore, if the court found it could provide justice to individuals only 'by using means that tend to the hurt of society' (that is, by evading general rules), 'a court of equity ought not to interpose'.[105]

If Kames in these observations presented a view of equity practice coincident with that of such English lawyers as Blackstone and Hargrave, he had in fact reached this position by a rather different route. And this reflected their antagonistic assessments of equity's place in the legal system as a whole. For the English lawyers accounted for equity's emerging status as a settled system of case law in historical terms, and in drawing attention to this feature of the Court of Chancery's practice they emphasized the more restricted aspects of equity's impact on the English legal system. Kames, in contrast, was clear that the Scots common law required a nearly lethal dose of equitable correction. 'The imperfections of common law are so many and so various', he maintained, that it was almost impossible 'to bring them into any perfect system'.[106] By justifying the general rules of equity practice on utilitarian grounds, he effectively eliminated just those jurisdictional limitations which the English

[104] Ibid., pp. 46-7.   [105] Ibid., p. 268.   [106] Ibid., p. 56.

authorities sought to impose on their equity courts. For Kames's general rules in equity, while restricting the actions of an individual judge, did not permanently restrict the equity court as an instrument for legal change and correction. As he explained, at a later stage of social development the court might again be called upon to advance the law by enforcing a new range of social obligations, and these extensions of its authority would again be legitimate provided they were formulated as a system of general rules.[107]

Kames's system of equity thus existed as a separate, supplementary body of general rules of law, fashioned according to the dictates of justice and utility, and adjusted to the particular legal demands posed by commercial life. Moreover, by supplying a new set of legal rules, equity enabled the court to advance the law without recourse to legal fictions (a device Kames criticized elsewhere) and without reshaping antiquated legal forms to new social purposes (a procedure he broadly condemned in the *Historical Law Tracts*).[108] And when this conception of equity as a system of general rules designed to advance the common law is considered along side Kames's own ambitions that his work would encourage the expansion and regularization of the Court of Session's equity practice, then the *Principles of Equity* begins to bear an uncanny resemblance to a programme of legislative law reform.

It is important not to overstate the case. Kames never directly compared his general rules of equity to legislation, and he of course never suggested that what his equity judges were doing was legislating. Nonetheless, the resemblance is not entirely in appearance. This becomes clearest in Kames's account in the *Principles* of the operation of statutes 'as they regard matters of law'. These he divided into classes: 'First, those which have justice for their object by supplying the defects... of common law. Second, those which have utility for their sole object.' By presenting the function of legislation in these terms, Kames had ascribed to it just the same role through which he had first defined the province of equity. Both legislation and equity served the administration of justice by correcting the common law and both were authorized to promote social utility. The principal difference between them was that equity could only further utility by negative means, by preventing acts which produced social mischief. Statute, however, could also effect projects 'calculated for promoting the positive good and happiness of society'.[109] Thus, the equity court, for example, could never undertake such programmes as the improvement of the Scottish highways or the reform of the royal burghs, to name but two of Kames's own favoured projects.[110] But with regard to private jurisprudence, their functions were plainly analogous, and indeed characterized in almost exactly the same terms.

[107] *Ibid.*, p. 47.
[108] Kames, *Essays concerning British Antiquities*, p. 147, and 'Securities upon the Land', pp. 244–51.
[109] *Equity*, pp. 185–6, and see pp. 261–6.
[110] 'Government of Royal Boroughs in Scotland' and 'Plan for Improving and Preserving in Order the Highways in Scotland', *Sketches*, iv, pp. 464–92.

All this fully indicates just how much Kames thought he could extract from an equity theory which acknowledged and pursued the dictates of utility. But what deserves equal attention is the altogether bizarre notion of equity this commitment engendered. For in his utilitarianization of equity jurisprudence Kames had eliminated precisely that judicial function which orthodox theories of equity explained and justified. This was the judicial authority to grant exceptions to legal rules where their application would result in injustice. Kames, in his analysis of the utility of general rules, firmly denied to the equity judge just this sort of discretion, even though he readily conceded that even general rules of equity 'must often produce decrees that are materially unjust, for no rule can be equally just in its application to a whole class of cases'.[111]

Not only did Kames sacrifice justice to the utility of general rules, he further specified a range of cases in which the equity court was again to ignore the justice of individual claims and adhere to the principle of utility. These cases reflected the special demands on law created by commerce; for were the equity court to pursue the demands of justice in such situations, it would altogether fail to support that system of rapid property exchange upon which the existence and prosperity of a commercial society depended. On this basis Kames even suggested that in a mercantile nation the principle of justice might be entirely subsumed within the dictates of utility. The two principles were indeed such 'good friends' that 'utility' was 'inseparable from justice', and this 'must always be understood when we talk of justice'.[112] In short, commercial society demanded utilitarian jurisprudence.

Apparently, however, commercial society did not demand any simple system of utilitarian morals. Whereas in the *Principles of Equity* Kames argued that justice was to be maintained only to the extent that its maintenance promoted utility, in his moral theory he insisted upon the autonomy of the virtue of justice – a virtue formed by the immediate injunctions of the moral sense, and a virtue which could never be reduced to the mere calculation of consequences. And whereas in his equity theory he identified a system of legal policy which ensured the 'advancement of commerce', in the *Sketches* he was equally concerned to identify the moral dangers which invariably attended 'successful commerce'. If the equity court served to further commerce and wealth, the achievement of this end inevitably opened 'a wide door to indolence, sensuality, corruption, prostitution and perdition'. If the self-interested commercial agent was well served by the *Principles of Equity*, a society whose members were exclusively motivated by the self-interested pursuit of material gain was one already lost to luxury and corruption.[113]

To return to Kames's larger anxieties regarding the ultimate moral consequences of commercial life is in one sense to point out the limited moral sphere

---
[111] *Equity*, p. 46.
[112] *Ibid.*, p. 267.
[113] 'Progress and Effects of Luxury', *Sketches*, ii, pp. 153–4, and 'Manners', *Sketches*, i, p. 347.

occupied by his legal doctrines. The equity court was not empowered to create patriotism, and like all political institutions it could never permanently check the forces which threatened it. Moreover, it was only in considering that part of morality which came before the equity court that Kames was moved to a notion of justice which seemed to lose its distinct identity and emerge as a mere appendage to utility and the interests of social well-being. Still, it often remains unclear how Kames's enthusiasms for improvement are to be squared with his broader moral commitments; and in the case of the *Principles of Equity*, he at least felt the need to explain why a work which began by invoking the 'refined duties of morality' ended up with contract and commercial law. Yet, revealingly enough, he could only make sense of the matter by returning to the dictates of utility. If the equity court dispensed with the 'more substantial ties' and devoted itself instead 'to the grosser connections solely, *viz.* those of interest', this was not to be taken to signify an excessive 'attachment to riches'. Rather, it only reflected the inability of the court to bring these 'more substantial' moral duties 'under general rules'.[114]

Kames's legal theory, then, had not solved all the problems posed by commercial society. But, through his historical investigations, he had relentlessly and exactingly demonstrated the unsuitability of much of Scots law for that society. In the *Principles of Equity* he had developed a systematic, theoretical account of the manner in which legal principles operated to create a law responsive to that society's needs. And, at the same time, he had identified in the Court of Session an effective instrument for lifting Scots law into the utilitarian world of law in commercial society – a feature of the theory of equity Kames himself could scarcely have undervalued.

[114] *Equity*, p. 47.

9 Cambridge paradigms and Scotch philosophers: a study of the relations between the civic humanist and the civil jurisprudential interpretation of eighteenth-century social thought

J. G. A. POCOCK

This essay is designed to study two approaches to the interpretation of early modern political and social thought, and of Scottish historical and economic theory in particular. The title chosen for the essay suggests that Cambridge is a ground on which both approaches are flourishing, as was clearly demonstrated by the King's College symposium out of which this volume grows; and I shall take the opportunity to comment upon some recent developments in Cambridge study of the history of political and social thought. The essay itself, however, is written at a distance from Cambridge, and reflects some of the current preoccupations of American and Canadian scholarship in the field.

I

The so-called civic humanist paradigm, with which the author of this essay is associated, makes its starting point a certain early modern articulation of the idea of virtue. In this sense, the term 'virtue' referred not simply to morally desirable practices or the inner disposition of the self towards them, but to the practice of citizenship in the classical or Graeco-Roman sense of that term. It entailed the maintenance of a civic equality among those who passed the often severe tests prerequisite to equality, and the moral disposition of the self towards the maintenance of a public (a better adjective than common) good, identifiable with the political association, *polis* or *respublica*, itself. It affirmed that the human personality was that of a *zōon politikon* and was fully expressed only in the practice of citizenship as an active virtue; man (the male bias of this ideal bordered on the absolute) was by nature a public being, and his public action was less that of a magistrate exercising authority than that of a citizen exercising equality. Authority occurred either as that of a master over an inferior, an equal over a non-equal – the classical republic was an open conspiracy of equals – or in a more moral sense, within the republic itself, as that of a few to which the many deferred without sacrificing their equality. And as the result of historical processes which need not be rehearsed again here, virtue in this sense had acquired material as well as moral preconditions. To qualify for equality and citizenship, the individual must be master of his own household, proprietor along with his equals of the only arms permitted to be borne in wars which must be publicly undertaken, and possessor of property whose function was to bring him not profit and luxury, but independence and leisure. Without property he must be a servant; without a public and civic monopoly of arms, his citizenship must be corrupted.

It has been often enough told how this ideal – I shall reserve the term 'paradigm' to denote its employment as an interpretative matrix – was articulated by Florentine thinkers including Machiavelli, established in English thought by Harrington, and subsequently modernized by those whom some call neo-Harringtonians. Before proceeding, it is worthwhile to note the important tensions between civic and Christian morality. The citizen (or 'patriot') did not forgive or love his city's enemies, and Machiavelli had carried this distinction so far that even the public character of virtue began to appear morally ambivalent. In a universe where everything was civic, the practice of religion would be a function of citizenship and there would be no room for an autonomous clergy; the possibility fascinated post-Puritan Erastians and deists, but such worship might be directed towards the gods of a classical city rather than the creator of the *civitas Dei*. Lastly, the public self which was that of the citizen practised a virtue of *ataraxia* very far removed from *agape*. The anti-Christian possibilities latent in the civic ideal help account for its role in the Enlightenment, but only begin to account for the profound ambivalences of the Enlightenment's vision of the self.

The civic humanist ideal is applied as a paradigm in the interpretation of social thought in the eighteenth century by particularizing the ways in which it was used as a mode of criticism against the 'Whig oligarchy'.[1] This regime, which took shape by degrees in the half-century following the Exclusion crisis, was marked by a series of characteristics: a system of public credit, established in the 1690s, which was thought to stabilize government, facilitate the expansion of trade and the growth of military and naval power in Europe, America and India; a system of political patronage, associated in the public mind with the growth of credit and standing armies, and reinforced by the Septennial Act and other measures aimed at the restriction of political activity, which were believed to ensure the executive's control of the legislature; and the creation of the Kingdom of Great Britain by the 1707 Act of Union, which seemed to have established Scotland as a province or dependency of the English parliamentary oligarchy. It was in the course of criticizing, attacking and

---

[1] A Cambridge paradigm in its own right; we now study eighteenth-century ideologies as reactions against the processes described by J. H. Plumb.

defending these perceived realities that the classic oppositions between virtue and fortune, virtue and corruption, were joined by a third, that between virtue and commerce. The Whig regime, whose pillars were credit, patronage and office, was perceived as facilitating the growth of trade, a thing indeed almost universally desired; but it was perceived as ruling through the creation of a system of aristocratic dependencies, modern and commercial in their character rather than traditional or feudal, but no less aristocratic for all that. The growth of commerce was therefore associated with the growth of oligarchy, and perceived as the expansion of dependency long past the point where dependency became corruption – a line of thought perhaps culminating in the Virginian doctrinaire John Taylor of Caroline, for whom it was axiomatic that capitalism was a mode of aristocracy and that aristocracies employed capitalism to their own ends.[2] And Taylor was right, at least to the extent that the defence of commerce and capitalism, to 1776 and far beyond, tended to be a defence and not a criticism of aristocratic government in its Whig and even in its Federalist form; the notion that the 'bourgeois' and 'aristocratic' principles were at war in eighteenth-century Britain is wide of the mark.

The deployment of the paradigm continues in the following terms. The critics of the emerging Whig regime assailed its dependencies in the name of independence. They asserted the ideal of the classical citizen, head of his household, proprietor of his arms and direct participant in his own government; and they depicted him in Harringtonian or neo-Harringtonian terms, as the master of property in its natural form – which was land appropriated for cultivation – discharging its classical function, which was to endow him with the independence necessary to leisure, citizenship, self-mastery and virtue. His property was agrarian because its prime function was political rather than chrematistic; if Marxist categories were worth revising, one could say that the 'ancient' mode of production was being pitted against the 'feudal' and the 'bourgeois'. His morality was neo-Stoic, and more likely to lead to a deist than a Christian religious expression. His politics were in principle republican, because the classical republic was the paradigmatic form of political association for independent individuals desiring to affirm their virtue against corruption; and the Whig regime, employing patronage, credit and commerce in the service of parliamentary monarchy, represented corruption in its modern shape.

The classical and agrarian critique of Whig values intersected with dominant reality in a diversity of ways, which are seen to vary as one passes from province to province of the eighteenth-century British empire. In England the ruling oligarchy and the Tory and Old Whig oppositions to it had both first taken

[2] John Taylor (1753–1824), *Arator: being a series of agricultural essays, practical and political* (Georgetown, 1813); *An Inquiry into the Principles and Policy of the Government of the United States* (Fredericksburg, 1814).

shape; and here a quasi-republican language, which attempted to state alternatives to the ancient if turbulent association between king and parliament, had existed since the middle of the seventeenth century. It derived from the misguided endeavour of Sir John Culpeper (or whoever it was) to employ republican theory as a defence of Charles I's monarchy in *His Majesty's Answer to the Nineteen Propositions of Parliament*.[3] A number of writers, culminating in James Harrington, had retorted that if king, lords and commons aimed at maintaining an equilibrium between monarchy, aristocracy and democracy, they were doing so with outstanding inefficiency, and that if a true balance was desired it must be found in the orders of a true republic – which Harrington contended were also the orders of an agrarian balance. But the neo-Harringtonian writers, of whom Henry Neville was the first, began the conversion of republican theory into a means of restating the historical and constitutional relations of king, lords and commons; and from that time on – though a republican underground can usually be discovered if we look for it – the doctrine survived as the ideology of a series of parliamentary oppositions, within and without doors, of varying but seldom exalted levels of integrity. On the plane of reflection, this ideology maintained throughout the age of oligarchy a steady polemic against corruption, credit and commerce which – if the promptings of the paradigm be followed – was the occasion for the great revaluations of history that mark the eighteenth century. On the plane of action, however, it was hamstrung by English society's ineradicable commitment to the parliamentary institution, which as Montesquieu remarked played Byzantium (a not inappropriate image) to the Chalcedon of the republican ideal.[4] We may look upon the years 1780–4 – the years of Herbert Butterfield's 'revolution that did not happen'[5] – as marking the failure of the last attempt to move the Country against the Court, to create a classic alliance between Yorkshire gentlemen and London radicals that should have recalled the convergence of Tory and Old Whig notions to form the Country or Commonwealth ideology. Since ideas outlive movements, the extent of this ideology's role in forming the changing radicalisms of the next half-century remains on the agenda for historical investigation; but the complexity of the terms in which the history of English political thought must necessarily be written means that its role, however important, is likely to be less than paradigmatic.

In the thirteen British colonies which became the United States of America, we encounter a scene at once more simple and more dynamic. Increasingly autonomous elite and popular political movements found Old Whig language

---

[3] The definitive study remains that of Corinne C. Weston, *English Constitutional Theory and the House of Lords* (London, 1965).
[4] '...he [Harrington] built a Chalcedon, though he had a Byzantium before his eyes' (Montesquieu, *The Spirit of the Laws*, trans. T. Nugent (1750), Bk. XI, ch. 6).
[5] Herbert Butterfield, *George III, Lord North and the People* (London, 1949).

greatly to their taste and highly expressive of their values and experience; they became overwhelmingly (if not exclusively) responsive to the argument that the parliamentary institution in Britain was itself corrupt and attempting to foist corruption on an innocent but vulnerable America. The Whig mind's enduring concern with seventeenth-century precedents ensured that the Declaration of Independence presented George III as a Charles or a James, not as a Sir Robert Walpole;[6] but the equally persistent concern with virtue and corruption helped ensure that the republic which emerged rejected parliamentary monarchy in favour of the separation of powers. The debates of the Philadelphia Convention are notoriously the highest point ever reached by civic humanist theory in practice; and though the relative naïveties of English opposition ideology were transformed by, and into, the Federalism of Hamilton and Madison, they continued to inform the criticisms of the Federal institution that arose within its own workings. The polemic which Madison and Jefferson conducted against Hamilton in the 1790s was quite self-consciously a replay of the polemic against Walpole seventy years previously;[7] and the themes which it developed included every one of the great ambivalences of the dialogue between virtue and commerce. The civic humanist paradigm – known here as 'the republican synthesis'[8] – continues to find acceptance among historians as an operational guide to the growth of American values and an American perception of history.[9] It remains irreplaceable as a means of explaining why this is the only political culture which recurrently laments the corruption of its virtue, the loss of its innocence and the end of its dream, and then sets about renewing them; the 'Puritan origins of the American self'[10] blend perfectly at this point with the republican paradigm. Those European historians whose deepest wish is that America should never have existed – since it compromises the uniqueness they claim for their own history – are driven to the unconvincing strategy of condemning the paradigm as ideology precisely because it works as historiography;[11] while in America – pending the next revival of the Hamiltonian mode of interpretation – its only challengers are those, from Marxists on the left to Straussians on the right, so obsessed with

[6] But John Taylor regularly insisted that it had been the intention of the British to impose the Walpolean system on America, after independence as well as before; and this is the point of most accusations against Hamilton and Adams of wanting to install 'English' principles of government.

[7] Lance Banning, *The Jeffersonian Persuasion* (Ithaca, N.Y., 1978).

[8] A useful if no longer up-to-date bibliography is in Robert E. Shallhope, 'Towards a Republican Synthesis: The Emergence of an Understanding of Republicanism in American Historiography', *William and Mary Quarterly*, 3rd Ser., 19 (1972), 49–80.

[9] See John Higham and Paul Conkin (eds.), *New Directions in American Intellectual History* (Baltimore, 1979); John M. Murrin, 'The Great Inversion', in J. G. A. Pocock (ed.), *Three British Revolutions: 1641, 1688, 1776* (Princeton, N.J., 1980).

[10] Sacvan Bercovich, *The Puritan Origins of the American Self* (New Haven, Conn., 1975).

[11] See Cesare Vasoli, '*The Machiavellian Moment*: A Grand Ideological Synthesis', *Journal of Modern History*, 49 (1977), 661–70.

their hostility to a Lockean 'modern' or 'bourgeois' 'liberalism' that they can see nothing on the stage of history but the arrival and triumph of their antagonist.

It is when we arrive, by this circuitous route, at the interpretation of Scottish thought in the eighteenth century that we encounter the problems of describing the alternatives to the civic humanist paradigm which existed in that age. In *The Machiavellian Moment* and elsewhere may be found the deliberately coat-trailing assertion that the indictments of the Whig regime and its dominant values are a good deal easier to discover than the countervailing vindications.[12] That assertion – though its author has not yet seen reason to abandon it – was designed to elicit responses, while pointing out that the true structure of eighteenth-century argument was still to be discovered. Since it was made, there has been rapid development of a thesis which presents Scottish political economy as the effective alternative to the nostalgias of agrarian republicanism; at the same time there has come forward a counter-thesis which argues that Scottish thought evolved largely outside the maxims and language of the paradigm. It is this circumstance which has made the present essay necessary.

The writings of Nicholas Phillipson[13] and John Robertson (see pp. 179–202 and 137–78 above), as well as of others, present the means of treating Scottish thought as responding to the civic humanist challenge. They take their departure from the writings and oratory of Andrew Fletcher of Saltoun, a key figure in the neo-Harringtonian lineage, who from 1698 to 1707 argued the cause of a Scottish form of civic virtue, to be preserved by safeguarding an autonomous parliament and militia. With the defeat of his advocacy of a federal rather than an incorporating Union, came the realization that Scottish participation in the English *Wirtschaftwunder* had been bought by the sacrifice of civic virtue, and that an alternative form of virtue was an ideological and practical necessity. This was met by the massive and rapid adoption of an Addisonian Whig political, or rather social, culture; Edinburgh saw a proliferation of Spectatorial clubs and societies, practising the virtues of polite conversation and enlightened taste while discussing the economic, cultural and even – given an age in which manners seemed no unimportant part of morality – the moral improvement of Scottish life. The locus of virtue shifted decisively from the civic to the civil, from the political and military to that blend of the economic, cultural and moral which we call the social for short.

---

[12] Pocock, *The Machiavellian Moment: Florentine Political Thought and the Atlantic Republican Tradition* (Princeton, N.J., 1975), pp. 467, 487–8, 508.

[13] N. T. Phillipson, 'Towards a Definition of the Scottish Enlightenment', in P. Fritz and D. Williams (eds.), *City and Society in the Eighteenth Century* (Toronto, 1973), pp. 125–47; 'Culture and Society in the 18th Century Province: The Case of Edinburgh and the Scottish Enlightenment', in L. Stone (ed.), *The University in Society*, 2 vols. (Princeton, N.J., 1974), ii, pp. 407–48.

In thus taking up Addisonian politeness as a substitute for Fletcherian patriotism, the new Unionist elites attached themselves to such themes as the quarrel between ancients and moderns, or that tension between republican and imperial values which renders any concept of the 'Augustan' problematic;[14] but did so in ways which placed them conclusively, if never exclusively, on the 'modern' or 'Augustan' side of the rift. 'Taste' and 'politeness', for most of the eighteenth century, were concepts freighted with a heavy ideological load. To latitudinarians and *philosophes* they connoted that reasonable and civil Anglicanism, Arminianism or deism, with which it was hoped to replace the enthusiasms and fanaticisms of Puritanism or Christianity; but they were no less effectively employed in answer to the challenge (itself often non-Christian) of civic and republican virtue. Andrew Fletcher himself had declared that it was the growth of commerce and culture, towards the end of the Middle Ages, which tempted the warrior freeman to entrust government and defence to professionals, thus losing his liberty and virtue in the pursuit of leisure and refinement. Taste and politeness had been among the causes of a harmful specialization of functions. In reply to Fletcher, Defoe (and later by implication Addison) asserted that liberty had been worth modifying, and had not been truly lost, when the processes of government had been entrusted to representatives and specialists, leaving the individual free to strengthen his economic and cultural, and in consequence his political, resources. The liberal paradigm thus made its appearance in answer to the civic. There had been – it began to be said – a fanaticism of virtue no less than of religion; just as the enthusiast flung himself into fantasies of faith for lack of taste and polite discrimination, so – declared Montesquieu – Lycurgus and Plato had promulgated harsh disciplines and rigorous metaphysics to the inhabitants of a restrictive and under-specialized antique economy.[15] With the growth of trade and more under-specialized antique economy.[15] With the growth of trade and more complex exchange relationships, manners began to be softened and passions refined, *le doux commerce* made its appearance,[16] and 'conversation', 'intercourse' and 'commerce' could be used synonymously to denote economic, cultural or sexual transaction. Commerce was the parent of politeness, and of an altogether non-classical conception of liberty. The philosopher of antiquity, exponent of an *esprit de système*, could be replaced by the *philosophe* of modernity, whose *esprit de méthode* abandoned metaphysical system in favour of that faculty of judicious discrimination known by the names of 'taste and science'.[17] When

---

[14] Howard D. Weinbrot, *Augustus Caesar in 'Augustan' England* (Princeton, N.J., 1978).
[15] Montesquieu, *The Spirit of the Laws*, Bk. IV, ch. 8.
[16] Albert Hirschman, *The Passions and the Interests: Political Arguments for Capitalism before its Triumph* (Princeton, N.J., 1977).
[17] The language here is Gibbon's; *esprit de système* and *esprit de méthode* (though not originating with him) are key terms in his *Essai sur l' Étude de la Littérature*, and 'taste and science' conclude a notable quotation from the *Decline and Fall*, given below at note 27.

the failure of the *Treatise of Human Nature* caused Hume to take up belles-lettres, essays and histories, his withdrawal was a highly strategic one by the canons of his day.[18]

By considering Scottish thought in this way, as a response to the civic humanist paradigm, we gain a fuller understanding of how Adam Smith moved from the *Theory of Moral Sentiments* to the *Inquiry into the Nature and Causes of the Wealth of Nations*. A crucial step in the emergence of Scottish social theory is, of course, that elusive phenomenon, the advent of the four-stages scheme of history.[19] The progression from hunter to shepherd to farmer to merchant offered not only an account of increasing plenty, but a series of stages of increasing division of labour, bringing about in their turn an increasingly complex organization of both society and personality. Given an epistemology of sense-impressions and ideas, a psychology of passions and sympathies, it must become evident that the human personality took shape through interaction with the objects it encountered; and the four-stages theory placed at the centre of perception a historical typology of the objects it gathered, appropriated, exchanged and produced in seeking its own sustenance and perpetuation. The refinement of the passions and the growth of politeness were central to the process; it is not by accident that Kames, Millar and (with modifications) Smith and Robertson preface their accounts of social development with a chapter on the condition of women,[20] based on the virtually materialist assumption that sexuality is historically conditioned by the means of production and their effect upon social and personality structures. Savages, thought Robertson, were sexually cold;[21] shepherds, thought Millar, were socially conditioned to the emotionalisms of pastoral poetry.[22] In each case, the distribution of goods determined social relations, and both determined the appearance and expression of the passions. The Scottish theorists were not far removed – though the distances may need stressing – from the hypothesis that men create themselves in history through their modes of production.

Our paradigm presents the Scottish Enlightenment as directed less against the Christians than against the ancients. It replaced the *polis* by politeness, the *oikos* by the economy. In place of the classical citizen, master of his land, family and arms, practising an austerely virtuous equality with his no less independent

---

[18] See the essays by James Moore, George Davie and Peter Jones, in David F. Norton, Nicholas Capaldi and Wade L. Robison (eds.), *McGill Hume Studies* (San Diego, Calif., 1979).

[19] Ronald L. Meek, *Social Science and the Ignoble Savage* (Cambridge, 1976); Peter Stein, *Legal Evolution: The Story of an Idea* (Cambridge, 1980).

[20] Lord Kames, 'Progress of the Female Sex', *Sketches of the History of Man*, 4th edn, 4 vols. (Edinburgh, 1788), ii, pp. 1–97; John Millar, *The Origin of the Distinction of Ranks*, in William C. Lehmann, *John Millar of Glasgow 1735–1801: His Life and Thought and his Contributions to Sociological Analysis* (Cambridge, 1960), pp. 183–228; Smith, *LJ(A)* iii.1–77.

[21] William Robertson, *The History of America*, in Robertson, *Works*, 2 vols. (Edinburgh, 1824), i, pp. 292–3, 295–6, 317–22.

[22] Millar, *Ranks*, pp. 203–8.

peers, appeared a fluid, historical and transactional vision of *homo faber et mercator*, shaping himself through the stages of history by means of the division and specialization of labour, the diversification and refinement of the passions. The political image of man was replaced by a social and transactional image of man and politics. In the historical (and in that sense 'modern') process which was now man's habitat, republican citizenship was no more than a crucial episode; a moment in the transition from agriculture to merchandise when propertied independence made possible the growth of patriot virtue but, at the same moment, of commercial relationships which might all too easily corrupt it. It was not clear, however, that Lycurgus or Plato, Diogenes or Cato were figures to whom one should look back with overwhelming nostalgia. In a perfectly serious sense, they lacked politeness; and there was an alternative ideal of liberty and virtue, in which property and specialization were protected by authority and law, more appropriate to the commercial stage of history and perhaps ranking higher in the human scale.

The paradigm rejects or modifies a number of wisdoms once conventional and still persistent. Since it presents the ideal of republican virtue as an ideological assault upon the Whig regime, it presents Scottish social theory as the latter's ideological defence; from which it follows that the delineation of commercial society was not a criticism of aristocracy, but a vindication of it in its Whig form. Conservatives such as Josiah Tucker, agrarian radicals such as John Taylor and William Cobbett, saw this with peculiar clarity, both before and after urban radicals began attacking the management of public finance by an aristocracy acting in its own interests. Any thesis that in eighteenth-century Britain 'aristocracy' and 'bourgeoisie' were generally at strife has to be given up as unhesitatingly in the history of ideology as in that of political management; the history of the ideology of commerce would be better written with an extremely sparing application of the term 'bourgeois' formerly used to connote it. Most collisions between the humanist paradigm and Marxian interpreters occur because the latter are compulsively addicted to employing 'bourgeois' in and out of season; if it could be shelved for a while we should find much to agree about.

The paradigm also encourages us to look questioningly on the convention that the ideology of commerce sprang from the political and epistemological individualisms of Hobbes and Locke – a position long held by Marxians and other nineteenth-century romantics, and currently reinforced in North America by a series of neo-classical and neo-Aristotelian schools, on the whole conservative and varyingly linked with the names of Arendt, Strauss, and (elsewhere on the spectrum) Voegelin and Wolin.[23] The rise of the social to pre-eminence over the political (to denote which is at present one of the cant

---

[23] For a short introduction to these schools, see John G. Gunnell, *Political Theory: Tradition and Interpretation* (Boston, Mass., 1978).

usages of the term 'liberalism') seems to have rested on a psychology of sentiment, sympathy and passion, better equipped to account for politeness, taste and transaction than was the rigorous individualism of self-interest. At least one notable political economist, Josiah Tucker, bracketed Locke's theory of property with classical republicanism and stamped him an essentially archaic and pre-commercial thinker;[24] and it was only at the very end of the century that romantics of the left and right began denouncing commercial ideology as founded on the 'cold', 'mechanical' philosophies of Hobbes, Locke, Newton and Hume. It is possible, however, that Reid and the Aberdeen school began the practice of writing the history of British philosophy as organized around the advent of Locke, and that this in turn had something to do with that still obscure process, the movement from the Scottish Enlightenment to the 'philosophic radicals' (who were not polite and cared little for the refinement of the passions).

The last-mentioned phenomenon raises the question whether we are to think of the commercial ideology as having at any period triumphed over the ideology of civic patriotism and virtue, and driven it from the field. Since historians are trained to think in linear, progressive and quasi-dialectical patterns, in which the movement is normally 'from' one state of affairs 'to' another, they are disposed to think in terms of one reigning paradigm at a time, and to see any tensions and contradictions which may have given rise to a successor as contained within the structure reigning at a given moment. It is conventional to think of the predecessor of a given paradigm as altogether superseded and submerged. But the civic humanist paradigm, whose rise as a tool of historical explanation we have been exploring here, encourages us to think of the civic and commercial ideologies as struggling with one another at least down to the lifetimes of Adam Smith and John Millar; and whatever may have happened in the next half-century, it is not yet obvious that we have found, or even that we should look for, a moment at which the former may be said to have disappeared entirely. In the United States, this is not even on the agenda; the persistence of Jeffersonian values, in no matter how attenuated and nostalgic a form, is a major fact of intellectual history and cannot be understood without constant reference to the agrarian republicanism of the founders. What America might have been remains a standing instrument of criticism of what it is. In the very different climate of the United Kingdom, nostalgia and the jeremiad are not cultural institutions; but the historian of pre-Victorian values must observe that denunciations of 'old corruption', paper money, the national debt and so on remain staples of radical criticism

[24] Josiah Tucker, *A Treatise Concerning Civil Government* (London, 1781). See Pocock, 'Natural Right and Commerce: Josiah Tucker's Critique of Locke', unpublished paper presented to the 'John Locke and the Political Thought of the 1680s' symposium of the Conference for the Study of Political Thought and the Folger Institute for Renaissance and Eighteenth-Century Studies, Washington, D.C., 21–23 March 1980.

and that debates over the historical role of the landed and monied interests figure prominently in the Reform controversies of 1832 and 1867.

At a higher level of systematic theory, the question which the paradigm obliges us to raise is that of the success which Scottish social thought enjoyed in winning acceptance for the view that division of labour and diversification of personality were the natural and desirable lot of historical man. We see this as originating in the effort to legitimize the standing army; the original specialization of function denounced by Fletcher and defended by Defoe was that between citizen and soldier; the virtue of the citizen – whether rigorous in Sparta or versatile in Athens – was the virtue of unspecialized man. In the era of Smith and Millar the effects of specialization on the personality of the labourer were beginning to arouse concern. If it is possible to establish linkages here, to show that it was in some real sense civic capacity and virtue which employer and labourer were thought in danger of losing, we may end by establishing a kind of continuity between the days of Swift and those of Marx, and showing that there was in fact no moment at which the ideology of commerce was immune from the criticisms which the neo-Harringtonians had set in motion. This possibility, which has yet to be tested in research, seems at present to provide the civic humanist paradigm with its outer limits.

II

So much – and it is a good deal – for the project of explaining Scottish social thought as a theory of the diversification of personality through the processes of history, presented as an ideological alternative to the classical ideal of personality unified in the practice of civic virtue and by a relatively static economy. Both England and Scotland (Fletcher's seminal *Discourse of Government in Relation to Militias* was published in both London and Edinburgh and evoked responses mainly in the former) can be made to yield ideological settings in which this interpretation seems plausible. But there is an alternative, and largely Cambridge, paradigm to which we now turn: one which selects different threads in the texture of eighteenth-century thought, and in so doing draws attention to the cultural limitations of the civic humanist paradigm. The latter is republican in its premises; it presents eighteenth-century social theories as organized for and against an ideal of virtue which, as stated at the outset of this essay, was rigorously civic in character and denoted the public relations between equal and independent political animals. There are many other ways of using the word 'virtue'; and, what is far more important, it has never been suggested by anyone that the whole tradition of western political thought has been constructed around the civic ideal in its expressly republican form. The function of such monographs as Fink's *The Classical Republicans*, Bailyn's *The*

Ideological Origins of the American Revolution[25] and the present writer's *The Machiavellian Moment* has been to show how a civic humanist or classical republican politics was evolved by Florentines and restated by Englishmen and Americans, receiving from the Scots a reply which helped constitute the new science of political economy. The works just mentioned form a 'tunnel history', selecting a single theme and pushing it through until it emerges in the daylight of new country; they do not and cannot claim to have told all that there is to tell.

The alternative paradigm starts driving its tunnel from that point at which Scottish social thought differed most in character from English: the central position which it accorded to the study of civil jurisprudence. To familiarize themselves with this pillar in the edifice of European intellectual training, Scotsmen regularly, as Englishmen seldom, studied at Dutch universities, and in the age of Pufendorf and Barbeyrac they encountered natural law, the law of nations and the civil law, not merely as a professional training but as a principal mode of organizing great traditions of moral, social and political philosophy. Even those, like David Hume, who had no vocation for the law, studied human nature and polite letters in a climate pervaded by what was once known as 'the modernised theory of natural law'[26] and was rapidly becoming, by one route and another, the attempt to establish the principles of social living by empirically establishing the principles of human nature. Since human society could now be studied in much geographical and historical diversity, the way lay increasingly open to studying these principles as manifest in variety, change, process and even development. And since, for reasons which go back at least to the Stoics, the study of law has been associated, far more closely than has the study of civic virtue and the *vivere civile*, with moral and epistemological philosophy, the way also lay open to the integration of Cartesian, Lockean, Shaftesburean or Humean theories about perceptions, ideas, sympathies and passions into what became a science of man and society, founded on the unity of human nature in the diversity of human history. Even the newly important cults of politeness and taste could be incorporated into this science, and could appear, as they increasingly did, a historical phenomenon of great if problematic significance.[27]

The alternative paradigm, therefore, considers the growth of Scottish social thought in the eighteenth century as an evolution within a tradition of civil jurisprudence which Scotland shared with adjacent Europe rather than with England. It may do something for nationalist sentiment by laying emphasis on

---

[25] Z. S. Fink, *The Classical Republicans: An Essay in the Recovery of a Pattern of Thought in Seventeenth-Century England* (Evanston, Illinois, 1945); Bernard Bailyn, *The Ideological Origins of the American Revolution* (Cambridge, Mass., 1967).

[26] G. H. Sabine, heading to ch. 21 of *A History of Political Theory* (New York, 1937).

[27] Gibbon: '...and after the revolution of ten centuries, freedom became the happy parent of taste and science': *Decline and Fall*, ed. J. B. Bury, 7 vols. (London, 1902), i, p. 53.

Scottish cosmopolitanism rather than provincialism, on membership in Europe rather than on self-doubt and self-affirmation in an age of involvement within Britain. It may even attract the intellect of an England currently in search of means of affirming some unity with Europe. There are signs of a tendency to play down the historic importance of both the common law mind, as overstressing English autochthony, and civic humanism, as making England too marginal to Europe; the present writer may soon find himself acused by English as well as European colleagues of exaggerating for ideological purposes the uniqueness of the Anglo-American Atlantic.[28] But though the debate between the paradigms, like other historiographical controversies, may not be free of ideological overtones, these will not assist us in evaluating the arguments advanced. The jurisprudential paradigm possesses great strength and attraction, and performs services which the civic humanist paradigm does not. The study of civil law was central to the Scottish intellect, and merely to explore the opposition between Whig commercialism and Tory or Old Whig neo-classicism is not to explore the whole field over which it exercised force. Scottish thought is not reducible to – though it may at times be usefully characterized as – a debate between Court and Country,[29] and Scottish culture must be seen as operating within its own conditioning structures, even though provincialism within the Union was obviously one of these.

There is also a far broader perspective, in which the approach through jurisprudence obliges us to move from paradigm to canon. It permits us to study Scottish social thought in the context of a generalized history of western political theory, which everything encourages and even enjoins us to organize, and to see as having been organized, along jurisprudential and philosophical lines. We approach even Hume (that 'terrible campaign country')[30] through the broad fields of Aquinas and Ockham, Suarez and Grotius, Hobbes and Locke and Pufendorf; the swiftly-moving horsemen of moral philosophy skirmish and regroup along our line of march; and we even find, accompanying us as heavy auxiliaries, a separate troop of civic humanists, Ciceronian and Stoic rather than Catonian and Machiavellian in character, whose understanding of an active social morality is a good deal easier to integrate with the moralist and juristic traditions than is that studied in *The Machiavellian Moment*. It would not be hard to feel that the tendencies of research, in the few years since that book was published, have been to emphasize the distinctiveness and even the isolation of the themes it explored.

If writing the history of civic humanism (or classical republicanism) may be compared to the driving of a tunnel, it is understandable that there should

---

[28] Vasoli, '*The Machiavellian Moment*: A Grand Ideological Synthesis'.
[29] H. T. Dickinson, *Liberty and Property: Political Ideology in Eighteenth-Century Britain* (London, 1977).
[30] Duncan Forbes, *Hume's Philosophical Politics* (Cambridge, 1975), p. viii.

follow an attempt to restore the history of political thought in general to the high road so long marked out by philosophy and jurisprudence. This has been the achievement of a sequence of scholars – Duncan Forbes, Quentin Skinner, Peter Stein, Richard Tuck, James Tully[31] – who may be collectively considered the authors of the second 'Cambridge paradigm'. It is when we come to apply the several paradigms to 'Scotch philosophers' that it becomes peculiarly necessary to inquire how they are related to one another, and the indications at present are that this may not prove an easy problem to solve. Everyone is anxious to avoid the 'two-buckets fallacy', which presumes rival explanations to be mutually exclusive, so that to strengthen one is necessarily to weaken the other; but we are to some extent pushed in that direction by what appears to be a marked hiatus or discontinuity between the vocabulary or language of civic humanism and that of civil jurisprudence.

It is hard to find juristic terminology or assumptions in Machiavelli, Guicciardini or Harrington – though the second was a doctor of laws and the third lived in the iron age of the common law mind – and the reason is not far to seek: so at least the premises of the civic humanist paradigm strongly suggest. The basic concept in republican thinking is *virtus*; the basic concept of all jurisprudence is necessarily *ius*; and there is no known way of representing virtue as a right. To say – as no doubt many have said – that the prince, the magistrate or the individual must exercise virtue if right is to be done is to utter a principle which does not deliver us from our difficulty; for virtue, once we cease to describe it merely as a disposition to righteousness and begin to define it in a strictly political sense, becomes a quality of the relations between persons equal in citizenship, and between them and the republic, *polis* or *vivere civile*, which is the form of that equality. It pertains so directly to those relationships that it does not require that they be mediated through the proprietorship of things; property is the precondition of virtue, but not the medium in which it is expressed. We may say that the citizens grant one another an equality of rights, somewhat as we say that they rule and are ruled; but the rights exist for the sake of the equality and the virtue which is its expression, not the other way round. Civic virtue may entail the presence of all manner of rights, but it is neither necessary nor appropriate to premise a right in order to explain its presence.

If *virtus* (in the rigorously political sense) pertains exclusively to the relations between persons, *ius* takes its departure from a myriad starting points in the possession, distribution and administration of things. *Ius ad rem* and *ius in re*[32] are premised in explaining the rights demanded of one person by another,

---

[31] Forbes, *Hume's Philosophical Politics*; Quentin Skinner, *The Foundations of Modern Political Thought*, 2 vols. (Cambridge, 1978); Stein, *Legal Evolution*; Richard Tuck, *Natural Rights Theories: Their Origin and Development* (Cambridge, 1979); James Tully, *A Discourse on Property: John Locke and his Adversaries* (Cambridge, 1980).

[32] I am much indebted to Tuck, *Natural Rights Theories*, pp. 14–15, for these useful terms.

recognized in one person by another; and to the extent to which this is so, the things are the medium of contact between the persons and the grounds of the rights which they recognize in one another. Jurisprudence, with its inbuilt concerns for *meum et tuum* and for *suum cuique*, has been from its historic beginnings the fundamental expression of possessive individualism, in which the individual and his social and moral world are defined in terms of the property transactions in which he is engaged. As we pass from the civic humanist to the jurisprudential paradigm, therefore, the relation of property to politics changes, and with it the definition of the political itself. Since – for example – the civic humanist supposes men to be *kata phusin* the inhabitants of *poleis*, he has a different need from the jurist's to envisage a pre-civil or pre-natural state, in which men are not yet men because not yet citizens. Stoics and others have imagined a wilderness of savage men as prelude to the appearance of the legislator, who by speech, divine afflatus or benevolent imposture, awakens them to the possibility of virtue; but this is a profoundly different process from that imagined by the jurist, through which in a diversity of ways individuals come to have *ius et dominium* over things and other persons, rights which they then transfer to others or retain in their own possession. The classical republic, in which *ius, dominium* and sovereignty have been transferred by all men to all men, is a rare and inconspicuous product of the jurist's state of nature, though Richard Tuck claims to have found some Dutch contemporaries of Spinoza in whom this phenomenon is more important than we have hitherto noticed.[33] He has not yet told us, however, whether the Dutchmen's republic existed in order to safeguard right or to practise virtue, and until this point is cleared up we shall not know whether they had bridged the gap between *ius* and *virtus*. *Prima facie*, it would seem that the function of the jurist's state of nature was to generate *ius* and transfer it to a magistrate or sovereign who might exercise absolute or conditional authority, and might represent the individual but could never be identical with him; and that even when the whole people was ruled and represented by the people as a whole, the distinguishing attribute of that *populus* was the exercise of *maiestas* rather than *virtus*. The child of jurisprudence is liberalism, in which the disjunction between individual and sovereign remains, no matter how close the two are brought to one another; whereas republican virtue pertains immediately to the individual, not as proprietor or rights-bearer but as citizen, sharing self-rule among a number of equals without the need of any prior *translatio*.

This theoretical differentiation is designed to explain a result which is predicted of further research: namely, that some aspects of Scottish social thought in the eighteenth century will continue to answer to the civic humanist

---

[33] Tuck, *Natural Rights Theories*, p. 141n. I am sorry Richard Tuck thinks I 'chose not to discuss' these theories in *The Machiavellian Moment*; as he might have guessed, I was unaware of their existence before reading his footnote.

paradigm, while others yield better results when treated by the jurisprudential. If this is so, we shall find the vocabulary and language of civic humanism, together with others derived from it, existing side by side with the language of civil jurisprudence; and we shall be in a position to account for their simultaneous presence, but not as yet to determine the relationship between them. One possible strategy to use in confronting the latter problem will be to declare that the civic humanist and jurisprudential vocabularies entailed distinct and opposing structures of political value, so that the relation between them was one of ideological tension. Criticism of the Whig regime was best expressed by invoking the virtue of the Roman republic; its defence by invoking the law of the empire. The individual who found his rights in the possession and conveyance of property was easier to depict as the inhabitant of a commercial and polite society, held together by the exchange of goods and sympathies, than the individual who affirmed his virtue in the austere equalities of purely civic action. Josiah Tucker – who was an English Whig well-acquainted with Scottish thought – was clear that men's natural sociability found expression only in modern commercial society;[34] Edward Gibbon – who was another – seems to have shaped the *Decline and Fall* around the proposition that while the corruption of virtue explained the decay of the ancient world, it was irrelevant to the diagnosis of the modern.[35] This projection does not oblige us to suppose that the ideological motive was always and unvaryingly present. We shall find cases where the thesis of a progressive division of labour and diversification of personality was openly advanced as a means of escaping the grip of the ideal of civic virtue; but should we find others where it seems to have evolved out of the autonomous development of civil jurisprudence and no reference to the civic humanist critique can be found, we need not affirm an ideological motive – and we are free to look for other motives – while continuing to examine the ideological effect.

But this broadly binary presentation must not be allowed to become too tidy and elegant. The civic humanist and jurisprudential paradigms had, as Quentin Skinner has shown,[36] existed side by side since at latest the thirteenth century, when the liberty of Italian republics could be defended simultaneously by rhetoricians such as Brunetto Latini, chanting the praises of civic virtue, and by jurists such as Bartolus of Saxoferrato, tracing the peregrinations of *imperium* and *ius*. If Skinner has not produced much in the way of intertraffic between these two modes of speech, there is clearly no need to present them as ideologically opposed at that period. Moving to the sixteenth century, he

[34] See Pocock, 'Natural Right and Commerce: Josiah Tucker's Critique of Locke'.
[35] See Pocock, 'Between Machiavelli and Hume; Gibbon as Civic Humanist and Philosophic Historian', in G. W. Bowersock, J. Clive and S. Graubard (eds.), *Edward Gibbon and the Decline and Fall of the Roman Empire* (Cambridge, Mass., 1977), and 'Gibbon's *Decline and Fall* and the World-View of the Late Enlightenment', *Eighteenth-Century Studies*, 10 (1977), 287–303.
[36] Skinner, *Foundations*, i, chs. 1 and 2.

has done much to remind us of the existence of Ciceronian and Senecan modes of humanism, in which the tensions between virtue and commerce – and conceivably the gap between *virtus* and *ius* – were already a good deal reduced.[37] It is highly possible that these or their successors figure in eighteenth-century ideologies of sociability, sensibility and politeness, and there serve to reduce the starkness of the opposition between citizenship and culture. In the age of the Anglo-Scottish Union, when the reaction against the Whig regime in its various forms led to many dramatic restatements of the virtue-commerce tension, there is plenty of evidence for the persistence of the civic humanist paradigm. In such American phenomena as the confrontation between Jeffersonian and Hamiltonian values, it appears to be the dominating presence; but in the very different climate of Scotland, it may be that we shall find both theorists who thought they had overcome the tension and theorists who had hardly felt it, and that these will prove difficult to tell apart. It is certainly not the case that the Scottish theorists in general regarded republican and jurisprudential language as distinct and ideologically opposite rhetorics. Their methods were highly syncretic, and work remains to be done on how and why the first generation of Enlightened professors – Carmichael, Turnbull, Hutcheson[38] – set about integrating with their systems of modernized jurisprudence and social morality the works not only of Locke, but of such republicans and Commonwealthmen as Harrington and Sidney. Here again, we must investigate how far the concept of 'virtue' – above all in its rigorously civic significance – was at tension with that of 'moral sense', and how far the tension was overcome if it ever existed.

The effect of approaching the birth of political economy through the alternative paradigms of civic humanism, Addisonian morality and natural jurisprudence is that it appears to have had far more to do with morality than with science. We see it as part of an immensely rich and multi-faceted civil or social humanism, intimately related with the civic or military–political humanism which it was intended to replace. This gain in vision, however, leaves us confronting a problem which is not unlike the old 'Adam Smith problem' in a more complex historical form. How did the complex synthesis of 'moral sentiment' with 'the wealth of nations' evolve or degenerate into the science of classical economics; how did it come to be denounced as cold, mechanical and dismal, founded on a restrictive and reductionist theory of the human personality it had sought to liberate from classical restraints? What, if any, is the relationship between Smith's or Millar's criticisms of the effects

---

[37] *Ibid.*, chs. 8 and 9.
[38] See Donald Winch, *Adam Smith's Politics: An Essay in Historiographic Revision* (Cambridge, 1978); and James Moore, 'Locke and the Scottish Jurists', unpublished paper presented to the 'John Locke and the Political Thought of the 1680s' symposium of the Conference for the Study of Political Thought and the Folger Institute for Renaissance and Eighteenth-Century Studies, Washington, D.C., 21–23 March 1980.

of specialization on the labourer's personality, founded as they are on civic humanist premises, and the apparently similar criticisms put forward by Marx, to whom the perception of man as naturally political meant so little? These questions persist at the end of the inquiry we have been conducting.

A common strategy is to invoke Mandeville and suppose that this vindication of egotism and greed somehow unmasks commercial society and prefigures its reductionism. Yet this hardly seems convincing in the light of Hume's, Smith's and Robertson's labours to demonstrate the proliferation and diversification of personality under the conditions of commercial growth, an enterprise in which they incorporated all that Mandeville had had to say. Another strategy would be to go back to the proto-economists such as Petty or Child, and study those older conceptions of 'the wealth of nations' in which the generation of value and the circulation of goods were explored because they contributed to national power. To the first Chinese students of western values, a century after Smith, it seemed inescapable that this was the root of the matter, and that liberal individualism was a means to the pursuit of power;[39] and if we are to seek a dismal science latent in Scottish thought, this might be a way of finding it. The pursuit of virtue was never, as Machiavelli stressed, separable from the pursuit of power.

But the analysis and unmasking of ideology seem inferior, as means of solving the problems we are left confronting, to the further study of history. If we are to understand whether political economy did become a reductionist science, or why it was denounced for doing so, we must write or rewrite the whole ideological and philosophical history of the half-century of counter-revolution, industrial revolution and war that separate the time of Smith from that of Ricardo. Outside America,[40] it seems unlikely that the history of thought in this period can be organized with the clash of virtue and commerce at its centre; but the arguments and perceptions generated in that debate will prove to have been powerfully present.

[39] Benjamin Schwartz, *The Search for Wealth and Power: Yen Fu and the West* (Cambridge, Mass., 1964).

[40] Drew R. McCoy, *The Elusive Republic: Political Economy in Jeffersonian America* (Chapel Hill, North Carolina, 1980).

10 Adam Smith's 'enduring particular result': a political and cosmopolitan perspective*

DONALD WINCH

The initial premise of this paper is stunningly obvious: the main prize in any attempt to establish connections between the civic tradition, natural jurisprudence, and political economy, considered within an eighteenth-century Scottish context, must be awarded to an interpretation that succeeds in capturing the *Wealth of Nations* and whatever else seems essential to secure that summit once reached. This military-cum-mountaineering metaphor accords with some harmless competitive features of the present state of scholarly debate, and I shall continue the theme by defending a particular interpretative route, while suggesting that various rocks obstruct one of the alternative paths. But in so doing, I shall certainly not be claiming any prizes for reaching the summit; and in upholding a particular side in the dialogue now joined, I shall not question John Pocock's wisdom in pointing out that there may be more than one route, and that the connections between routes have yet to be established.[1] Indeed, in the present state of Smith scholarship it would be unwise to assume that we are anywhere near the end of the process of understanding the connections between the overlapping sub-systems that compose Smith's highly ambitious and systematic enterprise – the most ambitious enterprise to be carried through to near-completion in an age and place that was notable for the compendious quality of its intellectual projects.

Walter Bagehot was nearer the truth than either he or his readers could perhaps have appreciated in 1876 when he said of Smith that 'scarcely any philosopher has imagined a vaster dream'; and that Smith was that rare creature who had 'produced an enduring particular result in consequence of a comprehensive and diffused ambition'.[2] We are now far more likely to be

---

* This paper is a modified version of a talk given in Edinburgh in 1979, and is in turn based on an extension of my book *Adam Smith's Politics: An Essay in Historiographic Revision* (Cambridge, 1978), and correspondence with Nicholas Phillipson after the King's College Research Centre colloquium on 'Civic Humanism and Scottish Classical Political Economy', May 1979. [1] See pp. 235-52 above.
[2] Walter Bagehot, 'Adam Smith as a Person', in *The Collected Works of Walter Bagehot*, ed. N. St John-Stevas, 10 vols., iii (London, 1968), p. 86.

impressed by the second-order difficulties and opportunities opened up by Smith's methodological and historiographic writings, particularly his essay on astronomy and the student notes on his lectures on rhetoric and belles-lettres. These show that Smith held sophisticated theories not only about what we would call the psychology and sociology of scientific discovery, but also about the didactic and rhetorical conventions which govern scientific, historical and other forms of discourse.[3] At the very least, this means that we can no longer assume that we are dealing with an implicit philosophy of knowledge that can be made explicit by the imposition of our own favoured categories – a practice that has been all too common in the past two hundred years, as both critics and claimants to Smith's methodological mantle have variously described his procedure as deductive, inductive, rationalist, empiricist, historical and even historicist, not to mention such dimensions as apologetic, ideological and even plain explanatory. While I shall not be directly concerned with such issues here, I shall pay particular attention to Smith's own characterizations of his work. Intentions may not be everything in intellectual history, but we are unlikely to get very far if we ignore them at the outset.

For generations of scholars *the* problem of interpreting the connections between Smith's various writings was, of course, that of reconciling the sympathetic ethic of the *Theory of Moral Sentiments* with the selfish ethic of the *Wealth of Nations*. Few scholars now believe that this is how the problem should be posed, though there is still scope for discussion of how Smith's complex interpersonal approach to morals and social ethics should be reconciled with the more impersonal and anonymous world depicted in the *Wealth of Nations*; and whether, and in what respects, it is legitimate to use the ethical work as a court of appeal for resolving difficulties in the economic work. In this volume, for example, one of the underlying issues is how far a knowledge of the *Theory of Moral Sentiments* will carry one in attempting to comprehend the *Wealth of Nations*.[4]

While the importance of such questions should not be minimized, they can be misleadingly posed if insufficient account is taken of a major and largely novel source of challenge, namely that created by the gap in Smith's project

---

[3] Among the more notable of recent attempts to use the essay on 'The History of Astronomy' and the *Lectures on Rhetoric* to understand Smith's other works are: J. R. Lindgren, 'Adam Smith's Theory of Enquiry', *Journal of Political Economy*, 77 (1969), 897–915; T. D. Campbell, *Adam Smith's Science of Morals* (London, 1971); and A. S. Skinner, 'Science and the Role of the Imagination', as reprinted in his *A System of Social Science* (Oxford, 1979), a collection of papers that represents the most sustained attempt so far to interpret the interconnections between Smith's works, making use of all the evidence now available in the Glasgow edition.

[4] Thus Nicholas Phillipson, agreeing with the basic position of Ralph Lindgren's *The Social Philosophy of Adam Smith* (The Hague, 1973), accords primacy to the *Theory of Moral Sentiments* and concludes that 'the science of economics and the four-stage theory of history appear as by-products of a model that was designed to deal with problems peculiar to the serious Scottish moralists'; see p. 194 above.

left by his failure to complete, or allow to be published, the 'account of the general principles of law and government' which he promised at the end of the *Theory of Moral Sentiments*. Although we now have two sets of students' notes on the lectures on jurisprudence, there is a great deal of disagreement about the nature of the missing element and whether Smith simply failed to complete it or found himself incapable of doing so for reasons that have nothing to do with the Great Reaper.[5] Moreover, the main effort so far has been addressed to two separate questions, namely, what light do the lectures shed on the economics of the *Wealth of Nations*, and what do they tell us about the peculiarities and significance of what the late Ronald Meek described as the 'theory of the four stages', around which so much of the historical evidence in the lectures appears to be organized.[6] As yet, the lectures have not been fully exploited as the basis for an understanding of Smith's views on the science of jurisprudence and on the science of politics – the 'science of a statesman or legislator' of which the political economy contained in the *Wealth of Nations* was merely to be a branch.[7] And while this middle part of the enterprise remains obscure, most attention is still likely to be focussed on reconciling the two ends of Smith's spectrum, the ethics of the *Theory of Moral Sentiments* at one end, and the *Wealth of Nations* at the other. The problem of the missing science of politics and jurisprudence will be faced later, but my present point can be summarized by saying that even if we can now claim to understand all the components of the *Wealth of Nations*, and how they fit together to form an extended economic argument, we are still no closer to knowing what kind of book the *Wealth of Nations* is when seen as part of Smith's larger enterprise.

In spite of endless work on Smith's 'enduring particular result' by generations of economists, and by those historians of economic thought who write with economists chiefly in mind, it seems unlikely that they will supply answers to this kind of question. Even when they wish to do more than simply retrieve modern economic meanings, often by stripping away what seem to be mere period residues, they regard the *Wealth of Nations*, first and foremost, as an *economic* classic, the magnificent opening speech in a largely autonomous form of discourse that has continued to the present day. In consequence, their reaction to this and other papers collected here is likely to be one of impatience. Or, to return to an earlier image, the routes mapped out here may seem too circuitous, wasting energy that could best be used to make a frontal assault on the summit. Although it can be said in reply that some of the economists' methods seem more like helicopter landings than mountaineering, their point of view will eventually have to be accommodated. A brief and unsatisfactory

---

[5] The positions that have been adopted towards Smith's 'missing politics' are surveyed in Winch, *Adam Smith's Politics*, pp. 9–27.

[6] See R. L. Meek, 'Smith, Turgot and the "Four Stages" Theory', in his *Smith: Marx and After* (London, 1977), pp. 18–32; and the same author's *Social Science and the Ignoble Savage* (Cambridge, 1976).   [7] *WN* IV.i.138.

indication of the space occupied by what we now call economic theory will be given at the end of this paper, but the space itself will not be filled.

But if for one reason or another students of Smith's economics seem unwilling or unable to shed new light on his project taken as a whole, the same cannot be said of those for whom the appropriate context within which Smith's work should be viewed is pre-eminently a Scottish one. Highly sophisticated treatments of post-Union political and cultural debate in Scotland have recently been employed as a means of interpreting the philosophical concerns of most of the leading figures of the Scottish Enlightenment. Such work is well represented in this volume, where, despite differences of emphasis, a unifying stress is placed on what can be called a persistent civic moralist or civic humanist dimension to Scottish debate.[8] It is with the application of this particular Scottish ideological perspective to Smith that I should like to take friendly issue in what follows. It can hardly be anything other than friendly when I share with those I shall be treating as my opponents a profound debt to John Pocock, whose work on the civic humanist tradition constitutes a common point of departure.[9] But before rehearsing my doubts as to the chances – to change images – of landing such a large fish as Smith by means of a Scottish ideological net designed along purely civic lines, I should first like to confront two questions mentioned earlier: what kind of a work was the *Wealth of Nations* intended to be, and how does it relate to the missing parts of Smith's enterprise?

Smith's description of political economy as 'a branch of the science of a statesman or legislator' continues to prove troublesome to economists and historians of economic thought. This reference to some kind of statecraft seems to belie the very nature of the *Wealth of Nations*, whether considered anachronistically as 'positive' economics or as a critique of contemporary economic policies from a position we now call economic liberalism.[10] If, however, we take Smith's description to be an informative statement of both his intentions and achievements, he becomes a major contributor to the eighteenth-century science of politics, and this provides the natural link between the *Wealth of Nations* and the lectures on jurisprudence from which it sprang. Smith created a system of political economy based on the principles of 'natural liberty and justice' which was a branch of a more ambitious inquiry into law and government that was variously described by its devotees as the

---

[8] See, for example, the papers by I. Hont, P. Jones, N. Phillipson and J. Robertson in this volume.

[9] See J. G. A. Pocock, *Politics, Language and Time* (London, 1972), and *The Machiavellian Moment: Florentine Political Thought and the Atlantic Republican Tradition* (Princeton, N.J., 1975). For my own use of Pocock's thesis see *Adam Smith's Politics*, esp. pp. 31–5, 86–7, 122, 126, 175–7.

[10] See, for example, Mark Blaug's remark that 'The introduction to Book IV defines political economy as a branch of statecraft, a definition in violent opposition to the whole tenor of the *Wealth of Nations*' (Blaug, *Economic Theory in Retrospect*, 3rd edn (Cambridge, 1978), p. 59).

'science of politics', the 'science of jurisprudence', and, more comprehensively, as the 'science of the legislator'. He was not, therefore, simply making ritual academic obeisance to ancient precedent in dividing moral philosophy into its two Aristotelian components, ethics and politics; he was constructing in parallel with Hume, and on a foundation laid by the Continental natural lawyers, by his teacher Frances Hutcheson, and by Montesquieu, a science of law and politics of considerable significance and modernity, within which political economy occupied a crucial but by no means dominant role.

The statement that Smith is a significant contributor to the science of politics might appear to be a banal claim to those who regard economic liberalism, the doctrine with which Smith's name is still most closely associated, as pre-eminently a political doctrine in its own right – one that had considerable nineteenth-century import and is clearly alive and well in some circles today. To say that economic liberalism was merely an instrumental doctrine concerned solely with the efficient allocation of economic resources and the conditions for achieving maximum economic growth would be to adopt a naïvely economistic position. Whatever modern economists may say about such matters, Smith cannot be treated as a mere economic instrumentalist; he was advancing far more ambitious claims.

Nevertheless, I wish to maintain that we cannot grasp the nature of those claims if we place undue and proleptic emphasis on Smith's economic liberalism. The deficiencies of *laissez-faire* as a translation of what Smith meant by speaking of 'the natural system of liberty' – the full implementation of which, it should be remembered, he regarded as a utopian dream – are well known.[11] For present purposes, however, the main oversight lies in the failure to appreciate the complex reciprocal relationship which Smith established between economy and polity, between commerce and liberty.[12] Smith provided us with an historical and economic analysis of this relationship, and used it as the basis for his recommendations for bringing economic and political institutions into harmony with one another. Even when imperfectly realized, liberty defined as personal security under the rule of law was a precondition for commercial advance. Commerce had been favourable to liberty, but only under circumstances in which a political and legal order existed that was capable of being consciously adapted and extended to take account of the increasing complexity of the social relationships and processes of change released by the advent of a society in which 'every man is in some measure a merchant'.

But even when Smith is granted the status of theorist of social change rather

---

[11] The classic interpretation is still that contained in Jacob Viner's 'Adam Smith and *Laissez-Faire*', in his *The Long View and the Short: Studies in Economic Theory and Policy* (Glencoe, Illinois, 1958), pp. 213–45. See also Skinner, *A System of Social Science*, ch. 9.

[12] For a fuller treatment of this relationship see Winch, *Adam Smith's Politics*, ch. 4.

than mere economist, he is still regarded as a theorist for whom the underlying factors remain predominantly economic. I am, of course, referring here to the interpretation, chiefly associated with Ronald Meek, to the effect that Smith's originality as a social theorist lay in combining an economic analysis of capitalism with a materialist theory of social change which explained the emergence of commercial society in terms of a theory of four stages – hunting, pastoral, agricultural and commercial – in which each stage is characterized by its mode of subsistence. Ronald Meek regarded this theory as 'an organising principle of considerable power'; it entailed 'a conscious acceptance of the more general environmental or materialist approach which underlay that theory'. It involved giving novel emphasis to modes of subsistence and to economic forces generally in generating social change. It was *a* materialist version of history, if not yet *the* materialist interpretation that we find in Marx.[13]

Ronald Meek's position has been a persuasive one, and has acquired a number of influential adherents over the years. It also has the great virtue of linking the *Wealth of Nations* to the lectures on jurisprudence, even though Ronald Meek was disappointed to find that the four stages apparatus, as he saw it, made only a limited appearance in the *Wealth of Nations* itself. Another virtue of Ronald Meek's interpretation is that it makes a genuine attempt to encompass the historical dimension of Smith's work – something which was remarked on extensively by Smith's contemporaries, and has always been treated with respect by students of the Scottish Enlightenment, even though most economists have either ignored or dismissed it as a mere digression from the main analytical themes.[14]

Nevertheless, if we take the 'science of a statesman or legislator' seriously, materialist interpretations of Smith's use of the four stages, with their more or less mono-causal overtones, have unfortunate implications: they place severe limitations on any genuinely *political* vision of society. Political and legal institutions are treated as epiphenomenal to underlying economic forces, leaving little or no scope for a science of the legislator designed to show what active steps should be taken to remove injustices and adapt institutions to changing circumstance. The ultimate effect of such interpretations, therefore, is to confirm the conventional stereotype of Smith as an advocate of *laissez-faire* or strictly limited government, thereby failing to recognize Smith's consistent

[13] See Meek, *Social Science and the Ignoble Savage*, pp. 120, 125.
[14] See, for example, S. Hollander, 'Historical Dimension of *The Wealth of Nations*', in Gerald P. O'Driscoll, Jr (ed.), *Adam Smith and Modern Political Economy* (Ames, Iowa, 1979), pp. 71–84, where a large variety of arguments is deployed to show that there is 'no clash' between Smith's history and economic analysis; that history is a 'digression', or 'scaffolding'; that the *Wealth of Nations* 'as a whole is not governed by the [Scottish historical] tradition'; and that Smith's use of history was basically deductive. Much of this reappears in Hollander's *The Economics of David Ricardo* (London, 1979), ch. 2, where the object is to minimize differences between Smith and Ricardo on questions of method.

concern to demonstrate how actual practices or outcomes in modern commercial societies require the attention of the legislator.

But materialist interpretations of the four stages are by no means obligatory. It may be significant that the temporal sequence which Smith uses for taxonomic purposes has labels which refer to modes of subsistence, but that could be all there is to say for materialist interpretations.[15] Thus, even when Smith deals with the two earliest stages, where societies are more primitive and hence more under the direct influence of their immediate environment, topographical and military considerations are often treated as being as important as economic circumstances. And as Smith approached modern times, the range of explanatory variables increased to encompass accidents and acts of political will, as well as the personalities of monarchs. Add to this the various cyclical themes of rise and fall which feature in the story, and Smith's recognition of the possibilities that societies may become arrested at certain stages as a result of the absence of favourable political institutions, and the whole unilinear stadial sequence begins to seem highly contingent on circumstances that are by no means traceable merely to economic causes.

When Smith dealt with the different canons of historical composition in his lectures on rhetoric and belles-lettres, he distinguished between 'a knowledge of the causes of events', and 'a science no less useful', namely 'a knowledge of the motives by which men act'.[16] It was by means of such history, if written on the basis of accurate psychological observation, that 'future conduct' could be regulated. Once the focus is shifted towards motives and conduct it should become clear that the author of the *Theory of Moral Sentiments* is hardly likely to give economic motives an exclusive role in history. Compared with the persistent desire for vanity, social status and love of dominance, man's purely material wants are easily satisfied.

Smith's use of the two final stages in Book III of the *Wealth of Nations*, where he discusses the emergence of commercial society from the urban interstices of feudal Europe, is designed to point up the contrast between the 'natural progress of opulence' and the actual course of change produced by political intervention, thereby focussing attention on those institutions and policies of his own day that were no longer adapted to the requirements of expediency

[15] In recent years there has been a steady retreat from materialist interpretations, especially those of a more determinist variety. See D. Forbes, 'Sceptical Whiggism, Commerce and Liberty', in A. S. Skinner and T. Wilson (eds.), *Essays on Adam Smith* (Oxford, 1976), pp. 179–201; Winch, *Adam Smith's Politics*, pp. 56–65; and K. Haakonssen, *The Science of a Legislator: The Natural Jurisprudence of David Hume and Adam Smith* (Cambridge, 1981), esp. ch. 8, 'Natural Jurisprudence in the Face of History', pp. 178–89. The whole debate has recently been surveyed in relation to Ronald Meek's work by A. Skinner, 'A Scottish Contribution to Marxist Sociology?', in I. Bradley and M. Howard (eds.), *Classical and Marxian Political Economy: Essays in Honour of Ronald L. Meek* (London, 1982), pp. 79–114.

[16] *Lectures on Rhetoric and Belles Lettres Delivered in the University of Glasgow by Adam Smith, Reported by a Student in 1762–63*, ed. J. M. Lothian (Edinburgh, 1963), p. 109.

and justice. The purpose of Book IV's 'violent attack' on mercantile policies was to show how policy had continued to operate in a direction that was neither expedient nor just when judged by the more enlightened criteria which Smith was expounding. Finally, in Book V the full four stages reappear precisely where one should expect them to on the basis of the lectures, namely when dealing with two of the most important duties of the sovereign with respect to defence and justice, on both of which Smith was lending his active support to new policies and institutions – standing armies and the separation of the administration of justice from the executive arm of government.

None of these counter-arguments in favour of a political rather than economic interpretation of Smith's use of history would be necessary if due attention had been paid to Smith's own claims in the first place – if we had started out from the basic fact that the theory of the four stages was introduced in the lectures to explain how law and government, in Smith's phrase, 'grew up with society'. This enables one to avoid assuming at the outset – as materialist interpretations invite us to do – that the *actual* purpose of the lectures was merely the *ostensible* one, behind which lurk other, more fundamental, concerns, or what may seem more fundamental to a post-Marxian generation. The subject of the lectures was, to repeat, law and government, depicted not simply as a passive response to circumstances but as 'the highest effort of human prudence and wisdom' – a prudence exercised by men in differing physical and economic circumstances but driven by natural wants and passions that were common to all men at all times and places. Moreover, as has been indicated, it was Smith's view that the scope for prudence and wisdom increased rather than diminished with the development of society into its more complex forms. Centralized forms of government and the regular administration of justice separate from the executive arm of government were essential preconditions for the continued progress of opulence. They provided the necessary stability for the accumulation of capital, and hence for the extension of the division of labour in society; they also protected the more complex forms of property that arise in advanced commercial societies. And just as the need for impartial methods of administering justice grew with opulence, so did the requirements for defence against increasingly jealous external enemies. Hence the enhanced contemporary significance of cultivating the science of the legislator.

I am suggesting that we take seriously another of Smith's descriptions of his work, the one he used in a letter to the Duc de la Rochefoucauld in 1785, when he said that he was engaged in writing 'a sort of theory and History of Law and Government'.[17] And if we then ask ourselves what the 'theory' component was, and how it related to 'History', I very much doubt if the answer will be a materialist *theory* of progress. As Knud Haakonssen has shown, it is far more

[17] Smith to Le Duc de la Rochefoucauld, 1 November 1785, in Smith, *Correspondence*, pp. 286–7.

likely to be the theory of natural justice, the social and psychological foundations for which were laid in the *Theory of Moral Sentiments*.[18] At this point, therefore, we see how the lectures on jurisprudence act as a bridge to carry us backwards and forwards between the *Wealth of Nations* and the *Theory of Moral Sentiments*.

We know that Smith regarded rules of justice in some form or other as the essential prerequisite for any type of social existence. We also know that he regarded the negative or prohibitory rules of justice as being capable of precise formulation, largely because they dealt with pains or injuries that could be more easily discerned than their virtuous opposites – those embodied, for example, in codes of beneficence. The theory of natural justice provided a normative basis for the 'general principles which ought to run through and be the foundation of the laws of all nations'. It was designed to show that universal rules could be established on the basis of constant principles of psychology or morals – principles which explained the resentment aroused by acts of injustice and sanctioned punishment for injuries to persons, reputations and property, the three main categories of natural and adventitious rights which form the subject matter of the lectures on jurisprudence proper.

But the rules of justice and the rights they were designed to protect could not be known or proclaimed in the abstract, in a social and historical void. Both the relationships between persons and the nature and forms of property were subject to change and hence variation across time and space. Thus no theory of justice could have content if it was not supplemented by a history of social development (or anthropology of social types) capable of illustrating and locating the precise forms of injury that it was possible for men to inflict upon one another, and of revealing the kinds of positive legal institutions which had evolved to deal with such injuries. Since property constitutes a major and growing source of injury, this alone would be sufficient grounds for a history directed at 'how' questions in which the property relationships connected with different modes of subsistence were stressed. History performs a similar function in giving content to Smith's theory of political obligation. The twin psychological principles on which civil obedience is based, namely deference to authority and a sense of public utility, require an empirical or historical study of the relations of wealth, property, rank and dependence in society. Without such a study we cannot know to whom deference is shown – the old, the strong, the wise, the rich and powerful – and why a sense of public utility dictates obedience in some circumstances but not others.

As Knud Haakonssen has further shown, history was not required in order

---

[18] See Haakonssen, *The Science of a Legislator*, pp. 182-4. A recent treatment of Smith's jurisprudence can be found in P. Stein, 'Adam Smith's Jurisprudence – Between Morality and Economics', *Cornell Law Review*, 64 (1979), 621-38.

to *justify* the principles of natural justice; there is no recourse to any Burkean argument to the effect that mere antiquity has prescriptive force. By itself, history could only provide 'the records of the sentiments of mankind in different ages and nations'. But when used in conjunction with the theory of natural justice it was capable of serving as a flexible and powerful instrument that was at once positive and normative, causal yet critical, explanatory on one level, but preserving the moral stance on the other.

But where has the civic tradition gone in all this talk about natural jurisprudence and the science of the legislator? That indeed is my question. Where and how can civic humanism or Scottish civic moralism be brought into the picture? What does it add to or subtract from an interpretation based largely on the science of the legislator?

As I understand it, John Pocock's approach to such questions has been to posit a dialectical relationship between the values embodied in the civic tradition and those concerns with historical change which, according to the view sketched here, provide an 'experimental' basis for Smith's science of politics. In his earlier essays and in *The Machiavellian Moment*, he counterposed the historicization of Scottish political thought against the more atavistic preoccupations of civic humanism. The language of corruption and virtue, therefore, appears in a novel historical scheme as an expression of those citizenly values threatened by specialized commercial society for which modern substitutes could not readily be found; it features as a set of criteria for judging the point at which progress worked to the disadvantage of man as citizen or political animal.[19] In this way the civic humanist perspective and the associated idea of a Court–Country spectrum in eighteenth-century political thinking serve a valuable heuristic purpose in helping to locate the civic or republican implications of Smith's vocabulary and agenda. That it enables one to pose issues that otherwise could not be seen to advantage has certainly proved to be the case with regard to Smith's analysis of, and remedies for, the effect of the division of labour on martial spirit and in producing 'mental mutilation'. It helps us to appreciate the more or less residual civic concerns we find in Smith – those places where, as an English follower of Smith, Sir Frederick Morton Eden, put it, the 'negative exertions of government' with regard to natural liberty and justice are insufficient 'to impress the people with the energy of character which constitutes a great nation'.[20]

It serves a no less valuable *negative* purpose in indicating just where Smith is to be found standing the civic vocabulary and agenda on its head, and failing to endorse the 'boy-scout virtues' of civic humanism – to borrow a phrase coined by my colleague at the University of Sussex, John Burrow – to put some

---

[19] See Pocock, 'Civic Humanism and its Role in Anglo-American Thought', in *Language, Politics and Time*, pp. 101–3; and *Machiavellian Moment*, pp. 498–505.
[20] F. M. Eden, *The State of the Poor* (London, 1797), p. 424.

distance between Edward Gibbon and the same ideas.[21] The most obvious example here is to be found in Smith's advocacy of standing armies over militias, where, characteristically, he continued to treat the fears of 'men of republican principles' with respect, but largely, it could be argued, because they constituted an important element in the climate of opinion within which, he believed, all governments, and particularly 'free' governments, operated. In this respect it is interesting that those contributors to this volume who approach Smith's texts from the vantage point of a post-Union Scottish ideology in which the civic dimension is stressed find it necessary to speak of '*post*-civic man', and of Smith escaping from or standing at the *limit* of the civic tradition.[22] The next step, surely, is to ask whether Smith was ever sufficiently part of that tradition for escape to be an informative description of what happened.

John Pocock takes this step in his contribution to this volume by warning against trying to explain *everything* by reference to the dialectic of the civic humanist debate. He goes even further towards accommodating the position outlined in this paper by recognizing the possible autonomy of the natural law alternative; that it could have had an existence quite independent of its role as antithesis to the civic thesis; that the language of virtue might not be capable of being translated into the language of right.[23] I have nothing to add to his fertile suggestions concerning alternative languages and their possible inter-relationships, but I would like to underline the consequences of the present impasse as far as the interpretation of Smith's project is concerned.

As things stand at the moment we appear to be faced with a straight choice between alternative interpretative routes, with a further consequence that the intellectual context appropriate to one will probably not be appropriate to the other. Those of us who choose to stress the natural jurisprudential underpinnings of Smith's science of the legislator, of which political economy was merely a branch, find ourselves facing the upholders of a civic moralist interpretation across a divide. But it would be highly unsatisfactory to find ourselves facing a new and equally artificial version of *Das Adam Smith Problem* by suggesting that a civic moralist context fits the *Theory of Moral Sentiments*, whereas the *Wealth of Nations* requires an approach via natural law. The former work contains the theoretical basis for the ideas on justice that are applied in an experimental fashion in the lectures and in the *Wealth of Nations*, as well as much else that is helpful in understanding Smith's science of the legislator. Similarly, those who adopt a civic moralist interpretation are unlikely to concede that the lectures and the *Wealth of Nations* are permanently beyond their grasp.

I have hinted at possible ways of reconciling the two positions, but it does not seem as though such hints are likely to prove satisfactory to either group.

[21] In a bi-centenary lecture on Edward Gibbon's *Decline and Fall of the Roman Empire* delivered at the University of Sussex, 4 November 1976 (unpublished).
[22] See for example pp. 198-9 above.   [23] See pp. 137-78 above.

There are those on the natural jurisprudence side of the divide who find it unnecessary to mention the civic tradition, even heuristically, except perhaps as part of a 'vulgar' alternative to the 'scientific' position which Smith (and Hume) were attempting to sustain.[24] Similarly, on the civic side there appears to be a disinclination to come to terms with the insights provided by natural law and the science of the legislator. Once joined, however, the debate could be an instructive one, largely because it appears that all parties accept, in principle at least, that disputes must be resolved historically – by which I mean that they are not engaged in a bid to recruit Smith into one or other of the favoured modern ideologies. Both sides recognize that they must prove that the alternatives were actually available to Smith before showing which he chose and how he made use of it.

This could be a means of bringing some of the issues to a point. Thus when we examine what Smith's 'never-to-be-forgotten' teacher, Frances Hutcheson, had to say about law and politics in his lectures, we find what could be a rare combination of natural law doctrines derived from Locke and the Continental natural jurists together with a thoroughly neo-Harringtonian treatment of forms of government. In other words, Hutcheson combined contractarian ideas on the moral themes of obligation, obedience and rights of resistance with a Real Whig, republican or civic humanist treatment of forms of polity, their advantages and disadvantages. Since Smith began by following his teacher closely in the order and basic subject matter of his lectures, we can say with some certainty that both of the relevant alternatives were available to him.

How then did Smith exercise his choice? On slightly starker lines than Hume, Smith rejects the idea of social contract while retaining Hutcheson's classification of rights and duties, as modified by the doctrine that such rights must be placed within a setting of social approval and mutual understanding. More significantly for my purpose, we find Smith rejecting the neo-Harringtonian treatment of forms of government, agrarian laws and the like in favour of an approach which Montesquieu and Hume had pioneered before him, but which Hutcheson had explicitly ruled out, namely a comparative historical treatment of law and government considered as social phenomena – a four-stages account of how law and government 'grew up with society', with all that that entailed for the historicization of Scottish social and political theory.[25]

The four-stages framework not only enabled Smith to organize evidence in a way that complemented his theory of justice, it also furnished the historical setting within which he deployed with such skill the explanatory device of contrasting the private intentions or professed aims of individuals with their unintended social or public consequences. This Mandevillian device serves a distinctive didactic purpose in the *Wealth of Nations*, but it is also employed

---

[24] See Forbes, 'Sceptical Whiggism, Commerce and Liberty', p. 180.
[25] Hutcheson and Smith are contrasted in Winch, *Adam Smith's Politics*, ch. 3.

there with a cynicism, acerbity, even world-weariness that
to that of Mandeville himself, and has, to my knowledge, r
work of other Scottish historians of civil society. This could
Stewart's (semi-apologetic?) decision in writing his me...
emphasize the connections between the *Wealth of Nations* and 'those specula...
of his earlier years, in which he aimed *more professedly* at the advancement of
human improvement and happiness'.²⁶ But the case for making the doctrine
of unintended consequences central to any interpretation of Smith does not
turn on qualities of personal style or mood. It adds an ironic dimension to
Smith's treatment of motivation in human affairs, but it also provided him with
a method that was well-adapted to the task of analysing a commercial world
increasingly characterized by impersonal and anonymous relationships – a
world of hidden interdependencies rather than of direct dependency, the
leading characteristic of its feudal predecessor.

This could be seen as Smith's contribution to an earlier Augustan debate
about the foundations and consequences of modern propriety and civility.
Samuel Johnson had spoken of the satisfactions to be derived from contemplating 'the secret concatenation of society that links together the great and
the mean, the illustrious and the obscure'.²⁷ Hume had dealt with the same
problem in his essays on commerce, luxury and refinement, and when he
announced that 'the same age, which produces great philosophers and
politicians, renowned generals and poets, usually abounds in skilful weavers,
and ship-carpenters'.²⁸ The doctrine of unintended consequences was at the
heart of the cynical paradoxes with which Mandeville plagued his generation
on these matters, and it was one of the keys used by Smith to reveal Johnson's
'secret concatenation'.

Since Nicholas Phillipson's portrait of Scottish civic moralism stresses the
Addisonian connections, there could be an area of convergence here that is
worthy of further exploration, especially when it is remembered that Addison
was one of Mandeville's chief targets.²⁹ At present, however, the doctrine of
unintended consequences, with its characteristic attempt to prove that private
vice and virtue and public benefit and loss are connected in ways that defy
a more conventional morality, does not figure prominently in accounts which
see Smith as being engaged in an ideological defence of commercial society,
demonstrating that its fruits – moral autonomy, propriety and civility – were

---

²⁶ Dugald Stewart, 'Account of the Life and Writings of Adam Smith LL.D', in Smith, *EPS*, p. 314 (my italics).
²⁷ '[On the Trades of London], *The Adventurer* no. 67, 26 June 1753', in Samuel Johnson, *The Idler and The Adventurer*, ed. W. J. Bate, J. M. Bullitt, L. F. Powell, *The Yale Edition of the Works of Samuel Johnson*, 11 vols., ii (New Haven, Conn., 1963), p. 386.
²⁸ Hume, 'Of Refinement in the Arts', *Philosophical Works*, iii, p. 301.
²⁹ See M. M. Goldsmith, 'Public Virtue and Private Virtues', *Eighteenth-Century Studies*, 9 (1976), 477–510.

ore than adequate compensation for the loss of more active political virtues. This approach seems necessary in order to show how Smith can be seen responding to persistent themes in post-Union debate in Scotland. But while Smith undoubtedly drew attention to the improvements associated with commerce, and was anxious to show how its potentialities for enhancing liberty and communal (including cultural) enrichment could best be realized, a *defensive* interpretation seems optional. Moreover, those of us who stress the political dimension of Smith's work are likely to be suspicious of the reintroduction, via a more sophisticated route, of the standard portrait of Smith as an apolitical thinker concerned to justify quietist or what Phillipson calls 'para-political virtues'.

Rather than ideological defence or apology, the science of the legislator approach sees Smith as engaged in a clinical analysis of commercial society, and therefore concerned to record losses as well as gains. The 'invisible hand' example encourages us to think most readily of cases where Smith demonstrates how unintended social benefit arises from private selfishness and vanity; how, in policy contexts, the patient recovers in spite of the absurd nostrums of doctor–politicians. But exactly the same method is applied to the debit items – to explain, for example, the undesirable unplanned consequences to society of the division of labour; to show how the 'natural' consequences of commerce in weakening the defences of rich nations can be, but have not always been, overcome; to reveal the serious political dangers, in the form of the extra-parliamentary pressures exerted by an interested mercantile community, which are associated with those very mercantile proclivities that are essential to commercial society.

The apolitical, or para-political, implications of the civic moralist reading are more difficult to respond to briefly, if only because of the various meanings that can be attached to 'political'. But if driven to characterize Smith's politics rapidly, I would have to say that, like Hume's, it was a politics that relied more on machinery than men; that government is seen largely as a matter of balancing, checking and harnessing interests rather than calling forth public spirit and virtue. Like beneficence in men's social dealings, public spirit added lustre to society; but it should not be relied upon in a science of politics, except perhaps during rare crises of legitimacy – when, of course, no *science* could be called upon.

We can call this reliance on constitutional machinery apolitical by contrast with a more romantic conception of political action, but it should not be characterized as a mere attitude of mind, a purely contemplative vision. Civic humanism enables us to detect values, but we also need to register analysis and system. Nathan Rosenberg, in a seminal article published in 1960, drew our attention to Smith's persistent concern with institutions, and to the extraordinary fertility he showed in proposing new institutional mechanisms for containing harmful proclivities.[30] We also need to appreciate Smith's acute understanding of the role played by ambition and 'sense of importance' in activating the 'natural aristocracy' of any society; and his analysis of faction, conflict and pathological states of opinion in politics. How else can we explain his desire to find ways of moderating or harnessing such political forces? How else can we understand his discussion of 'influence' and political management, his emphasis on the role of leadership and political sagacity in removing abuses and adapting institutions and laws to changing circumstances? The same qualities of realism to be seen in Smith's consistently non-utopian cast of mind should also make us wary of extrapolating his diagnoses far beyond his present into a future which he believed, in principle, to be unknowable. That his 'particular result' was 'enduring' encourages this, but nineteenth-century usages underline how tenuous the connection between actual future and intended present can be.

The other feature of Smith's science of the legislator which appears to conflict with Scottish civic moralist interpretations is its commitment to the cosmopolitan standpoint. This highest level of discourse dealing with 'the great society of mankind', after man as individual, member of a family and citizen, was one that Smith believed was the peculiar domain of the philosophical observer. It was, of course, a concomitant of the natural law perspective and any attempt to distinguish natural from positive law, morals from mere manners, universal principles from local adaptations.

Cosmopolitanism could be an affectation – perhaps even a peculiarly Scottish affectation. Smith could well have been referring to himself when he said that the provincial spectator removed from 'the great scramble of faction and ambition' was peculiarly well-placed to observe metropolitan affairs impartially.[31] But if this describes the location and stance, it can hardly be said to describe the method or its rationale. Anybody bold enough to accuse Smith of mere affectation in such matters must come to terms with the immense range of comparative-historical material which he so skilfully employed in the lectures and in the *Wealth of Nations*.

Smith's cosmopolitanism is the chief source of my doubts about Nicholas Phillipson's view that the province was the locus of so much that Smith valued.[32] After all, it was only by being part of a much larger political unit that Scotland, Ireland and the American colonies could be released from the 'rancorous and virulent factions' that dominated provincial political and social life.[33] Smith's lack of attention to such features of his own society as the existence of serfdom among Scottish colliers, especially in view of his interest

---

[30] See N. Rosenberg, 'Some Institutional Aspects of the *Wealth of Nations*', *Journal of Political Economy*, 68 (1960), 537–70.
[31] *WN* V.iii.90.
[32] See pp. 194–7 above.
[33] *WN* V.iii.89–90.

in slavery in the West Indies and North America, has also been attributed to the same commitment to a cosmopolitan point of view.[34]

Finally, there is the *economic* analysis of the *Wealth of Nations*, which has a shadowy existence in recent discussions on civic humanism or moralism and its bearings on Smith, and which I have also ignored here. By emphasizing that political economy was merely a branch of the science of the legislator, I have, by implication, treated it as unproblematic – as not requiring any special effort to explain its presence or form. This is a fair reflection of my present position: Smith did not invent what is now called economic analysis, though he did extend and give it academic respectability by absorbing it into a larger class of metaphysical and humane speculation. Its use parallels that of the theory of natural justice; it provides the criteria by which the expediency or public utility, as opposed to the justice, of institutions and policies can be judged.

In this respect the *Wealth of Nations* seems ideally suited to an approach which stresses the Scottish academic context. It emerged as a natural by-product of the Glasgow moral philosophy curriculum, a framework which Smith was remarkably content to use for all his writings. Smith never appears in mufti; he is always in full academic dress. Unlike most of his contemporaries he never wrote a topical pamphlet or a popular essay. The posthumously published essays are more like minor treatises than Hume's delightful exercises in the Addisonian art. But while this suggests that a Scottish context is highly relevant, it also suggests that, in Smith's case, broader ideological considerations will have to be introduced via the academic context.

On the other hand, the *Wealth of Nations* has strong maverick qualities. With one exception, it is difficult to think of any other Scottish author who conceived and executed a work remotely like the *Wealth of Nations*, either in scope or character. Hume's economic essays are, after all, *essays*. The exception, of course, is Sir James Steuart's *Principles of Political Oeconomy*; but the difficulties in making this part of Smith's context are well-known. To put it bluntly, one has to take on board a Jacobite traitor tainted with Continental notions, and an author whose work was largely ignored by his Scottish contemporaries, including, notoriously and self-consciously, Smith himself.[35] It would have been more fitting from a Scottish perspective if Smith had wished to dedicate his work to his friend Hume. In fact, he chose François Quesnay; and the Physiocrats are the only group of authors recognized by Smith as operating on the same plane of discourse.[36] There was more than conventional flattery

---

[34] For discussion of this question see J. Viner, 'Guide to John Rae's Life of Adam Smith', in John Rae, *Life of Adam Smith* (New York, 1965), pp. 114–16.

[35] Smith to W. Pulteney, 3 September 1772, Smith, *Correspondence*, p. 164: 'I have the same opinion of Sir James Stewart's Book that you have. Without once mentioning it, I flatter myself, that every false principle in it, will meet with a clear and distinct confrontation in mine.'

[36] The authority for Smith's intention to dedicate *WN* to Quesnay is Dugald Stewart, who claimed to have been informed by Smith himself; see Stewart, 'Account of Smith', p. 304.

in Ferguson's remark to Smith after publication: 'You are surely to reign *alone* on these subjects.'[37]

Before I am accused of resorting to the opaque doctrine of historical uniqueness, I had better draw my argument to a close. The indispensability of context to the establishment of the meaning of texts is a common point of departure for all the contributors to this volume, though there may be lingering differences between those like myself who work, initially, from text to context, rather than vice versa. The danger of an ideological approach which moves from collective context to text is a tendency to stress correspondences while overlooking dissonances. There could also be an element of over-determination in the shape of a belief in *necessary* dialectical engagement between text and context which makes it difficult to tell just where an author passes beyond the grasp or limits of the posited ideology. Hence the no doubt unworthy suspicion that history is sometimes being forsaken for meta-history.

The sophisticated Scottish civic moralist interpretations offered in this volume have many advantages over 'vulgar' boy-scout versions of civic humanism. I have tried to show how such interpretations might be fitted into Smith's science of the legislator. What seems necessary now is for those who stress the civic dimension to confront the evidence in favour of the alternative more directly than they have done so far – if only to show what parts of Smith's 'diffused ambition' it fails to capture.

[37] A. Ferguson to Smith, 18 April 1776, Smith, *Correspondence*, p. 193 (my italics).

11 The 'rich country–poor country' debate in Scottish classical political economy*

ISTVAN HONT

'where the Necessaries of Life are cheap, there also will Labour and Art be cheap'
This is disputed
(Jonathan Swift's marginalia to John Browne's
Essays on the Trade and Coin of Ireland, 1729)[1]

There would be no novelty in arguing that the eighteenth-century Scottish 'inquiry into the origin and causes of the wealth of nations' can *a posteriori* be seen as a series of considerations on why certain countries were rich and others were poor, whether the rich were getting richer while the poor were getting poorer or whether they were all marching together into some common future of 'abundance'. The thesis of this paper is both more specific and more historical than that. It argues that there was a distinct debate in eighteenth-century Scottish political economy about the relationship of rich and poor countries as they coexisted and fought for international markets in historical time. While only the bare outlines of this debate can be presented here, these alone may serve to indicate how crucial this debate was to the shaping of classical political economy in the Scottish Enlightenment.

The terminal dates of this Scottish debate are 1752 and 1804. It was provoked by the publication in 1752 of David Hume's *Political Discourses*, and came to an end in the last major work of eighteenth-century Scottish political economy, Lord Lauderdale's *Inquiry into the Nature and Origin of Public Wealth*. Lauderdale was the last writer who felt it necessary to argue his case against what he believed to be Hume's original thesis. In the debate, political economy's new analysis of commercial society as the first historical formation capable of extending wealth even to its lowest ranks met the challenge of a

---

* I am grateful to Lord Dacre, George Davie, John Dunn, Aladár Madarász, Nicholas Phillipson and John Robertson for their comments on various versions of this paper. My research on the subject, which is now embodied in a larger manuscript, has been generously supported by the British Academy, the Institute of Advanced Studies in the Humanities of the University of Edinburgh and the King's College Research Centre.

[1] Jonathan Swift, *Miscellaneous and Autobiographical Pieces, Fragments and Marginalia*, ed. Herbert Davis (Oxford, 1962), p. 256.

civic humanist discourse concerned above all with the ability of human societies to preserve their virtue in the flow of time.

The nascent historicism of this Renaissance civic humanist tradition, John Pocock has explained to us, was implied in its attempt to analyse the preconditions for virtue and *fortuna* in a conceptual matrix of time. 'The republic or Aristotelian polis', Pocock argued,

as that concept re-emerged in the civic humanist thought of the fifteenth century, was at once universal, in the sense that it existed to realise for its citizens all the values which men were capable of realising in this life, and particular, in the sense that it was finite and located in space and time. It had had a beginning and would consequently have an end; and this rendered crucial both the problem of showing how it had come into being and might maintain its existence, and that of reconciling its end of realising universal values with the instability and circumstantial disorder of its temporal life.[2]

In order to express these tensions in the republic's fight to preserve its virtue and the stability of its institutions, this Aristotelian–Machiavellian tradition of political understanding developed its own powerful vocabulary, which became widely dispersed in the various languages of social thought in early modern Europe. This vocabulary was very much in vogue in Britain at the time when Hume decided to present his thinking about commercial society and political economy to a wider public in the form of polite essays. In his *Political Discourses*, crucially, Hume used this vocabulary to raise questions not only about the political virtue and the probable stability of the British constitution in time, but also about the very stability of the *commerce* of commercial society itself. He inquired about the ability of a rich commercial country to confront her *fortuna* by superimposing the language of civic humanist historicism on the language of eighteenth-century political economy, the language of money, wages, prices and markets. In view of the traditional tension between wealth and virtue in the civic vocabulary, this transposition was intensely paradoxical. For this was a vocabulary used by those who had doubts about the lasting happiness and the utility of commercial society, about its effect on the morals and virtues of free people, rather than that of those who argued *for* it. In contrast, instead of writing in the language of luxury about 'poor and virtuous' and 'rich but corrupt' nations, Hume now saw the issue in terms of the historical fate of the 'virtue', as it were, of rich countries, the stability of their wealth, their polite culture and their propriety. For him poverty was in no sense the nursemaid of virtue.

In the essay 'Of Commerce', the first essay of the *Political Discourses*, Hume gave the first account of the long-term prospects for a rich country, when he spoke about 'the great advantage of *England* above any nation at present in

[2] J. G. A. Pocock, *The Machiavellian Moment: Florentine Political Thought and the Atlantic Republican Tradition* (Princeton, N.J., 1975), p. 3. The theme is developed brilliantly in depth in Part I of the book: 'Particularity and Time: The Conceptual Background', pp. 3–80.

the world, or that appears in the records of any story'.[3] England's historically unique greatness consisted not simply in the possession of a 'multitude of mechanical arts' but in the 'great number of persons to whose share the productions of these arts fall'. The 'riches' of English 'artisans' were advantageous for the health of her polity, but first and foremost lent 'virtue' to her commercial society. 'Every person, if possible' – Hume laid down the moral axiom –

ought to enjoy the fruits of his labour, in a full possession of all the necessaries, and many of the conveniencies of life. No one can doubt, but such an equality is most suitable to human nature, and diminishes much less from the *happiness* of the rich than it adds to that of the poor.

On the other hand the disadvantage of a rich country like England was the loss of competitive edge on international markets which flowed from 'the high price of labour, ...as well as the plenty of money'. However, Hume argued, the desire to remain competitive on foreign markets was 'not the most material circumstance' of the greatness of a rich country and thus had no priority over the richness of the artisans, 'the happiness of so many millions'. The rich country, Hume explained, herself caused the loss of her own markets, by rousing the inhabitants of poor countries into 'fermentation' through the desires generated by the luxuries which the rich country was so eager to sell them.[4] Once these desires seized the people of the poor country 'imitation soon diffused all those arts', 'domestic manufacturers' started to 'emulate the foreign in their improvements' until they managed to substitute for the imports from their rich neighbour.

Even though the new competition damaged her export markets, Hume argued, a rich country could still 'continue a great and powerful people'. If there was no market for a particular commodity, its production for export must necessarily cease. Since without exports imports could not take place, the skilled labourers of the rich nation had to turn towards the production of 'other commodities, which may be wanted at home'. Hume could see no reason why the 'springs of well being' should ever wind down in an already rich and developed country even if she was cut off from foreign markets. New opportunities for production would always be generated at home 'till every person in the state, who possesses riches, enjoys as great plenty of home commodities, and those in as great perfection, as he desires; which can never happen'.[5] If, Hume continued, high wages and 'plenty of money' barred the country from competing on foreign markets, instead of pushing down the wages of her artisans she must give up foreign trade. The '*virtù*' of the rich country manifested itself in her ability to review her commercial structure, to switch

[3] Hume, 'Of Commerce', *Philosophical Works*, iii, pp. 296–7.
[4] Hume, 'Of Refinement in the Arts', *Philosophical Works*, iii, p. 301.
[5] Hume, 'Of Commerce', p. 296.

her skilled artisans to supplying for the home market.[6] Given this flexibility, the welfare of the rich country could be maintained because the home demand of a rich country was potentially open-ended. The impossibility of satisfying all of commercial man's desires put the decline of the rich country beyond the finitude of time.

The 'rich country–poor country' argument in 'Of Money', instead of simply continuing the praise of the riches of England and their wide dispersion among the lower ranks, picked up the threads of the analysis offered in 'Of Commerce', but now from the point of view of a poor country. Hume's rather compressed statement offered an apparently self-contained argument in the following steps:[7]

1. Thanks to 'a happy concurrence of causes', international trade had an in-built self-correcting mechanism which worked for the benefit of mankind.
2. The happy benefit accruing from the 'checks' upon 'the growth of trade and riches' was that it prevented a world monopoly of commerce, i.e. the benefits of commerce 'being confined entirely to one people'.
3. Such a monopoly was what 'might naturally at first be dreaded from' considering exclusively 'the advantages of an established commerce'.
4. These advantages were indeed formidable: thus 'where one nation has got the start of another in trade, it is very difficult for the latter to regain the ground it has lost'.

---

[6] Following Pocock's usage, *virtù* is used here in a Machiavellian sense to refer to the skill and courage by which men are enabled to dominate events and conquer *fortuna*.

[7] Hume, 'Of Money', *Philosophical Works*, iii, pp. 310–11. It was in relation to this passage in 'Of Money' that Eugene Rotwein introduced the rich and poor countries terminology to describe Hume's position: David Hume, *Writings on Economics*, ed. E. Rotwein (Edinburgh, 1955), pp. 194n, 189n. The label 'rich country–poor country issue' was invented by George Davie in his 'Anglophobe and Anglophil', *Scottish Journal of Political Economy*, 14 (1967), pp. 295–6. Elsewhere he described the argument as 'David Hume's economic question as to whether backward Scotland, under the free-trade conditions provided by the Union, could ever catch up with the immense superiority of her predominant partner': 'Hume, Reid and the Passion for Ideas', in *Edinburgh in the Age of Reason*, ed. George Bruce (Edinburgh, 1967), p. 33. The first substantial account of the eighteenth-century Scottish debate, in a pioneering article by Joseph Low in the early 1950s, did not yet use the 'rich country–poor country' terminology: J. M. Low, 'An Eighteenth Century Controversy in the Theory of Economic Progress', *Manchester School of Economics and Social Studies*, 20 (1952), 311–33. Low defined the debate as a controversy on 'the theory of economic progress of an internationally trading community'. Despite his historical insights, Low's language and the intellectual framework he had chosen for his analysis could not do justice to his topic. His classification of the positions as optimistic or pessimistic with regard to progress eliminated the dialectic of looking at the issue from either the rich or the poor country's point of view and resulted both in a simplification and a misrepresentation of the historical material. Henry Spiegel continued this tradition by presenting Hume's argument as 'a law of the migration of economic opportunity': *The Growth of Economic Theory* (Englewood Cliffs, N.J., 1971), p. 210. As so many times in history, the contemporaries did not care to attach any short-hand label to the controversy in which they participated. Nonetheless, the debate was undoubtedly conducted in the language of rich and poor *countries*. Hume used the word 'country' interchangeably with 'people', 'state', 'nation' and most significantly with 'province'.

5. These advantages of the rich country included 'superior industry and skill', 'greater stocks', while as a consequence of greater capital and a higher volume of production, a rich country could also viably trade at 'much smaller profits'.
6. These advantages could only 'in some measure' be 'compensated...by the low price of labour in every nation which has not an extensive commerce'.
7. This partial advantage of undeveloped countries existed only in such 'poor' countries which did 'not much abound in gold and silver'.
8. As a result of the 'happy concurrence of causes' in international trade, 'manufactures...gradually shift their places, leaving those countries and provinces which they have already enriched', 'flying' to those places 'whither they are allured by the cheapness of provisions and labour'.
9. The relative advantage of the poor country over the rich was self-cancelling in time. Once the new industry 'enriched' the formerly poor country, the same shift towards low-wage, low-subsistence-cost countries would repeat itself, the 'same causes' being in operation again.
10. On balance, despite all her great advantages, every rich country suffers from a key 'disadvantage', i.e. 'the dearness of everything' which 'sets bound to' an 'established commerce...in every country'.
11. This dearness of everything eventually appears because of the 'plenty of money' in rich countries.
12. Finally, the working of the self-regulating mechanism of world trade could be observed in the 'poorer' 'states' underselling 'the richer in all foreign markets'.

Hume's model immediately aroused controversy. In the two direct clashes on the 'rich country–poor country' issue in his correspondence, first with James Oswald in 1750 and then with Josiah Tucker in 1758,[8] Hume added an

---

[8] It should be noted that the exchange with Oswald had taken place a year before Hume sent the manuscript of the *Political Discourses* to the printers. Significantly, he had carried the letter with him to the house of William Mure of Caldwell before he finalized the essays in September 1751, and Oswald's long letter in fact survived in Mure's possession: 'Correspondence and Miscellaneous Papers of Baron Mure, 1753–1764', in *Selections from the Family Papers preserved at Caldwell*, 3 vols. (Glasgow, 1854), Part II, i, pp. 93–107. For the dating, see the letter of Hume to Robert Wallace, 22 September 1751, *New Letters of David Hume*, eds. R. Klibansky and E. C. Mossner (Oxford, 1954), pp. 28–30, and 'Correspondence of Baron Mure, 1753–1764', plate 116. A shortened version, omitting some important passages, has been reprinted in Hume, *Writings on Economics*, pp. 190–6. For Hume's answer to Oswald, see *The Letters of David Hume*, ed. J. Y. T. Greig, 2 vols. (Oxford, 1932), i, pp. 142–4. The Hume–Tucker correspondence was conducted through the mediation of Henry Home, Lord Kames. Tucker asked Kames to pass on a manuscript of his to David Hume on 11 February 1758: 'Correspondence of Henry Home, Lord Kames', Scottish Record Office, Abercairny Muniments, GD 24/I/558, fols. 4–5. Hume's answer to Kames was dated 4 March 1758. The whole letter, including remarks addressed to Kames, reached Tucker. Later it got into the possession of Lord Shelburne, who after the death of Tucker permitted its publication by T. B. Clarke in the latter's *A Survey of the Strength and Opulence of Great Britain, wherein is shown the Progress of its Commerce, Agriculture, Population, etc., before and since the Accession of the House of Hanover: with Observations by Dean Tucker and David Hume, Esq. in a Correspondence with Lord Kaimes, now first*

essential clarification to his statement in the essay 'Of Money'. In the text of the essay Hume was discussing the flight of 'manufactures' from the rich country to the poor, but the expression was ambiguous enough to leave it unclear whether he meant individual products or industries rather than 'manufactures' in general. Nor did he specify which types of 'manufactures' would go first and which later. In the correspondence, when pressed, he admitted that what he had in mind was a partition of labour between rich and poor countries.[9] 'The rich country', he wrote to Oswald, 'would acquire and retain all the manufactures, that require great stock and great skill; but the poor country would gain from it all the simpler and more laborious.'[10] Writing in 1758 to Lord Kames, who mediated the communication between Hume and Tucker, Hume repeated the basic idea: 'The finest arts will flourish best in the capital: those next in value in the more opulent provinces: the coarser in the remote countries.'[11] Hume's failure to add these one or two sentences of clarification later to the original text of the essay helps to explain why his arguments were so poorly understood later on. Real debates between historical actors often were and are 'comedies of error'.

Quite apart from this weakness in Hume's presentation of his argument, the 'rich country–poor country' passage could only be understood adequately when seen as part of a very complex intellectual strategy for uniting different facets of his political economy into a single self-sustained argument about the historical dynamics of market relations between rich and poor countries. As we have seen earlier, Hume maintained that the inconvenience of dear provisions and dear labour should not be avoided by pushing down wages, because high wages are 'the very effects of that public wealth and prosperity which are the end of all our wishes'. He also stated, in no less categorical language, that the 'rich country–poor country' argument cast a substantial doubt 'concerning the benefit of *banks* and *paper-credit*'.[12] In ruling out John Law's strategy of paper money and banks as instruments of development (since

---

published (London, 1801). It is now reprinted from this source in Hume, *Letters*, i, pp. 270–2. Tucker's riposte was first published by A. F. Tytler, Lord Woodhouselee, *Memoirs of the Life and Writings of the Honourable Henry Home of Kames, on of the senators of the College of Justice, and one of the lords commissioners of justiciary in Scotland: containing sketches of the progress of literature and general improvement in Scotland during the greater part of the eighteenth century*, 2 vols. (Edinburgh, 1807), ii, Appendix, pp. 4–6, and is reprinted in Hume, *Writings on Economics*, pp. 202–5.

[9] In fact, Hume never used the phrase 'division of labour' in the context of the 'rich country–poor country' debate or for that matter in any of his economic writings. For the sole example of a parallel expression, 'partition of employments', see the jurisprudence section of the *Treatise of Human Nature*, p. 485.

[10] Hume's examples were the following: 'The manufactures of London, you know, are steel, lace, silk, books, coaches, watches, furniture, fashions. But the outlying provinces have the linen and woollen trades' (Hume, *Letters*, i, pp. 143–4).

[11] Hume, *Letters*, i, p. 271. Writing to Tucker, Hume also emphasized the importance of transport costs.

[12] Hume, 'Of Money', p. 311.

they raised the amount of money in the country over its natural level and thus undermined the low-cost, low-wage advantages of the poor country), he was not simply adopting a firm position against the use of credit and paper money in the ideological context of the Mississippi and South Sea bubbles and the new mobile property of the 'Financial Revolution'. He was also arguing against Law's heritage as it survived in 'our darling projects of paper-credit' in Scotland.[13] As Adam Smith noted in the *Wealth of Nations*, the opinion of the famous Mr Law was 'that the industry of Scotland languished for the want of money'.[14] When formulating his ideas during the Union debate in Scotland in the first years of the century Law was deeply preoccupied with the problem that the Dutch were able, because of their 'great Quantity of Money' and 'their great Oeconomy...to under-sell other Nations' who were in fact better-endowed with natural resources and population but were poor.[15] Law clearly saw that in a monetized economy the circulation of money facilitates the production cycle, and he drew the conclusion that if resources were in fact available, the wheel of circulation could be brought into motion by the artificial injection of money.[16] The crucial technical question was how to determine the amount of paper money the economy could naturally carry.[17] Over-issue could lead to runaway inflation and the ruin of the market competitiveness of the country. Hume, who according to his notebook read Law's book and studied the *Articles of the Union* of 1707,[18] drew the conclusion, in the light of the later French debate between Melon, Dutot and Duverney on the historical lessons of the great English and French disasters, that the supply of paper money in fact could not be controlled.[19] The answer

[13] Hume, 'Of the Balance of Trade', *Philosophical Works*, iii, p. 340.
[14] *WN* II.ii.78.
[15] John Law, *Money and Trade considered, with a Proposal for Supplying the Nation with Money* (Edinburgh, 1705), p. 112.
[16] On Law, see Charles Rist, *Monetary and Credit Theory: From John Law to the Present Day*, trans. Jane Degras (London, 1940), and Douglas Vickers, *Studies in the Theory of Money, 1690–1776* (London, 1960).
[17] For a discussion of the difficulties involved, see J. K. Horsefield, 'The Duties of the Banker I: The Eighteenth Century', in T. S. Ashton and R. Sayers (eds.), *Papers in English Monetary History* (Oxford, 1945), pp. 1–15, and also his *Early British Monetary Experiments* (Cambridge, Mass., 1957). Hume firmly held the view that there was a natural ratio between a society's commercial capacity and the quantity of money needed for its smooth functioning. The clearest expression of this notion can be found in a footnote added to the essay 'Of the Balance of Trade' in which Hume responded to Oswald's complaint that the language of the essay was ambiguous (pp. 335–6n).
[18] 'Hume's Early Memoranda, 1729–1740: The Complete Text', ed. E. C. Mossner, *Journal of the History of Ideas*, 9 (1948), notes 80–2, p. 507. On the compilation of the philosophy sections of Hume's notebook, see J. P. Pittion, 'Hume's Reading of Bayle: An Inquiry into the Source and Role of the Memoranda', *Journal of the History of Philosophy*, 15 (1977), 373–86.
[19] Hume used Dutot's book as a source of data in his 'Early Memoranda'. See section III, entries 15, 68–74, 125–7. In a footnote to the essay 'Of Public Credit' which he dropped in 1772 he referred to the trio Melon, Dutot and Law. In the same footnote he distanced himself from the central concept of 'circulation' employed by these writers, remarking that though he had

given by Law and by other Scottish projectors that a socially responsible virtuous elite could supervise the bank experiment was not a solution which he was prepared to accept.[20]

His refusal to endorse the Scottish enthusiasm for banking experiments was, however, inconsistent with his own monetary analysis, however convincing it might be as a political analysis of human institutions. Hume shared two of Law's basic propositions. In a brilliant analysis of the effect of the influx of a given amount of money through trade into a poor country, he demonstrated how the new demand created by the influx of money could breathe a spark of life into the economy.[21] He then generalized this model into a continuous one, arguing that it was vital for a country marching from poverty to riches that money should be on a constant 'gradual increase' and have a 'thorough concoction and circulation through the state'.[22] The conception of money underpinning the demand-stimulation model was very close to Law's. Money was considered as a mere exchange facility. Its intrinsic value was immaterial. Thus, in principle Hume had no good economic reason to oppose a strategy for poor nations which tried first to obtain stimuli from credit creation through a banking experiment. Indeed Hume himself, in a footnote, did in fact concede the economic point but immediately and firmly restricted its practical application. 'Money, when increasing', he argued

gives encouragement to industry, during the interval between the encrease of money and the rise of prices. A good effect of this nature may follow too from paper-credit;

'sought for its meaning...ever since I was a school-boy, I have never yet been able to discover it' (p. 363n). While during his stay in France in the 1730s Hume was in an advantageous position to follow the French debate, he was certainly not alone in Britain in paying attention to it. Both Melon's *Political Essay upon Commerce* and Dutot's *Political Reflections upon the Finances and Commerce of France* were published in English translation in 1739, in Dublin and London respectively. The *Scots Magazine* published extracts from both books and from an English pamphlet answering Dutot; see *Scots Magazine*, 2 (1740), 276–7, 335–7; 4 (1742), 298–304, 365–7. On Melon's and Dutot's role in the debate on Law's heritage, see Paul Harsin, Introduction to Dutot, *Réflexions politiques sur les finances et le commerce*, ed. P. Harsin, 2 vols. (Paris, 1935), i, pp. xi–lv, and Michel Foucault, *The Order of Things: An Archaeology of the Human Sciences* (London, 1970), ch. 6. On their important contribution to the luxury debate, see Joseph J. Spengler, *French Predecessors of Malthus. A Study in Eighteenth-Century Wage and Population Theory* (Durham, North Carolina, 1942), and Ellen Ross, 'The Debate on Luxury in Eighteenth-Century France: A Study in the Language of Opposition to Change' (Ph.D. thesis, University of Chicago, 1975).

[20] For Law's planned supervisory body, see ch. 7 of his *Money and Trade*. The Scottish origins of Law's famous project were difficult to forget. Dutot reminded his French audience that the plan of Law's bank was first submitted to the Scottish Parliament in 1705 (*Political Reflections*, p. 62).

[21] Hume, 'Of Money', pp. 313–14. Hume's model was confined to the description of a single cycle of increased economic activity coming to an end when the once-and-for all influx of money finally affects wages as well as prices. For an analysis of the Humean model, see Michael I. Duke, 'David Hume and Monetary Adjustment', *History of Political Economy*, 11 (1979), 572–87.

[22] Hume, 'Of Money', p. 320.

but it is dangerous to precipitate matters; at the risk of losing all by the failing of that credit, as must happen upon any violent shock in public affairs.[23]

In rejecting this option he opposed a distinct strain of Scottish polite opinion on how a poor country could help herself. More importantly, from the point of view of the 'rich country–poor country' debate, he did not leave himself room for any other solution for the problems of the poor country but that of securing a toe-hold in the international division of labour by working on its low-wage advantage.

The simplicity of this argument, however, was overshadowed by the language Hume used in 'Of Money'. His talk about 'checks' in human affairs, 'shifts', and trade 'flying' from one country to another invoked the image of historical flux, renewal and decay, all too familiar to his readers. It was no innovation itself to apply this language to the *fortuna* of markets. Seventeenth-century and eighteenth-century tracts and pamphlets on trade constantly discussed the relationship of countries in terms of one underselling the other. Low price of provisions, low wages, low interest and low profits were all advantages which resulted in the ability to sell cheaper. Wealth and greatness in trade were understood as being inherently volatile. Serious trade theorists such as Sir William Petty argued that there was no point in making long-term projections into the future 'since 'tis not unlikely, but that before that time we may be all transplanted from hence to *America*, these Countreys being overrun with Turks, and made waste'.[24] Cantillon argued fifty years later that if one looked at how in history 'the Republic of Venice, the Hanseatic Towns, Flanders and Brabant, the Dutch Republic, etc. ... have succeeded each other in the profitable branches of trade' one would realize that 'when a State has arrived at the highest point of wealth ... it will inevitably fall into poverty by the ordinary course of things'.[25] Luxury and corruption were the staple concepts of these theories of the volatility of trading wealth. Sir William Temple, an author Hume quoted several times in the *Political Discourses*, saw the seeds of decay in Holland already in the seventeenth century and not only explained it in terms of corruption and luxury but also pointed out that when poorer nations come 'to set up' in competition with the rich 'some must give over, or all must break'. 'So, as it seems to be with trade', he concluded

as with the sea (its element) that has a certain pitch above which it never rises in the highest tides, and begins to ebb, as soon as ever it ceases to flow; and ever loses ground in one place, proportionable to what it gains in another[26]

---

[23] Hume, 'Of the Balance of Trade', p. 337n.
[24] William Petty, *A Treatise of Taxes and Contributions* (1662), in C. H. Hull (ed.), *The Economic Writings of Sir William Petty*, 2 vols. (Cambridge, 1899), i, p. 42.
[25] Richard Cantillon, *Essay on the Nature of Trade in General* (1730–4), ed. and trans. Henry Higgs (London, 1931), pp. 246–7.
[26] William Temple, *Observations upon the United Provinces of the Netherlands* (1672), ed. George Clark (Oxford, 1972), pp. 123–6. Hume quoted at length Temple's famous example of the diverse

Not only credit but trade itself was depicted as *Fortuna*, a lady of easy virtue. Trade, as Gordon wrote in *Cato's Letters*, was

a coy and humorous Dame, who must be won by Flattery and Allurements, and always flies Force and Power; she is not confined to Nations, Sects, or Climates, but travels and wanders about the Earth, till she fixes Residence where she finds the best Welcome and kindest Reception; her Contexture is so nice, that she cannot breathe in a tyrannical Air.[27]

Hume himself said something similar in his essay 'Of Civil Liberty', published ten years before the *Political Discourses*. 'If we trace commerce in its progress', he argued, 'through Tyre, Athens, Syracuse, Carthage, Venice, Florence, Genoa, Antwerp, Holland, England, etc., we shall always find it to have fixed its seat in free governments.'[28]

This Machiavellian invocation of the pendulum of historical change with which Hume ornamented his treatment of the relations between rich and poor countries seems to have cancelled out, at least in some of his contemporary readers' minds, his insistence that the decline in the first instance applied to individual industries only, and that he was not prophesying the fall of the rich nation. Although he described the 'concurrence of causes' for the poor country's opportunities as a happy one, it was easy to read him as asserting that the rich country could not escape decay. In the essay 'Of Luxury', which immediately preceded 'Of Money', he had made a determined attempt to break out of a theory of historical change centred on luxury and corruption. The severe Roman moralists whom 'we peruse in our infancy', he insisted, should not be believed. It was not in fact 'Grecian and Asiatic luxury' and ensuing

---

incentive effects of the different natural endowments of Ireland and Holland and called attention to Temple's enumeration of 'places where trade has most flourished, in ancient and modern times': 'Of Taxes', *Philosophical Works*, iii, p. 357. For his own list of the great commercial nations of history, see *ibid.*, p. 356. For an interesting account of seventeenth-century English views on the economic success of Holland, see J. O. Appleby, *Economic Thought and Ideology in Seventeenth-Century England* (Princeton, N.J., 1978), ch. 4.

[27] Thomas Gordon, 'Trade and Naval Power the Offspring of Civil Liberty only and cannot subsist without it', Cato's Letters, No. 64, 3 February 1721, in *Cato's Letters: or essays on liberty, civil and religious, and other important subjects*, 4th edn, 4 vols. (London, 1737), p. 267.

[28] Hume, 'Of Civil Liberty', *Philosophical Works*, iii, pp. 159-60. Hume was familiar with the analysis which associated commercial success with free and Protestant countries, and while travelling in Germany in 1748 he investigated whether it was true that there was a difference in riches between the Protestant and Catholic provinces; see the letter to John Home of Ninewells, 2 April 1748, *Letters*, i, p. 125. Seeing Germany, he expressed disillusionment with the liberty-based English 'vulgar Whig' analysis of commerce: "Tis of this country Mr Addison speaks when he calls the People "Nations of Slaves, as Tyranny debas'd: Their Makers Image more than half defac'd"... If any Foot Soldier cou'd have more ridiculous national Prejudices than the Poet, I shou'd be much surpriz'd... John Bull's Prejudices are ridiculous, as his Insolence is intolerable' (letter to John Home of Ninewells, 26 March 1748, *Letters*, i, p. 121). See Duncan Forbes, 'The European, or Cosmopolitan Dimension in Hume's Science of Politics', *British Journal of Eighteenth-Century Studies*, 1 (1978), 57-60.

corruption which had ruined poor, rustic and virtuous Rome.[29] Yet his analysis of the issue of 'rich and poor countries' was read as a general historical statement about the finitude of any country's wealth within the flux of time. The Aberdonian David Skene, for example, summarized Hume as saying that 'Trade has its natural limits beyond which it cannot pass, it circulates from one nation to another and poverty and industry continually draw it from Wealth'. Continuing with his own thoughts, Skene then concluded:

If this is a just representation of things, I cannot forbear calling it uncomfortable. I must regret the lot of Humanity, where principles seemingly opposite are so nearly connected as to be productive of each other; where every advance towards wealth is likewise a step to Poverty and where the destitution of Trade is the immediate consequence of its perfection.[30]

The paradoxical result of Hume's optimism over the chances of poor countries in international trade was thus a general despondency about the forlornness of men's efforts to establish a lasting commercial society for themselves.

David Skene, James Oswald and Josiah Tucker all misread the methodological purpose behind Hume's attempt to prove the unimportance of money *in itself* for the wealth of nations. A main theme of Hume's essays was that the real riches of a country were in her people, skills and materials. Hume realized that the old balance-of-trade theory, with its focus on money crossing and recrossing the country's borders, could 'never be refuted by a particular detail'. The only way to prove that the amount of money in a country taken in itself did not matter was 'to form a general argument' which would prove the 'impossibility' of the loss of a country's money as long as her people and industry were preserved.[31] It is ironical that this abstract argument about the

[29] Hume, 'Of Luxury', p. 305. In 1760 the title was changed to 'Of Refinements in the Arts' and at the same time the epithet 'Grecian' was also dropped from 'Grecian and Asiatic luxury'.

[30] David Skene, 'Extracts from Wallace's *Considerations of the Present Political State of Great Britain*', in 'Literary Essays: Dr. D. Skene', Aberdeen University Library, MS. 475, fols. 95–6. Skene's views were clearly influenced by the civic humanist ideas of his Aberdeen circle. See his essay 'Of the Dutch Trade', which was most likely written as an answer to Beattie's question put to the members of the Aberdeen Philosophical Society: 'What are the advantages and disadvantages of an extensive commerce' (MS. 475, fols. 179–94). On Skene, see Bernhard Fabian, ' David Skene and the Aberdeen Philosophical Society', *Bibliotheck*, 5 (1968), 81–99. For an opposite ideological use of a Skene-type 'rich country–poor country' model within the same Aberdeen circle, see Alexander Gerrard's lecture 'Of Commerce'. According to Gerrard, the difference between rich and poor countries was self-corrective. Once a nation enriched itself wages started to rise; thus 'its Poorer Neighbours can undersell it, and by this draw back to themselves the Advantages of Commerce': 'Philosophy Lectures, written by Robert Morgan, Marischal College, Aberdeen, 1758–1759', Edinburgh University Library, Dc.5.62, fols. 487–8.

[31] Hume, 'Of the Balance of Trade', p. 332. Oswald's critique of Hume's polemical strategy was sharp: '*People and industry*, tho' mentioned in your first proposition, enter for nothing into the argument which is adduced to prove it...This proposition, which is certainly new, is established by *one single argument*, tho' it is illustrated by a number of curious observations.' As a consequence Oswald held that 'the argument was inconclusive, from not embracing the

self-levelling mechanism operating in international markets, distributing to every country the appropriate amount of money in proportion to its trade – a 'scientific' argument in the Newtonian fashion if ever there was one – was read by Hume's readers as an endorsement of the Machiavellian image of growth and decay in the flow of time.

The argument itself was very simple. According to his so-called quantity theory of money the general price level of a country was determined by the 'proportion between commodities and money... Encrease the commodities, they become cheaper; encrease the money, they rise in value.'[32] In a two-country model, accordingly, under *ceteris paribus* assumptions (i.e. that people and their industry remain the same), a sudden disturbance in the quantity of money in the economy would create a price movement whose impact on the country's trade position, if it continued with its export–import trade, would in time cancel out the results of this aberration. 'All water', Hume argued

> wherever it communicates, remains always at level. Ask naturalists the reason; they tell you, that, were it to be raised in any one place, the superior gravity of that part not being balanced, must depress it, till it meet a counterpoise; and that the same cause which redresses the inequality when it happens, must for ever prevent it.[33]

The source of the misunderstandings of Hume's argument was again its rhetoric. He set out the model in figurative language, couching a *ceteris paribus* condition in terms of a figurative hypothesis of what would happen if 'four-fifths of all money in Great Britain were to be annihilated in one night' or, conversely, supposing that 'all the money of Great Britain were multiplied fivefold in a night'. The point was that overnight changes did not affect the real strength of the economy; all that changed was the quantity of money. He

whole subject' ('Correspondence of Baron Mure', pp. 94–5, and also p. 93). Adam Smith followed this line of criticism when he argued that the mercantilist fallacy of money was present in 'the systems of Mun and Gee, of Mandeville who built upon them, and of Mr. Hume who endeavoured to refute them': 'Early Draft of Part of the *Wealth of Nations*', in Smith, *Lectures on Jurisprudence*, ed. R. L. Meek, D. D. Raphael, P. G. Stein (Oxford, 1978), p. 36. Compare Oswald's critique of Hume with *WN* IV.i.34: 'Some of the best English writers upon commerce set out with observing, that the wealth of the country consists, not in its gold and silver only, but in its lands, houses, and consumable goods of all different kinds. In the course of their reasoning, however, the lands, houses, and consumable goods seem to slip from their memory, and the strain of their argument frequently supposes that all wealth consists of gold and silver.' See also *LJ(B)* 253.

[32] Hume, 'Of Money', p. 317. Hume's aim was to state a self-evident relationship rather than a *theory* of market price, although the *Political Discourses* as a whole attempted to state a price theory. See Andrew S. Skinner, 'Money and Prices: A Critique of the Quantity Theory', *Scottish Journal of Political Economy*, 14 (1967), 276–7; Joseph Schumpeter, *History of Economic Analysis*, ed. E. Boody Schumpeter (London, 1954), pp. 312–17; and Hugo Hegeland, *The Quantity Theory of Money: A Critical Study of Its Historical Development and Interpretation and a Restatement* (Göteborg, 1951), pp. 34–7, 44–5.

[33] Hume, 'Of the Balance of Trade', p. 333. Hume's first exposition of the self-balancing specie-flow model was in a critical remark on the *Spirit of Laws* in a letter to Montesquieu, dated 10 April 1749, *Letters*, i, pp. 136–7.

then showed that the rise in money raised prices, reducing the competitiveness of exports and creating an outflow of money to pay for the continuing imports until the level of money was restored to its natural level. This imagery readily evoked the rhetoric of the pendulum movement in his statement of the 'rich country–poor country' model.[34] This resonance led naturally to the presumption that the so-called 'automatic specie-flow adjustment mechanism in international trade' was the conception behind a model which in reality centred on the international division of labour between rich and poor countries through sharing out the production of simpler products to the poor and of more sophisticated products to the rich countries.

It was in discussion of Hume's automatic specie-flow distribution model that James Oswald was led to suggest to Hume his own contention. Since he received only the manuscript of the essay 'Of the Balance of Trade', he cannot have been aware of the arguments of either 'Of Commerce' or 'Of Money'.[35] Failing to realize that Hume's metaphor of an overnight miracle was simply a figurative expression of a *ceteris paribus* condition, he speculated about the real consequences of a sharp increase of money in a country. Following the steps of Hume's argument, he realized that in reality he could not discover the constant flows of money from high-price to low-price regions and vice versa which Hume's argument apparently assumed. The capital cities of countries seemed to be able to retain more money than the poor provinces, and similarly a rich country could perpetually gain on the poorer. The rich nations in fact could keep their wages low by buying cheap food in season from the poor provinces and by storing it to overcome seasonal fluctuations in food prices. Artisans from all over the world would come to the capital city or rich country and thus their competition for work would also keep wages low. Poor countries could never produce as cheaply as the rich, because they had only a few natural resources on which they could work cheaply, while most products needed a larger variety of components. They had no strong demand to support their manufacturers and thus were always left to the vagaries and fluctuations of international markets. Wide fluctuations in their corn prices from year to year would make the poor countries' wages unstable.

Summing up his arguments, Oswald concluded that 'the advantages of a rich country compared with the disadvantages of the poor one, are almost infinite... and notwithstanding... a balance of treasure arising in its favour... it would soon appear, that... it could make up manufactures cheaper than any

---

[34] Hume, 'Of the Balance of Trade', p. 333. Hume's rhetoric in these passages blurred the fact that the instantaneous overnight changes in the money supply were simply figurative expressions of a *ceteris paribus* condition. An interesting reading of the polite Humean metaphor was that of Joseph Harris, who interpreted it as an allusion to the South Sea Bubble; see his *Essay upon Money and Coins* (London, 1757), p. 86 and n.

[35] There is no reason to suppose, as does Eugene Rotwein, that Oswald was shown the other essays as well; see Hume, *Writings on Economics*, p. 190n.

other part of the world'. The poor countries could not starve the rich by refusing to supply food, materials and labour 'unless the rich country co-operated with them'.[36] In Oswald's analysis the rich country's ability to buy and store food cheaply and her ability to attract a constant flow of immigrant labour were the keys to her success. He agreed with Hume that the right way of thinking about commerce was to concentrate on real riches, not on the quantity of money. But there was no trace of reflection in Oswald's whole letter on how poor countries could break out of the vicious circle which he described so well.

While Hume was grateful to Oswald for his observations on the essay 'Of the Balance of Trade', he pointed out that a division of labour between the rich and poor countries provided a solution to the problem. His difficulty, as he made clear to Oswald, was not in admitting the advantages of rich countries, but in admitting that these could extend indefinitely. 'I cannot agree with you', he wrote, 'that barring ill policy or accidents, the rich might proceed gaining upon the poor forever', and then repeated his contention that 'the growth of everything, both in arts and nature, at last checks itself'.[37] Confronted with the idea of a world trade-monopoly totally immune to decay Hume was immediately spurred into reintroducing a language which emphasized the finitude of all particularities in time. In 1758, answering Josiah Tucker's attack, Hume reacted in precisely the same way. The question was not whether the advantages of a rich country were real. They were. 'The question is', he wrote

whether these advantages can go on, increasing trade *in infinitum*, or whether they do not at last come to a *ne plus ultra*, and check themselves, by begetting disadvantages, which at first retard, and at last finally stop their progress. Among these disadvantages, we may reckon the dear price of provisions and labour, which enables the poorer country to rival them, first in coarser manufactures, and then in those which are more elaborate. Were it otherwise, commerce, if not dissipated by violent conquests, would go on perpetually increasing, and one spot of the globe would engross the art and industry of the whole.[38]

For six years Tucker has been occupied with writing a comprehensive treatise on trade and commercial society for the education of the Prince of Wales.[39] The thesis of this major work, the *Elements of Commerce*, the first large

[36] 'Correspondence of Baron Mure', pp. 96-7.
[37] Hume, *Letters*, i, p. 143.   [38] *Ibid.*, p. 271.
[39] For Tucker's biography, see Schuyler's Introduction to Josiah Tucker, *A Selection from his Economic and Political Writings*, ed. R. L. Schuyler (New York, 1931), and George Shelton, *Dean Tucker and Eighteenth-Century Economic and Political Thought* (London, 1981). On Tucker's political background in Bristol, see Linda Colley, *In Defiance of Oligarchy: The Tory Party, 1714-1760* (Cambridge, 1982), pp. 171-2; his brand of 'Court' Whiggism is discussed in J. G. A. Pocock, 'The Ideology of Commerce: Josiah Tucker's Critique of Locke', unpublished paper presented to the 'John Locke and the Political Thought of the 1680s' symposium of the Conference for the Study of Political Thought and the Folger Institute for Renaissance and Eighteenth-Century Studies, Washington, D.C., 21-23 March 1980. Tucker received the commission to write the *Elements of Commerce* in early 1752 and by the summer he had already

section of which was ready in 1755 and distributed privately in a hundred copies for private criticism, was that the Glorious Revolution would remain incomplete until the old mercantile system of monopolies had been dismantled.[40] Without monopolies, a market equilibrium could arise through the continuous creation of new artificial needs whose satisfaction had become possible in a system of increasing division of labour.[41] In his free market model, Tucker boldly presented the development of the division of labour, leading to the introduction of machinery. Contradicting Montesquieu on the dangerous effects of machines on levels of employment, he argued that with their help one could continuously cut prices and thus create a mass market amongst those ranks of the population which were until then outside the limits of market sociability.[42]

By 1757-8 Tucker's project had run into political difficulties and the paper which he sent specifically for the attention of Hume was a fragment of the never-completed second part of the *Elements of Commerce* in which Tucker set out to refute 'vulgar prejudices'.[43] The vulgar error which he had in mind was 'that rival nations cannot all flourish at the same time; that poor nations will draw away trade from rich, that low wages create cheap manufactures'.[44]

drafted the preliminary dissertation which set the tone of the whole enterprise. On his thinking in this period see his correspondence with Lord Townshend in *The Manuscripts of the Marquis Townshend*, Historical Manuscripts Commission, Eleventh Report, Appendix, Part IV (London, 1887), pp. 371-82. That Tucker does not seem to have been affected by the appearance of Hume's *Political Discourses* is suggested by the successive editions of his *Brief Essay on Trade*. See Salim Rashid, 'Economists, Economic Historians and Mercantilism', *Scandinavian Economic History Review*, 28 (1980), 12. The early parts of the *Elements of Commerce* rather reveal the marked impact of Montesquieu on Tucker's thinking.

[40] Josiah Tucker, *The Elements of Commerce and the Theory of Taxes* (London, 1755), pp. 88-9, 135. One of the last of these privately circulated volumes reached Hume through Lord Kames. See Tucker's letter to Kames, 28 March 1757, S.R.O., GD24/I/558, fol. 3, and Hume's letter to Lord Elibank, 6 April 1758, in 'New Hume Letters to Lord Elibank, 1748-1776', ed. E. C. Mossner, *Texas Studies in Literature and Language*, 4 (1962), 442. Hume discovered a similarity between some of his ideas and those of Tucker, but the point seems to be a rather trivial one compared to the issues at stake in their controversy on rich and poor countries. Compare Hume, *The History of Great Britain*, ed. D. Forbes (Harmondsworth, Middlesex, 1970), p. 235, and Tucker, *Elements of Commerce*, pp. 105-6.

[41] Tucker, *Elements of Commerce*, p. 41.

[42] Tucker, *Instructions to Travellers* (London, 1757), pp. 20-2. Tucker remarked that the fact that by the use of machines 'the Price of Goods is...prodigiously lowered from what otherwise it must have been...is a position universally assented to' (*ibid.*, p. 21). The *Instructions* were a part of the original *Elements of Commerce* project and were likewise privately printed by the author. Tucker sent copies immediately after its printing to Lord Kames and to Dr James Home, a Glasgow physician. See S.R.O., GD24/I/558, fol. 3.

[43] On Tucker's troubles in formulating a system of commerce attacking monopolies in the political environment of an English port city, see his letters to Kames, 18 October 1761 and 10 December 1763, in Tytler, *Life of Kames*, ii, Appendix, pp. 7-10, and Tucker's Introduction to his *Four Tracts on Political and Commercial Subjects* (Gloucester, 1774).

[44] See the handwritten contents list of the planned second part of the *Elements of Commerce* in the copy which Tucker had sent to his bishop in Bristol, Thomas Secker, later Archbishop of Canterbury. The copy is in the New York Public Library; the list was published in W. E. Clark, *Josiah Tucker, Economist* (New York, 1903), p. 239. The eventual title of the answer

Unwittingly, Tucker in fact managed to prove Hume's own point. He started from a reconstruction of Hume's self-regulating specie-flow mechanism and interpreted it as a model of the distribution of wealth.[45] In an effort to prove that low wages in the poor country could not cause shifts in trade and manufactures through an equilibrating mechanism of international trade, he reached the conclusion that the advantages of the rich country would enable her to retain the high-skill 'operose' manufactures, while the poor would have to content herself with the ruder arts.[46] Wages in themselves told little about prices, argued Tucker; it was cheaper to pay 2s 6d to a skilled man than to pay 6d to an awkward bungler.[47] He recognized the connection between the division of labour and the extent of the market and argued that in the rich country

where the demands are great and constant, every Manufacture that requires various processes, and is composed of different Parts, is accordingly divided and subdivided into separate and distinct Branches; ...whereas in a poor Country, the same Person is obliged by Necessity...to undertake such different Branches, as prevent him from excelling, or being expeditious in any.[48]

The same was true in agriculture, he continued. Growing corn required considerable skill, and accordingly English corn was cheaper than Scottish.[49] Tucker thus turned his initial abstract model of neighbouring rich and poor countries into the example of England and Scotland. His conclusion was that 'the manufacturing Counties of England...Sheffield and Birmingham are in

---

to the vulgar prejudice when it was published as 'Tract I' of the *Four Tracts* echoed Tucker's first formulation: 'A Solution to the important Question, Whether a poor Country, where raw Materials and Provisions are cheap, and Wages low, can supplant the Trade of a rich manufacturing Country, where raw Materials and Provisions are dear, and the Price of Labour high'.

[45] 'Tract I', in *Four Tracts*, pp. 17–18. Bernard Semmel, championing Tucker's claims against Hume, recently himself repeated Tucker's confusion: 'The pride of the Scottish Enlightenment, David Hume – philosopher, historian, economist – had argued in one of his tracts that, under conditions of a free trade, wealth would inevitably be transferred from a richer to a poorer state until the riches of both states were equal' ('The Hume–Tucker Debate and Pitt's Trade Proposals', *Economic Journal*, 65 (1955), pp. 759–60). Jacob Viner, ignoring the evidence of the text of 'Of Money' and the Oswald–Hume correspondence, argued that the 'rich country–poor country' debate between Hume and Tucker was a confused product of Tucker's initial misreading of Hume's self-correcting *ceteris paribus* specie-flow model, since 'Hume, in an unsatisfactory reply, himself follows this shift in issues' (*Studies in the Theory of International Trade* (New York, 1937), p. 87).

[46] 'Tract I', pp. 35–6. Tucker sharply criticized the common-sense association of high wages with high prices: 'For the Argument proceeds thus, The more Labour, the more Wages; – the more Wages, the more Money; the more Money paid for making them, the dearer the Goods must come to Market: And yet the Fact itself is quite the Reverse of this seemingly just Conclusion.'   [47] *Ibid.*, p. 34.

[48] *Ibid.*, pp. 33–4. See also the parallel passage in *Elements of Commerce*, p. 12. In the *Instructions to Travellers* Tucker also hailed the piece-rate wage system of England as providing a further incentive 'to exert on Industry, Dexterity, or Skill superior to others' (p. 19).

[49] 'Tract I', p. 36.

The 'rich country–poor country' debate 287

the Possession of the Trade, and will ever keep it, unless it be their own Faults',[50] and that the wealth of the rich country 'will promote still greater Industry, and go on, for anything that appears to the contrary, still accumulating'.[51] While he suggested that the poor country could protect her infant industries with a tariff barrier and that by 'the very Largeness of their Capitals... the English might be able to assist the Scotch in various Ways',[52] he believed that the gap between the rich and the poor country would remain constant despite the developing division of labour between the two. Tucker's judgement on the future of the rich country was optimistic. Why should one suppose that

> our Children cannot as far exceed us as we have exceeded our Gothic Forefathers? And is it not much more natural and reasonable to suppose, that we are rather at the Beginning only, and just got within the Threshold, than that we arrived at the *ne plus ultra* of useful Discoveries?[53]

Tucker's direct comparison between England and Scotland brought the debate on to home ground and Hume immediately took up the challenge to vindicate the prospects for his native Scotland. 'I am pleased when I find the author insist on the advantages of England', he wrote in a solemn tone to Kames

> and prognosticate thence the continuance and even further progress of the opulence of that country, but I still indulge myself in the hopes that we in Scotland possess also some advantages, which may enable us to share with them in wealth and industry.

And he repeated his policy advice to the Scots: 'It is certain that the simpler kind of industry ought first to be attempted in a country like ours'.[54] It was in this perspective that Hume repeated to Tucker that no 'one nation should be the monopoliser of wealth'. In any case, despite all appearances, such an eventuality was impossible:

> the growth of all bodies, artificial as well as natural, is stopped by internal causes,

---

[50] *Ibid.*, p. 40.
[51] *Ibid.*, p. 44.
[52] *Ibid.*, p. 42.
[53] *Ibid.*, p. 31.
[54] Hume, *Letters*, i, p. 273. Hume and Kames shared a feeling of Scottishness. In the same month as the Hume–Tucker exchange Kames wrote to Gilbert Elliot: 'No union can make me forget that I am a Scotchman': Kames to Elliot, 6 February 1758, Minto Papers, National Library of Scotland, MS. 11014, fol. 111. It was also Elliot who was on the receiving end of Hume's outburst in a letter from Paris, 22 September 1764: 'Some hate me because I am a Tory, some because I am not a Whig, some because I am not a Christian, and all because I am a Scotsman. Can you seriously talk of my continuing an Englishman?' (Hume, *Letters*, i, p. 253). Elliot, a Westminster M.P., saw also the other side of the coin: 'Notwithstanding all you say we are both Englishmen – that is true British subjects, entitled to every emolument and advantage that our happy constitution can bestow' (Elliot to Hume, 6 November 1764, Minto Papers, National Library of Scotland, MS. 11009, fols. 134–6). Didier Deleule, in his *Hume et la naissance du libéralisme économique* (Paris, 1979), overstates his case when he argues that Hume's critique of Tucker anticipated a critique of *européocentrisme* (p. 117).

derived from their enormous size and greatness. Great empires, great cities, great commerce, all of them receive a check, not from accidental events, but necessary principles.[55]

Tucker resented being described as a 'monopolist' and protested in reply that he was not speaking about 'infinite', only as yet 'indefinite', prospects for the rich country.[56] Tucker thought that the facts of the matter were on his side, even if he was not quite sure whether he could 'rightly account for this phenomenon or not'.[57] But Hume's pendulum-of-growth argument was used precisely to counter such intellectually complacent extrapolations into an indefinite future from the apparently widening gap between rich and poor countries in his own day. In modern commentaries on Hume this 'check on growth' argument is interpreted as a sign of his inability to break out from the 'growth and decay' commonplaces.[58] In the 'rich country–poor country'

[55] Hume, *Letters*, i, p. 273. The source of Hume's notion is difficult to pinpoint exactly. However, its first appearance in Hume's *oeuvre* is almost certainly in a jotted-down note in the 'Early Memoranda' which provided Hume with an alternative explanation of the fall of Rome from the luxury-corruption model: 'There seems to be a Natural Course of Things, which brings on the Destruction of great Empires. They push their Conquests till they come to barbarous Nations, which stop their Progress, by the Difficulty of subsisting great Armies. After that, the Nobility & considerable Men of the conquering Nation & best Provinces withdraw gradually from the frontier Army, by reason of its Distance from the Capital & barbarity of the Country, in which they quarter: they forget the Use of War. Their barbarous Soldiers become their Masters. These have no Law but their Sword, both from their bad Education & from their Distance from the Sovereign to whom they bear no Affection. Hence Disorder, Violence, Anarchy, & Tyranny, & Dissolution of Empire' ('Early Memoranda', pp. 517-18). Hume later repeated this passage with minor alterations in the essay 'Of the Balance of Power', *Philosophical Works*, iii, p. 355.
[56] Hume, *Writings on Economics*, p. 203. See the Postscript to 'Tract I', p. 49. Tucker discounted Hume's 'checks to growth' argument as an idea 'borrowed from the State of Natural Bodies, and from thence metaphorically transferred to political Constitutions', and also expressed disbelief in the civic humanist analysis of the 'absolutely incurable' corruption of the body politic ('Tract I', pp. 55-6). In fact, Tucker had an English national monopolist streak in his thinking which he preserved from his early admiration for Charles King's *British Merchant*. Tucker quoted approvingly the aim of this famous Whig argument against Tory free-trade policies, i.e. to make 'Great Britain the *General Center* of Trade and a *Magazine* for other Nations'; see Tucker, *Reflections on the Expediency of a Law for the Naturalisation of Foreign Protestants* (London, 1751), pp. 58-9 and note. According to Lord Shelburne, the narrow views of the *British Merchant* formed the principles of nine-tenths of the British public even later in the century; see the letter of Shelburne to George III, 26 July 1782, as quoted in Kirk Willis, 'The Role in Parliament of the Economic Ideas of Adam Smith, 1776-1800', *History of Political Economy*, 11 (1979), 530. On the *British Merchant*, see E. A. J. Johnson, *Predecessors of Adam Smith: The Growth of British Economic Thought* (London, 1937), ch. 8.
[57] Tucker to Kames, 6 July 1758 in Hume, *Writings on Economics*, pp. 202-3.
[58] Duncan Forbes, who generally opposes civic humanist interpretations of Hume, see this argument of Hume as an aberration. Disregarding its economic context he diagnoses it as a 'swinging pendulum variety of determinism' of the Machiavellian type 'which suggests a cyclical view of history that cannot be squared, among other things, with the progress of commerce and the arts and the rise of the middling rank and growth of liberty in modern Europe' (*Hume's Philosophical Politics* (Cambridge, 1975), pp. 189-90). For similar views, see Giuseppe Giarrizzo, *David Hume Politico e Storico* (Turin, 1962), pp. 75, 61; Peter Burke, 'Tradition and Experience: The Idea of Decline from Bruni to Gibbon', in G. W. Bowersock,

argument, however, especially in Hume's hope for a rich Scotland sharing the wealth of Tucker's England, this old commonplace of the Aristotelian–Machiavellian discourse was deployed as a firmly optimistic argument.[59] One might have expected that in Scotland Hume's argument for a rich commercial future for poor countries would be well-received. This was true in some cases. Lord Kames, for example, who was privy to the arguments involved in the Hume–Tucker correspondence, paraphrased Hume as saying 'It appears the intention of Providence that all nations should benefit by commerce as sunshine'. Although 'an ambitious country would willingly engross all to themselves', Providence had a solution for that by 'making an overgrown commerce the means of its own destruction'.[60] But for others, incapable of unravelling their dual identities as Scots but also as North Britons and subjects of the United Kingdom of Great Britain, the argument for the necessary decline of rich countries proved double-edged.

The language of corruption and renewal, historical decay and riches was particularly associated for a brief period in the late 1750s with the immensely popular *Estimate of the Manners and Principles of the Times* of John Brown.[61] Brown's tract was answered in Scotland by Robert Wallace, Hume's antagonist in the debate on the decline of population in modern times. Wallace's defence of the commercial well-being of Great Britain and of Scotland in particular caught Hume in a crossfire. Wallace dismantled every bit of Hume's 'rich

John Clive and Stephen R. Graubaud (eds.), *Edward Gibbon and the Decline and Fall of the Roman Empire* (Cambridge, Mass., 1977), pp. 143, 146. Joseph Low in his 'Eighteenth Century Controversy in the Theory of Economic Progress' also mispositioned Hume as the leading pessimist in the debate.

[59] It is in the nature of cyclical arguments of historical change that they cannot be judged to be pessimistic or optimistic without a knowledge of the overall time-frame. Downswings are followed by an upswing, a *renovatio*. The double-edged nature of rotation theories is shown in Hans Baron, 'The Querelle of the Ancients and the Moderns as a Problem for Renaissance Scholarship', *Journal of the History of Ideas*, 20 (1959), 3–22, and Jochen Schlobach, *Zyklentheorie und Epochenmetaphorik: Studien zur bildlichen Sprache der Geschichtsreflexion in Frankreich von der Renaissance bis zur Frühaufklärung* (Munich, 1977). See also John D. Scheffer, 'The Idea of Decline in Literature and the Fine Arts in Eighteenth-Century England', *Modern Philology*, 34 (1936), 155–78, and H. Vyverberg, *Historical Pessimism in the French Enlightenment* (Cambridge, Mass., 1958).

[60] Lord Kames, 'Origin and Progress of Commerce', *Sketches of the History of Man*, 2 vols. (Edinburgh, 1774), i, pp. 34–5. For commentary see Viner, *Studies in the Theory of International Trade*, p. 103, and Tytler, *Life of Kames*, ii, pp. 117–18.

[61] John Brown, *An Estimate of the Manners and Principles of the Times*, 2 vols. (London, 1757–8), and *An Explanatory Defence of the Estimate of Manners and the Principles of Times being an Appendix to that Work, occasioned by the Clamours lately raised against it among certain Ranks of Men, written by the Author of the Estimate, in a Series of Letters to a Noble Friend* (London, 1758). Brown abused Hume and in violent attacks on him associated his name with that of Bolingbroke and Mandeville; see *Estimate*, ii, pp. 20–1, 86. On 'Estimate' Brown, see Simeon M. Wade Jr, 'The Idea of Luxury in Eighteenth-Century England' (Ph.D. thesis, Harvard University, 1968). Significantly, Tucker condemned Brown's 'indecent' attack on Hume and welcomed William Temple's *Vindication of Commerce* as the best answer to the *Estimate*. See his letter to Kames, 6 July 1759, in Tytler, *Life of Kames*, ii, Appendix, p. 6.

country–poor country' argument and found its apparent 'historical pessimism' in contradiction to Hume's praise of commercial society. For him Hume's idea 'that trade gives a check to itself; and there is a limit, beyond which it cannot be increased', that 'poorer nations... can work cheaper than those that are richer; and must therefore carry away their trade',[62] was very similar to Brown's argument, which 'naturally tends to dispirit our countrymen'.[63] Hume was mistaken: the well-fed Englishman who earned 'higher wages' could work 'many things *by the piece*, as cheap, or cheaper than a Frenchman'.[64] He seemed to be familiar with Hume's polemic with Tucker, or at any rate phrased his position in Hume's own terms:

trade is, indeed, limited because the earth and everything in it is limited. One nation can never extend its trade *in infinitum*, or over all the earth. But a richer nation, by a proper management, may always maintain its superiority in trade over the poorer.[65]

Wallace also revived the idea that a poor but growing country stood in need of paper money and credit to boost her economy. He wisely refrained from referring to John Law, but drew instead on Berkeley's *Querist* which pointed out that a paper-money experiment might have helped poor Ireland to break out from its poverty.[66] Hume's opposition to paper money and banks made Wallace doubt whether he really did care about the well-being and high wages

---

[62] Robert Wallace, *Characteristics of the Present Political State of Great Britain* (London, 1758), p. 41.
[63] *Ibid.*, p. xviii.   [64] *Ibid.*, p. 41.
[65] *Ibid.*, p. 42. Wallace as a Commonwealthman is discussed by Caroline Robbins, *The Eighteenth-Century Commonwealthmen: Studies in the Transmission, Development and Circumstances of English Liberal Thought from the Restoration of Charles II until the War with the Thirteen Colonies* (Cambridge, Mass., 1959), pp. 202–11. Wallace's civic humanist sympathies are evident in his polemic against Hume in the population debate; see his *A Dissertation on the Numbers of Mankind in Ancient and Modern Times* (Edinburgh, 1753). His sympathies remained the same in the *Characteristics*. Nevertheless, he now argued for the acceptance of the realities of the eighteenth century and embraced the spirit of Montesquieu's differential analysis of luxury under different systems of government: 'After all, a poorer State chiefly addicted to agriculture and pasturage, and less employed in procuring the elegancies and ornaments of life by an extensive trade, may be, in many respects, preferable to a richer commercial nation. The inhabitants of such a poorer country may be more numerous, more healthy, and more virtuous. They may, by being more war-like, be more able to defend themselves at home; and may likewise be abundantly provided with the real necessaries and conveniences of life. In such a case they may adopt every frugal scheme. They will not need Paper-credit, and but very little money. At the same time, they may be very happy; happier, perhaps, than richer commercial nations. But, if they will not be satisfied with such simplicity; if a people must have delicacies and ornaments, and the trade and manufactures that are necessary to procure them; they must not exclude those maxims, that are suitable to such an end' (*Characteristics*, pp. 56–7; also pp. 16, 20, 25, 30). For a life of Wallace, see Norah Smith, 'The Literary Career and Achievement of Robert Wallace (1697–1771)' (Ph.D. thesis, University of Edinburgh, 1973); on the debate with Hume on population, E. C. Mossner, *The Forgotten Hume: Le bon David* (New York, 1943), ch. 5.
[66] Wallace, *Characteristics*, pp. 55–6. Wallace even defended the institution of public debt and invoked Berkeley's queries 223–5, 242, 296–9 and 303 to support his case; see *Characteristics*, pp. 27, 55–6, 59–60. Berkeley's *Querist* was reprinted by the Foulis Press in Glasgow, and Wallace recommended it 'to be perused by every lover of this country, and of mankind'

of the common labourers of Scotland. 'It is ridiculous', Wallace argued, 'to be perpetually extolling trade and manufactures, while we are constantly railing at what is evidently connected with them, or necessary to procure them. This is to act inconsistently, and aim at impossibilities.'[67]

The sharp criticism that his 'rich country–poor country' argument attracted did not cause Hume to amend the formulations of the essay 'Of Money'. But he realized that he must say more about the position of rich countries if he was to get his claims about that of poor ones accepted. He stood by his original idea that the ultimate strength of the rich country lay in its strong home market, but he no longer presumed that the choice to protect the high wages of its artisans entailed the loss of its foreign markets. The very nature of trade, including foreign trade, was its mutuality: to sell your goods you needed a buyer. If the rich country isolated itself from the poor, the latter could not enjoy the benefits of an international division of labour and receive the stimulus of foreign trade. Conversely, if the rich country tried to pre-empt the loss of its foreign trade by suppressing its poor potential competitors, the result would also be the loss of its foreign trade. By suppressing poor neighbours the rich would simply lose their own foreign markets. 'The encrease of riches and commerce in any one nation', Hume argued, 'instead of hurting, commonly promotes the riches and commerce of all its neighbours.'[68] In the new essay which he added soon after the clash with Tucker and Wallace, 'Of the Jealousy of Trade', Hume generalized his optimistic statement about the rich countries' future to the future of the whole international trading community. If the spirit of industry was kept alive by interaction with other nations, a rich country keeping its borders open to the products of the poor did not have to 'dread' that it would lose its industries one by one. Its manufacturers might have to

(*Characteristics*, p. 27). On the similarities between Low's and Berkeley's ideas, see Vickers, *Studies in the Theory of Money*, ch. 8; for a comparison with Hume's monetary theory, see Joseph Johnston, *Bishop Berkeley's Querist in Historical Perspective* (Dundalk, 1970). Berkeley can also be seen as a protagonist of the case of poor countries; see T. W. Hutchinson, 'Berkeley's Querist and Its Place in the Economic Thought of the Eighteenth Century', *British Journal of the Philosophy of Science*, 4 (1953), 52–77, and I. D. S. Ward, 'George Berkeley: Precursor of Keynes or Moral Economist on Underdevelopment?', *Journal of Political Economy*, 67 (1959), 31–40, and the ensuing debate between Hutchinson and Ward. Berkeley played an important role in the shaping of Wallace's generation in Scotland in general; see George Davie, 'Berkeley's Impact on Scottish Philosophers', *Philosophy*, 40 (1965), 222–34.

[67] Wallace, *Characteristics*, p. 57. Compare it with pp. 45–6. Hume was condescending towards Wallace and did not bother to answer even to the accusation of Jacobitism. He also noted to Elibank that poor Wallace 'was quite surprizd, when I assurd him, that no Bank in Europe but that of Scotland, usd that Practice' (letter of Hume to Elibank, 12 April 1758, in 'Letters to Lord Elibank', p. 445).

[68] Hume, 'Of the Jealousy of Trade', *Philosophical Works*, iii, p. 361. That in this essay Hume was not arguing the English viewpoint of 'imperialism of free trade' but rather tried to distance himself from the monopolistic tendencies of rich England was clearly seen by both Benjamin Franklin and Turgot. See the letter of Franklin to Hume, 27 September 1760, in *The Papers of Benjamin Franklin*, ed. L. W. Labaree, ix (New Haven, Conn., 1966), p. 229, and Turgot to Hume, 23 July 1766, in Hume, *Writings on Economics*, p. 205.

switch to new products but would not be 'in danger of wanting employment'. If they themselves prospered, and let their poorer neighbours also prosper, the whole international trading community of nations could face the future with optimism. In a system of free world-trade no state had to

> entertain apprehensions, that their neighbours will improve to such a degree in every art and manufacture, as to have no demand from them. Nature, by giving diversity of geniuses, climates, and soils, to different nations, has secured their mutual intercourse and commerce, as long as they all remain industrious and civilised.[69]

Hume's free-trade explanation of how a rich country could escape decline was now entirely predicated on the flexibility which alone could permit that great nation to remain commercial and industrious. This '*virtù*' could save even such a rich nation as England which relied only on a few stable commodities to maintain her trade. A rich country, Hume explained, could only gain her advantage in these staple branches of trade because she had 'some peculiar and natural advantages for raising the commodity' in the first place. If the corruption of her commerce, Hume went on, did in fact occur, 'if notwithstanding these advantages, they lose such a manufacture, they ought to blame their own idleness, or bad government, not the industry of their neighbours'.[70] Clearly, Hume believed even more strongly that poor countries should start up first in the simpler industries while the rich retained the more 'operose' ones. He also demonstrated that the chimera of a world trade-monopoly was a contradiction in terms. When all the neighbours of the monopolist country were impoverished, trade had to stop. If 'they could send us no commodities: they could take none from us'.

[69] Hume, 'Of the Jealousy of Trade', p. 364. Hume also added that even a pure trading nation, like the Dutch, can survive for a very long time, since 'the advantage of superior stocks and correspondence is so great, that it is not easily overcome; and as all the transactions increase by the increase of industry in the neighbouring states, even a people whose commerce stands on this precarious basis, may at first reap a considerable profit from the flourishing condition of their neighbours' (*ibid.*, pp. 347–8). For a criticism of Hume's 'rich country–poor country' argument as 'conventional optimism' and a 'superficial construction' stemming from a 'spontaneous impulse of Cosmopolitan sympathy', see P. Chamley, 'The Conflict between Montesquieu and Hume. A Study of the Origins of Adam Smith's Universalism', in A. S. Skinner and T. Wilson (eds.), *Essays on Adam Smith* (Oxford, 1975), pp. 303–5.

[70] Hume, 'Of the Jealousy of Trade', p. 365. Bad government for Hume was primarily one which ran up a huge public debt, since at the end this could lead to the country being conquered by her enemies in war. Hume's logic here was again to refuse to accept that things can go on *ad infinitum*. However, he was not so pessimistic if the government had the courage to declare voluntary bankruptcy in order to use the funds to finance the army. No 'everlasting destruction of credit' was to be feared and Hume also maintained that one 'must still suppose great commerce and opulence to remain, even after every fund is mortgaged', as had been demonstrated by the Dutch. See 'Of Public Credit', *Philosophical Works*, iii, p. 368, and 'Of Jealousy of Trade', p. 348. Compare this with J. G. A. Pocock, *The Machiavellian Moment*, pp. 496–7, and 'Hume and the American Revolution: The Dying Thoughts of a North Briton', in D. F. Norton, N. Capaldi and W. L. Robison (eds.), *McGill Hume Studies* (San Diego, Calif., 1979), pp. 323–43.

The new essay on the futility of trade rivalries failed to lay to rest the criticisms of Hume's 'rich country–poor country' argument. Tucker, who – as Hume himself acknowledged – also saw the mutuality of markets, but unlike Hume argued for pronounced protectionism and selective tariff policies for poor countries in legitimate self-defence against the rich, claimed that he had managed to convert Hume to his view of the poor prospects of the backward countries in the face of the accumulating advantages of the rich.[71] When he actually saw the new edition of Hume's essays, he must have been acutely disappointed. The original 'rich country–poor country' formula in 'Of Money' was reprinted alongside the new essay 'Of the Jealousy of Trade'. Hume himself plainly regarded the two models as compatible. Applying Duncan Forbes's interpretative yardstick, that 'if...in the numerous carefully revised editions Hume left anything vital unaltered, one must surely presume that he still held to that opinion, unless a note to the contrary is appended', Tucker's claim of conversion must surely be questioned.[72] When the last volumes of Hume's *History of England* came out, Tucker once again interpreted its appendixes on economic history as signalling a change of heart and hastened to communicate the 'discovery' to Lord Kames:

> I think I may gather from several passages in the two volumes of History last published, that I have had the honour of making him [i.e. Hume] a convert, in regard to the notion, *That cheap countries do not produce cheap manufactures.* The more he reflects on the matter, the more he will be convinced, that a rich industrious country can never be overtaken, much less outdone by a poor one; equal industry operating in both.[73]

As we have seen earlier, Hume had never hesitated to admit that the rich

---

[71] Tucker to Dr Birch, 19 May 1760, British Library, Add. MS. 4329, fol. 269. He also claimed that the truth about the origins of Hume's ideas in 'Of the Jealousy of Trade' was known to Lord Kames, Dr Robertson and many others. In contrast, P. Chamley claims that Hume might have taken the point from Montesquieu, *Spirit of the Laws*, 20.2: 'The nations who traffic with each other become reciprocally dependent: for if one has an interest in buying, the other has an interest in selling; and thus their union is founded on their mutual necessities'; see Chamley, 'The Conflict between Hume and Montesquieu', p. 304. Hume himself also advocated a limited tariff protection of home industries; see 'Of the Balance of Trade', pp. 343–4. It is difficult to see, however, how this advocacy of protection could have been 'the logical outgrowth' of the 'law of growth and decay presented in the essay "Of Money"' as Rotwein claims in Hume, *Writings on Economics*, p. 76n.

[72] Forbes, *Hume's Philosophical Politics*, p. 187. Disregarding Tucker's own 1763 correction of the conversion claim, several modern commentators inferred that Tucker must have meant 'Of the Jealousy of Trade' and Hume's only addition to his economic essays after 1758, and have accepted Tucker's point of view. See Rotwein in Hume, *Writings on Economics*, p. 204n; A. W. Coats, 'Changing Attitudes to Labour in the Mid-Eighteenth Century', reprinted in M. W. Flinn and T. C. Smout (eds.), *Essays in Social History*, p. 90; Bernard Semmel, *The Rise of Free Trade Imperialism, 1750–1850* (Cambridge, 1970), p. 15; R. L. Meek in Meek (ed.), *Precursors of Adam Smith* (London, 1973), p. 176; Samuel Hollander, *The Economics of Adam Smith* (London, 1973), p. 78; and G. Shelton, *Dean Tucker*, p. 132.

[73] Tucker to Kames, 26 December 1763, in Tytler, *Life of Kames*, ii, Appendix, pp. 16–17. Tucker's corrected conversion claim was referring to Hume's *The History of England from the Invasion of Julius Caesar to the Accession of Henry VII*, 2 vols. (London, 1762).

country's advantages were enormous in refined products. In the *History*, indeed, he had gathered long-term price data in order to prove that despite the 'price revolution' the real price of 'operose' products was continuously falling in England over the preceding centuries. The price of those 'commodities...such as required little Art to raise them, such as Cattle, Poultry, etc....would most rise'.[74] To prove his point, Hume used corn as a proxy for manufactures which 'require a great deal of Art' and compared corn prices with the price of cattle in the English Middle Ages. It was the proof of the poverty and unrefined civilization of medieval England that corn bore a much higher price than cattle. 'So great a difference between the prices of corn and cattle as that of four to one, compared to the present rates', Hume argued, 'affords important reflections concerning the very different state of industry and tillage in the two periods.' A few chapters later he drew his conclusion: 'It may thence be inferred' – he looked back to his earlier argument – 'that the raising of corn was a species of manufactory, which few in the age could practice with advantage.'[75] What Hume wished to demonstrate was that all manufactured products 'must become cheaper in times of industry and refinement, than in rude, uncultivated ages', a consequence which he attributed to the beneficial market effects of the new 'imaginary wants of men, which have since extremely multiplied'.[76] In addition, he established as the cornerstone of his argument the conclusion that the same beneficial effect would not apply to primitive products, and that poor countries which were also able to produce them could thus obtain a foothold in international trade by exporting them to rich countries where their price, in comparison with the fall in the price of manufactured goods, would remain relatively high.

Tucker's illusion that he had convinced David Hume was reaffirmed in print, when in 1774, in his *Four Tracts*, he published the fragment of the *Elements of Commerce* which he had originally sent to Hume in 1758.[77] Thus the debate, and Hume's position in it, remained very much in the public eye.[78] Indeed,

[74] Hume to Elibank, 23 May 1758, 'Letters to Lord Elibank', p. 562.
[75] Hume, *History of England from the Invasion*, i, 'Miscellaneous transactions of the reign of Henry III', p. 56; 'Miscellaneous transactions during the reign of Edward II', p. 152.
[76] Hume, *The History of Great Britain*, ed. D. Forbes, p. 235.
[77] Tucker and Hume met in the 1760s in France and had an amicable relationship; see Tucker's letters to Hume in the 'Hume Papers', Royal Society of Edinburgh, vol. 7, letters 79–81. Thus, when Tucker announced his conversion claim publicly, he knew well that Hume did not accept it: 'The first Piece itself arose from a Correspondence in the Year 1758, with a Gentleman of *North Britain*, eminently distinguished in the Republic of Letters. Though I cannot boast that I had the Honour of making the Gentleman a *declared* Convert, yet I can say, and prove likewise, that in his Publications since our Correspondence, he has wrote, and reasoned as if he was a Convert' (Preface to the *Four Tracts*, p. vii).
[78] Hume's essay 'Of Money' containing the striking 'rich country–poor country' passage as the trump card against paper money and banks was provocatively reprinted by the editors of the *Scots Magazine* as the first piece of a public debate on banking in 1762, amidst the severe Scottish exchange and banking crisis of the time: *Scots Magazine*, 24 (1762), 33–9. As a result of the heated controversy, Hume significantly modified his position on banks in a long addition to

The 'rich country–poor country' debate 295

one finds that its echoes can be found almost everywhere in the writings of the Scottish Enlightenment. The ambiguity in Hume's use of the two contrasting discourses was highlighted by a renewed Scottish preoccupation with prophecies of premature decline. The writer who reintroduced into the debate of the 1760s the Machiavellian themes of growth and decay, virtue and corruption, was Adam Ferguson. The *Essay on the History of Civil Society* with its play on these Machiavellian chords caused Hume to fear for the reputation of the Scottish circle of literati,[79] despite his own earlier flirtation with such language in the course of his analysis of the relations between rich and poor countries.

In fact Ferguson's focus on the 'decline of nations' and particularly of commercial, 'polished' nations elided what for Hume himself was the central issue: the historical fate of the commerce of 'polished society' itself. Ferguson ignored such issues as the dynamic interrelationship of rich and poor countries in trade, although he noted the facts of the division of labour with great interest.[80] His main preoccupation was the effect which this division produced upon political personality. While he emphasized that in the modern division of labour men became 'like the parts of an engine, to concur to the purpose',[81] his main fear was that this 'dismemberment' of personality could spread to 'the higher departments of policy and war'.[82] The internal decay of the political fabric in Ferguson's account truncated the main question which Hume wished to resolve.

Whatever may be the natural wealth of people, or whatever may be the limits beyond which they cannot improve on their stock it is probable, that no nation has ever reached those limits, or has been able to postpone its misfortunes, and the effects of misconduct, until its fund of materials, and the fertility of its soil, were exhausted, or the numbers

---

the essay while leaving the 'rich country–poor country' statement intact. On the banking crisis, see H. Hamilton, 'Scotland's Balance of Payments Problem in 1762', *Economic History Review*, 2nd ser., 5 (1953), 344–57.

[79] Hume was in Paris when Ferguson's book came out. He had serious misgivings about it and feared for the reputation of Ferguson as a moral philosophy teacher at Edinburgh University; see his correspondence with Hugh Blair, *Letters*, ii, pp. 11–12, and David Kettler, *The Social and Political Thought of Adam Ferguson* (Ohio, 1967), pp. 57–60. Ferguson's arguments were heavily influenced by Montesquieu; see Alan Baum, *Montesquieu and Social Theory* (Oxford, 1979), pp. 113–15.

[80] See Ferguson's lecture heads concerning machines and the steam engine in the synopsis of his natural philosophy course in *Analysis of Pneumatics and Moral Philosophy for the use of Students in the College of Edinburgh* (Edinburgh, 1766), Appendix 'Of Natural Philosophy' [separately paginated], pp. 12–13, 26.

[81] Adam Ferguson, *Essay on the History of Civil Society*, ed. D. Forbes (Edinburgh, 1967), p. 182, and also p. 183: 'Manufactures...prosper most, where the mind is least consulted, and where the workshop may, without any great effort of imagination, be considered as an engine, the parts of which are men.' Ferguson repeated and further developed his critique of the division of labour at the end of his life in his essay 'Of the Separation of Departments, Professions and Tasks Resulting from the Progress of Arts in Society', in 'Collection of MSS Essays in the Possession of Sir John Macpherson, Bt', Edinburgh University Library, Dc.1.42.[15]

[82] Ferguson, *Essay*, p. 230.

of its people greatly reduced. The same errors in policy, and weakness of manners, which prevent the proper use of resources, likewise check their increase, or improvement.[83]

Thus, while Ferguson prophesied an inevitable decline, mainly as a result of the separation between the politician and the soldier, his discussion of commerce and the growth of riches contained no hint of limit in the mechanics of commerce itself. For him, 'the separation of arts and professions' laid open the 'sources of wealth',[84] and the mushrooming of new desires kept the 'engine' going. 'Corruption', he argued, did 'not arise from the abuse of commercial arts alone': 'it must be owned, that as the materials of commerce may continue to be accumulated without any determinate limit, so the arts which are applied to improve them may admit of perpetual refinements'.[85] In Ferguson's picture there were no strictly economic bounds to the future of commercial society.

Sir James Steuart's analysis of political economy was published in 1767, in the same year as Ferguson's. His terminology of corruption, luxury and decay resembled that of Ferguson, but his interest lay far more in the stability of commerce than that of manners. From his Jacobite exile, Steuart followed Hume's writing with the closest attention. Like Oswald and Tucker, he also misunderstood Hume's specie-distribution model and tried to argue out in full detail a situation which Hume had modelled only under *ceteris paribus* conditions. His view of what would happen under a general system of free trade was the opposite of Hume's:

Laying...trade quite open would have this effect; it would destroy at first at least, all the luxurious arts; consequently, it would diminish consumption; consequently,

[83] *Ibid.*, p. 233. For an analysis of the historical dynamics in Ferguson's model, see Pocock, *The Machiavellian Moment*, p. 501. Ferguson's personal vantage point in looking at the rise of commercial society in Scotland is discussed in David Kettler, 'History and Theory in Ferguson's *Essay on the History of Civil Society*: A Reconsideration', *Political Theory*, 5 (1977), 437–60.

[84] Ferguson, *Essay*, p. 181. Ferguson strongly emphasized the necessity of division of labour in the 'political oeconomy' sections of his 'Lectures on Pneumatics and Moral Philosophy, 1776–1785', Edinburgh University Library, Dc.1.84–6, lectures 89–95, fols. 458–91; and also in the conjectural history lectures on 'the history of the species', lectures 18–23, fols. 192–237. The same emphasis is also present in the textbooks based on these lectures: *Institutes of Moral Philosophy* (Edinburgh, 1769), Pt. VII, ch. II, 'Of Public Oeconomy', section III, 'Of Riches and Wealth', and in the *Principles of Moral and Political Science: being chiefly a retrospect of lectures delivered in the College of Edinburgh*, 2 vols. (Edinburgh, 1792), ii, ch. VI, section IV, 'Of the Wealth of the People', where he remarked that in rich countries ambition as well as necessity fuels the accumulation of wealth, 'so that nations who are forward in the accumulation of wealth, proceed in it with a double ardour from the effect of advances that they have already made' (p. 423).

[85] Ferguson, *Essay*, p. 255. Ferguson explicitly denied that his argument had been based on the premise of need constraints: 'The use of morality on this subject [i.e. refinement bestowed on the means of subsistence, or the conveniences of life] is not to limit men to any particular species of lodging, diet, or clothes; but to prevent them considering their conveniences as the principal objects of human life' (p. 247).

diminish the quantity of circulating cash; consequently, it would promote hoarding; and consequently, would bring on poverty to all the *states* of Europe.[86]

'Nothing, I imagine', he added, 'but an universal monarchy, governed by the same laws, and administered according to one plan well concerted, can be compatible with an universally open trade.'[87] He could see no reason to suppose that the pattern of history had changed with the appearance of commercial societies. 'We perceive in history', he stated, the fate of rich countries in the past:

the rise, progress, grandeur, and decline of Sydon, Tyre, Carthage, Alexandria and Venice, not to come nearer home. While these states were on the growing hand, they were powerful; when once they came to their height, they immediately found themselves labouring under their own greatness.[88]

Because he set no store by the dynamism of a free-trade system, Steuart advocated trade isolation for a rich country wherever it ran into competitive difficulties. He made his prediction of the rich country's future conditional on her following the right policies. But he had no doubt that if the dexterity of her workers was maintained, it was almost impossible to compete effectively with a rich country which could sell more cheaply than others. 'The trading nations of Europe', he wrote

represent a fleet of ships, every one striving who shall get first to a certain port. The statesman of each is the master. The same wind blows upon all; and this wind is the principle of self-interest, which engages every consumer to seek the cheapest and best market... [The] natural advantages of each country represent the degree of goodness of each vessel; but the master who sails his ship with the greatest dexterity, and he who can lay his rivals under the lee of his sails, will, *ceteris paribus*, undoubtedly get before them, and maintain his advantage.[89]

Since Steuart saw that 'dexterity increasing diminishes the price of work', he remarked that provided machines are introduced with care not to cause unemployment, their advantages were 'so palpable' that there was no 'need to insist upon them'.[90] Machines, he said, could be considered 'as a method

---

[86] Sir James Steuart, *Inquiry into the Principles of Political Oeconomy*, ed. A. S. Skinner, 2 vols. (Edinburgh, 1967), ii, p. 365. For Steuart's analysis and critique of Hume's automatic specie-distribution model, see *ibid.*, pp. 357–65. For Steuart, international free trade was no more than a thought experiment and added that if he discussed the possibility at all, it was 'to apply principles only, and show how the consequences *may* follow one another: to foretel what *must* follow is exceedingly difficult, if not impossible' (p. 365).

[87] Steuart, *Political Oeconomy*, ii, p. 365.

[88] *Ibid.*, pp. 195–6. For a discussion of this passage in comparison with Hume, see A. S. Skinner, 'Sir James Steuart: International Relations', *Economic History Review*, 2nd ser., 15 (1963), 445–7, 449.

[89] Steuart, *Political Oeconomy*, i, p. 203.

[90] *Ibid.*, p. 123. Steuart, like Montesquieu, discussed the use of machines in the context of the depopulation controversy. Montesquieu was against the use of machines for their own sake:

of augmenting (virtually) the number of the industrious, without the expense of feeding an additional number'.[91] Machines, in short, were 'found to reduce prices in a surprising manner'; they could assist in 'accumulating the wealth of a trading nation, by enabling the industrious to feed themselves at the expense of foreigners'.[92] Theoretically, of course, Steuart saw that a wealthy nation could easily ruin herself in luxury, particularly in the dangerous variety which 'consolidated' itself into the high wages of artisans.[93] But the examples which he had in mind were not industrious nations but rather countries like Spain, the type of country Hume called poor but abounding in money.[94]

Looking at the chances of poor countries, he could see only the same trade options as Hume. But looking beyond foreign trade Steuart was more favourably disposed towards the Scottish tradition and he approved well-regulated banking experiments.[95] In trade the advantage of a poor country was in her miserable wages. Starting from her cheap-provision, cheap-wage advantage, the poor country could produce the simpler products, and perhaps in time, 'if a plan of oeconomy, equally good with that of the rivals, be set on foot and pursued', she could gain riches in proportion to her natural advantages of 'climate, soil, situation and extent'.[96] This process required patience and Steuart advocated not only the establishment of banks but also protection for infant industries from the vagaries of open markets.

In the case of Adam Smith, it is remarkable that his position on the central issue was restated virtually unchanged from his jurisprudence lectures and the 'Early Draft' through to the *Wealth of Nations*. Smith was a close friend of both Hume and Oswald and followed Tucker's publications with interest.[97] Although there is no evidence of his participating directly in the debate, the phrasing of his views was more consistent with those of Hume's polemical opponents.[98]

'If a piece of workmanship is of a moderate price, such as is equally agreeable to the maker and the buyer, those machines which would render the manufacture more simple, or, in other words, diminish the number of workmen, would be pernicious' (*Spirit of the Laws*, 23.15). But he supported the use of 'ingenious machines' in mines in place of heavy physical labour (*ibid.*, 15.8).   [91] Steuart, *Political Oeconomy*, i, p. 124.

[92] *Ibid.*, p. 256.   [93] *Ibid.*, p. 256.   [94] *Ibid.*, pp. 259–60.

[95] *Ibid.*, Bk. IV, Pt. II, 'Of Banks'. Steuart was also arguing in the context of the Scottish public debate on banking ensuing on the 1762–3 exchange crisis. His discussion of Law's bank shows the importance of the issue for Scottish thinking in the 1760s and 1770s.

[96] Steuart, *Political Oeconomy*, i, p. 259. It appears that Steuart was not more radical on the issue of poor countries than Hume, nor is it apparent how his political oeconomy can be correlated with his Jacobite politics in the mid-1740s, though a case is made for both these contentions in George Davie's interesting essay, 'Anglophobe and Anglophil', pp. 295–6.

[97] John Rae, *Life of Adam Smith* (London, 1895), pp. 37–8, and Jacob Viner, 'Guide to John Rae's *Life of Adam Smith*', in Rae, *Life of Adam Smith* (Fairfield, N.J., 1965), pp. 53–4. For Tucker, see Smith's holding of copies of Tucker's works in his library.

[98] See S. Hollander, *The Economics of Adam Smith*, p. 291. Smith's covert attacks on Hume were apparent to their contemporaries; see John Playfair's letter to the son of William Robertson, William Jr: 'I cannot but observe that Dr. Smith is superior to the most acute writer that

Smith certainly possessed powerful reasons for rejecting the Machiavellian pendulum of inevitable decline, had he supposed Hume's analysis of the relations between rich and poor countries to imply this. The opening argument of his political economy, advanced consistently in every version of it, implied a time-framework wholly incompatible with the language of corruption and decay and particularly at odds with a view which attributed the seeds of decay to the high wages of the common people. Smith's cherished paradox of commercial society stressed that direct experience had proved such a society able to provide higher living standards for the labouring poor than any previous society in history. For Smith it was wrong to imagine that the conveniences of the modern poor were 'extremely simple and easy'. They were in fact the products of a complex division of labour between a large number of producers. The way the ordinary labourer could get his share from the 'immense multiplication of the production of all the different arts' was by receiving high wages, a 'liberal reward of labour' which for Smith was 'the very thing in which public opulence' consisted.[99]

The whole elaborate edifice of Smith's 'paradox of commercial society'[100] would have been destroyed if the historically unprecedented opulence of the English and Dutch labourer had endured no more than the 200 years since the reign of Elizabeth, a 'period', Smith remarked, 'as long as the course of human prosperity endures'.[101] The second main claim of the opening argument of his system of political economy was thus that the same extensive division of labour which created this wealth would also protect countries against the vagaries of international markets. It was 'vulgar prejudice and superficial reflection' to imagine as 'altogether incompatible' that 'in an opulent and commercial society labour becomes dear and work cheap'. However counter-intuitive this appeared to the vulgar, these apparently irreconcilable facts were 'found in experience to be perfectly consistent'.[102] The co-existence of 'these two things', Smith pointed out, was 'evidently very consistent, as the improvement of arts render things so much easier done that a great wage can be afforded to the artisan and the goods still be at a low price'. By subdividing labour, raising the dexterity of workers and introducing machines the wage

have touched on this subject before him, and that he corrects David Hume on innumerable occasions, which his own delicacy, and respect for his Friend have not suffered him to mention': 12 December 1977, 'Robertson Macdonald Papers', National Library of Scotland, MS. 3943, fols. 52–3.

[99] Smith, *LJ(A)* vi.81.
[100] On the 'paradox of commercial society', see *WN*, 'Introduction and Plan of the Work', and the introductory essay in this volume written by Michael Ignatieff and myself (pp. 1–44 above).
[101] *WN* III.iv.20. Smith's *obiter dictum* was a roughly correct generalization of medieval and early modern European experience. To attribute to Smith a 'profound pessimism', as R. L. Heilbroner did in his 'The Paradox of Progress: Decline and Decay in the *Wealth of Nations*', in Skinner and Wilson, *Essays on Adam Smith*, is misleading. For a critique of Heilbroner, see Donald Winch, 'Not by Economics Alone', *Times Literary Supplement*, 12 March 1976, p. 280.
[102] *ED*, 11–12.

cost embodied in the price of individual products became much lower than in any previous time. Now the 'master of the works' in a new model industry could 'afford both to increase the workmans wages and to sell the commodities cheaper'.[103]

Thus a rich country was potentially well protected from her low-wage competitors. 'As a rich merchant can always afford to under-sell a poor one so can a rich nation one of less wealth.'[104] The paradoxical greatness of commercial society was that it did not have to pay for the well-being of its poor with the loss of its markets. Wealth was rather self-reinforcing than self-destructive:

The more opulent therefore the society, labour will always be so much dearer and work so much cheaper, and if some opulent countries have lost several of their manufactures and some branches of their commerce by having been undersold in foreign markets by the traders and artisans of poorer countries, who were contented with less profit and smaller wages, this will rarely be found to have been merely the effect of the opulence of one country and the poverty of the other. Some other cause, we may be assured, most have concurred. The rich country must have been guilty of some error in its police.[105]

What led him, perhaps, to give such prominence in the design of the *Wealth of Nations* to the chapter on the division of labour was precisely its need to carry this double weight; to answer both the question of the justice and 'virtue' of commercial society and that of its future prospects in international trade with poor but increasingly successful rivals.

But Smith's analysis was not exhausted by this apparently simple statement. The possible 'errors of police' in the rich country, after all, were many. It was not for nothing that he chose to write the *Wealth of Nations* as a 'very violent attack' on the 'whole commercial system of Great Britain'.[106] The connection of the issue with the 'mercantile system' itself became obvious on its first reappearance in the *Wealth of Nations* after the division of labour chapter, not as a question of wages, but as one of profits. For Smith, profit did not mean the income or 'wages' of the artisan, as it had for James Steuart. Instead it

---

[103] *LJ(A)* vi.33; *LJ(B)* 214; *ED* 10-11; *WN* I.i.10. In the 'Early Draft' Smith candidly added the following cautionary remark to the argument: 'I do not mean that the profits are divided in fact...in the above manner, but that they may be divided in such manner.'

[104] *LJ(A)* vi.34; *LJ(B)* 215; *ED* 13.

[105] *ED* 12-13; *LJ(A)* vi.34; *LJ(B)* 215. Andrew Skinner reconstructed Smith's argument on the division on labour in *LJ(A)* in thirteen consecutive steps omitting the 'rich country–poor country' argument. A full reconstruction of Smith's text should contain it between steps seven and eight of the Skinnerian sequence. See A. S. Skinner, *A System of Social Science: Papers Relating to Adam Smith* (Oxford, 1979), pp. 135–7. The passage is omitted from the *Wealth of Nations*, but its equivalent, including also the contrast between the agricultural prices of rich and poor countries, was preserved; see *WN* I.i.4, and compare with 'Early Draft', 9–10.

[106] Letter of Smith to Andreas Holt, 26 October 1780, *Correspondence*, p. 251.

meant the merchants' and master-manufacturers' share in the price of the product.[107]

The greatest problem which faced the rich country was the baneful influence of merchants on her policies. Their interest was 'never exactly the same with that of the publick'.[108] They always contrived ways to push up their profits. The merchants of the rich country 'raising the price of her produce above what otherwise would be' enabled 'the merchants of other countries to undersell her in foreign markets, and thereby to jostle her out of almost all those branches of trade, of which she has not the monopoly'. This behaviour endangered the rich commercial country. As Smith explained, 'in countries which are fast advancing to riches' it was 'the low rate of profit' which could 'compensate the high wages of labour, and enable those countries to sell as cheap as their less thriving neighbours among whom the wages of labour may be lower'.[109] No country could hope to preserve her wealth if her policies were influenced by profit-hungry merchants. 'Our merchants frequently complain of the high wages of British labour as the cause of their manufactures being undersold in foreign markets', Smith mordantly observed, but 'they say nothing of their own extravagant gains'.[110]

The merchants of course thought that they had a recipe for keeping their high profits and still preserving their foreign trade. One way to achieve that was to suppress competition. The more cunning had advocated a system of dependent foreign markets. The creation of dependent poor countries as outlets for the trade of the rich invited Smith's most damning comments:

The sneaking arts of underling tradesmen are thus erected into political maxims for the conduct of a great empire: for it is the most underling tradesmen only who make it a rule to employ chiefly their own customers...By such maxims as these...nations have been taught that their interest consisted in beggaring all their neighbours. Each nation has been made to look with an invidious eye upon the prosperity of all the nations with which it trades, and to consider their gain as its own loss.[111]

Smith, like Hume in the 'Jealousy of Trade', realized that the selective trading policies of the rich would prevent the poor countries from benefiting from their

---

[107] On Adam Smith's notion of profit, see R. L. Meek, 'Adam Smith and the Classical Concept of Profit', in *Economics and Ideology and Other Essays: Studies in the Development of Economic Thought* (London, 1967), pp. 18–33. According to Dugald Stewart, the famous Smithian adding-up formula of value was suggested by James Oswald. See Stewart, *Lectures on Political Economy*, in *Collected Works*, ed. Sir William Hamilton, 10 vols. (Edinburgh, 1854-60), ix, p. 6.

[108] *WN* IV.iii.c.10; I.xi.p.10.

[109] *WN* I.ix.23. Smith also observed that 'the rate of profit does not, like the rent and wages, rise with prosperity, and fall with the declension of society. On the contrary, it is naturally low in rich, and high in poor countries...' (*WN* I.xi.p.10).

[110] *WN* IV.vii.c.29; I.ix.24. On Smith's general opposition to high profits, see Nathan Rosenberg, 'Adam Smith on Profits - Paradox Lost and Regained', in Skinner and Wilson, *Essays on Adam Smith*, pp. 377–89.

[111] *WN* IV.iii.c.8–9. The context of Smith's statement was the regulation of English trade with Portugal. See also *WN* IV.viii.52.

various advantages. He maintained that only free trade between nations could eventually lead to the wealth of all. The mutuality of markets would guarantee this 'A rich nation surrounded on all sides by wandering savages and poor barbarians', he added in characteristic vein, 'might, no doubt, acquire riches by the cultivation of its own lands, and by its interior commerce, but not by foreign trade.'[112]

Smith's new description of rich and poor countries interlocked in a system of free trade reflected the realities of a changing world. He could see the possibilities of development, both for rich and poor countries, offered by a system of natural liberty in foreign trade. He did not simply impose a grid of advance, stagnation and decline on the trajectory of nations, as James Steuart did, but also took account of the rate at which individual nations were moving along their historical trajectory. England was richer than France, France was richer than Scotland and the Lowlands of Scotland were richer than the American colonies. But in growth rates the picture was very different. North America was growing the fastest, England was second, and Scotland came ahead of France. The combination of wealth *and* a high growth rate was the key to England's dominant position.[113]

However, Smith was aware that a fast-growing rich country would easily keep her advantages over a poor country whose growth was not significantly faster. Comparing England and Scotland he pointed out that for Scotland 'the steps by which it advances to a better condition... seem to be much slower and more tardy'.[114] It was easy for the rich country to grow faster using her advantages. 'Money' – Smith cited the proverb – 'makes money. When you have got a little, it is often easy to get more. The great difficulty is to get the little.'[115] Then, even if the poor country had acquired some capital, it had usually to perform too many tasks. 'The man who employs either his labour or his stock in a greater variety of ways than his situation renders necessary', Smith observed at another place, 'can never hurt his neighbour by under-selling him. He may hurt himself, and he generally does so. Jack of all trades will never be rich.'[116]

Smith, unlike his friend Hume, advocated the use of paper money to overcome the initial lack of capital stock.[117] But when discussing the trade

---

[112] *WN* IV.iii.c.11. Smith was cautious in his advocacy of free trade and suggested that it 'should never be introduced suddenly, but slowly, gradually, and after a very long warning'. As to a complete freedom of trade he warned that to hope for its introduction was 'as absurd as to expect that an Oceana or Utopia should ever be established' (*WN* IV.ii.43–4).

[113] *WN* I.ix.9–11; I.viii.23; I.xi.e.34; II.v.21; III.iv.19; IV.iii.c.12.

[114] *WN* I.ix.8; I.xi.e.34. Smith's statement on Scotland was clearly phrased in the language of the 'rich country–poor country' issue, England being a rich, Scotland a poor *country*.

[115] *WN* I.ix.11.

[116] *WN* IV.v.b.16.

[117] *WN* II.ii.86–7. See S. G. Checkland, 'Adam Smith and the Bankers', in Skinner and Wilson, *Essays on Adam Smith*, pp. 504–23.

advantages of rich nations, he followed Hume's analysis of long-term price trends in the *History of England*. Moreover, he also regarded the relative prices of rude products and manufactures as the indicator of whether a country was rich or poor.[118] As a result of the modern division of labour and the use of machinery, the real price of manufactures was constantly falling. The same was not true for natural resources and rude products. While the changing terms of trade thus worked against the manufacturers, other factors worked against the poor countries. Smith emphasized the impact of transport costs upon selling prices on foreign markets. The 'diminution of price' due to the division of labour, he argued, was most notable 'in those manufactures, of which the materials are coarser metals', such as watches, cutlery, toys, etc., like those manufactured in Sheffield and Birmingham. These products were very easy to transport, certainly much easier than corn and cattle. This gave further advantages to the rich manufacturing nations to conquer international markets.[119]

Yet Smith did not pin his hopes for the rich country remaining rich simply on the industry of the towns. Precisely because the transport of manufactured products was cheap, 'in manufactures a very small advantage will enable foreigners to undersell our own workman, even in the home market'. On the other hand, because of the bulkiness and high transport costs 'it requires a very great one to enable them to do so in the rude produce'.[120]

Smith's fundamental historical argument on development in Book III of the *Wealth of Nations* has clear implications for the 'rich country–poor country' problem. Although he considered that the history of Western Europe had departed from the 'natural course of things' in reversing the primacy of agriculture in the successive stages of development, he insisted that their development of a highly sophisticated agriculture in response to the economic incentives of the towns had been to the great advantage of rich countries.[121] He also expressed some concern about the balance and harmony which he thought necessary between manufacturing and agriculture. In agriculture, division of labour had its obvious limits. Therefore, for agricultural products the effects of price competition were somewhat more complicated than they were for manufactures. Smith's example in the context of the 'rich country–poor country' issue was that it was not necessarily the case for a given quality of corn that the rich country's prices were cheaper. For low-quality corn, the prices of poor Poland were as cheap as those of France and in the higher quality range, the French, despite being poorer in general, could match the English price. Nonetheless, it remained true that the richer nation produced better-quality corn than the poorer:

most opulent nations, indeed, generally excell all their neighbours in agriculture as well

[118] *WN* I.xi.n.3.
[119] *WN* I.xi.o.4; I.xi.c.37-8.
[120] *WN* IV.ii.16.
[121] *WN* III.iii.20.

as manufactures... their lands are in general better cultivated, and having more labour and expence bestowed upon them produce more, in proportion to the extent and natural fertility of the ground.[122]

Given the burden of transport costs on agricultural exports, Smith did not think that poor countries presented a real competitive challenge. He stressed, however, that the condition for preserving the advantages of the rich was that capital should be invested in agriculture as well as in manufacturing industry.

A developed agriculture had a further important feature which made it more resilient than manufacturing in the face of foreign competition. The division of labour, despite its favourable effect on prices, had undesirable side-effects. It disaggregated the steps of the artisan's work into a few 'very simple operations' and thus reduced the skill of the labourer, making him 'as stupid and ignorant as it is possible for a human creature to become'.[123] In competitive terms this meant that it was easier to compete against such a labour force. The simplification of most of the 'mechanical trades' entailed that 'all the operations' could be 'compleatly and distinctly explained in a pamphlet of very few pages' or through pictures as it was done in the various French encyclopedias.[124] It was only one step from here to argue that imitation became quite easy. In contrast, Smith observed, 'the art of the farmer requires much more skill and experience than the greater part of the mechanick trades'. As a result, the country poor were 'really superior to those of the town'. Their practical knowledge was not easily transferable. 'From all those volumes' which were written in many languages on agriculture it was still a 'vain attempt to collect knowledge of its various and complicated operations, which is commonly possessed even by a common farmer'.[125]

The importance of attracting capital into agriculture was shown by Smith to be vital to the long-term future of both manufacturing rich countries and poor countries aspiring to have new industries. Acquiring manufacturing through short cuts, such as special subsidies, might bring fruits to the poor country, in the sense that after a certain time she would be able to produce those products as cheaply as the rich.[126] But it would not necessarily help the

---

[122] *WN* I.i.4; *ED* 25. For a commentary on the language of Smith in these passages, see Vincent Bladen, *From Adam Smith to Maynard Keynes: The Heritage of Political Economy* (Toronto, 1974), pp. 15–16.

[123] *WN* V.ix.45.   [124] *WN* I.x.c.23.

[125] *WN* I.x.c.23–4. For a contrast, see Smith's harsh words on the slothfulness and laziness of the country workman, who constantly has to break his work rhythm by moving from agricultural labour to domestic industry and is thus 'obliged to change his work and tools every half hour' (*WN* I.i.7). There is a sharp critique of this Smithian exaggeration in J. S. Mill, *Principles of Political Economy*, ed. J. M. Robson, 2 vols. (Toronto, 1965), ii, pp. 126–8.

[126] *WN* IV.ii.13–14. For an analysis of the relationship between Smith's foreign-trade theory and his understanding of the development strategies open to poor countries, see Hla Myint, 'The "Classical Theory" of International Trade and the Underdeveloped Countries', in his *Economic Theory and the Underdeveloped Countries* (London, 1971), pp. 118–46, and particularly his emphasis on Smith's notion of free trade 'as a method of bringing out more fully the

country as a 'sum total' to develop faster. 'The capital...that is acquired to any country by commerce', he argued, 'is all a very precarious and uncertain possession, till some part of it has been secured and realised in the cultivation and improvement in land.' The Hansa towns which failed to do this disappeared without trace. Italy lost most of her early manufactures but remained one of the most populous and best-cultivated parts of Europe owing to her attention to agriculture. 'The solid improvements of agriculture' could last.[127]

By emphasizing the crucial importance of agriculture as well as the effects of the division of labour in manufacturing, Smith created a model which could answer the questions raised by the Physiocratic doctrine of the relations between rich and poor countries. Smith, in the *Wealth of Nations*, gave an excellent summary of the Physiocratic view and of the contrast which the Physiocrats drew between the futures of rich 'manufacturing' countries and those of 'poor' landed ones. They presupposed free international trade on the one hand and a 'natural course' of development in the landed nations on the other, commencing with a concentration of investment in agriculture. Through free trade the landed country would be exposed to foreign stimuli and once she had generated a sufficient surplus in agriculture she would be able to start up her own manufacturing operations in imitation of the mercantile countries. Her manufacturers could by then acquire a cheap and abundant supply of subsistence and raw materials at home which a mercantile country was obliged to import in exchange for her manufactures. A stronger home base would operate so much to the advantage of the advancing agricultural country that, in Smith's summary of the Physiocratic model, her artists and merchants even

with inferior art and skill...would be able to sell...as cheap in foreign markets as the merchants of...mercantile nations; and with equal arts and skill they would be able to sell it cheaper. They would soon, therefore, rival those mercantile nations in this branch of foreign trade, and in due time jostle them out altogether.[128]

Obviously, only if nations heeded Smith's policy advice that 'the increase of stock and the improvement of land are two events which must go hand in hand',[129] could they live without fear that a newly industrialized agricultural country would 'jostle them out' of their markets.

The publication of the *Wealth of Nations* radically changed the public framework of this Scottish debate. What had been until then a matter for discussion among the cognoscenti of the group around Hume, Smith and Kames now became available for every reader of Smith's book. If they wanted

longer-run productive potentialities of countries provided by an increasing division of labour, capital accumulation and changing supplies of factors of production' in 'Adam Smith's Theory of International Trade in the Perspective of International Development', *Economica*, N.S., 44 (1977), 231–48.

[127] *WN* III.iv.23–4; III.i.3; III.i.7. [128] *WN* IV.ix.20–4.
[129] *WN* I.xi.1.3. For an account of Smith's analysis of investment priorities, see S. Hollander, *The Economics of Adam Smith*, pp. 277–304.

to know what Smith thought about the 'rich country–poor country' question, it was there for everybody to read. But the *Wealth of Nations* was far too complex and elliptical to fit easily into the rather sketchy terms of the debate as this had been conducted in the clubs and debating societies of Edinburgh, Glasgow and Aberdeen.[130] Nor would one expect that well-established currents and undercurrents of thinking about society would be readily displaced simply by the publication of even 900 pages on what had until then been no more than a singular and controversial position.[131]

To trace the trajectory of the Scottish debate after the publication of Smith's *Wealth of Nations*, we must now turn to the contribution of three individuals whose opinion on political economy and on the issue of rich and poor country relations were closely connected. John Millar, Lord Lauderdale and Dugald Stewart influenced each other on the issue and there is evidence of personal discussions about it, first between Millar and Lauderdale, two Foxite Whigs and radicals, and later between Lauderdale and Stewart, who became close friends.[132]

The lectures of John Millar, who taught law at Glasgow and studied under Smith, amply demonstrate the influence of the *Wealth of Nations*. Millar took up his professorship in the early 1760s before Smith himself had given up teaching at Glasgow. He devised a lecture course on 'public law' or 'government' which he ran concurrently with his jurisprudence lectures and with his exegetical classes on the *Institutions* and *Pandects* of Justinian.[133] The government lectures contained Millar's theory of commercial society. The original eleventh

---

[130] See Hugh Blair's advice to Smith after the publication of the first edition of the *Wealth of Nations* to add a short summary of the main arguments to the full text in order to 'gather together the Scatter'd Ideas which many of your Readers will form' (Blair to Smith, 3 April 1776, Smith, *Correspondence*, p. 189).

[131] See Kirk Willis, 'The Role in Parliament of the Economic Ideas of Adam Smith, 1776–1800', *History of Political Economy*, 11 (1979), 505–44.

[132] Lauderdale was a favourite pupil of Millar. According to John Craig, 'it is to their frequent and unreserved communication of sentiment, that a similarity, observable between their opinion of the nature of the profit of stock, may be ascribed. Which of them first suggested this ingenious idea, it would have been difficult, even for themselves, to determine; it is likely to have occured in some of their conversations on political oeconomy': 'Account of the Life and Writings of John Millar, Esq.', in John Millar, *The Origin of the Distinction of Ranks*, 4th edn (Edinburgh, 1806), pp. xc–xci. On the essence of the so-called 'productivity theory of profit', see E. V. Böhm-Bawerk, *Capital and Interest: A Critical History of Economic Theory*, trans. W. Smart (London, 1890), pp. 142–8. Millar's brief mention of the idea occurs in the posthumous essays added to his *An Historical View of the English Government*, 4 vols. (London, 1812), iv, p. 120 and note. Lauderdale's version is in chapter III, 'Of the Sources of Wealth', of his *An Inquiry into the Nature and Origin of Public Wealth and into the Means and Cause of its Increase* (Edinburgh, 1804). This history of Dugald Stewart's and Lauderdale's friendship after Millar's death is described in John Veitch, 'A Memoir of Dugald Stewart with Selections from his Correspondence', in *Collected Works of Dugald Stewart*, ed. Sir William Hamilton, 10 vols. (Edinburgh, 1854–60), x, pp. lxxix–lxxx.

[133] See William H. Lehmann, 'Some Observations on the Law Lectures of Professor Millar's at the University of Glasgow (1760–1801)', *Juridical Review*, N.S., 15 (1970), 56–77.

lecture of his course, entitled 'The Decline of Nations', contained his analysis of the 'rich country–poor country' debate, where he analysed what would happen to a commercial country in competition with other nations.[134] As Millar's nephew, John Craig, reported in his biographical sketch of his uncle: 'After having followed the progress of civilization, Mr. Millar in his government lectures examined at some length whether this advancement could be continued without end, or whether, from the nature of human affairs it was not subjected to certain limitations.'[135]

Millar's treatment of the 'rich country–poor country' issue in terms of the Machiavellian preoccupation with temporal finitude and the consequences of luxury was far from being Smithian, despite the exemplary analysis of the effect of the arts and sciences which he had given in the preceding lectures and his firm endorsement of the four-stages theory. Instead, Millar appears to have been following his first teacher in jurisprudence and moral philosophy in Glasgow, Francis Hutcheson. Hutcheson, who concluded his own lectures with an examination of the dissolution of states, used to offer his students a treatment of the relations between rich and poor countries which followed the conventional lines of civic humanist analysis. After roundly denouncing luxury as 'venal' he conceded that it still might have been necessary to 'encourage arts and manufactures' and accordingly that 'men of higher fortunes may without any luxury purchase the most ingenious and nice manufactures' without corruption. But it was difficult to confine these customs to the rich. 'As lower orders are always imitating the manners of the superiors', Hutcheson observed

> the plague of luxury will soon infest the very lowest, and even the mechanicks. Then they cannot subsist without higher prices for their labours; the manufacturers must consequently rise in their prices, and cannot be vended abroad, if any more industrious and sober country can afford the like in foreign markets at lower prices.[136]

Millar blandly repeated this analysis a quarter of a century later. In an earlier section of his lectures he noted that the division of labour made commodities cheaper and that the price paid in the deformation of the personality of the worker was a high one.[137] But he connected the decline of commerce not with the stultifying effects of the division of labour on the worker, but with the

---

[134] Later the eleventh lecture became the thirteenth in the expanded syllabus. See [Millar], *A Course of Lectures on Government; given annually in the University* (Glasgow, 1787), p. 4.

[135] Craig, 'Life of Millar', pp. xlvii–xlviii. This account corroborates the evidence of the student notes of Millar's lectures.

[136] Francis Hutcheson, *A Short Introduction to Moral Philosophy in Three Books containing the Elements of Ethicks and the Law of Nature* (Glasgow, 1747), pp. 321–2.

[137] This was covered in Millar's lecture on the 'change produced in the state of society, by the improvement of manufactures, commerce, and the liberal arts'. Compare this with the fourth essay in vol. iv of the *Historical View*, 'How far the Advancement of Commerce and Manufactures has contributed to the Extension and Diffusion of Knowledge and Literature', pp. 144–6, and with the review of the Scottish character in vol. iii, pp. 92–4.

contracting by the workers and the lower ranks of the habits of luxury from the retinue and servants of the prodigal landlord and from the manners of 'the Great Towns whither all the Idle or rich will flock to'. Rotation of fortunes and property, he argued, could not avert this outcome, since the tradesmen 'once rich now poor retain nevertheless their habits of Idleness'.[138]

Literature would suffer first – Millar repeated the time-honoured commonplace – but eventually the blight would reach even the mechanical arts. Idleness and luxury would result in the loss of dexterity. The final outcome would be as disastrous as it was edifying: the artisans were 'obliged to heighten the price' of their products. This process, Millar explained, could

soon come to so great a length that they cannot find a market to vend them at. Their poorer neighbours being easily enabled to undersell them. And when they are not able to vend them, they will be dropt of course. The history of Mankind shews that this is the tendency of luxury.[139]

Millar's analysis of luxury cited the fate of Greece and Rome, as well as that of Italy as a proof. He believed Holland still to be virtuous. But the decline of literature in France and England was the harbinger of their gloomy future. Scotland's literature, Millar told his students, was just at its height.

---

[138] John Millar, 'Lectures on Government, delivered by Mr. J. Millar, an: 1771–72', extended by George Skene, 2 vols., Mitchell Library, Glasgow, MS. 99, fol. 57. Compare this rotation theory with the version in 'The Advancement of Manufactures, Commerce, and the Arts, since the Reign of William III, and the Tendency of this Advancement to diffuse a Spirit of Liberty and Independence', *Historical View*, iv, pp. 129–32.

[139] The account of Millar's government lectures given here is based on the analysis of ten surviving student lecture-note sets deposited in various Scottish libraries. In chronological order they are the following: 'Lectures on the Public Law of Great Britain', Glasgow University Library, MS. Gen. 203 (probably the earliest set, although not dated); 'Lectures on Government, delivered by Mr. J. Millar, an: 1771–72', extended by George Skene, 2 vols., Mitchell Library, Glasgow, MS. 99; 'Notes from Professor Millar's Lectures on Publick Law or Government', 1780-1, National Library of Scotland, MS. 3931; 'A Course of Lectures on Government', 1782, Aberdeen University Library, MS. 133; 'Lectures on Government, delivered in the University of Glasgow, written from notes taken by Alexander Campbell, 1783', actually 1785, G.U.L., MS. Gen. 179; 'Lectures on Government, taken by James Moncreiff', Moncreiff of Tulliebole Collection, catalogued by N.R.A. (Scotland), Survey 0333, Box 12; 'Lectures on Government given in the University of Glasgow, 1787–88', 3 vols., G.U.L., MS. Gen. 289–91; 'Lectures on Government in the University of Glasgow, taken down by William Rae, 1789', 3 vols., G.U.L., MS. Gen. 18 (1–3); 'Lectures on Government, 1789–90, taken by David Royle', 3 vols, G.U.L., MS. Murray 88–90; [Lectures on the Science of Government]', 1797–98 (title given by the library catalogue), G.U.L., MS. Hamilton 116. Compare this list with Hans Medick, *Naturzustand und Naturgeschichte der bürgerlichen Gesellschaft: Die Ursprünge der bürgerlichen Sozialtheorie als Geschichtsphilosophie und Sozialwissenschaft bei Samuel Pufendorf, John Locke und Adam Smith* (Göttingen, 1973), p. 136n, whose 'begriffgeschichtliche' scheme of the putative change in the title of Millar's lecture series suggests a misleading image of 'progress' in Millar's intellectual achievement. The passage quoted in the text above is from 'Lectures on Government, 1787–88', vol. 1., G.U.L., MS. Gen. 289, fol. 153. This set, the so-called Hamilton copy, is in the handwriting of Millar's son James and considered to be the most authentic one.

After the publication of the *Wealth of Nations*, Millar's lectures changed. He left the chapter on 'decline' in place, as the conclusion of the course, but he extended its scope, dividing the issue into two distinct topics. He retained his emphasis on the need 'to apprehend that the *luxury* arising from great wealth, may, when it comes to certain pitch, destroy the *industry* and *frugality*, of a people, and thereby put a stop to their progress in the arts', but added to this a novel line of thought:

it has been supposed that commerce and manufactures, by introducing wealth tend to raise the price of provisions and consequently, the wages of labour, so that commodities are rendered dearer in every country in proportion to its improvement in arts. Hence a poor nation will be enabled to undersell one that is rich; and whenever a country had advanced in improvement far beyond its neighbours, it will be deprived of a market, and its trade will begin to decay.[140]

Here the tired litany of luxury and effeminacy, of barbarous and polished nations confronts the new debate in political economy. As Millar explained to his students, the view in question had been maintained by Mr Hume, who demonstrated that 'poorer nations where Labour cheaper will be able to undersell the Richer' and who notoriously inferred from this that no nation should be jealous of another. But Hume, Millar claimed, has been answered by 'Tucker and Smith'.[141] There was no reason to believe this argument for necessary decline well-founded. The two philosophers had proved that a clumsy labourer could be no match for the degree of division of labour in rich countries, where labour could be dearer while the manufacture itself remained cheaper. Millar believed the advantage of rich countries to have shown itself not merely in manufacturing industry, but also in the case of common labourers, country artificers and agricultural hands.[142] The latter improvement would lead to higher yields on farms and thus to a higher income, while the merchants of the rich country would be able to pay higher wages to the labourer because they could trade on lower profits. 'For this reason', he concluded, 'it should seem a nation which has grown rich by trade is while it retains its industry

---

[140] Millar, 'Lectures on Government, 1787-88', G.U.L., MS. Gen. 289, fol. 149. The new passage already appears in 'Lectures on Publick Law, 1780-81', N.L.S., MS. 3931, fol. 87. Millar's grasp of Hume's political economy was uneven. He understood Hume's automatic specie-flow model well; see 'The Advancement of Manufactures, Commerce, and the Arts', p. 109.

[141] Millar, 'Lectures on Publick Law, 1780-81', N.L.S., MS. 3931, fol. 89. This is the most detailed set of notes on Millar's lectures and the only one mentioning names in connection with the various positions discussed. Smith, of course, appears in all sets, but the mention of Tucker was not totally isolated, either. In the previous lecture of the same set Millar referred to another piece by Tucker in the *Four Tracts*, 'The Case of going to War for the Sake of Trade'; see fols. 87-8. This 1780-1 lecture set is interspersed with a primitive shorthand abbreviation system, but the crucial passages are legible.

[142] Millar, 'Lectures on Government, 1787-88', G.U.L., MS. Gen. 289, fol. 150-3. A further refinement on the prospects of division of labour in agriculture is in 'Lectures on Government, 1797-98', G.U.L., MS. Hamilton 116, vol. 2, fols. 26-8.

and continues its improvements, in no danger of being cut out of market by poorer neighbours.'[143] He made no claim to be in a position to demonstrate the economic decline of English industry. Apart from the decline of literature, the luxury of merchants and the spirit of stockjobbing were the only worrying signs.[144] In Millar's case, the antiquated Machiavellian discourse of growth and decay had been brusquely interrupted by the new debate on the future of the commerce of commercial society. He had aligned himself with Smith and Tucker against the position which he believed to be Hume's. But he retained the framework of his lectures intact. Commerce was something which could not go on infinitely or even indefinitely. The experience of his own age was judged by Millar to be as yet too precarious to cancel out the long experience of mankind.

First in his moral philosophy class, and later in separate graduate classes on political economy, Dugald Stewart in Edinburgh resolved the technical issue of rich and poor country relations in the same fashion as Millar, but he based his conclusions upon a somewhat different Scottish tradition. Not only did he cast his answer in different terms; he also reached an ultimate conclusion on the overall future of commercial society which was the opposite of Millar's civic humanist gloom. The lectures which he gave on government, property, the history of rank and subordination as well as on political economy[145] addressed Montesquieu's celebrated question of the utility of machines. Stewart's primary answer to Montesquieu's concern for unemployment was drawn from Sir James Steuart's *Principles of Political Oeconomy*. If population grew up to the limits of the resources available, the most favourable population growth could be induced by the use of machinery, since 'the invention of a machine of this kind has the same effect as employing additional hands in the service of the public without the attendant expense of consuming part of the fruits of Labour'. Stewart, like Millar, noted the negative effects of commerce; machines and manufacturing 'crowd men into large cities whereby their health

---

[143] Millar, 'Lectures on Government, 1787–88', G.U.L., Gen. 289, fol. 153. Compare it with Craig's paraphrasing of his uncle's thought. Millar did not suppose that the 'high wages of labour, arising from the general diffusion of wealth, could so far counter-balance the advantages resulting from superior capital, from improved machinery, and from the division of labour, as to enable a poor nation to outstrip a richer, in the commercial competition' ('Life of Millar', p. xlviii).

[144] Millar, 'Lectures on Government, 1787–88', G.U.L., MS. Gen. 289, fol. 159: 'After all it seems impossible to determine what precise degree of wealth will produce a decay of industry in any particular country.'

[145] See the headings of Part III, 'Of Man considered as the Member of a Political Body', appended to the *Outlines of Moral Philosophy* (Edinburgh, 1792), pp. 297–302. 'Of Political Oeconomy' was the first chapter in the second section 'Of the General Principles of Legislation'. In 1792 Stewart indicated that 'as soon as my other engagements allow me sufficient leisure for such an undertaking, I shall attempt a separate course of lectures on this very extensive and difficult subject' (p. vii). He actually gave a course of graduate evening classes on political economy from the academic year 1799–1800 to that of 1808–9.

is impaired and their morals corrupted'. But in his view the implications of the 'rich country–poor country' analysis resolved the debate decisively in favour of the use of machinery. 'Let us consider a nation as connected by foreign commerce... If we produce these manufactures by men's hands which other nations produce by machines, those nations will be enabled to undersell us.'[146]

In his political economy lectures proper, some twenty years later, he repeated this argument to the generation of the 'Edinburgh reviewers'. To criticize machinery was to miss the key to commercial society. As Benjamin Franklin had said, Stewart recalled, man was a 'tool-making animal, or engineer'. 'How have mankind been enabled to emerge from barbarism to civilisation but by the introduction and progressive improvement of machinery?'[147] Nor was it sufficient merely to speculate and philosophize about the disadvantages or benefits of machinery. For to consider the role of machines in the context of the whole economy was to grasp clearly their 'infinite importance, or rather, indeed, their *absolute necessity* to maintain the national prosperity of a commercial country like Great Britain':[148]

it is only by such contrivances, combined with the division of labour which is intimately connected with them, that nations, among whom the wages of labour are comparatively high, can maintain competition in foreign markets; and to what an extraordinary extent the productive powers of industry may thus be multiplied, the commercial history of our own island affords a proof hitherto unequalled among mankind.[149]

Stewart had read Smith with care and noted the challenge which the *Wealth of Nations* offered to the Physiocratic model of relations between rich and poor countries. He insisted that Britain could preserve its advantages only if it devoted sufficient attention and protection to agriculture. It was indispensable to adopt every means to raise the productivity of agriculture, first and foremost the 'consolidation of farms'. While this might be 'unfavourable to the agricultural population of the country', it must be accepted without reservation if the Physiocratic argument were to be answered. This 'evil', Stewart insisted, 'is not to be compared in magnitude with a dependence on foreign nations for the means of subsistence'.[150]

While Millar had presumed that the multiplication of new wants which first

---

[146] Stewart, 'Lectures on Moral Philosophy', 1786, Aberdeen University Library, MS. 191, fol. 67. 1786 was Stewart's first year as full Professor of Moral Philosophy at Edinburgh.
[147] Stewart, *Lectures on Political Economy*, ed. Sir William Hamilton, in *Collected Works*, vols. viii–ix (Edinburgh, 1856), viii, p. 192.
[148] *Ibid.*, p. 195. Stewart did not refer to either Hume or Tucker in this context. On the intellectual relationship of the two, however, he remarked that 'the same liberal principles of trade, which were advanced by Mr. Hume, were soon after adopted, and very zealously enforced, by Dean Tucker... particularly in a small work entitled *Four Tracts*...' (*Lectures on Political Economy*, ix, p. 33). [149] Stewart, *Lectures on Political Economy*, viii, pp. 195–6.
[150] *Ibid.*, p. 197. For the Physiocratic model, see *ibid.*, pp. 267–8.

create industry and all the beneficial effects of the arts and sciences would end naturally and inevitably in a relaxation of industrial spirit, for Stewart the mighty engine was not to be easily wound down. While he fully acknowledged that the truism that 'A Jack of all trades is master of none' was 'one of those maxims of common sense which the slightest survey of human life forces on the most careless observer', he also remembered the lesson taught by his predecessor in Edinburgh's moral philosophy chair, Adam Ferguson, whose *Essay on the History of Civilisation* had been first published when the young Stewart was attending his classes.[151] For Stewart it was not luxury, but the blighting impact upon the worker of the division of labour which endangered the bright future of commerce. Machinery indicated the way out of this dilemma. Smith had been wrong to lay such emphasis on the extent to which subdivision of labour raised the dexterity and speed of the worker. Stewart agreed with Lauderdale that it was not an ever deeper division of labour but the use of machines that offered the way forward. It was hopeless to expect newer inventions to come from the 'living automatons' produced by Smith's system.[152] Machines could take the place of men, since they not only enabled 'one man to perform the work of many', but 'produced also an economy of time, by separating the work into its different branches, all of which may be carried into execution at the same moment'.[153]

In this way Stewart felt able to present machines and the economy of time as an alternative to the 'system of national instruction' in counteracting the dire effects of the division of labour which Ferguson had described so luridly. The 'evil', argued Stewart, was only transitional and it could lead the way 'to its own correction'. When the simplification has been carried so far

as to convert, according to Dr. Ferguson's metaphor, a workshop into an engine, the parts of which are men, the next step is that which converts it into an engine, literally so called, where the place of men is supplied by mechanical contrivances. The ultimate tendency, therefore, of this process, is to substitute mechanical contrivances to manufacturing work, and to open a field for human genius in the nobler departments of industry and talent.[154]

Stewart's eulogy of machines in a polemical contrast to Smith's emphasis on the gains obtained by the division of labour supplied him also with the ultimate solution to the 'rich country–poor country' problem. The danger of emphasizing the advantages in human skills which the rich countries acquired through the extension of division of labour was, as Stewart realized, that it

[151] *Ibid.*, pp. 310–11.   [152] *Ibid.*, p. 318.
[153] *Ibid.*, p. 319. Stewart's critique of the Smithian theory of division of labour was comprehensive and he even ventured 'to substitute, instead of the phrase "*division of labour*", as employed by Mr. Smith, the more general phrase, "*economy of labour*", a phrase which points out with precision the common qualities from which the division of labour, the invention of machinery, the facilities afforded to commerce, and the application of chemistry, derive all their value' (*ibid.*, p. 332).   [154] *Ibid.*, p. 331.

could raise again the spectre of a world monopoly of commerce and wealth: the very chimera which led Hume to oppose so violently linear projections of the future of rich countries. Indeed, in Stewart's view, the 'division of labour' argument itself had been hailed by some precisely because it made difficult 'the transplantation of manufactures from one country to another, tending thereby to preserve to a nation which has once outstripped its neighbours, the superiority which it has gained'. If, however, mechanical trades could be learnt from pamphlets, the transfer of new technology to poor countries through the export of machinery could 'accelerate'. This might prove inconvenient for the rich country, Stewart noticed, 'with respect to the stability of some branches of foreign trade', but its advantages to mankind would be enormous. He concluded his argument in authentically Humean vein. The rapid proliferation of machines would not merely exert a beneficent influence 'on the fortunes of the human race'; it would also help 'to support manufactures over the whole face of our own country', obliterating the differences between richer and poorer provinces.[155]

By his insistence that commercial society contained a self-correcting mechanism in the very long run and could thus check with due attention to agriculture the disadvantages which stemmed from the rise of the arts and sciences, Stewart had at last broken decisively with the temporal framework and the obsession with growth and decay of the Machiavellian tradition. His dominating emphasis upon machinery in his later lectures was the result of a fruitful dialectic between his own views and those of Lord Lauderdale. It was Lauderdale, a one time Foxite Whig and friend of liberty like Millar, who after reading an anonymous pamphlet entitled *Letters on the utility of employing Machines to shorten labour*,[156] had advanced the argument that machinery offered the key to the future of commercial society. This pamphlet, which Dugald Stewart himself plagiarized heavily in his lectures,[157] was cited approvingly in Lauderdale's 1804 *Inquiry into the Nature and Origin of Public Wealth*. Its author had argued that when

the price of labour comes to be advanced in a manufacturing and commercial country, more than in those of its commercial competitors, then the expensive nation will lose

---
[155] *Ibid.*, p. 331.
[156] Anon., *Letters on the Utility and Policy of Employing Machines to Shorten Labour; Occasioned by the late Disturbances in Lancashire; to which are added Some Hints for the further Extension and Improvement of our Woollen Trade and Manufactures* (London, 1780); Lauderdale, *Public Wealth*, pp. 297-8.
[157] Stewart, *Lectures on Political Economy*, viii, p. 325, and particularly pp. 192-3. Both the anonymous author of the pamphlet and Stewart cited the *bon mot* that the best definition of man is 'a *tool-making animal* or *engineer*', Stewart adding the attribution to Benjamin Franklin, presumably on the authority of James Boswell, who was the source of the anecdote on Franklin's famous formula: see Boswell, *The Journal of a Tour to the Hebrides, with Samuel Johnson, LL.D.*, in Boswell's *Life of Johnson*, ed. Birkbeck Hill, rev. L. F. Powell, v (Oxford, 1950), p. 33n. See Anon., *The Utility of Employing Machines*, pp. 2-3.

its commerce, and go to decay, if it doth not counterbalance the high price of labour, by the seasonable aid of mechanical inventions.[158]

Lauderdale took this hint and directed it against what he understood to be Hume's 'rich country–poor country' argument. Quoting for his readers almost the whole of Hume's famous passage in 'Of Money', he put forward his own 'unlimited human ingenuity' thesis:

> When Mr Hume, in the middle of last century, supposed that the progress of human industry, in any country, was bounded and confined by the check it must receive from the augmentation of wages, and 'that manufactures gradually shift their places, leaving those countries and provinces which they have already enriched, and flying to others, whither they are allured by the cheapness of provisions and labour, till they have enriched these also, and are again banished by the same causes;' he did not sufficiently attend to the unlimited resources that are to be found in the ingenuity of man in inventing means of supplanting labour by capital.[159]

On this basis, however, Lauderdale himself in fact embraced in a new guise the very model which Hume had set out in 'Of the Jealousy of Trade'. If Smith was right in supposing that the potential sources of improvement which conferred 'on the frugal European peasant, comforts and accommodations exceeding those of many an African king, the absolute master of the lives and liberties of thousands of naked savages' were 'common to all mankind', how could it happen, Lauderdale inquired, that not every civilized country was in fact rich?[160] With the help of machinery a country could escape the finitude of her commercial prospects by relying on man's 'infinite' capacity to invent. But some doubts remained as to just who would buy all the products of these marvellous machines. Would there necessarily be an adequate demand for all the products of machinery? If so, it had to be an 'effective demand' which could exist only 'on the part of those who possess wealth beyond what enables them to acquire the things which the habits of mankind induce them to regard as necessaries'.[161]

Since industry followed the dictates of demand only, and since demand was created by the ability to purchase, its extent in any country must in the end depend on the distribution of property. Industry might easily find itself in the position of overproducing if it had to rely on the consumption of a single country with its settled distribution of property and inequality of wealth.[162] The solution to this problem of under-consumption on the home market lay, in Lauderdale's view, in 'promoting the interchange' between different

---

[158] Anon., *The Utility of Employing Machines*, p. 22.
[159] Lauderdale, *Public Wealth*, pp. 298–9.
[160] *Ibid.*, pp. 303–4.   [161] *Ibid.*, p. 310.
[162] *Ibid.*, pp. 316–21. Introductions to Lauderdale's 'underconsumptionist' political economy can be found in Morton Paglin, *Malthus and Lauderdale: The Anti-Ricardian Tradition* (New York, 1961), ch. 4, and Michael Bleaney, *Underconsumption Theories: A History and Critical Analysis* (London, 1976), ch. 2.

nations. It was the mutuality of markets which ensured that trade, 'by exciting a quantity of industry that would otherwise have remained dormant', would benefit both partners.[163] As a consequence the wealth of a rich country no longer depended only on the 'internal distribution of its wealth'. In addition it could be founded also upon 'the growing wealth of rising countries'.[164] Echoing Hume's sentiments, Lauderdale completed his argument by declaring that the obstruction of free trade by 'ignorant jealousy'[165] would harm the rich country as much as it was intended to harm her neighbours. Her fortune now rested in the hands of those who were able to offer effective demand for the products of her industry and machines. Anxiety about the inequality of wealth at home and attention to the 'progressive wealth' of neighbouring nations, Lauderdale concluded, had to be on the mind of every man who was seriously 'concerned for the prosperity and aggrandisement of the British Empire'.[166]

In 1804 Lauderdale still deemed Hume's 'rich country–poor country' argument worthy at least of a refutation. He quoted once again Hume's ambiguous language with its odd fusion of the Machiavellian vocabulary of growth with an analysis of the internal stability of the commerce of a rich and high-wage society. Lauderdale's over-production or under-consumption argument and his attempt to raise the spectre of excess accumulation transformed the status of Hume's argument in the mind of his readers. When the superficial Henry Brougham, deploying the political economy he had learnt in Dugald Stewart's classroom, wrote his famous attack on Lauderdale's book for the *Edinburgh Review*, he now understood Hume as arguing 'against unlimited accumulation'.[167] But his translation of a travesty of Hume's 'rich country–poor country' argument into the language of the post-Smithian political economy of the early nineteenth century probably stretched the formula to its limits. The riches and poverty of nations of course remained in the centre of political economy's debates. But debate on their determinants was conducted in the language of excess accumulation, imperial markets, under-consumption, population growth, the wisdom or otherwise of the export of machinery, and the stationary state. Political economy's discussion of the temporality and prospects of commercial society in the language of civic humanism had come to an end.

---

[163] Lauderdale, *Public Wealth*, p. 353.   [164] *Ibid.*, p. 356.
[165] *Ibid.*, p. 359.   [166] *Ibid.*, p. 358.
[167] Henry Brougham, 'Lord Lauderdale's *Inquiry into the Nature and Origin of Public Wealth*', *Edinburgh Review*, 4 (1804), p. 373. See also S. Hollander, *The Economics of David Ricardo* (London, 1979), p. 72 and note. Brougham's review created a minor scandal and Lauderdale gave a sharp answer in his *Observation by the Earl of Lauderdale, on the Review of His Inquiry into the Nature and Origin of Public Wealth Published in the VIIIth Number of the Edinburgh Review* (Edinburgh, 1804). Brougham's new 'political economy' language found disfavour with many of his contemporaries; see the letter of Dr J. Currie to Thomas Creevey, 2 October 1804, in *The Creevey Papers: A Selection from the Correspondence and Diaries of the late Thomas Creevey, M.P.*, 2 vols. (London, 1904), i, p. 30.

12 John Millar and individualism
MICHAEL IGNATIEFF

I

Since his death in 1801, Millar has lived on in fitful and contradictory reincarnations. Sombart, Pascal and Meek have laid claim to him as the pioneer of the materialist interpretation of history, while Lehmann and Schneider have revived him as the father of mainstream sociology.[1] Millar's politics are no less divergently interpreted. To Duncan Forbes, he is a Smithian 'scientific' Whig, while to Hans Medick he is the social scientist of the radical petty bourgeoisie in the transient heyday of petty commodity production.[2] To John Pocock, on the other hand, he is a latter-day civic republican and Commonwealthman, his categories imbedded in the language of corruption and virtue.[3] There is equal disagreement about his legacy. For A. L. Macfie and for Duncan Forbes, Millar is the 'bridge' between Smith and the Utilitarians, while others such as Donald Winch and John Burrow have wondered aloud whether Scottish conjectural history and science of government, as Millar practised them, find any echo at all in the *Edinburgh Review* or the Utilitarians. Does Millar transmit a tradition, or does he announce its end?[4]

[1] W. Sombart, 'Die Anfange der Soziologie', in Melchior Palyi (ed.), *Errinnerungsgabe für Max Weber*, 2 vols. (Munich, 1923), pp. 5–19; Ronald L. Meek, 'The Scottish Contribution to Marxist Sociology', in *Economics and Ideology and Other Essays: Studies in the Development of Economic Thought* (London, 1967), pp. 34–50; Roy Pascal, 'Property or Society: The Scottish Historical School of the 18th Century', *Modern Quarterly*, 1 (1938), 167–79; William C. Lehmann, *John Millar of Glasgow 1735–1801: His Life and Thought and his Contributions to Sociological Analysis* (Cambridge, 1960); Louis Schneider, 'Tension in the Thought of John Millar', in *Studies in Burke and His Time*, 13 (1972), 2083–98.
[2] Duncan Forbes, 'Scientific Whiggism: Adam Smith and John Millar', *Cambridge Journal*, 7 (1954), 643–70; Hans Medick and Annette Leppert-Fogen, 'Frühe Sozialwissenschaft als Ideologie des Kleinen Bürgertums: John Millar of Glasgow, 1735–1801', in H. U. Wehler (ed.), *Sozialgeschichte Heute: Festschrift für Hans Rosenberg* (Göttingen, 1974), pp. 22–48.
[3] J. G. A. Pocock, *The Machiavellian Moment: Florentine Political Thought and the Atlantic Republican Tradition* (Princeton, N.J., 1975), p. 503.
[4] A. L. Macfie, 'John Millar: A Bridge between Adam Smith and the 19th Century Figures', in his *The Individual in Society: Papers on Adam Smith* (London, 1967), p. 141; Donald Winch, 'Political Economy and the Science of Politics: Dugald Stewart and his Pupils', paper delivered to the Political Economy and Society Seminar at King's College, Cambridge, March 1979; John Burrow, *Evolution and Society: A Study in Victorian Social Theory* (Cambridge, 1966), p. 16.

Any new look at Millar has to begin with these interpretations and their contradictions.

The emphasis placed by Sombart, Pascal and Meek on Millar and Smith's 'materialism' does capture the radicalism of their challenge to a historiography of kings and queens and to an ethical rationalism which looked down upon 'hunger, thirst and the passion for sex' as aspects of human nature unfit to be placed at the centre of historical process.[5] 'Materialism' is the right word for a theory which made the satisfaction of basic human needs, rather than conscious intention, the motor of historical change, and which interpreted laws, manners and rank systems as dependent upon stages of subsistence. Materialism of course need not imply determinism. They were well aware, as Millar put it, that 'among nations advanced very nearly to the same degree of civilization, very opposite laws often prevail'.[6] His 'materialist' model of the progress of authority in *The Origin of Ranks* was balanced with a second model, in the lectures and the *Historical View*, of the particular trajectories of national legal and political systems, accounting for their deviations from 'the natural course of things'.

Treating Millar as a precursor of Marx is at least more specific than calling him a 'father of sociology'. But both have the defects of any 'anticipatory' reading. Millar's 'ranks' do not translate straightforwardly into the language of 'class'. He operated on the now forgotten terrain of civil polity jurisprudence, inherited from Hutcheson and his teacher, Smith. This interpreted civil society as a network of relations between husbands and wives, parents and children, masters and servants, bound together by the obligations of natural justice and by the 'adventitious rights' of positive law.[7] In so far as it dealt with economic relationships, it treated them under the law of contract. The household rather than the market was the implied frame of reference. Even though his own analysis showed that wage relations were passing out of the dependency nexus of the household into the independency of market relations, Millar continued to follow the Hutchesonian treatment of master and servant as a household relation. The *Origin of Ranks* is not a work in 'political economy', implying a market of free exchangers, but a treatise in the '*oeconomicks*' of the household.[8]

This is not to ignore the historical dimension which Millar, following Smith,

---

[5] The quotation is from *LJ(B)* 300; see also *LJ(A)* vi.20–1; Hume, *Treatise*, p. 491; A. O. Hirschman, *The Passions and the Interests: Political Arguments for Capitalism before its Triumph* (Princeton, N.J., 1977).

[6] John Craig, 'Account of the Life and Writings of John Millar, Esq.', in Millar, *The Origin of the Distinction of Ranks*, 4th edn (Edinburgh, 1806), p. xxxvii. Millar, *The Origin of the Distinction of Ranks*, in Lehmann, *John Millar of Glasgow*, pp. 176–7.

[7] F. Hutcheson, *A System of Moral Philosophy*, 2 vols. (Glasgow, 1755); see esp. vol. 2, Bk 3, 'Of Civil Polity'. *LJ(A)* iii.1–147.

[8] F. Hutcheson, *A Short Introduction to Moral Philosophy* (Glasgow, 1747), p. xi. On the usage of 'oeconomy', see Keith Tribe, *Land, Labour and Economic Discourse* (London, 1978), ch. 5, 'The Structure of Political Oeconomy'.

gave to the categories of natural jurisprudence. Millar was modest about his own contribution, claiming Montesquieu as his Bacon and Smith as his Newton in pointing the way to a historical method capable of solving the key quandaries of jurisprudence.[9] These concerned the so-called 'adventitious rights', created by human institution. While there were clear grounds in natural equity for our (rather few) rights as human beings, there was no such 'natural' rationale for our right to property, and for those rights conferred by primogeniture and entail, which reproduced inequality of condition.[10] Smith was able to explain these laws of succession as contingent exigencies of 'the feudal government', by means of a stadial history of property derived from hints and anticipations in Mandeville, Temple and Locke.[11] In the 1766 report of his lectures, stadial theory was deployed instead to explain the origins of government and to provide a historical account of the emergence of the rights of citizenship to set against a consent theory in Locke which seemed implausible as an account of the origins of government.[12]

Besides property and citizenship, the laws and customs concerning marriage and paternal authority over the household were the third set of 'adventitious rights' which showed wide divergence from the principles of natural equity in different times and places. In his treatment of these, Hutcheson denied that male heads of households had a natural right of dominion over their charges, and argued that servants, children and women had a natural right to humane usage.[13] These rights were 'natural', according to Hutcheson, because families were held together by 'natural connection', by bonds of innate feeling. Smith was scathing about this natural psychology. The 'force of blood', the 'natural connection', he tartly observed, 'exists nowhere but in tragedies and romances'. The feelings of family connection were the work of historical socialization rather than innate propensity. Thus, for example, the intensity of kinship bonding in the clan systems of the Highlands had to be explained in terms of the weakness of central legal authority and the political necessity of joint mutual defence by clan members. In commercial countries, 'where the authority of law is always perfectly sufficient to protect the meanest man in the state',

[9] John Millar, *An Historical View of the English Government*, 4 vols. (London, 1812), ii, 429–30n.
[10] *LJ(A)* i.25; Donald Winch, *Adam Smith's Politics: An Essay in Historiographic Revision* (Cambridge, 1977), p. 51.
[11] F. B. Kaye, Introduction to his edition of B. Mandeville, *The Fable of the Bees*, 2 vols. (Oxford, 1924), i, pp. lxv–lxvi; W. Temple, 'An Essay upon the Origin and Nature of Government' (1672), in *Works*, ed. J. Swift, 4 vols. (London, 1770), i, pp. 29–57; John Locke, *Two Treatises of Government*, 2, para. 105; on the origins of conjectural history within the natural jurisprudence tradition, see James Moore, 'Locke and the Scottish Jurists', unpublished paper presented to the 'John Locke and the Political Thought of the 1680s' Symposium of the Conference for the Study of Political Thought, and the Folger Institute for Renaissance and Eighteenth-Century Studies, Washington, D.C., 21–23 March 1980.
[12] *LJ(B)* 12–13; on Smith's and Hume's engagement with Locke, see John Dunn's paper in this volume, pp. 119–35 above.
[13] Hutcheson, *System*, ii, pp. 149, 164–5.

intergenerational allegiance and respect for family authority were correspondingly weaker. This demolition of the 'innateness' of family feeling opened the way for Millar's historical treatment of family rights and customs.[14] It seemed obvious to Millar that these family rights of Hutcheson's were nowhere observed, and indeed to speak of them as 'rights' at all was to confuse the boundaries between law and morality, between our absolute obligation to justice, and our merely voluntary obligation to be 'benevolent'. Natural jurisprudence was powerless to explain the changing relation between justice and ethics. Indeed it confounded the two, and in so doing, it was unable to explain why laws antithetical to principles of natural justice had been accepted as rational and humane in times past.[15]

The ambiguous, sometimes antithetical relation between positive law and moral manners was at the centre of another decisive influence on Millar's thought, the civic humanist vocabulary whose revival in the 1698–1714 period John Pocock has taught us to associate with the Fletcherian opposition to the Union in Scotland, and with the Whig Commonwealthman and Country Party opposition.[16] In this tradition, it was axiomatic that good laws could not save a polity from corruption if a people's morals were vicious. The jurisprudence of both Hutcheson and Montesquieu was full of references to the unstable relation between private manners and public law, but Millar and Smith believed that neither had been able to specify the analytical connection between changes in one and changes in the other. To do so would require an excursion beyond law itself to the determinants of manners, which Montesquieu and Harrington too had seen as the modes of subsistence and the distribution of property.[17] It was of little use, from Millar's point of view, for Hutcheson to have specified the relations of natural justice which ought to inhere in the private sphere unless one could also specify the social conditions in which such relations could actually come to pass. Smith's jurisprudence lectures, the decisive event in Millar's intellectual life, seemed to provide a theory of the relation between law, manners and property which the civic tradition had always emphasized in its conception of the conditions for virtuous citizenship.

Smith himself did not offer a historical account of the household in his jurisprudence, but his method did point the way for his pupil to 'finish' the job. The key move was to treat 'civil polity', not as a juridical nexus of rights and duties, but as a set of social and economic relations directed in the first instance to the production of subsistence and the reproduction of life. Law

---

[14] *TMS* VI.ii.1.10; Millar, *Ranks*, p. 243. 'The Effects of Commerce and Manufactures and of Opulence and Civilisation upon the Morals of a People', *Historical View*, iv, pp. 255–6.

[15] Craig, *Life*, pp. xxiv–xxv; 'The Progress of Science relating to Law and Government', *Historical View*, iv, pp. 283–4; see also Hume, *Treatise*, p. 482; *TMS* II.ii.1.6–10.

[16] Pocock, *The Machiavellian Moment*, pp. 426–35; for Fletcher, see the contribution by John Robertson in this volume, pp. 137–78 above.

[17] Montesquieu, *Spirit of the Laws*, Bk V, ch. 6; Bk XII, ch. 1; James Harrington, *The Commonwealth of Oceana*, in *The Political Works of James Harrington*, ed. J. G. A. Pocock (Cambridge, 1977), pp. 158, 164.

and rights were then interpreted as deriving from these relations. Craig signalled this decisive switch in terminology when he wrote that

> Millar confined himself altogether to the changes produced in the several relations of society by the gradual progress of civilization and improvement. He neither intended to give any account of the laws and institutions springing from these relations...nor to investigate in a detailed manner the effects produced upon them by particular systems of government.[18]

In the *Ranks*, Millar used old English and Scottish statutes as anthropological evidence of the manners and social relations of feudal agricultural peoples, in the same way as he used Old Testament quotations as wholly secular testimony about the marriage practice of semitic pastoral peoples.[19]

Given Smith and Millar's own sensitivity to unintended consequences, they would have appreciated the irony that their own theory, created in the first instance to solve certain problems in jurisprudence, ended up by displacing law as the constitutive element of social order, and relegating it to a dependent position as an artefact of social relations. Meek, Pascal and Sombart, as well as the Schneider-Lehmann account, miss this irony by taking it for granted that the categories of modern social science were 'available' for use in the 1760s. Their account fails to explain how such categories were created, how it became possible to conceive of order in social relations apart from their judicial form, and how the new language inscribed within itself a conception of civil society dependent upon the legal armature of the state, but essentially autonomous.

This new language did continue the jurisprudential practice of joining together the study of 'oeconomics' and 'politics', the study of the 'various plans of civil government'. This linking up of private and public spheres was also inscribed in the civic humanist vocabulary, which Millar inherited from Hutcheson, from Montesquieu, and from Commonwealthman and Country Party writing – in their belief that moral virtue and propertied independence in the 'oeconomic' or household sphere were decisive to the maintenance of liberty in the 'political' sphere. Millar's history of civil society meshed together jurisprudential and civic humanist concerns, in a theory linking changes in sexual authority, wage relations and forms of state power in one over-arching historical process. It is this synoptic integration of family, economy and state spheres which makes the *Ranks* such subversive reading for anyone whose mental categories are bounded by the sociology, economics and political science which descend from the original Scottish project. Millar's syncretic view was possible, not because he 'anticipated' our disciplines but precisely because he was *not* working within their precincts, but instead within a jurisprudential and civic humanist mode which treated private and public spheres together, which unified 'oeconomics' and 'politics' in one historical synthesis.

[18] Craig, *Life of Millar*, p. lxxvi.
[19] Millar, *Ranks*, pp. 205-8.

'Anticipatory' readings also fail to pay attention to the conceptual development between *The Origin of Ranks*, a work dependent upon Smith's jurisprudence lectures, and the *Historical View*, which took on board the categories of the *Wealth of Nations*. The *Ranks* took the household as its theoretical object, while the dissertations at the end of the *Historical View* clearly presume a market society divided into landlords, labourers and a third category comprising traders, merchants, manufacturers and 'capitalists' (variously described as 'mercantile adventurers', 'monied men' and 'speculators' to distinguish them from employers).[20] When viewed in terms of its impact on Millar, the *Wealth of Nations* appears as a revolution in social language, specifying civil society, not as a network of households, but as a nexus in which 'every man lives by exchanging'.[21]

II

'Anticipatory' readings of Millar as 'father' and 'precursor' also miss the extent to which his thought was given shape by his political purposes and by his immediate social milieu. The most ambitious attempt to interconnect Millar's theory, his politics and his milieu has been Hans Medick's. He sees Millar as a social scientist seeking to validate artisanal radicalism in the high noon of petty commodity production. According to Medick, he endorsed free trade, the abolition of corporate privileges, monopolies, primogeniture and entail, for the same reasons as Paine – that is, to help the small producer and tenant farmer against large merchants, monopolists and landlords. Medick interprets Millar politically as a latter-day civic republican seeking to emancipate Fletcherian and Harringtonian republicanism from its elitist gentry form and redefining its conception of civic personality and independence to legitimize the petty commodity producer's claim to the suffrage. Millar's historical theory was designed, in turn, to free artisanal radicalism from its dependence on the simplistic rhetoric of 'the ancient constitution' and to argue their political claims on the basis of an economic analysis of their rising 'independence' within commercial society. Millar's one distinctive economic argument, the treatment of profit in the *Historical View* as the wage of the manufacturer and as a saving achieved by investment in the division of labour, is seen by Medick to speak precisely for that 'early bourgeois small entrepreneur whose capital does in fact largely increase in proportion to his personal economy'. The tensions in Millar's thought, his endorsement of free market relations side by side with his invectives against monopoly, corruption and inequality in commercial states are ascribed by Medick to the 'petty bourgeois'

---

[20] 'The Advancement of Manufacturing, Commerce, and the Arts, since the Reign of William III, and the Tendency of this Advancement to diffuse a Spirit of Liberty and Independence', *Historical View*, iv, pp. 118 26. [21] *WN* I.iv.1.

horizon of his outlook. His was a vision which sought to 'stop time' at the apogee of the artisanal mode, at the moment of the petty commodity producer's 'independence'.

Medick's account has the great merit of offering a 'social' explanation of the tensions in Millar's thought which Schneider and others have only pointed to. Yet it has its difficulties. First, Medick bases his reading of Millar on the *Letters of Sydney*. These letters, however, can only be attributed to him by ignoring the footnotes which refer explicitly to the influence of 'Professor Millar's lectures'.[22] It is unlikely that an author would refer glowingly to the experience of having heard his own lectures. If we treat these footnotes seriously, they would incline us to attribute *Sydney* to one of his students, perhaps his nephew and biographer John Craig, whose own *Elements of Moral and Political Science* of 1814, Medick argues, 'plagiarized' from Millar. How much more likely that Craig himself wrote *Sydney*, using Millar's lectures as his authority.

The correct attribution of *Sydney* is important because its scathing attack on wastrel landlords, on 'the illiberal monopolizing spirit of merchants', on 'stockjobbers' and 'great capitalists' and its Harringtonian appeal for an equalization of property through the abolition of primogeniture and entail is more Jacobin than any text which can be definitely attributed to Millar. *Sydney*'s argument does draw on sources of thought which were Millar's own – Harrington, Smith's *Theory of Moral Sentiments* (on the idleness of the rich), the *Wealth of Nations* (on the wasteful investments of the great landlords), and Hume's *Essays* (on the aristocratic prejudice against the 'useful professions').[23] *Sydney* shows that a petty bourgeois Jacobinism *could* draw its intellectual charter from a radical reading of the Scottish Enlightenment. The question, however, is whether it did, and more specifically, whether Millar is the bridge between Hume and Smith and Paine, Cartwright and Cobbett.

Millar may have attended the meetings of the Glasgow Friends of the People and one of his former pupils, Thomas Muir, was singled out for political martyrdom in one of Pitt's notorious state trials.[24] Yet Millar could not be called a Jacobin. Medick does pay attention to his repeated disavowal of forcible 'levelling', but he misses his emphatic endorsement of 'our mixed constitution', his rejection of Cartwright's manhood suffrage in the lectures and his condemnation of Paine's atheism.[25] As for Paine's politics, if we are to

---

[22] Anon., *Letters of Sydney on Inequality of Property* (Edinburgh, 1796), pp. 47, 55.
[23] *Letters of Sydney*, pp. 6, 18, 22, 71.
[24] H. W. Meikle, *Scotland and the French Revolution* (Glasgow, 1912), ch. V; *An Account of the Trial of Thomas Muir* (Edinburgh, 1793); P. Mackenzie, *Life of Thomas Muir* (Glasgow, 1831); Medick cites Public Record Office, Home Office Papers 102, V, fol. 389 (12 October 1792), for evidence of Millar's presence at the Glasgow (as opposed to Edinburgh) meetings of the Friends of the People.
[25] Anon., *Letters of Crito on the Causes, Objects and Consequences of the Present War* (London, 1796), pp. 12, 48–9. John Millar, 'Lectures on Government given at the University of Glasgow, 1787–8', 3 vols. Glasgow University Library, MS. Gen. 289–91, vol. 3, fols. 16–18.

believe Craig, Millar 'ridiculed the idea of an imprescriptible, indefeasible right in the people to conduct the affairs of Government'. Indeed, he conceived of the enfranchisement of artisans as a 'solid refutation' of popular doctrines then afloat, as a strategy of conciliation to 'rally the great body of the nation around the constitution'.[26] This is not the language of the London Corresponding Society, but that of Charles James Fox, Millar's lodestar in politics, and of Lord Grey, whose London Friends of the People Millar joined as a charter subscriber in 1792.[27]

Millar's horizons were not defined by the political demands of the petty bourgeoisie but by the Foxite Whigs of the middle class and gentry in the 1790s. His was not a social vision of reform, an artisanal republic, but a narrowly political reformism, aiming at maintaining the constitutional balance between executive and legislative achieved in 1688.

At the same time, Millar did bring something very new to the defence of the Revolution settlement – a theory of the economic determination of the political. In the *Historical View*, he argued that capitalist economic development since 1688 had required a steady expansion of state power – in the form of navies to protect maritime commerce, 'standing armies' to prosecute campaigns against European rivals, excise agents to protect domestic commerce, tax collectors to raise revenue, and an expanding system of 'police' to ensure the security of property and exchange transactions in a national market. In this respect, the coming of commercial society, he argued, undoubtedly increased the influence of the crown within the constitution.[28] Millar endorsed the Smithian attack on state interference in the economy, not, as Medick argues, in the name of the petty commodity producer, but because of his concern to maintain the balance of the constitution against the growing power of the executive.

Like Hume and Smith, Millar believed that the coming of a commercial economy was essentially ambiguous in its political consequences. If a market economy required a steadily expanding state structure, the 'independence' of contractual relations in the market sphere created the conditions for new demands for political freedom. In the passage from relations of status to relations of contract, everyone in a commercial economy became freer to make political decisions on the basis of personal interest rather than deference to authority. 'Independency' in the economic sphere, Millar argued (following Hume), gave rise to new habits of mind – 'utility' came to replace 'authority' as the basis of decision in political matters.

Millar especially noticed that in modern commercial politics, 'the bond

[26] Craig, *Life of Millar*, p. cxiv.
[27] Society of the Friends of the People; associated for the purpose of obtaining a Parliamentary reform, *Proceedings, 1792* (London, 1793).
[28] 'Political Consequences of the Revolution', *Historical View*, iv, pp. 90–5.

between the workmen and their employer' had been loosened by freedom of contract. His endorsement of this trend was surprisingly emphatic, given the strength of the fears, particularly within the civic republican tradition, about the social stability of a society based on free labour. Fletcher, for example, had insisted that free labour meant beggary for some, and idleness and vagrancy for many, and had argued in the Union debates that the only stable path towards commercial improvement in Scottish agriculture lay in gentry exploitation of a labouring population held in slavish tutelage. As late as the 1760s, James Steuart can be found musing, before dismissing the idea as an anachronism, that an updated and paternalistic system of slavery would avoid beggary, unemployment and estrangement between ranks in the new commercial economy.[29] That Millar broke emphatically with this authoritarian strain in Scottish civic republicanism is a sign of his confidence in the equilibrating function of a social psychology of sympathy, the universalization of the possibility of accumulation, and the persistence of 'natural' deference for the rich in a commercial economy. 'Independence' in a free-labour economy created the material conditions for the vindication of political as well as private rights. Liberty was thus a modern condition, not, as in the ancient constitution rhetoric, a heritage bequeathed by Anglo-Saxon simplicity.

Medick is quite right to point out that Millar's analysis of the 'independence' of wage relations was viable only on the assumption of a petty commodity mode of production as the implied point of social reference. Neither Millar nor Smith was so naïve as to assume that the day labourer, buried under the weight of necessity, could be called 'independent', and they even admitted that artisans were increasingly hard-pressed to maintain their freedom. As Smith remarked in 1776, for every independent master, there were twenty dependent journeymen. Yet their concept of 'independence' did not refer exclusively to the petty commodity producer, but to all of the middling ranks, the professionals, the merchants, the traders, the large capitalists, rendered free of clientage relations by the dissolution of the 'feudal government'. In seeing the centre of Millar's social thought in his contingent assumptions about the 'independence' made possible by the artisanal mode of production, Medick gives Millar's thought a 'productivist' bias. For Millar, it was not the mode of production which defined commercial society as a social formation, but rather the generalized principle of exchange, permeating all social relations of authority in the household, in the economy and in the polity. 'Independence' was the generalized social condition of all men in a society based on contract rather than status relations. It was the rising 'independence' of all of the 'middling ranks', and not simply of the petty commodity producer, which Millar looked to for the defence of the legislative power in maintaining the balance of the

[29] Sir James Steuart, *An Inquiry into the Principles of Political Oeconomy*, ed. A. S. Skinner, 2 vols. (Edinburgh, 1966), i, p. 148.

constitution. If any particular social allegiance can be read from his economic theory of politics, it is to the 'middling ranks', a heterogeneous formation which, in Millar's mind, included everyone from the independent tenant-farming gentry to the independent small master. Medick's account seems to have read Millar, not in terms of the social vocabulary available in the 1790s, but according to the schema of Marx's *18th Brumaire*.

If Millar had subscribed to a social vision of an artisanal republic, as Medick implies, we might have expected his economic history of politics to have passed into the vernacular of early-nineteenth-century English radical republicanism. As Duncan Forbes has pointed out, the *Historical View* is in the Humean tradition of 'scientific Whiggism'. It was a demolition job on the witangemote, on the myth of the original Anglo-Saxon liberties, and the 'ancient constitution' so dear to every strand of the Whig tradition, from James Burgh to William Blackstone, from Christopher Wyvill to Cartwright.[30] Millar's argument that political liberty was an entirely modern result of market 'independence' was an attempt to rid Whiggism of its simplistic nostalgia and to ground its principles on a 'scientific' history of commercial society. Yet all of the mythology of 'vulgar Whiggism' survived the 1790s unscathed by Hume, Millar and Smith's historicism. Wyvill, nearing the end of his life, wrote admiringly of Millar as an 'upright patriot', but there is no evidence that the Scot's historical work dislodged his old Country Party belief in the ancient constitution.[31] Of Fox's opinions of the *Historical View*, we have no record, even though the work was dedicated to him. As for the Scottish Jacobins, however, there is clear evidence that they had learned nothing from their teacher. Had Millar been at Muir's trial he would have squirmed in his seat to hear Muir asserting that the rights of free-born Englishmen were 'substantially enjoyed in the times of the immortal Alfred' and that he wished to 'restore the Constitution to its purity in King Alfred's time'.[32]

While the lingering half-life of 'ancient constitution' rhetoric in Cobbett's *Register*, in the Hampden clubs and the *Black Dwarf* would take us beyond the limits of this paper, it should be asked if Edward Thompson was right to contend that Paine's 'natural right' arguments succeeded in emancipating English radicalism from its recursive appeal to vanished traditions.[33] The artisanal radicalism which has its birth in the 1790s drew on traditions impervious to Millar's 'scientific' historicism: the gentry opposition of the

[30] Forbes, 'Scientific Whiggism'; Duncan Forbes, *Hume's Philosophical Politics* (Cambridge, 1975); James Burgh, *Political Disquisitions* (London, 1774); Society for Constitutional Information, *Tracts* (London, 1783), p. 91; Christopher Wyvill, *Political Papers*, 6 vols. (York, 1806), iii, pp. 40-5; John Cartwright, *The People's Barrier Against Undue Influence* (London, 1780).
[31] Letters between Millar and Wyvill, 27 July 1800 to 20 February 1801, in Wyvill, 'Political Correspondence', *Political Papers*, vi, pp. 95-108.
[32] Mackenzie, *Muir*, p. 7; Meikle, *Scotland and the French Revolution*, p. 143.
[33] Edward Thompson, *The Making of the English Working Class* (Harmondsworth, Middlesex, 1963), pp. 70-98.

Country Party of the 1720s, the rational deism of Priestley, and the older millenarian strain of Commonwealthman and Dissenting sectarianism of 1640. Thus when Marx rediscovered the *Ranks*, it was not through the medium of Owenism or Chartism, the source of so many of his ideas, but by reading in 'the dismal science' and by uncovering the materialist theory of history which it had jettisoned by the time of Ricardo. In making these points we begin to see why Millar had so few nineteenth-century heirs.

III

If Millar is not to be inscribed at the beginning of the artisanal radical tradition, are we then to read him as the last of the 'sceptical Whigs'? This is Duncan Forbes's position, and it aligns Millar with Hume and Smith. But there are obvious difficulties here. Forbes admits that Millar was a more 'militant' Whig than Smith, but he puts this down to Millar's more pugnacious temperament. Surely the relations between pupil and teacher are more complicated and ambivalent than Forbes's account, or Millar's own reverent remarks about Smith, would suggest.

In the 1760s and early 1770s, as a young lecturer at Glasgow, Millar *could* still be described as being within the precincts of the sceptical Whiggism of his mentor. He believed that the property qualification was already low enough to give political voice to the growing power of the middle ranks, and he even wondered aloud in his lectures whether, in enfranchising petty tradesmen as city burgesses, the English franchise had 'descended too low to the dregs of the people'.[34] On the vexed question of parliamentary privilege he took an anti-Wilkesian line, maintaining that Parliament had the right to expel members, and with the Wilkes and Liberty riots of the 1760s in mind, he agreed with Smith that a standing army was necessary to 'quell any insurrection that may happen' now that 'the people are everyday acquiring more and more the spirit of liberty'.[35] He also rejected the traditional Commonwealthman and Country Party call for triennial Parliaments, arguing that more frequent contests would only provide additional pretexts for election debauchery by the poor. Millar's account of royal prerogative and executive power was benign and Humean in tone. The settlement had fixed a just balance between executive authority and parliamentary independence and social change had acted to secure the stability of the balance. While the power of the executive had been swelled by a century of imperialist war, the rising independency of the 'middling ranks' had frustrated executive attempts to suborn middle-class M.P.s from keeping the power of ministry and crown under scrutiny. As a

[34] John Millar, 'Lectures on Government delivered by Mr J. Millar, 1771-2', extended by George Skene, Mitchell Library (Glasgow), 2 vols., MS. 99, vol. 1, fol. 247.
[35] Millar, *Government Lectures*, 1771-2, vol. 2, fol. 252.

result, England had achieved a 'popular government after the best model, perhaps, which is practicable in an extensive country'. While Hume's account of Millar as a 'republican' may be true to his opposition to the patrician domination of the Scottish burghal franchises, it was a republicanism at peace with the *status quo* of *English* metropolitan politics.[36] As Millar himself implied, full 'republicanism' was not practicable in 'an extensive country' requiring coordination from the top. At the outbreak of the American War, therefore, Millar is to be found squarely with Smith, among the Rockingham Whigs.[37] Thereafter, while the teacher remained more or less as he was, the pupil was forced to change, adapting a Humean and Smithian science of politics to a radically new configuration. The catalyst, of course, was the American War. On both sides of the Atlantic, the conflict revived the dormant rhetoric of the Commonwealthmen. The old denunciations of standing armies, war finance and executive despotism, first formulated during 'King William's war' in 1698 regained plausibility as the ministry blundered into an imperial campaign against what the Americans insisted were 'the rights of free-born Englishmen'. The disastrous course of the war put parliamentary and fiscal reform upon the political agenda once again.[38] Millar took the unpopular line of favouring the 'total separation' of the colonies in a town tied hand and foot to the Virginia tobacco trade. Until 1784, however, 'the leading article of his political creed', according to Craig, was the idea of 'a union of talents and ranks' 'to limit the growing influence of the Court'.[39]

The ministerial crisis of 1784 dislodged his faith in this old Country Party nostrum. As a devout partisan of the North–Fox coalition, he watched with indignation as the King secured the defeat of Fox's India Bill by circulating a note in the Lords indicating that 'he should consider all who voted for [the bill] as his enemies'. Millar regarded this as a 'highly illegal' breach of the independence of Parliament. When Fox resigned, the King chose Pitt as his first minister. The Commons remained under Fox's control and between December 1783 and March 1784 passed sixteen successive motions of non-confidence in the Pitt ministry. Pitt and the King refused to cede and Pitt used blandishments and bribery to chip away at the Foxite majority until he had secured passage of a major piece of legislation. With this victory in hand, he secured a dissolution from the King, went to the country and by liberal

---

[36] *Ibid.*, fol. 247; David Hume, to David Hume the Younger, 8 December 1775, *The Letters of David Hume* ed. J. Y. T. Greig, 2 vols. (Oxford, 1932), ii, pp. 305–7.

[37] Craig, *Life of Millar*, p. cii; D. Forbes, 'Sceptical Whiggism, Commerce and Liberty', in A. S. Skinner and T. Wilson (eds.), *Essays on Adam Smith* (Oxford, 1975), pp. 185–91.

[38] Caroline Robbins, *The Eighteenth-Century Commonwealthman: Studies in the Transmission, Development and Circumstance of English Liberal Thought from the Restoration of Charles II until the War with the Thirteen Colonies* (Cambridge, Mass., 1961); Ian Christie, *Wilkes, Wyvill and Reform* (London, 1962).

[39] Craig, *Life of Millar*, p. cii.

application of the grease of 'Treasury influence', or so Millar believed, returned with a majority.[40]

It was the electorate's apparent vulnerability to corruption in 1784 which convinced Millar, as Craig put it, 'of the necessity of henceforward founding national liberty on a much more general diffusion of political power'.[41] In his government lectures of 1787, Millar gave his first explicit support to triennial Parliaments and to the enfranchisement of every male 'with as much property as a good labourer can earn by his daily labour, suppose £20 or £25 a year'.[42]

According to Craig, the French Revolution 'from its first appearance riveted Mr. Millar's attention, and in its early progress, excited his fondest hopes'. While his aging teacher was writing, in apparent reference to the Revolution, that 'a real patriot' had the perilous choice of deciding whether to 're-establish the authority of the old system' or to 'give way to the more daring but often dangerous spirit of innovation', Millar was welcoming the Revolution in his lectures as the liberation of civil society from the shackles of feudal legal encumbrances.[43]

Millar's denunciation of Pitt's war policy – the quartering of a standing army in barracks in the manufacturing towns, the corrupt linkages between the ministry and war financiers, the spiralling increase of the national debt – gave voice again to the language coined a century earlier by Whig Commonwealthmen and Country Party opponents of King William's war.[44] Smith's defusing of the standing army and public debt issues had sounded apposite to Millar in his student days, but in the charged atmosphere of the 1790s, his position would have seemed complacent. Likewise Smith and Hume's insistence that the French monarchy ought to be considered a 'regular government' might have been a welcome riposte to vulgar Whig parochialisms about 'French despotism' in the 1760s, but in the wake of the Revolution their views seemed to ignore the *lettres de cachet*, the Bastille and the feudal privileges struck down on the night of 5 August.[45]

The heart of Hume and Smith's political position rested on a distinction between 'personal freedom', the passive rights of enjoyment of property, and 'civil liberty', the exercise of sovereignty by the citizenship.[46] They objected

---

[40] J. S. Watson, *The Reign of George III* (Oxford, 1960), p. 256; T. B. Macaulay, 'William Pitt', *Miscellaneous Writings and Speeches* (London, 1889), pp. 395-432.

[41] Craig, *Life of Millar*, p. ciii; *Letters of Crito*, p. 17.

[42] Millar, *Government Lectures, 1787-8*, vol. 3, fol. 18; see also J. R. Balow, '"Scientific Republicanism" in David Hume, Adam Smith and John Millar', paper delivered to the New Zealand Historians' Conference, University of Canterbury, N.Z., August 1979.

[43] Craig, *Life of Millar*, p. cxii; *TMS* VI.ii.2.10-13; Millar, *Government Lectures, 1787-8*, vol. 2, fols. 34-44 (an interpolation into the 1787 text of material delivered in 1792).

[44] *Letters of Crito*, pp. 84-101.

[45] Millar, *Government Lectures, 1787-8*, vol. 3, fol. 40; *Letters of Crito*, pp. 1-3; Forbes, *Hume's Philosophical Politics*, pp. 141-61.

[46] Craig, *Life of Millar*, p. cxi; on the distinction between 'active' and 'passive' conceptions of liberty, see J. H. Hexter, 'Republic, Virtue, Liberty, and the Political Universe of J. G. A.

to the vulgar Whig label of French 'despotism' because, in their view, the French had as much 'personal freedom' as the English. While a commercial society absolutely required 'personal freedom' in the private sphere, they argued, it did not require 'civil liberty'. A monarchical absolutism like France was becoming 'a commercial society' as rapidly as 'free' England. Is it going too far to argue that the nub of their 'sceptical Whiggism' consisted in believing that 'personal freedom' was more important than 'civil liberty'? Hume said that if faced with the choice of joining in the factious, conflict-ridden politics of a popular (as opposed to oligarchical) republic and enjoying tranquil security under the rule of law in an absolute monarchy, he would choose the latter.[47] Smith for his part believed that popular participation in government was also less important for the happiness of a state than equitable administration of law. Dugald Stewart reported Smith as having believed that

> the happiness of mankind depends not on the share which the people possess directly or indirectly in the enactment of laws, but on the equity and expediency of the laws which are enacted. The share which the people possess in the government is interesting chiefly to the small number of men whose object is the attainment of political importance; but the equity and expediency of the laws are interesting to every member of the community.[48]

Dugald Stewart's own 'Lectures on Political Economy' emphatically downgraded 'civil liberty' at the expense of 'personal freedom' as the proper goal of modern politics:

> Happiness is in truth the only object of legislation of intrinsic value; and what is called political liberty is only one of the means of obtaining this end. With the advantage of good laws, a people though not possessed of political power may yet enjoy a great degree of happiness; and on the contrary where laws are unjust and inexpedient, the political power of the people, so far from furnishing any compensation for their misery, is likely to pose an insurmountable obstacle to improvement by employing the despotism of numbers in support of principles of which the multitude is incompetent to judge.[49]

These positions marked sceptical Whiggism's decisive break with the political theory of civic republicanism. Property was morally approved, in Harrington, in *Cato's Letters*, in Hutcheson and Montesquieu, primarily because it conferred the material independence necessary for the unencumbered exercise of citizenship and only secondarily because it provided the legal basis for the private satisfaction of needs. Justice and the rule of law, important as

---

Pocock', in his *On Historians* (London, 1979), pp. 293–303; also Knud Haakonssen, *The Science of a Legislator: The Natural Jurisprudence of David Hume and Adam Smith* (Cambridge, 1981), p. 140.

[47] Hume, 'Whether the British Government inclines more to Absolute Monarchy, or to a Republic', *Philosophical Works*, iii, p. 126.

[48] Dugald Stewart, 'Account of the Life and Writings of Adam Smith LL.D', *EPS*, p. 310.

[49] D. Stewart, *Lectures on Political Economy*, in *Collected Works*, ed. Sir William Hamilton, 10 vols. (Edinburgh, 1854–60), viii, pp. 23–4.

they were for social stability and commercial development, could not prevent the corruption of a state if property-holders were unwilling to engage in that 'self-renunciation, ever arduous and painful' which went by the name of Virtue.[50] Justice and Virtue, law and public spiritedness, were conceived to be in tension with each other. The rule of Justice was no substitute for the rule of Virtue. Indeed, in a despotism, the rule of law was perfectly consistent with the utter extinction of civil liberty, and hence with the extinction of all possibility of virtue. Adam Ferguson summed up this critique of the tendency to value 'private freedom' more highly than 'civil liberty':

> Liberty is never in greater danger than it is when we measure national felicity by the blessings which a prince may bestow, or by the mere tranquility which may attend on equitable administration.[51]

Ferguson and Millar were at opposite ends of the spectrum over the American War, over the French Revolution and over the enfranchisement of the people, but they both valued civic participation more highly than passive enjoyment of property. As Millar told his students, 'liberty is more valuable than riches'.[52] In the 1790s a government like Pitt's could be said to have guaranteed rights of private accumulation while going some way towards extinguishing rights of citizenship altogether. Unless the active rights of citizenship were defended and strengthened by franchise reform, Millar believed that 'the euthanasia of the British constitution' which Hume had predicted if the executive gained predominance would be at hand.

Millar did not deny that 'regular government' and the rule of law were crucial to progress. Modern commercial peoples *were* more honest, more just in their dealings than 'rude tribes', who thought cattle-stealing, for example, was an acceptable practice. Yet this justice of 'commercial peoples' hardly required moral courage at all. It was merely 'that coarse though useful virtue, the guardian of contracts and promises, whose guide is the square and the compass, and whose protector is the gallows'.[53] A society which valued only justice, only the security provided by regular government, might become wealthy, but it had less reason to be proud of itself than one which valued liberty and virtue.

---

[50] Montesquieu, *Spirit of the Laws*, Bk IV, ch. 5; Harrington, *Oceana*, p. 158; Hutcheson, *System*, ii, pp. 259–60; J. Trenchard and T. Gordon, 'Of the natural Honesty of the People, and their reasonable Demands. How important it is to every Government to consult their Affections', Cato's Letters, No. 24, 8 April 1721, and 'Considerations on the destructive Spirit of arbitrary Power. With the Blessings of Liberty, and their own Constitution', Cato's Letters, No. 25, 15 April 1721, in *Cato's Letters: or essays on liberty, civil and religious, and other important subjects*, 4th edn, 4 vols. (London, 1737), i, pp. 177–94.

[51] Adam Ferguson, *An Essay on the History of Civil Society*, ed. D. Forbes (Edinburgh, 1966), pp. 269–70.

[52] Millar, *Government Lectures, 1787–8*, vol. 3, fol. 18; on Ferguson's position over the American War, see his *Remarks on a Pamphlet Lately Published by Dr Price*.... (London, 1776).

[53] 'Political Consequences of the Revolution', *Historical View*, iv, p. 94.

Surely this preference for 'virtue' over 'justice', for 'free government' over 'regular government', took Millar out of the 'sceptical Whiggism' in which he began his intellectual career. In conflating Millar with Smith, Duncan Forbes has missed the real divergences which opened up between teacher and pupil in the generation after 1776. In one sense Millar's radicalization represented a 'return' to Commonwealthman and Country Party vocabulary. But if it was a 'return', it was a highly complex one, adopting the language of virtue and corruption, while jettisoning the historical crudities of the Anglo-Saxon myth, interpreting liberty as a modern consequence of commerce while condemning the selfishness and hedonism of modern individualism.

IV

In order to get closer to these contradictions in Millar, to the unreconciled layers of discourse in his thought, we should take a detailed look at the most original and interesting part of his theoretical work, the history of sexual authority to be found in the *Ranks*.

Millar's attention to the condition of women and to the transformation of sexual relations within the family was neither idiosyncratic nor unusual in his time. The impact of commercial society upon the condition of women and upon family authority was a matter of controversy and speculation in Edinburgh's Select Society, and in provincial centres of Enlightenment throughout Europe.[54] Those like Michel Foucault who have speculated on the reasons why sex is 'put into discourse' in the eighteenth century have not paid sufficient emphasis to the decisive influence of classical Stoicism, in its modern neo-Harringtonian form, in pairing the passions of sex and gain as the 'private' desires most inimical to the public good.[55] As John Pocock has argued, sex became visible by means of a political economy of desire created by early-eighteenth-century moralists to assess the implications of the liberation of private instinct in market society.[56] Their problem was that, while they admired Cicero's condemnation of 'the mere pursuits of sensual gratification', they found it psychologically unrealistic, 'too rigid to be popular', as Trenchard and Gordon put it.[57] It was 'the highest stupidity', they went on, 'to talk of subduing the passions'. The political virtue appropriate to modern as opposed to ancient polities would have to consist in an ambiguously poised self-repression, 'an equal administration of the appetites by which they are

---

[54] 'Minutes and Procedures of the Select Society', National Library of Scotland, MS. 23.1.1.
[55] M. Foucault, *The History of Sexuality*, vol. 1: *An Introduction*, trans. R. Hurley (London, 1979).
[56] Pocock, *The Machiavellian Moment*, pp. 452–3; also his 'The Mobility of Property and the Rise of 18th Century Sociology', in A. Parel and T. Flanagan (eds.), *Theories of Property: Aristotle to the Present* (Calgary, 1980), pp. 141–66.
[57] Cicero, *De Officiis*, Bk I, xxx. 105–6; Trenchard and Gordon, 'Of the Passions, that they are all alike good or all alike evil, according as they are applied', Cato's Letters, No. 39, 29 July 1721, in *Cato's Letters*, ii, pp. 43–9.

restrained from outrunning one another'. The classical and Christian ideal of self-abnegation for the sake of the public good was also economically naïve, in that the spiral of human wants was the very motor of modern economic growth. Even a man as hostile to 'luxury' as Bishop Berkeley knew well enough that 'the creating of wants is the likeliest way to produce industry in a people'. Yet the strain of his effort to come to terms with the force of private need becomes evident, pages later in *The Querist*, when the Bishop denounces 'women of fashion' as the chief begetters of those luxurious wants which 'enslave' men to their private passions.[58]

If, as nearly every eighteenth-century thinker of consequence realized, there was no 'natural' or as we would say 'biological' distinction between luxury and necessary needs, how was it possible to develop an ethic of private behaviour and consumption which would help men to chose the public over the private good? At what point on the needs spiral ought a man in conscience to stop? Francis Hutcheson's discussion of luxury epitomized the struggle to salvage an ethic of public obligation from the beckoning opportunities for private gratification offered by the coming of a commercial economy. Luxury, he said, was to be defined as

an excessive desire or use of the lowest pleasures as is inconsistent with discharging the offices of life. Luxury lavishes out men's fortunes and yet increases their keen desires, making them needy and craving, it must occasion the strongest temptations to desert their duty to their country whenever it is inconsistent with pleasure – it must lead the citizens to betray their country either to a tyrant at home or to a foreign enemy.[59]

But as Hume pointed out, while vicious private gratifications could be defined and punished by law, how *was* one to identify the moment when *harmless* private gratification passed over into neglect of public duty? Men could be compelled to observe the rules of justice in the satisfaction of need, but how could they be compelled to be virtuous?[60]

Eighteenth-century civic moralists increasingly presented public-spirited citizenship as a leap from the necessity of need into the freedom of ethical choice, but, in doing so, left themselves vulnerable to a Mandevillian and Humean counter-attack that such a conception of virtue contradicted the truth about old Adam. Unable to give psychological plausibility to virtue, civic moralists increasingly portrayed it as a vanishing reproach to the decadence of the age.

In England public calamity tended to revive these anti-modernist jeremiads. In the wake of the '45 the Whig Commonwealthman, James Burgh, and Robert Wallace, the Scottish republican, ascribed the martial supineness of the English

[58] George Berkeley, *The Querist*, in *Works*, ed. A. A. Luce and T. E. Jessop, 9 vols. (London, 1948–57), vi, pp. 20, 308–9.
[59] Hutcheson, *Short Introduction*, p. 321.
[60] Hume, 'Of Commerce', *Philosophical Works*, iii, pp. 294–5; 'Of the Original Contract', p. 454.

to the 'irregular and exorbitant sexual desires awakened among the elite by leisure and luxury'.[61]

At the onset of the American War, Richard Price and other Unitarian and Dissenting opponents of the war interpreted the ministry's imperial blunders as a divine visitation upon a commercial society so immersed in private pleasure as to be incapable of devoting itself to sober scrutiny of public measures.[62] What is significant here is the linkage in Whig oppositional thought between alarm over sexual libertinism and the militia-debate rhetoric about the effeminacy and martial timidity of commercial peoples.[63]

Converging with this political discourse on sexuality was a tendency in European Enlightenment thought to read the flood of anthropological evidence about the simplicity of 'primitive' sexuality as a judgement on the neurotic and rapacious sexual behaviour of 'civilized' societies.[64] Diderot's 'Supplement to Bougainville's Voyages', perhaps the most famous of the genre, found several Scottish echoes – for example, in Ferguson's remark that the German tribes 'even in their native forest paid a kind of devotion to the female sex', and in Gilbert Stuart's denunciation of modern sexuality perverted from natural frankness by 'the cares, corruptions and the distinctions of property'.[65] In Ferguson, we can see that the anthropological evidence was read through civic humanist spectacles. Lafitau's Iroquois were seen as virtuous Roman freeholders, alike in their martial virtue, sexual asceticism and contempt for trade:

It was not among the ancient Romans alone that commercial arts or a sordid mind were held in contempt. A like spirit prevails in every rude and independent society. 'I am a warrior, not a merchant', said an American to the governor of Canada who proposed to give him goods in exchange for some prisoners he had taken.[66]

This odd mixture of primitivist naturalism and civic humanist stoicism was

[61] James Burgh, *Britain's Remembrancer* (London, 1746), pp. 18, 43.
[62] Robert Wallace, *A Dissertation on the Numbers of Mankind in Antient and Modern Times; in Which the Superior Populousness of Antiquity is Maintained. With an Appendix Containing Additional Observations on the Same Subject, and Some Remarks on Mr. Hume's Political Discourse, Of the Populousness of Antient Nations* (Edinburgh, 1753), p. 19; John Brown, *An Estimate of the Manners and Principles of the Times* (London, 1757), p. 91; R. Wallace, *Characteristics of the Present Political State of Great Britain* (London, 1758); see also Robert Wallace, 'Of Venery', ed. Norah Smith, *Texas Studies in Literature and Language*, 15 (1973), 429–44.
[63] Anthony Lincoln, *Some Political and Social Ideas of English Dissent, 1763–1800* (London, 1938), p. 133; for the militia debate, see John Robertson, 'The Improving Citizen: The Militia Debates and Political Thought in the Scottish Enlightenment' (D.Phil. thesis, University of Oxford, 1980).
[64] Denis Diderot, 'Supplément au voyage de Bougainville', *Oeuvres philosophiques*, ed. P. Verniére (Paris, 1964); M. Duchet, *Anthropologie et Histoire au siècle des lumières* (Paris, 1971); J. Lafitau, *Moeurs des Sauvages Americains comparées aux Moeurs des premiers temps*, 2 vols. (Paris, 1724).
[65] Ferguson, *Civil Society*, pp. 201, 146–7; Gilbert Stuart, *An Historical Dissertation Concerning the Antiquity of the English Constitution* (Edinburgh, 1768), pp. 23, 36, 92, 131, 276; William Robertson, on the other hand, dissociated himself from this sort of primitivism; see his *History of America*, 2 vols. (Edinburgh, 1777), i, pp. 317–24.
[66] Ferguson, *Civil Society*, p. 93.

widely associated with Rousseau, or at least was attributed to that cardboard Rousseau who was the dart-board of eighteenth-century polemic. In Rousseau's *Discourses*, there is in fact no explicitly sexual critique of modernity. The real object of his attack was the threat to personal moral autonomy posed by the universalized scramble for riches and status. In this critique of the spiral of human needs, the problem of sexual self-control was seen as only one dimension of the personal struggle to maintain moral integrity in a heedless and self-deceiving rat race. As we know from Smith's letter to the *Edinburgh Review* in 1755, an encounter with Rousseau was an essential preliminary in his formation of the sceptical and measured endorsement of competitive individualism to be found in the *Theory of Moral Sentiments*.[67] For Millar too 'a cool examination' of Rousseau's 'declamations' was an unavoidable theoretical task.[68]

If primitivist naturalism and civic humanist modes of thought defined the terms in which the moral assessment of modern individualism had been raised, Smith and Hume self-consciously sought to transpose these terms from a moralizing to a historical plane, changing the question from how people *ought* to behave in commercial society, to the question of how commercial society was making them behave, whether they willed it or not. Millar followed Smith and Hume in 'historicizing' the moral problem of commercial society, and in doing so was able to see through the primitive naturalism of Diderot and Gilbert Stuart. By reading the anthropological evidence through the interpretative grid of Smith's stadial theory, Millar was able to interpret the sexual manners of primitive peoples as the cultural form appropriate to a hunting and gathering stage. It was neither martial stoicism nor natural simplicity, but hunger, poverty and the brutal uncertainty of their mode of subsistence which prevented primitive peoples from abusing their natural liberty in sexual matters. Equally sentimental, in his opinion, was Ferguson and Diderot's belief in the egalitarianism of primitive sexual relations. A hunting and gathering economy naturally favoured masculine strength and hence allowed men's 'natural love of dominion' to range unchecked.[69] It was only when tribal groups settled down, appropriated property in land and began to generate surpluses that women began to be treated with the dignity appropriate to their natural rights as human beings. The leisure and physical comfort made possible by surpluses heightened sexual desire, while the pacification of these societies by central authority devalued the cultural stress on masculine martial prowess. Settled agricultural economies also afforded women an important economic role in storing, managing and consuming the surplus. For all of these

[67] J. J. Rousseau, *A Discourse on the Origin of Inequality*, in his *The Social Contract and Discourses*, trans. G. D. H. Cole, rev. J. H. Brumfitt and J. C. Hall (London, 1973), pp. 27–113; Adam Smith, 'A Letter to the Authors of the *Edinburgh Review*', *EPS*, pp. 250–4; *TMS* I.iii.2.
[68] Millar, *Government Lectures, 1787–8*, vol. 1, fol. 83.
[69] Millar, *Ranks*, pp. 192–3.

reasons, 'progress in the arts and manufactures' favoured the condition of women.

As a result of these improvements, Millar argued, there was

in refined and polished nations the same free communication between the sexes as in the ages of rudeness and barbarism. In the latter women enjoy the most unbounded liberty because it is thought of no consequence what use they shall make of it. In the former they are entitled to the same freedom upon account of those agreeable qualities which they possess and the rank and dignity which they hold as members of society.[70]

The most estimable consequence of modern individualism Millar argued, was that modern marriage was premised on the free choice of partners, and on expectations of obligation, friendship and desire.

Up to this point Millar clearly endorsed the sexual correlates of market freedom. But he went on, and here his ambivalence became evident:

It should seem, however, that there are certain limits beyond which it is impossible to push the real improvements arising from wealth and opulence. In a simple age, the free intercourse of the sexes is attended with no bad consequences; but in opulent and luxurious nations, it gives rise to licentious and dissolute manners, inconsistent with good order, and with the general interest of society. The love of pleasure, when carried to excess, is apt to weaken and destroy those passions which it endeavours to gratify, and to pervert those appetites which nature has bestowed for the most beneficial purposes. The natural tendency, therefore, of great luxury and dissipation is to diminish the rank and dignity of the women, by preventing all refinement in their connection with the other sex, and rendering them only subservient to the purposes of animal enjoyment.[71]

What troubled Millar was the dialectic between improvements in the mode of subsistence and the spiral of human need. Like Smith and Hume, Millar accepted it as axiomatic that human needs were insatiable. This indeed was the motor of historical progress. Yet in the case of sex the liberation of desire from backwardness and repression had paradoxical consequences. In modern urban centres of 'great opulence', men and women were brought into constant contact, while the rapid rotation of property broke down the distinction of ranks and the taboos of caste. Leisure and 'opulence' heightened people's erotic sensibilities. Paradoxically, however, when the 'commerce between the sexes' was made free, people were soon 'too much dissipated by pleasure to feel any violent passion for an individual'.[72] Erotic gratification itself was diminished by the removal of obstacles to its satisfaction. Hence the perversion of 'those appetites which nature has bestowed upon mankind for the most beneficial purposes'.[73] Men and women turned towards extra-marital or homosexual entanglements to recover the inciting dialectic between taboo and desire. Hence, too, the frequency of divorce. Marriage was threatened by the

[70] *Ibid.*, p. 225.   [71] *Ibid.*, p. 225.   [72] *Ibid.*, p. 227.   [73] *Ibid.*, p. 225.

universalization of erotic possibility. Paradoxically, it was not freedom but denial which propelled the spiral of need:

> The restraints... thus laid upon the sexual correspondence contribute in a high degree to improve and augment the pleasures which result from it. The difficulties, the delays, the disappointments which we experience in pursuit of a favourable gratification, cannot fail to enhance its value, by fixing our attention for a length of time upon the same object, by disposing us to estimate the attainment in proportion to the distress which we feel from the want of it, and by rousing the imagination to paint every circumstance in such colours as may flatter our prevailing inclinations.[74]

These ideas, in no sense original to Millar, led him to argue, for example, that it was the repression enjoined by the chivalric code which made possible the flowering of romantic troubador poetry. Desire, far from being extinguished by restraint, was inflamed by it and through what we would call the ruses of sublimation, but which he called 'the great expedients of nature', a 'simple desire or appetite is often converted into a violent passion'.[75] The obstacles thrown in the way of modern couples, by courting rituals, by the restrictions on marriage across the divide of 'ranks', helped to forge between lovers 'a sincere and lasting attachment'.[76] The stability of marriage thus depended on the maintenance of social obstacles to pre-marital erotic gratification.

What is particularly interesting is Millar's account of the relation between external social prohibition and internal restraint. In an analysis taken from the *Theory of Moral Sentiments*, Millar argued that our natural human modesty in sexual matters was not so much imposed by outside social prohibition as generated from within by a rational act of distancing which enabled us to see the 'extravagance' of our own desires. Our sexual passions, when soberly considered, were 'ridiculous', Smith argued, because they were purely private emotions incapable of being shared with a society larger than one other person. Here we can detect just a hint of the classical categorization of sexual desire as a privatizing emotion which takes men and women away from the public life. As Smith said of love, 'it is almost always attended with an incapacity for labour, a neglect of duty, a contempt of fame and even of common reputation'.[77] Through the psycho-social mechanism of sympathy we learned to see our own desire in this disparaging light and hence to control our public exhibitions of erotic feeling according to conventions of propriety. Or as Millar put it

> Those who are not actuated by the same desires must behold our enjoyment with disgust – those who are, must look upon it with jealousy and rivalship. It is to be expected, therefore, that according as men become sensible of this, they will endeavour to remove such disagreeable appearances. They will be disposed to throw a veil over

---

[74] *Ibid.*, pp. 189–91; 'Effects of Commerce', p. 221.
[75] 'Effects of Commerce', p. 221.
[76] *Ibid.*, p. 224.   [77] *TMS* I.ii.2.5.

those pleasures and to cover from the public eye those thoughts and inclinations which they know by experience would expose them to contempt and aversion.[78]

So accustomed are we, by Freud's *Civilization and its Discontents*, to feel our sexual id at war with our social superego, that it is surprising to come across a theory which insisted that our control of our sexual being was 'a dictate of nature', inculcated by the force of education and sustained by a comparison of our feelings with 'those of the people around us'. As moderns we feel more at home with Mandeville's wry insistence on 'guilt and shame' as the major instruments of sexual socialization. 'This was the manner', he observed drily, 'after which savage man was broke.' And 'broke' was the right word. Mandeville insisted that the social cost of such 'public goods' as the prohibition on female sexuality outside of marriage was paid for in 'distemper', hypochondria and mental illness among women.[79] In Millar's and Smith's unusually social conception of character formation, sexual sanctions were internalized with little pain or conflict. The mechanism of sympathy gave inner psychological legitimacy to those 'rules of decency and decorum' which constrained men and women's sexual behaviour. The external force of law merely ratified conventions already felt as binding.

Modern licentiousness originated precisely when the social customs of propriety no longer commanded internal assent. In this breakdown of the legitimizing linkage between social norm and private conscience, sexual commerce became a theatre of duplicity: outward 'politeness' and 'refinement', inward lust and private licence. This breakdown occurred in modern commercial society because sexual desire was subordinated to sordid motives of gain. When these two most powerful of the private passions were paired together in harness, no force of public propriety was powerful enough to restrain them. In the 'highest and most opulent ranks' of modern society, Millar argued, marriage had degenerated into a mercenary bargain in which sexual rapacity and commercial lust joined in an unholy alliance against female chastity.[80] 'The effects of opulence and luxury', Millar went on, were 'no less hurtful to the parental and filial affections':

> The father immersed in the sordid pursuits of the world is apt to look upon his family as a tax upon his pleasures and to find himself elbowed by children who as they grow up in years, require from their increasing demands, a suitable retrenchment of his own personal expenses.

In an economy which encouraged fathers to apprentice their sons and send their daughters out to service, Millar warned, 'the members of a family will be raised to greater independence than is consistent with good order, and with a proper domestic subordination'.

[78] Millar, *Ranks*, p. 190; see also *LJ(A)* iii.20–1.
[79] Mandeville, *The Fable of the Bees*, i, p. 46. [80] 'Effects of Commerce', pp. 256–7.

'The commercial spirit' was legitimizing the replacement of 'generosity' by market calculation as the prevailing language of family life. Fathers and sons haggled over the terms of inheritances, daughters wheedled their allowances and dowries. In family life we had become anxious calculators, measuring all interactions in the mean coinage of 'justice' rather than 'generosity'.

Significantly, therefore, the moral problem of commercial society lay in the impoverishment of social relations in the family sphere, not in the injustice of the economic sphere. Following Smith, Millar argued that the exchange system imposed its own discipline of 'equivalent' or 'just' exchanges. Millar made the familiar contrast between primitive peoples who did not distinguish strictly between *meum* and *tuum* and who did not establish rigid conceptions of monetary equivalents, and commercial peoples who measured each transaction in the shrewd coinage of equivalent exchange. Undergirding this conception of the modern market as a realm of justice was the Smithian sympathy ethic which interpreted market actors as being motivated primarily by a concern to maintain their reputations for 'probity'. The concern for reputation, the desire to observe the proprieties constituted a kind of moral homeostatic mechanism for market society. Undergirding the sympathy mechanism in turn lay the laws of competition. Anyone caught disobeying the laws of equivalent exchange, through the artifices of fraud or deception, would inevitably be punished by market failure, at least in conditions of free competition. Exploitation of the consumer or the labourer could only persist in conditions of monopoly or weak demand. Competition, much more than the law of the state, was made the real guarantor of 'justice' in market relations.[81]

This blithe confidence that competition would ensure equivalent exchange shifted Millar's moral concerns away from the economic sphere altogether, towards what he regarded as the pitifully insufficient and fragile character of market calculation as the basis for moral behaviour in the private or family sphere. In a society in which individuals measured their obligations only in terms of personal advantage, family life risked becoming as brittle a human engagement as a business deal.

Ironically, what was sacrificed in a society devoted to maximizing individual satisfaction was the real happiness of individuals. Millar followed Smith in believing that human happiness consisted, not in material acquisition *per se*, but in the social esteem and prestige conferred by material success. Paradoxically, therefore, the driving force of our aggressive, elbowing competition with our fellows was our need, ultimately, to win their approval. By arguing that our admiration for those who have scrambled to the top was disinterested and unmixed with envy, Smith could maintain that it was possible to achieve the love of our fellows through the rat race.

---

[81] *Ibid.*, pp. 249-55.

Millar's assessment of competitive individualism insisted much more than Smith's on the envy and bitterness of the scramble:

> ...in a country where nobody is idle and where every person is eager to augment his fortune, or to improve his circumstances, there occur innumerable competitions and rivalships, which contract the heart and set mankind at variance. In proportion as every man is attentive to his own advancement, he is vexed and tormented by every obstacle to his prosperity, and prompted to regard his competitors with envy, resentment and other malignant passions.
>
> The pursuit of riches becomes a scramble in which the hand of every man is against every other.[82]

While man's deepest satisfaction consisted in 'generosity', in giving and receiving non-market gifts of affection, commercial society only rewarded equivalent exchanges. Unlike feudal or gothic societies, in which a man's social esteem was judged by his capacity for free spending on retainers, commercial societies never rewarded the giver of the free gift, only the maximizer of private returns. Millar concluded:

> That there is no friendship in trade is an established maxim among traders. Every man for himself, and God Almighty for us all, is their fundamental doctrine.

Only in the moral injunctions of the Christian religion and in the chivalric code of behaviour towards women could Millar detect forces of custom capable of sustaining a non-market rationale for personal behaviour in a commercial society, and these he regarded as vestigial survivals from ruder 'modes of subsistence'. Millar put little trust in law as a means of moral regeneration. Once manners had given way to the corruptions of commerce, there was little that legal enactment could do to recall men and women to virtue. In this pessimism, he stood against the argument in Hume and Mandeville that good laws were capable of reforming a corrupted people. As a system of thought which placed such emphasis on political activism, the civic republican strain in Millar delivered him up, paradoxically, to a thorough-going fatalism about the effectiveness of political reform in regenerating manners. At the same time, Millar placed little faith in the moral autonomy of the individual conscience, the 'impartial spectator within the breast'. Millar's assessment of competitive individualism was significantly bleaker than Smith's because he doubted that conscience could make a stand against the force of 'the commercial spirit'.

Millar also drew a significantly more pessimistic picture of the economic consequences of modern hedonism than Smith. While Smith admitted the disjunction between happiness and material satisfaction in commercial society, he was sure, for that very reason, that the economic machine created to serve our insatiability would never run down. Millar was less hopeful. In a section of his government lectures of 1771 devoted to the decline of nations, Millar

---

[82] *Ibid.*, pp. 248–9; *TMS* I.iii.2.1–12.

wondered aloud whether the spiral of human wants would indeed proceed indefinitely. The idleness and profusion of the 'great' seemed to suggest that once men had succeeded in scrambling to the top of the ladder of status, they tended to renounce 'business' and settle back to enjoy long-deferred gratification. To be sure, the 'profusion' and wastefulness of the great would result in their eventual ruin, but there would always be poor men, drawn by the force of fashion, to emulate the striving of the great for idleness. The emulative cycle, which Smith considered the driving motor of economic progress, became in Millar's hands the psychological mechanism through which the work ethic was gradually poisoned in a commercial society:

> This want of labour and application is soon communicated so that all the other arts and professions idle in like manner for as they are more and more remiss at work they will manage the work with less dexterity and consequently will not be able to produce so much as before.[83]

In international competition for markets, 'luxurious' rich nations, given over to gratification, would lose out to leaner, low-wage competitors from poor nations. Miller stuck to this pessimistic long-term prognosis for commercial society even after Smith had argued in the *Wealth of Nations* that the productivity advantages of rich nations, owing to their more advanced division of labour, would offset the low-wage advantages of poorer nations. Millar continued to insist that the productivity advantages of rich nations would be undercut in the long run by the leisure preference of an idle and luxurious populace.[84] This suggests how fully Millar's encounter with modernity remained enclosed within the classic Stoic paradigm of the decline of nations, and within a theory of needs as satiable and corruptible. For Millar the dynamic of needs in commercial society was the Achilles heel of acquisitive men. Lulled into present enjoyment, they would forswear the strategies of deferred gratification essential for the continuance of progress. Liberation of instinct in commercial society, in other words, contained the seeds of its own destruction.

V

Millar's contradictions were those of a theorist caught between two languages which bifurcate in his own lifetime – civic humanist moralism and political economy. I see no reason why his inability to choose between the evaluative premises of these two discourses should be referred to a 'social' explanation. Smith and Millar both lived at approximately the same social moment and in the work of both there are deep tensions between the language of corruption and the language of markets and interests. But only one of them had the

---

[83] Millar, *Government Lectures, 1771–2*, fol. 57; on the 'rich country–poor country' problematic in Scottish thought, see the contribution by Istvan Hont in this volume, pp. 271–316 above.
[84] Millar, *Government Lectures, 1787–8*, vol. 1, fol. 159.

resolution to force his way to an internally consistent discourse. This is surely a matter, not of differences in 'social' positioning, but in tenacity of mind. The same tensions which Smith was able to hold under control broke Millar's work into irreconcilable layers.

The intellectual disarray of the final pages of the *Historical View* suggests one reason for Millar's relative lack of influence. His work palpably did not hold together and it did not speak in the new language of economics. The jurisprudential framework in which *The Origin of Ranks* was written became out of date with the appearance of the market analysis of the *Wealth of Nations*. Here was a rare case in which the teacher made the pupil into an anachronism.

More subtly, Millar's own analysis acted to marginalize him. As we have seen, he agreed with Smith and Hume that commercial society had civilized manners in the 'economic sphere'. A free market encouraged relations of justice. And in the 'political sphere', the independence of the rising ranks could be relied on to counterbalance the increasing proliferation of 'police' and bureaucracy. It was in 'the private and intimate relations of human life' that the 'commercial spirit' was working its ravages.[85] To split public and private realms in this way was to reduce the old civic humanist language to an innocuous moralism. If the moral dangers of individualism and the 'commercial spirit' were confined to the private sphere, if neither the economic system nor public liberty were threatened by the untrammelled satisfaction of private needs, it became easier to read Millar's pessimism as a 'vestigial' and 'romantic' jeremiad. This was, I think, how Jeffrey reacted to the final pages of the *Historical View*. Complacently dismissing Millar's fears about the mental mutilation of operatives in the division of labour, Jeffrey argued that liberal sentiments among the leisured middle class were bound to be 'spread by contagion through every order of society'.[86] This sort of remark makes it evident why Dugald Stewart's airy optimism about the march of the mind, coupled with his agnosticism on the franchise question, were much more to the taste of the sophisticated and disenchanted young gentlemen of the *Edinburgh Review* than Millar's pessimistic and old-fashioned republicanism.[87]

It is significant that the *Edinburgh Reviewers* found his historical work 'conjectural' in a new and pejorative sense of the word. He was, Jeffrey said, more tenacious in argument than in the marshalling of fact. Who can deny that this was true of the dissertations at the end of the *Historical View*? Indeed, as history, Millar's work seems to slide from the minutely documented, self-conciously 'scientific' *Ranks* to the sweeping moral jeremiad of the final pages

---

[85] 'Effects of Commerce', p. 255.
[86] *Edinburgh Review*, 3 (1803–4), 154–81; *Edinburgh Review*, 9 (1806–7), 84–7; for the reviewers see John Clive, *Scotch Reviewers* (London, 1957).
[87] Dugald Stewart, *Dissertation Exhibiting the Progress of Metaphysical, Ethical and Political Philosophy since the Revival of Letters in Europe*, in *Collected Works*, i, p. 509; *Elements of the Philosophy of the Human Mind*, in *Collected Works*, ii, pp. 198–9.

of the *Historical View*. It is almost as if the force of his moral disquiet swept him beyond the canons of a new historical method, back to the polemical style of an older vernacular, closer to Ferguson's moralizing in the *History of Civil Society*, than to Book III of the *Wealth of Nations*.

If Millar himself plays a part in 'marginalizing' the moral critique of commercial society which features so prominently in the work of Smith, Ferguson and Millar himself, we can begin to see why, beginning with Horner and Mill and continuing through Ricardo, the 'economics' in Hume and Smith was paired away from their history of manners. If Millar's history of civil society went to show that the moral problem was confined to the private and familiar sphere, it could be hived off as essentially irrelevant to the economic. The Smithian synthesis of economics, politics and history of civil society then began to seem, as Horner put it, like system-building, much better broken down into separate 'treatises'. It would then not be accidental that the moralizing critique of the 'commercial spirit' splits away from the 'dismal science' altogether, finding expression in the vernacular of the Evangelicals, and, in a different register altogether, in the Romantic poets.[88] If this were true, then Millar helps us to see how the Scottish synthesis, momentarily achieved in Smith, contains the seeds of its own disaggregation.

[88] W. Wilberforce, *A Practical View of the Prevailing Religious Systems of Professed Christians* (London, 1797); Coleridge, 'The Present Discontents' (1817), *The Political Thought of Samuel Taylor Coleridge: A Selection*, ed. R. J. White (London, 1938), p. 200.

13 Scottish echoes in eighteenth-century Italy

FRANCO VENTURI

In his *Historical Memoirs of the Life of Suard*, published in Paris in 1820, Dominique-Joseph Garat referred to the arguments aroused in Paris in the 1760s by the publication of Cesare Beccaria's *Of Crimes and Punishments*. He recalled how Suard – one of the most active intermediaries between the Paris of the Encyclopedists and the other European centres of the Enlightenment – dwelt particularly on the impact of the final part of the Milanese philosopher's famous treatise, chapter 41 of the French translation by Morellet. 'This chapter, which Suard re-read in the last days of his life, seemed to possess the prescience of an oracle and Suard, an admirer of the Scottish philosophical school, almost preferred it to Ferguson's *History of Civil Society*, a work remarkable for its merit and utility.'[1] Beccaria's chapter was a dense and compact sketch of the history of human society from the age of 'primitive peoples' to the 'formation of large societies', from the age of faith to the dawn of reason. So tragic and arduous had this passage been that there was good reason to regret all that man had had to abandon in order to make it possible. Particularly 'difficult and terrible' had been the passage from the age of error to the age of reason: 'entire generations' had been sacrificed for the sake of the happiness of those destined to make the sorrowful but necessary transition from the darkness of ignorance to the light of philosophy, from the age of tyranny to the dawn of liberty.'[2] Beccaria's philosophy of history read into the past the anguish of his own age, poised as it was between reform and reaction, an age, therefore, all the more in need of the inspiration of philosophers and men of letters.

It was not surprising that Suard saw parallels between Beccaria's and

---

[1] Dominique-Joseph Garat, *Mémoires historiques sur la vie de M. Suard, sur ses écrits et sur le XVIIIe siècle* (Paris, 1820), ii, pp. 204ff.
[2] Cesare Beccaria, *Dei delitti e delle pene. Con una raccolta di lettere e documenti relativi alla nascita dell'opera e alla sua fortuna nell'Europa del Settecento*, ed. Franco Venturi (Turin, 1973), pp. 96ff. Ch. 41, 'Come si prevengono i delitti', and ch. 42, 'Delle Scienze', were combined into a single one, ch. 41, 'Des moyens de prévenir les crimes', in the Morellet version entitled *Traité des délits et des peines* published in 1767, pp. 267ff. This version was republished in 1797, pp. 173ff.

Ferguson's history. The similarities between Beccaria's ideas and those of the Scottish Enlightenment impressed other contemporaries. The great debate on the death penalty stimulated by Beccaria during his journey to Paris in 1766 drew interventions not only from Voltaire, Morellet, Marmontel and Grimm, but also from the Scottish painter and writer, Allan Ramsay. In January 1766, Ramsay sent to Diderot 'some reflections on the treatise of Crimes and Punishments which you and Suard mentioned at the Baron d'Holbach's during my stay in Paris'. Ramsay could not accept the Lockean and Rousseauian elements in Beccaria's work. He despised its egalitarian spirit, and dismissed the idea of a social contract as 'the product of all the petty grumbling that the liberty of each individual can engender'. Ramsay wished to counter such metaphysical abstractions with historical fact. Instead of indulging in abstract speculations, Beccaria should have tried to establish 'the real origins of different governments and their different laws'. The Beccarian social contract was a fragile foundation on which to build 'an edifice of civil liberty'. 'Political questions cannot be treated by means of geometrical and mathematical abstractions. Laws do not take shape *a priori* from general principles drawn from human nature. Everywhere laws have arisen from the particular needs and circumstances of individual societies.' Reforms had to be suited to each specific society. Hence, for instance, 'those who advocate the suppression of torture, the wheel, impalement, the rack, as well as arbitrary imprisonments and executions, would deprive themselves of their surest means of security and would abandon the state to the mercy of the first bunch of rebels who like better to command than to obey'. A mere fiftieth part of the conflicts which, over twenty years, had led to the fall of Walpole, would have been sufficient in Constantinople to provoke 'the overthrow of the Divan'. Laws were drawn up, not by well-intentioned reformers, 'theoretical philosophers, witty intellectuals, cold examiners of human nature', but always 'at the point of a sword wet with human blood'. It was mere foolishness, therefore, to expect a total transformation of society, 'a universal revolution', a 'general reform' which, in any event, could only be brought about by 'very violent means'. Beccaria's ideas were typical of utopias like Plato's Republic. Certainly the light of reason was not entirely useless: it helped to civilize manners, though even in this case the price to be paid was an ever-increasing corruption. 'In my opinion, the pleadings of sages and philosophers are cries of innocence on the rack, cries which have not and never will save them from perishing, their eyes turned towards the sky. Theirs is a torment which perhaps will excite the enthusiasm, the religious delirium or some other vengeful folly which will accomplish all that their wisdom could not bring about. It is never the sage's pleading which disarms a strong will, but the unintended combination of fortuitous events.'[3]

---

[3] Beccaria, *Dei delitti e delle pene*, pp. 537ff.

This marked hostility to Enlightenment reformism would be worth following in other works by Allan Ramsay – a writer who should, in general, be studied more closely, though in this context he interests us because somehow he was accepted by the Encyclopedist *par excellence*, Diderot himself. It was he who translated and circulated the letter. He did not take responsibility for Ramsay's opinions, but he circulated them because he had his own, more radical reservations about Beccaria's position. Diderot was convinced that the reform of criminal law could not cure society of its inequality, misery and disorder. Giving such importance to the death penalty was to ignore the deaths attributable to medicine itself and to unhealthy cities in which so many people were compelled to live. As he wrote in his 'Observations on the Nakaz [Instruction] of Catherine II', 'In our capital city as few as 150 men are sentenced to death every year. In all the tribunals of France, as many again are sentenced to death. That makes 300 men in a population of 25 million, or one in every 83,000. How much more damage is caused by vice, fatigue, dancing, feasting, common hazards, diseased prostitutes, carriage accidents, falling tiles, common colds, incompetent doctors.'[4] These were serious dangers which everyone ignored in their denunciation of bad criminal laws. In this way Diderot sought to shift attention from Beccaria's immediately attainable reforms towards vague and distant horizons. Only the transformation of the whole society, of humanity itself, would cure the evils which Beccaria had denounced. Not new legislation but a revolution in social relations: so far did Diderot's condemnation of his world take him.

Beccaria's reformism by contrast led him towards an evolutionary and historical vision of human society, towards an increasingly detailed study of the stages through which previous generations had passed, and finally towards a kind of social history of humanity. This paralleled the way of thinking of his Scottish contemporaries and had many points in common with them. Morellet perceived this, reading the *Historical Law Tracts* of Henry Home, Lord Kames, in the French translation by Mathieu-Antoine Bouchaud.[5] The words with which Bouchaud began his *Advertisement* to the French translation could not have been more characteristic: 'the immortal Montesquieu has given us *The Spirit of the Laws*. I introduce an unknown Scottish author who has tried to write their history.' In these pages there was to be found 'the progressive evolution of law in the different periods of world history and in different nations'. However, the translator had decided not to include Kames's chapter on 'the development of English and Scottish law', a subject bound to be 'of only meagre interest to French readers'. Instead he concentrated on the

---

[4] D. Diderot, 'Observations sur le Nakaz', in *Oeuvres politiques*, ed. P. Vernière (Paris, 1963), pp. 395ff.

[5] On this Encyclopedist, see Frank A. Kafker, 'An Encyclopedist Victimized', *Modern Language Review*, (1964), pp. 25ff.

sections in which 'the author expounded the subject from a general point of view'.[6] When Morellet read the Bouchaud translation he immediately noticed the 'family resemblance' the book seemed to have with *Of Crimes and Punishments*. 'Kames is Beccaria's brother', he wrote. But the parallel seemed exaggerated to Bouchaud. 'Mr Beccaria is a philosopher who deals with his subject from the most useful point of view for humanity. My Scot is no more than a jurist who describes with a feeble and sometimes insecure hand the progressive evolution of law in most nations.'[7] Essentially Beccaria was a philosopher and Kames an historian. Morellet, however, was not wrong. A 'family likeness' did connect the Milanese and the Scot. The common element consisted in their attempt to construct a general history of human development based on economics and law, a typology of the systems of production and legal organization in the progress of humanity. In the most recent attempt to describe the eighteenth-century origins and development of this philosophy of history – Ronald Meek's *Social Science and the Ignoble Savage* – Lord Kames is, of course, strongly emphasized while Beccaria is scarcely mentioned, as if he were outside this current of thought.

On the subject, as a matter of fact, Morellet and Suard were right. The proof lies in the notes and fragmentary writings which Beccaria wrote on his return to Milan in 1767. They provide vivid illustration of the parallel development of the Milanese and the Scottish philosopher. These notes, entitled 'Thoughts on the barbarous and civilized state of nations and on the primitive state of man' and 'Thoughts on manners and customs', represent a typically Beccarian attempt to give a utilitarian and almost mathematical definition to the idea of the barbaric and savage stages of society. The first was characterized by ignorance 'of the means available to promote individual happiness', while in the primitive state 'the progress of knowledge made it possible to satisfy such needs as people could conceive', but still denied them 'the order and happiness they were capable of achieving'. 'The greatest happiness of the greatest number', a formula of Scottish origin, was employed by Beccaria and by Verri, not simply to justify reform, but also as a means of interpreting the fundamental forms taken by human society in its development. From this perspective, Beccaria examined the available examples of the 'barbaric' and 'primitive' stages, concluding that 'a nation can be barbaric and primitive, can be primitive and not barbaric, can be very barbaric and highly sociable at the same time'. In the first case ferocity and cannibalism were the norm. An 'equilibrium' of needs characterized the second type of society. The third – combining barbarism and sociability in various forms – posed again the issue

---

[6] *Essais historiques sur les loix. Traduits de l'Anglois par M. Bouchaud, censeur royal et docteur aggregé de la Faculté de Droit, avec des notes et une Dissertation du traducteur* (Paris, 1766).

[7] Morellet's letter is lost. Bouchard's one which quotes the opinions of his correspondent is published in C. Beccaria, *Scritti e lettere inediti*, ed. Eugenio Landry (Milan, 1910), pp. 262ff.

which had constituted the foundation of *Of Crimes and Punishments*, the passage from barbarism to civilization in all its diverse, difficult, even tragic forms. Beccaria's vision was by now sociological and his notes set out a descriptive sketch of all the possible stages of human society.[8]

Beccaria lacked the strength and determination to develop his brief intuitions. But he did not lack external stimulation, particularly from Scotland. Thus on 15 March 1767, the Baron d'Holbach had written to him from Paris: 'In England, a *History of Civil Society* by M. Ferguson is expected shortly, of which they speak very highly -- we shall see if the author has freed himself from the national tendency to Platonism, which makes it very difficult to write good philosophy.'[9] We do not know, however, if Beccaria read Ferguson's work. Beccaria continued on his solitary way, withdrawing increasingly from the friends with whom he had collaborated in the literary journal, *Il Caffè*. He searched for a way to bring together his restless and tormenting ideas into a general vision of the 'science of goodness, usefulness and beauty'.[10] His attention was drawn not to ethics but to aesthetics, to the science of beauty which he set out in his *Studies on the Nature of Style*, published incomplete in 1770, and above all to the science of utility or political economy, to which he dedicated a great part of his efforts in the years after 1769, when he was nominated professor in the subject in Milan. Though recognizing their obvious differences, it is hard not to think of the evolution of Adam Smith's own work, from *The Theory of Moral Sentiments* to the *Inquiry into the Nature and Causes of the Wealth of Nations*. For Beccaria, as for the Enlightenment as a whole, the 'maximum happiness' which seemed to be the core of their conception of mankind eventually revealed its essentially economic content. Beccaria's effort to apply a mathematical approach to social realities proved particularly fruitful and promising when dealing with the wealth of nations. While the historical reconstruction of the passage from rudeness to refinement was arbitrary and conjectural, the dynamics of the economic growth of society could be examined in simple and measurable terms. 'Public economics' was the logical outcome and in some ways the conclusion of Beccaria's research.

In Lombardy the influence of Scottish thinking found echoes in the periodicals of the 1760s and 1770s which continued the tradition of Beccaria and Verri's *Il Caffè*. In the *Estratto delle letteratura europea*, a periodical begun in Switzerland by Fortunato de Felice and subsequently continued in Milan, we find a review of Ferguson's *Essay on the History of Civil Society* in 1767. The reviewer observed, 'Our century has been the first to study man in all his relationships. The book under review fulfils the promise of its title in a highly enlightening manner.'[11]

---

[8] See *Riformatori lombardi, piemontesi e toscani*, in F. Venturi (ed.), *Illuministi italiani* (Milan and Naples, 1958), iii, pp. 106ff.   [9] Beccaria, *Scritti e lettere inediti*, p. 148.
[10] C. Beccaria, *Ricerche intorno alla natura dello stile*, part 1, 'A chi legge', in Venturi, *Illuministi italiani*, iii, p. 125.   [11] *Estratto della letteratura europea*, no. 4 (1767).

Some years later Ferguson's influence reached Milan indirectly through Germany. The *Gazzetta Letteraria* of November 1773 reviewed Christian Garve's German translation of Ferguson's *Institutes of Moral Philosophy*. 'The success of the original work has induced Mr Garve to popularize it in his country, and he has done so in a manner not undeserving of praise.'[12] A year later, in 1774, Lord Monboddo's *The Origin and Progress of Language* was extensively reviewed. 'For a real philosopher there is no subject more suitable and interesting than the one which is announced in the present title.' It was certainly not easy to accept Monboddo's idea that 'speech is not a gift of nature but an aquisition like the arts, so that in his opinion society not only precedes the emergence of language but indeed other arts precede her too'. 'I do not know if this thinking is accepted with much approbation in scholarly circles.' Monboddo's polemic with Locke and his nostalgia for the ancient world also surprised the reviewer. Everything regarding the 'language mechanism' interested the reviewer, as did the paradoxical comparison which Lord Monboddo made between human and animal societies. 'This work', he concluded, 'combines thought and research with paradoxical ideas more fanciful than true. In it appear sparkles of illumination, some new discoveries, and a number of interesting arguments. While this treatise may not give us an exact account of the origin and development of language, its excellent material will make it possible one day to tackle this almost impossible subject.'[13]

Similar interest was aroused by the *Sketches of the History of Man* by Lord Kames, published in 1774 and mentioned the same year in the *Gazzetta Letteraria* of Milan. The question which the author had asked himself was interesting: 'Are there different races of man, or is there a common origin for them all?' The monogenetic origin suggested by Lord Kames seemed 'strange and more pleasing than true'. The reviewer thought that the treatment of the problem of property was more persuasive, even though he was sceptical about the possibility of writing the history of such a principle in all its stages of progress. The material on commerce was convincing but when the author dealt with the 'development of taste and the fine arts', it did not appear 'as interesting' and indeed often seemed 'very superficial'. 'Among the essays, the best was the last, full of meaning and elegance.' 'The author describes the gradual progress of women from their unhappy condition in primitive society to the present status they enjoy in civilized nations.' 'This work', he considered, 'deserves to be read, though it could have been improved.'[14] Editorial carelessness perhaps allowed a second review of this work to appear in the same magazine a year later. This time, the pages in which Lord Kames dealt with population attracted attention. The reviewer also pointed out

[12] *Gazzetta letteraria*, no. 46 (17 November 1773).
[13] *Ibid.*, no. 18 (4 May 1774).   [14] *Ibid.*, no. 41 (12 October 1774).

Kames's treatment of the slow and halting development of technology in the medieval period, making frequent reference of his own to the work of Muratori. Sometimes the moralism of the author struck the reviewer as excessive: 'if mothers do not feed and bring up their children, it is the fault of society and its customs, which they can do nothing to change'.[15]

The history of man in society was at the centre of Beccaria's and the Lombard writers' attention when they turned to the Scottish Enlightenment for stimulation, debate and suggestion. In Venice, by contrast, the economic and political dimension was the central focus. It is above all David Hume's echo that we can hear in Venice.[16] In 1767, two important Venetian booksellers, Gianmaria Bassaglia and Luigi Pavini, published a collection of Hume's essays which deserves to be closely examined and to be placed in the political context of the Serenissima Republic of those years. First of all, it is striking that the collection was bilingual.[17] The translator himself sent a copy to the author with a note in French: 'Your political essays on commerce are read extensively by all scholars. This has prompted me to translate them into Italian to render a service to the public... I also hope to publish your essay on population, which it will be my pleasure to present to you.'[18] In the most important Venetian magazine of those years, the *Giornale d'Italia*, this work was mentioned as a 'noble example of patriotic devotion, worthy of a young descendant of the ancient and illustrious Dandolo family'.[19] The *Magazzino Italiano* also congratulated the 'young gentleman, Matteo Dandolo, noble Venetian' for his edition and translation before going on to an extensive analysis of Hume's ideas.[20] The Scottish philosopher's thinking fitted in at a particularly important moment in Venetian life, in the decade which began with the 'correzione' or constitutional reform of 1760–1. The 'correzione' was intended to give back power to the Maggior Consiglio (Great Council), while diminishing or even eliminating the authority of the Inquisitori (state Inquisitors) and of the

---

[15] *Ibid.*, no. 35 (30 August 1775).
[16] On Hume's work in Italy, see G. Tarabuzzi, 'Echi italiani settecenteschi della storiografia inglese', *Archivio storico italiano*, 505 (1980).
[17] The permit to print had been granted on 18 March 1767 by the public censor Natal delle Laste and by the *riformatori dello studio* of Padua, Sebastiano Giustinian, Andrea Tron and Girolamo Grimani. On the censorship policy of those years, see F. Venturi, *Settecento Riformatore*, ii, *La chiesa e la repubblica dentro i loro limiti* (Turin, 1976), pp. 122ff. On the most famous of these *riformatori*, see G. Tabacco, *Andrea Tron (1712–1785) e la crisi dell'aristocrazia senatoria a Venezia*, 2nd edn (Udine, 1980).
[18] The letter is in 'Hume Papers', Royal Society of Edinburgh, vol. 4, fol. 50, and it is published by Ronald Grimsley and Daisy D. Ronco, 'Corrispondenti italiani di David Hume', *Rivista critica di storia della filosofia*, 20 (1965), 411ff. The authors of this article have read the date of the letter as 2 May 1762. It should probably be changed to 2 May 1767.
[19] *Giornale d'Italia spettante alla scienza naturale e principalmente all'agricoltura e al commercio*, no. 10 (5 September 1767). The review continued in no. 11 (12 September), and in no. 15 (10 October).
[20] *Magazzino italiano*, no. 3 (June 1767); no. 4 (July 1767). On this and other magazines, see M. Berengo (ed.), *Giornali veneziani del settecento* (Milan, 1962).

Consiglio dei Dieci (Council of Ten). This was the decade in which Marco Foscarini, the most influential intellectual in the Republic, was nominated as Doge, without being able to carry through a real reform of Venetian institutions. It was then that a complex reform movement developed both in the provinces and in the city itself to modify the economic structure of the Republic, to modernize agriculture and to replace the antiquated system of craft guilds. After 1765 the reform movement became engaged in a challenge to the relationship between church and state, making Venice the centre of the anti-clericalism which in those years was alive all over Italy and throughout the whole of Catholic Europe from Portugal to Poland.

The Venetian edition of Hume's political essays began with a letter to 'his excellency Alvise Emo, son of the late Giovanni, procurator of San Marco' – the brother of Angelo Emo, the reformer and admiral of the Venetian Navy, famed for his successful expeditions against the Barbary pirates and for other campaigns in the Mediterranean. Alvise Emo was also to play a leading role in Venetian political life. In 1774–5 he was to be the champion of another 'correzione' of the old political structure of the Republic. Nobody else, Matteo Dandolo told him, could have understood Hume's political economy better than 'you a citizen of a country which was the emporium of Europe and which thanks to our workmanship and our ancient enterprising spirit was able to attain glory and wealth from all over the world'. Undoubtedly these 'happy days' when Venice was 'great, rich and glorious' were now over, with the discovery of the Cape route. This alone, however, was not responsible for the change in Venice's fortunes. 'Her decline would not have been so rapid if our merchants had cared to maintain the balance of trade.' Now that centuries had gone by, the only way forward lay in 'improving our products'. Why do we not try to 'revive our commerce on foreign markets and make it flourishing and strong once again'? This was not a rhetorical question. 'I think I can see the reason very clearly', Dandolo wrote. 'Three centuries ago, to be a merchant was the privilege of wealthy and great men.' Then with the acquisition of new possessions on the Venetian plain, the Venetians had turned their energies and investment towards the land and had preferred to live there even on less income as secure estate proprietors than to expose their wealth to the risks of the waves. Nowadays, 'as the most enlightened can attest', commerce is all 'in the hands of strangers who lack the necessary boldness or in the hands of Venetians who lack the necessary capital'. 'Boldness was lacking.' 'Our merchants...when they have gained sufficient wealth disdain further effort, persuaded that by renouncing trade, they will rise to a superior condition.' Thus an increasingly harmful gap had developed between 'estate proprietors' and 'merchants'. 'Our indifference...leads me to suspect that proprietors have lost interest in promoting commerce.' They had not considered the depopulation and the general impoverishment which would finally afflict their own lands as well. How could one fail to understand that a flourishing commerce increased 'the value of our estates'? The economic responsibility of the landowners required them to shoulder a political one as well. 'Finally let us consider that we are bound to our country with stronger feelings than those who do not possess estates... We are the most deeply established of our countrymen.' Matteo Dandolo, however, did not propose a programme of agricultural improvement or a transformation of social relations in the countryside, but a resumption and reorganization of commerce. 'I believe that commerce with other foreign countries is the real barometer of public wealth and strength.' For this reason he turned to the 'illustrious Emo family', 'whose love of the Republic runs in their blood'.

By introducing Hume's essays, therefore, Dandolo intended to promote a new economic relation between proprietors and merchants. The glorious Venetian past held his gaze for a moment, but it was to England that he turned for a model of the future. England had been able to combine agriculture and exports, landed property and manufacture, sharing political responsibility among the aristocracy and merchants alike. He hoped that his two small volumes – either in English 'the language of fashion' or in translation – would be read in this light. His edition included the essays 'Of Commerce', 'Of Refinement in the Arts', 'Of Money', 'Of Interest', 'Of the Balance of Trade', 'Of Taxes', and 'Of Public Credit'. As one can see, the economic essays are the same ones which Rotwein published under the title *Writings on Economics* in 1955. The only difference is that Rotwein also included 'Of the Populousness of Ancient Nations', arguing that demography formed part of the modern conception of economics. Dandolo had also intended to translate this essay. Hume's political writings were excluded partly perhaps for censorial reasons, but more probably because Venetian preoccupations in those years guided Dandolo to a selection of the economic rather than the political essays. Only through economics would it have been possible to restore Venice's strength. As Hume himself pointed out, a new relation between 'husbandmen' and 'manufacturers' was crucial. At the centre of his ideas, as Guiseppe Giarrizzo has written, was 'the conflict of interests between merchants and landed gentry'.[21] How could the Venetian aristocracy not be interested in the second essay, 'Of Luxury', later retitled 'Of Refinement in the Arts', in which Hume tried to trace the historical origins of the military weakness and 'degeneracy' of the Italian people? Or in which he tried to establish the relationship between luxury and political liberty? Or again, in his essay 'Of the Balance of Trade', in which he examined what had happened 'when Lisbon and Amsterdam got the East Indian trade from Venice and Genoa'.[22] On page

---

[21] G. Giarrizzo, *David Hume politico e storico* (Turin, 1962), p. 47.
[22] *Ibid.*, p. 70, note 39. On all these problems see D. Forbes, *Hume's Philosophical Politics* (Cambridge, 1975).

after page of his writings, however difficult they were to interpret, the Venetian people could project their own preoccupations. Nor could they fail to notice the admiration Hume expressed for their Republic. If in Hume's opinion the Polish represented the worst of aristocracies, the Venetian seemed to him the most stable, as he had written in the essay 'That politics may be reduced to a science', which Dandolo did not include in his collection.

Dandolo's edition had considerable success even outside Venice. A second edition was published in 1774 in Palermo, edited by Andrea Rapetti, a Venetian bookseller who had emigrated to Sicily, and edited by Isidoro Bianchi, a Cremonese professor at Monreale. In his 'Preliminary Discourse' Isidoro Bianchi recalled the glories of Sicilian commerce in centuries past and concluded with a passionate exhortation to reform all aspects of the island's economic life. It was with commerce that they would have to start, just as in Venice. This was 'the real source of our riches and our splendour'. If commerce were not expanded and crafts improved, 'merchants and artisans will languish and so too will the estate owners, till the decline of the whole state ensues'.[23] Many years after in 1798, a new edition of Hume's essays was published with introductions by Matteo Dandolo and Isidoro Bianchi.[24]

Matteo Dandolo's further activity after 1767 reveals more clearly the ideas and motives which had prompted him to translate and publish Hume's essays. In 1769 he edited a collection of Rousseau's writings, with the title *Thoughts of an Illustrious Modern Philosopher*.[25] In 1771 there appeared his selection from the Encyclopédie, *The Spirit of the Encyclopédie chosen from the famous Dictionary with notes and illustrations by Matteo Dandolo, Venetian nobleman*.[26] In 1773, when he was 32, he was elected to the Consiglio dei quaranta (Council of Forty) and took an increasingly active part in the growing conflicts which divided the Venetian aristocracy. An active member of the Masonic Lodge of Padua, a follower of Georgio Pisani, the leader of the impoverished aristocracy and the most energetic organizer of the struggle against the senatorial oligarchy, Dandolo was to be arrested and confined for six months in a villa in the village of San Bruson near Dolo. It seems that he was the author or at least a contributor with Luigi Gonzaga di Castiglione to a pamphlet which appeared in 1780, entitled *Political and Philosophical Reflections on the ancient Democracy of Rome, addressed to all free nations, dedicated to the English people*. He praised 'the brave and noble Italian tribes' who in their war against Rome had been 'precursors of the Anglo-Americans' in founding a federation in the name of the common good against the exclusive ambition of the Roman Senate. Their just determination to uphold their rights served as a memorable example of

[23] *Saggi politici sul commercio del signor David Hume*, 2nd edn (Venice and Palermo, 1774), p. xii. See the review in the Roman magazine *Efemeridi Letterarie* (28 May 1774).
[24] *Saggi politici sopra il commercio del signor David Hume* (Reggio and Parma, 1798).
[25] See the review by Domenico Caminer in *Europa letteraria* (May 1769).
[26] See the review in the Palermo magazine *Notizie di letterati* (3 November 1772).

national courage.²⁷ In this pamphlet we can detect a trace of an atmosphere not alien to Hume's own. The pamphlet included a letter written from Geneva on 14 October 1780 by an English writer, Pat Clason, maintaining that the defence of the people in these pages 'was above suspicion'. 'It is not envy which has inspired you, as it has often inspired common men against great ones. It is a magnificent spectacle to see the most noble aristocracy of Europe aroused in the defence of humanity.'²⁸ These words referred to Luigi Gonzaga di Castiglione, but they could also have been addressed to Matteo Dandolo. It is sufficient to recall Lafayette to understand the importance that American events had for the European aristocracy. In Venice, the constitutional reform movement led by Giorgio Pisani, Carlo Contarini and Matteo Dandolo mobilized the descendants of the most ancient and illustrious families of the Republic in the name of an ideal that Gonzaga did not hesitate to call 'democratic liberty'. We ought not to be surprised to find Matteo Dandolo, a few years later, aligning himself with those in Venice who wished to follow the example of the French Revolution.²⁹

As far as Tuscany is concerned, we shall confine our attention to a single but significant point. It was Tuscany which first welcomed the historical writings of William Robertson, later to enjoy extraordinary success in Italy. Gianfranco Tarabuzzi, who has recently reconstructed this event, has written that 'in 1765 William Robertson's *Preliminary Notes Concerning the History of Scotland Before the Death of James V* was published in Siena with a false Amsterdam imprint. It was the translation of the first book of his *History of Scotland*. The translation was by the Tuscan Pietro Crocchi, who in those years was the Italian teacher of the young John Mountstuart, eldest son of Lord Bute.'³⁰ In his 'Notes to the Reader', Crocchi said that surely in Italy, a 'country famed for its historians', Robertson's work would be welcomed, as he had examined the feudal system 'with masterly strength and veracity, in such a way that the picture of the whole situation deserves to capture the attention of any reader who likes to think for himself; it can still be useful in showing the origins of nearly all of the monarchies of Europe founded on the ruins of the Roman Empire in those centuries in which feudal institutions were in force'.³¹

²⁷ Quoted by Piero del Negro, 'Il mito americano nella Venezia del settecento', *Memorie della classe di scienze morali, storiche e filologiche* (Rome, Accademia dei Lincei), 8th ser., 18 (1975), 538ff.
²⁸ *Riflessioni filosofico-politiche sull'antica aristocrazia romana* (Venice, 1780), p. 128. On Pat Clason, see the letter of D. Hume to A. Smith, 1772, in *The Letters of David Hume*, ed. J. Y. T. Greig, 2 vols. (Oxford, 1932), ii, p. 262.
²⁹ Marino Berengo, *La società veneta alla fine del Settecento* (Florence, 1955), pp. 267ff. A brief biography of Matteo Dandolo can be found in Girolamo Dandolo, *La caduta della Repubblica di Venezia* (Venice, 1855-7), p. 99. On his Masonic activity, see Carlo Francovich, *Storia della massoneria in Italia dalle origini alla rivoluzione francese* (Florence, 1974).
³⁰ Gianfranco Tarabuzzi, 'Le traduzioni italiane Settecentesche delle opere di William Robertson', *Rivista storica italiana*, 91 (1979), 487ff.
³¹ *Notizie preliminari alla storia di Scozia avanti la morte di Giacomo V nelle quali si contiene un succinto*

In the introduction, Crocchi also referred to the work of David Hume, 'one of the most vivid geniuses of this century'. Through James Boswell, whom Crocchi had taught Italian, he transmitted a copy of his translation of Robertson's work to David Hume, and in the accompanying letter he wrote that by introducing the Italian people to the work of the Scottish historian, he intended to 'make Italy acquainted with the genius and merit of so famous a writer'.[32]

Venice and Siena contended for the honour of publishing the Italian version of another and more famous work by Robertson. Already in 1771, while announcing the French translation of his *View of the Progress of Society in Europe*, the Florentine *Notizia Letterarie* reported that this work contained 'the most exact history of feudal law yet written'.[33] However, the reviewer could not help criticizing the anti-Catholic polemic in the Scottish historian's work. This constituted the major obstacle in Italy to the acceptance of his *History of the Reign of Charles V*, a version of which was published in Venice in 1774. However, in Venice, intelligent Italian readers were struck mainly by Robertson's interpretation of feudalism. The Vicenzan lawyer Giovanni Scola, in an important review in the *Giornale Enciclopedico* which appeared in Venice in 1775, compared Robertson with Vico.[34] Scola recommended Robertson's description of the historical evolution of 'political institutions' to statesmen, while to jurists he commended the light cast on the feudal mind in barbarous centuries; and he also recommended it to 'noblemen who did not let themselves be puffed up by adulation and pomp'. They would certainly find material in it 'to gratify their minds'. After having compared the interpretation of feudalism offered by Vico, Hume and Robertson, Scola gave a lively picture of the political and social transformations which had allowed 'the Italian cities to break their chains and to revive the municipal self-government enjoyed under the Romans'. Then the Italian spirit of liberty had passed to other European nations.[35]

Between 1778 and 1780 a Sienese bookseller, Francesco Rossi, published Robertson's *History of Scotland under the Reigns of Mary Stuart and James IV* in four volumes. The anonymous translator was a great admirer of Robertson, even if his reservations about his religious views made him leave out some pages of

ragguaglio dell'origine, de' progressi e della decadenza del sistema del governo feudale, del sig. dottore Guglielmo Robertson rettore dell' Università di Edimburgo (Amsterdam [Siena], 1765), 'Avviso al Lettore'.

[32] Tarabuzzi, *Le traduzioni italiane settecentesche*, p. 488. The quotation of Crocchi's letter is taken from Grimsley and Ronco, 'Corrispondenti italiani di David Hume', p. 410.

[33] *Notizie letterarie*, no. 43 (26 October 1771). For an argument on the same problems from a different point of view, see F. Venturi, 'From Scotland to Russia: an eighteenth-century debate on feudalism', in A. G. Cross (ed.), *Great Britain and Russia in the Eighteenth Century: Contacts and Comparisons* (Newtonville, Mass., 1979), pp. 2–24.

[34] *Giornale enciclopedico*, no. 3 (March 1775); no. 4 (1775). This text has been reprinted in the anthology edited by M. Berengo, *Giornali veneziani*, pp. 376ff.

[35] Tarabuzzi, *Le traduzioni italiane settecentesche*, p. 497.

the original. Nevertheless, the Scottish historian was in his opinion 'a patriotic citizen who had devoted his life to the noble ambition of writing the first accurate history of his country'.[36] The complete edition of the *History of Scotland* was published in Venice a few years later and not without various kinds of difficulties. In 1778 Pietro Antoniutti from Friuli completed a translation, but only three years later the public censor, Gasparo Gozzi, and the reformers of the university of Padua, Alvise Vallaresso, Andrea Tron and Gerolamo Guistiniani, granted permission to the Venetian editor, Giovanni Gatti, to print it with a false London imprint. Another bookseller interfered and tried to obtain this authorization for himself. It was only in 1784 that Giovanni Gatti was able to market his *History*. The translator maintained that Robertson's work, in contrast to those of other historians, contained 'philosophical reflections on human feeling and action'. Its philosophical character interested him particularly, and this fact led him to translate Hume's *History of England*, although the translation never saw the light.[37] The vivid interest which greeted the historical works of Scottish philosophers in those years found a further confirmation in the great success enjoyed by Robertson's *History of America*, translated by Antonio Pillori, published in Florence by Allegrini and Pisoni in 1777 and 1778 in four volumes.[38]

As far as Rome is concerned, the example I will cite might appear unexpected. It was in the capital of the Papal States itself that Smith's *Wealth of Nations* was discussed for the first time, and with particular depth and intelligence.[39] In 1776 a writer named Luigi Riccomanni succeeded in setting up a weekly magazine entitled *Diario economico di agricoltura, manifatture e commercio* (Economic diary of agriculture, manufacture and commerce), making it into one of the best magazines published in Italy on the various economic and social problems of the Peninsular States. Riccomanni was born in Sabina and came to Rome towards the end of 1766 to practise law. Nominally he was a cleric but there was nothing ecclesiastical about him, since he was a married man with children. In 1775 we find him involved in the diffusion of technical knowledge in connection with the agricultural academy of Treja, one of the most energetic of the economic societies established everywhere in Europe, even in the Papal States in that period. He was in contact with Turin, Florence and the Veneto, and he took his models from England, France and Poland as well. In his examination of the Italian past he argued that in former centuries the 'revival of literature and arts' had corresponded with the resumption of agriculture and commerce. In his *Diario* he published the latest news of discoveries and promising experiments on everything from the potato to the

[36] Mentioned *ibid.*, p. 490.
[37] *Ibid.*, pp. 491ff.   [38] *Ibid.*, pp. 501ff.
[39] See Oslavia Vercillo, 'Della conoscenza di Adamo Smith in Italia nel XVIII secolo', *Economia e storia*, 3 (1963), 416ff., and F. Venturi, 'Elementi e tentativi di riforme nello Stato pontificio del Settecento', *Rivista storica italiana*, 75, no. 4 (1963), 800ff.

improvement of vineyards, from peat to drainage. What was more important to him, however, was to relate technological renewal to more general economic and political problems. Already in the issue of 10 February 1776 of his *Diario* we find an article on English and French manufactures in which, following Hume, he underlined the importance of developing manufactures in France and praised Colbert's work. But he insisted on the price France had had to pay for Colbert's success. His policies had 'driven the farmers to desert the countryside for the production of luxuries and the development of a precarious commerce, thereby weakening the agriculture which the great Sully had made into a source of wealth for France far more secure than that of the mines of Mexico and Peru'. Thus, Colbert or Sully? As in the Paris of the 1770s, where Colbert and Sully were made to stand for Turgot and Necker, in Rome too the ministers of Henry IV and Louis XIV became the symbols of two different policies. Riccommani knew how difficult it was to choose, but he ended up cautiously siding with a policy which considered agriculture as of primary importance, as the *sine qua non* of general development. Thus Sully rather than Colbert.[40] But in which direction and at what price? Riccomanni turned with great interest to 'the real principles of economic science' of Le Trosne, a typical Physiocrat.[41] However, he also looked favourably on the attempt to introduce new manufactures, woollens in particular, into the Papal States.[42] In his reading of Pietro Verri, Hume and Condillac he searched for a middle path between agriculture and commerce. And he was the first Italian to place particular faith in 'an illustrious work published this year in London by Adam Smith, doctor in laws and member of the Royal Society, in two volumes in quarto with the following title: *An Inquiry into the Nature and Causes of the Wealth of Nations*'.[43] He found confirmation in it of his conviction that it was not gold but an improved agriculture, an active and enlightened industry and constant and wisely distributed labour which constitutes the real wealth of nations. This was a maxim which he would have liked to see 'engraved in the hearts of our statesmen and specially of those (and there are many!) who choose to languish in indolence and inactivity'. He could only approve of Smith's concept of economic value.

He observes with great wisdom that the annual labour of every nation is the only foundation on which she can rely for the necessities and comforts of life, either by the product of labour itself or by what it enables her to import from other nations. And thus in consequence a people will be supplied with all their natural or artificial needs according to whether the supply of such products or what can be brought with them is in proportion to its population.

Riccomanni was also convinced by what he had read about the division of

---

[40] *Diario economico di agricoltura, manifatture e commercio*, no. 6 (10 February 1776), and no. 26 (28 June 1777).
[41] *Ibid.*, no. 44 (2 November 1776).
[42] *Ibid.*, no. 1 (4 January 1777).
[43] *Ibid.*, no. 3 (18 January 1777).

labour, and he quoted extensively from the famous example of pin-making. He paid attention to Smith's remarks on the distribution of labour 'and the importance of the size of the market'.[44] He approved of the passage in which the Scottish philosopher had described 'the deplorable state of Europe after the fall of the Roman Empire' and in which he had charted 'the origin and growth of towns', as well as 'the influence of their commerce on the culture of the countryside'. On this point he saw a problem which interested him particularly: should merchants invest their capital in the countryside? Did the merchants have the capacity to become able landowners? 'Pardon us, Mr Smith, if this conviction of yours seems a little weak to us. Is a merchant, who leaves his counter to cultivate the land, acquainted with the laws of agriculture? A landowner born in the countryside will make double the improvements on the same amount of capital.' And yet Smith seemed to be right on one point; 'the merchant who abandons commerce generally has much more capital than the ordinary run of landowner'. Surely history had demonstrated the importance of investment and initiative issuing from the cities. 'Mr Smith presents his views with such clarity that he deserves praise.'[45] Besides 'almost all modern historians had pointed out the positive effects which had followed the emancipation of the municipalities'. The same spirit had inspired the best legislators, such as 'the last king of Sardinia, of glorious memory, who had ordered the emancipation of those of his people still subjected to various forms of slavery' – a reference to Carlo Emmanuele III's abolition of feudal slavery in Savoy in 1770. Adam Smith had written that feudal law 'far from extending the authority of the allodial lords had reduced and limited it'. A questionable idea, wrote Riccomanni, but one which could be clarified by deeper research into the 'origin of feuds'. 'The differences of opinion on this subject are sufficient proof that it has not yet been fully investigated.'

From these historical and legal aspects of Smith's work, Riccomanni turned to economic problems, repeatedly citing Smith's views on 'the mercantile and agricultural systems'. Here, too, especially on the role of state intervention in the economy, the reviewer was not without his doubts. He concluded that 'fixed and perpetual bounties do not generally cause the effects one expects, while temporary bounties strengthen a weakened economy or one which has taken a bad turn'.[46] As far as Smith's ideas on 'the agricultural system' were concerned, he thought they could serve as a common ground for reconciling the various schools which till then had divided France and other countries. 'As a result we should neglect neither cultivation nor commerce': a wise policy would certainly reconcile the supporters of Sully and Colbert in France. On this subject, too, a historical view was indispensable. When Sully had come to power, 'France was uncultivated and in a state of complete devastation.'

[44] *Ibid.*, no. 4 (25 January 1777). [45] *Ibid.*, no. 5 (1 February 1777).
[46] *Ibid.*, no. 6 (8 February 1777).

It would have been folly to make her rich through commerce before first giving her the bread which she needed. Can one trade before possessing the raw materials which are essential to commerce? Under Colbert's government France already had food in abundance, and he would have been foolish to have increased the production of agriculture without thinking how to provide a market for its product. On the other hand, Riccomanni found Smith's section on the public debt defective and disappointing. 'Without a doubt it would have been better to get rid of it altogether, but Smith was unable to devise suitable means.'

Scottish thought had a complex influence on the ferment of the Neapolitan Enlightenment in the 1770s and 1780s. The disciples of Antonio Genovesi, the whole of the second generation of southern Enlightenment thinkers – from Giuseppe Galanti to Francesantonio Grimaldi, from Gaetano Filangeri to Francesco Mario Pagano – tried to fuse Hume, Ferguson and Robertson's insights with the local historical tradition of Pietro Giannone and Giambattista Vico as well as with Montesquieu, Voltaire, Rousseau and Nicolas-Antoine Boulanger. Scotland was an indispensable point of reference and comparison. In Giuseppe Galanti's opinion, Vico did not explain 'the progress of nations' even though his work displayed 'the highest wisdom, deep research and enormous erudition'. Nor could Giannone, for all his merit, be chosen as a guide. 'We have admired the *Civil History* for want of a better model.'[47] In France as well as in Great Britain, a new conception of history was coming to light thanks to Hume, Robertson, and Voltaire, and he (Galanti) intended to follow and develop it. Accordingly he translated the *Éléments d'histoire générale* by a follower of Voltaire, Claude François Millot. Beginning with the first volume, Galanti added observations taken from authors such as Condillac, Chastellux and from 'an English work entitled *Essay on Civil Society* by M. Ferguson, professor of moral philosophy in Edinburgh University'. Of this work, he chose a part of the third chapter of the second book to underline how 'important it is to understand the customs and principles of the barbarians who have founded so many of the modern monarchies'. Other sections, taken from Robertson's *History of Charles V* 'translated from the English', formed another indispensable complement. Then in 1782, when he reached the medieval period, he found Millot's work totally inadequate. Galanti published an appendix to clarify the meaning of feudalism. He turned once again to Condillac and Chastellux but above all to Hume, translating the dissertation on feudal government from the *History of England* and drawing at length from Robertson's *A View of the Progress of Society in Europe*.[48] Galanti's work was an

---

[47] These and other similar judgements are found in the *Elogio storico del signor abate Antonio Genovesi* which Giuseppe Galanti published in Naples in 1772 after long arguments with the censors. See 'Nota introduttiva' on Giuseppe Maria Galanti in *Riformatori napoletani*, in Venturi, *Illuministi italiani*, v, pp. 941ff.

[48] Tarabuzzi, *Le traduzioni italiane settecentesche*, pp. 498ff.

important attempt to shift the problem of feudalism from the field of law to that of history. The editor's foreword stressed that the 'nature of feudal government had stimulated an infinite number of modern writers to investigate its laws and to analyse its constitution'. Feudalism had become 'more interesting in our age than any other remote period'. The dissertation written by 'the immortal Hume' on the same subject seemed particularly illuminating. 'The name of the author is sufficient praise for the work and guarantees the excellence of its standards and the profundity of its doctrines.' Hume's was a historical vision with a conservative element in it, too, a polemic against the hopes and the most extreme ideas of the Enlightenment. Scottish thinking was for Galanti not only a historiographic model, but also an example of political moderation.

We could say something similar about Francesco Grimaldi, the author of *Reflections on Inequality among Men*, published in Naples between 1779 and 1780.[49] Starting from the contrast between the necessity of equality and the hard reality of inequality, he found a way out in the idea of progress in history. Human society was founded on inequality, but some steps could be taken towards greater social justice. Guided by Voltaire and Ferguson, he attacked the idea of a state of nature and 'natural man' at the beginning of his second volume. For several years, he wrote, the philosophical mania for natural man and the state of nature had shown signs of subsiding. Voltaire and Ferguson were the first to declare this idea a useless dream. From Ferguson he drew the fundamental ideas of his psychology: 'the natural state of man is in society, in this state we need to study him, to know him as he really is, for outside of it he is a chimera, or the sole exception to the laws established by nature'. Rousseau would have been on the right track if he had said that 'nature progresses from the savage to the civilized state'. Grimaldi dedicated most of his volume to an outline of the general history of humanity, describing 'the moral state of the first family groups', 'the savage tribe', 'the barbarous and civilized nations', widely quoting travellers and philosophers as well as historians such as Hume and Robertson.

More tortuous was the path taken by Francesco Mario Pagano, one of the central figures of the southern eighteenth century, a philosopher and jurist destined to give his life in the attempt to carry the reforming ideas of the Enlightenment into the Neapolitan revolution of 1799.[50] Pagano's own thought derived from the humanism of Vico, but until the 1780s his work still bore the tone and colour of remote provinces and stagnant traditions. Nevertheless, an exceptional moral and political conviction inspired him. Under the influence of Antonio Genovesi, Pagano became a reformer committed to a profound transformation of southern society. In 1783 he published the first

---

[49] 'Nota introduttiva' on Francesco Grimaldi, in Venturi, *Illuministi italiani*, v, pp. 509ff.
[50] 'Nota introduttiva' on Mario Pagano, in *ibid.*, pp. 785ff.

edition of his *Saggi politici* (Political Essays), his most original work. It began with a passionate study of the social consequences of the dreadful earthquake which that year had destroyed Calabria. He sensed that an overpowering demand for equality and justice was rising from the depths, amidst the ruins and the mourning. Boulanger helped him to understand the elemental and powerful instincts in men thrown back into savagery by the unleashing of the earthquake. From Vico he took the idea of the *ritorno*, the eternal cycles of development and recurrence in social change. Hume and Ferguson, whom he only quoted in the second edition of his essays in 1792, guided him towards the ideas of development and progress. In 1785 the *Novelle letterarie*, the most important literary magazine in Florence, remarked upon the influence of Scottish thought in Pagano's writings. In the issue of 23 September, they compared his writings to Hume's 'except for a certain historical thread which does not appear in Hume's *Essays* and which it seems the lawyer Pagano owes to the *Essay on Civil Society*, the much praised work of Ferguson, another professor of moral philosophy'.[51]

In reality, the Scottish influence on Pagano was more than a matter of literary connections. It was in the logic of his position itself. Fired both by curiosity about the primitive world and by his reformist convictions he could not avoid meeting the Scottish philosophers. There was in him something of the 'Platonism' which d'Holbach had noticed in the thought of the Edinburgh writers. Nor was it alien to Pagano's thought to rediscover through the study of art the relation between primitive and civilized which could not be grasped simply in terms of the progressive development of humanity. The power of the imagination came into its own again, in various forms, in a world that wanted to be dominated by reason. Introducing the second edition of his *Saggi*, he declared himself a follower of 'the divine science' created by Voltaire, Robertson, Hume, Gibbon, Mably and Ferguson, to follow the order in which he listed them. Through them he found his political faith reaffirmed. Profoundly democratic, he denounced every kind of oligarchy or privilege for the most powerful and wealthy. For him reform represented an attempt to establish legal rather than economic or political equality. Everyone had the right to live and prosper, but the virtuous, the enlightened alone had to be in charge of public welfare. Platonic in his vision of justice and humanity, Pagano was Aristotelian in his search for virtue 'among middle-class citizens': he sought, not privileges, for the enlightened strata, but rather the precise definition of their function as the political and social leaders of Naples and of eighteenth-century Italy as a whole.

[51] *Novelle letterarie*, no. 38 (23 September 1785).

Index

Aberdeen, 56, 67; *see also* Aberdeen Philosophical Society: King's College; Marischal College
Aberdeen Philosophical Society, 105, 110, 281n
Addison, Joseph, 180, 188–9, 198, 199, 200, 202, 241, 265, 280n; Addisonian morality, 182, 251
agriculture: balance between manufacturing and, 21–2, 71, 303–5, 358–60; reform of Scottish, 46–7, 55, 57–8, 142, 144–5
allegiance, theory of, 80, 81, 84, 153
American independence, 51, 239, 328, 331, 334
American perception of history, 239–40, 244, 252
Amhurst, Nicholas, 95
ancient constitutionalism, 145–6, 147, 325, 326
Antoniutti, Pietro, 357
Appleby, J. O., 122n, 280n
approval, need for, 11–12, 183–6, 339
Aquinas, Saint Thomas, 26–8, 36n, 79, 247
Arbuckle, James, 94–5, 96, 97
Arendt, Hannah, 243
Aristotle, 26, 27, 33, 34, 139n; Aristotelianism, 138, 257; neo-Aristotelians, 243
artisanal radicalism, 322–4, 325, 326–7
atheism, 119–20
Avery, Benjamin, 105
Ayr Bank crisis, 51, 66, 70

Bacon, Francis, 96, 106, 113, 148n, 206
Bagehot, Walter, 253
Bailyn, Bernard, 245–6
bankruptcy, 168, 169, 292n
banks, banking, 276, 278, 290, 294n, 298; Scottish, 56, 69–70, 278, 294n, 298n; *see also* credit; paper money

Bankton, Lord (A. McDouall), 224–5
Barbeyrac, Jean, 36n, 38n, 40, 76, 77n, 78, 81, 82, 83, 84
Basil of Caesarea, Saint, 27
Bassaglia, Gianmaria, 351
Bayle, P., 84
Beattie, James, 181, 281n
Beccaria, Cesare, 214, 345–9, 351
Bell, George Joseph, 224
benevolence, 8, 11, 23, 24, 31, 266, 320; *see also* charity
Bentham, Jeremy, 210, 214, 215, 221n, 222
Berkeley, George, 11, 93, 99, 100, 101, 290, 291n, 333
Bianchi, Isidoro, 354
Birch, Thomas, 105
Black, Joseph, 58
Blackstone, William, 205, 207, 208, 215, 220, 221, 225, 226, 227, 231, 326
Blackwell, Thomas, the younger, 105, 106, 108
Blair, Hugh, 100, 306n
Bolingbroke, Henry St John, Viscount, 206
Boswell, James, 119, 313n, 356
Bouchaud, Mathieu-Antoine, 347–8
Boulanger, Nicolas-Antoine, 360, 362
Bracton, Henry de, 207n
British Linen Company, 69–70
Brougham, Henry, 315
Brown, John, 289, 290
Buchanan, George, 94, 98, 111, 145
Burgh, James, 326, 333–4
Burke, Edmund, 182
Burrow, John, 262, 317
Butterfield, Herbert, 238

Caffè, Il, 349
Campanella, Tommaso, 33
Cantillon, Richard, 279
Carlyle, Adam, 100

Carlyle, Alexander, 58, 91-2, 104, 114
Carmichael, Gershom, 40n, 73-87, 251
Carre, John, 101
Carstares, William, 81, 97, 111
Cartwright, John, 323, 326
Cato's Letters (*London Journal*), 94, 100, 280, 330
cattle trade, Scottish, 46, 55, 56, 57-8, 69; prices, 52, 53, 54-5
charity, 24, 26n, 37-8, 49; *see also* benevolence
Charles I, King, 145, 238
Checkland, S. G., 56, 69
Child, Sir Josiah, 252
Christian morality, 2, 6, 78, 236, 241, 333, 340
Cicero, Ciceronianism, 38, 100, 140, 181, 251, 332
civic humanism, 2, 6, 13, 138-41, 177-8, 242-52, 315, 334-5; and criticism of Whig oligarchy, 236-40; 243; in Fletcher's thinking, 7, 141-51, 152, 240, 241; hiatus between language of civil jurisprudence and of, 248-51, 263-4; Hume and, 151-77, 181, 272, 288n; Kames and, 222; Millar and, 320, 321; Smith and, 7-8, 44, 177, 179, 181-202, 256, 262-4; and wealth as public good, 156, 158; *see also* luxury; militias; republicanism; virtue
Clarendon, 1st Earl of, 206
Clark, Alexander, 103
Cleghorn, William, 115
Clerk, Sir John, of Penicuik, 54, 59, 105
clubs and societies, literary and improving, 93, 98, 102, 110, 198-200, 201, 220, 240; *see also* Aberdeen Philosophical Society; Easy Club; Honourable Society of Improvers; Rankenian Club; Sophocardian Club; Spectator Club
Cobbett, William, 243, 323, 326
Coccejus, S., 40n
Cockburn, John, of Ormiston, 46
Colbert, Jean Baptiste, Colbertists, 4, 22, 358, 359, 360
common law, 221, 226-9, 231
Commonwealth, Commonwealthmen, 6, 7, 90, 94, 95, 238, 320, 321, 327, 328, 329, 332
community of goods, 2, 6, 22, 28, 29, 32-3, 35-6, 40n, 42, 81-2
Condillac, Étienne Bonnot de, 358, 360
Condorcet, Marquis de, 17, 26
conjectural history, 4, 28, 42, 43, 214, 317, 319n, 342; *see also* 'four stages'
consent theory, 34, 36, 82, 84, 85, 129, 319

contract theory, *see* original contract, property theory
Corn Laws, 19-20
'correzione', 351-2
corruption, *see* luxury
cosmopolitanism, Scottish, 247, 267-8
Coste, Pierre, 81
Country Party, 6, 22, 238, 320, 321, 326, 327, 328, 329, 332
Court of Chancery, 224, 225, 226-8, 231
Court of Session, 218, 219-20, 224-5, 228, 231, 232, 234
Covenanters, 145, 146
Craig, John, 306n, 307, 310n, 321, 323, 324, 328, 329
Craig, William, 103
credit, public, 154-5, 169, 236, 237, 238, 276-8, 290; *see also* banks; paper money
Creech, William, 62
Crochi, Pietro, 355-6
Cromarty, Earl of, 146
Cropsey, Joseph, 180
Cumberland, Richard, 82

Dalrymple, David (Lord Hailes), 99
Dalrymple, James, *see* Stair
Dandolo, Matteo, 351, 352-4, 355
Darien scheme, 89-142
Davie, G. E., 101
de Felice, Fortunato, 349
debt, payment of, 230; *see also* national debt
Defoe, Daniel, 201, 241, 245
deism, 236, 241, 327
dependence, 13, 126, 127-8, 133, 188, 237, 265; *see also* independence
Devine, T. M., 50
Diario economico di agricoltura, manifatture e comercio, 357-8
Diderot, Denis, 17, 22, 334, 335, 346, 347
Dissent, 327, 334
division of labour: between town and country, 9-10, 21-2; early expositions of theory, 5-6; effect on labourers, 192-3, 245, 262, 304, 307, 312, 342; Ferguson's concern over, 295-6; Hume and, 5, 276, 279, 283, 284; Locke and, 41, 42; Millar's position on, 307, 309, 322, 342; Smith and, 2, 4-5, 6, 7-8, 9, 43, 191, 262, 299-300, 303, 304, 359; Stewart and, 311, 312, 313; Tucker's theory of, 285, 286
Doddridge, Philip, 105, 109
Dodsley, Robert, 108
domestic servitude, 143, 144, 145, 147, 150
dominium, 80, 85, 249
Drummond, George, 59

Index

Du Pont de Nemours, Pierre Samuel, 17
Duncan, William, 108
Dundee, 48, 56, 67
Dunlop, Alexander, 103, 104
Dunlop, Jean, 70n
Dutch universities, 81, 108, 246
Dutot, Charles de Ferrare, 277, 278n

Easy Club, 199
economic development and political institutions, relation between, 137, 140-1, 151-77, 257
Eden, Sir Frederick Morton, 262
Eden, William, 214-15
Edinburgh, 147n; clubs and societies, 58, 91, 99, 199, 220, 240; economic growth and prosperity, 56, 58-9, 61, 62, 64, 67, 71; University and professoriate, 58, 91, 94, 97, 99, 102, 104-5, 107, 111
Edinburgh Medical School, 91
Edinburgh Philosophical Society, 111, 112
Edinburgh Review, 10, 199, 315, 317, 335, 342
Eliot, Sir Gilbert, 58, 59, 99, 100, 104, 287n
enclosure, 46, 68, 72
entails, 68, 215-17, 218, 219, 319, 323; 1685 Statute, 216
equality: civic, 170, 235-6, 248; of property, 6, 24, 157, 158, 323
equity jurisprudence, 221, 225-34
Erskine, John, 99
Evangelicals, 99, 204, 343
exports: bounty system, 19, 21; Scottish, 47, 52, 53, 65-6

Faculty of Advocates, 68, 218
family relationships, 75n, 187-8, 318, 319-20, 339
famine: property rights in times of, 20, 22, 27-30; Scottish, 19n, 45, 47, 49
federalism, 147, 170, 239
Ferguson, Adam, 58, 179, 180, 185, 269, 331, 334, 335, 361; *Essay on the History of Civil Society*, 295-6, 312, 343, 345, 346, 349, 360, 362; *Institutes of Moral Philosophy*, 350
Ferguson, William, 146n
feudalism, 13, 355, 356, 360-1; feudal law, 208, 216
Filmer, Robert, 30, 32n, 36, 37n, 126
Fink, Z. S., 245
fish trade, Scottish, 65-6
flax imports, Scottish, 52, 53, 62-3, 66
Fletcher, Andrew, 140, 141-51, 152, 156, 158, 165n, 195-6, 201, 240-1, 320
Fonblanque, John, 225-6

Forbes, Duncan, 7, 114, 167, 208, 219, 248, 293, 317, 326, 327, 332
Fordyce, David, 105, 108-11, 112, 115, 116
Forster, James, 105
Foscarini, Marco, 352
'four stages' theory of history, 7, 242-3, 254n, 255, 258-60, 264, 307, 335, 347, 348-9
Fox, Charles James, 324, 326, 328
France: debates over liberalisation of internal grain trade, 15-18; education, 181; monarchic government, 166, 167, 175-6; *see also* Ferench Revolution
franchise, 170, 323, 324, 327, 328, 329, 331, 342
Franklin, Benjamin, 102, 108, 291n, 311, 313n
Fraser, James, 75
free trade, 38, 151n, 291-2, 296-7, 301-2, 315, 322, 342; *see also* 'police' of grain; 'system of natural liberty'
French Revolution, 14, 18, 329, 331, 355
Friends of the People Society, 323, 324
friendship, 127, 188, 189, 199, 340

Galanti, Giuseppe, 360-1
Galiani, Ferdinando, 14, 17 18, 19, 26n
Garden, Francis, 101
Garve, Christian, 350
Gatti, Giovanni, 357
Gauthier, David, 119
Genovesi, Antonio, 360, 361
gentry, *see* 'middling ranks'
George III, King, 239, 328
Gerard, Alexander, 105, 106, 110, 113, 281n
Germany, 18, 280n
Giannone, Pietro, 360
Giarrizzo, Giuseppe, 353
Gibbon, Edward, 241n, 246n, 250, 263, 362
Gilbert, Jeffrey, 228
Glasgow: population, 56, 67; trade, 20n, 49n, 50, 51, 59, 67; University, 73, 74, 91, 94-5, 97, 98, 102-5, 106, 112, 114, 115, 268, 306
Gonzaga di Castiglioni, Luigi, 354, 355
Gordon, Thomas, 280
government: Hume's discussion of, 161-9, 176; social function of, 130-1; *see also* allegiance; economic development; monarchic government; political obligation; republics
Gozzi, Gasparo, 357
grain trade, eighteenth-century debates on, *see* 'police' of grain

Index

grain trade, Scottish, 47, 66, 69; prices, 19n, 48, 49, 50, 51, 52, 53, 54, 60, 71
Grant of Monymusk, 46
Gray, Malcolm, 54, 57n
Grey, Lord, 324
Grimaldi, Francesco, 360, 361
Grimm, Jacob, 17, 346
Grotius, Hugo, 2, 25n, 26, 28–31, 33, 35, 76, 204, 225, 226
Guicciardini, Francesco, 248

Haakonssen, Knud, 260, 261
Hadow, James, 89
Hailes, Lord (David Dalrymple), 99
Hamilton, Alexander, 239, 251
Hamilton, Gavin, 62–92
Hamilton, Henry, 59–60
Hamilton, William, 103
Hamilton, Sir William, 73
Hardwicke, Lord (Philip Yorke), 218, 219, 228
Hargrave, Francis, 227, 231
Harrington, James, 86, 139, 148n, 170, 174, 200, 236, 238, 248, 251, 320, 330
Hartlib, Samuel, 95
Henderson, Robert, 102
Hepburn, Robert, 92, 93, 99
Hexter, J. H., 139
history: cyclical view of, 288n, 289n; materialist version of, 258–9, 260, 317, 318, 327; uses of, 261–2; *see also* conjectural history; 'four stages'; luxury, corruption and decline
Hobbes, Thomas, 31, 76, 119, 125–6, 243, 244, 247
Holbach, Paul Henri Thirty, Baron d', 349, 362
Holland, 166, 167, 279, 280n, 292n; *see also* Dutch universities
Home, Henry, *see* Kames
Honourable Society of Improvers, 68, 91, 199
Hope, Thomas, of Rankeilor, 91
Hopetoun, John, 4th Earl of, 104
Hume, David, 11, 64, 104, 179–80, 191, 205, 246, 247, 252, 268, 324, 331, 342, 343; clash with Robert Wallace, 289–91; commitment to justice, 7, 212; and dependence and independence, 13, 133, 159; discussion with James Oswald, 275–6, 283; and distinction between 'personal freedom' and 'civil liberty', 329–30; *Essays Moral and Political*, 153, 160, 161, 323; *History of England*, 293–4, 303, 357, 360; 'Idea of a Perfect Commonwealth', 25n, 169–75, 177, 197n; influence in Italy, 351–4, 358, 360–2; monetary theory, 70, 277–9, 281–3; 'Of Civil Liberty', 166, 280; 'Of Commerce', 9, 154–5, 157, 158, 164, 272–3, 353; 'Of the Jealousy of Trade', 291–3, 301, 314; 'Of Refinement in the Arts' ('Of Luxury'), 157, 164, 265, 280–1, 353; 'Of Money', 274–6, 279, 291, 314, 353; 'Of the Origin of Government', 176; 'Of the Original Contract', 131; 'Of the Populousness of Ancient Nations', 164–5, 353; 'Of Public Credit', 155, 353; 'Of the Rise and Progress of the Arts and Sciences', 161–4; polemic with Josiah Tucker, 5, 275, 276, 281, 284–9, 290, 293–4, 309, 311n; *Political Discourses*, 154, 157, 160, 168, 169, 271, 272; and political obligation, 86, 129–31, 132; and regionalism, 196; and relation between political institutions and economic development, 137, 140–1, 151–77; religious opinions, 78, 79, 119–20; and 'rich country-poor country' debate, 5, 272–96, 298, 301, 309, 313, 314, 315; and social causation of human beliefs, 120, 121–2, 129, 134–5; *Treatise of Human Nature*, 130–1, 152–3, 155, 242; *see also* civic humanism; division of labour; government; luxury; militias; property; specie-flow model; virtue; wages
Hutcheson, Francis, 73, 115, 131n, 211, 251, 318, 319, 320, 321, 330; academic influence of, 91, 93, 103, 104–5, 108, 179, 257, 264; his appreciation of Gershom Carmichael's work, 74, 82, 85, 86, 87; on luxury, 307, 333

impartial spectator theory, 185–7, 189, 191, 197, 340
imperium, 80, 84, 85, 250
imports: duty on, 19, 21; Scottish, 52, 53, 66–7
improvers, improving societies, 46, 68–9, 71, 91, 93, 199
independence: civic humanist ideal of, 165, 236, 237, 330; in commercial society, 13, 63, 86, 159, 188, 189, 199, 324–6, 327, 342; *see also* dependence
individualism, 156, 158, 159–60, 243, 244, 249, 252, 332, 335, 336, 339–40, 342
Industrial Revolution, 63, 71
'invisible hand', 8–12, 13, 21, 266; *see also* unintended consequences
Ireland, 62–3, 290
ius, 248–9, 250, 251

Jacobinism, 323, 326
Jacobitism, Jacobite risings, 46, 48, 114–15, 147n, 291n

Index

Jansenists, 26n
Jardine, George, 108
Jefferson, Thomas, 239; Jeffersonian values, 244, 251
Jeffrey, Francis, 199, 342
Jesuits, 26n
Johnson, Samuel, 108, 265
jurisprudence, *see* law; natural jurisprudence
justice, 320, 331; Locke and distributive, 38–9; Lord Kames and 209, 211–12; Smith's concern with, 7, 8, 24–5, 26, 29, 42, 43, 44, 211–12, 256, 260, 261–2, 263, 268

Kames, Lord (Henry Home), 69, 82, 179, 203–34, 242, 275n, 287n, 289, 293, 350–1
Kindleberger, Charles, 55, 57, 63
King's College, Aberdeen, 105, 107
Knox, John, 89

laissez-faire, 257, 258
land management, Scottish, 46; *see also* agriculture; enclosure; landowners
land surveyors, Scottish, 52, 53, 67
landowners, landownership, Scottish, 19n, 68, 69, 71, 116–17, 192; *see also* entails
Latini, Brunetto, 250
Lauderdale, 8th Earl of (James Maitland), 271, 306, 312, 313–15
Law, John, 70, 276, 277–8, 290, 291n
law: contract, 229–30; criminal, 212–15, 221n, 347; historical treatment of, 206–10, 212, 214; Lord Kames's theory of, 202–34; reform, 205–6, 210, 214–15, 218–21; *see also* civil polity; common law; entails; equity; justice; natural jurisprudence; Roman law
Le Clerc, Jean, 81
Le Trosne, Guillaume François, 358
Leechman, William, 103
Lehmann, William C., 317, 321
Leibniz, G. W., 77, 78, 80
Leven, Alexander, 5th Earl of, 112
liberty: 'active' and 'passive', 44, 138, 140, 159–60, 173, 175, 176, 329–31; growth of commerce and, 86, 157, 241, 243, 257, 325, 326, 332
Liberty riots of 1760s, 327
Lindgren, Ralph, 180, 185, 194
linen industry, Scottish, 46, 49, 50, 51, 52, 53, 62–5, 67, 69, 72
Linguet, Simon-Nicolas-Henri, 17, 22, 23n
Liston, Robert, 101
Loch, David, 64
Locke, John, 2, 87, 119–35, 243, 244, 251, 264, 350; and dependence, 126–8, 133; 'ethics of belief', 122–6; and political obligation, 129–30, 133; property theory, 35–41, 42, 81, 82, 83, 85, 244, 319; theocentrism, 119, 120, 122, 127–9, 134–5; theory of consent, 84, 85, 129; *Two Treatises of Government*, 5, 36, 80–1, 85, 129
Locke, John, Senior, 126
London Journal, 94, 100
Loudon, John, 74
Lounger, 199
luxury, corruption and decline, cycle of, 34, 44, 100, 138–9, 250, 262, 278n, 290n, 313; Ferguson and, 295–6; Fletcher and, 148, 149–50; Hume and, 154, 156, 157, 279, 280–1, 284, 288–9; Hutcheson and, 307, 333; Kames and, 222–3, 233; Locke and, 40–1; Millar and, 306–10, 311–12, 317, 340–1; Smith and, 4, 6, 8–9, 299; Steuart and, 296–7; and Whig regime, 237, 238, 239
Lycurgus, 241, 243

Mably, Gabriel Bonnot de, 17
McCosh, James, 73
Macfie, A. L., 317
Machiavelli, Machiavellianism, 139, 236, 248, 252, 280
machines, use of, 41n, 285, 295n, 297–8, 299, 303, 310–11, 312, 314
Mackenzie, Sir George, 90
Mackenzie, Henry, 199
Mackie, Charles, 99, 102, 108, 111–12
MacLaurin, Colin, 91, 93, 99, 101, 102, 104–5, 111, 112, 114, 115
Madison, James, 239
Malebranche, Nicholas, 11, 79
Mandeville, Bernard, 11, 12, 83, 252, 264–5, 340; *Fable of the Bees*, 5–6, 319, 338
manufacture, balance between agriculture and, 21–2, 71, 303–5, 358–60
Marischal College, Aberdeen, 91, 94, 97, 102, 105, 106, 107, 109, 113
markets, Scottish, growth of, 47–8, 49
Marmontel, Jean François, 346
Marx, Karl, 1, 245, 252, 258, 318, 326, 327; Marxism, 239, 243
Medick, Hans, 308n, 317, 322–3, 324, 325, 326
Meek, Ronald, 28n, 255, 258, 259n, 317, 318, 321, 348
Melon, Jean François, 277, 278n
Melville, Andrew, 89, 111
merchant guilds, 59
'middling ranks', gentry, 69, 158–9, 165, 167, 169, 179, 192, 197, 288n, 325–6, 327

368 Index

militias, 7n, 116, 138, 178, 200, 334; Fletcher's proposals for, 143, 146, 147, 148, 150, 196, 240; in Hume's 'perfect commonwealth', 171, 173, 176; Smith's view of, 7–8, 263; *see also* standing armies
Mill, James, 343
Millar, Andrew, 92
Millar, John, 43, 83, 180, 204, 208, 242, 251–2, 317–43; and competitive individualism, 332, 339–40, 342; *Historical View of English Government*, 204, 226, 318, 322, 324, 326, 342; and the household and 'adventitious rights', 318–19, 320–2, 325; and independence in free-labour economy, 13, 324–6, 327, 342; on luxury and decline of commerce, 306–10, 311–12, 317, 340–1; *The Origin of the Distinction of Ranks*, 204, 318, 321, 322, 327, 332, 342; political position, 323–4, 327–9, 331–2
millenarianism, 95, 327
Millot, Claude François, 360
Milton, John, 95, 96
Mirror, 199
Mitford, John (Lord Redesdale), 226, 227
Molesworth, Robert, 1st Viscount, 90, 93–5, 96, 97, 98, 99, 100, 103
monarchic government: and civic tradition, 139; Fletcher on, 148–9; Hume's approval of, 140, 162–4, 166–8, 172, 175, 330
Monboddo, Lord (James Burnet), 350
monetary theory, 33–4, 39, 70, 122n, 277–9, 281–3; *see also* banks; credit; paper money
monopolies, 193–4, 196–7, 274, 285, 291n, 292, 313, 322, 339
Montesquieu, 168n, 204, 214, 238, 241, 257, 264, 290n, 293n, 295n, 319; and relation between private manners and public laws, 223, 320, 321, 330–1; and utility of machines, 285, 297n, 310
Moor, James, 103–4
More, Thomas, 33, 170
Morellet, André, 17, 345, 347, 348
Muir, Thomas, 323, 326
Muratori, Lodovico Antonio, 351
Mure family of Caldwell, 102–4; Elizabeth, 102–3; William, 103, 104, 275n
Musgrave, Sir Christopher, 146

national debt, 168, 244, 292n, 329, 360
natural jurisprudence tradition, 246–51; Carmichael and, 73–87; Millar and, 306, 318–21, 340; property theory in, 7, 22–44, 80–7; Smith's engagement with, 6, 7, 22–8, 43–4, 255–69; *see also* law
'natural man', idea of, 361
Neapolitan Enlightenment, 360–2

Necker, Jacques, 17, 26n
neo-Harringtonians, 236, 237, 238, 240, 245, 264, 332
Neville, Henry, 238

oat prices, Scottish, 49, 50, 51, 52, 53, 54
Old Whig neo-classicism, 237, 238, 247
original contract, 28, 30, 33, 40, 84–6, 132, 264, 346; *see also* community of goods
Oswald, James, 275, 276, 277n, 281, 282n, 283–4, 298, 301n
Oxford University, 95

Pagano, Francesco Mario, 360, 361–2
Paine, Thomas, 322, 323, 326
Paisley, 56, 57
Paley, William, 209
pamphlets, economic, 5, 41, 42
paper money, 70, 71, 244, 276–7, 290, 294n, 302; *see also* banks; credit
paper trade, Scottish, 52, 53, 61–2
Pascal, Roy, 317, 318, 321
patriotism, 222–3, 234, 241, 244
Pavini, Luigi, 351
personality: classical ideal of, 7–8, 235; diversification of, 242, 243, 245, 250, 252, 295
Perth Academy, 114
Petty, William, 5n, 252, 279
Philadelphia Convention, 239
Phillipson, Nicholas, 220, 240, 265, 266, 267
Physiocrats, 14, 16, 18, 21, 22, 268, 305, 311, 358
Pisani, Giorgio, 354, 355
Pitcairne, Archibald, 89
Pitt, William, the younger, 323, 328, 329, 331
Plato, 170, 241, 243, 346; Platonism, 349, 362
pneumatology, 76, 130n
Pocock, J. G. A., 210, 240, 246, 247, 253, 256, 262, 263, 272, 317, 320, 332
Poker Club, 116
Polanyi, Karl, 13–14
'police' of grain, 2, 13–14, 15–21, 26
politeness, 108, 200n, 241, 242, 243, 244, 246, 251
political obligation, 129–33, 261
Polizeiwissenschaft, 18–19
population: of ancient republics, 164–5; statistics for eighteenth-century Scotland, 56, 67; use of machines and, 310
Presbyterian Church, 75, 98, 113
Price, Richard, 334
Priestley, Joseph, 327
primitive societies, 1–3, 33, 185n, 334–5, 348

Index

Pringle, Sir John, 74, 102
Privy Council, 224
professoriate, Scottish, 89-117
profit, 301, 322
property theory: of Aquinas, 26-7; of Carmichael, 80-3, 85; and civic humanism, 236, 237, 248, 249, 330; of Grotius, 28-30, 31, 33; of Hume, 20-1, 23-4, 82, 83, 130, 152, 158, 175; labour, 37, 41, 82-3, 85; of Locke, 35-41, 42, 81, 82, 83, 85, 244, 319; of Pufendorf, 30, 31-5, 37, 42, 80-2; of Smith, 20-6, 42-3, 82, 83, 260, 261, 319
propriety, 189-91, 199
Pufendorf, Samuel, 2, 38, 76-8, 246; original contract theory, 84-6; and origins of modern money-economy, 34, 39; property theory, 30-5, 37, 42, 80-2
punishment, 213-14
Puritanism, 239-241

Quesnay, François, 16-17, 268

Ramsay, Allan, 346, 347
Ramsay, John, of Ochertyre, 91, 92, 203, 206
Rankenian Club, 99, 100-1, 102, 104, 110, 111, 115
Rapetti, Andrea, 354
Raphael, D. D., 185-6
Redesdale, Lord (John Mitford), 226, 227
regenting system, university, 74, 106-7
regionalism, 194-7
Reid, Thomas, 20n, 94, 105, 106, 116, 179, 180-1, 244
republicanism, 139-40, 237-8, 240, 244, 245-6, 325, 326, 328, 330; American, 239, 244, 246; republican virtue, 241, 243, 245, 248-51; in Scottish universities, 90
republics, ancient and modern, 162-9
Revolution of 1688, 324
Ricardo, David, 252, 258n, 327, 343
Riccomanni, Luigi, 357-60
'rich country-poor country' debate, 271-315, 341
rights and duties, 31, 78, 264, 318-21
Ritchie, David, 107
roads, Scottish, 48, 232
Robertson, William, 58, 91, 99, 115, 203, 207, 242, 252, 293n, 334n; *History of America*, 357; *History of Scotland*, 355, 356-7; influence in Italy, 355-7, 360, 362; *View of the Progress of Society in Europe*, 356, 360
Roman law, 81, 85, 111, 140
Romantic poets, 343
Rosenberg, Nathan, 266

Rosse, George, 104, 108
Rossi, Francesco, 356
Rotwein, Eugene, 274n, 283n, 293n, 353
Roubaud, Pierre Joseph André, 17, 22n
Rouet, William, 104
Rousseau, Jean-Jacques, 10, 11, 12, 41n, 335, 354, 361
Rule, Gilbert, 107
Russell, John, 112

St Andrews University, 107
Schneider, Louis, 317, 321, 323
scholasticism in Scottish universities, 107, 108, 113
Schoolmen, Scholastic tradition, 26, 79-80, 81, 83
'science of a legislator', 255-69
Scola, Giovanni, 356
Scotland: economy, 19n, 45-72; Highlands, 54, 55, 57, 59; independence, 200-1; Lowlands, 55, 57, 65; *see also* agriculture; banks; landowners; Union; universities
Scots Magazine, 97, 102, 106, 278n, 294n
Scott, Sir Walter, 92
Selden, John, 76, 221
Select Society, Edinburgh, 44n, 58, 68, 90, 91, 93n, 100, 112, 115-16, 151, 199, 332
self-improvement, 12, 110
self-love, 8, 11-12
Septennial Act (1716), 236
Seton, William, 201
sexual relations: eighteenth-century discussion of, 242, 332-8; primitive, 242, 334, 335
Seymour, Sir Edward, 146, 147n, 150n
Shaftesbury, 3rd Earl of, 73, 90, 94, 96, 100, 104, 105, 108, 125n
Shelburne, Lord (William Petty), 68, 69, 275n, 288n
shipping, Scottish, 48, 67
Sibbald, Robert, 90
Sidney, Algernon, 132, 251
Simson, John, 93, 98
Simson, Robert, 104
Skene, David, 281
Skinner, Quentin, 248, 250-1
slaves, slavery, 2, 6, 13, 44, 87, 144, 165, 268, 325, 359
Smellie, William, 205
Smith, Adam, 1-26, 29, 41-4, 121-2, 134-5, 179-202, 203n, 242, 251-69, 282n, 318, 328, 335, 337-43, 349; and balance between agriculture and manufacturing, 303-5; and dependence and independence, 13, 134n, 188, 325; and distinction between 'personal freedom' and 'civil

Smith, Adam (*cont.*)
  liberty', 329–30; and 'improving' landlords, 68–9, 192; *Lectures on Jurisprudence*, 86, 185, 188, 204, 208, 213n, 255, 258, 261, 263, 267, 320; and paper money, 70, 277, 302; and paradox of commercial society, 1–15, 18, 20–6, 29, 41–4, 299; and political obligation, 129, 131–3, 261; and regionalism, 194–7; and relation between political institutions and economic development, 137, 141, 177; religious opinions, 119–20, 128–9; and 'rich country–poor country' debate, 298–306, 341; and Scotland's economy, 50–1, 54, 55, 57, 63, 65, 67, 72, 302; and Scottish universities, 107, 112; theory of history, 7, 255, 258–60, 264; *see also* civic humanism; division of labour; impartial spectator; 'invisible hand'; justice; luxury; natural jurisprudence; property; sympathy; 'system of natural liberty'; *Theory of Moral Sentiments*; virtue; wages; *Wealth of Nations*
Smith, William, 106
societies, literary and improving, *see* clubs
Sombart, W., 317, 318, 321
South Sea Bubble, 93, 95, 277, 283n
specie-flow model, Hume's, 282–3, 286, 296, 297n, 309n
Spectator, 188–9, 199
Spectator Club, 198, 240
Stair, Viscount of (James Dalrymple), *The Institutions of the Law of Scotland*, 30n, 221, 224, 226
standing armies, 156, 236, 245, 327, 328, 329; Fletcher's view of, 143, 148, 149; Smith's attitude towards, 3, 7, 260, 263; *see also* militias
Statistical Account of Scotland, 56, 59, 60, 62
Steele, Sir Richard, 188, 198
Stein, Peter, 205, 210, 248
Steuart, James, 64, 70, 72, 296–8, 300, 302, 325; and 'police' of grain, 13, 14, 18–19, 20n; *Principles of Political Oeconomy*, 268, 296, 310
Stevenson, John, 91–2, 99–100, 101, 102, 108, 111; Stevenson class essays, 99–101
Stewart, Dugald, 72, 87, 91, 100, 181, 214, 301n, 342; 'Account of the Life and Writings of Adam Smith', 182, 187, 265, 330; and issue of rich country–poor country relations, 306, 310–13; *Lectures on Political Economy*, 330; pedagogic aims and influence, 108, 116, 179, 180, 315
Stirling, Professor, Principal of Glasgow University, 94
Stoics, Stoicism, 10, 27n, 140, 181, 186n, 246, 249, 332, 341
Strachey, John, 127
Strauss, Leo, 239, 243
Stuart, Baillie, 114
Stuart, Gilbert, 334, 335
Suard, Jean Baptiste Antoine, 345, 346, 348
Suarez, Francisco, 32, 247
Sully, Maximilien de Béthune, Duc de, 358, 359
Switzerland, 165, 171
sympathy, theory of, 181–8, 193, 194, 195, 196, 197, 198, 254, 337, 338, 339
'system of natural liberty', Adam Smith's 12, 13–14, 15, 18, 20–1, 25, 26, 257

Tarabuzzi, Gianfranco, 355
tariff protection, 287, 293; *see also* exports; imports
'taste', 241, 244, 246
Tatler, 188, 199
Tatler of the North, 92
tax yields on beer and malt, Scottish, 52, 53, 60–1
Taylor, John, of Caroline, 237, 239n, 243
Temple, Sir William, 279, 289n, 319
Terray, l'Abbé, 18
textile industry, Scottish, 65; *see also* linen
theft, in cases of necessity, 26n, 27–30, 37
theology: Carmichael's theory of natural, 77–80, 81; theocentrism of Locke, 119–29, 134–5
Theory of Moral Sentiments (Adam Smith), 24–6, 43, 120n, 128, 133n, 181–91, 211, 335, 337; discussion of pursuit of wealth in, 8–9, 10, 11, 12, 13; relationship with Smith's other works, 254–5, 259, 261, 263, 349
Thom, William, of Govan, 112–14, 115
Thompson, Edward, P., 14–15, 326
Titius, Gerhard Gottlieb, 84
tobacco trade, Scottish, 46, 49–50, 51, 52, 53, 66, 67
Toland, John, 90
Tory neo-classicism, 237, 238, 247
Tron, Andrea, 351n, 357
Tuck, Richard, 221, 248, 249
Tucker, Josiah, 243, 244, 250, 284–5, 294, 298; polemic with Hume, 5, 275, 276, 281, 284–9, 290, 293, 294, 309, 311n
Tully, James, 248
Turgot, A. R. J., 17, 18, 291n
Turnbull, George, 40n, 82, 93–5, 96–8, 99, 101, 105, 108, 251
Tytler, Andrew Fraser (Lord Woodhouselee), 203n, 205, 210, 276n

Index

underconsumption, 314–15
unintended consequences, doctrine of, 11, 44, 264–5, 266, 321; *see also* 'invisible hand'
Union, Parliamentary (1707), 137, 141–2, 145, 151, 152, 218, 236, 320; and Scotland's economy, 45, 48, 54
universities, Scottish, 74, 75, 81, 89–117, 220; *see also* Edinburgh; Glasgow; King's College; Marischal College; St Andrews
urban growth, 22, 67, 194–5
utility, principle of: and authority, 132, 133, 324; and equity, 229, 230–1, 233, 234

Venice, 165, 166n, 170, 351–4, 355, 356, 357
Venturi, Franco, 17
Verri, Pietro, 348, 349, 358
Vico, Giambattista, 356, 360, 361, 362
virtù, 273, 274n, 292
virtue: in civic humanist discourse, 6–7, 138, 235–6, 237, 241, 243, 244, 245, 248–51, 272, 320, 330–1; and commerce, 159, 237–9, 241, 251, 252, 262, 272, 273; Hume and, 159, 160, 181, 189, 190, 196, 273, 292, 333, 340; Millar and, 317, 320, 331–2, 335–43; Smith and, 179, 181–202; *virtus* and *ius*, 248–51; in voluntarist language, 200–2
Voegelin, Erich, 243
Voltaire, 17, 346, 360, 361, 362
voluntarism, 198–200, 202

wage-labourers: effects of division of labour on, 192, 245, 304, 307, 312, 342; 'independence' of, 13, 63, 188, 324–5; *see also* wages
wages: Hume's endorsement of high-wage economy, 5, 276, 283, 291; of Scottish day-labourers in eighteenth century, 52, 53, 60; Smith and, 4–5, 299, 301; Steuart and, 298, Tucker's observations on, 285, 286
Wallace, George, 99
Wallace, Robert, 13, 99, 289–91, 333
Walpole, Robert, 93, 346
Watts, Isaac, 105
Wealth of Nations (Adam Smith), 1–24, 41–4, 128, 134n, 177, 185, 188, 191–7; in context of Smith's other works, 253–69, 300–6, 342; influence in Italy, 357, 358–60; Scottish context of, 55, 63–4, 68–9, 72
Webster, Charles, 96
Whig regime, 236–7, 239, 240, 243, 250, 251
Whigs, Whiggism: 'Old', 238, 247; 'Real', 90, 264; 'sceptical', 327, 330, 332; 'scientific', 326; 'vulgar', 7, 129, 131, 326; *see also* Whig regime
whisky industry, 61
Whyte, Ian, 46, 47
Wilkesite campaigns, 176n, 327
Winch, Donald, 4n, 131n, 200n, 255n, 317
Wise Club (Aberdeen Philosophical Society), 105, 110, 281n
Wishart, George, 99, 103, 104, 105
Wishart, Sir James, 97
Wishart, William, the younger, 94, 95, 96, 97, 98, 99, 102, 103, 104, 105
Wodrow, Robert, 74n, 75n, 95, 98, 103
Wolin, S. S., 243
women: condition, 242, 332, 335–6; education, 109; employment, 60, 64, 65, 71; *see also* sexual relations
Wyvill, Christopher, 326

Printed in the United States
76581LV00003B/73